*National Portrait Gallery*
David Garrick.
Portrait by Thomas Gainsborough, ca. 1770.

# DAVID GARRICK

## A Critical Biography

.

By George Winchester Stone, Jr.
and George M. Kahrl

SOUTHERN ILLINOIS UNIVERSITY PRESS
CARBONDALE AND EDWARDSVILLE
FEFFER & SIMONS, INC.
LONDON AND AMSTERDAM

Library of Congress Cataloging in Publication Data

Stone, George Winchester, 1907–
David Garrick, a critical biography.

Bibliography: p.
Includes index.
1. Garrick, David, 1717–1779. 2. Actors—
England—Biography. 3. Dramatists, English—
18th century—Biography. I. Kahrl, George Morrow,
1904–      joint author. II. Title.
PN2598.G3S67      792'.028'0924 [B]      79-9476
ISBN 0-8093-0931-9

cc

# Contents

.

## Contents

# Illustrations

·

# Preface

.

THIS BIOGRAPHY of David Garrick might well be titled *Garrick 14*, since it marks the fourteenth full treatment of the life of that remarkable actor, playwright, manager—one who elevated the profession of acting, who displayed a genius for theatre administration unknown up to his time and seldom since, who was an extraordinarily successful dramatist and versifier, whose death in Samuel Johnson's words "eclipsed the gaiety of nations." Garrick was also the embodiment of the best in an eighteenth-century gentleman, socially, morally, and personally.

The previous biographies are anecdotal in the extreme, mingling fact with fiction, and showing the man bouncing off the surface of eighteenth-century social life, making the rounds of the elite, lionized in society at home and abroad, vilified by authors whose plays he rejected and by rival actors, careful of his money, jealous of his reputation, vain, tyrannical as a manager, brilliant as an actor, frothy as a playwright, engaging as a letter writer and conversationalist—the antithesis of Dr Johnson, the foil for Goldsmith, and a target for Horace Walpole.

The story told by biographers from Thomas Davies and Arthur Murphy (his contemporaries) to Carola Oman (some 20 years ago) makes pleasant reading. Why then another biography? The very early writers had biases which have over the years become entrenched in the Garrick lore. Some distortions thus set can now be corrected in view of abundant evidence and new facts to which the first biographers were not privy. For we are the immediate heirs to a wealth of sources, including three great collections pertinent to the man which none of the previous 13 writers had available. The largest collection of Garrick's writings and records came to light when the Folger Shakespeare Library opened its doors in 1932. Since the writing of Garrick's latest biography (1958) the day-by-day account of *The London Stage, 1600–1800* has appeared with its organized wealth of theatrical material known only in fragments earlier. And in 1963 David M. Little and

xiii

George M. Kahrl, aided by the resources of the Harvard Theatre Collection, published the full edition of *The Letters of David Garrick*, which together with the annotations reveal the man in his professional, human, and social relations with his contemporaries.

The Folger materials range widely, including acting copies of plays, unpublished verse, diaries, letters of Mrs Garrick, portraits, prints, and memorabilia essential to the depiction of a life. The London stage documentation is basic to Garrick's professional life. For 29 years he managed Drury Lane Theatre and cared passionately for its well being. He realized that the lives, hopes, and families of a company of some 140 actors, actresses, singers, dancers, musicians, and house servants depended upon the successful operation of that theatre. He was determined that it not fail (as it often had in the past). It must become the most brilliant performing theatre in Europe, as it did under his administration. His own acting set the pace of performance, his discipline carried it on, his innovations and writings and adaptations of older plays freshened the repertory. We profit today from a dozen advances he made in that period of great English acting. The Garrick *Letters*, some 1,400 of them, reveal one side at least of his correspondence with over 300 persons, about 30 of whom became close friends —some of them prominent public figures, some not—the quality of whose friendship can now be seen in a new light.

We the present authors have experienced no difficulty in the general division of labor in this collaborative study. One of us catalogued the Garrick collection in the Folger and spent 35 years editing that part of *The London Stage* covering the period of Garrick's management (1747–76), thus following his professional career in intimate detail. The other spent 35 years helping to assemble, edit, and annotate thoroughly *The Letters of David Garrick*, tracking down his acquaintance with his 300 correspondents, the circumstances, the pressures and the pleasures of his personal and social life.

We debated the nature of a collaborative biography, and the structure it should take—but not for long. For we long ago agreed that biography is not charted with adequacy or imagination by the stark record of hours and days in routine sequence. Involvements grow, widen, interlock, and return upon themselves—their meaning revealed, perhaps, only as a continuum, best unbroken by the clock or by constant mention of the passage of weeks and months. Even Boswell, with all his minutiae, lost sight of the dull sequence of days, believing that increments of experience and simultaneous groupings of actions often count more than a strict calendar of unfolding events.

A substructure, however, keyed to the calendar of Garrick's 60 years occurs in our treatment first of his early years in Lichfield, succeeded by his four periods of management, broken by his grand tour of France and Italy, and his years of retirement from the stage. But in the narrative he is revealed topically, so to speak, as actor, as poet, as dramatist, as a stimulator of scholarship by the use to which he put his extensive dramatic library, and as an engaging conversationalist with and respecter of women of distinction and with his closest friends. The process often gets us way ahead of the calendar. But the combination seems to work well in the delineation of the man in his many, many activities, his remarkable accomplishments, friendships, battles, gracious and effective living, cool business sense, and in the artistry with which he touched all he came in contact with. Mr Stone is responsible for those chapters on Garrick the professional man; Mr Kahrl, for those on Garrick the private figure and his social relationships off stage and out of the theatre.

In the following pages Garrick often speaks for himself, as we quote him from his letters. We hope not over much, but he was such an articulate and charming letter writer that paraphrase of content to make a point often belies the flavor of the man. We likewise encourage some of his contemporaries to speak for themselves. All published letters are documented by date, or by letter number (indicated by numbers in parentheses throughout the text) in the Little-Kahrl, *The Letters of David Garrick*, 3 vols. (Cambridge, Mass., 1963), or in James Boaden's *The Private Correspondence of David Garrick with the Most Celebrated Persons of His Time*, 2 vols. (London, 1831) or in *The Letters of David Garrick and Georgiana Countess Spencer, 1759–1779*, edited by Earl Spencer and Christopher Dobson (Cambridge, 1960). Unpublished correspondence from other sources, such as the Forster Collection in the Victoria and Albert Museum, are documented in appropriate notes. Reference to *The Letters of David Garrick* assume reference to the full annotations provided therein. A list of all referenced sources is provided in the back matter of the biography, hence all notes use short titles only.

Dates of performances may be substantiated by ready reference to *The London Stage, 1660–1800* (Southern Illinois University Press, 1960–68), wherein all entries appear in chronological order, voiding the need for page reference.

Since readers may wish to see at a glance the roles Garrick undertook, or certain management statistics (employment interviews), or the ramifications of the Garrick family, or the provisions of his will, we have included such matters in a number of appendixes. The fullest published account of Garrick iconography has been recently set forth

in volume 6 of *A Biographical Dictionary of Actors, Actresses . . .
1660–1800* (Southern Illinois University Press, 1978) by Philip H.
Highfill, Jr, Kalman A. Burnim, and Edward A. Langhans, which lists
accounts of some 282 separate paintings and engravings. No need
to repeat the listing here. Instead we have included 18 of the Garrick
portraits from the earliest by Van Loo in 1741 to the death mask by
Robert Edge Pine in 1779, as well as portraits of his close friends and
associates, along with illustrations of the actor in various roles. He was
one of the most be-pictured men in the whole eighteenth century,
outdistancing Alexander Pope, Voltaire, and even King George III.
Artists sought to paint his portrait. He sought engravers to depict him
in his roles. The illustrations yield vividness to many points of biographical significance discussed in the text. They bear witness to Garrick's remarkable and penetrating eyes, his mobile face, his carriage,
the thoughtfulness of his expression, and the various stages of his life.
They provide in sequence a running view of the effects of the passage
of time on the actor's physical appearance.

The life of this actor and eighteenth-century gentleman has been
long in the making, and has laid under contribution the cumulative
scholarship of generations. To the great private and public libraries
here and abroad and to their staffs we owe a debt of particular thanks
—to the British Museum, the Folger, the Clark, the Huntington, the
Harvard and Yale libraries, to the New York Public, the Library of
Congress, to the Garrick Club our debt is very heavy. And special
collections have been opened to us for which we make grateful acknowledgment: The James M. Osborn Collection at Yale, The Four
Oaks Collection of Donald and Mary Hyde, The Malone Collection
at the Bodleian, the Enthoven and Forster Collections at the Victoria
and Albert Museum, the Charles Burney Collection at the British Library, the Harvard Theatre Collection, and McGraw Hill for Boswell.

Financial support over the years has come from the Guggenheim
Foundation, The American Council of Learned Societies, Elmira College, New York University, and Kenyon College. Support for much
research and for final preparation of the manuscript has come from a
liberal grant from the National Endowment for the Humanities. To all
our thanks are sincere.

And we wish to make particular acknowledgment to Marie Edel,
whose expert advice, coming from years of editing scholarly manuscripts, enabled us to bring disparate chapters into some unity of design, and whose eye and relish as a third reader, unencumbered by
the thousand details with which we have been living for 15 years,
profited the undertaking immeasurably.

## Preface

A serious blow to the publishing of eighteenth-century studies in drama and theatre fell with the death, 26 February 1979, of Vernon Sternberg, sensitive Director of the Southern Illinois University Press. He was in the midst of copy editing this biography at the time. Our special thanks go now to Miss Joyce Atwood, Chief Editor of the Press, and to Vernon Sternberg's competent staff for their unstinting efforts to move on with the volume so that it might appear in 1979 as a tribute to Garrick on the two-hundredth anniversary of his death.

GWS, Jr
GMK

1 March 1979

# Chronology

.

| | |
|---|---|
| 19 February 1717 | Birth at the Angel Inn, Hereford. |
| 28 February 1717 | Baptized in All Saints' Church, Hereford. |
| 1717–37 | Resides in Lichfield. |
| 1735 | Attends Edial Hall School, two miles west of Lichfield, under Samuel Johnson. |
| 2 March 1737 | Journeys to London with Samuel Johnson. |
| 9 March 1737 | Enrolls as prospective law student at Lincoln's Inn. |
| Summer 1737 | In Rochester being tutored by the Reverend John Colson, mathematician. |
| 1738–41 | Engages in the wine trade in London. |
| June–July 1741 | Acts at Ipswich in Henry Giffard's company under the name of Mr Lyddall. |
| 19 October 1741 | Makes London debut at Goodman's Fields Theatre in *Richard III*. |
| 1741–42 | Acts at Goodman's Fields Theatre, with his own name in the bills from 23 November. |
| Summer 1742 | Plays at Smock Alley Theatre in Dublin. |
| 1742–45 | Acts at Drury Lane Theatre. Resides in "Great Piazza in Covent Garden," in Bow Street, and in James Street. |
| Fall 1743 | With Charles Macklin leads the walkout of actors at Drury Lane. |
| December 1743 | Is reinstated in Drury Lane. |
| Ca. 1745 | Begins collecting his library of old plays. |
| 1745–46 | Comanager of Smock Alley theatre in Dublin with Thomas Sheridan. |
| 1746–47 | Engages with John Rich for the season at Covent Garden. |
| 9 April 1747 | Contracts with James Lacy as joint patentee of Drury Lane. |
| 22 June 1749 | Marries Eva Maria Veigel, dancer from Vienna. |

| | |
|---|---|
| 1749–72 | Resides at 27 Southampton Street. |
| Summer 1751 | With Mrs Garrick visits Paris. |
| 1754 | Purchases the Lacey Primatt house at Hampton on Thames. |
| 20 April 1757 | Purchases the manor house and estate at Hendon. |
| 1763–65 | With Mrs Garrick makes a grand tour of France, Italy, and Germany. |
| September 1769 | Organizes and administers the Shakespeare Jubilee at Stratford. |
| March 1772 | Moves from Southampton Street to his new residence in Adelphi Terrace. |
| 1775–76 | Final season of acting. |
| 18 January 1776 | Sells his portion of the patent to Sheridan, Linley, Ford, and Ewart. |
| March 1776 | Incorporates the Theatrical Fund by a bill in Parliament. |
| 10 June 1776 | Gives his final performance, and takes leave of the stage forever. Assigns the night's income (£311.12.6) to use by the Theatrical Fund. |
| 20 January 1779 | Dies in London just short of 62 years of age. |
| 1 February 1779 | Buried in Westminster Abbey in Poets' Corner. |

# Part One
## The Apprentice

.

# The Lichfield Years

THE STRUCTURE AND MEANING of David Garrick's life was predominantly cultural, developing in waves and interlocking circles of associations. He shared, of course, the plodding chronological movement of time with all mankind, but what he made of it was what counted. To see him day by day from birth to death, from an inn at Hereford to a tomb in Westminster Abbey is to miss the essence and focal impact of a rare personality and an artistic professional man. He had an extraordinary capacity for assimilating, as well as enriching the social and artistic resources of the eighteenth century with few subjective questionings, and no obsession with the relative values of progress. Unconsciously he accepted all cultural creativity as cyclical, the unit being the life of the individual amid several generations of a family.

He became an actor because early he was conscious of a gift for pantomime, which he developed, and an abiding taste for dramatic poetry, not as a means of cultivating an individual identity, but as a social and civilizing art. His relish was great for the diversity of human personality, and he sought an audience both from a circle of close friends and from the widening circle of crowded theatres. From each he drew exhilaration. He excelled as an actor because he tirelessly cultivated his capacities, and was well paid for doing so. His steady and handsome income as actor, playwright, and theatre manager enabled him to satisfy the aspirations he shared with his generation for family, property, friends, society, the fine arts, and literature. The values to be found in his biography are not to be found in a particularly complex or highly original or eccentric personality, but in a sustained mastery of his profession, that is his public career. He showed, however, acute sensibilities in his private life that sustained his professional one, and his activities in each enriched both English life and literature.

Garrick was fortunate in growing up in the community of a Lichfield of 3,000, which offered him almost the full range of English life outside of London, resources for a maturing boy to which he responded positively and gratefully. Small though it was, Lichfield was supported and distinguished by two major national institutions—the army and the church. As a garrison town, the social life centered in part around the officers and their families, generally younger sons of the gentry with leisured interests that only education and privilege can support. That Garrick was descended from a Huguenot wine merchant from Bordeaux meant far less to him and the community than that he was living in a garrison town, and that for 30 years his father was an officer in three of the top-ranking regiments in the aristocracy of the established army.

On 12 April 1706, the grandfather, David Garrick, bought for his son Peter a commission as ensign in Colonel James Tyrrel's (later Sir Robert Bradshaigh's) Regiment of Foot. At David's birth (19 February 1717) Peter, his father, was a lieutenant in Tyrrel's New Raised Regiment of Dragoons. That young David was born in the Angel Inn in Hereford was incidental to his parents' temporary residence there while the lieutenant was on a recruiting mission. Ten years later the father attained the rank of captain in Major General Percy Kirke's Second Regiment of Foot, the Queen's Own. All three regiments were garrisoned at various times in Lichfield. London was far away.

As a lieutenant in the Dragoons, the father, Peter, received £109.10.0 a year; as a captain in a ranking foot regiment, £182.10.0, supplemented as always in the eighteenth century by allowances for clothes, maintenance, recruiting, perquisites, all of which so add up that the purchase of a commission, running into thousands of pounds, was actually a very remunerative investment. Captain Peter Garrick was unfortunately a career officer when the Crown did not "busy giddy minds With foreign quarrels" sufficient to employ all established regiments at full pay, with the consequence that Captain Garrick for about 30 years as an officer was on half pay, though with the advantage of residing with his family in Lichfield. Eventually with a wife and seven children to support, he sought active service in August 1729 in Kirke's Second Regiment of Foot stationed at Gibraltar, and he continued at Gibraltar for five years until he returned to Lichfield less than a year before his death (1737).

Eighteenth-century incomes must not be estimated by the sum but by the purchasing power of the pound; a shilling then was equivalent to 30 shillings and more in the 1970s. Though the Garrick family lived on a basic annual income that varied from £1,000 to £2,000 to as much as £5,000 or more, in recent purchasing equivalent, and though the half pay of an officer may not have always been adequate for a large family, it was certain and honorable. Garrick later often emphasized that he grew up accustomed to strict habits of economy, as Johnson remarked "to make four-pence do as much as others made four-pence halfpenny do." This good habit laid the foundation and sustained Garrick's later fortune and bounties, though much resented by the indigent who abused his charity.

With Captain Garrick stationed at Gibraltar for five years, and the eldest son Peter in the Mediterranean and the West Indies as an ensign in the navy, under the command of Sir Chaloner Ogle, David became the resident head of the family in Lichfield. In 11 of what must have been more, letters to his father, carefully preserved by the father and later by brother Peter, David endeavored, between the age of 13 and 18, to cheer the lonely watch at Gibraltar with family news, village gossip, and some flourishes of his own wit. He noted the expenses for doctors for Mrs Garrick in her long illness, bills for rent and the baker, the clearing up of small debts—all in all half a dozen references in 11 letters in great good humor, with no apprehensions. David's request for "some hansome thing for a wastecoat & p$^r$ of Breeches . . . they tell me Velvet is very cheap at Gibralter"; the sisters' request for some money for lace for their heads to distinguish them from the "Vulgar Madams" (8,9)* are hardly cries of distress. Whether or not Captain Garrick sold his commission shortly before his death for £1,100, the approximate value of the commission, has not been settled. The sum may have been a part of the estate of £2,500 he willed (1 January 1737) his children. That Mrs Garrick is not named in the will, however, implies that Captain Garrick retained his commission whereby his widow would receive a pension, as apparently she did. David was willed one shilling, for his father anticipated a legacy of £1,000 to come to him from an Uncle David, when the boy would come of age.

In fact the Garrick family's relations to the armed forces were so satisfactory that Captain Garrick provided a commission for Peter, his eldest son; later William, the youngest son, bought a commission as an ensign in the regiment raised by Lord John Leveson-Gower, lord lieutenant of Staffordshire, to fight the Scots in 1745. Two Lichfield cousins and/or uncles, Captain Hugh Bailye and Lieutenant John Kynaston, as well as other Lichfield acquaintances, were in Captain Garrick's regiment. What is more David, age 18, enthusiastically wrote his father: "I was in great hopes I should have Recruited my Self this Spring [1735], For M$^r$ Hervey who is a Cornett in my Lord

---

*Numbers in parentheses throughout the text refer to letter numbers in David M. Little and George M. Kahrl, eds., and associate editor Phoebe DeK. Wilson, *The Letters of David Garrick*, Harvard University Press, 1963.

5

Car's Reg^nt has given me & M^r Walmisley a promise for his Commission, If his Brother in Law S^r Tho^s Aston had died," a commission worth £600 (8,10). Two months later, 24 April 1735, he continued: "I can tell my Papa I stand a good chance to get into y^e Army, I have the promise of three Lieutenant Colonells to provide for me . . . & Col. Pyot who has swore to make [me] Chaplain to his Reg^t if I should be in orders" (10). Of all the officers, with families, garrisoned in Lichfield, the Garricks were on the most congenial social relations with the Herveys. Henry Hervey, the fourth son of the Earl of Bristol, and a coronet in the King's Own Regiment of Horse (Kerr's Dragoons) had married in 1730 Catherine Aston, the daughter of Sir Thomas Aston and sister to Magdalen whom Gilbert Walmesley, about whom more shortly, was to marry in 1736. The ladies exchanged visits; Garrick wrote his father as early as 21 January 1733: "I am [a] great favourite of both of [the Herveys] and am with them every Day . . . M^r Hervey . . . Has lately come from London and has brought me two Pair of large Silver Buckles . . . and M^r Walmisley a fine Snuff Box" (1,2). Henry Hervey also noticed fellow townsman Johnson and was so kind to him that Johnson became devoted to Hervey in his dissolute and charming life and later asserted, "If you call a dog Hervey, I shall love him."

Captain Garrick, a gentleman, gave his son the sophisticated life of professional officers in a garrison town, the security of an honored profession, paternal care and affection, and the prospects of a university education, and to all these opportunities Garrick responded with a sense of personal responsibility, good humor in the circumstances in which he found himself, a relish for social life, and gratitude to friends and family. All of his later life Garrick was at ease with military friends and acquaintances. All in keeping with this inheritance Garrick produced at the age of 12, in the bishop's palace, Farquhar's *The Recruiting Officer* (currently the most popular comedy in London), with David in the lead as Kite, and at the age of 18 he was "set on to answer" by the officers some verse at their expense, "having a little smattering y^t way," some 57 lines in all in the vein of the comedy of manners (10).

Ever since John Forster obtained from William Upcott, the extensive files preserved by Garrick of his drafts and the letters of his correspondents, biographers have been grateful for ten letters, and an eleventh in the William Salt Library, which Garrick wrote his father at Gibraltar from 21 January 1733 to 25 April 1735. These letters have been almost too eagerly summarized and quoted ever since as revealing Garrick's personality as a boy or young man. Nearly all the references are to older people, not his age contemporaries in Lichfield; in these older gentry he had found an audience for his conscious and precocious sallies at wit, his mimicry, his reciting passages of dramatic poetry, his already exceptional memory, and his linguistic facility. With all the affection for the father, his mother, and brothers and sister, still one can sense a somewhat overdeveloped or exploited loquacity, what later biographers have celebrated as vivacity. It is well to recall that Johnson considered vivacity as a habit that might be cultivated. Though the remark was made years later, in 1776, Johnson was certainly thinking of the young David when he remarked, "Sir (said he) I don't know but if Peter had cultivated all the arts of gaity as much as David has done, he might have been as brisk and lively. Depend upon it, Sir, vivacity is much an art, and depends greatly on habit."[1] Clearly Garrick was self-consciously cultivating what later on the stage might better be identified as a conscious vitality and animation, and his early letters were as much addressed to an audience as to a father: He sought to cheer up the father by a kind of vivacious sparkle.

Had Garrick continued in this manner, he might very well have turned out to be the village bore; but fortunately the sort of Pickwickian dramaturgy was chastened and disciplined in the company of Walmesley and Johnson, and by an apprenticeship that began early in Lichfield and was energetically pursued in London for four years before he ventured on the stage. Some of the old Lichfield adolescence lingered on, and again and again Garrick responded to the invitation and flattery to put on as a sort of parlor stunt, passages or scenes from his popular plays—when the applause was uncritical and flattering, unlike the competitive responses of an audience in a theatre. The temptation many years later lead him to accept the invitation from the royal family to "recite" his *Lethe*, which turned out to be one of the most distressing experiences for Garrick simply because court etiquette forbad applause. No career is so brief and often pathetic as that of the child actor. Most fortunately, thanks to some of the mature members of the Lichfield community, such as Walmesley and Johnson, Garrick as a boy developed a chastening sense of comedy, glimpsed in the two short satiric pieces he sent his father. It is much to be regretted that brother Peter in his dotage destroyed the longer piece, which would have certainly reinforced the evidence for Garrick's early practicing a saving grace of wit and laughter.

Lichfield was not only a garrison town; it was also a cathedral town. As a cathedral town, there were always the chapter and diocesan officials resident in the close and a succession of young clergy fresh from the universities, almost all sons of wealthy gentry, who in the worldly wisdom of the times sought the preferments, social standing, and the leisure which the church could offer. As a result, much of the stimulating intellectual life of the community centered in the cathedral close, and there was all the drama of the yearly cycle of services in an imposing cathedral. Garrick from his mother, a granddaughter and daughter of choral vicars, inherited an entrée into the intimate and established social-intellectual community of the close.

As with so much that has to do with the 12 choral vicars in Lichfield Cathedral, the life of Garrick's maternal grandfather is a mystery. In the subscription books of the cathedral, Anthony Clough, on 25 April 1681, took the oath as "Vicar Choral belonging to the prebend of Ufton *ex parte decanti* of Cloughton als Ufton," presumably in succession to Anthony Clough, though there is no record of Anthony Clough's death in the cathedral register or in St. Mary's or St. Chad's, both in Lichfield. Though humble, the position as a choral vicar was one of the more lucrative sinecures held by many respected in the cathedral close.

There is little to recall of Mrs Peter Garrick, née Arabella Clough (d. 1740), other than David's reports on her chronic illness that was eventually fatal. She was emotionally devoted to and dependent on her husband and apparently had little influence on her children. After seeing the captain off for Gibraltar, she stayed on in London for six weeks, with the result that it was no wonder she found the children in rags when she returned to Lichfield. Davies, who never met her, has left this brief characterization, almost certainly from Samuel Johnson, even in Johnson's words: "Mrs. Garrick, though not beautiful in her person, was very attractive in her manner; her address was polite, and her conversation sprightly and engaging: she had the peculiar happiness, wherever she went, to please and to entertain."[2]

The house on Bird, now Beacon Street, occupied by the Garricks was opposite and second door to the south from the cathedral gate, and belonged to the prebend of Wolvey, apparently for the organist. The house, rebuilt after the destructive siege of the Civil War, was located at the end of the causeway and on an acre, "more or less," of land that reached down to the old marshes to the west and south. Garrick once called the house, his home, "y$^e$ Castle on y$^e$ Bridge" (114). In the 1730s when Garrick was writing to his father, the grandmother, Arabella Clough, was living with the family, though she may have been the tenant (as widow of a vicar-general) and the family living with her. Garrick mentions paying a rent of £10 to Richard Rider, the deputy registrar of the cathedral. In Garrick's boyhood the house must have been a substantial dwelling with accommodations for eight to ten persons and conveniently located in a respectable neighborhood near the close.[3]

Garrick had other ties with the cathedral and the close. The births and deaths of some of his brothers and sisters and the deaths of his parents are recorded in the cathedral registers, and presumably the parents and some of the siblings were buried in the close. Nor is it surprising that 12 relatively unoccupied and securely endowed choral vicars should beget a numerous progeny, and that many Lichfield families should be interrelated in the close. Through his mother's family, Garrick had three uncles, or great uncles, choral vicars, named Morgan, Kynaston, and Bailye, and quite a few acquaintances who were sons of choral vicars.

In the 20 years of his life as a boy and adolescent in Lichfield, Garrick profited most of all by the guidance, patronage, and society of Lichfield's most respected gentleman-scholar, Gilbert Walmesley, registrar of the ecclesiastical court, who lived in the bishop's palace. Well-born, wealthy, a graduate of Trinity College, Oxford, called to the bar at the Inner Temple, he read widely, cultivated liberal tastes, and enjoyed good conversation. Walmesley and Captain Garrick were good friends; his kindnesses to David were to a member of a respected family. "Davy was in and out every day." "This young gentleman," Walmesley wrote to John Colson, 5 February 1736[?7], recommending David to him as a tutee, "you must know, has bin much w$^{th}$ me, ever since he was a child, almost every day;, & I have taken Pleasure often in Instructing him & have a great Affection & Esteem for him."[4] In eight of the 11 letters Garrick wrote to his father at Gibraltar, David mentions Walmesley 16 times, generally in connection with petitions for Captain Garrick to return from Gibraltar. The one personal reference affords some sense of the quality of a long association: "I have been to M$^r$ Ofleys who sent a Man & horse for me with M$^r$ & M$^{rs}$ Harvey & M$^r$ Walmisley, were I got acquainted with his two Sons, who are fine young Gentlemen, M$^r$ Walmisley gave me slyly, half a crown for y$^e$ Butler & another for y$^e$ Groom, for my self, which made me look very grand" (1). Tradition, doubtless founded on idle speculation, singled out David as Walmesley's heir, until in the spring of 1736, at the age of 56 he married Magdalen Aston. Walmesley introduced Garrick to a library such as he certainly did not find at home, to literature as embodying ideas, and to a respect for humane letters.[5] One small bibliographical momento has survived of Walmesley's supervision of Garrick's education, giving some insight into Garrick's classical education (which Johnson never allowed anyone to question). Walmesley inscribed to David *Le Jardin des Racines Grecques* (1701), a new edition (1719) by Claude Lancelot and L. J. LeMaistre de Sacy—an alphabetical listing of Greek roots with French meanings, cast in some 216 stanzas of from nine to 12 lines each, plus additional lexicographical material. The inscription reads in part: "D.D.D.G.G.W ca vero conditione, ut unam quoque die paginam memoriter ad verbum ediscat; postq, quovis tempore sine scripto verbis eisdem reddere ac pronunciare paratus promptusq, fuerit. Lichf. 30 Julii a,d, 1732."[6] From the careful underlinings on each of the pages in Section I, and the annotations giving the Latin equivalents in the margin, one gathers that Garrick used the book energetically to gain some command of Greek, particularly in relation to his studies of Latin and French.

Contemporaries in Lichfield and subsequent biographers have always associated Samuel Johnson with Garrick and Walmesley. Michael Johnson, with all his industry and ambition, opened for his son Samuel only the Lichfield communities of the Market Place, the Guildhall, and St. Mary's, with little security and less guidance and help in finding a livelihood. According to Boswell, Johnson had "a kind reception in the best families at Lichfield. Among these I can mention Mr. Howard, Dr. Swinfen, Mr Simpson, Mr Levett, Captain Garrick . . . Mr. Gilbert Walmisley." The earliest anecdote of Johnson and Garrick is the oft-repeated query of Mrs Garrick "how little David went on at school," to which Johnson replied "he would probably come to be hanged, or come to be a great man." When some young people certainly including David and his sisters proposed acting Ambrose Philips's *The Distressed Mother*, Samuel wrote a special prologue. This was followed by Garrick's production, as noted above, of Farquhar's *The Recruiting Officer*. David and Samuel had in common the superior Lichfield Grammar School, but Johnson, seven years older, was no longer a pupil when Garrick entered. For over a 100 years, however, university graduates as tutors and master had been preparing local boys there for Oxford and Cambridge, and in Garrick's own day under the Reverend John Hunter, headmaster, a remarkable number of later distinguished men were educated at the school.

Gilbert Walmesley was also the moving spirit in Johnson's venture as headmaster of the school at Edial, where Garrick and brother George were to be pupils, and where Garrick, as Walmesley remarked, might perfect his Italian and French. Of the Edial schooling, we are now bothered that Garrick later caricatured Johnson and his wife, Tetty, in a bedroom scene, so much so that a distinguished Johnson scholar recently journeyed to Edial to inspect the size of the keyhole through which Garrick spied on his master, moved by the pathos of the union, rather than the comedy as Garrick and others regarded it. Johnson presumably told Davies, Garrick's first biographer, that while at Edial Garrick's "thoughts were constantly employed on the stage; for even at that time he was very busy in composing plays . . . he showed [Johnson] several scenes of a new comedy, which had engrossed his time; and these, he told him, were the produce of his third attempt in dramatic poetry."[7] On the other hand Garrick inspired, if he did not actually assist Johnson in the latter's drafting his own tragedy *Irene*. The sooner one minimizes the Johnson-Garrick relationship as that of master to pupil (they never referred to each other in these terms) the better one sees their friendship in the more enduring common devotion to the theatre and humane letters.

Close as Garrick was to Lichfield in his early years and to his mature friends there, he did have a chance at about age 15 to see briefly the London metropolis, and cross the Channel to Lisbon, where his uncle, for whom he was named, a considerable wine merchant, invited him. Presumably David was to make a connection, enter a business, and pursue a way of life in the trade. His stay, however, endured but a year, for while there he did more to entertain the English merchants in town by reciting passages from plays at their banquets than to apply himself seriously to the wine business. Yet he made a connection which stood him in good stead in his venture several years later in partnership with his brother Peter in a London wine and spirits business. His uncle did later bequeath him 1,000 pounds, but Garrick returned to Lichfield and to school.

While much of the cultural history for which Lichfield is famous developed after Garrick left it for good, the sources were all vigorous in his boyhood, and through family and boyhood ties, Garrick maintained a lively interest in all that was going on in his native village, and Lichfield in turn kept very much in touch with Garrick. Perhaps the most effective and sustaining support of Garrick's decision to embark on a theatrical career, came from two clerical Lichfield acquaintances, with whom he maintained a lifetime friendship, though both like Garrick ceased to continue to reside there. Joseph Smith (1687–1781), whom Garrick addressed in 1776 as "an old friend & school fellow," was ordained in Lichfield and became for life rector of Great Stanmore, near Hampton, he assisted Garrick in finding and restoring his residence there and was long Garrick's neighbor in Hampton. After attending Garrick's first performances at Goodman's Fields Theatre he wrote (25 January 1742) "You Surpass all whom I ever remember to have seen upon the Stage . . . you are not made for tragedy only: the Sock becomes you as much as the buskin" (20,1012,792, 805).[8] The other, Thomas Newton (1704–82) ordained in his native

Lichfield in 1730 and later (1761) bishop of Bristol, as a young man was very fond of the social life in Lichfield and of versifying. When Newton was conducting services at the Grosvenor Chapel in London (1741) he also attended Garrick's first season performances at Goodman's Fields, and wrote Garrick seven very full, analytical, and commendatory letters in praise of his acting: "You need make no apology for your profession, at least to me. I always thought you was a born actor, if ever any man was so." Garrick carefully preserved the letters grateful for Newton's encouragement and excellent critical advice. They braced him as he wrote to Peter—"I have receiv'd Several very pretty Letters for M$^r$ Newton, y$^e$ Clergyman who has been Several Times to See Me" (20). Later in 1743 Newton dined with Garrick and solicited his assistance in persuading Jacob Tonson II and Somerset Draper (Garrick's friends) to publish his edition of Milton. He also asked Garrick's judgment on the illustrations being prepared by another Garrick friend, the artist Frank Hayman (10,11,20,32).[9] When Garrick was seeking a scholar to complete the editing of what was eventually to be a ten-volume edition of Beaumont and Fletcher (originally undertaken by Oldys in 1745) he interviewed and engaged Thomas Seward (1708–90), canon of Lichfield and Salisbury. Years later the Lichfieldian connection was still lively when James Wickins, a church warden in Lichfield, sent Garrick (1772) "a small pedistal and vase" carved from the wood of Shakespeare's mulberry tree, the "finishing stroke of which was given by M$^r$ Peter Garrick with *his* Varnish." Garrick thanked him in a pleasant note (721).

The roll call might be lengthened of natives and residents whom Garrick knew and kept in touch with over the years, and who in turn both introduced and welcomed Garrick to intellectual and cultural interests and social circles, well above and beyond the resources of a small country village. No more revealing example of Garrick's standing in Lichfield and his respect for his fellow natives exists than his long unknown letter to his brother George of 30 August 1766, wherein he requests that he not be nominated for Parliament from that town: "The Seat at Lichfield is too costly a one for Me—Lord G[ower] has too much Interest, & tho' I may have half a Dozen Loving friends for Me, yet I sh$^d$ be oblig'd to sneak with my tail between my Legs, out of y$^e$ Town Hall, up Bow-Street, & pass by the Free School as Miserable, as I once was Merry" (426).

Nor as resident in London did Garrick forget his Lichfield friends and acquaintances, warmly inviting and welcoming them to Drury Lane or to his home. A delegation of Lichfieldians attended the Stratford Jubilee to greet him in 1769. Of all the responses to his acting and hospitality, the one most often recalled was recounted by William Cooke in his *Memoirs of Charles Macklin* of the Lichfield grocer, who came to London with a letter of introduction to Garrick from Peter Garrick, saw him act Abel Drugger, and returned without calling on him. He said to Peter: "I saw enough of him on the stage. He may be rich, as I dare say any man who lives like him must be; but, by G–d, . . . Tho' he is your brother, Mr. Garrick, he is one of the shabbiest, meanest, most pitiful hounds I ever saw in the whole course of my life."

To return from the lasting friendships with Lichfieldians to Garrick's departure for London 2 March 1737, aged 20, we come again to Johnson. With the failure of the school at Edial, and Garrick unable to go on for a university degree for lack of finances, Johnson and Garrick set out to make their way in London, once again supported by the patronage of Gilbert Walmesley. He had written to the Reverend John Colson, son of a Lichfield choral vicar and head of the Free School at Rochester, in part: "My neighbor, Captain Garrick (who is an honest and valuable man) has a son who is a very sensible young fellow, and a good scholar, and whom the Captain hopes, in some two or three years, he shall be able to send to the Temple, and breed to the Bar. But at present his pocket will not hold out for sending him to the University. I have proposed your taking him, . . . and instructing him in mathematics, and philosophy, and humane learning. He is now nineteen, of sober and good disposition, and is as ingenious and promising a young man as ever I knew in my life."

Colson replied he would take Garrick on, and Walmesley wrote again the day Johnson and Garrick set out: "He and another neighbor of mine, one Mr. Johnson, set out this morning for London together: Davy Garrick to be with you early the next week, and Mr. Johnson to try his fate with a tragedy and seek to get himself employed in some translation, either from the Latin or the French. Johnson is a very good scholar and poet, and I have great hopes will turn out a fine tragedy writer." [10]

This ended Walmesley's direct influence on the two, but years later Johnson in his *Life of Edmund Smith* paid tribute of special gratitude to Gilbert Walmesley—a tribute that Garrick also might well have rendered, for Johnson closed, "It may be doubted whether a day now passes in which I have not some advantage from his friendship."

Seeking to glamorize the momentous adventuring up to London by the two men, biographers, undoubtedly with the analogy of Tom Jones and Parson Adams in mind, have repeated two remarks preserved by Boswell, which Garrick and Johnson humorously concocted to sentimentalize the occasion. "Garrick, evidently meaning to embellish a little, said one day in my hearing, 'we rode and tied.'" Johnson on another occasion when he and Garrick were dining together "in a pretty large company, Johnson humourously ascertaining the chronology of something, expressed himself thus: 'that was the year when I came to London with two-pence half-penny in my pocket.' Garrick over-hearing him exclaimed, 'eh? what do you say? with two-pence half-penny in your pocket?'—Johnson, 'Why yes; when I came with two-pence half-penny in *my* pocket, and thou, Davy, with three half pence in thine.'" [11] On Garrick's initiative, they are reported to have borrowed £5 from Wilcox, a secondhand-book dealer, with whom Garrick was slightly acquainted but who later became one of Johnson's best friends. Johnson continued in London for around three months, cultivating the art of living there on 30 pounds a year, and then returned to Lichfield for the summer. Garrick was not a stranger in London; he had passed through on his way out and return from his sojourn with his Uncle David in Lisbon, and tradition has it that his Lichfield friends raised a purse that he might for a while attend the theatres in London; besides he had some of his father's family resident in London. After enrolling at Lincoln's Inn on 9 March, he went on to study under Colson in the Free School at Rochester, presumably only until the autumn. The death of Captain Garrick on 19 March, left Garrick unsettled until Peter came up to London in late summer and the two entered upon a partnership in the wine trade on their combined inheritance.

When Garrick and Johnson settled in London, they by no means broke with Lichfield; rather home ties were almost tragically tightened by the death of Johnson's brother Nathaniel, two days after their departure and of Garrick's father a week later. Peter, Garrick's older brother, had apparently left the navy and returned to Lichfield by 1736 when Johnson borrowed from him Richard Knolles's *General History of the Turks* and began writing his tragedy *Irene*. Peter, nine months older, had been with him in the Lichfield Grammar School. In the autumn of 1737, Peter was in London with David to launch their partnership in the wine trade and Johnson sought out Peter to whom he read his play in the Fountain Tavern. Peter in turn solicited Charles Fleetwood, the manager of Drury Lane, and tried to prevail upon him to produce the play, but to no avail. Just how Peter knew Fleetwood is a minor mystery. Peter apparently continued to live off and on with David in London, and during the three years from 1737 to 1741, Johnson was often with the Garrick brothers in London and occasionally must have been with Peter in Lichfield. Garrick staged

Fielding's *Mock Doctor* at Johnson's bequest for Edward Cave and his staff of the *Gentleman's Magazine* in St. John's Gate, and Garrick and Johnson certainly were often in each other's company in the Hervey home. One evening, at a tavern, Johnson composed his moving epitaph on Claudy Philips, the wandering musician whom both had known in Lichfield—an epitaph that Garrick recalled from memory 25 years later for Boswell. Finally Johnson mediated between Peter and David in the friction that arose from David's increasing absorption in the theatre to the neglect of the wine business.

Peter became for both David and Johnson their one common sustaining bond with Lichfield. After four years back and forth between London and Lichfield, Peter settled in Lichfield (10 June 1741) and prospered in his wine trade, 20 years later forming a partnership (1761–69) with a cousin, Richard Bailye. At first he may have resided with his spinster sister(s); later at a date not determined, he moved north next door, in a house also belonging to the choral vicars, directly opposite the cathedral gate, hence called to this day Westgate House.[12] The handsome residence, with the later addition of a fourth floor, is now a dormitory for girls. During Peter's occupancy there was an extensive garden which was Peter's and a part-time gardener's special care for 37 years. With the passing of the years, Peter prospered, leased and bought freeholds, served on a jury, headed up the Lichfield Volunteers raised to resist the invasion of Prince Charles in 1745, signed the will of Frances Gastrell (1772), often borrowed books from the cathedral library, but above all else he supported the St. Cecelia Society.

From its founding in 1739, the St. Cecelia Society became the sponsor of the most important musical concerts and social gatherings in the close. The most honorable and responsible office was that of steward, which Peter, honored with an Esquire, held a number of times from 1741 on. He kept the manuscript records of the society, a partial transcript of which is in the William Salt Library, copied by Thomas Fernybough, verger in the cathedral, who lived opposite Peter in Beacon Street. In 1742 Peter ordered through David musical instruments for the orchestra; in 1745 David attended the concert and ball; later he sent Peter sconces for the Vicar's Hall, used as a theatre; in 1747 the St. Cecelia library included some 30 volumes of music.[13]

In 1740, after three years as partners, David was writing Peter in Lichfield accounting for his transactions in the wine trade, but the autumn of 1741 brought the partnership to a crisis. David was overwhelmed by the praise of his first acting season at Goodman's Fields that confirmed his inclinations and abilities as an actor that he had been nervously and almost surreptitiously cultivating for three years, yet all the while he was apprehensive and distressed over what he knew was the very low opinion of actors. Above all else he sought to win Peter's approval, and when Peter wrote reprobating David's decision, David responded: "My Dear Brother. The uneasiness I have receiv'd w$^{th}$ Y$^r$ Letter is inexpressible; however 'twas a Shock I expected & had guarded Myself as well as I could against it, and y$^e$ Love I sincerely have for You togeather with y$^e$ prevailing Arguments You have made Use of were enough to overthrow My Strongest Resolutions did not Necessity (a very pressing Advocate) on My Side convince me that I am not so much to blame as You Seem to think I am . . . & as My Genius that Way (by y$^e$ best Judges) is thought Wonderfull how can You be so averse to My proceedings when not only my Inclinations, but My Friends who at first were Surpriz'd at my intent, by seeing me on y$^e$ Stage, are now well convinc'd twas impossible for Me to keep off " (17). He elaborates how he has been losing the money of his inheritance in the wine trade, but more to the point, he should be able to make a most satisfying income as an actor and be accepted into the best company. David continues his defense in several most affectionate and considerate and persuasive letters, adding that his cousins the Fermignacs from Carshalton and Mr Charles Sudall with Lichfield people had been to see him and were persuaded of the wisdom of the decision. These half a dozen letters to Peter, thoughtful, documented, and containing patient apologia and defense of his determined choice of the career in which he triumphed as no other English actor ever has, reveal both Garrick's command of himself and his command of his career for the ensuing 30 years and more, and move us to honor the high calling of the theatre. Within six months after the first of these letters to Peter, Peter responded on 21 February 1742: "You know your good fortune is as pleasing to me as my own, I wonder you did not give me my share of pleasure, & let me know all your good fortune, however for the future beg you'l let me hear from You once a fort-night at least, & I assure you will never trouble you with more Commissions."[14] Of the ensuing correspondence only one other of Peter's letters survives (1 June 1765), but there are 38 of David's, full of London, theatrical, family, and Lichfield news, greetings to the Walmesleys, and all graced with affection. So much in these letters is fraught with meaning to the brothers, especially the Lichfield allusions, and yet they are almost meaningless now to us unless we dip deeply into the community life of Lichfield where the brothers had their roots and flourished. Peter engaged a gardener for David, made inquiries about the possibility of buying a local estate that involved

Brooke Boothby and John Taylor; visited with David, the Burlingtons at Londesburgh, and Sir Watkin Williams Wynn in Wales. One example of Garrick's letters, 1740, shows the spirit, though not the identity and relations of mutual friends as it comes through to us.

Pray my best services to M$^r$ Sudal [a neighbor on Beacon Street] & tell him his Nephew is at present very well tho he has been troubled with his old Disorder, I have got Drapar [an apothecary and a brother of Garrick's good friend, Somerset Draper] to take him to D$^r$ Pellet a very Eminent Physician [fellow and recently president of the Royal College of Physicians] who has prescrib'd for him & I dont doubt but he will relieve him; he is a very honest, sober, sensible Young fellow & I dont doubt but will turn out well, he cannot get into y$^e$ Hospital till Michelmas, he is therefore advis'd till then to Attend D$^r$ Nichols Lectures [physician to George II] which will be of infinite Service to him & Serve by way of preparation for y$^e$ hospital Studies, I will take care of him till then & preach up Oeconomy & Virtue to him; I have already given him a just detestation for y$^e$ lewd Night Walkers & vile polluters of Youth; he always smiles when I begin my Lecture & cries FLEE Y$^e$, You talk WELLY [well-nigh] as well as M$^r$ Hinton, (a favourite Clergyman of his at Lichfield) Drapar gives him all y$^e$ Instruction he can & sends him to visit his patients every Day; he likewise tells me he is an understanding Youth & wants Nothing but a little polishing of his Dialect which has much of y$^e$ Staffordshire twang with It. I would advise M$^r$ Sudal to Let him attend D$^r$ Nichols Lectures, tell him I say so, & that Damn him I have a small veneration for his rotund Paunch & no despicable opinion of his Brains & that Likewise I have a much greater for [the] Rest of his family (12).

If Peter in his occasional visits to David and perhaps Johnson in London, expanded under the fame and fortune of his brother, David did no less when he often returned to Lichfield, at first alone and then with Mrs Garrick. There he was received into a well-appointed residence of a prospering and respected brother who lived at ease as a member of the increasingly distinguished society of the close. And when Johnson after 1769 began making his visits every year or two to Lichfield, he was often received and entertained by Peter, who also welcomed the Thrales, and later was called on by Boswell in search of biographical material, some of which is recorded in his *Journals* and embodied in the *Life of Samuel Johnson*. In his final illness Peter was attended by Dr Erasmus Darwin and his approaching death memorialized by Anna Seward: "It is melancholy that the light of reason and comic originality should be utterly darkened with poor Peter Garrick, before the long and mornless night descends." [15]

In the 40 years that Garrick and Johnson were both in London, each going his own way professionally and socially, it is remarkable how the friendship endured, how much they were together, how much they assisted each other, how many friends they shared. Their correspondence is no measure of their diverse relations; their rivalries were subordinate to their devotion. From first to last the Lichfield ties endured. Johnson wrote Boswell from Ashbourne after a visit to Lichfield on 1 September 1777: "The friends which merit or usefulness can procure us, are not able to supply the place of old acquaintances, with whom the days of our youth may be retraced, and those images revived which gave the earliest delight." [16] Garrick and Johnson each had his own circle of friends and family in Lichfield, in London, and elsewhere. This is not the occasion to enumerate the continuing relationships they shared with Lichfield acquaintances, such for example as Dr Robert James and Joseph Simpson, whose biographies, meaningless now to us, were fraught with memories for the two men.

With the successful production of Garrick's *Lethe* on 15 April, and Johnson's return from his wanderings to labor for Cave, from that year, 1740, they were not together in Lichfield again except perhaps in 1761–62 when Johnson returned after an absence of 22 years and the Garricks were on a visit to Peter. From then on Johnson returned semiannually; but not until 1775, after entertaining Lichfield friends in London, did Garrick write one of his guests, cousin Richard Bailye: "Tell all my Lichfield friends that I long to be with them, & that I certainly intend to shake Every dirty fist from Bacon Street to Green hill some time in y$^e$ Summer" (968). And on 21 March, with the sale of the patent, that is of Drury Lane, to be completed on 24 June, he wrote Peter: "I wish from my Soul I could tell You when I shall be in Lichfield . . . I really feel y$^e$ Joy, I us'd to do, when I was a boy at a breaking up" of school. He then continues: "D$^r$ Johnson & M$^r$ Boswell will be at Lichfield almost as soon as this—he is coming to take his leave of you all before his departure for Italy [with the Thrales—prevented by illness]. You are Johnson's prime favourite" (995). On the next day, 23 March, and again on the twenty-fourth, Johnson and Boswell called on Peter several times, recorded in the well-known passages in the *Life*, where both Johnson and Boswell remark on the "family likeness of the Garricks." Johnson and Garrick were back in Lichfield in 1776 and 1777, but not at the same time, yet we may be sure not without reminiscences about old Lichfield and acquaintances and memories of each other.

Finally, one other circumstance in the community of Lichfield reinforced if it did not originate Garrick's familial loyalties that made heavy claims at times on his patience and resources. Anyone who has looked into the records, antiquarian and historical publications, or consulted

Aleyn Lyell Reade's *Johnsonian Gleanings*, all covering Lichfield biography, must be impressed above all else how everyone thought of himself and his fellow townsmen in terms of family. Basic to this attitude, to be sure, was the eighteenth-century correlation between property and family. Marriage was a legal contract, and children were heirs to property; in fact the ownership of most property originated in a will and not in a deed of sale. Also there was a pervasive social classification by family origins and professions and trades, a structured class system that cultivated and enforced familial obligations.

To what extent Garrick inherited his sense of family obligations and affections from his French origins is most conjectural. His forebears were among the French refugees who for generations preserved memory and habits of their origins in the Huguenot community in London. The family still extant originated in the barren country (as the name *Garrique* implies) near Castres, and the grandfather, David, was in Bordeaux when driven to England in 1685 by the revocation of the Edict of Nantes. His son, Peter, was too young for the hazardous journey by sea and it was not until 1687, when he was 18 months old that he was smuggled out of France in the arms of a nurse. How much David's grandson David's affections were intensified by familial memories of persecution and exile and poverty, as stoically chronicled in his grandfather's diary, Garrick never revealed. One of his aunts, Mary Magdalene, married a Fermignac cousin; and Jane, another aunt, married a French compatriot Louis La Condé. Both families settled at Carshalton, and with the descendants of these two families Garrick kept in touch all his life. Furthermore, his uncle, David, in an episode that is obscure, invited him when he was about 12 to Lisbon to be an apprentice in the wine trade. Just why nothing came of this apprenticeship is not known, though it has been conjectured that the uncle found the boy too spirited to be congenial. In 1737, however, Garrick inherited from the Lisbon uncle a thousand pounds, partly in compensation for the time lost in his education and partly because he was the namesake.

As for Garrick's immediate family, following the death of his father in 1737 and his mother in 1740, David, in affection, and with the resources his success brought him to show this affection, became the virtual head of the family, though his brother Peter, as already remarked long held up the family name in Lichfield but without heirs. Of the three sisters who lived on in Lichfield, Jane (born 4 January 1718) died unmarried in 1745 and Magdalene (1715) in 1764, while Merrial married Thomas Docksey and survived until 1799, often dependent on David's loans and later Peter's benefactions. The Dockseys had only one daughter, Merrial. David's brother William, after an unsettled beginning in the army, drops out of Garrick's letters.

Garrick's family affections were put to the severest tests by George (1723–79). Little is known of George's life in Lichfield before 1746 when David wrote Peter he had obtained through his friend John Paterson, the London city solicitor, a place for George in his office. With all of David's recommendations and hopes and advice, nothing came of this opportunity, and by 1750 George had become for life David's assistant in all the routine management of Drury Lane and the mollifying mediary between the exacting standards of his brother and the irresponsibility of some in the company of actors. Just what compensation George received at first is uncertain, but by 1767 he was receiving an annual allowance of £100 from David plus £200 from the theatre. From the first George exceeded his income and survived on the bounty of David, though under the guise of loans. Typical is the entry made by David in his diary on 26 July 1755: "the same Day I cancell'd another Bond due to me from George date y$^e$ 20th of April 1750 for 200£ w$^{ch}$ he is to pay me when he grows rich."[17] It was a thankless job that George had at Drury Lane, yet he carried on season in and season out with the tolerance of the company and gratitude from David.

What irritations arose between the brothers grew mostly out of George's domestic life. Sometime in 1751–52, in the Savoy Chapel, whose records are now lost, George married Catherine, the daughter of Nathan Carrington, a king's messenger for 50 years. Garrick wrote out for George the draft of the letter of proposal George sent (99). Carrington, by exploiting every privilege of the office, amassed a small fortune on an annual salary of £45. In 1752, undoubtedly with Carrington's influence, George became a stablekeeper in the royal household and moved into Somerset House. Here, under the influence of an ambitious grandparent, also resident in Somerset House, George's five children grew up, and after their father's second marriage in 1771, were entirely dependent on the bounty of the grandparent and uncle.

Carrington, George's eldest son, was sent to Eton and Cambridge, ordained by the Bishop of London in 1776, and shortly thereafter instituted vicar at Hendon on presentation of Garrick, who owned the advowson—all pretty much at Garrick's expense. David, the second son, early settled upon an army career and was sent by his uncle to study in The Academy, which later became the University of Geneva. All the while he held a commission as a cornet in the Royal Regiment of Dragoons, presumably purchased by his grandfather. Asthma and obesity necessitated resignation of the commission, and for a while he resided with his aunt and uncle, appearing in amateur theatricals. Later Garrick tried in vain to obtain another commission for this nephew. In the end, when David married Emma Hart in 1778, Garrick settled upon him as a wedding gift an estate that he had bought in 1757 in Essex. Even the third son, Nathan, though as a namesake favored by the grandfather, enjoyed his uncle's bounty, notably while at Eton. Without exception, George's sons little merited their uncle's continued kindness, and not one of them amounted to anything.

Destined to be childless himself, Garrick took an even more personal interest in George's two daughters, Arabella and Catherine. Not only did he make the arrangements for their education in Paris but also guided their tastes and included them in parties at Hampton. When Arabella married Captain Frederick Schaw in 1778, Garrick assumed the role of father, and with all that involved financially in the eighteenth century. In his will he left the girls £6,000 apiece.

As if to cap a profitable career of dependency, in 1771, George married Elizabeth Tetley, an actress, and moved out of Somerset House. Their only son, George, was for many years an actor and left numerous descendants, some of whom are now living in Canada.

Over the years Garrick took his brother George more and more into his confidence, demanded an increase in his salary, and gave him added responsibilities. The later letters of the brothers were generally written when one or the other was ill at Bath, and though taken up mostly with theatrical matters, they are affectionate on family affairs, except for a brief interlude when Garrick felt that George had not treated him with complete candor about his finances. This was in 1771, when in a letter of clarification and reconciliation Garrick wrote George (25 January): "did I Ever keep any Concern of any kind from You, have I not always open'd my heart, & designs to You, have You not had permission to open my letters, & know Every thing about me, & my affairs?" (621,336,337,605). Two months later Garrick concluded a letter packed with instructions, comments, reports, covering Hampton, artists, actors, playwrights, tickets for various productions, management of property, studies of a nephew. "I must intreat when you go to my house to do y$^e$ above business, that you will see my poor cat fed with y$^e$ milk we have sent for her—if you don't see her dip her whiskers in it, that unfeeling devil [maid] in y$^e$ house, will make up a Sack posset to dip Cautherly's chin in. Should you discover anything—pray put somebody into y$^e$ house & turn her out *directly*. Ask for y$^e$ milk, & say you promis'd Me to see her fed" (626).

"George was always in anxiety," according to Charles Dibdin in his autobiography, "lest in his absence his brother should have wanted him; and the first question he asked on his return was, 'Did David want me?'." George died two weeks after his brother, in 1779, which circumstance being remarked in the greenroom at Drury Lane, as Dibdin reports, and noticed as extraordinary. "Extraordinary," said old Bannister, "not at all—David wanted him." [18]

If Johnson conferred upon Lichfield his fame, Lichfield endowed Garrick richly in family, in friends, in education, in devotion to literature, and with a sense of comedy and tragedy—logistics and qualities that supported the actor and patterns that remained with him throughout his brilliant career—a career of growing triumph from London, to Paris, to Rome, to Munich, and back to London again. Yet in the thoughts of many, including his own reflections, he was Lichfield's David Garrick. There, in the cathedral, Mrs Garrick chose for the memorializing inscription the few famous lines, identified only as the observations of a friend, Johnson's tribute to Garrick: "I am disappointed by that stroke of death, which has eclipsed the gaity of nations, and impoverished the public stock of harmless pleasure." [19]

While the customs and qualities of Lichfield prevailed and flourished, David Garrick, with all his talents and ambitions, matured and succeeded in London in ways far beyond the horizon or imaginings of his Lichfield home community.

# Garrick and the Acting Tradition

·

Just before Garrick went up to London as many as five theatres were in some manner flourishing and competing there, as well as many booths during the Mayfair and Bartholomew Fair seasons. Entertainment was wide-ranging, often experimental, and especially during the 1730s fraught with political satire against the Walpole regime. The Licensing Act of 1737, just when Garrick and Dr. Johnson came to the great city, reduced the legal operation of entertainment to the two royal patent theatres in Dury Lane and Covent Garden, with opera sanctioned at the Haymarket. In 1729, however, Thomas Odell had erected a new theatre in Ayliffe Street, Goodman's Fields, the management of which he gave to Henry Giffard, an actor from Dublin. Giffard in 1733 erected a larger one in Leman Street, Goodman's Fields, far from the central theatre district. Giffard's hopes were high for years of success.

The Licensing Act was a blow, for it not only limited the number of theatres, but also controlled the plays acted in them, stating that no new play, interlude, farce, or other entertainment could be performed for gain without the sanction of the Lord Chamberlain's Office, nor could any new act, scene, or other part be added to any old play without similar sanction. Penalty for not complying was a £50 fine for "every person so offending, and for each offense."[1] Scores of actors were thus disadvantaged, and the patent theatres gained a near monopoly which they were not anxious to relinquish.

Loopholes in the act were sought out immediately, and bold managers made haste, for several years, to slip through them. The act had specified that "no person shall for *hire, gain* or *reward* act, perform, or represent, or cause to be acted . . . any new play." Giffard, and some others, therefore devised the "concert" formula, whereby admission was charged for the music, but during the intermission gentlemen would perform "gratis" a play or interlude for the diversion of those attending the music. By this device Giffard and the Goodman's Fields theatre were able to carry on for five seasons, until the royal patentees, John Rich and Charles Fleetwood, were able to have the house closed down.

Garrick as soon as he arrived in London enrolled to read law at Lincoln's Inn (9 March 1737), but very soon attended the theatres and made friends easily with the actors. To these he revealed his stage interests while he was a working partner with his brother Peter in the wine business. One such acquaintance was Henry Giffard, who was still trying to obtain a license for his theatre. Garrick wrote to Peter (5 July 1740) in Lichfield asking him, among items pertinent to the wine trade, to speak to his neighbor John Webster who knew Charles Maddockes, deputy secretary to the Lord Chamberlain, and to ask him to put a favorable word for Giffard's pending appeal for the license. How far young Garrick was in with Giffard, who was within a year to launch him as an actor, is indicated by the fact that during the preceding March Garrick had written a skit called *Lethe*, and had given it to Giffard as an after piece for his benefit at Drury Lane 15 April 1740. It was accepted by Fleetwood—that is by Charles Macklin, his stage manager—and proved to be a continuing success thereafter season upon season. The piece was a boon not only to Giffard, but to the two prominent actor-singers of Drury Lane John Beard, the great tenor, and Catherine Clive. They sang the songs Garrick had written into the piece for them, both on stage and off, again, and again, and again. Garrick was also getting further acquainted with Charles Macklin, some of whose concepts of acting appealed to him.

In March 1741 Giffard, operating his "concert" formula at Goodman's Fields, launched a new pantomime *Harlequin Student*, featuring the introduction of a Monument to Shakespeare, with the gist of the performance showing the fall of pantomime and the restoration of true speaking drama. Tradition has it that Richard Yates, in the part of Harlequin, was ill one night, so Giffard asked young Garrick to mime the part. He was masked, of course, so no identity was revealed. During the summer season that year Giffard took a group of actors to the theatre in Ipswich, Garrick with them. There Garrick played the role of Aboan in Southerne's *Oroonoko*, where his face was blackened to make him up as the royal slave. Under the name of Lyddall he also appeared as Duretete in Farquhar's *The Inconstant*.

Garrick's excitement was great. He had written for the stage, and acted upon it, but tied as he was to his Lichfield family and friends in the cathedral close he felt he must keep these activities secret, so as not to embarrass them until he could prove successful. This, his actual apprenticeship, had been short in the art that had attracted him since the age of 12, back in his town in Staffordshire.

Were he to continue seriously as an actor he knew that he must compete ultimately with the then leading men on the stage. Theatre management in London was still having its difficulties after the break-up of the regime of Barton Booth, Robert Wilks, and Colley Cibber, but performances continued and audiences were pleased with a James Quin, whose lovely rich voice, declamatory style, and statuesque stance dominated role action. Quin's competitor, the lusty fat actor John Harper pleased in Falstaff, and in the roles of booby country gentlemen, Dennis Delane's star was rising, though soon to be sunk by the bottle. His rant and eye-rolling in Othello, and his similar action in *Alexander the Great* drew a following, as did his gentler portrayal of Bevil, Jr, in Steele's *Conscious Lovers*. William Havard, the graceful, reliable wheelhorse for excellency in supporting roles, and the old versatile John Mills, who could act 50 different roles well (and was but beginning to yield parts such as Dominique in *The Spanish Fryar* to Quin), and William Milward, a Hamlet of stature, but who (as Davies notes) could not distinguish noise from passion, and rant from sensibility, were highly accepted in the public eye. John Dunstall, who had risen from a start in the booths at the London fairs was becoming a success at Covent Garden. The solid Roger Bridgewater, a huff-bluff Ventidius in *All for Love* and a raging Tamerlane was well spoken of in comic parts as well. John Hippisley the comedian of low parts, precise in his study and performance, especially as a drunken man, had top billing. James Taswell, scholarly and careful, was a great Polonius, and also a credible Dogberry. He was being advanced by Macklin. There was Lacy Ryan who had begun playing as a youth with Betterton, and among many others stood Charles Macklin himself, craggy, opinionated, devoted to the art, who was breaking new ground in an absorbing sort of realistic rather than stylized performance. Theophilus Cibber, though an annoyance to everyone, could still carry a group of actors with him, and perform many parts with conviction. And Garrick knew that he had to perform sympathetically with Catherine Clive, Hannah Pritchard, Christiana Horton, Mrs Dunstall, Mrs Richard Cross, Susanna Maria Cibber, and Margaret Woffington. He observed the performances of male and female in the companies, sized up their skills, and with the daring of youth backed by courage born of conviction of his own budding talents moved into the profession—but still as an unidentified "young Gentleman."

On 19 October 1741 at Goodman's Fields Theatre King Richard III became the most frightening royal villain of the eighteenth century, and chilled spectators 80 times more in word, in appearance, and action until the evening of 3 June 1776 at Drury Lane, 35 years later.

Under the anonymity of "a Gentleman who never appear'd before," Garrick in this role struck his audience with astonishment that first night. "[His] Reception," wrote a journalist next day, "was the most extraordinary and great that was ever known upon such an Occasion."[2] The art of the acting was what counted, in this off-limits theatre by an unknown actor. Within a week the benches of Drury Lane and Covent Garden were emptied, as the coaches of the great packed about the little theatre in Goodman's Fields.

This Richard III was not a flash in the pan. Within a month after the first performance Londoners flocked to see the unknown and unnamed prodigy do Clodio in Cibber's *Love Makes a Man* (28 October), Chamont in Otway's *The Orphan* (6 November), and Jack Smatter in an adaptation of Richardson's *Pamela* (9 November). Garrick was doing comedy, tragedy, and farce, in young, middle-aged, and old men's parts. The versatility pleased, because he did not set a Garrick stamp on each, but played each for its own peculiar humor. The "Garrick fever" which built up for him in Dublin the following summer lasted, more or less, for the rest of his career.

The excitement that this first month offered Garrick was countered by genuine concern for what the members of his family would think of it all. The temper of this concern appears in his letter to Peter about 20 October 1741, which reads in part: "I . . . am now to tell You what I suppose You may have heard of before this, but before I let you into y$^e$ Affair, 'tis proper to premise Some things that I may appear less culpable in y$^r$ Opinion than I might Otherwise do. [He then notes that his accounts in the Wine business are all straight.] My Mind (as You must know) has been always inclin'd to y$^e$ Stage, nay so strongly so that all my Illness & lowness of Spirits was owing to my want of resolution to tell You my thoughts . . . I know You will bee much displeas'd with Me yet I hope when You shall find that I may have y$^e$ genius of an Actor without y$^e$ Vices, You will think Less Severe of Me & not be asham'd to own me for a Brother . . . Last Night I play'd Richard y$^e$ Third to y$^e$ Surprize of Every Body & as I shall make very near £300 p Annum by It & as it is really what I doat upon I am resolv'd to pursue it" (15).

He wrote in similar vein on the same day to his cousin Peter Fermignac: "My Mind lead me to y$^e$ Stage, w$^{ch}$ from being very Young, I found Myself very much inclining too . . . The only thing that gives me pain . . . is that My Friends I suppose will look very cool upon Me . . . but w$^t$ can I do, I am wholly bent upon y$^e$ Thing." Brother Peter replied, somewhat shocked at the news. Garrick's answer, worth

*Walker Gallery, Liverpool*
Garrick as Richard III.
Painting by William Hogarth, 1745.

repeating in part as expressive of his deep family concern, noted: "y^e Love I sincerely have for You togeather with y^e prevailing Arguments You have made Use of were enough to overthrow My Strongest Resolutions did not Necessity (a very pressing Advocate) on My Side convince me that I am not so much to blame as You Seem to think I am. . . . I have not yet had my Name in y^e Bills" (17). Half a dozen more letters register the concern, but the motif in them growing stronger and stronger about his success overcame the family prejudice in about three months, and after the curious neighbors in Lichfield came to London, saw several performances, and reported good tidings at home.

"Oh what a pity it is," wrote Colley Cibber, "that the strong and beautiful strokes of a great actor should not be as lasting as the strokes of the pencil or the chisel of inferior artists."[3] A biographer's task, however, is not to lament a patent fact, but to recapture where possible the life and force of the man who perfected a kind of acting that electrified his spectators from his very first appearance, and "raised the character of his profession," in Burke's words, "to the rank of a liberal art." Five years after that first appearance William Hogarth sought to capture the awakening of Richard in the tent at Bosworth field, as Garrick conveyed the confusion, the fear, the bravado, and the villain's insight into his own character in a moment of gripping action. Thirty-five years later (as Garrick bowed out of the role on the eve of his retiring) one would expect adulation, but Garrick left his audience speechless. "It is vanity to endeavour to describe Mr. Garrick's merits they beggar all description, suffice it to say that he was what he represented," wrote William Hopkins, prompter, and an eyewitness of some authority.[4]

Hogarth's painting, and Hopkins's comment prompt us to explore the acting further. The extended right hand with five fingers spread as a fending off gesture in the Hogarth painting comes directly from the acting manuals of the rhetorical tradition, familiar to actors and audiences alike in the 1730s and 1740s. The belief that Richard himself walked the stage, in Hopkins's phrase, that the personator was the man personated, emphasizes what for 30 years had been perceived in Garrick's "new" acting—the triumph of the sympathetic imagination in preparing the role, the attention to detail in the idiosyncrasy of characterization, the particularization of a villain, rather than the generalized universal appearance of villainy. The matter is important, for Garrick wrought a change significant to all acting.[5]

Richard Cumberland writing his memoirs many, many years later gives a vivid example of the distinction between the older conventional style and the new one developed by Garrick. His instance comes from what he seems to have recollected of the manner of Quin's motions on stage, wherein one character was little distinguished from another "save by costume and outbursts of fury."[6] Wrote Cumberland, "with very little variation of cadence and in a deep full tone, accompanied by a sawing kind of action, which had more of the senate than of the stage in it, he rolled out his heroics." The result—interpretations of Brutus, Cato, Richard III, and King Lear rather than displaying individual differences all bore a common or universal tragic similarity, a noble, statuesque quality in which the rich tones of Quin's cultivated voice were the most memorable elements.[7] Aaron Hill, who watched Quin nightly and liked much of his acting, berated him, however, in his periodical *The Prompter*: "You . . . lose the advantage of your deliberate articulation, distinct use of pausing, solemn significance of look, and that composed air and gravity of your motion. For though there arises from these good qualities an esteem . . . of your friends . . . to be always deliberate and solemn is an error. . . . To pause where no pauses are necessary is the way to destroy their effect where the sense stands in need of assistance. And tho' dignity is finely maintained by the weight of majestic composure, yet there are scenes in your parts where the voice should be sharp and impatient, the look disordered and agonized, the action precipitate and turbulent."[8]

Cumberland was remembering from a boyhood glimpse of Quin and Garrick as they played together in Rowe's *The Fair Penitent* (14 December 1746), and he suggested that the change from the older to Garrick's newer style was wrought quickly: "But when, after long and eager expectation, I beheld little Garrick, young and light, and alive in every muscle and feature, come bounding on the stage, and pointing at the wittol Altamont (Lacy Ryan) and the heavy-paced Horatio (Quin)—Heavens, what a transition! It seemed as if a whole century had been stepped over in the transition of a single scene."[9] Audiences by 1746, indeed, sensed the different styles competing—the traditionally formal and the new—for Davies writes, "The shouts of applause, when Horatio and Lothario met on the stage together in the second act, were so loud, and so often repeated, before the audience permitted them to speak, that the combatants seemed to be disconcerted. It was observed, that Quin changed colour, and Garrick seemed to be embarrassed."[10] But the change, as applicable to an acting company, was not a complete and sudden turn about. Came the shock of the Garrick first appearance, then the long road of gradualism which Garrick worked at and worked with his company as a group in mastering rather than as single individuals. And during all the span of Garrick's stage life trailing clouds of the traditional, formal way of doing things turned up. When well done, in proper plays—by a Quin— excellent! When mechanically done by second- and third-rate actors— poor and subject to the withering derision of a Charles Churchill.[11] But several succeeding generations caught their acting cues from Garrick.

To follow the steps by which the resourceful and imaginative Garrick moved in upon this state of acting and modified it, maintaining always the artistry and control of true professionalism, is to see genius at work. The story has its own fascination, but can be viewed in better perspective if one observes the nature of acting theory which prevailed when Garrick first appeared.

The "conventional style" which Garrick was witnessing as he engaged in the London wine trade was founded on a theory which rests in the English rhetorical tradition, springing from deeper roots in the classics and reinforced by painting and sculpture theory from France.[12] Discussion of acting theory falls naturally into two parts, for distinction must be made between theories of the *effect* sought in acting style upon audiences (which is what acting is all about anyway) and the *process* (method, if one will) of obtaining that effect. Descriptions of both abound. Our care must be to define the ideals of both the "conventional" and the "new" schools and the best practices of both, rather than fall into the trap of comparing second-rate performance of the first (hence damnation of its theory) with first-rate performance of the second (hence indiscriminate praise for its theory and accomplishments). For Garrick, a thorough professional, mastered the "conventional" style, used it with consummate ease when necessary, but emphasized some new departures.

The conventional (rhetorical) theory in brief conceives of the universal nature of the emotions in mankind, and seeks ways to communicate them in stylized and often symbolic fashion. "Every passion has its peculiar and appropriate look, and every look its adopted and peculiar gesture," wrote Aaron Hill.[13] Fear is fear; anger, anger; and love, love among humans across the boundaries of time and geographical lines—so went the theory—and expression of these comes out about the same in any time and in any country. No human is apt to laugh in anger, grind his teeth in tender love, or smile in rage. Could one but abstract appropriate facial expression, typical accompanying gestures, postures, and attitudes which, in varying degrees, convey the passions, actors might have models for conveying the essences of moods and of basic natural emotions.

Belief in the universality of the passions combined with a theoretical need to individualize them in acting different characters was deeply rooted in English dramaturgy. The schoolmasters who taught the fledgling actors in Elizabeth's days relied upon the rhetoricians Cicero (*De Oratore*) and Quintilian (*Institutio Oratoria*),[14] who rather emphasized patterned ways of expressing the emotions—aversion "by turning the head away and thrusting out our hands as though to repel the thought." But Thomas Heywood in his germinal account of acting, although he gave a bow to the rhetoricians, also urged an approach—later termed use of the sympathetic imagination—by which the actor studied the individual characteristics of the role he played and *became* the person personated. He there spoke of avoiding "forced motion in any part of the body . . . but to qualify everything according to the person personated." In such an approach he found rewards of recognition and/or easy identification on the part of the spectators: "to turn to our domestic histories, what English blood seeing the person of any bold English man presented, and doth not hug himself . . . and offer to him all prosperous performance, as if the personater were the man personated, so bewitching a thing is a lively and spirited action, that it hath the power to new mold the hearts of the spectators, and fashion them to the shape of any noble or notable attempt."[15]

But the anonymous writer of a preface to *The Cyprian Conquerer* (1635) veered again to the traditional display of universals by the patterning of voice and gesture: "we must be various as required; as in a sorrowful part the head must hang down; in a proud the head must be lofty; in an amorous, closed eyes, hanging down looks and crossed arms; in a hastie [part] fuming and scratching the head."[16]

The traditional theory of patterned style prevailed when acting resumed after the restoration of Charles II. The spectator's enjoyment came from viewing the "passions" going through their paces, or being exquisitely delineated in a series of isolated actions and declamations, rather than from enjoying the development of a "whole" character, or the complications of a full plot. Set speeches were helpful, and soliloquies seemed made for exhibiting virtuosity. The star performer could declaim both, and rivet attention on his individual performance. Supreme art showed in his doing it well. A parallel comes to mind in our present-day experience with grand opera, sung in tongues alien to the comprehension of half the audience, presented with little consecutive action, but with great concentration (by the singer) upon the quality of his or her lyrical outpourings. Enjoyment comes from hearing the trained voice come forth with power and appropriate modulation, rise to unthinkable heights and descend with perfection to moving depths. A Madam Caballé can thus stop the performance of *The*

*Sicilian Vespers* with her aria in the third act for five minutes while the audience yields volumes of applause, bravas, and approbation—not for the plot, not for the characterization, but for the pure quality of her performing the aria.

For the spectator on into the Garrick era pleasure in seeing the "passions" well performed also paralleled his pleasure in reading the "beauties" of a long poem rather than the whole work. Florilegia such as Edward Bysshe's *Art of English Poetry*, which reached seven editions by 1725, and William Dodd's *The Beauties of Shakespeare Regularly Selected from Each Play, with a General Index Digesting Them under Proper Heads* (1752) are apposite, and help define the atmosphere of expectancy to which audiences were attuned.

Reaffirmation of the validity of the patterned approach came to England's restoration theatre and reinforcement of the value of presenting universals, as well as clear exemplification of how to present them, came from France, by way of exposition in the sister arts of painting and sculpture. Evidence of the transfer of art theory to stage practice is seen in the translation and adaptation of Charles Le Brun's *A Method to Learn to Design the Passions*. Chief painter to Louis XIV, Le Brun addressed the French Academy of Painting and Sculpture in 1697, explaining (according to his master Descartes) the psychology of expression and the beauty and utility of universals.[17] He provided therewith a set of remarkable drawings of the emotions, both simple, complex, and in varying degrees. "Hatred" for example, "is an emotion caused by the animal spirits [cf. Descartes] which move the soul to shun such objects as she apprehends to be harmful to her. . . . In hatred the pulse beats are irregular, lower, and frequently quicker than ordinary; the breast feels a heat intermixed with a certain sharp and piercing fire, and the stomach ceases to perform its function." But the outward manifestation of the state is what counts with the artist. "Contempt," for example, "is expressed by the eyebrows knit and lowering towards the nose, and at the other end very much elevated; the eye very open, and the pupil in the middle; the nostrils drawing upwards; the mouth shut, and the corners somewhat down, and the under lip thrust out farther than the upper one." "Horror" knits the brows more, lowers the pupil from the center to the lower part of the eye, mouth half open and compressed in the middle, wrinkles in the cheek, pallor spreading over the whole contenance." These expressions of the passions and the soul could, of course, be learned by education, and be perfected by exercise. Good actors knew and practiced them.[18]

Quintilian, father of much such theorizing, though writing primarily to instruct orators, recognized that both innate ability (nature) *and* training were important: "I quite realize that there is a question as to whether eloquence derives most from nature or from education. . . . If we make an absolute divorce between the two nature will ill be able to accomplish much without the aid of education, while the latter is valueless without the aid of nature." His ambiguity, however, gave some encouragement to those followers who were to emphasize the value of method. "If on the other hand they are blended in equal proportion, we shall find that the average orator owes much to nature, while the *perfect* orator owes most to education."[19]

Charles Gildon, probable author of *The Life of Betterton* (1710), acknowledges reliance upon the French, and the French reliance upon Quintilian. His key premise, which he ascribes to Betterton, is that "motion is what catches the eye of the spectator, so that even an indifferent actor can draw attention by an outlandish one. Therefore skill, address, refinement of motion yield the true elevated art of acting." For Gildon, who had watched Betterton, two phases in the art interact. First the actor must transform himself into every person he represents (since he is to present all sorts of actions and passions) and second he must be master of appropriate gestures, voice, and attitudes to represent the passions of the man he acts. If the role is for a choleric, hot, jealous man "he must be thoroughly acquainted with all the motions and sentiments productive of these, motions of the feet, hands, and looks of such a person in such circumstances." But Gildon makes it a cardinal principle that the display of jealousy might be different in the role of a prince from that in the role of a beggar. Betterton though knowing the appropriate gestures and expressions for declaiming in all the passions is praised for his "naturalness" (in conveying them), probably because of applying and adjusting his style to the station of the character he was presenting.[20]

William Oldys, in 1741, just when Garrick first appeared, codified more tightly the expression of universals as he reproduced Gildon's "Betterton papers." "Every passion or emotion," he quotes, "has from nature its peculiar and proper countenance, sound and gesture; and the whole body of man, all his looks and every tone of his voice, like strings on an instrument, receive their sounds from the various impulses of the passions. . . . A lifting or tossing of the head is the gesture of Pride and Arrogance. Carrying the head aloft is a sign of joy . . . a bold front is looked upon as a mark of obstinacy," and so the patterns of action are spelled out. "When you speak of yourself, the right hand, not the left must be apply'd to the bosom, declaring your own faculties and passions; but this action . . . should only be apply'd

. . . by laying the hand gently on the breast, and not by thumping it." Quality of performances, that is to say apt and recognized gesture, living up to audience expectation, counted as much for him as it did for Hamlet or for Heywood. "Your arm should not stretch out sideways above half a foot from the trunk of your body; you will otherwise throw your gesture quite out of sight, unless you turn your head to pursue it, which would be ridiculous."[21]

Aaron Hill in *The Prompter* (1734–36) helped concentrate his readers' attention on what to look for in stage representation. Though he seemed to advocate a new style, his papers served to crystallize impressions for his public about how the "passions" should be expressed.[22] Another of his critical works, *The Art of Acting*, makes clear, however, that his "natural acting" referred to the quality of presenting universals. Versified, and later expanded in prose (1746),[23] it specified ten basic dramatic passions, that is "those that can be distinguished by their outward marks of action."—joy, grief, anger, fear, pity, scorn, jealousy, hatred, wonder, and love. These he defined and described appropriate gestures for expressing them. "Joy is pride possessed with triumph—forehead raised and open, eye full and sparkling, neck expanded and erect, breast inflated and thrown back, vertebrae linked and straightened, and all joints (arm, wrist, fingers, hip, knee and ankle) connected and boldly braced." He advised practice before a mirror. He preferred his descriptions to be just starters, arguing that the actor generate the passion (as step one in his "new" principles) within himself before trying to externalize it—a practice which Garrick, presumably, was to adopt. "The actor should utter no word until he has first assayed and embraced the idea of what his look and nerves must then be adapted to express. As soon as this pathetic confidence is mustered, let him then, but not a moment before, attempt speech."[24]

Among the unskillful this "on your mark, get set, go" method became obvious—a Prufrockian "preparing of a face to meet a face." Skillfully done it displayed the passions well. Enjoyment for audience after audience lay in watching the passion move from degree to degree of intensity. The fault which discriminating critics expressed (from the early Dryden era to that of Macklin) lay in the ease with which universals neatly stereotyped could and did become hackneyed in repeated performances of actors. Those of middling talent seemed to be the ones who relied most heavily upon the manuals. As to voice, ranting (unrestrained, loud, bombastic discourse, tearing a passion to tatters), entoning (carrying on in a nasal monotony slightly elevated), whining (reciting in a plaintive, high pitched manner—a specialty of

Colley Cibber) by rule surely marked some actors, but were not characteristic of many for very long, yet a series of stereotypes must have
developed against which the oncoming waves of so-called "natural
actors" reacted.[25] Though the extremes of formula-techniques bored
some spectators, they were liked by many. For a time, at least, excellent artistic display of the passions almost as virtuoso arias was what
acting was supposed to be about—where mighty characters were
thrown into mighty predicaments, and conveyed their thoughts by
heightened action and heightened (nonconversational) speech. Garrick
entering this field was no naturalistic bumbler. He mastered the techniques of conveying universals, and performed them in closet-drama
circumstances—as he did in the drawing rooms of Paris later in 1763.
At a dinner there "the conversation turned upon the delineation of
the passions, in the course of which Mr. Garrick made many judicious
observations, and illustrated them by alternately throwing his features
into the representations of Love, Hatred, Terror, Pity, Jealousy,
Desire, Joy in so rapid and striking a manner as astounded the whole
country [Buttoni, Cochin, Dance, and his brother the architect] who
acknowledged it was the finest instance of 'nature' they had ever met
with." But upon the public stage Garrick was seeking other artistic
values.[26]

Given the expectancy that tragic action was not to be played in
everyday fashion, one may be unsound to condemn a Quin's tragic
performance as the imposition of book theory over lifelike verisimilitude. Furthermore the very conditions of the theatre often administered to declamatory style. Although none complained of theatre and
stage lighting, the Reverend Thomas Newton asked Garrick to procure
seats in a stage box for him the second time he was to see *Richard III*.
"All that we wanted was to see more of your face and the expression
of your countenance . . . where we may see your looks in the scene
with Lady Ann . . . that is, that we may sit with the stage on our right
hand, and the pit on our left."[27] Also the theatres were often filled
with noisy audiences, with gentlemen sitting on the stage and wandering behind the scenes. The actor had to come down stage, assume a
stance, and declaim (with proper gestures) a long and effective moral
sentiment from a *Cato* or heroic play. Otherwise he could not be
heard. Ensemble performance in Quin's day counted for less than it
did after Garrick became manager.[28] And weak ensemble performance
encouraged star performers to perfect the aria technique. Garrick was
going to change this radically—but later—and offer a stage where
audience pleasure in recognizing a deep rooted "expectancy-fulfilled,"
gradually would yield to the pleasure of discovery and recognition

35

in a new mode, as the individualizing of characters replaced universal abstracts of the passions, and where all on stage worked together.

Hackneyed performance in the late 1730s and in 1740 had been relieved by a fresh breath of innovation in some of the acting of Charles Macklin, who on 14 February 1741 startled Londoners by his interpretation of Shylock, "the Jew that Shakespeare drew" in *The Merchant of Venice*. Shylock, traditionally a buffoon on stage, became with Macklin a serious, revengeful man, but *not* an example of abstract vengeance. Macklin abandoned the guidelines of the manuals and, as Garrick wrote, "has been observed constantly to attend the 'Change for weeks together before he exhibited one of Shakespeare's most inimitable and difficult characters, and so far succeeded by his great attention and observation of the manners, dress and behavior of a peculiar tribe of people—that crowded theatres and unequalled applause greeted him."[29] Macklin had begun his march toward a new art in acting. Nine years later John Hill wrote: "There was a time when that extravagance recommended for farce had its place in tragedy, both in action and delivery: the gestures were forced, and beyond all that ever was in nature; and the recitation was a kind of singing. We are at present [1750] getting more into nature in playing, and (if the violence of gesture be not quite suppressed) we have nothing of the recitative of the old tragedy. It is to the honour of Mr. Macklin that he began this improvement. . . . It was his manner to check all the cant and cadence of tragedy; he would bid his pupil first to speak the passage as he would in common life, if he had the occasion to pronounce the same words, and then give them more force, but preserving the same accent, to deliver them on stage."[30] And Macklin advised further that the young actor know intimately each character, sink himself in it, and not impose upon it his own stamp. Garrick's continuing example led this art of acting to perfection.

Garrick, though skilled in conveying the universals, and working to do so in seemingly effortless manner, saw the novel value of particularization, individualizing, playing out the unique and idiosyncratic humors of the roles he took on. He submerged the aria effect (with its special concentration on ability to do a "turn" of passion) and brought to the fore the character as it moved through the play, contributed to the plot, and to the total tragic (or comic) impact of the piece. When he became manager and had to read new plays submitted to him, again and again he rejected those in which the plot (or story line) was unclear. He wanted no timberyard full of arias (even though their poetry might be fine) masking under the name of plays, as he wrote to Boswell 2 March 1772 (677). Within the plot, characterizations, for him, had to be well done, capable of acting development. Some now see in Garrick's attention to detail in preparing his own parts the triumph of the sympathetic-imagination theory, which has been defined as a "faculty whereby the imagination through attendant emotional sensitivity, succeeds in identifying itself with the object of its attention, and consequently enters with almost intuitive force into the distinctive character of the object."[31] Perhaps the feat is akin to what Heywood envisioned as "to be the man personated" and not a stereotype of him. In Garrick's time the triumph was called that of "natural acting" as opposed to acting by formula. We, wary of the many conflicting uses of the term *natural* in the century, see it as the "new" as opposed to the "conventional" form.

The actor is supposed to create an illusion. *Question*: How? By a fiction achieved through artful deception, by parading the passions in their universal aspects, or by authentic realization via sympathetic imagining? Horace was much quoted in regard to communicating feelings on stage: "We weep and laugh as we see others do, / He only makes me sad, who shows the way / And first is sad himself." Echoes of the *Ion* of Plato were also heard, when the actor, possessed, as it were, electrifies and magnetizes the spectator: "Here lies the golden secret [wrote Robert Lloyd] learn to feel / Or fool or monarch, happy or distress'd— / No actor pleases who is not possess'd."[32] Granted that love is love, anger, anger in some universal sense, the manner of communicating the passion convincingly came to depend, with Garrick, upon the details, rather than the universal essences, the realistic rather than the conventional, in order to bring off an effect so well expressed by Pope—to yield "Something whose truth convinc'd at sight we find / That gives us back the image of our mind."[33] Pope was describing the effect of something achieved by art, not by impulse. Garrick further agreed with him that the total effect of the work of art was what counted—"the *eye* and the *lip*, and the *joint force* and full result of all"[34]—not just a "turn." Professor Cecil Price defines the "turn" as a "psychological revelation in the moments of transition from one aspect of character to another."[35] What the whole cast did throughout the play, including what each character contributed (even in turns and arialike speeches) became under Garrick new and fascinating to audiences. With the new acting and emphasis upon ensemble performing the old revived plays took on refreshing newness. Thus Garrick's creative adaptations and productions bred excellent theatre.

From the outset leadership by force of example counted most highly. And this Garrick carried out brilliantly. He amazed his fellow actors during his first year by tenaciousness in maintaining a role—not falling out of character even when off stage during a performance. Nor did he fall out of character *on* stage (as some actors did) even when realism demanded that he occasionally not face the audience. He heeded the lines of the other actors. He modulated his voice, he moved gracefully, yet took an unconventional stance when proper character delineation demanded. His attention to the details of acting, wherein the lines were but the first point of departure, swept the Drury Lane company into fond allegiance, and toned up the performing of all others.[36]

John Hill, who had so complimented Macklin, spoke also of Garrick's creativity. "The great thing in which [excellent] players distinguish themselves is the expressing to the audience such sentiments as are *not* deliver'd in the play, yet are not only agreeable but necessary to be understood of the character they represent." He referred not to "gagging" (a source of bad acting) but to stage business—the meaningful emphasis, the gesture, the hint in body language by which the creative actor interprets a part, and seems to be the character he represents. He instances Garrick in Iago, and Macklin in Shylock.[37] Years later the conservative Francis Gentleman attacked Garrick for this sort of creativity. "Fond of something critical and new [he] A meaning gives beyond the author's view."[38]

Midway in time between Hill and Gentleman an author in the *Universal Museum* (1762) called attention to new revelations by Garrick in playing Bayes in *The Rehearsal*. "He has in it such an infinite fund of original humour, not to say nature, that he actually does the highest justice to so original a piece, or to use Mr. Walpole's expression *creation*. Was there ever anything better spoken than Bayes's telling the plot of his play? He amplifies himself into a full stop of confusion, and unable to go a step further cries—'In fine you'll understand it better when you see it' and runs off to call the players . . . every syllable is spoke in such an admirable manner that the audience have hardly the power to clap they are so engag'd in laughing."[39] The governing words here are "admirable manner," for Garrick came to be every inch a professional, studying and practicing effects for his performance—an essential artist, in no way a rude, offhand, ad-libbing player.

Drama as the art of concentration demands that characterization (of one or many persons) be developed—hinting at layer upon layer of depth, even in comedies—within a two-hour period. Novelists can luxuriate, doing the same in 500 pages, as they enjoy the art of amplification. Vignettes seriatim, or "turns," have had their appeal for dramatists and actors in the shorthand nature of the art. But characterization rather than exquisite "turns" interested Garrick. He revealed the character of Archer in *The Beaux Stratagem* as the play developed, so that in the last act where characterization and "turn" coincide he could create a capital performance. John Hill was so impressed that he noted "Till this excellent performer play'd this part we never knew what beauties it was capable of in the sudden transitions from passion to passion in the last act."[40]

More on this characterization when we discuss Garrick in his leading comic roles,[41] but though Hill may have had eyes only for a display of "turns," attitudes of a series of critics veered toward concern with total characterization, and one senses Garrick's influence upon them. One need instance but two from many. Joseph Warton: "I should be guilty of insensibility and injustice if I did not take this occasion to acknowledge that I have been more moved and delighted by hearing this single line [well along in the acting text of *Lear*], 'O, me, my rising heart—but down,' spoken by the only actor of the age who understands and relishes those little touches of nature, and therefore the only one qualified to personate this most difficult character of Lear, than by the most pompous declaimer of the most pompous speeches in Cato or Tamerlane" [1754].[42] And George Steevens ten years later, while preparing his edition of Shakespeare: "I am contented with the spirit of the author you first taught me to admire, and when I found you could do so much for him, I was naturally curious to know the value of the materials he had supplied you with; and often when I have taken my pen in hand to try to illustrate a passage, I have thrown it down again with discontent when I remembered how able you were to clear that difficulty by a single look, or particular modulation of voice, which a long and laboured paraphrase was insufficient to explain half so well."[43]

What of Garrick's method of preparing a part—by art and artifice, or by sympathetic imagination? It was a mixture no doubt, but the odds just may be in favor of the latter. Two more witnesses suggest it: Joseph Pittard, "A player who personates in every part the living manners of a supreme character, manifests beyond all contradiction that he has conceived the true idea of the author."[44] *True idea of the author* would seem to suggest "character concept," not just ability to shine in conveying a single emotion. He then compliments Garrick on his art that conceals art, "He is the only man on any stage where I have been who speaks tragedy truly natural. The French tragedians mouth it too much—they lose resemblance to humanity; a hero on that stage seems to be a creature just arrived from another planet. To be angry is easy. To be angry with superior sovereignty is difficult." Garrick's Lear had that dignity.

Three years before Pittard's publication Jean Georges Noverre, the ballet master, came under Garrick's influence. Mightily impressed Noverre wrote, "He studied the characters of his personages, and still more their passions. Strongly attached to his profession, he shut himself up and would see no one on the day he played important parts. His genius raised him to the rank of the prince he must portray, he assumed all his virtues and his frailties, he assimilated all his character and its foibles, and was a man transformed. It was no longer Garrick whom we heard: the change once effected, the actor disappeared and the hero was revealed, and the actor did not become his natural self until his task was done." Carlyle reminds us that *genius* is nine-tenths made up of hard work. Noverre thought Garrick's preparation for a part came from mimesis in the market place, so to speak. "There is no man more sprightly than he the day he is to act a poet, a tradesman, a character in low life, a newsmonger. . . . To diction, declamation, fire, natural ease, wit and subtlety he joined that force of pantomime, and that rare power of dumb show, which characterizes the great actor and perfect comedian."[45]

The German visitor Lichtenberg observed the details of Garrick's deportment on stage, and the resulting quality of his performance. To bring this off with apparent ease, Garrick turned observation and mimicry into art, giving as a result of study, pains, and infinite practice the appearance of unforced realism in detail. "When he turns to some one with a bow," marked Lichtenberg, "it is not merely that the head, the shoulders, the feet and arms, are engaged in this exercise, but that each member helps with great propriety to produce the demeanor most pleasing and appropriate to the occasion . . . with him are no extravagant gestures. . . . It is therefore refreshing to see the manner of his walking, shrugging his shoulders, putting his hands in his pockets, putting on his hat, now pulling it down over his eyes and then pushing it sideways off his forehead, all this with so slight a movement of his limbs as though each were his right hand. . . . Man was his study from the cultured and artificial denizens of the salons of St James's down to the savage creatures in the eating houses of St. Giles."[46]

Garrick lived for 22 years in Southampton Street, within walking distance of the theatres. Record of a by-election in the parish in 1749 lists the names and occupations of 442 residents who voted, including himself.[47] These with whom he daily walked and often talked followed 113 different trades, with largest concentration on tailors (39), victuallers (35), peruke makers (25), gentlemen (among whom he, Spranger Barry, and John Rich characterized themselves) (25), shoemakers and apothecaries (15), jewellers (14), staymakers (11), and so on with bakers, distillers, and haberdashers. Garrick literally rubbed elbows with everyone, and from the daily surge of London life (along with extended week-end visits to the houses of the great) he observed and picked up by studied imitation and sympathetic understanding a hundred recognizable mannerisms for use in exhibiting stage characters, and bringing them home to the business and bosoms of his audiences. "Something whose truth convinc'd at sight they find, that gave them back the image of their mind."

Ways to imitate and ways to adapt precepts from rhetorical manuals always combine with the instincts and personal conceptions of every actor. The question, presumably, is one of emphasis and accentuation. Garrick believed that acting was an art—a studied way of doing things, involving emotional response and control. The art lay in the happy ability to combine the two, but at base lay capacity for sympathetic imagining. John Hill's *The Actor*, taken as he acknowledged somewhat from St Albine's *Le Comédien* (1747), was retranslated by Antonio Fabie Sticetti as *Garrick ou les Acteurs Anglais*, which in turn influenced Denis Diderot to develop his theory of acting in *Le Paradoxe sur le Comédien* (1773). Diderot saw in Garrick one who studied his role well, yet while playing never lost control of himself. His art lay in the perfection of this control, so that he was able to make the audience *believe* he *was* the character he was portraying. The paradox of the actor, wrote Diderot, is that in touching or amusing scenes he must be devoid of feeling; whilst seeming to grow excited he must remain cool. He must possess such judgment that he carries within himself an unmoved disinterested onlooker. He must have penetration, but no sensibility; the art of mimicking everything, the art of rendering so exactly the outward signs of feeling that the audience falls into the trap.

The complexity of Garrick's art (as commented upon by all sorts of observers) comes as clear as does his effort to move acting (by the powers of management and personal example) into a new status—one more compelling and more refreshing than it had been when it was dominated by the conventions extant when he first appeared. Observers tell us much, and may in the long run be the safest guides, for they were the ones impressed. Yet Garrick had some things to say himself on the art he was embracing—and these reveal the man.

Although Garrick was no consistent essayist on the theory of acting his letters abound with specific commentary on the why and how of his interpretation of many characters. For he got the articulate public so interested in his presentations from the very beginning that members rushed to correspond and thus participate in a way in the new movement, asking about his stops and starts, his pronunciation, and under-

41

standing of the texts he used. The most impressive fact emerging from these letters is the openness of Garrick's mind, and his willingness to accept suggestion, especially during the early formative years.

Aside from commenting in letters he published a full essay, jotted down two important memoranda, compared at full length (in a letter to a foreign correspondent) great French acting and his own, and produced an interlude on the subject of misbegotten stereotypes. The five documents begin in 1744 and appear at about seven-year intervals until the approach of his retirement. Garrick speaks therein about acting techniques and requirements, the importance of audience reaction, the effect of spontaneous leaps beyond the reach of art, the abuse of stereotypes, and the reluctance of audiences to abandon pleasure in them.

In 1744 he floated anonymously, in a London pamphlet, a characteristic mock attack upon himself in order to focus attention upon his new departure in acting the role of Macbeth. Entitled *An Essay on Acting* its preface focuses upon the different concepts and proper manifestations of fear—in the gullible tobacconist Abel Drugger's reacting to dropping a urinal (in Ben Jonson's *The Alchemist*), and Macbeth's afterthoughts of the murder of Duncan. The urinal sequence, not in Jonson's text, came about originally when Colley Cibber playing Drugger, during a flow of some 50 lines between other characters on stage (Act III), instead of standing idly by fiddled about the Alchemist's table and took up a urinal, which accidentally slipped through his fingers and crashed. He had the presence of mind to put on an expression of comic distress which so pleased the audience that succeeding audiences demanded that that piece of stage business be retained in all performances. Garrick developed this bit fully.[48]

"When Drugger has broke the urinal," writes Garrick, "he is mentally absorbed with the different ideas of the invaluable price of the urinal and the punishment that may be inflicted in consequence of a curiosity no way pertaining or belonging to the business he came about." Garrick then describes how he would communicate the complex tensions of the tobacconist by action and without a word—body language giving "the compleatest low picture of grotesque terror imagined by a Dutch painter." As for Macbeth, Garrick first analyses for himself the essence of the Scotsman's character, and the compulsions that are upon him. "He is an experienced general, crowned with conquest, innately ambitious, and religiously humane, spurred on by metaphysical prophesies, and the uncontrollable pride of his wife, to a deed horrid in itself, and repugnant to his nature, but it is the ladder to the swelling act of the imperial theme; his milk soon becomes gall, embitters his whole disposition, and the consequence is the murder of Duncan." His action in communicating the fear and awe in Macbeth would differ vastly from the grotesque, but again would be done in pantomime—riveting the attention of the spectators on him, as "his faculties are intensely rivited to the murder alone . . . a moving statue . . . a petrified man, whose eyes must speak, tongue metaphorically silent, ears sensible of imaginary noises, and deaf to the audible sound of his wife's voice."[49]

In the comparisons Garrick is not setting up models (universals) of the grotesque and the awesome. He is particularizing *after* the actor has through sympathetic understanding of relevant experience of his own and sympathetic imagining put himself into the two different characters he is to portray. These are the obvious first steps. Clues follow about the manner thereafter of arriving at the level of performance which impressed his audiences. The important element of the essay is its revelation of the study and thought about the total characterizations to be portrayed, as well as how to suit action to word in order to particularize meaning. For Abel Drugger's eyes "must be reversed from the object he is most intimidated with. By dropping his lip at the same time to the object, it throws a trembling languor upon every muscle, and by declining the right part of the head towards the urinal, it casts a most comic terror and shame over the upper part of the body that can be imagined; and to make the lower part equally ridiculous, his toes must be inverted from the heel, and by holding his breath give himself a tremor in the knees, and if his fingers, at the same time seem convuls'd it finishes the picture."

How were the different members of the body to be agitated? Not by standard techniques of terror set forth by Le Brun and the rhetorical guides, but by the kind of terror this particular fellow might show in this particular circumstance—but relevant to his total character.

Similar particularization reveals the way of Garrick's showing the awestruck Macbeth, "attitudes quick and permanent, his voice articulately trembling, and confusedly intelligible . . . cork heels to his shoes, as in this scene he should seem to tread on air."

Garrick then generalizes on his penchant for portraying the humor, the idiosyncratic in character: "The only way to arrive at great excellency in characters of humour, is to be very conversant with human nature. . . . Would the painter produce a perfect piece in the world, let him copy from the life. . . . Would a player perform equally excellent in his profession, let him be introduced into the world, be conversant with the humours of every kind, digest 'em in his mind, let 'em be cherished by the genial warmth of his conception, transplanted into

43

the fair garden of his judgment, there let 'em ripen into perfection and become his own. *Hic labor! Hic opus!*" [50] Garrick was not exactly feeling his way; he knew where he was going, even at the age of 27. But the public is never completely tractable.

Some event in about 1754—possibly the increased rush of the public to Covent Garden pantomimes—prompted Garrick to jot down in a brief paragraph "Miscellaneous thoughts upon the Stage, Authors, Actors, &c."—concerned about actor and author innovations relative to public demands. "There are no hopes of seeing a perfect stage, till the public as well as the managers get rid of their errors and prejudices—the reformation must begin with the first. When the taste of the public is right, the managers and actors must follow it or starve. I speak of those who understand something of their business—there are and have been managers and actors who are so naturally blind that they cannot find the right way tho' the finger of the public point it out ever so strongly to 'em." [51] This fragment of momentary depression (perhaps notes for a larger document) tells us not a greal deal save for the impression it yields that new styles in acting (as well as in repertory) must receive continuing support from the mainstay of the theatre—the public. Public taste can dominate practice, if not theory. But actors just might take the lead.

Practices in the profession varied of course in London and in the provinces. By the 1760s Garrick's recruitment and training programs had pretty well outlined what was expected in achievement for actors he wished to bring to Drury Lane. He saw that a total changeover from the rudely conventional to the expertly new was a Herculean task. His thoughts on the subject crystallized in a letter memorandum to his brother Peter in Lichfield (1762). He condemned conceit and affectation in actors' minds, and spoke his dislike of the older stereotyped acting which he had still found operating in the country circuits. "I don't know how it is, but the Strollers are a hundred years behind hand —We in Town are Endeavouring to bring the Sock & Buskin down to Nature, but *they* still keep to their Strutting, bouncing & mouthing, that with Whiskers on, they put me in mind of y^e late Czar of Russia, who was both an Ideot & a Madman" (297, 528).

The way of achieving particular characterization continued to intrigue him. On 3 January 1769 he wrote his Danish friend Helfric Peter Sturz his most intimate thoughts about this central element in acting, as well the sensibility component. And he added a point of great interest scarcely mentioned in the texts on acting—the matter of subconscious creativity, which comes in a flash, unanticipated by the

44

actor.[52] The thought was basic to Longinus's theories of persuasive oratory, and was also reflected in general in Edmund Burke's *Inquiry into the Origins of the Sublime and the Beautiful* (1756).[53] Garrick was commenting to Sturz on the acting of Mme Clairon, as he remembered seeing performances of the great French actress from his time in Paris:

> She has every thing that Art and a good understanding, with great Natural Spirit can give her—But then I fear . . . the Heart has none of those instantaneous feelings, that Life blood, that keen Sensibility, that bursts at once from Genius, and like Electrical fire shoots thro' the Veins, Marrow, Bones and all, of every Spectator—Mad^m *Clairon* is so conscious and certain of what she can do, that she never (I believe) had the feelings of the instant come upon her unexpectedly.—but I pronounce that the greatest strokes of Genius, have been unknown to the Actor himself, 'till Circumstances, and the warmth of the Scene has sprung the Mine as it were, as much to his own Surprize, as that of the Audience—Thus I make a great different between a great Genius, and a good Actor. The first will always realize the feelings of his Character, and be transported beyond himself, while the other, with great powers, and good sense, will give great pleasure to an Audience, but never
>
> ————pectus inanitor angit
> Irritat Malis & falcis, terroribus implet
> Ut Magus.
>         [With airy nothings wring my heart,
>      inflame, soothe, fill it with vain alarms
>      like a magician.]
>
> I have with great Freedom communicated my Ideas of Acting, but you must not betray me . . . ; The Clairon wou'd never forgive me, tho' I call'd her an excellent Actress, If I did not swear by all the Gods, that she was the greatest Genius too" (528).

Garrick was making specific what John Gilbert Cooper in the first of his *Letters Concerning Taste* (1755) had generalized about audience reception of geniuslike acting: "The effect of a good taste is that instantaneous glow of pleasure which thrills through our whole frame, and seizes upon the applause of the heart before the intellectual power of reason can descend from the throne of the mind to ratify the approbation."

The fifth direct comment Garrick made on the art of acting came towards the close of his stage career, reaching hundreds of people, for he drafted it as an interlude, *The Meeting of the Company*. He had been mulling over the skit since 1771, and produced it at the opening of the 1774–75 season. He sketched the scenario in a letter to John Hoadly (4 January 1772): "Bayes gives them his Art of Acting—which will shew all the false manner of acting Tragedy & Comedy w^ch I have collected in about 30 or 40 comical Verses" (671). The show is topsy-turvy, for in it Bayes turns Hamlet's advice to the players upside down advising:

> First Gentlemen, turn Nature out of Door
> Than rant away, 'till you can rant no more,
> Walk, talk, & look as none walk'd, talk'd & look'd before.
> Would you in Tragedy Extort applause
> Distort *Yourselves*,—now Rage, now Start—now pause,
> Beat breast, roll Eyes, stretch Nose, up brows, down Jaws,
> Then strut, stride, start, Goggle, bounce, & Bawl,
> And when you're out of breath—pant drag, & drawl.[54]

He thought of it as a merry purgative, if acted with second- or third-rate quality, to the old conventional art. Hopkins caught the method, noting in his diary, "It is full of fine satire & an excellent lesson to all performers, it was received with very great applause." For 11 performances Garrick was thus beating a second-rate, but not dead horse, for the rhetorical and stereotyped returned for another heyday at the close of the century, with the enlargement of the theatres—well after his time. Though aimed at players, Garrick was speaking to audiences, urging them to continue to demand the sort of performing he had practiced and had long stood for.

In that first month of the 1741–42 season a nonpareil seemed to have appeared, whose vigor and intensity and concentration on the movement of the whole play was matched by his sprightliness, impudence, and nonchalance in comedy, along with his refreshing attention to detail. His revelation of layers of character complexity in Richard III opened up new visions of stage characterization. What did this young man of 24 look like, what physical advantages did he possess, what limitations had he to overcome from the outset?

We know what he looked like in still-life portraiture (for he was the most bepictured man in Europe in the eighteenth century) at a good many periods of his career. Prints of portraits and roles abound, which when laid out seriatim show the young, graceful form thickening up and growing old, but the common denominator of each portrait is the bright, piercing quality of his remarkable eyes, and the potentially mobile quality of his face—two of the greatest assets an actor can have. Le Brun had concentrated on using the eyes. Garrick was naturally endowed with splendid ones, enabling him to command on stage, to enliven all roles, and within the intimacy of the small theatres of the time to flash upon and hold in concentration spectators from all parts of the house.

The portraits and prints of Garrick in various roles tell much to the theatre historian and suggest something new to any viewer, but in the long passage of time hardly match the 1,000 words that simultaneously poured from the presses, and flowed from the pens of letter writers and diarists. To the word pictures which tell of his size, grace of movement, mobile face, eyes, quality of voice, each reader can add from his own imagination what pleases or displeases most, and so the actor can live in a partial way century after century as biographers re-create from descriptions.

Many contemporaries who had not yet seen Garrick on stage learned about him from his first commentator, who wrote up what he saw for a column of *The Champion*.[55] It was picked up and widely circulated by the *Gentleman's Magazine* in October 1742:

> Mr. Garrick is but of middling stature, yet, being well-porportioned and having a peculiar happiness in his address and action is a living instance that it is not essential to a theatrical hero to be six feet high. His voice is clear and piercing, perfectly sweet and harmonious, without monotony, drawling, or affectation; it is capable of all the various passions, which the heart of man is agitated with, and the Genius of Shakespeare can describe; it is neither whining, bellowing, or grumbling, but in whatever character he assimilates, perfectly easy in its transitions, natural in its cadence, and beautiful in elocution. He is not less happy in his mein and gait, in which he is neither strutting or mincing, neither stiff nor slouching. When three or four are on stage with him, he is attentive to whatever is spoke, and never drops his character when he has finished a speech, by either looking contemptibly on an inferior performer, unnecessary spitting, or suffering his eyes to wander through the whole circle of spectators. His action corresponds with his voice, and both with the character he is to play.

Samuel Foote thought he strained his voice in tragedy, so that it became hoarse in the last act. Others thought he retained harmony throughout. In 1757 a writer for the *Theatrical Review* was still impressed with his marvelous facial expression, and noted the piercing quality of his stage whispers, or asides, which sent distinct sounds to the farthest bench of the galleries without losing the appearance of a whisper. All writers were amazed at the range of his characters (he performed over 90 in his time)—young, old, noble, common, comic, and tragic. "Garrick," wrote one in 1760, stands as "the most universal theatrical genius in Europe" with one perfection in both tragedy and comedy absolutely unique: "that of delivering himself with the unconstrained ease of an Italian player, and not seeming to utter a studied part."[56]

Garrick cared greatly about the quality of his voice—its harmony in

*Maugham Collection, the National Theatre*
David Garrick, 1741.
From a painting by Jean Baptiste Van Loo.

scenes of tenderness, its explosiveness in stage anger. He feared catching colds—of which he had many. He learned to control and conserve his voice magnificently. In his time great fame came from excelling in tragedy, and he achieved it over and over again. But in his natural gaiety and ebullience of spirit he preferred to play comedy. The strain was less, the fun was there, and opportunities abounded for shrewd and amusing interpretations of the roles he took on. Of the more than 90 roles he played, however, a nearly equal balance obtained—42 tragic and the rest comic, but in performance five comic roles far outdid, numerically, performance in any tragic part.[57]

He took on no new roles after his return from France in 1765, because of the strain of artfully bringing a new one up to the standard of his performance. The strain in preparing and acting the tragic ones during his last five years he commented on, and meant what he said. In turning down a prospect of a command performance he wrote, "I am really not yet prepar'd for Macbeth [and he had played it 50 times before], 'tis the most violent part I have, & I don't think myself able yet to obey his Lordship's Commands as I ought. . . ." This was in 1772. He intended to do a Hamlet, then a Lear, and after these Macbeth, but never did play the Scots king again after Mrs Pritchard's death, his Lady Macbeth. His state of physical health concerned him throughout his life, though it never became a major preoccupation, for it directly affected his professional activities. But more on this in a later chapter.[58]

This general view of an exciting new actor with new views of his own, who, despite the strain, maintained on stage his freshness of appeal for 35 years whets us, perhaps, to see him as we shall through the eyes of skillful observers in his great specific roles. Review of his general theory and illustrative practice sets the stage for a clearer view of his comic and tragic performances.

One senses from abundant generalizing by foreign visitors, as well as by inveterate theatre goers of London that audiences lagged in commentary upon total performance, seeing brilliancies still in spots and commenting upon specifics with more vivid recollection than they did on total effects—Lear's curse and Macbeth's air-drawn daggers stuck in their memories. Yet one must remember that the theatres were not filled nightly with aesthetic theoreticians but with people from a wide range of society. For the populace an evening's entertainment was satisfied by the "whole show"—music, a prologue, a main piece movingly performed, entr'acte singing and dancing, and an after piece of farce, pantomime, or procession to usher them into the night air and dimly lit streets. The central event was the main piece—tragedy, comedy, or opera—but the economics of theatre activity allowed entrance after the third act of the main piece for half price. Garrick recognized, played to, and when manager fostered the joys of the whole show, writing with great creativity his own prologues and after pieces, all of them successful. Writers of all stripes called his acting "natural" in all these parts, and the pages of journals from Dublin to London spoke out again and again their admiration. "Tell me," wrote a versifier for the *Dublin Journal* (14 June 1746), while Garrick was acting a season in that city,

> Tell me thou informing pow'r
> Tell me where the difference lies
> Twixt the actor of an hour
> And of life. The Dame replies
>
> In the force, the fire, the feature
> Usher'd from a feeling heart
> Garrick is the child of Nature
> Mankind only acts the part.

Despite the ambiguity of the term "nature" as used in the century,[59] when "natural" was applied to Garrick's acting people understood the effects of ease, particularization, and credible depth, a freedom from the influence of convention, self-expression without self-consciousness, seeming freedom from premeditation and deliberate design, fidelity in representing attitudes or events, along with seeming spontaneity. His particularizations released the imaginations of onlookers. His Tancred in the 1750s "surpasses everything I have seen on the stage . . . the languid appearance when he is raised from the side of Sigismunda in the last scene. It was said by a French connoisseur upon viewing the famous Magdelene of Le Brun, '*elle pleure aux boits doights*,' signifying that the expression of grief was not confined to the countenance, but extended itself over the whole body. Something similar to this is observable in Mr. Garrick's in the instance referred to. He not only shows affliction painted on his visage in the most picturesque manner, but represents his whole figure broke down with sorrow and every nerve unstrung."[60] Or again, "Mr Garrick has that almost unparalleled qualification of conveying his character into what one would imagine the most trifling and insignificant parts of it, and very often doing more justice to an author in a single and seemingly simple expression, than players of inferior talent could in the most laboured scenes."[61] This care and particularization extended to speaking prologues and epilogues—integral parts of the whole show, as he wrote to John Arthur, manager of the Bristol theatre, for whom he had written an epilogue—"take pains to give the full Effect of it in y$^e$ speaking . . . mimic the *Prude* drawing up herself & speaking affectedly . . . pronounce y$^e$ french *Madame* not like our *Madam*—but broad & Long *Mawdawme*."[62]

But a footnote in all this to Garrick the understanding man interested in having members of his company (as Arthur had been) excell in his manner. "He hoped," wrote Davies, "that [Thomas] King would comprehend his idea of the character of Lord Ogilby [in *The Clandestine Marriage*] and catch from him the manner of executing it." He fixed a day for secret rehearsal in his library, King attended, reluctant to take the part. But he complied and "*in his own way* went through the whole. As soon as he had finished Garrick said, 'Now Mr. King I am perfectly satisfied; you have followed your own conception, and have struck out a manner that becomes you better than if you had imitated me. The audience would have traced you treading in my steps, whereas at present your idea is original. It becomes you, and I beg you will persevere.'"[63] Fixed in his opinions for his own professional self-discipline, desirous for the success of others, but no tyrant where he saw quality and originality! Warm, Garrick was, and understanding in his leadership.

# 3

# The Beginning Manager

AFTER A SUMMER'S APPRENTICESHIP and a year's burgeoning success at the theatre in Goodman's Fields, Garrick entered fully into the swirl of theatrical relationships with rising young actors, with veterans, with differing managerial types, with the facilities of three stages and their theatre audiences. For a period of five years—from 1742 to 1747—submersion in this world with its triumphs and its setbacks matured him immensely.

He spent the summer season of 1742 in a series of performances at the Smock Alley theatre in Dublin, to the delight of the Irish, but not before he set foot on the stage of Drury Lane, England's leading theatre, for three specially contracted performances in late May—as Bayes in *The Rehearsal* (26 May), King Lear (28 May), and Richard III (31 May). He set out for Ireland with an agreement in his pocket from Charles Fleetwood, the Drury Lane manager, that he should article himself there for the 1742–43 season. Options were opening up to the young actor. He wanted to root himself at Drury Lane, but wisely kept the avenues clear for a longer tour of Dublin (which he made in the 1745–46 season) and a trial at least on the boards of Covent Garden (1746–47).

During the period Garrick had grown from a remarkable stage neophyte of 24 to an accomplished actor of 29. He had done more. As a trouper in Dublin and a citizen of London he cultivated friends both in and out of the profession, especially cool-headed friends in London's business community, and leading actors and actresses in two cosmopolitan capitals.

The veteran actor Charles Macklin was attracted to him from the start, and he to Macklin. The elder man saw budding genius there, as yet imperfect in development, but capable of polishing under proper tutelage. The younger man saw in Macklin an original—one strong, very strong in personality, and a source of power at Drury Lane, whose concepts of performance appealed. The actors Dennis Delane and James Quin watched Garrick, and he watched them—mutually affable, but mutually quizzical they were. Thomas Sheridan, the Irish actor born somewhat earlier, had quickly learned of Garrick's attractiveness to London audiences. Garrick respected the accurate, classical, and scholarly approach Sheridan had for the stage. Peg Woffington, the spirited, liberal-minded beauty of the London and Dublin theatres, was attracted to the young man (five years her junior), while her colleague Catherine Clive, Hannah Pritchard, and Susanna Maria Cibber came to feel especially happy in their early coacting with this vivacious, agreeable man of ability and clear dramatic vision. William Havard at once came into and remained within the Garrick orbit. The lives of all these, among others, became closely interwoven professionally with Garrick's.

Macklin, the durable and rugged Irishman, had begun his acting during his school days in Dublin, where in a school play he studied and performed to everyone's astonishment Monimia, the heroine of Otway's *The Orphan*.[1] Subsequently as a strolling player he had to master all sides of theatrics, knocking "up the stage and seats in a barn," writing a prologue, adapting a song and singing it, rebuffing (for he was strong and athletic) stage intruders, appearing in harlequinades as well as in comedy and tragedy.[2] He knew the value of a brogue in dialogue, and worked his precarious way up from farces at London fairs to a term at Lincoln's Inn Fields, where he arrived about the year 1720. When Drury Lane fell apart in 1733 after Colley Cibber's retirement, Macklin became attached there, and was the man-to-be-called-upon in stage matters by John Highmore, then the manager, and his follower, Charles Fleetwood. He was irascible in temper. In a nonsensical dispute in the greenroom over the use of a wig he poked his cane into the eye of fellow actor Thomas Hallam, who died the day after from the blow. Indicted for murder, Macklin was saved from death himself by the intercession of Fleetwood, who led into court a group of character witnesses. The jury found him guilty of manslaughter, but the judge sentenced him only "to be branded on the hand and discharged."[3] He dominated Drury Lane when Garrick was employed there. In the early years he advised Garrick, especially in his performing King Lear, and the younger man improved to Macklin's recorded great satisfaction.[4] The bond between the two seemingly was close.

Thomas Sheridan, the gentleman son of a gentleman schoolmaster and classical rhetorician, was also a Dubliner. Three years Garrick's junior he began his own stage career in the role of Richard III at the Smock Alley theatre 29 January 1743 advertised, as Garrick had been, as "attempted by a young Gentleman." Dublin took to him readily, and when Garrick heard of his success he invited Sheridan to alternate some roles with him in the winter of 1743.[5] Sheridan, in declining, suggested that, "like Castor and Pollux," they should play in different hemispheres. In 1744 he was at Drury Lane working in Fleetwood's company, where report of his added success sufficiently impressed people in Dublin to recall him to become manager of the new theatre in Smock Alley. Before leaving London he engaged Garrick to be his comanager for the 1745–46 season. Their cooperation and their rivalries in various parts became the talk of actors and commentators throughout the rest of their lives. Their sharp evaluation of each other was tempered by their mutual respect.[6]

Although Garrick had enjoyed a fairly sophisticated intellectual upbringing in Lichfield among the choral vicar families, and with the books of Gilbert Walmesley always accessible, nothing there had prepared him to meet and greet the likes of Margaret Woffington. But a short apprenticeship at the London theatres drew him inevitably into her circle. She, already established as the reigning wit and beauty of the stage, captivated all men. He watched her play at Covent Garden during the 1740–41 season, and actually played King Lear opposite her Cordelia at Drury Lane in May 1742. None were surprised when the two of them crossed over to Dublin together that first summer to play at Smock Alley. Thus commenced a theatrical alliance which year in and year out for a time attracted comment from writers, and has since caused speculation by all biographers of each, for David Garrick the rising star was in love with Mistress Woffington the most accomplished actress from Dublin, charmer of all. The relationship indeed affected Garrick personally as well as professionally. The Dublin summer season was a great success, but there also, at the rival theatre was Susanna Maria Cibber.

Later that autumn Peg Woffington joined Garrick in the Bow Street house of Charles Macklin in what some supposed to be a triumvirate housekeeping arrangement. Ostensibly each was to train up aspiring actors, but each was free to pursue his and her own dramatic career. Each was for a stated period to manage the household details and finances. That Macklin could have participated in a *ménage à trois* with whatever sexual overtones the phrase suggests seems a remote possibility, for he was then married, with a child, Maria, eight years old, and was appearing regularly with his wife on the stage at Drury Lane.[7] The arrangement between Peg and Garrick soon collapsed, we know not why, but presumably over management of the finances perhaps on both sides. The two continued to act together at Drury Lane, through three successful seasons. Late in May 1745 Garrick retired for

Margaret Woffington.
Painting by Henry Pickering.

some rest to Teddington, where Peg had established a home, and where at one time Garrick had assisted in some private theatricals. He was about to propose marriage, but in the autumn they terminated all social relations. The following season (1745–46) when Garrick at Sheridan's invitation went again to Smock Alley, he and she acted there often together, and again in 1746–47 at Covent Garden. But when Garrick arose to comanagership of Drury Lane in April 1747, he neither acted with her thereafter, nor engaged her after that season to come to the Drury Lane company. For her last ten years on stage she performed at Covent Garden or in Dublin.

Yet for three crucial years in his professional development Garrick was in love with Peg Woffington, and their love affair became public property for comment by all hack writers, rivals, and admirers. On stage, however, Peg was a superior and versatile actress, one who not merely exploited her physical charm, but one who developed by intelligence and application a superior dramatic skill. According to Arthur Murphy she possessed every "honor, truth, benevolence, and charity" and above all else the charm of a vivacious conversationalist. Garrick in an early love poem to her conveys a sense of his genuine recognition of her beauty, brains, and charm, and his wish to love her all his life. In this courting verse he notes that if his love were only infatuation, possession would "cure the wounded heart / Destroy the transient fires." Contemporaries assumed that he did possess her in the conventional sense, but only as so many had possessed her. Her promiscuity became notable with men of the theatre as well as with titled and social adventurers, but with all an almost masculinelike relish. This transitory inconstancy, as she encouraged and satisfied a succession of lovers—the Lord Darnleys and Sir Thomas Hanbury-Williamses of the world, distressed Garrick, and became the source of conflict within himself for the three years of their relationship. Nothing has been recorded of Peg's attitude toward Garrick. Although they exchanged gifts and letters, none of the letters survives, yet two versions of the final break do. The first, mentioned half a century after the event by William Cooke in his *Memoirs of Charles Macklin*, is a long poem presumably written and sent by Garrick to her in June 1745, proposing to expose the naked truth of her lovers and his distress:

> I know your sophistry, I know your art
> Which all your dupes and fools control;
> Yourself you give without your heart—
> All may share *that* but not your soul[8]

The second version of the break comes from Garrick himself (an item saved, incredibly, by Mrs Garrick) in a letter written to his close friend Somerset Draper (bookseller, brewer, and financial advisor) on 23 October 1745, appropriately from Lichfield where Garrick had gone to regain his bearings: "*Woffington,* I am told, shews my letters about; pray have you heard any thing of that kind? What she does now, so little affects me, that, excepting her shewing my letters of nonsense and *love* to make me ridiculous, she can do nothing to give me a moment's uneasiness—*the scene is changed—I'm alter'd quite*" (37). Bitter though he may have been, Garrick honored his memory of her. He returned her letters and gifts, keeping only the diamond buckles she had once given him, and which he wore to the end of his life.

Survival of another kind for this love has beguiled the imaginations of more recent biographers. Though no eighteenth-century record has come to light to support the allegation, it was proposed by gossips late in the century that Peg bore an illegitimate son to Garrick, one Samuel Cautherly, who died in 1805. No record or even rumor occurs that Peg ever bore a child. But as to Cautherly, Garrick engaged him as a child actor 29 April 1755, after which Cautherly became his special protégé. He sent him to Hawkesworth's school in Bromley, took him into his household, sent him to France for further schooling, and paid his expenses there. "The boy is a Sweet Lad," he wrote 17 March 1759 to Hawkesworth, "& of a most insinuating disposition, & his follies are those of Idleness & Indulgence." Cautherly stayed with the Drury Lane company until 1775, and years later (in 1805) wrote to the aged Mrs Garrick: "The Gratitude I shall ever feel for the many kindnesses confer'd on me, while under your Hospitable roof (for almost Twenty years) can never be effaced" (228n.2).

*If* Cautherly were Peg's son (and who knows who the father could have been) all that can be concluded is that Garrick cared for the boy in past affection and memory of three years of happiness, hope, and wretchedness with her. His preservation (if this be so) of the identity of the boy as Cautherly was all in keeping with a regard for the mother and the boy.

The experience with Peg had great influence upon Garrick in his relationships with the other women he knew and was to know. Though he found other actresses often trying as prima donnas, he never belittled them as women. He treated all with a respect due their individuality and their attainments. He took advantage of no young actresses. He involved himself in no social scandal. His decision to forgo the life-style offered him by Peg Woffington and her lovers was all to the advantage of the English theatre, and to the women he came to know, care for, and support by his friendship.

As mentioned, when Garrick and Peg played their first summer at Smock Alley, Mrs Cibber was competing at the theatre in Aungier Street. Just when Garrick became acquainted with Susanna Maria Arne (Mrs Theophilus Cibber) is uncertain, but she was to become a major figure in his acting career. After a three-year absence from the London stage (1738–41), during which she was escaping the persecution of her husband, she had (probably with her protector, William Sloper, and their daughter) gone in the company of Handel and James Quin for a season's performing in Dublin. They arrived on 5 June 1741, some four months, that is, before Garrick made his debut in London. In Dublin Susanna made a triumphal comeback on the stage especially in her singing in Handel's *The Messiah*. Word about this reaching London, she was again sought after to return. She let Quin, who returned in the spring of 1742, arrange for her articles of employment. She stipulated, however, that she was *never* to play opposite Theophilus, or in any theatre where he was engaged. Comfortable in a social group in Dublin she asked her brother Thomas Arne, the musician, and his wife, Cecilia Young, to come over in June 1742 for a summer season of concerts,[9] at the same time Garrick and Peg Woffington arrived. Garrick was then completely absorbed with his attachment to Peg. Mrs Cibber's Dublin admirers engaged in no sexual sparring for her, or in seeking to supplant William Sloper. Where Margaret Woffington was sparkling, sophisticated, challenging in all senses, and capable on stage in spirited parts, Susanna Cibber was subdued, languishing, patient, quiet, and though possessing a fine sense of humor, excelled in tragic heroines and put-down females.

Presumably, however, on the trip back across the Irish Sea Garrick and Mrs Cibber met, for he and the Arne contingent were aboard the same small vessel in the crossing—the packet *Lovely Jane*, which left Dublin 23 August.[10] During the upcoming season Garrick played at Drury Lane, and Mrs Cibber at Covent Garden. She did not play at all during the next season (1743–44). But both found themselves in Drury Lane's company during 1744–45, along with Peg Woffington. For the 1745–46 season she moved again to Covent Garden, while Garrick went to Dublin to share managership with Sheridan. During the season of 1746–47 (and after Garrick had broken with Peg) they were both playing (and in many of the same plays) at the Covent Garden house.

An obvious friendship had sprung up between the two but on a pattern of emotional relationship of tender understanding and mutual respect, which was to mark Garrick's attitude towards the women of his acquaintance for the rest of his life. Often the two were professional rivals, more often they were acting partners in the same company, at which times she was his leading lady, most highly paid, and a special friend. He told Horace Walpole later that he could easily control a noisy complaint from Mrs Pritchard or Mrs Clive, but Mrs Cibber could persuade him out of anything.

Born in 1714 she was three years Garrick's elder. In 1734 her ambitious father, a Covent Garden upholsterer who had given her and her brother a musical education, presented her in marriage to Colley Cibber's son Theophilus, thus opening to her opportunity for a stage career. The Cibbers trained her well for suitable parts, as did Quin and Handel, her great admirers and devoted friends. Four years later she deserted Theophilus, with the approval of the jury who heard her rather despicable husband's two suits for infidelity (into which he had pushed her), and for the rest of her life lived with, and bore children to William Sloper, a gentleman of fortune, quiet and steady, whose home, Woodhay, near Burnham was on the way from London to Bath.

In their personal relations Garrick visited Susanna in her home on Craven Street in Scotland Yard,[11] with all her theatrical and musical friends, and the Garricks often visited her and Mr Sloper at Woodhay on journeys to and from Bath. Their correspondence survives from 1745, when for this and the following two years Garrick was involved with ticklish negotiations for management of Drury Lane. In the negotiations Garrick turned for advice to Somerset Draper and urged him (while Garrick was in Dublin) to keep in touch with Mrs Cibber. "Mrs. Cibber," he wrote, "proposes a scheme for our acting with *Mr. Quin* gratis in the Haymarket; in order to raise a sum of money to enlist men for His Majesty's service" (38), and again "She has written me two letters, and talks much of *buying the patent*, and thinks we may purchase it immediately" (41). Elsewhere he wrote Draper "*Mrs. Cibber* writes me word, that she is turned out of Drury Lane, and that the schemers intend sending Theophilus to her to force her compliance; she still presses me to *visit her*, that we may *settle something*; but my head runs on the *buck-basket* [where Falstaff ended up in *The Merry Wives of Windsor*] and no more intrigues for me" (32).

Garrick and Susanna, however, continued their correspondence in much the same tone and manner as that of Garrick and Draper—frank, virtuous, and personal on the progress of the negotiations at Drury Lane. A mutually rewarding friendship lasted between them for 25 years in which Susanna desired Garrick early on (November 1745) "to be my lover upon the stage, and my friend off it."[12]

Garrick in turn was solicitous about her acting roles, and about her health and increasing spells of illness. As he was about to leave the stage for a long vacation in France (September 1763) he concluded a letter to her: "If Your or M$^r$ Sloper have any Commands to France or Italy I shall Obey them with pleasure Mrs Garrick desires her best Comp$^{ts}$ to all about You" (315). To which she replied on 8 September, "Though I had read a paragraph in the papers that you intended going abroad, I gave no credit to it. However sorry I am for my own sake, I think you do right, and wish to God I could do the same: my best wishes and compliments wait on you and Mrs Garrick. Mr. Sloper and my daughter join in the same." She hoped he would write, and offered to carry out any request from him for errands in England.[13]

When Mrs Cibber was first in Dublin, wrote Davies, she had conquered even clerical prejudice against her reputation in the Sloper arrangement when she sang so sweetly and with such feeling the "he was despised" aria from the *Messiah*, for Dr Delaney, chancellor of St. Patrick's, remarked "Woman for this thy sins be forgiven thee." Pale and slender always from the trials of her life she could at the age of 50 play effectively the part of a girl of 17 in Whitehead's *School for Lovers*, "owing," said Benjamin Victor, "to that uncommon symmetry and exact proportion of form that happily remained with her to her death."[14] Her quiet, sensible, but affectionate friendship for Garrick, particularly at a time of his life when he needed such, bespeaks the quality of her character. In conversation extremely agreeable, civil without constraint, and polite without affectation—accomplishments which rendered her "dear to persons of the first quality of her own sex," wrote Davies, "there was ever such an engaging decency in her manners, that, notwithstanding a peculiarity of situation, she charmed and obliged all who approached her. She was a perfect judge of music, vocal and instrumental; and though she was not mistress of a voice requisite to a capital singer, yet her fine taste was sure to gain her the applause and admiration of the best judges."[15] When she died in 1766, age 51, and was buried in the cloister of Westminster Abbey, Garrick lamented that "half of Tragedy is dead," and closed the theatre that night in her memory.[16] He had acted with her 426 times.

Garrick's first five years of experience as an actor under several different managers were both useful and confining to the independent spirit and practical imaginings of the young man. Knowing his own strengths and accepting challenges in all sorts of roles he early sensed that acting was not a solo profession. The greatest artistic impact of a play lay in its excellent ensemble performance. The resulting satisfactions to the players could be great, and the advantages for the profession were tremendous. How could he best select, shape, and command his fellow actors to this end? Not under Highmore, or Fleetwood, or Rich, certainly, whose theatre involvements were keyed primarily to the business profits resulting from whatever cartel they could arrange and preserve under the Licensing Act. Management was the chair to seek, for management, as he had tasted it in Dublin, involved all aspects of theatre performance. Management he knew required capital for assured backing, which for him as he was aspiring to the chair meant a partnership.

Aesthetic, but pragmatic considerations had become important to him as he mused about his future in Dublin in 1745. News, as was hinted in Mrs Cibber's letters, came across the Irish Sea that the bankers Norton Amber and Richard Green—the backers of James Lacy, the then new manager of Drury Lane—had extended themselves too far at the time of the Jacobite rebellion, and had declared bankruptcy. Mrs Cibber hoped the actors would act betimes to secure their own futures. Thereupon Garrick wrote to Draper (December 1745): "Sure some thing must happen in the theatrical state, that may turn to my advantage; can Lacy support the House without them [the bankers]? I am positive he cannot; therefore my dear Draper, look about a little, and *if you can conveniently wriggle your little friend into the patent upon good terms, you make me for ever*" (42).

The actual offer to manage Drury Lane came only a season and a half later, after Garrick ended in Dublin and completed a season with Rich at Covent Garden (1746–47). When it did come Garrick found himself forced to join with James Lacy. Brief recall of some theatre history and of Garrick's scars from brief encounters with Fleetwood and Lacy management practices throws light on Garrick's cautions and priorities as he came into the power and responsibilities of his new management.

Garrick had been primarily an actor. Adversary situations were not uncommon between actors and management even as far back as Betterton's day. Actor self-assertion against nonactor patentees and businessmen managers had a long history in London. Betterton had led a group of rebellious players, back in 1695, to seek a new theatre and get a license to perform on their own. Within a decade the project disintegrated, only to be picked up by the remarkable triumvirate of actors Barton Booth, Robert Wilks, and Colley Cibber for a golden period of prosperity from 1708 to 1733.[17] Cibber later in his *Apology* put his finger on the basis for a sure breakup of theatre affairs, namely when the chief actors and the owner managers were at variance.[18] Garrick knew the history and the comment.

When the Cibber triumvirate disbanded from deaths and retirement

in 1733, with the patent being sold to the businessman John Highmore, rather than descending to Colley's son Theophilus, a new 15
year phase of confusion and disintegration set in. Young Cibber
seemed resolved to wreck the new manager. He made exorbitant demands for salary increases (all in the name of his fellow actors), and
unsuccessful in this, led a group of his compeers in a walkout to set
up a rival company. The revolt lasted but a single season, for Theophilus could not obtain a license to perform longer. Most of the actors
returned, but Highmore's legal problems coupled with loss of theatre
income prompted him to sell his interests to another businessman,
Charles Fleetwood.[19] Although Macklin straightway became Fleetwood's stage manager, many of the financial decisions fell into the
hands of Pierson, the treasurer, whose skill in alienating people of all
types and ranks was unsurpassed. Even the affable Garrick had refused
to act in Pierson's benefit—the only occasion in his life in which he
turned down such a request. By the spring of 1743 actors' salaries and
those of the house servants, seldom regularly paid, came into arrears
of several thousand pounds. Garrick and Macklin, not willing to tolerate such a state of affairs led a walkout with a group of other actors.[20]
It had seemed to Garrick, as it had to Colley Cibber, that fiscal and
artistic division in the theatre bred decay unless lines of authority
and a rational division of labor were clearly drawn.

The Garrick-Macklin group was as unsuccessful in obtaining a license as Theophilus Cibber's group had been. The members held out
as long as they could—until December 1743, when Garrick yielded to
pressure from the really distressed minor actors, and returned with
them to Fleetwood's employ. All were accepted back save Macklin,
who had incurred Fleetwood's enmity for ingratitude, and for supposedly instigating the walkout—after all, Fleetwood had saved his life
in the Hallam trial. A spate of furious pamphlets ensued, as members
of the town grew interested and took sides, spurred on by a cartoon
"The Theatrical Contest" (24 October 1743).[21] In this poster-sized picture the seceders, carried upon the watery flood of uncertainty by the
bladders of their performance of favorite parts, appeal to the Lord
Chamberlain for a new license against Fleetwood, who kneeling pleads
also while manager John Rich watches with pleasure the crowds of
theatregoers pour into his competing house.

The revolt, justified by 11 years of chaotic conditions, ran to its
last endurable moment. Garrick's return, traumatic to Macklin by his
exclusion forever from any stage managed by Fleetwood, left an indelible impression on the 26-year-old Garrick. He was caught in an
insoluble power struggle. For Fleetwood had first used Macklin to at-

tract Garrick to Drury Lane, and Macklin, turning against the manager, bound Garrick in a two-way compact that they should hold out to break Fleetwood, or leave together for Ireland. But Macklin and Garrick had persuaded eight other good but lesser actors to join them to thwart Fleetwood's proposed reduction in salaries. These seceders, now without a license to act, arrived at a point of starvation, and some were elderly.

Fleetwood would take the eight back *only* if Garrick came with them. Garrick wanted to help them, and proposed three compromises to help Macklin. The proud Macklin obdurately refused, and accused Garrick of reneging on a personal bond to him regardless of the fate of the others.[22] The moral dilemma must have made Garrick's heart ache, but it also apprenticed him in the severest emotional way to the perils of management, the human problems involved, and the need for regularizing stage operations in a fair and agreeable fashion.

Macklin, enraged, broke his story in a two-page broadside to the press—"Case" he called it—on the Tuesday morning of Garrick's return to play Bayes in *The Rehearsal*. Anger engendered by the "Case" prompted the audience to a near riot, driving Garrick off the stage. Two days later appeared Garrick's "Answer" to Macklin's "Case," in a four-page pamphlet, wherein the young actor cried "foul," corrected misstatements in Macklin's text, deplored his "going public" for timing a riot before allowing Garrick a response to his contentions. He quoted a letter from the starving eight, the main point of which was that the pact had been made *on the assumption* that they *would* receive a license. When the license was refused the pact ended, and everyone was on his own. To this Macklin replied scathingly, boring in on two points, in effect, "you Garrick deserted me, you did not continue to hold out by going with me to act elsewhere, and the dissolution of the pact with the eight does not release you from the obligation to remain with me."[23] But Fleetwood held the trump card: no Garrick, no return of the eight.

The presses busied themselves. Garrick and London town had some serious thinking to do, when an anonymous writer in 34 specific *Questions to Be Answered by the Manager of Drury Lane for the Satisfaction of the Public in Regard to the present Disputes between Him and the Actors* came to the basic issue in overall theatrical business. *Question 16* focused on the fate of actors who, when old and disabled, had to rely upon the whim of a manager. *Question 20* spoke of the issue of nightly theatre costs: If expenses were mounting could not the best of Shakespeare be acted by the best actors at their present salaries at less expense than £50 per night? *Question 21* spoke to the issue of open dealing: Should not the financial books of the theatres be made public, if the public is to be thrust into such an embroilment as this one? *Questions 25* and *26* sought to sort out the principles of action versus managerial resentments: Is not the reprisal against Macklin a blind for the real purpose of reducing actor salaries, and for abetting a theatre cartel? *Question 34* raised the problem of essential humanitarianism: Have not the under members of the company suffered intolerably by nonpayment of wages, only to be laughed at by the treasurer?

The pamphlet concluded by defining a good manager as one who "ought to have *good sense* to regulate a body of people; *good nature* to appease animosities within doors; and *prudence* to prevent tumult without; *Judgment* in the choice of his plays; *decency* in the conduct of them; *taste* in his decorations; *impartiality* in disposing of his characters; *good manners* in his treatment of authors; *generosity* to regard merit; and above all *honesty* to perform his contracts."[24] These points Garrick engraved on the tables of his memory, for the whole theatre public was now thinking of the lack of pensions for actors, of managerial accountability to the profession as well as to the public, of meeting payrolls regularly, and of a practical standard of managerial attributes which would assure favorable public response.

Hardly a fortnight passed, however, before a set of counter arguments reached the public in the anonymous *Queries upon Queries to Be Answered by the Male-content Actors*.[25] To each of the 34 "Questions" first proposed it responded negatively upon the sole argument that actors formed no more privileged a class than any other members of the community. To carry out for *every* trade and profession the suggestions implied for the actors would tear apart the fabric of society. The sought-after collective bargaining would amount to a cartel in reverse.

Garrick returned to Drury Lane and saved the eight, and was accepted by the audience after the first riotous night. Macklin was excluded and brooded bitterly. Catherine Clive could return only at a reduced salary, which she refused and found herself excluded also from Covent Garden, and eventually too late to apply for acting the rest of the season at Dublin. Garrick thereafter praised Macklin wherever he could, as in his *Essay on Acting*,[26] in which he commended Macklin for the careful study of the people he was to impersonate, for his natural acting, and for eschewing preconceived attitudes. "I shall not enter into the reasons why he is excluded at present, but shall only say as an advocate for the public, that I wish for their sake there were many more such actors as him upon both theatres." Any brashness that might have appeared in the young and successful Garrick was sobered by this experience. The whole episode emphasized his ultimate need to be his own master, and to manage in such a way as to obviate causes for repetitions of such disastrous actor walkouts.

By 1747 this traumatic experience had dimmed in its details, though Fleetwood's managerial problems had multiplied. He borrowed heavily from bankers Amber and Green, and freed himself from other problems first by finding a deputy, James Lacy, then by departing to France. Lacy, an Irish actor, had for years been in and out of theatrical enterprises. He had come to London as a young man about 1720, and by 1738 was studying ways to get around the Licensing Act by putting on shows for one-night stands here and there about town. He knew the theatres, and had a care for limiting expenses and husbanding cash. Amber and Green thought his talents would work in their best interests.

Garrick's and Lacy's initial relationship was not the happiest for either. Garrick found arrearages in salary from Fleetwood not made up by the late Spring of 1745 so left to comanage Smock Alley with Sheridan the next season. Lacy accused him of breach of contract in the frequency of his performing and had been testing out his authority over him by determining the number of nights he was to play. He found that he could not manipulate Garrick, and learned from Garrick's long and detailed letter of mid-October not only that he had mistaken his man, but that his relationship should chart a different course were they ever to be together again. The tone of Garrick's letter left him no doubt that his tactics had been wrong. Wrote Garrick, "What I had already experienced of your proceedings had given me such an insight into your character that I was not surprised in the least to find you fallacious in reasoning & bold in the misrepresentation of facts" (36). Garrick kept a copy of the letter for possible future use, endorsing it "The story of Lacy's offering . . . to make a sham quarrel to redu[ce] the other actors salaries."

Garrick had in fact been extremely ill, and, outraged by Lacy's treatment, explained, "I was but just recovering from my illness I asked the physicians who had honour[ed] me with their attendance whether I might venture to play a character or two before the season ended. Their opinion was I should run great hazard of my life & that if I continued to act so much as I had done the consequences might prove fatal. This was a caution I had already had from the most eminent physician in Dublin; & has been often repeated to me. I will appeal to any body who has seen me play but yourself whether I am capable of undergoing more fatigue in a week than the characters of Hamlet,

Richard or Macbeth give me." He added that he had played and would play comic parts whenever Lacy scheduled them. As to Lacy's assertion that he had played only thrice a week, Garrick told him to check the playbills, and see that his facts were wrong—he had played four and five times a week, "& tho by my articles I was not obliged to play laborious capital parts two nights successively, yet I have done it often at your desire to my own prejudice." The final sentences of his letter showed the firmness of his mind: "I shall abide by my last agreem<sup>t</sup> which I have not broke in the smallest article. *if the conditions are comply'd with on your part. I will return to Drury lane, & will to the [u]tmost of my power endeavour to entertain the town & adva[nce] the interest in the manager.* for there can be no reason given why I should suffer by the schemes of Managers. [who] by breaking the most legal & equitable contracts. make new ones among themselves to evade the first" (36).

Lacy, though tightfisted with finances, was no fool. He knew what he had lost in Garrick's departure and was to come with a different frame of mind to a new relationship two years later. The tone and content of this letter is basic to our understanding of the subdued and secondary role that Lacy played in the comanagership with Garrick that subsequently took place.

Garrick felt sure that he could, if given authority in a joint partnership, clarify management procedures and spell out in some written form (for clear guidelines) the obligations and responsibilities of actors vis-à-vis managers; but as a start he wanted clear definitions to be written down and understood between managers themselves. During the Smock Alley season he sized up the advantages and pitfalls of the option of comanagement, and was not sanguine, since there both he and Sheridan were to work for a set of proprietors, and since their specific areas of operation were not spelled out. He wrote to Draper from Dublin 1 December 1745: "My brother Manager and I at present are civil. . . . I intend to behave in such a manner, that no blame shall light upon me, but (*entre nous*) he is as shifting as Lacy, and has got an indifferent character among people here" (40).

Mrs Cibber wanted very, very much to join with Garrick in some kind of professional partnership for the better running of Drury Lane. She proposed 24 October 1745 combining the three obvious acting strengths of Garrick, Quin, and herself. In another century such a partnership might have worked, but the now experienced and natively shrewd Garrick shied away from it for two very good reasons. First, he wanted no three-way arrangement, preferring to join with a single good businessman, and second, laws and customs being what they

66

JAMES LACY ESQ.
(Late Patentee of the Theatre Royal Drury Lane,
From an original Portrait in the Possession of W. Lacy

*Harvard Theatre Collection*
James Lacy.
Engraving from an original portrait.

were in 1745, he feared that if Mrs Cibber were involved in any way, most certainly her estranged husband Theophilus would somehow muscle in, or make such a pest of himself that hours and weeks of administrative time would be taken up with him, and none could doubt that he, litigious as he was, would go to the public press upon the least provocation.[27]

Garrick at one time hoped that Hutchinson Mure, a prosperous London merchant, might buy Lacy's share. He thought he could work with him, but Mure was interested only in laying out money for mort-gages—both at Drury Lane and at Covent Garden, and partnership with him would have involved yet a third party, probably Lacy, to whom Fleetwood had signed over the patent (41).

Affairs came to a head, however, in the spring of 1747. Partnership, if partnership were to be, would have to be with Lacy. Garrick moved from a position of strength, for no theatre that wanted to survive could do without his acting talents,[28] and moved from knowledge, gained early under Giffard, seasoned under Fleetwood, and polished with Sheridan.[29] The two eyed each other carefully, and each entered the partnership with distinct reservations about the other.

After a long period of negotiation, and Garrick's refusal to put up a penny more than £12,000 as his share, a contract was signed (9 April 1747) with Lacy for the joint management of Drury Lane theatre. The contract laid responsibility upon Lacy to obtain the new patent for both, granted Garrick £500 annually as proprietor (for his managing activities) and 500 guineas annually as an actor. It forbade Garrick's acting elsewhere, and provided a clear benefit night for him each year. A "clear benefit' meant that all the cash came to the actor and that the normal house charges would be absorbed by the theatre. It stated that he would "enter into & execute proper Articles of Copartnership for the carrying on & managing the Business of the s^d Patents for their joint & equal benefit" (III, app. B). A subdued Lacy accepted. The articles defining the separate responsibilities of each seem not to have got onto paper until 1750, when Garrick's solicitor, John Paterson, drew up the seven-point specifications to obviate any future misunder-standings. They provided that Garrick alone should "settle or alter" the business of the stage, that hiring of all hands and stipulations about salaries should be joint, that George Garrick be deputized to act for Garrick in the business office of the theatre, that all differences be-tween the managers be laid before Paterson as arbitrator, and that irreconcilable ones be settled by an auctioning off of the property, that when either partner died, a similar auction be carried out for the bene-fit of the heirs and assigns, and that these specified agreements remain confidential. The documents and Garrick's letters to Lacy leading up to the contract are calm, rational, tight, and businesslike. Garrick at 30, dedicated to the theatre, reveled in being at the very center of dramatic and theatrical activity. His was a business and a profession, and a devotion to an art that he was daily practicing. Given his business, acting, writing talents, and his experience, order was bound to assert itself and the theatre to prosper.

A first, major, and continuing concern of the young manager was for the artistic supremacy of his theatre. Such supremacy involved mastery of a corporate attitude, so to speak, toward morality, artistic production, novelty, variety, and appropriate topical reference. Plays and their performance should entertain. That is comedy should provide amusement and escape from the humdrum of life; tragedy, release from the tensions built up and aroused in it, hence satisfaction of emotional concerns. Both should be salted now and again with a note reflecting or refracting of current events or topics uppermost in the drift of the current of ideas. Grand strategy in these matters involved the repertory, scheduling, casting, costuming, and mounting appropriate remarkable scenery. His company was playing before a generation fascinated by watching, after the first raising of the curtain, the movement of the sets as part of the progress of plays on stage. To these tasks of management were added the providing of music and dance.

Garrick was familiar with Dryden's remarks that "In the playhouse everything contributes to impose upon the judgment: the lights, the scenes, the habits, and above all the grace of action, which is commonly best where there is most need of it, surprise the audience and cast a mist upon their understanding." He knew, as Dryden knew, "that these false beauties of the stage were no more lasting than the rainbow," and that when the actor ceased to shine in them and gild them no more with his accomplished presence they would "vanish in a twinkling." [30] But the fascination was there, and the challenge was there, and the joy of individual fulfillment was there. And the anonymous definition of managerial attributes from the "Queries" in the Macklin "Case" came again and again to his mind, calling for good sense, good nature, prudence, judgment, decency, taste, impartiality, good manners, generosity, and scrupulous honesty.

Garrick also knew from six years of experience that implementing artistry, novelty, variety, morality, embroidered with topical commentary was not within the powers of a single person—though his individual leadership must count and count heavily. He also knew that for Londoners the "whole show" of an evening counted, a fact which disappointed authors, who, arrogating central stage to their own works, could not, or would not understand. Implementing the "whole show" depended upon the specific behavior of the theatrical personnel more than on anything else. His company—the entire company—actors, actresses, singers, dancers, musicians, supernumeraries, and 20 to 30 house servants (treasurers, boxkeepers, lobby keepers, wardrobe keepers, carpenters, painters, sweepers, lamplighters, checkers, concessionaires, and bill stickers) could be cajoled, persuaded, or ordered into cohesive useful action. But the forward movement, he would come to discover, was never a single wave of joyous cooperation. When Mrs Abington at the last minute balked at a part, Garrick wrote "we shall not mount Much, if your cold Counter Acting discourse is to pull us back at every Step" (865). The reprimand came late in his career, but typifies a personnel problem he encountered from the start. His comment was sharp and exasperated, yet gentle and apt, typical of his managerial tone.

Had Garrick not become manager of Drury Lane but remained at Covent Garden in 1747, the course of stage history might have changed radically. For that season Rich's theatre boasted one of the strongest companies of actors in the century, one which with little development could have blanked all competition. There among others were John Beard, singer, William Havard, all-round actor, John Hippisley, everyone's comedian, John Rich, harlequin, James Quin, tragedian and comedian, Henry Woodward, equal in most categories with all the rest, and Garrick. The actresses were stellar, including both Mrs Cibber and Mrs Pritchard. Great singers and a remarkable group of dancers rounded out the complement. Suddenly the balance changed in Drury Lane's favor when Garrick took with him Mrs Cibber, Mrs Pritchard, and Havard; when Quin sulked at Bath; and Woodward departed for Smock Alley.

At Drury Lane he could count on the support of Macklin, Mrs Woffington, and Mrs Clive. There also was Dennis Delane, who had commenced his acting career in Smock Alley, Dublin, as early as 1729. Two years later he had been engaged by Giffard at Goodman's Fields, where his fine figure and rich voice, his interpretive ability in the older style of acting gained him credit with London audiences, though some felt he lacked variation and modulation in his speaking. He did well in loud, angry parts in tragedy, especially in Alexander the Great. He had moved back and forth from the Dublin to the London theatres spending a good number of years with his friend Quin at Covent Garden. He was a Trinity College, Dublin, man originally intended for the law. He would be useful, but soon, unfortunately, he grew portly, sluggish, and took to the bottle, dying in 1750.[31]

At Drury Lane Garrick could also count on Spranger Barry, Lacy's one major appointment there for the previous year, who too came from Ireland. Thomas Gray wrote to Walpole about him. "He is upwards of six feet in height, well and proportionably made, treads well, and knows what to do with his limbs . . . a graceful figure. . . . His voice is of a clear and pleasing tone, something like Delane's, but not so deep-mouthed, not so like a passing bell . . . when it sinks into any softer passion, particularly expressive and touching . . . in the scenes of rage and jealousy he was seldom inferior to Quin, in the parts of tenderness and sorrow far above him." [32] In Othello he was remarkable.

At Drury Lane was a promising actor Thomas Mozeen, formerly bred to the law, but who had quit it for the stage in the mid-1740s. He had first appeared in Giffard's company at Lincoln's Inn Fields, where he became an all-around actor in tragedy and comedy, competent in supporting roles and second lords—Sir Charles Freeman in *The Stratagem*, Stanley in *Richard III*, the Player in *The Beggar's Opera*. The faithful William Havard came also with Garrick. They had been together in Giffard's company. Son of a Dublin vintner, in his youth apprenticed to a surgeon, he had left that profession early for an acting career in London. He became the accomplished wheelhorse of each company he had been with—always decent, sensible, perfect in understanding his roles. He played fine gentlemen with ease and grace, comely and genteel in person. Contemporaries thought he lacked passion for some tragic roles, and that his voice, though clear and articulate, tended toward a certain monotony. But he became a staple at Drury Lane, where he wrote prologues and plays to boot. [33]

In a year's time Garrick was also to attract Henry Woodward back from Ireland. He had been born the same year as Garrick and was educated at the Merchant Taylor's School. His father hoped he would follow his trade as tallow chandler, but Rich took him on as a child to perform in his experimental *The Beggar's Opera* with an all-child cast. He performed Peachum with such success that he stayed on in the profession. As a young man he had become an excellent comic performer in Touchstone, Petruchio, the Fine Gentleman in Garrick's *Lethe*. Garrick later cast him as Bobadil in the revived *Every Man in His Humour*, one of his outstanding parts. [34] *The Theatrical Review for 1757* records for us Woodward's paradoxical qualifications as comedian —his figure perfectly genteel, voice smart and agreeable seeming to point him for genteel roles which he naturally would grace, "yet he never pleases his audience more than when he is oblig'd to distort that figure into the awkward deportment of a Scrub, or to swell his voice to hectoring accents of a Bobadil." He played second to Garrick, and car-

ried his comic parts when he did not play. His Mercutio was outstanding.

Edward Shuter was also a member of that opening company. Young
at the time he had come from being a pot boy in the taverns near
Covent Garden to make his debut as Master Shuter at Rich's theatre,
in 1745. He was to grow into a fine Falstaff, Obediah Prim (in *A Bold
Stroke for a Wife*), and Lovegold in *The Miser*. *The Theatrical Review
for 1757–58* writes about him ten years after he started with Garrick.
"Mr. Shuter owes everything to nature, to nature unimproved. . . .
Art and education have left his natural parts untainted by imitation.
He is undoubtedly an original actor He has strong features and is happy
in a peculiar turn of face, which he could throw into many very ridiculous shapes. Tho' bordering on grimace they were seldom disagreeable. His eyes were expressive and could put on a ridiculous demure-
ness, the soul of humour, which caused great laughter. He was often
too droll and apt to laugh at his own jests. His favorite epilogue was
in the character of Joe Haines riding on an ass." John Rich, depleted,
indeed saw need for new starts and new recruits even to measure up
to his young competitor.

Garrick had been sure that Mrs Cibber would come with him. He
had wanted very much to attract Hannah Vaughan Pritchard as well,
which would give his company the four absolutely leading ladies of the
age. Hannah Pritchard, six years older than Garrick, had begun her
career singing in Fielding and Hippisley's Booth during Bartholomew
Fair in 1733, from which she graduated to the Haymarket Theatre,
singing as Nell in the popular *Devil to Pay*. There as a 22-year-old
actress she quickly took on a great variety of roles in tragedy and
comedy, as well as in musicals. Thence she moved to and from Drury
Lane and Covent Garden until the 1747 season, but was Garrick's
thereafter until her retirement. Dr Johnson found her not the conversationalist or intellect he found in Mrs Woffington, Mrs Clive, or Mrs
Cibber, but was amazed at her ability on stage to rise from common
mispronunciations in daily conversation (saying *gownd* for *gown*) as
though being inspired to "gentility and understanding."[35] Edward
Gibbon commented on "the surprising versatility of [her] talents, who
rehearsed almost at the same time the part of a famous Queen in the
greenroom, and that of a coquette on the stage; and passed several
times from one to the other with the utmost ease and happiness."[36]
Garrick saw in her what the audiences saw and what Davies described
—a slender woman with an attractive countenance, expressive yet
simple in manner whose unembarrassed deportment and proper action

*Harvard Theatre Collection*
Mrs Hannah Pritchard.
From a portrait by Francis Hayman.

charmed. Her delivery of dialogue appealed especially to Garrick's sense of realism. "She uttered her words as the great poet advises the actor, smoothly and trippingly from the tongue, and however voluble in enunciation her part might require her to be, not a syllable of articulation was lost."[37]

Her family, the Vaughans, was one of professional actors and theatre people, and her daughter Prudence as a young girl played a happy performance of Juliet to her mother's Lady Capulet and Garrick's Romeo (9 October 1756), and thereafter married John Palmer, a Drury Lane actor who became manager of the theatre at Bath. Mrs Pritchard was remarkable among actresses for leading a "wholly blameless and respectable life."[38] She was the greatest Lady Macbeth of her time, but could do equally well in the part of Doll Common.

Garrick, aware of the jockeying prevalent among actresses for roles of prominence (even Mrs Cibber was a bit haughty in such exchanges) wanted Mrs Pritchard and wanted harmony in his theatrical household. The first intimation of a management problem in fulfilling this desire came at the outset as one sees from his long letter to her husband William Pritchard, 11 July 1747. The Pritchards had been with Garrick in the walkout on Fleetwood and were partial to him, but Pritchard gleaned from greenroom rumor that Garrick intended himself to play exclusively with Mrs Cibber. Garrick allayed his fears, and set him up as Drury Lane's treasurer to boot. "I have dealt by You as One of my *own* Family. . . . I have not engag'd Mrs Cibber as yet, & if I shou'd You may depend upon it that no such stupid Article as *playing with her alone* shall be part of the Agreem$^t$, if You will consider the Falsehood You may know that such Clauses are incompatible w$^{th}$ my Interest & Inclination, & I am sorry they shou'd be thrown out to Spoil the Harmony, I intend shall subsist in our Company. . . . It is my Interest (putting Friendship out of the Case) that your Wife should maintain her Character upon the Stage." William Pritchard had an accountant's mind, so Garrick's final point to convince him was "nor shall it be in the power of *any haughty Woman* to injure her, . . . [if so] shall not the Managers be great Losers?" And so her career was maintained for the next 20 years. She retained her roles, and when Garrick projected new plays he cast her in appropriate leading parts. He performed with her 652 times.

At the outset Garrick also took the privilege of establishing the benefit sequence, as he explained in no uncertain terms to Prudence Pritchard in a letter of 13 March 1762, who had questioned her place in such a schedule. He felt she and her father were invading his turf

74

by even raising the question, but he said, "I don't include Mrs Pritchard in this, for She deserves Everything we can do for her" (287). While he was in France he was concerned about her maintaining her successes, writing both to George and his deputy manager, George Colman, about it (329).[39] In 1767 he saw Mrs Pritchard growing old and puffy, and with ailing dentures, but still sure of her acting ability, planned to make Colman's *The English Merchant* succeed by starting her in the leading role, and to relieve her "in case of Indisposition" by Mrs Hopkins (445,447). For her final performance 25 April 1768, Garrick played Macbeth to her Lady Macbeth, and wrote a "Simple, modest, short & pathetick" epilogue for her farewell speech, asking her to change and amend it in any way she liked, and to have her daughter add any lines she wished:

> Before I go, and this lov'd Spot forsake,
> The all I have to give, my *Wishes* take:
> Upon Your hearts may no affliction weigh,
> Which cannot by the Stage be chas'd away;
> . . . . . . . . . . . . . . .
>
> Like *Me* in this, may ev'ry future Play'r,
> Supply the want of Genius, by their Care;
> And may Your Bounty flow, as full & free
> To *Them*, as many Years it flow'd to *Me* (498).

She outlived retirement only a few months, dying at Bath in August. A monument to her was placed in Westminster Abbey in the Poets' Corner. No letters flow from her to Garrick, for they saw each other constantly in the theatre, but his choice of her for his stage was sound, and her loyalty to him utterly pleasing.

Garrick was fortunate in inheriting at Drury Lane Mrs Pritchard's good friend Catherine Raftor Clive, who, everybody agreed, was the best "romp" (Dr. Johnson), "a mixture of combustibles, passionate, cross, and vulgar" (Tate Wilkinson), "always inimitable" (Benjamin Victor), sprightliest in humor, and the most amusing singer the stage had seen up to that time.[40] Throughout his career Garrick found her articulate and frank, outspoken and argumentative, but gracious, ultimately admiring, and friendly. Six years older than he, she had come to the stage in 1728 at the age of 17 to play a page in Lee's *Mithridates*, where she sang a song so well she was encouraged to continue, like Mrs Pritchard, in the part of Nell in *The Devil to Pay*. She had progressed rapidly to various comic parts, becoming the very top performer in comedy, farce, and musicals. She once tried tragic and serious parts but without success. Along the way she married a young

75

Mrs Catherine Clive.
Engraving by W. J. Alais from a painting by Joseph Van Haecken.

barrister, George Clive, but separated from him soon and lived thereafter an exemplary, respectable life, ending up in a house provided
by Horace Walpole on his estate at Strawberry Hill.

In 1740 Garrick had written his *Lethe* for the stage in which Mrs
Clive played Lucy and sang a song which she made immensely popular, "The Life of a Belle." Garrick's knowledge and appreciation of her
talents were of long standing. The two had been companions in arms
for a while as she joined the 1743 walkout on Fleetwood. Her spunk,
however, and desire to stick by her principles about combating the
then theatre cartel kept her from returning at reduced pay with Garrick and the others. Finding herself also excluded by Rich she placed
her "Case of Mrs Catherine Clive" before the public in 1744.[41] This
significant document made clear to all that Catherine Clive had a mind
and a courage of her own. Its analysis of the theatre cartel was sharp,
and it pleaded for the profession as a whole which was in the hands
of faulty and domineering management at all points. She had been just
as firm and understanding when ten years earlier she had refused to
separate from Drury Lane under the attempted boycott led by Theophilus Cibber. Whoever took Catherine Clive into his company knew
he was to be possessed not only of an excellent actress, but of a contending personality. In 1745 she was rehired at Drury Lane, where she
remained. During her career her talents for writing as well as for acting
appeared in four *petites pièces* which she wrote, and played in, but
did not publish.[42]

She fussed a great deal with Garrick and their managerial controversies nearly always came to a draw (337).[43] They understood each
other perfectly, and basically admired one another. Garrick in his letters to her was always gracious but firm, while she in turn, after his
return from France, paid him the frankest and highest compliments
he ever received from one in the profession. Once in February 1768,
Garrick, as a help to her, fixed her benefit a week earlier than she had
anticipated. She flared up. He calmly explained his motive and held
his ground. "You always chuse to have some quarrel at your Benefit,
& without reason, but I do not;—I am Surpriz'd that You have not
thank'd the Managers for their kindness instead of writing so peevish
a Letter. Your Benefit is now Settled, upon the best day in the Week,
. . . Therefore if You will not Advertise, & fix your play, Your folly be
upon your own head." In his next response—"How can you be so ridiculous, & still so cross to Mistake every word of my Letter, . . .
however I have still such a regard for You, that I promise You for the
future, that you shall be no more troubled with any Nonsense of
Mine" (487,488). The following November, when Garrick again fixed

her benefit night she wrote, "How charming you can be when you are good." Garrick endorsed the letter "A love-letter, the first I ever had from that truly great comedian, Mrs Clive." [44]

When Mrs Pritchard retired in 1768, Mrs Clive thought she ought also, though Garrick tried to dissuade her. After all he had written the part of Mrs Heidelberg in *The Clandestine Marriage* for her (in 1766) wherein her "malapropisms" (ten years before Sheridan's in *The Rivals* and his Mrs Malaprop) moved audiences to merriment. But she remained firm and set the date for her final benefit 24 April 1769. The play was to be *The Wonder*, with Garrick as Don Felix and her as the maid Flora. The after piece was to be Garrick's *Lethe*, in which she would play the role of the Fine Lady. Thinking about this sure-fire combination she wrote on 14 April to Garrick: "I could not stay till the 24th to thank you. . . . I am *glad* you are well for the sake of my audience, who will have the pleasure to see their own Don Felix. What signifies fifty-two? they had rather see *the* Garrick and *the* Clive at a hundred and four, than any of the moderns;—the ancients, you know, have always been admired." [45]

Five years later Garrick asked her for a character reference for one Mr Crofts who had sought his influence in getting a job in the Excise Office. She provided one from Crofts's minister, but began: "Wonderful Sir, Who have been for these thirty years contradicting an old established proverb—you cannot make brick without straw; but you have done what is infinitely more difficult, for you have made actors and actresses without genius; that is, you have made them pass for such, which has answered your end, though it has given you infinite trouble:—you never took much with yourself, for you could not help acting well." [46]

After Garrick himself had retired she wrote—"never think of being a justice of the peace, for the people will quarrel on purpose to be brought before you to hear you talk, so that you may have as much business upon the lawn as you had upon the boards." [47] This fine cordiality and genuine affection from a person as strong minded and outspoken as Catherine Clive, no doubt cheered Garrick in the 1770s, but he knew in 1747 the strength she would continue to give his company. She was indispensable. He acted with her on 415 occasions.

Every action as Newton pointed out has its reaction. Garrick's appointment of Pritchard as treasurer of Drury Lane caused him to pass over John Powel, an under treasurer in Lacy's company. Powel, expecting the position and bitterly disappointed prepared a devastating account which he called "Tit for Tat," purporting to lay bare to the public the trammels of management in which he found himself, as well as the financial condition of the theatre. "Then let the stricken deer go weep," he quoted, "the hart ungall'd go play." The document, though never printed, turns out in many ways to be a grudging tribute to Garrick, whose charm and business skill and acting support drew his admiration. Powel's gun was for Lacy, who should have stood firmly, he thought, for appointing him to first treasurer's position.[48]

That Powel's bitterness was tempered, accountant that he was, by the rich inflow to the box office but symbolized one kind of life which the new manager-actor gave to the company. Precepts were fine, but example was magnetic. Powel noted that Garrick himself played more frequently when manager than he had when "under management." The fact surprised because it displayed commitment on Garrick's part rather than the evident satisfactions of power. The recorded performances of Garrick's initial year of administration show a marked increase over those of the preceding one—in play, after piece, or delivery of the famous Johnson Prologue. From an average of 65 appearances he moved up to 116. These included 13 of the 31 benefit nights for actors—for Barry, Macklin, Mrs Pritchard, Mrs Woffington, of course; but also for dancers, boxkeepers and members of the house staff. All in all many, many, many individuals profited by his drawing power. The next season he played in 18 of the 31 benefits. During his first season he played 13 different roles, and gave a packed-house benefit for sufferers from a destructive fire in Cornhill. This leadership by the new manager was not a ploy, merely to win friends at the outset. It marked a deeper strain of character proving the sincerity of his commitment to the company he was leading, for he made a similar all-out attempt in 1757–58, and surpassed it in 1759–60.

During the early period he was also writing and producing popular plays—*Miss in Her Teens*, *The Male Coquette*—adopting Southerne's *Isabella*, and Shirley's *The Gamester*. The total involvement, the energy, the good humor, the good feeling generated endeared him to his fellow actors, his company, and his public. Support and exemplary involvement were also brilliant strokes of good management, for they inspired a confidence and willing cooperation that facilitated the administrative structural changes and the regularizing of procedures which he was determined to put into effect.

From our view 200 years after the heat of daily events perhaps conclusions and sweeping generalizations are sufficient. Perspectives count probably more than details. But to come at the man who was coping and leading and profiting from theatrical activity for 29 years of management, one must dwell for a time with the specifics. So statement after the fact yields to documentation of the fact.

A first problem in managing and possibly changing the routines of some 70 individualists (for so each was in his way) is that of communication. Mrs Clive in her "Case" had deplored in the public press "secret decisions and dark agreements." Assuredly arbitrariness continued as did some confidential decisions, but a fresh confidence born of a new sense of order operating at Drury Lane was established. Garrick was not responsible for the conglomerate of physical facilities that comprised Drury Lane Theatre when he took over (though he and Lacy improved them nine times during their long partnership).[49] But one must visualize the "house" and its many compartments which Garrick inherited, to which he adapted, and within which he worked.

Walk for a moment into that Drury Lane structure, which had been Garrick's training ground for a number of years, and which was about to be the centerpiece of his life for 29 years to come. It was not a single structure but a composite of ten buildings—a fairly large auditorium and stage area to which clung nine houses, or appendage structures providing rooms and apartments for the carpenter shops, paint shops, wardrobe storage and issuing facilities, scene room, and administrative offices of the managers, treasurers, boxkeepers and prompters. Practice rooms and dressing rooms were many, and loft space for stage machinery rose high, of course. A room for the library of acting copies of plays and one for record books and music scores, and a copying room formed essential parts of the conglomerate, which as a whole occupied the space of 13,134 square feet bounded by Drury Lane on the East, Brydges Street on the West, Great Russell Street on the North and Little Russell Street on the South. Each office was located in a different section of the conglomerate making instant communication with all hands difficult. The central meeting place, therefore, was the greenroom, located to the side of the stage. There actors lounged, waiting for cues summoning them to the stage, there they gossiped, there they entertained privileged guests, there they assembled for the reading and casting of a new play. One recalls Dr. Johnson's telling Garrick that he would come no more to the greenroom for the bosomy actresses excited his amorous propensities,[50] and one recalls Mrs Siddons's excitement and trepidation years later when Garrick first introduced her there to the company.[51]

The persons busy in these compartments made the theatre work. Its two central and complementary parts were an auditorium and a stage, the latter 45 feet wide and 30 feet deep, raked, that is elevated from the footlights back to the rear drop, at a gradually rising angle of one inch to every 24 so that an actor back stage would stand 15 inches higher than his partner at the footlights. Stage equipment was complete—wings and flats running in seriated grooves, trap doors, pulleys, winches, balances, a proscenium arch for masking the ceiling-hung machinery, and two huge girondels (wheellike structures) holding many candles and suspended from the stage ceiling to counterbalance the lights from foot lamps in sunken grooves at the front of the stage apron.[52]

Upon this space the stage curtain rose at the commencement of the show, and was not lowered until the end of the evening. Right- and left-hand doors stood at the front sides of the opening, above which were some stage boxes. Slips ran from either side to the side-box levels. A row of short spikes circled the narrow apron barring easy access from the pit and orchestra. The latter was a space just in front of the stage and extending a bit under the apron, where the 21-piece orchestra played the music necessary for all performances. A wide door at the rear of the stage could be opened out to give it a depth clear to Drury Lane.

One standing on stage viewing the auditorium would see in it four main portions which when packed could seat nearly 1,000 people (in 1747) and perhaps 1,200 (in 1776 when Garrick retired), with the largest numbers in the boxes, next in the first gallery and slips, next in the pit, and the smallest in the upper gallery. Occasionally seats were also erected on the stage proper to increase income for benefits.[53] A row of front boxes at the rear of the pit section and under the gallery faced the stage, others (side-boxes) rose in several tiers at the sides of the house. The first gallery rose above the front boxes, and a smaller upper gallery rose above that.

The occupants of the four sections ("estates") were divided mainly by the price of the tickets: 5s. for a box seat, 3s. for a seat on a backless bench in the pit (with 21 inches marked off for each bottom), 2s. for a seat in the first gallery, and 1s. for one in the upper gallery. Usually the nobility and wealthy gentry occupied the boxes, some gentry and the scholarly critics the pit, solid citizens the first gallery, and apprentices, footmen, sailors, and the less wealthy the upper gallery. Obviously various tastes distinguished the four estates, which all had to be attended to by the actors, managers, and playwrights.

Who precisely were these spectators whose tastes in a way determined so much of the fare presented? They came largely from nine sources in the community, and formed each night a mixed assembly: parliamentarians and their relatives; readers and subscribers to published books of plays and the dance; students and lawyers from the Inns of Court; apprentices from some 94 trades that supported the theatres in London and profited from the dealings; the tradesmen and merchants themselves who did a thriving business with the theatres; the renters (investors in theatre shares, each of whom held a free seat each night); visitors to London (especially ambassadors and envoys from foreign countries); Garrick's friends, neighbors, and correspondents from St Martin's Parish, from Lichfield, Bath, Hampton, the counties, and abroad; and the friends of all the other actors, as well as the intellectuals who wrote critiques for the *Monthly*, *Critical*, and other reviews.[54]

On nights when popular plays and actors performed, persons from these sources crowded into a structure planned by Christopher Wren back in 1674, and entry was not easy. Narrow passages led from Drury Lane under overhanging apartments around the stage door entrance into the complex, and around to the pit door, gallery door, and box lobby entrances. From the lobbies (with their bars and fruit concessions) passages led up to the galleries, and into the various seating sections. No seats were numbered. The first that came were the first served, so ladies usually sent servants well in advance of curtain time to hold places. The scramble of seat exchange as the curtain rose was often great, hence pieces of music and a prologue to quiet the house. Withal the Drury Lane house was rather intimate, and afforded good views of actors and their expressions.[55] This theatre space was an exciting place for three hours each evening, and the whole complex was busy and exciting throughout the day for Garrick the manager, and his company of 68 actors, singers, dancers, and 50 additional house servants, that is members of his operational staff. Some organization of the channels of communication had to be perfected.

The physical structure, then, aided a separation of powers, as it long had, and this separation in a way determined the organization of the company. It also seems to have rigidified the formalities of communication. Garrick was interested in definition of roles, delegation of responsibility, and a proper flow of messages and requests. Room locations set top management apart. He wished to be accessible, but required that appointments be made. Channels were set up, and the system began to work. Those with grievances went not directly to the managers. Notes had to be written and conferences held. Three regular mail drops operated, both for internal and for external matters: the prompter's office for theatre personnel; the Bedford Coffee House and Beckett's bookstore for authors; and Lacy, George Garrick, and Pritchard dealt largely with the tradesmen. Messages could also go directly to Garrick's house, but these were not encouraged.

Thomas King's letter to Garrick (30 April 1769) suggests the channels which had operated from the start. Garrick, in Bath recovering from illness, heard rumors of actor comment with the prompter about *Harlequin's Invasion* (Garrick's first pantomime). He wrote King to know more. To whom King: "As to what passed between Mr. Hopkins [prompter] and me . . . I have offended by giving my sentiments *to*, and sending a message *by* the prompter. . . . When Mr. Lacy and you are on the spot, if I have any thing that I think necessary to communicate to both, I always trouble Mr. G[eorge] Garrick, . . . as your representative; if I have any thing in the way of business to settle with the *managers*, I think it necessary to search for some other person to act for me. Who so likely to find the managers together as the prompter?"[56]

Yet regularization of channels did not mean for Garrick exclusion of advice from a wide range of his actors, as well as from others. It meant more effective use of it. A curious note in the *Covent Garden Journal* compares the theatre with the state, and speaks of the regular referring of major decisions in the theatre to a large council. "The Council assembles every morning in a chamber of state, which they call the greenroom, where the vacant places of the government are filled up, and all the affairs of the commonwealth debated. There is a very singular custom among these people, practised by no other nation, of admitting women to a seat in the Council, and a share in the management of public affairs."[57] The thought is a bit whimsical, but Garrick's actresses certainly communicated through all the channels available, and the greenroom was excellent common ground.

Although no love was lost between Garrick and Lacy when they joined in the management venture, they both realized that civilized behavior between them was healthiest for the company as well as for their particular interests. Lacy in general had authority in the physical structure and the materiel of the theatre. Occasionally he went, Garrick thought, too far in suggesting repertoire and kinds of performance. Arbiter Paterson was able to cool all differences, and Lacy was not keen to raise problems (III, app. B). Garrick soon developed his own coterie of advisers outside the theatre to whom he wrote, who visited him at his home in Southampton Street, or in his office in the theatre. For shrewd hard-headed business Somerset Draper (merchant, publisher), James Clutterbuck (merchant), John Paterson (lawyer), and later Albany Wallis (banker); for production and management Charles Macklin, George Colman, Thomas King, and at times in matters of taste, John Hoadly. But he realized that his own abilities were best exercised in a dominant leadership. In carrying this out his communications with Lacy were both delicate and important. Most of the Garrick-Lacy letters reveal Garrick's undercurrent of exasperation with his partner, but not all. Garrick made the effort in the early years to include Lacy in planning. Tensions, we know, built in 1750 and were relaxed by Paterson. By 27 July of that year all was running smoothly, for Garrick wrote to Lacy about preseason readiness. The point was to communicate enthusiasm, which Garrick had in abundant supply. "I assure you, I am in great spirits, and don't care how soon we are at work: I suppose you intend sticking to the resolution of opening the house the first Saturday in September." He was writing from Lord Hartington's place at Londesburgh, and assured Lacy that everyone there was his well-wisher. "I beg you will get forward the plays we intend shall be done by the Company." Getting ready meant having parts written out, lengths prepared, music copied, scenes made up. Here was a diplomatic concession involving Lacy in preseason thought so that Lacy would not feel he was losing stature in the eyes of the players. "The little parts too should be cast [he was thinking of a new *King John* and of *Romeo and Juliet*]; for, by alterations, many of them are undisposed of, I long to be with you; our company, I think, will pull at the oars with their heads and hearts." Barry and Mary Elmy had gone over to Covent Garden and King to Ireland, so Garrick was in a way regrouping his forces. "We shall have no false brothers I hope, nor intriguing sisters; and then—*that* for Goliah and the Philistines! . . . *Come what, come may,— / My Soul's in arms, and eager for the fray*" (93). His bubbling enthusiasm was contagious as he started a great decade of competition with the company at Covent Garden.

The ebullience of this letter reflects a cheerfulness and new sense of security born of Garrick's marriage (22 June 1749) and first happy year (in a long life of conjugal happiness and contentment) to Eva Maria Veigel, a beautiful Viennese dancer who had become the special protégée of the Earl and Countess of Burlington. More later about Garrick the husband and Eva Maria the wife respected by all. Here one only notes the beginning of a subtle but continuing influence of Mrs Garrick's high standards of professionalism, and the reflection of her interest in music, artistry, and the dance upon Garrick's subsequent theatre career.

John Rich, the manager of competing Covent Garden had moved his company into his new theatre in the Piazza of Covent Garden from its earlier location in Lincoln's Inn Fields in 1732. The proximity of the new theatre to the Theatre Royal in Drury Lane made competition easy and lively. In the unusual circumstance when identical plays were being performed at each theatre, patrons preferring a Garrick performance (for example, in 1750) of Romeo in his dying scene to Barry's

Romeo, who excelled in the first acts of the play, could nip over after the third act from Covent Garden and at half price finish the evening at Drury Lane.

Rich, a good businessman and a stellar performer in pantomimes, bore a somewhat eccentric personality. He met authors in his office or drawing room surrounded by a dozen well-fed cats, which purred as he caressed them during the interview, often to the distraction of the person being interviewed. He knew the quality of Garrick as actor, engaged him, as we know, for the 1746–47 season, and would have liked to keep him. Little if any correspondence exists between them, for what business they transacted as rival managers was done in oral conference.

Rich, though running a repertory parallel in essential respects to Garrick's, was rather addicted to spectacle, scenic effects, and song—a tradition carried on after he died (1761) by his son-in-law John Beard, England's greatest tenor of the time. Billed as Mr Lun, Rich made a name for himself on stage as Harlequin, where he could mince his steps 50 times within the space of three feet. In the masque and domino of that character his actions on stage astounded and pleased his audiences, the same audiences that also admired Garrick. Wordless pantomimes had been a staple at Lincoln's Inn Fields and the early Covent Garden houses in the 1720s and 1730s. During the 1750–60 decade Rich, to compete with Garrick's drawing power revived and expanded Harlequin's wand and pantomimes (which of course were all after pieces) galore. Garrick to meet the competition in kind enlisted Henry Woodward, who as pantomimic artist was second only to Rich. He produced a new one annually for Garrick for six years. His *Queen Mab, Harlequin Ranger, The Genii, Proteus, Fortunatus* and *Mercury Harlequin* not only confronted Rich's *Cheats of Harlequin, Merlin's Cave, Harlequin Statue, The Necromancer, Harlequin Sorcerer,* and *The Fair,* but carried on for decades in Garrick's Drury Lane repertory.[58] The two patent theatres also competed in the hiring of actors, and sought to bind each actor for a period during which he might not become a free agent, but might at the close renegotiate his articles or leave. It was not good form to break articles, either on the part of actor or manager. But the managers actually held the trump cards, for they, though competing, could and did refuse to employ anyone who had broken from the other house.

Despite Garrick's enthusiasm for the start of the 1750 decade his way of succeeding in competition and Lacy's for drawing in the box receipts were still at considerable variance. For in the summer of 1751 he was apprehensive of Lacy's proposals for increasing the revenues.

In a letter to Draper (again from Londesburgh) 17 August 1751, he suggested the difference in artistic taste between the two: "Have you seen the *Great Lacy* lately? I wish, when you have that pleasure, that you would hint your great surprise and dislike of *Maddox's* rope-dancing upon our stage. I cannot possibly agree to such a prostitution upon any account; and nothing but downright starving would induce me to bring such defilement and abomination to the *house of William Shakespeare*. What a mean, mistaken creature is this Par[tn]er of mine!" Either Garrick's suspicions were unfounded, or his caution prevailed, for Maddox did not appear there, though he performed in Rich's pantomime *The Fair* next season. And so Garrick, the younger, gained and maintained the dominant role in the partnership—consulting with many, accessible to all, but regularizing channels of communication. Later on Lacy got deep into an outside project of digging for coal on his Oxfordshire lands, and mortgaged his portion of the patent to Garrick to pay for the experiment.[59]

Had Garrick paused at the close of his first season of joint management to review the status of Drury Lane compared to what it had been the year before, and in comparison to what Covent Garden had done in a year of competition, he would have remarked upon a number of points in finance, in repertory, in company morale, and in management routines which augured well for the theatre's future. Income was nearly £800 over what it had been, and though salaries for prominent actors were high, the year-end profits rounded out at £6,334.[60] But changes in variety of entertainment, company morale, and strength were even more rewarding.

Under Lacy's lone deputy management the previous season, Drury Lane's performance was humdrum, save for the new face of Spranger Barry, whom Lacy engaged from Dublin. In 16 performances as Othello, several as Macbeth, as Anthony (in Dryden's *All for Love*), as Castalio (in Otway's *The Orphan*), and as Varanes (in Lee's *Theodosius*) he has attracted considerable attention. The company otherwise was solid, but in no way notable, for despite the presence of Barry the performances of 152 nights were undistinguished, and the plays were stock ones. Lacy towards the close of the season lamented the "falling off of business" as he was trying to assess the theatre's assets and arrears in hopes of engaging on a new partnership.[61] He had put on 40 performances of tragedy, 90 of comedy, and eight of musicals (mostly *The Beggar's Opera*), with Barry's *Othello* leading the serious plays, *The Provoked Husband* the comic ones, and Moses Mendez's *Double Disappointment* and Henry Carey's *The Dragon of Wanlty* outnumbering the rest of the after pieces. He managed to stage two new, but short-lived, after pieces—Joseph Dorman's *Sir Roger de Coverley*, and Macklin's *The Suspicious Husband Criticized* —both of which soon fell by the wayside. Sameness was all. Drury Lane badly needed new money and new direction. Lacy's liabilities included £1,275 of arrears in actors' salaries.[62]

In contrast, and prophetic of successful seasons to come, the theatre in Garrick's first managing year performed 172 nights, thus blanking out Covent Garden's 104, and adding 20 to the run of the previous year. It put on 61 tragic, 100 comic, and six musical performances. Garrick enriched the repertoire of main pieces by the popular new comedy *The Foundling* by Edward Moore, brought with him from Covent Garden Hoadly's new comedy *The Suspicious Husband*, revived Shakespeare's *King Henry V* (which had never been played there), Thomas Tomkis's humor comedy *Albumazar* (which he was to alter himself a number of years later), John Ford's tragedy *The Lover's Melancholy*, Dryden's operatic version of *The Tempest*, Rowe's pathetic tragedy *Jane Shore*, and Shakespeare's light and airy *Twelfth Night*. The face of his after pieces was freshened by a new *Club of Fortune Hunters*, and *A Will and No Will*, both by Macklin, the latter a farce taken from the French of Regnard, and the revival of John Gay's hilarious farce—a bone he had tossed to the critics—*The What D'ye Call It?*[63] As noted above Garrick himself played on over 100 nights during the season.

That year Drury Lane's stock, metaphorically speaking, was riding high over its previous performance, and Covent Garden's parallel stock was descending in the eyes of Londoners, for Rich put on there *no* new main piece that season, and only a single new pantomime—the anonymous *Perplexed Husband*, apparently for a single performance. Garrick's tempo in new-play selection, as well as new revivals and restorations, was to pick up and continue from then on, for by the close of his career he had put on 61 new main pieces to Covent Garden's 49; 96 new after pieces to Covent Garden's 42.[64]

He also had at Drury Lane for the moment the company of companies, whose morale was excellent. With Macklin (who agreed with him in matters of acting style and in the value of ensemble performance), with Barry, Mozeen, Havard, the singer Thomas Lowe, solid and experienced Astley Bransby, Edward Berry, Charles Blakes, with Mrs Clive, Mrs Cibber, Mrs Pritchard, and Mrs Woffington, the capability for a coming golden age of acting was upon him, an age of well-rehearsed ensemble acting, to be built up regularly with new faces, as the actors of the older style retired and vanished.

In the area of personnel management he had defined responsibili-

ties, regularized routines, and had set out upon clarifying articles of
agreement for all actors, which involved length of contract (one or
more seasons), salary and allowances, choice of assignment of roles,
frequency of performing, accountability (both on the part of the managers and the actors), place on the benefit schedule, periods of normal
renewal, attendance at rehearsals, temporary leaves of absence, and
dissolution of the contract by mutual agreement.[65] Garrick began that
first season with a company of about 68 actors, actresses, singers, and
dancers. Some prominent ones were missing from his roster the next
season—Delane, the Macklins, the Mozeens, Shuter, and Mrs Woffington among others. Many, except Peg, returned from time to time
in later seasons. But Garrick immediately set on foot plans for recruiting. New faces always intrigued theatregoers, and if the newly employed brought talent, their places on stage were assured. In his second season he added 36 new actors, the largest recruitment he made
in any year, save when he recruited dancers for Noverre's ballet in
1755.[66] The town saw strength flocking to Drury Lane. Beard and
Woodward came and stayed ten years, John Palmer came for 16, Mrs
James for seven, King for two, and after a hiatus, returned for 14 more.
Though all actors were supposed to be able to sing and dance, Garrick
gradually engaged an especially strong musical group. To Fredrick
Reinhold and Daniel Sullivan and Beard he added basso Samuel
Champness. By 1762 he had brought on a dozen more singers includ-
ing such favorites as George Mattox, Joseph Vernon, James Wilder,
Isabella Young, Master Michael Leoni, James Kear, and Thomas Nor-
ris. Also by that time he had engaged for several seasons 16 child
actors, actresses, and singers. They played specialty parts, charmed
audiences, and many grew up into theatre careers as did Cautherly,
Miss Pritchard, Master Leoni, and Norris.

Garrick scouted Covent Garden, as Rich did Drury Lane, and again
and again visited the theatre at Richmond, which had become a promising training ground for youngsters. In 1751 he engaged Henry Mossop, who remained for seven years then went to Dublin. Mossop's
occasional awkward motions were compensated, according to Davies
(who acted with him), by having a strong and harmonious voice, which
could rise from the lowest to the highest pitch of sound. Davies
deemed Mossop excellent in parts of turbulence and rage, in regal
tyranny, and sententious gravity. He had great audience appeal, as
did John Dexter and David Ross, whom though not well rounded,
Garrick brought on for special roles. Garrick was from time to time
criticized for not peopling his stage with a multitude of stars of equal
brilliance. "The argument would have some force," wrote Davies, "if

actors of genius were as easily raised as beds of tulips. But the genuine representer of nature on stage is as rarely to be found as the fine painter of manners in a dramatic story."[67]

Garrick's spirits were high, as we have seen, in the summer of 1750 as he contemplated the stiff competition which Rich was to give him at Covent Garden. His spirits were high again in the early summer of 1751 when he and Eva Maria crossed the straits of Dover for their first visit to France. A holiday was in the making, but mingled with the pleasures of sightseeing came an alertness in observing and noting down in his *Diary*[68] impressions of the three performing companies in Paris—the Comédie Française, the Comédie Italienne, and the Opera. He used the experience as a yardstick of comparison between what he was striving for and accomplishing in London and what a famed Parisian stage was offering. The notes in his *Diary* move not in scattered fashion, but in orderly progression. Molière's comedies, he found, scarcely drew a full house and were generally performed by second-rate actors. Novelty was the greatest incitement to attendance. Actors in general were inattentive at the close of their own lines. Only one piece of music was given before the play, and by an orchestra with only eight to ten pieces (he had double the quantity at Drury Lane). Singing and dancing at the Opera were indifferent, and the dancing at the Comédie Italienne would have been hissed off an English stage. Building (of seats) on the stage at the Comédie Française wholly destroyed "*vraysemblance*." He found Claude-Louis Chaussée the best singer, and was disappointed in Louis Dupré as a dancer. He remarked several times about the skill and evident feeling displayed by the new and upcoming actor Henri-Louis LeKain, but "he swallows his words, and his face is so ill made that it creates no feeling in the spectators from its distortions." Grandval pleased him in some characters, but Garrick felt he had no genius for tragedy, "Always when he endeavours at the high passion his expression is false, and he was inattentive to a degree," as was the pretty, but disappointing Coralline.[69]

Exaggeration he deemed a common fault, even Mme Claire Josèphe Clairon was "outrée in the parts of her character where she might be less violent, and [was] tame in the places of the highest and finest passages." Mme Marie Dumesnil could express terror and despair, but was "unequal and too violent at times." On the whole she seemed not up to the Clairon. He seemed in closer companionship with the actor Jean Sauvé (called *La Noué*), with whom he also visited and dined.[70]

He and Mrs Garrick had packed a great deal into the trip of just a day or so more than a month (30 May–2 July). Since Leviez, his Drury

*Devonshire Collection, Chatsworth*
David Garrick.
Pastel by Jean Étienne Liotard, 1751.

Lane ballet master, and Dévisse, one of his dancers, were in Paris at the same time, and since the commissioner of police in Paris was searching for both Frenchmen as persons possibly trying to lure French performers to England, and since Garrick is mentioned in the commissioner's correspondence, it would appear that Garrick cut his *Diary* short on Friday, 21 June, O.S. (2 July N.S.), and his trip also, returning to England before being questioned on the intent of his visit by the commissioner.[71] His correspondence picks up in England again in early July when he writes John Hoadly, "I am much, very much pleas'd with my Jaunt, & am ready & willing to take y$^e$ Same & for a Month longer, whenever Business will permit" (105). He had tucked away in his mind some possible singers and dancers for future consideration.

Garrick did not envision a continually expanding company. He had to keep it within manageable limits, but he thought of turnover and fresh input as a managerial obligation. He had his scouts in Paris to help with dancers, and in Rome for singers. In order to hold good actors he shared his roles with them, as he did with Mossop and Charles Holland, and the perceptive in the audience understood what his motives were. A writer for the *Covent Garden Journal* (4 February 1752) noted, "That Mr. Garrick is not immortal, whatever his fame may be, and that if no regard be had to the succession of actors, nor any care taken to bring those forward into the principal parts, who shall discover the greatest theatrical talents, the stage will fall with himself, as was the case when that famous triumvirate Booth Wilks and Cibber were in the management."

During his long term as manager (to look forward for a moment), Garrick engaged 156 new dancers, averaging six each year; 47 new singers; and 298 new actors and actresses. He built up several exceedingly competent companies—several because the opportunities calling away a number of his well-trained people to managerships of their own (in Bath, Bristol, Liverpool, Edinburgh, Covent Garden, and Dublin) coupled with attrition by death and marriage, and by the lure of temporary assignments to Covent Garden, and, later, by the coming on of a new generation, required him to shift and renew. Compared with the experiences of Drury Lane in previous regimes, his companies for all their fresh recruits were remarkably stable, but stable, as Garrick wished them to be in quality of performance. Employment at Drury Lane became a mark of distinction.

Garrick's preseason urging of Lacy about "getting forward the plays" planned for the coming year implies that a general ordering of the repertory was envisioned from the start of each season. But all such scheduling depended upon some constant factors in the calendar, and upon sufficient elasticity to allow for unanticipated contingencies. The season got underway by mid-September, but plays were scantily attended the first two weeks, so the theatres played but thrice a week until October. Thereafter certain preempted dates could be counted on. On the fourth and fifth of November, the anniversary of the landing of William III (1688) was celebrated by performing Rowe's *Tamerlane*. No plays were performed on Christmas, or on the Sabbath. A public charity benefit was scheduled just before Christmas, or just after—usually for a hospital. On 30 January the theatres were dark as public guilt was expiated for the beheading of Charles I. During Lent oratorios, but *no plays*, could be given on Wednesdays and Fridays. By the fifteenth of March benefit nights for actors and the house company members commenced. These were due to prominent actors, and clusters of house servants. On the 30 to 40 such occasions annually the managers received only the house charges required to light the theatre and pay the staff. Garrick increased the number of such nights by engaging benefit-quality performers. He had in mind the long-term success of the theatre as a national cultural institution. The season closed in late May, having run for from 170 to 180 nights.

Since by law entertainments were limited to two theatres, each had to offer the variety required by the public. A contest in 1750, to look forward a moment, when the rival companies both put on *Romeo and Juliet* for 12 successive nights drew excited interest for about a week, but soon drew caustic comment in the press: "Well, what's to-night? cries angry Ned, / As up from bed he rouses; / Romeo again! and shakes his head; / Ah! Pox on both your houses!"[72]

Both Garrick and Rich gave balanced repertoires—offering tragedy, comedy, and musical pieces, as well as farcical and pantomimic light after pieces, along with an abundance of entr'acte dancing and singing, and the recitation of prologues and epilogues. Garrick maintained variety in his main pieces by performing from 50 to 60 different plays annually. Three or four performances apiece each year of old standbys, such as *Hamlet*, or *The Provoked Wife*, served to maintain their popularity, and schooled audiences to develop critical understanding, as well as the enjoyments of comparison and recognition. Several new plays and new farces were called for, and Garrick provided them annually.[73]

But the schedule had to be elastic enough to account for last-minute illnesses of actors. Substitute plays would then be put on, or else a substitute actor would walk through the part reading it. Such a practice was seldom resorted to, but was received in good humor by the spectators. When new plays were mounted, the uncertainty of their run had to be allowed for. Managers hoped they would last out nine nights, so the author could be rewarded by the profits from the third, sixth, and ninth performances.[74] Garrick explained to his friend J. B. A. Suard 7 March 1776 what the managers had felt about the performing rights of new plays. "The managers of both theatres have agreed not to perform any of the new pieces which shall be done at either house, till the theatre where any new performance is first acted have enjoy'd it *two* seasons" (989). Thereafter the piece went into the public domain. Such had not always been the case earlier in the century, when piracies often occurred.

Upcoming plays were announced by notice in the leading newspaper, by handbills (small for issuance to patrons, and large for posting about town), and most importantly (because of contingencies—such as damning—which might arise) at the close of each night's performance. Make up of copy for bills and news notices was the final responsibility of the prompter, but as the curtain fell nightly Garrick or a leading actor would step forward and "give out" notice of the next evening's show. Conferences of the comanagers at the start of each season (and weekly thereafter) were held as to repertory, and such scheduling was a creative exercise, enjoyed by Garrick—not a routine matter. He requested the head prompter—at first Richard Cross, then William Hopkins—to keep *Diaries*, listing the plays and annotating audience reception. These provided guides for repertory selection the following season, and proved to be charts of actor reception and popularity. Garrick, who was not in the theatre every night, thus had his own judgment as to plays and actors checked by the expert observations of the prompters.[75]

Garrick's day in the theatre office was busy enough to occupy all the remarkable energy the man displayed—approving schedules (and keeping an eye on results), rehearsing and observing the rehearsals of others, reading play manuscripts, interviewing applicants, corresponding voluminously in a business as well as a social way, checking the use and availability of scenes, listening to orchestra practice, settling grievances which ascended to his level. The hum of the theatre during the day, and the applause (or groaning) at performance time animated his every act. He came early on to recognize his position as a public figure, and maintained it by living up to the concept. He loved praise, and he saw through flattery. Testimony in his letters is overwhelming. The underground press harped ad nauseam on the theme of his vanity and his need for flattery. Garrick's response was professional in the highest sense. He seldom engaged in public controversy, even in response to what now seem stinging statements. He relied, rather, on the views of the Burkes, Hoadlys, Warburtons, and Colmans of the world, as well as of his noble friends, and professional men—doctors, artists, publishers, and businessmen who carried on extensive personal correspondence with him.

In the wake of a successful first year Garrick pressed on with his theatre discipline, so that all performers, even leading actors and actresses, were required to attend rehearsals to get a fresh sense of their stage relationships, and of the thrust of the whole play. Mrs Clive, as late as 1765 protested stoppage of her pay for not attending. "I had my money last year stopped at the beginning of the season for not coming to rehearse two parts that I could repeat in my sleep, and which have cost me two guineas [travel time]. . . . The year Mrs Vincent came on the stage, it cost me about five pounds to go to and from London to rehearse with her, and teach her the part of Polly." But Garrick was firm. Five years before he had written Mrs Cibber, "The Comedy [*The Way to Keep Him*] will require four or five regular Rehearsals at least, and tho You may be able to appear with two, Yet I am afraid the rest of the Dramatis Personae will be perplex'd and disjointed if they have not the advantage of your Character to Rehearse with them" (247).[76] Garrick's emphasis upon well-timed acting and ensemble performance was new. His manner of getting it was diplomatic. The results were exciting.

With some satisfaction Garrick exhibited instances of theatrical sportsmanship within the competitive structure of the two theatres, for when, as happened infrequently, the sister theatre was distressed for want of a major performer for a special night, he would lend one from his company who knew the part, and Rich would reciprocate. Such amiable relations operated for the good of the profession as a whole. Even after his retirement he wrote Colman, then the manager of Covent Garden, hoping that such gentlemanlike agreements would continue between the competing managers (1057). He and his fellow managers came to view in statesmanlike fashion the well-being of the London stage as a cultural entity in London life. Garrick's sense of openness and of genuine concern for actors, house servants, good authors, and others show the man and the manager in the best light. When Mr Melmoth complained that Garrick played a fine part at Drury Lane the night when Dodsley's *Cleone* was opening at Covent Garden, he wrote to the author congratulating him on the success of his tragedy, adding, "I am certain that Your house was far from receiving any injury from Ours—however if You will call upon Me & let me know how I can support y$^r$ Interest, without absolutely giving up my

own, I will do it" (217).[77] Henry Mossop thanked Garrick from Ireland
for allowing some Drury Lane players to travel to Dublin before their
articles were up at the London house.[78] But on the whole Garrick was
protective of his whole company. His understanding of the value of
steady and good performance to all the workers in his company comes
clear in the negative reply he was to give to a proposal from Covent
Garden in 1775, a year of light attendance all round, that the two
houses play on alternate nights, or cut to five nights per week with
some alteration. Garrick's refusal was based on the hardship such an arrangement would place upon the lower members of the company,
some of whose articles indicated pay only for the nights they performed.[79]

Detailed documentation of a number of procedures in London stage
management as Garrick performed them sketches the nature of his
administrative care and brightness. The young Garrick was not animated by a laissez-faire attitude, but by a driving purposefulness. The
drive escaped tyranny because of the pleasantness of Garrick's personality, his diplomatic approaches, the essential rightness of his
regulatory progress for the cause of theatrical professionalism. Communication became businesslike through channels clear but not dead-
ening, terms of employment and expectancy of professional deportment became unequivocal, scheduling was pragmatic, cooperation
with the competing theatre occurred when necessary, and recruitment
vital to the company's best interests was wide-ranging. New faces and
voices, and new legs with dancing skills freshened the general assemblies in the greenroom. He was happy to accept advice both from within and from without, and he kept in close touch with the temper of his
audiences. He led by personal example, thus gaining the confidence
of his company and of a wide circle of theatrical supporters. He was
making the English theatre the most brilliant in the art form in all
Europe. But the road he was traveling, as soon to be seen, was not
a primrose path. He had to cope with many a disappointed author,
and with the increasingly articulate and critical friends of each. But
Garrick's commitment and drive, his tireless attention to acting and
management, remarkable as they were, did not preclude his pleasant
involvement with a dozen men friends in London's world of art, the
clergy, business, and the gentry.

# Part Two
## *The Manager*

.

# David Garrick, Esquire

WHEN GARRICK AND JOHNSON went up to London together in March 1737, Garrick, then 20 years old, by the standards of the time was a relatively mature young man, and had already acquired a social experience, sophistication in all levels of a thriving country town, a cathedral close, and a military station. The last two attracted university graduates, the sons of gentry with wealth and leisure for cultivated social living, some with taste for letters, and some with familiarity with London. Once a resident in London in the autumn of 1737 Garrick was not without acquaintances. He had family, the Fermignacs, Cazelets, and La Condés, cousins in and near London, and ties and introductions, which he shared with Johnson, to Lichfield men already settled in the city. While their professional ambitions were in separate areas, Johnson and Garrick were occasionally in each other's company, notably at the Honorable Henry Hervey's table, formerly resident of Lichfield, and in Edward Cave's premises over St. John's Gate in Clerkenwell. There with the help of Johnson and others Cave published the *Gentleman's Magazine*, and there Garrick may have first met several writers with whom he later became acquainted, such as Thomas Birch, Elizabeth Carter, and Mark Akenside, as well as with William Hogarth and Richard Savage.

Although he associated with a great many people only tangentially involved with the theatres, he became fast friends with but a select few, perhaps eight or ten. Surviving records are inevitably incomplete. Unsettled in any one residence, he did not file his correspondence, as he did later, nor had fame yet enhanced the value of his autograph.[1] The interrelated friendships begun in the early London days endured, hence sequential presentation involving day by day, or even year by year chronologies seems less to the purpose than presentation of Garrick's relationships with each separately.

## WILLIAM HOGARTH (1697–1764)

One such early acquaintance and longtime friendship sprang up with William Hogarth. Hogarth was an ardent theatregoer, finding in current dramatic theory and practice support for his emerging concept of historical painting, and in the actors, the action and concentration on facial characterization that he sought in his paintings.[2] Of all dramatists he liked Shakespeare and Jonson best. He had earlier made his first radical development in his own style when he undertook the six paintings of Gay's *Beggar's Opera* (1728) a decade before Garrick arrived in London. He moved into a second radical change in theory and practice in his life-size portrait of *Garrick as Richard III* sometime in 1745.[3] The production of this painting marked the beginning of a lifelong friendship in which Hogarth identified himself in his art with Garrick, and Garrick enthusiastically supported Hogarth's dramatic creations, honored the artist, collected his works, and loved the man.[4]

No evidence appears regarding when Hogarth began painting *Garrick as Richard III*, or whether in any way Garrick commissioned it. Presumably in the summer of 1745 Garrick posed for Hogarth in his studio in Pall Mall. Hogarth revised the face several times, and eventually engraved the face himself, the picture as a whole being engraved by Charles Grignion, and published in July 1746. "The subscription ticket for the engraved version shows jointly on one rope a manuscript hung with bayes (Shakespeare), a pallete (Hogarth), and a mask (a good likeness of Garrick's face)." The painting itself sold for £200, "more than any portrait painter was ever known to receive for a portrait."[5]

The two men became better acquainted during the sittings, and Garrick was both personally and professionally interested in the portrait. He may have encouraged Hogarth to take up and get ahead with the work. From mid-October (1745) Garrick resided for his health in Lichfield, where he inquired of Somerset Draper once (and again after he had gone to Dublin) regarding Hogarth's progress and asking "does he intend a print from it" (40). The print appeared in the month that Garrick accepted an invitation from the Reverend John Hoadly to accompany Hogarth and Benjamin Hoadly on a visit to Old Alresford, the Rectory near Southampton to be joined by Messenger Monsey, "there to be as Merry, facetious Mad & Nonsensical, as Liberty, Property & Old October can make Em" (45). Garrick composed for the gathering a bawdy parody, called "Ragandjaw," of the quarrel scene between Brutus and Cassius in *Julius Caesar*, very much in the Garrick-Hogarth manner. Whether or not another mutual friend, William Windham, was present is not recorded, but the manuscript of the skit in Garrick's hand, dated 20 July 1746 and dedicated to Windham, has been preserved by the Windhams at Felbrigg Hall. The part of Brutarse was played by Hoadly, Cassiarse by Garrick, and Caesar's Ghost (replaced by the Devil's Cook Grilliardo) was played by Hogarth, who had some difficulty in remembering his lines. The names of the characters suggest the tenor of the piece.

Less than a month later, in mid-August, Hogarth joined Garrick by invitation, for a farewell dinner before he left London for Cheltenham (47). The only reference to their association in the following half-dozen years lies in Hogarth's letter to his wife (6 June 1749) in which he remarks "I don't know whether or no you knew that Garrick was going to be married to the Violette when you went away. I supt with him last night and had a deal of talk about her." [6]

During the time of Garrick's contracting as co-manager of Drury Lane (8 April 1747), his marriage on 22 June 1749 to Eva Maria Veigel, their purchase and establishment of a residence in Southampton Street, and a villa in 1754 at Hampton, all of which involved him with an amplitude of new personalities, he simply had not the leisure hours to convene with early friends as often as he had formerly. But he terminated no real friendships, and never with Hogarth. In 1757 Hogarth, during an illness, complained to Benjamin Wilson that Garrick was remiss in his visits. Garrick got the word and responded with frankness and affection. The fullness and tone reveal the friendship:

"Dear Hogarth.                           Saturday Jan[y] 8th [1757?]
    Our Friend *Wilson* hinted to me this Morning, that I had of late been remiss in my visits to You—it may be so, tho upon my Word, I am not Conscious of it, for Such Ceremonies are to Me, mere Counters, where there is no remission of Regard & good Wishes—as *Wilson* is not an Accurate Observer of things, not Ev'n of those which concern him most, I imagine that y[e] Hint came from You, & shall say a Word or two to You upon it—*Montaigne*, who was a good Judge of Human Nature, takes Notice, *that when Friends grow Exact & Ceremonious, it is a certain Sign of Coolness, for the true Spirit of Friendship keeps no Account of Trifles*—We are, I hope, a Strong Exception to this Rule—
    Poor *Draper*, (whom I lov'd better than any Man breathing) once ask'd me Smiling—how long is it, since you were at my house?—how long? why a Month or Six weeks—a Year & some Days, reply'd he, but don't imagine that I have kept an Account; My Wife told Me so this Morning, & bid me Scold You for it—now if M[rs] Hogarth has observ'd my Neglect, I am flatter'd by it, but if it is *Your* Observation, Woe betide You—Could I follow my inclinations I would see You Every day

in y^e week, without caring whether it was in Leicester Fields or South-ampton Street, but what with an indifferent State of health, & y^e care of a large family, in which there are many froward Children, I have scarce half-an hour to myself—However Since You are grown a Polite Devil, & have a Mind to play at Lords & Ladies, have at You,—I will certainly call upon You soon & if you should not be at home, I will leave my *Card*

I am Yours Dear Hogy Most Sincerely" (299). [7]

Presumably Garrick did call on Hogarth and commissioned the famous double portrait *David Garrick and His Wife*, which Hogarth was at work on by April. In this as in other portraits of Garrick Hogarth had difficulty with Garrick's mobile features—Garrick shifting expression, perhaps to tease him. [8] Hogarth was also experimenting with the background, the upshot being that the artist retained the picture until his death when it was given by Mrs Hogarth to Garrick, though he had made a payment of £15 for it in August 1763 before he went to France. The picture is more than a portrait. As Paulson remarks, "Garrick is writing a prologue to Samuel Foote's *Taste*, a comedy that pursued Hogarth's tack about dealers duping collectors into buying faked old masters instead of works by contemporary Englishmen. Garrick is still serving the function he served in *Garrick as Richard III*. Knowing how Garrick loved to have artists paint him in his great roles, as a kind of self-advertisement, the artist chooses to show him ostensibly playing no role but in fact taking the Hogarthian stance of attacking connoisseurs." [9]

With the expanding obligations and pressures of his professional and social life, Garrick did not neglect Hogarth; rather more scattered and fragmentary records of their association survive from 1762 than for other years, some rooted in the past; others cover Hogarth's declining years and death. Both Garrick and Hogarth had known Fielding, and two almost apocryphal stories recount how Garrick "sat" for Hogarth's portrait of Fielding, used by Murphy as a frontispiece to his edition in 1762 of Fielding's works. The more reliable version goes "to the effect that Garrick and Hogarth 'sitting together in a tavern, mutually lamented the want of a picture of Fielding.' 'I think,' said Garrick, 'I could make his Face,' which he did accordingly. 'For Heaven's sake hold, David,' said Hogarth; 'remain as you are for a few minutes.' Garrick did so while Hogarth sketched the outlines, which were afterwards finished from their mutual recollection." [10] Hogarth's last picture of Garrick, the illustration of *The Farmer's Return from London* (a skit which Garrick dedicated to Hogarth), was published in March 1762, and sometime after April, Garrick out of compassion and gen-

*Royal Collection*
David Garrick and His Wife.
Painting by William Hogarth, 1752–57.

erosity paid offhand 200 guineas to Hogarth for his *Election* paintings to save him from having to auction them.[11] This same year Garrick purchased six wood blocks of the mulberry tree which Shakespeare was supposed to have planted in his garden at Stratford, and commissioned Hogarth to design the chair which Garrick placed in his Temple of Shakespeare in Hampton.[12] A lengthier episode that presumably came to a climax in January 1762 had its origins back in 1756, when Joseph Warton in his *Essay on the Writings and Genius of Pope*, commenting on Hogarth's paintings of *Paul Before Felix* and *Moses Before Pharaoh's Daughter*, remarked: "In the serious pieces, into which Hogarth has deviated from the natural bias of his genius, there are some strokes of the Ridiculous discernible, which suit not the dignity of the subject. In his PREACHING OF ST PAUL, a dog snarling at a cat; and in his PHARAOH'S DAUGHTER, the figure of the infant Moses, who expresses archness rather than timidity, are alleged as instanced, that this artist unrivalled in his own walk, could not resist the impulse of his imagination towards drollery. His picture, however, of Richard III is pure and unmix'd with any ridiculous circumstances, and strongly expresses terror and amazement."[13] Garrick must have remonstrated with Warton, who thereupon prepared for the second edition of his *Essay* an apology that Hoadly read to Hogarth in Garrick's presence, and for the time being Hogarth was mollified. Aroused, however, by subsequent irritations and misunderstandings, Hogarth reissued his plates, this time including Warton's comment. Eventually, when the second edition of the *Essay* appeared early in 1762, with Warton's apology printed, Garrick called on Hogarth with a copy, and read it to Hogarth, who humbly accepted the apology and offered to destroy the second set of plates (283).

A much more revealing test of Garrick's loyalty to Hogarth developed early in 1762, when Garrick was caught in the acrimonious political controversy between Hogarth on the one hand and the biting satirist Charles Churchill (among others) on the other. Hogarth focused the confrontation on his own support of the Bute administration's seeking for peace with France, in face of increasing opposition. He published a print, *The Times No. 1*, loaded with satire (on 7 September), depicting the city afire, and Bute struggling with hoses to dampen it, while Churchill and Wilkes sprayed water on Bute. To this John Wilkes, who was an open friend of both Garrick and Churchill, replied in the paper *The North Briton* on 11 September, with a bitter attack on Hogarth, to which Hogarth responded with a caricature of *Squinting Jack Wilkes*. Either by anticipation or from report of a pending collateral attack on Hogarth by Churchill, who was associating with Wilkes, Garrick took the initiative to write to Churchill, in reply to Churchill's request for a loan, that he could not make the loan for a week or two, and continued: "I must intreat of You by y$^e$ Regard You profess to Me, that You don't tilt at my Friend Hogarth before You See Me—You cannot sure be angry at his Print? there is surely very harmless, tho very Entertaining Stuff in it—He is a great & original Genius, I love him as a Man & reverence him as an Artist—I would not for all y$^e$ Politicks & Politicians in y$^e$ Universe that You two should have the least Cause of Illwill to Each other. I am sure You will not publish against him if You think twice—I am very unhappy at y$^e$ thoughts of it, pray Make Me quiet as soon as possibly by writing to me at Hampton or Seeing Me here" (296). All was ultimately to no avail, though Garrick's appeal did delay Churchill's attack for about nine months, for early in July of 1763 Churchill published his vicious attack *An Epistle to William Hogarth*. On 10 July Garrick wrote to Colman, "It is y$^e$ most bloody performance that has been publish'd in my time— I am very desirous to know the opinion of People, for I am really much, very much hurt at it—his description of his Age & infirmities is surely too shocking & barbarous—is Hogarth really ill, or does he meditate revenge?" (309) "On 1 August Hogarth retaliated with the caricature *The Bruiser, C. Churchill (once the Rev$^d$!)*" (309 n.2).

Six weeks later the Garricks went abroad to be absent for two years. He continued to send greetings to Hogarth through George Colman, and from Colman he learned of Hogarth's death on 26 October 1764. Some years later (1771) Garrick undertook an epitaph which he sent to Johnson, who commented unfavorably on the first draft and asked Garrick to revise and return the verses to him. On 4 January 1772 Garrick wrote Hoadly: "M$^{rs}$ Hogarth having desir'd me to write an Epitaph for her Husband our most Excellent friend—I have done it, as well as I can, & I am lucky Enough to have it approv'd by those I w$^d$ wish to please—here it is for you" (671).[14] A final version was engraved on the monument erected by Hogarth's friends in Chiswick churchyard:

> Farewell! great painter of Mankind!
>   Who reach'd the noblest point of Art,
> Whose pictur'd Morals charm y$^e$ Mind
>   And thro' the Eyes correct y$^e$ heart:
> If *Genius* fire thee, Reader, Stay,
>   If *Nature* touch thee, drop a tear,
> If Neither move thee, turn away,
>   For HOGARTH's honour'd dust lies here (666).[15]

## JOHN HOADLY (1711–1776)

As noted earlier the Reverend John Hoadly, LL.B., LL.D., invited his brother Benjamin, Dr. Messenger Monsey, Hogarth, and Garrick to Old Alresford in July 1746, when the party produced the parody "Ragandjaw." John, the son of the impressive religious controversialist Bishop Hoadly of Winchester, as a boy attracted attention acting in a school play, and later while at Cambridge began writing plays, which he continued to do without great success throughout his life. He took orders upon graduation to avail himself of his father's affluent patronage that afforded him for life the leisure and means to satisfy a passion for the stage in amateur acting, the collecting, reading, and writing dramatic pieces of all sorts, attending the theatres in London, Bath, and elsewhere, and seeking the company of actors.

Early he associated with Hogarth, assisting him with the verses for the engravings of "The Rake's Progress" (1734), while Hogarth in the early 1740s painted the portraits of his father the Bishop, and of John and his brother Benjamin. Presumably through Hogarth, Garrick met the brothers in London a year and a half before the party just spoken of. John in turn solicited a correspondence with Garrick. Garrick opened his first letter to him 29 December 1744: "Y$^r$ doubting my Inclination to write, is such a virulent Satire against my Head & Heart, that unless You Send immediately back Y$^r$ Recantation in form, I will never more suffer You to talk of Acting, Read Plays, write 'em, or laugh & be Jolly with Me in James Street [up] two pairs of Stairs," and closed, "You have desir'd me often to write to you" (29). Six months later (22 May 1745) Garrick acknowledged an invitation to Old Alresford, and continued, "I should think Myself very happy, for I have much to communicate of Schemes, Compositions, &c . . . finding I was much overcharg'd with Wit & Humour, I have let fly at a Comedy [*Miss in Her Teens*], in Short 'tis quite plan'd, & Some Scenes wrote, but more of this when I have y$^e$ pleasure of seeing You" (30).

Thus Garrick and Hoadly launched a lifelong friendship that soon included Mrs Garrick and Mrs Hoadly, pursued and enriched by exchanges of visits to Hampton and Old Alresford, and by perhaps the most extensive correspondence for both men on the full range of the literature, the writing, and the production of plays. This friendship included Dr Benjamin Hoadly (1706–57), a most distinguished London medical lecturer and practitioner and physician to the royal household. Garrick wrote many letters to him about his play *The Suspicious Husband*. The doctor had stipulated that the profits from the third, sixth, and ninth nights be turned over to Garrick, who was starring in the character Ranger. His widow in some anger at the assignment later burned these letters.[16]

Garrick discovered and cultivated in Hoadly perhaps the best informed nonprofessional scholar of English drama, past and present; a playwright whose judgments on after pieces, adaptations, and music were sound; a theatregoer who kept up with current drama, actors, and theatrical news; a liberal churchman with considerable insight into character. In Hoadly's company (and in correspondence) Garrick, uncommitted to him professionally, could discuss at ease, try out his thoughts on plays, actors, and critical evaluations. Garrick encouraged him to keep writing plays. Regarding a draft manuscript of a play in progress Garrick wrote, "Y$^e$ Alteration You intend in y$^e$ Comedy is quite judicious . . . let me See the Comedy finish'd Soon, or ne'er expect to see my laughing Face again" (29). Later he encouraged Hoadly in a projected tragedy, "You have A better Notion of Trage[dy] than any of Your Contemporaries" (49). In finally rejecting these two, and two later plays, Garrick was simply and sincerely stating what he wrote in rejecting several of Benjamin's plays (which his widow insisted he should produce), "I would not for all our Sakes, & for his Memory, that any thing unworthy of him should be expos'd, let who will be y$^e$ gainer" (632). On the other hand Garrick may well have proposed that Hoadly assist in several adaptations (not usually credited to Hoadly) that Garrick produced: *George Barnwell* (8 May 1749), frequently acted thereafter, and less successfully, Beaumont and Fletcher's *The Spanish Curate* (19 October 1749) (48,105).

As a playwright Hoadly made a promising beginning, collaborating with his brother in writing *The Contrast*, produced at Lincoln's Inn Fields 30 April 1731, but at the desire of the bishop the play was suppressed and never printed. The brothers somehow participated in the production the same year in the same theatre of George Jeffrey's *Merope*.[17] John collaborated with James Miller in completing his *Mahomet the Imposter* at Drury Lane 25 April 1744, produced later by Garrick "with improvements" 25 November 1765. He also completed George Lillo's adaptation of the Elizabethan play *Arden of Feversham* (presumably shortly after Lillo's death in 1739) although the play was not produced by Garrick until 12 July 1759.

Hoadly's most successful collaboration was with his brother Benjamin in *The Suspicious Husband* (C.G. 12 February 1747) with Garrick in the lead as Ranger and with a prologue by Garrick. Thereafter, Garrick produced the play almost every season at Drury Lane with Ranger as one of his favorite and famous roles.

Otherwise John Hoadly for 40 years hopefully and tirelessly turned out plays, parodies, farces, pantomimes, oratorios, adaptations often with musical accompaniment, all apparently rejected by Garrick. In his later letters Hoadly awakens sympathetic admiration in his repeated solicitation of Garrick to return all his pieces, "I would not have them appear in my hand after my or your death." [18] On 2 November 1772 he wrote Garrick: "I last week burn'd four acts of a *complete* comedy, and reserved the *first*, to be a momento of a young man's folly and vanity, who could bring it up from Cambridge himself, and send it without a name to John Rich, where by good luck *brother Ben* was and read it, and found out the ingenious author, and put a stop to his exposing himself." [19] Earlier in the same year he wrote: "Have you ever lighted on a farce of mine, from Molière's 'Mariage forcé,' called 'The lady her own Champion,' which I once read to you and Peggy Woffington at breakfast at her lodgings? I have lost it, and fear it is in my hand-writing." [20] As late as 10 September 1775 he wrote: "I here, as you desired, send you 'Love's Revenge,' hashed and slashed. I suppose not exactly the same with the former, but I think better. Part of the overture, we agreed, should be left out. That of the second interlude (minuet with French horns) I would certainly retain, as it is so pleasing and so adapted to the Satyr's appearance. (That gentleman's motions and songs would admit of something in the comic cast.) You may be able to abridge it a little, by leaving out some of the Da Capos. That will be best judged, when you hear it altogether. I think the repetition of the duet in chorus will be a good ending, without the intended grand chorus; and the few lines which I have taken from the songs, and added to the speaker, will be necessary." [21]

One may wonder what sustained Hoadly's spirit to persist. Obviously it lay in the hope Garrick, and Garrick alone, would act in one of his pieces, for when he heard rumor (falsely) that Garrick was going to retire in 1765, and after he had submitted a draft of *Cromwell*, he wrote: "Nothing but my entire friendship for you, and your conduct of the thing, and your inimitable performance, could induce me to break through the prudery of my profession, and the fantastical *decency* of my (too) exalted station in it, and bring the name of Hoadly again upon the public stage. I shall never forget your friendly advice at Hampton *against* my exhibiting it; and you cannot blame now my closing with that advice, when the main inducement to my rash resolution is vanished." [22]

Though not a successful playwright, Hoadly understood the realities of production. This with his wish for anonymity made him Garrick's most respected liberal and disinterested adviser in matters theatrical.

He was particularly familiar with the older drama—Shakespeare, Jonson, Congreve, Wycherley, as well as the acting abilities of contemporaries—Mrs Anne Dancer, Mr and Mrs James William Dodd, and John Henderson, and also of contemporary playwrights. "You seem now to give into Dr. Goldsmith's *ridiculosity* in opposition to *all sentimentality*."[23] He proposed older roles for Garrick to revive, warned against trying to bring *The Rehearsal* up to date, examined and approved Garrick's alteration of *Hamlet*, sharply criticized Cumberland for making the denouement in two of his plays dependent on an overheard soliloquy: "You must know, that a soliloquy is esteemed on the stage only as *thinking aloud*, and not supposed possible to be overheard; and I lament you have no more influence over Mr. Cumberland than to let such a fault pass in two comedies."[24] He recommended a play "Edwin" by the deceased Mr Jefferies, which might be redone profitably. When Garrick asked where to find it he replied: "I thought you had all the plays in the language. It was published when acted, and since in a quarto volume of Jefferies' Works."[25] Hoadly also sensed audience moods, and admonished Garrick against producing *Eastward Hoe* for a performance on Lord Mayor's Day, although at Garrick's request he had written a prologue for it. "As promises and pie-crust are made to be broken, so *opinions* and (I want a word beginning with an O) are made to be changed. Eastward-Hoe not on Lord Mayor's-Day. The Fair Quaker, which we agreed to be *skimmed milk*, (nay, hogwash) whipped up into *syllabub*, and swallowed by a foolish audience as if substantial as *roast beef*. You think you may do what you please with Mr. Town, so you give him but a *raree-show*; but take a litte care he does not revolt against absolute nonsense, however decorated."[26]

Garrick continued to discuss problems and air plans, telling him his hopes for succeeding as Othello (which were not fulfilled in 1745), and asking about Veranes in Lee's *Theodosius* (19 August 1946): "There is Something very moving in $y^e$ Character, but Such a Mixture of Sadness & Absurdity was never Serv'd up, upon $y^e$ Stage before, except by $y^e$ Same incomprehensible Nat Lee: I have been looking into Philaster, or Love lies a Bleeding [Beaumont and Fletcher]; there is good Stuff; but $y^e$ intrigue between Megra & Pharamond, upon $w^{ch}$ $y^e$ Whole turns, is very indecent & requires great alterations" (48).

In 1766 he thought Hoadly a valuable, objective reviewer of the scenario for *The Clandestine Marriage*, writing to George Colman: "$D^r$ Hoadly breakfasted with me this morning & longs to have a little theatrical Chat with Us—If You are disengag'd to morrow at Tea drinking about Six, or before, as you please, We shall Rejoice to burn our Shins w[th] Yours round a clear fire in Southampton Street—Townley has sent y[e] Farce [*The Clandestine Marriage*], but his opinion he reserves till I see him—D[r] Hoadly saw it, laugh'd at y[e] title & desir'd to read it—He'll bring it with him to morrow—he is ignorant that it is Yours" (387). In this last statement, Garrick had forgotten that Hoadly had written him more than a year earlier, 3 October 1765: "I am pleased to hear that Mr. Colman's comedy (two acts of which he showed me at Hampton some years ago) is in such forwardness; as I found by his talk at his own house last winter, he had not worked any farther upon it. I did not let him know I had seen any of it, or was privy to the scheme, which surely is a good one."[27] The example is here cited only as an insight into Garrick's intimate relations with Hoadly, and Hoadly's participation in the genesis of Garrick's and Colman's most successful comedy, *The Clandestine Marriage*. Garrick continued in his letter to Colman (above): "If you have a mind to oblige [Hoadly], He would be glad that you would read y[e] *Widow of y[e] Mill* which I sent you from D'Ancona [Italy], by his Brother, & w[ch] is now tickled up by y[e] Reverend for y[e] Stage—I have given him my thoughts, & he wishes for *Yours*. do as You please; You know You are safe with him, for he is all compliance, & takes Nothing amiss, & has a vast opinion of you."

The ultimate recognition of a lifelong friendship came when Garrick spontaneously and privately in letters announced first to his three oldest friends, Rigby, Clutterbuck, and Hoadly, his decision to retire; to Hoadly first of all, from Adelphi, 3 January 1776: "My dear Friend. I shall take my leave of the Stage, & bid Farewell to the plumed troops & the big Wars, & welcome content & the tranquil Mind—in Short—I will not stay to be Sixty with my Cap & bells—Active as I am, & full of Spirit, with the drawback of a *gravel-complaint*" (976).

Although Hoadly, Garrick's senior by 15 years, originally took the initiative to make Garrick's acquaintance, solicited the correspondence, and focused the substance of their relations on matters theatrical, Garrick's response was intellectual and personal. The friendship began in Garrick's "lodgings in James Street Cov[t] Garden . . . The Barber's Shop up two pair of stairs," and expanded in intimacy and affection with their wives and their several elegant residences. It included the "things" sought by Garrick: hospitality, mutual friends such as Joseph Warton at Winchester, personal and family life, health, books, charities, pastoral duties, the exchange of occasional verse: "It is so long since you sent me your epitaph on Hogarth, that I had forgotten what I owed to it and you. I have given it a niche in my temple

of immortality, *i.e.* inserted it in vol. 14."[28] Garrick kept up the conviviality of the early gatherings, and was unreserved in recounting the
inevitable concomitants of eighteenth-century conviviality, that is the
gastric disorders, such passages being omitted by Boaden in editing
Hoadly's letters as "calculated for private perusal only" but welcomed
by moderns: "Personal infirmities, and the contrivances to palliate
them, are but sorry subjects of jocularity; but we often find that, when
they are endured at home by delicacy and duty, the object of them
derives confidence from indulgence, and makes a favourite topic of
what should be a profound secret.—Ed."[29] From Paris in 1751, Garrick wrote Hoadly in response to such a passage in Hoadly's recent
letter: "I am sorry that son of a Bitch y^e Gout, likes the tenement so
well, that there's no routing him from thy Plump Body; the Bugs in
France would be glad to see thee there, & many a delicious Meal they
would make of thee; Beef & Pudd^g, tho at second hand, is a great
rarity, & therefore Thou are a *Feast fit for the Bugs*" (105). Twenty
years later from Hampton (9 May 1771), Garrick continued in the same
vein regarding his own illness. "My Dear Friend. As I was deaf, Gouty,
flatulent, dull &c &c &c in London, I chose to defer answ^g your very
kind letter [of April 28], till I return'd to Hampton & rigdum funnidos
[Garrick's nickname for Hoadly]: I was operated upon this morning, for
a Noise in my Head, it has had a surprizing Effect, for my disorder
is gone, & my Spirits are return'd—Ergo, I sit down to gallop over a
few pages of Nonsense to Thee, my dear D^r, who art y^e Genius of
Mirth & good fellowship—so have at The old Boy!

"I have been really blighted with y^e Spring, & till the Warm Weather came to make me bud a little with y^e trees, I was resolv'd to send no
cold-blooded prosing to Thee my Merry Wag of ten thousand! I am
tight in my Limbs, better in my head, & my belly is as big as Ever
—I cannot quit *Peck & Booze*—What's Life without Sack & Sugar! my
lips were made to be lick'd, & if the Devil appears to me in the Shape
of Turbot & Claret, my Crutches are forgot, & I laugh & Eat till my
Navel rosebud is as full blown as a Sun flower" (632,357).

On 22 February 1776, a month before his death, Hoadly wrote Garrick "another theatrical letter," on Garrick's discovery and production
of Fielding's lost play *The Father*, on plays by John Home,[30] Hugh
Kelly, and Mrs Hannah Cowley, and more at length on a bond that he
and Garrick had in common: "I hear the Poet Laureat has lately offered you a comedy, which you have refused. . . . I hear it had great
merit, but you did not care to hazard it; particularly objecting to a
character as unnatural, of a man who marries for love, and afterwards

wants to get rid of his wife. I take it for granted his management had made it unnatural; for there cannot be a character more in nature nor more frequent. It is seldom that men who marry for love have much more in their eye than the *person* of the lady, which is not foundation strong enough for a very lasting superstructure. . . . You will say I write this with no very good grace when I tell you, yesterday (Ash-wednesday, poor Ben's birth-day too) we two poor souls had been married forty years, and agreed we would do the same the next morning. And yet I think I married for love, as I never heard of fortune's being concerned. . . . I grieve that I cannot take my airings: I write now in a storm of wind, hail, snow, and rain; and a monstrous high tide, which is now overflowing my garden." [31]

Garrick had grown up in Lichfield participating and loyal to the institutions of the landed gentry, the church, and the army, which afforded the margin of income and supported the distinction between the public, professional life and the private, cultivated life of the gentleman, the amateur. The end of wealth was not to produce more wealth, the end of fame not to seek more fame; the ideal was that the margin of both afforded the opportunity to cultivate intellectual and social graces, to patronize the liberal and fine arts, in social life and conversation with a historical, literary, cultural content. Garrick, engrossed as the manager of Drury Lane and his fame as an actor, was seldom allowed by others to forget either professional role, nor did he always succeed in subordinating the actor-manager while cultivating the private image, the gentleman friend. In Hoadly he had an excellent example, a wealthy and influential churchman, who as a gentleman scholar cultivated the theatre. And Garrick responded first in private social life and then supplying as a content for that social life, not always the actor-manager, but more and more a love of the literature of the drama, the amenities of gracious social life.

## SOMERSET DRAPER (1706–1756) AND THE BRETHREN OF THE QUEEN'S-ARMS

Confronted and embroiled in the fluctuating state of the current theatre, Garrick himself, in his first ten years in London, was on occasion nervous, tentative, and irresolute, in regard to his acting, public relations, and contracts. Generally isolated in a competitive and

precarious profession, contending with the unpredictable tempera-
ments of actors, managers, the press and the public, Garrick fell back
on resources in his private life that supported him in his professional
ambitions. In the same manner in which he was reassured by the
cordiality of John Hoadly and his circle, Garrick attained a detachment
and stability in the company of "His Brethren in the Queen's-Arms"
Tavern in St Paul's Churchyard and in Batson's Coffee-House near the
Royal Exchange in Cornhill. In the former some of his personal
friends, among others Somerset Draper, James Clutterbuck, John
Patterson, and Samuel Sharp formed a club. They also rejoiced in
Batson's Coffee-House "much frequented by men of intelligence and
conversation."[32] In three of the men with whom Garrick thus associated, he found both immediate and lifelong, wise counsel and devoted
friends.

In two letters in 1740 from London to Peter in Lichfield, Garrick
makes two references to a "Draper," presumably to Nightingale
Draper, an apothecary in London, but from the tone of the letters,
both Garrick and Peter may first have known Nightingale in Lichfield.
Presumably he inherited the brewing business from his brother
Somerset Draper. If brothers, they were the sons of Somerset and
Anne Draper of Wadsworth, Surrey, not necessarily their place of
origin, more likely of their death (12,14). Some years later in 1745,
Garrick writing to Somerset Draper refers to "your friend Seward,"
that is Thomas Seward, canon of Lichfield and Salisbury (34). More
likely, however, Peter and David may first have met Draper when the
Garrick brothers were vintners in London and Draper was a brewer.
Around 1743 Draper became a partner of the publishers Jacob and
Richard Tonson. Thereafter Garrick and Draper were associated in the
patronage and publishing of a number of books, but Draper was to
take a far more crucial role in aiding the fulfillment of Garrick's ambition to become the actor-manager of Drury Lane.

In 1742 Draper married Elizabeth, "youngest sister to the friend of
his heart James Clutterbuck" (28), and shortly after, Clutterbuck, William Windham, and Draper became the three principal consultants,
advisors, and intermediaries for Garrick—often in his absence in Dublin, Lichfield, or elsewhere than London. In the protracted and fluctuating negotiations with managers, actors (notably with Mrs Cibber),
and bankers, Garrick gratefully accepted whatever offers and terms the
three proposed. "Into your hands I commit myself" (35). Garrick knew
that Draper was thoroughly conversant with the shifting theatrical
developments. This knowledge in addition to his friendship inspired

complete confidence on Garrick's part. The contract with James Lacy, though signed in April 1747, dragged on its final clarifications of details and misunderstandings until 1750, with Draper still involved. Garrick was persuaded it was essential and wise to commit his career at this juncture to those he trusted, rather than to become distracted, as other actors did, in wrangling confrontations. Eventually Garrick used the term *we* almost as though he and Draper were partners.

During Garrick's absence from London, he wrote Draper from Dublin, Londesburgh, and France in candor and gratitude on many subjects. Draper watched over the residence on Southampton Street, sending at Garrick's request articles he had left behind; he also handled Garrick's investments. Much of their correspondence was taken up with all sorts of theatrical news and business. There were inquiries after friends, Mrs Draper's health, how Hogarth was coming along with his picture (108,115,118,1299). Always generous where merited, Garrick wrote Draper from Dublin as early as 26 December 1745 about his friend Henry Harnage's failure in his banking house: "I beg you will enquire how affairs stand with him, and if this Bill of Exchange [enclosed with the letter] will be of the least service to him, pray let him have it immediately; I shall leave that business to your management; *if the sum were twenty times as much, and the whole of my fortune, he should have it*, for I know his worth and honour" (42).

The first surviving letter of Garrick to Draper (16 September 1744) opens with a profession of friendship that lasted throughout: "My Dear Draper, Though I have little to say to you of consequence, I must write you because I love you; we are generally most troublesome to our best friends" (28). This same unreserved profession of affection Garrick expressed again and again in salutations and complimentary closes, not the customary stereotyped flourishes, but varied and particularized to emphasize the quality of the friendship. In 1752 Garrick was much distressed by Draper's declining health, and inevitably Draper, Garrick's senior by 20 years, predeceased him in 1756. We know from a letter to Hogarth how much Garrick thought of Draper, and memory of the friendship lingered on in the 1760s, when he wrote to Colonel Bernard Hale: "I'll tell you a fact—the Man of all Men I lov'd the best, one *Draper* by name, & now an arch angel in Heav'n, was for many years Every Morning with Me at breakfast time" (1299). We can but regret that in a friendship which meant so much to Garrick, almost nothing is known of Draper outside of Garrick's letters. He seems to have been a most admirable man of affairs, counselor, and companion.

## James Clutterbuck (1704?–1776)

A prominent second member of the Queen's-Arms club, and one that helped negotiate Garrick's terms with Lacy, was Draper's brother-in-law James Clutterbuck. Very little is known about him personally, but a great deal about him financially. James Boaden called him "a much-valued friend of Mr. Garrick's, a man of business of considerable fortune. He kept a shop, the sign of the Three Angels in the Strand, and had a country-house in Richmond." [33] He seems to have been in partnership with Gastrell, a mercer, who often supplied Drury Lane with stage materials. [34] For some years he was a commissioner in Middlesex, and later in 1771 he was "enacting the parts of a Commissioner of the Land Tax, a Commissioner of a Turnpike Act, besides my ordinary role, as one of the quorum in the county of Gloucester," [35] all the appointments or offices requiring men of extensive property. He died in January 1776, and his will was registered in the Probate Court of Canterbury, 4 November 1776.

As early as 1744 Garrick and Clutterbuck were on terms of mutual confidence and of youthful conviviality. On 16 September that year Garrick wrote to Draper: "I hope poor Clutterbuck has found benefit from the bath; pray my sincere services to him, and let him know, that I called often at his house to overlook his servants, and preach up order, economy, and care to them. I am sorry he carried the key of his cellar with him; for I had a design before I left town to make the whole family drunk, by drinking bumpers to his recovery and return. However, I treated his household with some gallons of English brandy punch; and they were so mad and merry for a whole afternoon, as to excite a mob of four or five hundred people about the door" (28). A year later Garrick wrote Draper from Lichfield on 23 October 1745: "Clutterbuck has wrote me two devilish funny letters, and notwithstanding his colic, he has a pretty wit, I assure you; pray tell him I shall commit my stock wholly to his direction; and whatever he does (let what will be the consequence), I am sure will proceed from judgment, integrity, and friendship" (37). Though Garrick may have been determined to accumulate property, he certainly was not able to raise, after five or six years of acting, without Clutterbuck's help, the £8,000 he paid to Lacy for half the control of Drury Lane, and the £4,000 he contributed to Mrs Garrick's dowry when they were married in June 1749. In the 1750s and 1760s Clutterbuck was the responsible financial backer of Drury Lane. Sometime in the calendar year 1753

Garrick and Lacy drew up a mortgage on Drury Lane property for £10,000, which Clutterbuck held for a period of 21 years. Amortization was to come at £4 per acting night and permission to grant free seats in any part of the house (except on stage, behind the scenes, and in the orchestra) to 40 persons. These latter were to be named and location assigned ten days prior to the opening of any season.[36] He also handled the purchase and lease of the Rose Tavern, adjacent to the theatre for Garrick and Lacy (119), and later sensibly mediated a misunderstanding between the managers. He also mediated a misunderstanding between Garrick and Arthur Murphy in 1756, and another between Garrick and Colman over *The Clandestine Marriage* in 1765. The quality of his level headedness and real friendship appears in his letter to Garrick 9 November 1765: "Colman and you are men of most quick sensations, and are apt sometimes to catch at words instead of things, and those very words may probably receive great alterations by the medium through which they pass. I know you love one another, and a third person might call up such explanations as would satisfy ye both; I myself should not doubt being able to do it were we assembled together" (164,165,378,397).[37] A year later, after the resolution of that contretemps Garrick in a letter to his brother George remarked, "I see Colman often & we talk as usual: *Clutterbuck* & *Schomberg* would see Us on good terms—we all din'd with yᵉ former last Monday, & were merry" (452).

A collaboration of some magnitude and long duration developed when Garrick, through the agency and in the name of James Clutterbuck, purchased on 20 April 1757 the manor of Hendon, in Essex, for £13,038. Clutterbuck served as lord of the manor until 10 July 1767, when the property, excepting a small farm of £70 a year income, was conveyed to Garrick (337 n.6), the management of which continued to trouble him. On 10 January 1777, Garrick, who had the advowson, presented the vicorship of Hendon to his nephew Carrington Garrick (997). Exactly what the terms of agreement were between Garrick and Clutterbuck during his tenure have not been discovered, but in 1765 Clutterbuck wrote Garrick relative to Hendon: "I should not divest myself of it; because then I shall not have estate enough in Middlesex to qualify me to act as a commissioner in that county, which for your sake, at some future appeal day, I propose doing, if the same shall be thought necessary, and my health will permit me; however, I have in my will guarded against contingencies in relation to that article."[38]

When Garrick wrote to their mutual friends—Draper, Colman, and brother George—he often asked to be remembered to Clutterbuck in affectionate and friendly terms. They exchanged visits, dined together in London, were often together in Bath, and Garrick at least once (before the execution of the mortgage) supplied him with theatre tickets (127).[39] Each was interested in the other's health. Garrick made much of sending Clutterbuck from Munich (31 October 1765) a prescription for piles, from "MonS$^r$ Renaudin who was my Physician" (339). The last letter Clutterbuck wrote to Garrick (23 January 1776), though felicitating him on his upcoming retirement from the stage, sounded a sombre note: "The vulgar have in many places a notion, that whenever, after the bite of a mad dog, the hydrophobia appears, the unhappy patient, by virtue of an act of parliament, is to be smothered between two feather beds; and if so, methinks it is pity that the act were not extended to paralytic cases, which generally leave the object in such a condition as makes it cruelty to endeavour at a prolongation of his life."[40] Although Clutterbuck had been increasingly afflicted by declining health and the advance of age, he was sustained always by Garrick's thoughtfulness: "The dregs of life," he wrote in 1765, "are seldom palatable; but my spirits, and the kindness of those few friends that Providence hath spared me, take off the bitterness, and make the draught less nauseous to my dear, dear Garrick's ever affectionate and faithful friend."[41] Clutterbuck was glad to have a portrait of Garrick by Gainsborough in 1771 and thanked both profusely.[42] He already had a double portrait of Garrick and Mrs Garrick in his home, and once in gently chiding Garrick for long absence wrote: "I reap some comfort, by stepping now and then into my parlour, and holding a dumb conversation with you both."[43]

On the day, 18 January 1776, that Garrick signed the contract for the sale of Drury Lane, he wrote, "My dear Clut. You shall be the first Person to whom I shall make known, that I have at last Slipt my theatrical Shell. . . . I grow somewhat Older, tho I never play'd better in all my Life, & am resolv'd not to remain upon the Stage to be pitied instead of applauded . . . I hope I shall receive a Letter of felicitation from You—Love to Your better half & to the Sharps & all friends. Ever & most affect$^y$ Y$^{rs}$ D Garrick" (978). Clutterbuck responded immediately from Bath, January 23: "Joy! much joy! to my dear Garrick for having wound up his bottom so wisely. . . . I most heartily congratulate you upon the event, and thank you for authenticating the news so much like a true friend," endorsed by Garrick "My friend Clutterbuck upon the sale of my patent."[44] The following December, Clutterbuck died, having appointed Garrick as one of the executors of his will.

The records are more fragmentary of Garrick's enduring relations with four other members of the social gatherings or clubs already mentioned. If the *"plump Doctor"* who foregathered with Garrick and Hogarth as guests of Hoadly at Old Alresford in 1746, is to be identified as Messenger Monsey (1693–1788), physician, wit, and familiar figures in London social circles, reprobated by Johnson for profanity,[45] then Garrick early humored an almost notoriously gross or vulgar eccentric. Garrick later in their relations cultivated the tone of blunt familiarity of the doctor, of which many anecdotes survive. Long head of the Chelsea Hospital, he was for some years Garrick's and Mrs Garrick's doctor, she rather relishing his blunt wit, a sample of which Garrick imitated in reporting to the doctor the results of his prescription of a cathartic for Mrs Garrick (102). More in the spirit of the bawdy parody "Ragandjaw" acted out at Hoadly's, is the anecdote of Monsey's calling on Garrick on his way to see Garrick in *King Lear* only to find Garrick ill abed. Garrick assured Monsey that his stand-in, Marr, would be accepted as Garrick in the production that evening. In the course of the play Monsey began to have his doubts, and after the play hurried back to Southampton Street to find Garrick, who had barely returned before him, covered up in bed but still wearing his actor's robes.[46] Often in each other's company, they continued to "correspond" (102), Monsey even lending Garrick some books, but the wit of the doctor turned sour and defensive, and he bitterly complained that Garrick failed to return his books or a favor, and had made fun of him in company—Monsey's manner certainly provided an obvious target (1157). Yet the friendship endured after a fashion until in 1778 when Monsey wrote Garrick "Two peevish Letters" to which Garrick responded in part: "You as a Physician and I as a Manager of a Theatre, dealt in Tragedy, Comedy and Farce—You had always free Egress & Regress into my Shop, and why should not I have a peep into yours? —our Drugs indeed *work'd* in different ways, but I hope and believe that mine were as wholesome and Salutary as yours—however if you find that any ballance is due to you, for particular *favours*, I am ready to discharge it, notwithstanding Hudibras's Axion.—'When Friends begin to take Account / The Devil with such Friends may Mount'" (1157).

An early medical friend, of far different character, was Samuel Sharp (1700?–78), one of the brethren of the Queen's-Arms club (39,43), who in 1745 was delivering anatomical lectures in Covent Garden. Later he turned over his lectureship to his even more distinguished successor, the great William Hunter. There are no records of how often Sharp and Garrick were in each other's company; but in 1750 Garrick consulted Sharp after Mrs Garrick was bruised when a carriage overturned at Londesburgh (89). Later in 1765 Garrick recommended to Sharp his Italian valet, Antonio Carara, who was engaged by Sharp to accompany him on his Italian tour, recounted in his plainspoken *Letters from Italy*, 1766. Much earlier, in the 1720s, Sharp had passed much of his medical apprenticeship in France and became acquainted with Voltaire. In 1763, Garrick on his way to Italy, had been unable at the time to accept Voltaire's invitation to visit him at Ferney (318, 325),[47] though he presumably looked forward to calling on him on his return. Extended illness of both Garrick and Mrs Garrick obliged Garrick to return from Munich through Nancy, from which place on or before 10 November 1764, he wrote Voltaire, "My affairs are so circumstanc'd that I am oblig'd to go to Paris as expeditiously as my present weak state of health will permit me" (340). Garrick communicated to Sharp his regrets and uncertainties in his handling of Voltaire's invitation, with the upshot that Sharp called on Voltaire and wrote Garrick from Geneva, 18 August 1765: "I am just come from Mons. Voltaire's, and can give you the fullest assurance that neither your letter nor any other part of your conduct has given him the least umbrage. . . . Our chief topic was our English actor. When I signified to him that I should write this evening to Mr. Garrick, and that it would be the greatest pleasure I could do you, to say he was in good health; 'No, Sir,' said he, 'do not write an untruth, but tell him, *Je suis plein d'estime pour lui.*' When I represented how mortified you was in having lost the opportunity of paying him your respects, his answer was such, that I am persuaded you never offended."[48]

The fragmentary record of what was clearly a long and intimate friendship, ends, as so often in the eighteenth century in the lives of valetudinarian friends, in Bath, in a letter from Clutterbuck to Garrick, 21 June 1773: "Our valuable friend Sharpe is alarmed almost to despondency by a cataract formed upon one eye, and his fears that the other will share the same misfortune. He begs me to come as often as I can to him, and I purpose dining there to-morrow, in hopes of strengthening him in his wise resolution of laying in as many additional ideas as can be obtained while his sight lasts, and strive to imitate the feathered songsters, who are said to perform best when their eyes are out."[49]

Of all Garrick's early London friends who originally met at the Queen's-Arms or the Bedford, John Paterson (d. 1789) was the most trusted, enduring, and least known. On 24 May 1746 Garrick wrote Peter in Lichfield: "I have consulted my Friends about George: I spoke particularly to my very good Friend Mr Paterson the City Sollicitor who told me at once, that He should be in his office as long as he pleas'd & that he would use him as he would Me; which is so generous

an Offer & made with so much friendship & affection, that I desir'd
Drapar to Night at our Club (w^ch I could not attend on account of my
Illness) to let him know I should accept it. . . . He'll have an Opportunity of seeing vast variety of Business, & cultivating an Acquaintance
(by a proper Behav^r) with y^e most Amiable, sensible sweet fellow, that
ever the Law produc'd" (44). Paterson even dropped one of his clerks
in order to open a place for George (46) who, however, did not long
continue there, but joined the staff of Drury Lane as his brother's
trusted lieutenant. Ten years later Garrick solicited through Paterson,
then M. P. for Wiltshire, a member of the common council, and politically very active, a sinecure for Peter, but Paterson replied that he
thought "it too much for him," and Garrick readily agreed (421).

While Draper, Clutterbuck, and Windham may have participated in
negotiating the terms and financial arrangements in Garrick's contract
with Lacy back in 1745–47, the final contract of 9 April 1747 and the
subsequent formulation of several oral agreements, as we have noted,
were drawn up by Paterson, with the proviso, "That in case of any
future difference the Partner who shall think Himself injured shall . . .
state his complaint to M^r Paterson who shall decide theron & finally
settle the dispute between them," and if unsuccessful, then the partnership was to be terminated.[50]

In 1766 Paterson did mediate a dispute between Garrick and Lacy:
"I think [Lacy's] proposal fair and reasonable, and such as you should
agree to." Garrick immediately responded on 5 March 1766: "If M^r
Lacy, as you have told me, is sorry for our late quarrel, & sincere in
his desire of continuing in partnership with me—I shall at Once come
in to Your determination" (390). Paterson persevered and had "the
satisfaction of being the happy instrument in restoring [the] ancient
harmony and friendship."[51] This single incident exemplifies what was
certainly a pervasive stabilizing influence in the harrassing confrontations Garrick faced many a season as manager, an influence that transcended simply astute or prestigious legal advice, to an abiding association, and conversation, and affection of a much respected and
enduring friend. Garrick's trust in this quiet, level-headed friend
prompted him to name him as one of the executors of his will. Paterson was of all Garrick's pallbearers the senior in friendship.

Old friends sustained Garrick in his private life and subtly influenced him in his public one. These came from the business community, and from that community he grew into friendships with others
as time went on. In his later years Garrick enjoyed the company of
several bankers. Richard Cox (1719–1803) had built up a fortune as an
army agent and founded Cox's Bank, now Cox and King's Branch of

Lloyds Bank, Ltd, where Garrick's accounting is preserved and one of Garrick's letters to Cox of 12 March 1778. Cox was something of a *bon vivant* belonging to a group of 12 prominent figures in London who called themselves "The Gang" and acquainted with Goldsmith, Christopher Anstey, John Calvert, Rigby, Burke, and Burney.

By 1769 Garrick was addressing him as "Thou dear, dev'lish, agreeable, Confounded, best, & wickedest of Mortals!" "My dear Riccardetto," and in 1778, "my dear old Friend the Richard of all Richards" (552,1252,1161). They especially enjoyed dining together in London, Garrick sending Cox "two dozen of Burgandy, pray let it be kept warm. You will find it good, if not Send it again to Yours Ever most truly" (1252), and often at Cox's country seat at Aspenden in Hertfordshire. Garrick addressed one verse letter to him, a mark of favor exercised for only a few friends.[52]

As for the well-known banking house of the Hoare family, Garrick was a client in 1769; Henry Hoare, Jr, and his wife Mary were neighborly acquaintances in the Adelphi, guests at Hampton, attended the theatre, and journeyed together to visit Richard at Barn Elms, Barnes, Surrey; and to visit Henry in the magnificent country home at Stourhead, Wiltshire, where Sir Richard Colt Hoare (1758–1838), the Wiltshire historian, was to assemble his famous library of illustrations and records of local history.

Under circumstances, for which no records have been discovered, the Garricks met the Racketts who attended the Shakespeare Jubilee in 1769. Thomas Rackett, Sr (1717–79), was an army tailor (that is, contractor). An anonymous biographer of Garrick, for a sketch in *The Town and Country Magazine* (June 1779) asserted that ten years before Garrick had retired he had lost considerable money in loans to "R—," a Tailor. The Racketts lived near the Garricks, in King Street, Covent Garden, and in the London suburb of Wandsworth, Surrey, and were often hosts to and guests of the Garricks. Mrs Garrick was drawn to Mrs Rackett, who in 1777 cared for her niece Elizabeth Fürst, in an illness during their absence. She also visited and dined with Mrs Garrick during the actor's last illness.[53]

Thomas Rackett, Jr (1757–1841), as a boy of 14 so pleased Garrick by memorizing and reciting *An Ode upon Dedicating a Building and Erecting a Statue to Shakespeare at Stratford upon Avon*, 1769, that Garrick gave him an inscribed copy, followed the next year by a Shakespeare Folio, and shortly after *The Fables of La Fontaine*, in two volumes, illustrated. Curiously enough Garrick composed "Cupid and Damon; or The Siren Sisters. A Musical Family Drama. The Words by David Garrick, Esqr. The Music by Mr. Dibdin," to be performed at a Christmas party by young Rackett and the three daughters of the Reverend James Tatersall (309). Thomas, Jr, attended University College, Oxford, where Garrick was in touch with him, and whence he sent Garrick a brawn's head (877,960). He later became rector of Spotisbury, Dorsetshire, where he devoted much of his life to antiquarian studies. He kept up his ties with Mrs Garrick, becoming one of the executors of her estate, and with George Beltz writing her obituary notice in the *Gentleman's Magazine* in 1822. He passed on to his descendants a rich collection of Garrick memorabilia.[54]

Garrick's lively personality and friendly nature attracted not only the Hogarths, the Hoadlys, and the businessmen of his early acquaintance, but also young William Windham II, born into a long established landed-gentry family resident in Felbrigg Hall, near Cromer.

## WILLIAM WINDHAM II (1717–1761)

Garrick was perhaps first welcomed into cosmopolitan and aristocratic circles by William Windham II. Windham had the good fortune to have as excellent tutor Benjamin Stillingfleet, who directed his pupil's studies for 12 years and more in residence at Felbrigg Hall, where William grew up a vigorous, self-reliant, first-rate horseman, fencer, and boxer. He did not attend any school or university; rather, when he came of age, he and Stillingfleet, after a brief visit to Paris, established in 1738 a residence in Geneva, which they called the Common Room, and which became the center of their studies, travels, and friendship with several kindred spirits. During a year in Italy Windham began buying extensively a rather remarkable collection of pictures later displayed and preserved until the present in Felbrigg Hall. He also collected books and acquired the command of several continental languages. Among the activities of the small group in Geneva was the writing and production of plays, pantomimes, and harlequinades. In mid-July 1742 the Common Room broke up, and Windham and Stillingfleet set out on a leisurely journey to Felbrigg Hall through Germany and Holland, where Windham added some Dutch and Flemish paintings to his collection. He soon returned to London, to a residence in Panton Street, and made the acquaintance of the famous boxer John Broughton—hence the name "Boxing Windham." By December 1743 he had become so well known to Garrick that when Macklin, in his quarrel with Garrick, threatened to break up for the second time *The*

*Rehearsal* at Drury Lane on 2 December, Windham having recruited some 30 bruisers was admitted "by private way before the doors were regularly opened," challenged Macklin's mob, and drove them from the theatre.[55]

Windham rented a hunting lodge in Suffolk to be near his friend, William Henry Zuylestein, Lord Rochford, who was also cultivating Garrick's acquaintance, and to the lodge Windham invited Garrick in 1744. On this occasion Garrick and Windham visited Windham's friend Dr Thomas Dampier, with whom Garrick later in 1761 was appointed executor of Windham's estate and guardian of his son, William Windham III (288).

While at Eton with Dampier Garrick wrote Draper (16 September 1744): "My friend Mr. *Wyndham* . . . is a most ingenious, worthy, knowing young gentleman, and I think myself very happy and honoured with his friendship; he has travelled and read to some purpose; and he has so much good-nature, honour, spirit, and generosity, that I am confident when he is possessed of a great fortune, and sits in parliament, he will make an extraordinary figure" (28). The two were associated in the patronage of Francis Hayman, the artist, who painted a portrait of Garrick and Windham presumably while they were at Bath, 1745, and on the return journey Windham stopped by in Lichfield as Garrick's guest. Already, however, Garrick was alarmed by Windham's "indifferent state of health, and looks very ill; I have great fears about him—I should have the greatest loss of him—but I will not suppose it, nor think of it," forebodings of the tuberculosis that was to prove fatal (33,34,47). Having supported Garrick in the quarrel with Macklin, Windham took the initiative to collaborate with Draper in the drawn-out negotiations with Lacy, bringing up to London from Garrick in Lichfield, where they doubtless worked together, Garrick's initial offer to Lacy (36). Windham repeatedly conferred with Lacy, in particular when Garrick was in Dublin, 1745, when he wrote Draper: "My dear friend Mr. *Wyndham* will club judgment with you; . . . your mutual determination will be fate to me" (41,37). No other name is mentioned as often as Windham's in Garrick's letters to Draper.

Windham knew Hogarth and by late 1745 sent Garrick "a great account of *Hogarth's* picture," then in production of Richard III (37). The parody "Ragandjaw" was later dedicated to Windham by Garrick (45,48) in part in the words: "I must declare that the Choicest Flowers which I have added to this Poetical Nosegay, were all gathered and cull'd from your Private Conversation, Writings and Public Disputations on the Water, the Roads, in the Streets at Cuper's Gardens and Mr Broughton's ampitheatre."[56] Over the years, however, Garrick and

Windham did not agree on Hogarth. As late as 1758 when Hogarth published *The Bench*, Windham wrote Garrick: "You know my sentiments of him, though you and I have often disputed that affair," and then remarked on Hogarth's "no sure idea of caricature, which the blockhead writes car*acuture* . . . Since he has had the impudence to attack my friend the Colonel [Townshend] I will try at a dinner for him. I think I have material in my head: you shall be the sole confidant, and to your hands shall it be committed to burn or publish." [57]

In 1749 Windham negotiated for the Garricks the purchase of their first home, No 27 Southampton Street, which they were to occupy until they moved in 1772 to The Adelphi. In the same year, on the death of his father, Asche Windham, on 4 April 1749, Windham embarked on extensive restorations and alterations of Felbrigg Hall, in part to house his collection of paintings and his accumulating library, dividing his time for several years between London and Felbrigg. His account books of this period record his chief delight in London to have been to the theatre; "Garrick's name appears frequently, both in connection with the theatre and as a private friend." [58] On 16 July 1753, Garrick wrote from Booth Ferry to George: "I have sent two Tickets y$^e$ one for M$^r$ Clutterbuck, y$^e$ Other for M$^r$ Windham" (127). A year later Garrick with Mrs Garrick visited Windham at Felbrigg Hall: "We were indeed most happy at Windham's, all mirth, Joy, Love, Elegance & what not. . . . He seems thoughtfull at times, greatly so, & I don't absolutely like his Looks & Cough" (138). The Windhams in turn visited the Garricks in Lichfield. [59] Although Windham was less often in London as his illness increased, he was not forgotten by Garrick, who in 1758 sent him his two letters to Dodsley in response to Dodsley's indignation at Garrick's refusal to produce his *Cleone*, the brusque tone and wit much in Windham's manner. Windham in turn sent Garrick the manuscript of his most ambitious piece of writing, *A Plan of Discipline, Composed for the Use of the Militia of the County of Norfolk*, to be published in 1759, with the request: "Be so good as to mark for me what you think may be altered or retrenched, and what is ungrammatical in all expressed, for I am sensible there are many parts that are so." [60]

Windham died on 30 October 1761. Long aware of his approaching death, he prepared his will and codicils with great care, naming Thomas Dampier, his trusted friend from Geneva days, trustee of his estate, and Benjamin Stillingfleet, his devoted tutor and companion for 50 years, and David Garrick guardian of his son, William III, who was to realize what had been denied his father, a famous career as a statesman.

The churchman, the brewer and publisher, the artist, the lawyer, several doctors, the bankers, and the country gentleman with military interests and instincts for collecting books and pictures all shared interests in Garrick's profession. But the content of their mutual communications reached out embracing divergent areas and characters in eighteenth-century life. Through these friends Garrick transcended the limitations of his profession, and intellectually embraced the range of culture of his day—nowhere better reflected than in his own collected library. While Boswell was recording conversations, Garrick was observing, and exploring, and enjoying human personality. He was often flattered by the rank and fortune of those who flattered him, but his abiding initiative was the tireless enjoyment of the great diversity of all who came his way. None of the friends just described had attained any fame when they were drawn to Garrick, and he to them. Garrick had an almost uncanny intuition and admiration for ability and competence. In William Windham he saw a man of the world, well read, cultivated in taste, traveled, physically active and earthy, confident, open, and generous—in many respects the landed gentry at its best. It might almost be said that Windham stirred Garrick to seek a more cosmopolitan life, one which he was to find in Eva Maria Veigel and the circle into which she gave him access.

# 5

# Problems of Management

·

THE LIVELY CHALLENGES of early management, when even the daily routines seemed exciting, yielded in time, one must suppose, to a course of settled regularity. But Garrick's enthusiasm for his work maintained its high pitch as he dealt seriously with his contractual obligations "to settle and alter the business of the stage," and especially to be responsible for repertory. Drury Lane's library of prompt copies held a large and varied stock of plays, the continuing production of which the town would find amusing. But calls for variety and novelty persisted. A plethora of would-be suppliers came forth to meet demand.

Both the artist and manager in Garrick raised instinctive and pragmatic quality controls as to the new fare offered. He read and accepted or rejected many, many plays. He wrote and adapted many more. He experimented with musical performance and scenic enrichment. The activity involved him constantly with authors great and small, along with their articulate supporters and critic friends. His letters accepting or rejecting plays reveal his artistic standards. Back of all lay his knowledge of the cost and human effort required to bring a play from manuscript to production on stage. During his 29 years of management he read (and often more than once) the manuscripts of at least 162 new plays and after pieces which he accepted, and at least 83 more (along with revisions and second submissions) which he rejected. His letters are polite and diplomatic, for he was aware of the force of good public relations. They are more, for they give positive suggestions for improving texts, or valid reasons for rejection.

Authors, understandably, cherished their creations and were apt to be bitter when refusals came their way. They expressed dismay, and in close-knit, gossipy London passed the word to friends, who also expressed themselves. Grub Street buzzed, and it is important, in developing the biography of a remarkable manager to examine and evaluate authors' replies as Garrick himself spent hours doing. Garrick knew what many an author failed to recognize, that all the complicated

126

machinery of setting a performance in motion was not to be wound up lightly to give a try to a piece just to satisfy the ambition of an author. Selection based on probable success counted, not only for Garrick, but for the livelihood of his large company. Perhaps it is to his credit, however, that he *never* pled expense as a reason for rejection. Expenditure for fine production of worthy plays was what made theatre attractive. He often pointed out to an author what failure on stage would mean to his (not Garrick's) reputation. And he kept steadily in view the justification for holding a patent, namely to entertain the public, which would not be well served by a succession of failures. One senses a basic considerateness here on Garrick's part for the human ramifications of stage success or failure divorced from profit motive.

But the harangues went on. He was accused of delay in response, of hypocrisy, and of prejudice. The disappointed seldom stop with a single response. One comes to believe, however, in the sincerity of his remark to Arthur Murphy's irritation at the manager's delay in accepting his *Orphan of China*, 4 December 1758, "I have often said & do now again repeat it, that private pique should never interfere with public Entertainments, while I have any Concern in the Management" (218). Garrick's commitment as an artist was to the institution of the theatre as a cultural instrument in English society. The standards he marked out reveal his taste, and his taste in turn tended to set the tone for all London. Ninety percent of all critical writings about theatre policy after 1747 were addressed to Garrick—few pieces to Rich, Colman, Beard, or Harris. Garrick's standards reflected foundations of long-tried dramatic conventions first suggested by Aristotle. Plot and story line were important both for tragedy and comedy.[1] But in tragedy credibility in plot depended upon motivation among characters, and motivation had to be accompanied by the striking, the pathetic, and the terrible. The whole context had to signal the skilled actor ways to interpret character in a gripping manner. In 1754 he turned down John Cleland's *Vespasian* for lacking those qualities,[2] and on 2 March 1772 he wrote Boswell that friend William Mickle's play *The Siege of Marseilles* would not do: "Speeches & mere poetry will no more make a Play, than planks & timbers in yᵉ dock-Yard can be call'd a Ship—It is Fable, passion & Action which constitute a Tragedy, & without them, we might as well exhibit one of Tillotsons Sermons" (677). In 1757 he asked John Home to come in for a conference to see what could be done to relieve the heaviness, to perfect the timing, as well as to strengthen motivation and probability in his *Agis*. A dozen years later Home seems to have profited from Garrick's tutoring, for his *Fatal Discovery* then pleased the actor highly: "The Construction of Y$^r$ Fable is excellent, You leave the Audience at the End of Every Act, with a certain glow & in y$^e$ most eager Expectation of know$^g$ what is to follow" (509).

As a play reader he was conscious of many pressures, at times in conflict with his own artistic convictions. One such pressure had to do with the routines of management, another with those of finance, but a third had much to do with public relations and the weight of pleading by friends and by noble ladies and gentlemen for special treatment of manuscripts of their protégés. Garrick the man comes through refreshingly in his responses, true to certain aesthetic and practical principles as to text and successful performance.

Early in his career he had faced up to the problem of sponsor pressure and sought advice on 14 September 1746 from his good friend John Hoadly: "I have a Play now with Me, sent to Me by My Lord Chesterfield & wrote by One Smollet [*The Regicide*]; it is a Scotch Story, but it won't do, & yet recommended by his Lordship & patroniz'd by Ladies of Quality: what can I say, or do? must I belye my Judgment or run the risque of being thought impertinent, & disobliging y$^e$ Great Folks?" (49). He was reading the play for Rich, and advised rejection. Ten years later he wrote to the Earl of Bute in careful, detailed, and constructive fashion about rejecting Home's *Douglas*. The play succeeded in Edinburgh and later at Covent Garden. Its text may have profited from Garrick's suggestions, for we know that the published text is *not* in its details the manuscript that Garrick read (166).

In comedy, Garrick's major field of interest (if one judges from his own plays and adaptations) his most frequent requisite was *vis comica*. "If Caesar's criticism upon Terence was just (*Utinam scriptis adjuncta foret vis comica* [Would that thy graceful verses had force as well]," he wrote to James Murphy French turning down his comedy *The Brothers*, "surely a near imitation of his scenes will not have a proper effect upon a stage where a stronger comic force is expected" (187). Perhaps what Garrick had in mind, though he certainly cared not for the bland, occurs in his comment 12 September 1766 on Edward Thompson's *The Hobby Horse*. "It wants fable—*Action, Action, Action*, are words better apply'd to y$^e$ Drama, than to Oratory—be assur'd that without some comic Situations resulting from the fable, the *Hobby horse* will not run y$^e$ race we could wish it—all the knowledge of Character, with y$^e$ finest Dialogue would be lost without a proper Vehicle, to interest y$^e$ Audience. You will throw away much powder & Shot, if you don't ram down both, & comress them w$^{th}$ a good fable; there is y$^r$ great failure, & were I worthy to advise you . . . I would not write a line till I had fix'd upon a good Stoy & consider'd it well upon paper" (430). Comic force lay, in the active meld of situation, story, and lively dialogue offering opportunity and options for actors' interpreting character in either broad or subtle strokes, as eminently exemplified in his *The Lying Valet* and in *The Clandestine Marriage*.

Garrick sensed that though his *Lethe*, essentially a skit displaying a series of comical, satirical portraits, connected by only the thinnest thread of a fable, was doing well, and would do so as long as he continually added new characters, his *Lying Valet* and *Miss in Her Teens*, based each on amusing plots, would do better. And so they did.

Garrick knew that novelty sparked comedy and kept it flourishing. His rejection letters suggest his awareness of overdone patterns of speech, telling Mrs Griffith (August 1766): "*Civil* [character] is too like many Chambermaids of lat[e] who mistake Words, and I think that humour very near Exhausted" (422). In ten years Sheridan's Mrs Malaprop would revitalize such derangement of epitaphs afresh. To Charles Jenner he wrote, 26 April 1770, about his attempt to English Diderot's *Père de Famille*, "Your Wife is a great resemblance of M$^{rs}$ Heidleberg [*Clandestine Marriage*] & tho there are some good Scenes there wants Variety—they are all too Much of y$^e$ Same colouring" (582). To Joseph Cradock, "I fear that there is such a similitude between part [of your farce], and some scenes in the 'Country Girl,' not to say any thing of your friend Cumberland's 'Choleric Man'" (950). To Charles Jenner again, 30 April 1770, "The Comedie Larmoyante is getting too Much ground upon Us, & if those who can write the better Species of y$^e$ Comic drama don't make a Stand for y$^e$ Genuine Comedy & vis comic[a] the Stage in a few Years, will be (as Hamlet says) like Niobe all tears" (583).

What few authors of plays seemed then to understand, not themselves being actors, Garrick set forth simply in a letter to even such a practiced playwright as Arthur Murphy, suggesting a reordering of scenes in *The Way to Keep Him*: "The beginning of the third act . . . had better be spared, for fear it should take from the last act; and there is another reason for rejecting it, and a much stronger one, which is, that I shall never be able to change my dress from top to toe (as I must for Lord Etheridge) while the scene of the Ladies is acting. If I were to dress in the hurry I necessarily must to be ready, I shall be so blown that the following scene will suffer" (256). Practical, yes, but the aesthetics of a play for Garrick were not realized until it could be and was performed effectively on stage.

Whether he wrote to a high-ranking sponsor, Lord this or Lord that, to a contemporary playwright—a Cumberland, a Murphy, or a Kelley

—to a distinguished Lady—a Mrs Montagu or a Frances Sheridan—, or to a complete novice, unknown to the literary or social world of London or the provinces, he maintained his principles, wrote with kindness, tried to suggest the positive, and when in any doubt suggested that the author seek out a second or third reader. The drawing room at Hampton, at Southampton Street, or later at Adelphi Terrace was enlivened many an evening as Garrick read, semi-acted, and commented upon these manuscripts submitted—sometimes just to his wife, sometimes to a select company. Of Home's script for the *Fatal Discovery* (the second time around) he wrote 6 June 1768: "I drew y$^e$ tears last Night in great plenty from my Wife, & a very intimate friend of ours, who is now with us at Hampton, I read it with all my Powers & produc'd that Effect" (509).

Most plays were submitted to him under covering letters abounding in flattery which, indeed, was not unpleasing to the actor who so enjoyed his profession, who desired to please, and who had confidence in his powers as a professional critic of drama. When one reads in steady sequence some 50 Garrick letters rejecting plays and scenarios, one comes away with a sense of the actor's strict application of a formula for playwriting. Authors in effect must have a care for fable, character, dialogue, natural sequence of events, probability of circumstance, reasonable but evident motivation, and the development of amusing or passionate situations. True and probably sound, though not absolutely Procrustean advice. But each of Garrick's replies, save perhaps one, is responsive to the author and though businesslike, kindly. The atmosphere of kindliness which pervades removes the reply from that of a routine form letter. His most crisp turn-down (at least in the letters preserved) went to Elizabeth Ryves, 5 July 1770, who had written of her pathetic life, which reads in part: "Let me assure you, that I want No application to my humanity to do Justice, as far as in me lies, to every Lady or Gentleman who are pleas'd to Send me their performances; but on the other hand it would Not only be an Act of Cruelty to the Author, but a great injury to mySelf, Should I not judge of Plays from the little knowledge I have of such performances, more than from the circumstances of the Writer— The Tragedy of Adelaide, in my Opinion, could not answer the ends proposed by it, and of Consequence would hurt both the Author and the Managers" (595).

Earlier biographers seem to have exaggerated the Goldsmiths and the Smolletts of the age whose irritation (later to be sure smoothed over) at Garrick's rejection broke forth into print, and have tended to damn the actor for insensitivity to the writings of contemporary authors. Such authors accused him of aesthetic narrowness, guided by avarice and a tendency to yield to adulation expressed by powerful persons. One reads such accusations in Goldsmith's chapter on the English stage in his first edition of *An Enquiry into the Present State of Polite Learning in Europe*: "Are they [the plays in stock] sufficiently good? And is the credit of our age nothing? Must our present times pass away unnoticed by posterity?" The anger was directed at Garrick's reliance upon adaptations of past plays, which, according to the accusers, cost him little. Traces of Goldsmith's plea for his "now generation" exist even in his much revised edition of 1774. The facts of Garrick's acceptance of contemporary plays can at last be seen as a factual corrective. But the key to the aesthetic differences between actor and essayist emerges in both editions. "All must allow," wrote Goldsmith, "that the *reader* receives more benefit by *perusing* a well-written play than by seeing it acted . . . Nay I think it would be more for the interests of virtue if stage performances were read *not* acted; made rather our companions in the cabinet than on the theatre."[3] But as the letter-record shows (which indeed Goldsmith did not have at hand to consult) Garrick, though flattered by high and by low, by sycophants and sincere alike did *not* yield principles to power. The persuaders ringing in Garrick's ear were more apt to be the thunder of applause and the merriment of laughter within old Drury's walls, as well as the jingle of the shillings in the box office which would support his company. The stage was a business. It could be tawdry, or it could be artistically great. In the minds of most, the Garrick regime contributed daily to its greatness.

He found clear story lines in many old plays, hence adapted them—but he found more—certainly in Shakespeare's, where imaginative dialogue abounded also. F. A. Hedgcock, in his *David Garrick and His French Friends*, decided Garrick's was a French mind "positive, realist, and intellectual, [which] has never shown much sympathy for the visionary creations, so unlike anything in heaven or on earth, of our romantic, imaginative poets."[4] Certainly a half truth, this, but close study of the manager's adaptations of Shakespeare's plays, from *Romeo and Juliet*, through *A Midsummer Night's Dream*, *Antony and Cleopatra*, *Hamlet*, *Macbeth*, *Lear*, and *The Tempest*, throws heavy counterweights in the other side of the balance. His restorations of Shakespeare's poetry, his eliminations of Tate's dull prose, his bringing to his audiences passages in Shakespeare never heard on the eighteenth-century stage before, passages whose sheer magic weight of wording carries all emotion before it and lifts imagination to the sky, testify to a quality in the actor-manager-dramatist worth keeping in mind. He advised John Home, *re* his draft of *Agis*, 5 November 1757, "there are some affecting scenes in these three acts; and if your last two are gloriously poetical, I will assure you both fame and profit" (196).

All intelligent and sensitive readers since about 1800 have lamented the dearth of moving English tragedies written after the death of Nicholas Rowe. And so did Garrick. The challenge of reading manuscripts, as every editor long in the business knows, weighs one down ultimately. The process got to Garrick by the summer of 1775. Early in August of that year he wrote to George Colman (who had probably read nearly as many manuscripts—and some previously submitted to Garrick) "Damn all tragedies, the modern ones I mean, they are such mill-made matters that I sick at y$^e$ sight of 'em, however I shall read that you have sent me with great care, but if it were Shakespeare's, I could not perform it next Season, nor can I give a judgment on it till next Fryday" (928).[5]

But the authors who addressed Garrick in letters for his own eye occasionally (after rejection) released their spleen in open letters to the public—from 12 to 75 pages in length—justifying their works, and damning the theatre management in Garrick's hands, where they were joined by a minor host of other unhappy critics.

Scarred by the Macklin episode and the boycott which backfired, Garrick had generated a host of anonymous friends, and a host, at least equal in number of publications, of enemies. One group praised, warned, and advised him—apprehensive of the pool of piranhas into which managerial activities would plunge him. The other attacked, sometimes subtly, occasionally with humor, but most often with the virulence of frustrated pride, resulting from rejections of their works or those of their friends.

As one now reads half a hundred pamphlets from 1747 to 1763, one sees the sides shape up, and the terms of abuse and of praise repeat themselves, much as they were to do again after his return from the two-year vacation in France. Early on a well-wishing "Plain Dealer" friend wrote "An Open Letter to Mr. Garrick on His Having Purchased the Patent for Drury Lane Playhouse" (1747), complimenting him as a fine actor and a good dramatist, but warning him of the disturbing nature of management. His motto came from Dryden: "So blind we are, our wishes are so vain / That what we covet most, proves most our pain!"

"What possibly could induce you to such an undertaking," he wrote, "you abandon a certain and much more than sufficiency merely through vanity of a shadowy authority over your fellow comedians." He assumes avarice, notes that gold can be too dear a purchase, and advises the study of patience on the eve of the take-over. His lecture focuses on the envy and unreasonableness of the actors with whom Garrick must deal daily. He seems rather to have mistaken Garrick's motives and his aspirations.

The actor had been a-managing less than a month when one E. F. addressed another letter to the public, on *Mr. Garrick's Conduct as Manager. . . .*[6] He peppers forth his case in the rapid fire of half a dozen points for Garrick to abide by, in effect: "Play more often yourself, if *Albumazar* was worth reviving you should have taken a major role, when under management you were called upon frequently to entertain the town, now as manager do call upon yourself; only the upper gallery could have approved *The Scornful Lady* with its scandalous Parson, why therefore did you approve it; new management boded fair for a revival of the glorious stages of Greece and Rome here in England, but your repertory has let us down; give us the best, your Lears, Hamlets, Richards, not your Lying Valets and Fribbles." Samuel Foote was at him the same year in his *Treatise on the Passions*,[7] unconvinced that Garrick had merit as a playwright. His reputation as an actor has just spilled over, argues Foote, and only the thoughtless have cheered *Miss in Her Teens*. This Garrick play he sports with, suggesting it must have been composed by Stephen Duck, the thresher poet. Garrick could not have liked the comparison, but the long success of the play must have counteracted Foote's damnation.

Close on the following season a 24-page anonymous pamphlet, *Drury Lane Playhouse Broke Open*, was sold about town for sixpence (1748). "Sir, it is become the fashion (and I don't doubt you are vain of it)," wrote the author, "either greatly to abuse you or extravagantly to applaud you. The press swarms with pamphlets. I will speak impartially," he noted, "your assuming management was imprudent, your success hitherto has disappointed us your enemies, for you have introduced decency and regularity into the late state of confusion and anarchy. But the House has been plundered [broke open] by your stealing yourself away from more frequent acting." Cut down on prologues, abandon French dancers, appear more yourself. (This after 106 appearances on stage the previous season!) Garrick was amused. But he responded by continuing to average 95 performances each season.

In 1749 the pamphlet *Lethe Rehearsed* was pro-Garrick for 52 pages, praising Garrick's satire on persons as they are, but querying the form. The author approved the taking-off of persons more than dancing and pantomime, especially when the mimicry was set against types rather than individuals. Garrick's renting the theatre in 1751 to the Delavals and their noble friends for staging an amateur performance of *Othello* was criticized as a useless exercise, the money for which should have been given to the poor.[8] In the same season 63 more pages came forth in a dramatic satire called "*The Theatrical Manager*, presenting one Vaticide (obviously Garrick), power-hungry, ambitious, subservient to all who advance him, miserly, and hypocritical, who upon becoming manager hopes the poets will write bad plays which he can force on the public for profit. He will write lulling songs for new appearances of *Lethe* to put audiences into "a lethargy that they may forget they ever exposed their judgments by applauding such a ridiculous production." He hopes to recruit illiterate players whom he may train up to assure no competition.

Poets' pens wrote on, some seeking to redress the balance of criticism by overpraise. *Fortune, a Rhapsody Inscribed to Mr. Garrick* (1751), by Derrick(?) or Francis Gentleman(?) warned the actor not to let good fortune seduce him from alert watchfulness in rewarding merit where he could discern it in play and player. It was followed by the anonymous *Poetical Epistle from Shakespeare in Elysium* (1752),[9] unstinting in its praise of Garrick. Shakespeare notes therein that each nervous line, "each sentiment, each thought of mine, how happily thou hast inspir'd."

Garrick paid scant attention to both detractors and adulators, carrying on steadily his balanced repertoire to entertain the public.

For after pieces he produced, more often than not, farces light in touch, many of his own among them. Occasionally he varied them, in the 1750 decade more than before, by pantomimes to compete with those so pleasing at Covent Garden. Word came to him from Jean Monnet in 1754 about a capital ballet performance mounted in Paris by Jean Georges Noverre, whose splendid ballets had charmed audiences in Lyons, Marseilles, and Strasbourg. The novelty attracted his interest. Negotiations were set afoot for Noverre to bring over and present to Londoners his now famous *The Chinese Festival*, with its remarkable choreography, and elegant costumes.[10] Such an elaborate performance Rich did not have, and the ballet would be responsive, Garrick thought, to a growing eighteenth-century interest in the Orient. A contemporary spectator, J. de Boulmiers, described the scene of the Paris performance, and from it Garrick envisioned a whole new dimension of theatrical spectacle and scenic entertainment: "The stage represents in the first instance an avenue ending in terraces and steps leading to a palace on a height. The first scene changes and uncovers a public square decorated for a festival with, in the background, an amphitheatre on which are seated sixteen Chinese. By a quick change of positions, instead of sixteen Chinese thirty-two are seen on the gradins [steps] going through a pantomime. As the first group descend, sixteen further Chinese, both Mandarins and slaves, come out of their habitations and make their way to the gradins. All these form eight rows of dancers who, rising and dipping in succession, imitate fairly well the billows of a stormy sea."

What manager in his right mind could resist this in the 1750s! Garrick was quick to pick up the possibilities for his theatre as he read on: "All the Chinese, having descended, begin a character march. There are a Mandarin borne in a rich palanquin by six white slaves, whilst two negroes draw a chariot on which a young Chinese woman is seated. They are preceded and followed by a host of Chinese playing various musical instruments customary in their country. This march concluded, the ballet begins and leaves nothing to be desired either in the diversity or in the neatness of the figures."

Here sight, sound, and motion blend to contribute a pleasing effect upon which Garrick thought he could build (in a proper place in his nightly program) effects that would challenge many, many members of his company: "It ends in a *contredanse* of thirty-two persons whose movements trace a prodigious number of new and perfectly designed attitudes, which form and dissolve with the greatest of ease. At the end of the *contredanse*, the Chinese return to their places on the amphitheatre which is transformed into a China Cabinet. Thirty-two vases which rise up to conceal from the eyes of the spectators the thirty-two Chinese one saw before. . . . The costumes were made to the designs of Mr. Boquet." [11]

Noverre drove a hard bargain. Garrick met his terms, though the bargaining was a year in process. He scheduled the ballet for the night of 8 November 1755, and his initial enthusiasm was boundless. But between the start of negotiations and the scheduled date of performance, war clouds built up between France and England; hence, if extant newspapers make a proper barometer of the English mood, a wave of extreme nationalism developed which condemned anything French, or even attached to France. Noverre's name, his recent billings in Paris, and the French dancers in his company were bound to be suspect.

Feelings ran high. Noverre arrived and word of his rehearsals got about. He himself was actually 28-year-old Swiss Protestant, but in England indiscriminate emotions were taking over. Garrick felt himself heading into a storm, where he had hoped to provide a glorious novelty. On the eve of the performance he tapped his own resourcefulness and produced the longest playbill of his career, listing the names of 63 dancers, claiming that nearly all were either Swiss or

135

English—only four French—to becalm what seemed to be a rising protest.[12] All to no avail. The story is pretty well known: the theatre was nearly demolished in a several-day, stretched-out riot. The eye-witness report by prompter Richard Cross fairly puts us back into the pit on the first evening. Garrick had even procured the attendance of the king, who turned his back when the hissing began: "All our dancers appear. A good deal of hissing & Clapping and some cries of No french Dancers; a great clapping too—the Dance is fine!"

Garrick, wanting so to succeed in this new scenic venture, judged some hope from the scattered applause, and acquainted with the mercurial moods of audiences, let the ballet cool for three days, and scheduled it a second time for 12 November, hoping the supporters would distinguish between artistic performance and military events. Cross again: "A great deal of hissing—but the Boxes being on our side some swords were drawn, & several turn'd out of the Pit & Galleries. The officers of the Army are very busy in this Affair, on Account of their hissing when yᵉ King was there—saying it was an affront."

A pamphlet *The Dancers Damned* [13] describing the affair, and condemning mob patriotism appeared on the streets, describing how the leader of the opposition arose and called out: "These sixty dancers are come over with a design to undermine our constitution. This Navarre is Marshall Lewendhal, and the least amongst them is an ensign disguised in order to perpetrate our ruin. . . . Swiss, what the devil do we know of Swiss! a Swiss is a foreigner, and all foreigners are Frenchmen; and so damn you all!"

Garrick who had expended an estimated £2,000 on the staging and performance pushed on with it, appeared on stage himself on the fifteenth to hisses and cries of "Monsieur." He offered a compromise—the dance every other evening for the enjoyment of those who liked it, and abandoned other evenings to appease the anger. The compromise failed, and the blow fell on the night of 18 November, as noted by Cross. "This night the Riot was very Great, the Gentlemen came with Sticks, & tho' the play went on quiet till the last Act, we had there a great Stop, notwithstanding we ended it [*The Earl of Essex*] & then the rout went on, yᵉ boxes drove many out of the Pit & broken heads were plenty on both Sides; the dance began—was stopp'd—& so began again. While this was doing numbers were assembl'd in the Passages of the pit, broke down & were getting into the Cellar, but were repuls'd by our Scene men. . . . Justice Fielding—& Welch came with Constables and a Guard, but without effect."

Many of the bully boys began to make the affair a personal one rather than one of managerial policy. In a gang they walked a block or

two down Tavistock Street to nearby Southampton Street and broke
the windows in Garrick's house. They forced their points on all counts.
The dance was stopped, and total losses came to nearly £4,000. No
record appears of Dr. Johnson's attendance, but he, as did all London,
read about the affair. Perhaps from the experience he concluded that
"patriotism was the last refuge of scoundrels." [14]

One doubts that Garrick saw himself engaging in a power struggle—
the manager versus the people. He was too shrewd and too pragmatic
to involve himself in such essentially political maneuvers. His ambition was for good theatre, and he knew that success depended upon
basic rapprochement with the total audience. He must have been
stung by the massive demonstration which swept up an art form, as
he had undoubtedly been stung by the individual arrogance of a drunk
Irish Lord when he was performing Lear in Smock Alley theatre nearly
ten years earlier. What to do? He accepted the inevitable, considered
the outburst a cleansing of the spirit of the mob, refurbished the theatre and carried on—sadder but wiser, no doubt. Within a dozen years
he would pursue successfully in a different way experiments in scenic
design. Yet within eight he would go through another such riot,
planned by the critic and disappointed author Thaddeus Fitzpatrick.

The financial loss which he and Lacy sustained in the *Chinese Festival* fiasco was real. But no frets. No lamentations. No jeremiads were
manifested on his part. The satiric treatment of the affair by the press
in the succeeding weeks must somewhat have cheered his spirit, and
reinforced his resolve (shown on other occasions) to maintain sanity by
being as superior as possible to such events. Of the villifying pamphlets which came out, an *Epistle from Theophilus Cibber to David
Garrick* (1755) appeared, as one might have expected. He used the
*Chinese Festival* fracas as excuse to present his "Case."

Cibber's antipathy to Garrick had smouldered for some time. He
had not yet learned that the Licensing Act of 1737 was meant to operate for *all* parties. "I begrudge no man his feast," he wrote, "I only
wish to be sure of my own place at dinner. Justice to myself, therefore, not ill will to anyone occasions me to throw my case before the
town. I form no parties. I speak openly." He believed that Garrick had
had a hand in the Lord Chamberlain's long delayed negative to his
request for a license to operate the theatre in the Haymarket. His
Epistle mobilizes arguments for making the Haymarket the nursery for
training up new young players, but is based upon jingoism, ill will,
and threats. He finds it amazing that an Englishman, the son of an
Englishman, cannot get a license, when the son of a Frenchman
[obviously Garrick, though two steps removed] has one and makes a

great fortune by it. He notes that he long ago persuaded Fleetwood to take Garrick, who has now turned upon him with ingratitude. He threatens "by law to deprive you [Garrick] of a potent assistant" [Mrs Cibber], and concludes that Garrick's power is overstepping itself. The *Epistle* was signed on 20 November while shouts against the *Chinese Festival* were still in the air. An *Ode to a Player* (1755) written by an anti-Gallican extempore, was being hawked for sixpence:

> The Noverre's Dance
> And scum of France
> Made your ambition tool
> . . . . . . .
> 'Tis true you're great
> Have pacts and pate,
> Can mighty heroes brave,
> Yet high conceit
> And Friar's cheat
> Make you a Gallic slave![15]

No evidence occurs that Garrick felt threatened in any way by Cibber. But Cibber had breathed the fire of reckless nationalism, which was picked up by audience upon audience because of the impending war. The best way for Garrick to respond to the public on this matter was not to take issue with an individual, but to continue to use the amusing power of the prologue to bring the audience along with him and gently temper its moods. He himself had long pleased the taste of his audiences by gentle banter of all things French. He needed but to keep up this strain. One wonders in passing, however, whether Cibber's jibe may have elicited some jocund verses from him in 1756, published in *The Universal Visitor* under the title "A Recipe for a Modern Critic"—gay enough in tone in 16 couplets. Its flavor:

> Two drachms of stale sense, and a scruple of wit.
> A lump of old learning; of taste a small bit . . .
> Of Lethe's thick stream, a full gallon well shook,
> Of sarcasms two hundred from any old book;
> Of candour a grain, and of scandal a ton;
> Of knowledge two ounces, of merit not one . . .
>
> The brain of a calf, and the breast of a toad;
> The eye of a mole, and the nail of a cat,
> The tooth of a mouse, and the wing of a bat . . .
>
> Take this dose, my good author, you quickly shall do
> For the *Critical, Monthly,* or any *Review*.[16]

In situations, it seems, where the temper of a person less extrovert than Garrick might have been damped, he neither sought escape nor yielded to depression. "Impudence combined with a good understanding" (so recommended by Sharp in his *The Lying Valet*) seemed to sustain him. But perhaps his verses served further to challenge the authors.

Garrick's theatre, of course, had built-in possibilities for good public relations in the straight talk, bantering talk, cajoling or pleading talk in the prologues and epilogues to new and revived plays, and upon occasions such as seasons' openings. Prologues traditionally said something about the nature of the performance and about the author. They often reviewed (in mock pejorative fashion) the efforts within the recent memory of man of the opposing house, often catered to the nostalgia of the oldest living member seated in the pit (or supposed to be there) by noting that in the good old days things were different, taste masculine, intellects rather than eyes appealed to, and acting superior. Prologues railed gently at current taste, and bantered in a modified Aristophanic fashion audience, author, and performers, by taking the audience into confidence, assuming its collective intelligence to be brighter than that of the writing or performing crews, and setting it up to belittle the whole process. "While other culprits brave it to the last," Garrick had written in his prologue to *The Suspicious Husband*, back in 1747:

> Nor beg for mercy till the judgment's past;
> Poets alone, as conscious of their crimes,
> Open their trials with imploring rimes.
> Thus cram'd with flattery and low submission,
> Each trite dull Prologue is the bard's petition.
> A stale device to calm the critick's fury,
> And bribe at once the judges and the jury.

Garrick, past master of this form of public address, fell back upon it as he carried on with the public. But he kept his nationalistic commentary in the even and playful vein that had characterized it for many, many years. The recent French experience must blend, in any discussion, with the larger use of prologues as managerial public relations.[17]

France had long been the political bugaboo, because of its totalitarianism. Satiric jibes formed about its debilitating fashions, its lack of robustness in food, manners, occupations, and entertainments had become stereotyped.

Garrick was able to give just the right turn of novelty to repetitive points of view to make each comment seem fresh. Back in 1744, before the full heat of the Jacobite rebellion was felt, Garrick had framed the French theme in his prologue to James Ralph's *The Astrologer*:

> A modish frenzy so corrupts the town,
> That naught but *Alamode de France* goes down:
> We all submit to this fantastic yoke;
> Like them we dress, we dance, we eat, we joke;
> From top to toe they change us at their will;
> All but our hearts—and those are British still!

In 1754, on the eve of, but not yet seriously into, the Seven Years' War, Garrick's epilogue to *Barbarossa* had combined light raillery against the British (always pleasing to the sophisticated sports in the audience), justification for pantomimes by placing onus lightly, again, on audience taste, and a touch of jingoism:

> An English gentleman should never think—
> The reason's plain, which every soul might hit on—
> What trims a Frenchman, oversets a Briton.
> In us reflection breeds a sober sadness,
> Which always ends in politics and madness.
> I therefore now propose, by your command,
> That tragedies no more shall cloud this land;
> Send o'er your Shakespeare to the sons of France
> Let *them* grow grave—let *us* begin to dance!

How prophetic when the backlash came! And as the war actually drew on, and as memories of the strong brand of nationalism which had routed his theatre two months earlier, his prologue to Murphy's *The Apprentice* (January 1756) read ("to melt that rock of rocks the critic's heart"): "No mangl'd, pilfer'd scenes from France to show / 'Tis English—English Sirs, from top to toe." A year later a familiar change was rung in the prologue to Garrick's alteration of James Shirley's (1694) *The Gamester*:

> When this same play was writ that's now before ye,
> The English stage had reach'd its point of glory!
> No paltry thefts disgrac'd this author's pen,
> He painted English manners, Englishmen;
> And form'd his taste on Shakespeare and Old Ben.
> Then were French fashions, farces, quite unknown;
> Our wits wrote well, and all they writ their own.

Cibber was forgotten, and what minor splash he may have made subsided in the larger wave of Garrick's own banter. But a word more about the managerial use of the prologue.

Prices of seats then more than now grouped and classified audience components. Garrick the actor and manager had something to say directly, but separately to each of the four large sections of the theatre—box, pit, gallery, and upper gallery. And the occupants of each surmised they were receiving individual attention thereby from the manager. Each listened with pleasure as it was addressed, and with amusement as it heard the others spoken to. Example: Epilogue to Murphy's *All in the Wrong*, spoken by Mrs Mary Ann Yates:

> What shall we do your different tastes to hit?
> You relish satire [*to the pit*] you ragouts of wit [*to the Boxes*].
> Your taste is humour and high-fashioned joke [first Gallery]
> You call for hornpipes, and for hearts of oak, [upper Gallery].

So she sings 'em a song:

> Ye critics above and ye critics below,
> Ye finer-spun critics who keep the mid row,
> Oh, tarry one moment, I'll sing you a song
> Shall prove that like us—You are all in the wrong.
>
> Ye poets who mount on the fam'd winged steed,
> Of prancing, and wincing, and kicking take heed;
> For when by those hornets, the critics, he's stung,
> You're thrown in the dirt—and are all in the wrong.

A time for sobering thought came with the advent of a new king. Hence in 1761, just after the accession of George III to the throne, Mrs Pritchard, in the character of Queen Elizabeth, spoke a Garrick prologue to Henry Brooke's *Earl of Essex*:

> Since the most glorious time that here I reign'd
> An Age and half!—what have you lost or gain'd?
> Your wit, whate'er your poets sing or swear,
> Since Shakespeare's time is somewhat worse for wear.

After brief run-down praising the shape of laws, ecology ("your streams are good"), fashions, valor, justice and domestic peace, she concludes with a hope that George shall reign long undisturbed by unruly passions, such as those which disturbed her reign.

Garrick often assured audiences, via the prologue, that his policy was to retain a repertory balanced between tragedy, comedy, music and farce, procession and pantomime. Topics of the day were genially alluded to. Many a metaphor was used neatly to catch the imagination —food (especially a current fondness for turtle soup), culinary arts, drink, the marketplace, the theatre, the country, the town, minstrelsy —all to beget that feeling of mutual interest between audience and stage going before any restlessness on the benches might set in.[18] Garrick as manager mitigated the aftermath criticism of *The Chinese Festival*, cutting his losses, by directing his audience's attention elsewhere. But he would have been less than human had he not watched the papers for some cheering and sustaining note.

It must have been a relief for him to read one morning in 1757 *A*

*Letter of Abuse to D—d G—k, Esq*, probably by George Colman. "Shall Mr. Garrick engross the attention of the whole town?" it said. "I will admit that the British stage never received a better actor. I will acknowledge that the entertainment of the theatre has reached the utmost of perfection under your direction. I will not deny that many parts, even of the divine Shakespeare, were no more than a dead letter until your animating genius enliven'd their beauties and enforced their energy." It concludes, after 26 pages of amusing but positive comment, "The utmost of malevolence can fix nothing upon you to your disadvantage." Garrick soon found that a new youthful group of bright men was forming up as his supporters—George Colman, Bonnell Thornton, Robert Lloyd—who had access to the press.[19] But other critics kept sharpening their quill pens. Meantime Garrick was composing a play to comment on the contemporary scene in England— *The Male Coquette, or 1757.*

Garrick had never been one to live completely in the narrower confines of theatrical activity, gossip, and critical commentary. He read widely, and his circle of friends, both male and female, as we have seen, had more than normal concern for the interlocking fields of the economics, politics, and ethics of the nation, as well as its arts and international relations. Serious citizenry gave some thought during the Seven Years' War with France to the state of the moral fiber of the nation. The poetry and essays of the period address the problem of wealth and luxury, and the relation of affluence to the kind of living which Englishmen really wanted then. A popular book by the Reverend John Brown, writer also of a number of plays accepted by Garrick, became the subject of conversation at many levels of society. His *Estimate of the Manners and Principles of the Times* reached its third printing in 1757, and gained for the author the popular nickname "Estimate Brown." His thesis, developed over some 221 pages, was not encouraging. "Our situation seems most dangerous. We are rolling on the brink of a precipice that must destroy us." The public at large, he wrote, could ill afford to escape responsibility for the state of affairs by blaming certain individuals. The malady lay deeper—in permanent and established causes anchored in the principles and manners of the people. Three concepts needed examination and refreshed allegiance: the spirit of liberty, the spirit of humanity, and the spirit of civil administration. Humanity he defined as pity for distress along with adjustments of all punishments to their proper ends. What, he asked, are the ruling manners, and how do they contribute to the continuance or destruction of a nation? First among destructive forces, he found to be "vain, luxurious, and selfish effeminacy."[20] The schools and colleges of England abetted this, while affluence debilitated the manners of the upper classes and avarice was spreading like a stain through all classes. Garrick's *Male Coquette* satirized selfish effeminacy.

Perhaps a motivating clue for Garrick's satire lies in Brown's book, and Brown's fear of effeminacy as partial cause for decay probably helped the favorable response to the piece. At any rate Garrick needed to read no farther than page 48 in the *Estimate* to have felt some glow of satisfaction in its statement about his Drury Lane theatre as being one factor in the resurgence of positive taste in the country. The paragraph was considered worth quoting by James Ralph the following year in his *The Case of the Authors by Profession or Trade Stated* (1758): "Let us then search the theatre for the remains of manly taste, and here, apparently, at least, it must be acknowledged we shall find it. A great genius hath arisen to dignify the stage; who when it was sinking into the lowest insipidity restored it the fullness of its ancient splendor, and with a variety of powers beyond example establish'd Nature, Shakespeare and himself."

Garrick had, of course, lightly bantered masculine effeminacy earlier in his *Miss in Her Teens* (1747), and critic response then had focused upon what Brown conceived to be the problem.[21]

Whatever Garrick's thoughts may have been for Brown's accolade, he could not long bask in complaisance, for 1757 brought the tragedy of *Douglas* to Covent Garden from great success in Edinburgh, and to reach greater at Covent Garden. All the world seemed to know that Manager Garrick, reader and selector of new plays, had rejected it (at least the version which had been submitted to him). The effect for Garrick lay not so much in success at a rival house, as in the opening of floodgates of abundant correspondence and of public "Letters to . . . " him laden with advice from, as well as the recriminations of, many authors of other plays that he had turned down. He was on the griddle, and no mistake.

Factions hardened their lines. The preface of *The Theatrical Review for 1757–58*[22] described the scene, and proclaimed its own impartiality, "It is a very just observation that England is most properly characterized as the land of faction. Divisions among the people of other countries arise only from their higher concerns, but with us everything is made an affair of party, and the spirit of it is carried even into our diversions. . . . Nobody can talk or write about our theatres but he is immediately possessed with the demon of party, and praises or condemns not from his feelings but from his prejudices." The author in discussing Garrick at least blows a favorable trumpet for his *acting*, itemizing the quality of his eyes, face, symmetry of movement, and voice, concluding "Mr Garrick may have faults as an actor, but to me . . . they are as much lost as the spots in the sun, only visible to long-sighted astronomers." He was, however, but winding up to his main discourse. "Mr. Garrick as a *manager* appears to me in a very different light—the scarcity of new performances, the total deficiency of new performers are very strong prejudices against him," despite that is, "the fact that there never was in one season such a variety of entertainments of all sorts as we have had this winter." Upcoming writers seemed to be damped in their efforts to succeed on his stage. Garrick and sophisticated contemporaries must have roared with laughter at the journalist's solution, which became a repeated cry. "If a *committee* of ingenious men were selected to look into the demands and rights of authors, and appoint what dramatic pieces should be exhibited, the town would then be more satisfied, the poets less angry, and consequently our modern Roscius . . . would escape that continual torrent of resentment which disappointed writers shower upon him from all quarters."

William Shirley, whose play *Edward the Black Prince* Garrick had accepted and acted in back in 1750 but which lasted only nine nights, came forth with perhaps two contributions to cut down the manager, the first being 20 pages of *Brief Remarks on the Original and Present State of the Drama*, as preface to 20 more (bound with it) *Hecate's Prophecy, Being a Characteristic Dialogue Betwixt Future Managers and Their Dependents* (1758). He assumed that drama was formed to be beneficial to the world and proved to be so everywhere but in contemporary England. There power was "singly vested, and the channels of encouragement drained by the workings of vanity and circumvention."

Writing as a special pleader for the authors' group, showing a fine contempt for the "whole show" which Londoners wanted in the theatre, he lets Garrick have it with both barrels of his critical gun. The pellets by this time had become clichés, accusing Garrick of vanity, malice, envy, and hypocrisy. Garrick, it seems to him, has fricasseed Shakespeare's texts, has overloaded us with dancing, pantomime, and players' farces, and has employed writers of pamphlets to deify himself: "eternal changes rung upon eyes, legs, symmetry, voice, attitude, grace, melody, power, figure, tone, gesture, deportment, cadence, harmonies &c. all appropriated to his single self."[23] *Hecate's Prophecy* shows the modern stage declining as it is controlled by domineering, stuttering Fidget (Garrick) and his sycophantic prompter Crunch (Cross).

Another blast (1758) from Shirley came under the aegis of a Candid Observer entitled, *A Bone for the Chroniclers to Pick, or a Take-off from Behind the Curtain.* In ten pages of verse doggerel it "takes off" Garrick, as he purportedly once did some other actors. He is told, "You may do what you will with a prepossessed nation / So strong is the phrensy of infatuation," but hysteria takes over as Garrick looks at his riotous houses:

> G–d d–mn 'em screams David, they're groaning and hissing
> Hark they clamour like thunder! How dreadful the roar!
> Alas—O my benches, my windows, my doors,
> The sconces are smashing—the candles all fly,
> Damnation, I di-de, di, di-de, di-de, die.

Garrick was displeased but silent. Colman says he defended him,[24] but Garrick himself wasted little time in resentment, even putting an end to the quarrel later by recommending Shirley's *Roman Sacrifice* to Sheridan.

At the opening of the season 1758, with Woodward gone to Ireland, the Public might have expected what it received, namely, *A Letter to Mr Garrick on the Opening of the Theatre, with Observations on the Conduct of Managers to Actors, Authors, and Audiences.*[25] Purporting to speak for 10,000 London playgoers, it advised Garrick on the three points made in its title: performances, players, and authors. In brief it asked for Garrick to perform more himself, to train up a school of young performers, and get the advice of others than himself in selecting plays.

James Ralph presented the longest argument against Garrick's presumed antagonism to the works of contemporaries in his *The Case of Authors Stated* (1758).[26] In some 76 calmly written pages Ralph contends that Garrick has (in modern parlance) "psyched out" the audience so it will accept anything he does. On stage, therefore, "exhibition stands in the place of composition, the manager whether player or Harlequin [Garrick or Rich] must be the sole pivot on which the whole machine is both to move and rest. There is no draw-back on the profit from *old* plays, and any access of reputation to a dead author carries no impertinent claim and invidious distinctions along with it." Are we not theatre mad and so dazzled and bewitched as to become dupes, he asks. And have we not transferred the merits of the composer to the player? Rhetorical questions these, but preparative to his thesis (now becoming hoary with repetition) that the Society for the Encouragement of Learning be revived and a select committee of it be established to choose plays. Garrick had procured a pension of £200 for Ralph and, according to Davies felt his attack ungracious, so refused to speak to him thereafter, but the "committee" idea must have amused him.

It continued to come up, however. Even as late as 1772 Garrick jested with John Palmer, manager at Bath, about its implications. Palmer wrote his observations on committee action relative to managing the Pump Room and Ball Rooms at that resort, "The Committee got on pretty amicably, considering there were seven or eight of them; —a little of 'you lie,' and 'you lie;' and 'damme, I'm a Gentleman;' and 'damme, I'll tell guineas with you;'—'take care of your nose;' 'don't come within reach of my fist;' and such trifles as that; but not a word of gun-powder since their first meeting."[27]

Combined flattery and damnation breathes in H. W.'s (Edward Purdon's) *A Letter to David Garrick on the Opening of the Theatre in 1759*. The gist: Garrick discourages contemporary writers and must mend his ways. A committee of the whole audience should choose plays for the repertory by being able to see *every* play submitted. "It is better no doubt that twenty indifferent pieces should be represented than one good one be suppressed." Garrick and Lacy must have thrown up their hands at that one, just thinking about the wasted efforts that must be expended by managers, actors, and house company, and finance for mounting stuff, 80 percent of which would fail. Purdon pressed on, "You have acquired such a degree of importance that Nero was scarce more despotic in his theatre than you in yours." But he closed with flattery hoping to persuade Garrick to adopt his suggestion, "All will agree with me in thinking you the best performer in Europe, &c., &c."

A note about one more criticism in this period should underscore the magnitude of Garrick's task in public relations. *A Letter to the Honourable Author of the Rout*[28] (a new and unsuccessful farce) included a *Letter to G–rr–k* beginning "Sir, you have now been above ten years manager" and in the time have produced about six new pieces, but rejected six score. You have persuaded audiences to accept anything you put on, but such security cannot last. The author was grieved mostly by Garrick's delay in reading, and his rejecting of Dodsley's *Cleone*.

Comments continued not in a trickle but in steady flow from rejected authors, and would-be managers. But to one reading Garrick's calm, careful replies to authors themselves (and not meant for public display), to one thinking about the manager's responsibilities, and to one examining the flow of cash into the theatre treasury indicating the popularity of Garrick's repertory, the aroma of sour grapes in the public "Letters to . . ." becomes overpowering. Garrick did seek confirming judgment from others when in doubt.[29] He put on modern plays when they were improved. He did think texts were primarily for performing, not for reading, and that authors were but one-third of the triad which makes drama a distinctive art (along with actors and audiences). Friend Thomas Gray's "mute inglorious Miltons" theme as far as drama was concerned he deemed romantic in the extreme. Pope in the mood of the *Dunciad* would have denounced the authors and critics just mentioned as the reptiles of the literary profession. Yet Garrick as a public figure enjoying a royal patent, suffered them all and replied to each with exemplary polity. Though polite, he was firm; though often angered, he was conciliatory; and upon the whole, remarkably cheerful. A single instance of his dealing with a contentious but non-Grub Street author is instructive.

Of all contemporary playwrights Arthur Murphy was the most prominent and most prolific, save only for Samuel Foote. He outlived Garrick by a quarter of a century, but before Garrick's retirement had written a dramatic poem, four tragedies, eight comedies, and five farces.[30] Nearly all were successful, and most at one time or another came to Garrick for reading, rejection, or acceptance for production. The process in nearly all instances bred a sort of author-manager warfare, which kept the adrenaline flowing and begat a correspondence revealing the dominant characteristics of both men—Garrick on the whole rather even tempered, patient, and cool; Murphy, somewhat irascible, suspicious, and even angry. He was alternately an avid Garrick supporter and detractor.[31] The windup of the tensions between the two had begun early.

Coming from Ireland, and schooled well in the classics in France, Murphy settled in London in 1749 and by 1752 was producing the *Gray's Inn Journal*, which commented frequently on plays and actors, and at one point praised Garrick's acting against strictures made by MacNamara Morgan and John Hill.[32] Garrick was pleased. Within two years Murphy submitted a farce *The Young Apprentice* thinking Garrick would produce it before the end of the season. Garrick suggested it might do for the following year with some alterations. Murphy, confident of his talent and chagrined at the proposed delay, withdrew it, writing Garrick 27 February 1754, "It is not agreeable to a precipitance which I am sorry to find in my temper, to wait upon any body for a whole year, for so trivial a matter."[33] Garrick replied by offering him the freedom of the house, concluding "the mistake between us about the 'Young Apprentice' is, indeed, most mysterious and surprising; and as it was impossible to give you any promise for this season, on account of my other engagements with Mr. Foote, &c. so I most solemnly declare, that, however you may have mistaken me, I never hinted, or thought of performing it this Winter."[34] For most of Murphy's plays thereafter the adversary relationship continued.

When in 1754 Murphy was in debt up to about £300 he took the advice of his friend Foote to try a career of acting, presenting himself to Rich at Covent Garden, where on 18 October he made his debut as Othello. Endowed with an excellent memory for lines, he proved to be moderately successful. Garrick engaged him the following season to replace Mossop, who had gone to Dublin. But his acting career was short-lived, for not liking the parts Garrick wished to assign him during his second season, at its close he abandoned the stage forever.

From 1756 until 1759, when it was produced by Garrick, he wrote and rewrote his first tragedy, *The Orphan of China* (taken from Voltaire's *L'orphélin de la Chine*). The struggle to produce it was long—Garrick rejecting it, Murphy having Henry Fox and Horace Walpole read it and urge Garrick to review it again, Garrick's accepting it but stipulating alterations that must be made, Murphy angered, and finally both the men offering to let the laureate, William Whitehead, arbitrate.[35] Garrick played the principal role, but the play after a number of postponements made it for only nine nights, (which assured the author three benefit performances) but which exasperated Murphy. He thought Garrick had temporized too long to do the play full justice.

The year before he had dedicated his successful farce, *The Upholsterer* to Garrick, and the year before that he had turned to the law, entering Lincoln's Inn. Thereafter his career alternated between his legal practice, playwriting, and translating from the classics. When he published his most lasting work—a translation of the works of Tacitus—Garrick wrote asking him to be put down in the list of subscribers, noting that his partner Lacy, and his actors Powell and Holland would also like to subscribe. But another dispute was brewing over Garrick's alteration of William Wycherley's *The Country Wife* into his *The Country Girl*, which he put on after rejecting Murphy's *The School for Guardians* based upon Wycherley's same play.[36] Murphy was doubly perturbed because he was at the time forwarding the career of his young protégée (probably his mistress) Ann Elliott, for whom he wished to have a leading part. Isaac Bickerstaff seemingly helped smooth over this new break in their friendship. The tilting continued with Garrick rejecting this play and accepting that, and with Murphy wrangling over most of the negotiations. He disliked Garrick's revised text of *Hamlet* (1772), and argued a bit about Garrick's acting in Act II in *Macbeth* (1768). To which Garrick: "I am always happy to agree with You, & which I do most sincerely in Your opinion of yᵉ Scene with

Banquo—I was indeed not quite the Master of my feelings till I got to *clutching the air-drawn dagger*—I like your description of the State of Macbeth's Mind & Body. . . ." He concluded, "You have flatter'd me much by Your very Obliging letter—& I shall profit by y$^r$ Criticisms this Evening. . . . I am an Old Hunter . . . but stroke me, & clap me on the back, as You have kindly done, and I can make Shift to gallop over the Course" (485).

Murphy's sometimes latent as well as often exposed antagonisms to Garrick as manager were countered by his long and sincere admiration of Garrick as an actor. In his later years Murphy remarked to John Taylor about Garrick, "Off stage he was a little sneaking rascal, but on stage, Oh, my God!"[37] Surprisingly enough, after expressing such thoughts, in 1799, 20 years after Garrick's death, he started writing his *Life of David Garrick*, in which without trying to give a complete biography, he wrote of "Garrick in his profession."[38] He disposed of the work to the bookseller John Wright for 300 guineas in 1801.[39] Survey of the total correspondence suggests a lingering bias deriving from his contests with Garrick the manager and public figure with power, rather than with any preoccupation with Garrick the man, slighting though some of his remarks may have been. Garrick in turn, in the constant negotiations now loses a few points, now gains a few; stands firm, and again is conciliatory. Both gained something from the other.

But many another brooding author nursed his frustrations until they exploded. In 1760 a riot was brewing engineered by Thaddeus Fitzpatrick, leader of an antimanagerial group of young men who called themselves the "Town." With rising costs Garrick was trying gradually to abolish the half-price entrance charge after the third act. Fitzpatrick found a cause in this. Garrick probably hastened the maturation of the riot unwittingly by one of his very few public utterances in the form of a satirical poem on Fitzpatrick called *The Fribbleriad* (1761).[40] The object of the jibes sulked and bided his time. A dozen pamphlets pro and con tell the story.

For about a year in *The Craftsman*, and some other weekly papers Fitzpatrick, possibly William Shirley, and others masking under the initials X.Y.Z. wrote letters buzzing at Garrick's acting, or lack of acting, about his supposed false emphases in some lines, his ad-libbing and the like. The approach marked a shift in critical target from management *per se* to attack on the actor's vanity and prowess on stage. In late 1760 these were gathered into a reprint, together with Fitzpatrick's *An Inquiry into the Real Merits of a Certain Popular Performer*, the introduction to which states specifically that the collection is a chastisement of Garrick.[41] Promptly the author-grievance theme presents itself, "How much the public is endebted to you for your unequalled zeal in the revival of expiring and the introduction of expired plays," its indulgence "has enabled you to acquire a large stock of fame upon the credit of theatrical science which you never possessed." Long "Letters" filled with half-speeches, and many dashes indicating broken sequences sought to mimic and exaggerate Garrick's manner of speaking his lines, suggesting that he was unacquainted with the meaning of the speeches, and only stereotyped a monotonous hesitancy. One suspects that this turn about in the opposition strategy may have got under the skin of the actor, whereas complaints of prejudice and power-seeking, Garrick had taken as part of the task of management hence received with a degree of amusement and patience. For Garrick had written to Murphy (3 August 1759) "I despise the attacks & Misrepresentations of Blockwig, but shall be Ever Truly Sorry when I am misunderstood by a Man of Genius" (239).

The most amusing reply to the Fitzpatrick group came from Lawrence Sterne in chapter XII, vol. III, of *Tristram Shandy*, which appeared in 1761: "And how did Garrick speak the soliloquy last night? 'Oh against all rule, My Lord, Most ungrammatically! Betwixt the substantive and the adjective, which should agree together in number, case, and gender, he made a breech thus—, stopping as if the point wanted settling; and betwixt the nominative case, which your Lordship knows must govern the verb, he suspended his voice in the Epilogue a dozen times, three seconds and three fifths by a stop-watch, my Lord, each time!'—'Admirable grammarian! But in suspending his voice was the sense suspended likewise? Did no expression of attitude, or countenance fill up the chasm? Was the eye silent? Did you narrowly look?' 'I looked only at the stop-watch, My Lord.'—'Excellent observer!'"

To the attack on the actor's vanity about his skills, the X.Y.Z. group added a concerted one on his supposed avarice as a manager—the Nero of the profession. T. Gilbert's *Some Reflections on the Management of a Theatre* (1760) felt that management was exceedingly important because of "the great influence on the manners of the people" exercised by the stage, and the increased numbers in the audience affected. Gilbert had done his home reading of "Estimate Brown," for he thought plays were intended to "restrain our wild appetites, to give proper bias to our affections, to make us prudent by the misfortunes of others, and restore the tranquility of mind which can only result from the harmony of good actions." But the present management, he thought, is "so tainted with avarice as to make a sordid self-interest the invariable rule of action. . . . he [Garrick] is continually raking in the rubbish of antiquity to find out some old plays of sparkling wit, chaste diction and exemplary morals to improve the virtue of the present age and make them loath that obscene language which abounds in our modern comedies." Irony? The specifics of the rest of the essay appear more favorable to Garrick's stage.

But Garrick's production of Foote's *The Minor* stirred the Reverend Martin Madan's ire, who condemned the play for immorality, profanity, obscenity, and religious mockery. "I blush for my countrymen," he wrote.[42] But the criticism which moved Garrick to retort was that of the X.Y.Z. group, which had attacked his acting. His *Fribbleriad* (1761) was his response. Lacking quite the bite of a Churchill satire, it harks back to the 1757 campaign against effeminacy in England, and beyond that to Garrick's similar attack in his *Miss in Her Teens* of 1748. Light in touch, for Garrick always sought the Horatian rather than the Juvenalian in his social satire, it brands the X.Y.Z. writers as neuters, overfond of all *they* read and write:

> For playhouse critics, keen as mice,
> Are ever greedy, ever nice;
> And rank abuse, like toasted cheese,
> Will catch as many as you please.

The main character, Fitzgig, becomes Cock Fribble of them all. Ready identification must have been made by the public, for the name was attached to and stuck with Fitzpatrick thereafter. The scenario was modeled on Satan's assembly in hell (Book II, of *Paradise Lost*) but metamorphosed into a Fribble session debating how best to annoy Garrick—not by poison or by sword, but by ungracious theatre behavior (laughing at Lear) and by "swelling tiny faults to monstrous size" in squibs against the actor. Garrick's effort came out anonymously, as had the attacks upon him. His serious note in the poem is also characteristically light—but nonetheless heartfelt, one supposes: "For wit may have its ebbs and flows / But malice no abatement knows." That the verses lack force and sting, amid the bludgeoning satire of the day, says something about Garrick under fire, so to speak. Amusement takes over as he portrays the macaroni Fribble, and anger dissolves in the pleasure of caricature. But the humorless objects of the banter kept up their attack, and much of their malice continued in *The Muses' Address to D. Garrick* (1761) scoring the manager for producing harlequinade.[43] The year 1762 brought forth *The Battle of the Players*,[44] a heavy, heavy imitation of Swift's *Battle of the Books*, describing an inter-theatre skirmish with victory coming neither to the actors of Drury Lane nor to those of Covent Garden.

But Garrick's attention was centered not upon the leaflets and his reputation therein, but upon the effectiveness of the theatre. Hence just at this point he made stick one of his most excellent managerial changes in theatre operation—a cleansing of the stage from loungers during any performance, destroying at one stroke, also, plans of ready access for the annoyance campaign of the followers of Fitzpatrick. His timing was right, but the roots of the move ran deep, culminating a wish of three decades' duration.

Twenty years earlier Garrick, aged 25, had acted King Lear with Peg Woffington as Cordelia in Ireland. Thomas Sheridan recalls the incident in his *An Humble Appeal to the Public*:

> Just as they had prepared themselves for the drawing of the scene, which was to discover the old King asleep with his head in the lap of Cordelia, a Gentleman [lounger on stage] threw himself down on the other side of the fair princess, and without the least regard for her rank began to treat her with utmost indecency. Resentment followed on her part, and abuse on his. Mr. Garrick was silent, but could not help casting an eye of indignation at so brutal a scene, which was considered so daring an insult by the Gentleman, that he and two more of his comrades searched the house for him after the play was over, vowing with dreadful imprecations that they would put him to death.[45]

The incident rankled in Garrick's mind as an insult by the privileged and a deterrent to excellent ensemble performance. The stage should be player turf, even at the sacrifice of extra income which the stage loungers paid for the privilege. The problem was twofold: first banishing the "gentlemen" from *behind* the scenes, from wandering into the greenroom, the dressing rooms, and interfering with the stage machinery, and secondly banishing them from *sitting* in places built-up upon the stage on benefit nights which increased profits to the beneficiary.

His initial playbill as manager, 15 September 1747, spoke his determination (graciously) to abolish the first abuse.[46] By 1762 he felt sufficiently secure with the public to banish the loungers even on benefit nights. But he wished to provide alternatives so that actor-income would not be reduced by the action. This he did by persuading Lacy to redesign the auditorium and to increase seating capacity by placing seats in the slips and enlarging the boxes. When this was done he swept the loungers from the stage completely, but announced the move in customary diplomatic fashion: "As frequenters of the theatre have often complained of the interruptions in the performance, occasioned by the crowded stage at Benefit nights—the Performers will have no building on the stage nor take any money behind the scenes, being willing to forego that advantage, for the sake of rendering the Representation more agreeable to the Publick."[47] The action had a permanent effect in the London theatre, and is biographically important as evidence of Garrick's major and enduring interest (even amid a barrage of criticism from minor journalists in improving the theatre as a place where an art form could approach new excellences. For with a clear stage, subtle gesture, modulated tone, and group action could count more than it ever had before.

Even with this improvement in the wind the forces led by Fitzpatrick struck. On 25 January Garrick scheduled the sixth-night benefit for Benjamin Victor's modernized version of *The Two Gentlemen of Verona*. Although the customary ticket cost, with half-price taken from those entering after the third act, had operated for the first five performances, the play-notice for this night announced that "nothing under full prices would be taken." Therein Fitzpatrick saw his chance to extend his private pique to public cause, and to multiply aggravation for Garrick 300-fold. The issue he raised was "novelty" and the arrogance of the manager in charging full price for a revived piece, unaccompanied by a new pantomime.

On the night of the performance a person in center pit began "to pour forth his oratory," as reported in *An Historical and Succinct Account of the Late Riots*.[48] He was identified as Fitzpatrick, at least by Garrick who was hailed onto the stage. "I call upon you [to Garrick] in the name of the publick to answer for your rascally imposition!" The word *rascal* was immediately echoed through the house. The author had whipped up the riot possibility by circulating at the coffee houses earlier in the day a call to arms, so to speak. "Answer me Sir, Speak to the audience. Speak to the House," cried he. Garrick answered that he had a partner to consult who was not at the theatre that night. Pressure built up for an immediate reply. Garrick said he would publish one in next day's paper. Meantime a magistrate and guards arrived. The rioters left. Next day's paper noted that an appropriate answer would be published within a few days. The procedure was unsatisfactory to the audience assembled to see a performance of *Elvira*. Garrick was called for and forced to give a *yes* or *no* answer to the request for continuance of the half-price. John Moody and Ellis Ackman had the night before gone into the pit, and being seen were suspected of spying. Moody had prevented a feisty man from setting fire to the house. When the audience saw them the next night in a procession during the after piece, it demanded they step forward and apologize.

Ackman did so. Moody refused to drop to his knees, but with some sarcasm apologized for having saved their lives by avoiding a fire. Anger. The uproar was tremendous and the theatre demolished, even though Garrick had agreed to continue the half-price arrangement.

Of the many papers and reports on the riot three appeared quickly from purported eyewitnesses, all critical of Fitzpatrick. *Fitzgig, or the Modern Quixote, a Tale; Relative to the Late Disturbances* noted that Fitzpatrick's crowd, just to maintain the cause was public and even-handed, had approached the manager Beard of Covent Garden, extracting a promise from him to abide by the half-price custom. It demonstrated, however, that the satirical name taken from the mock epic had stuck to the perpetrator: I sing Fitzgig's wrath and ire / Say why, particular his rage / Against the actors and the stage? In thus attacking he had performed a Fribble part. But the hero comments:

> And thou, great Garrick, first I'll handle
> I'll treat you to contempt and scandal:
> But ah! Poor Fitzgig there was bit.
> His spite so far outran his wit
> That every man of taste and sense
> Despised his dull impertinence.[49]

Garrick again entered the public arena of pamphleteering (anonymously). He seems to have amused himself by drafting a parody of Dryden's long "Ode to St. Cecelia's Day" to add to the rioter's dossier —"Fitzgig's Triumph, or the Power of Riot, an Ode":

> Vex'd at the sound, the General's pride waxed low
> Too weak to ward off Reason's blow;
> Yet thrice he drown'd Fair Justice' voice, yet
> thrice he bawld
> YES or No![50]

The public benefited from several more pamphlets from authors outraged by the interruption the half-price riots had engendered. Benjamin Victor put the half-price cause in perspective in *Three Original Letters to a Friend in the Country* (29 January 1763) giving the history of ticket costs for the past 30 years. An anonymous author blasted the personal pique and operation of private revenge which animated the Fitzpatrick rioters.[51] But Garrick thought long and deeply about the total relationship of his theatre to the public and of both to himself.

Any establishment—regulated, orderly, profitable, and apparently satisfactory—hangs, of course, upon the thin thread of confidence and credibility. Drury Lane theatre was presumably pleasing in its schedule to the public at large. Its profits to actors and managers could be documented, but the pressure of satirical, sarcastic, resentful, and articulate authors was beginning to take toll psychologically, at least. The Fitzpatrick demolition of the house climaxed an attitude which might increase the tensions on that thread of confidence to another breaking point.

Garrick doubtless remembered, for he kept files on the various expressions of public opinion, the sharp attacks of the *Theatrical Examiner* made six years earlier (1757) on the tenth anniversary of his assuming managership. "Mr. Garrick," wrote the *Examiner*, "sits foremost and says and unsays—and distant Mr. Lacy says also the *same* things—and if the effective manager writes a play, farce, or prologue, or unwrites the work of another (no *uncommon* thing with him) the mum waiter manager subscribes to it, and freely follows the public in paying for them also; tho' I must allow they are in the point of handling a racket equally dextrous, and play the ball from one to another with great art and skill. Mr. Garrick always consults Mr. Lacy concerning the business of a new piece or performer, and Mr Lacy answers mechanically according to the humour of his political dictator. He will when alone most powerfully insinuate that *he* is the main politician, as Mr. Bayes says, but was I the one or the other, I should not be ambitions of that superiority, as it is well known their politics are often a *little dirty*." Dark hints, to be sure, but the anonymous author thought both managers exceedingly capable. Yet the *Theatrical Examiner* set forth their supposed practices of molding accepted plays to their own patterns, or leading young actors on with promises unfulfilled, and of holding in their own hands the strings controlling theatrical taste.

Garrick welcomed the close of the season in May 1763. He had had enough tension to string him up tight. To add to this a private quarrel obtruded itself in August with the actor Thomas Davies, which broke forth in a rather acrimonious correspondence. Odd that several years earlier (21 April 1759) Garrick had played Zamti, and Davies had played Miran in Arthur Murphy's *Orphan of China*. Though Garrick had no way of knowing it Davies and Murphy were to become his first and second biographers, unlikely candidates, one would think in the summer of 1762.

Thomas Davies, half a dozen years older than Garrick, having received a good classical education in Edinburgh, had made his first appearance on the London stage in 1736 in Henry Fielding's company at the Haymarket. The next year when the Licensing Act drove that company out of performing Davies entered upon his first venture as a bookseller. He carried on this trade for eight years before returning to the stage at Covent Garden (20 October 1746), where he soon played the part of King Henry to Garrick's Richard III. His success was moderate only, for Rich did not re-engage him for the following season. For the next four years he made the circuit of provincial playhouses until Garrick engaged him in 1752, along with his beautiful wife, Susannah Yarrow Davies, at Drury Lane, where he stayed for ten years. By 1760, however, he was reentering the book selling trade on the side, and retired to it completely in 1762.[52]

Garrick had loaned Davies £50 towards the purchase of a house. Davies sometime later wrote to George complaining that Garrick had, in effect, urged Colman to collect any sums owing to any loans Colman had made to Davies, thus, perhaps, impugning his credit and trust. Garrick seeing this letter wrote in a temper, "Upon my honour, I never once suspected Your integrity & till I heard of your last conversation w[th] my Brother I had not the least doubts of Your Veracity" (312). Davies hedged in his reply, complaining that he had been misunderstood. The argument then branched out into his reasons for quitting the stage, which he laid to his own sensitiveness under Garrick's harassment, and to his desire to devote himself full time to the book trade. He denied that Churchill's scathing lines in *The Rosciad* (that Davies "mouthed a sentence as curs mouth a bone") had anything to do with the decision. To which Garrick reminded him that his own "warmth" (not harassment) which had disturbed Davies's sensitiveness had been occasioned by Davies's ineptness during rehearsals. Garrick had earlier agreed to accept a set of Davies's *Museum Florentinium*, in 12 volumes, to settle his debt, and he stuck by the agreement— not hesitating to remind the actor-bookseller of the many favors he had done him (313). Whereupon Davies took his leave of Garrick in a long and detailed review of their relationship. The mutual ironical remarks and veiled scorn abiding in the correspondence suggest the need that existed for a parting of the ways.

Three years later Davies criticized *The Clandestine Marriage* (Garrick's and Colman's play) mildly complaining about some vulgarisms of dialogue therein. Garrick wrote Colman about this, not now in anger, but with gentle irony, "Pray when you see *Davies* the Bookseller, assure him that I bear him not the least Malice (which he is told I do) for having mentioned the *Vulgarisms* . . . and that I may convince him that all is well between us—let him know that I was well assur'd that he wrote his Criticism before he had seen y[e] Play. *Quod er[t] dem[m]*" (397). Garrick had, perhaps, been provoked with Davies as a whisperer and passer of ill-founded gossip back in 1756, when the suspicious Murphy was concerned about the faith of the Drury Lane managers in rehiring Mossop, "we intend to join him to our Comp[y] if we can . . . notwithstanding the Whispers of M^r Davies, or y^e Reports of this or that person," wrote Garrick (164).

And yet, and yet, and yet, when in September 1766 Joseph Reed accused Garrick of delay in reading his tragedy of *Dido*, which Garrick had not yet received, Garrick, who was in transit from Bath to Hampton, asked him to let him have the facts about the submission of the piece, noting "if you will send me a note of the particulars to my house . . . or leave them by word of mouth with M^r Davies the bookseller in Russel Street, I will make a proper inquiry & give you notice of my Coming to town that we may meet upon the occasion. I never had an accident of this kind before—Had the play been deliver'd to me you should have had my opinion of it immediately" (429). Terms between Garrick and Davies seem later, then, to have resumed on a cordial enough basis.

Both Davies and Garrick were, of course, friendly with Boswell and Dr Johnson, who seem at times to have arbitrated in the budding quarrel between the two. In 1778 Davies's business began to fail, even to the point of bankruptcy. Dr Johnson suggested, in 1779 after Garrick's death, that Davies write his *Life*, and supplied the first sentence for setting it going: "All excellence has a right to be recorded; I shall therefore think it superfluous to apologize for writing the life of a man who, by an uncommon assemblage of private virtue, adorned the highest eminence in a public profession." Published in 1780, the *Life* quickly ran through four editions, enabling Davies to clear his debts and resume his trade. But expression of the Davies-Johnson sentiment was years away from the summer of 1763.

At the close of that season a breather was called for. The public, the poets, and the players would benefit from a lull in the Drury Lane drive for continuing excellence on the scale hitherto followed. The theatre was on firm enough ground, despite the noisy few, to carry on and support its company, should Garrick take an extended leave of absence, if an equally capable person who would command the respect of the players could be seen in the manager's office. Garrick found such a person in George Colman—not an actor, but a playwright and theatre man of accepted experience.

At the close of the 1762–63 season Garrick and Eva Maria spent a fortnight delightfully with the Duke of Devonshire at Chatsworth, and there was Quin, and the Fitzherberts, with George and Peter Garrick invited. But Garrick's doctor advised him to slack off for a season in his dynamic expenditure of energy, and Garrick agreed that the time was right to do so. He asked prompter Hopkins to meet with him in

*Garrick Club*
Garrick Between Tragedy and Comedy.
Painting by Sir Joshua Reynolds.

mid-August (311), proposed and received permission from the Lord Chamberlain for a year's leave of absence, prepared for a visit to Paris, where he had built up a bank account in French livres sufficient to support him for many months, inserted a notice in the *London Chronicle* to alert the public, and wrote to some of his top actors telling them his plans (315). Mrs Cibber was surprised, but agreed the move was a good one. His attention to detail, and his consideration of the feelings of others was characteristic.[53]

Accompanied by Mrs Garrick he set out for France and Italy with great relief as the theatres were about to open for the 1763–64 season.

Sixteen years in the driver's seat of a vehicle constantly under the scrutiny of the mercurial public, as well as of the special-interest groups of proud authors, fairly tested the man's spirit. If also Garrick worked, as he often did, under the handicap of seizures of illness many many times throughout this span, one might expect to see signs of exhaustion. His doctors saw them, but the viewer of the documents 200 years after the fact hardly discerns such in this dynamic now 46-year-old man. Noverre described him in the late 1750s, after the *Chinese Festival* riot, preparing to act a new part, "There is no man more sprightly than he the day he is to act a poet, a tradesman, a character in low life, a newsmonger."[54] A leafing through his 265 extant letters during the period of induction to and carrying on management, supports the impression of movement, hard-headedness combined with graciousness, care for details without being swamped by them, flashes of spirit linked to moods of serenity, patience under provocation, planning followed by relaxation, hopes dashed but personality rebounding, learning from experience, leading others into new fields, evaluating success and confronting disaster.

These years actually were golden ones for the theatre—both in cash returns, sensible competition, relative stability, high-quality acting at both houses, and in impact upon a critical public. Garrick had probably, by 1763, met up with every aspect of joy in management as well as predicament therein. The experience in the arena and the marketplace was doubtless toughening. But an essential kindliness and thoughtfulness, something of self-searching, combined with some self-justification and self-confidence pervade his last letter from London—to Mrs Cibber—before his departure in early September 1763:

"I am sorry to hear that you are so thin, but congratulate You at y$^e$ same time upon y$^e$ return of Your Spirits . . . laugh and be fat all y$^e$ world over." He referred to the account in the papers about his trip abroad, and excused himself for not writing to friends about it until he had received permission from the Lord Chamberlain's office to absent himself for a long period. He added, truly enough "I have been advised by several Physicians . . . to give Myself a Winter's respite; I have dearly Earn'd it & shall take it in hopes of being better able to undergo the great fatigues of acting & Management" (315). He stretched the winter's respite into a two-year vacation. The *London Chronicle* (15 September) had lightly mocked his departure, but used to that tack in the press he paid no attention. The early letters from Paris are filled with the gaiety, joy, renewed energy, and excitement that the opening world of France promised.

The factor that seems actually to have made Garrick decide to take the winter's respite seems to have been medical advice that Eva Maria's arthritis might respond to a cure from the baths at Albano. But had he been of a turn of mind to think about his Drury Lane accomplishments from 1747 until the end of the season 1763, he would have noted that despite the complaints of the Goldsmiths and the Ralphs he had put on 29 new main pieces and 58 new after pieces to ten new main pieces and 20 new after pieces given at Covent Garden. Contemporaries Edward Moore, Samuel Johnson, William Shirley, William Whitehead, David Mallet, Philip Francis, Richard Glover, Henry Crisp, John Brown, John Slade, John Home, Arthur Murphy, John Hoadly, Samuel Foote, George Colman, John Delap, and Frances Sheridan, all had their pieces (from one to three each) staged as the main attractions. And none of the plays he turned down during those years succeeded elsewhere, save for Home's *Douglas*. Most of them in fact were never performed. In his spread of after pieces he had, besides five of his own, staged those of 26 other contemporary writers, each contributing from one to five pieces. The facts of production seem to belie the extreme complaints of the Ralphs and Goldsmiths that their generation would go unrecorded in performance. For fresh production and novel adaptation Garrick would have recalled the profitable runs of eight more main pieces in his *Romeo and Juliet*, *Every Man in His Humour*, *Cymbeline*, *The Tempest*, *The Winter's Tale*, *Catherine and Petruchio*, Southerne's *Isabella*, and Buckingham's *The Chances*. The record would be matched in the 11 seasons following his return until his retirement.

In spirit and action David Garrick had been and was a dynamo, expending his energy on living, acting, managing, and writing. Though this energy was controlled, it had indeed suffered again and again from physical setbacks. From his earliest stage years he knew that the art of his profession lay in a concealed but ever-present discipline of his vocal and bodily powers. The energy, psychic and physical, that he put into his performance of tragic roles was great, but must not, he knew, be overtaxed.

"My health is better than usual," he had written to Peter in April 1742, as he was planning his summer's trip to Smock Alley in Dublin (23). But while there he caught cold and a fever. By April 1745, his second season at Drury Lane, he performed 72 nights well, but on 6 April had fallen very ill, so that his parts had to be taken over by others. London, distressed, took note of the course of his illness through the papers: "Mr. Garrick lies very ill of a fever at his lodgings in Covent Garden," wrote the *Daily Advertiser* (11 April). The play-bills took note also: "Mr. Garrick's indisposition continuing, we have, at the particular desire of several ladies, chang'd our play" (23 April 1745) (44,48,49).[55] The siege lasted out the remainder of the season.

For this, we know, deputy manager Lacy had withheld wages, and had delayed payment of arrearages due for over five months.

In May 1746 he wrote to Peter "I have got a most Severe Cold & Sore Throat attended with a Small Feaver" (44). In August that year he was at Cheltenham taking the waters to improve his health, but got a set of irritating boils from the sojourn. In September he wrote to John Hoadly about the attack of scurvy he was curing: "I am drinking the Waters Here [as an antiscorbutic]. . . . I have certainly receiv'd a great deal of Pain from 'em w$^{ch}$ y$^e$ Doctors call Benefit, & if a Purgatory is as necessary for y$^e$ purification of y$^e$ Body, as the Soul, I am thoroughly cleansed; for Job had not More Sufferings, Nor perhaps more patience than I had" (48,49). Garrick was normally worried about such attacks, but was no hypochondriac. Customarily he passed off his illnesses, while mentioning them, with a characteristic lightness of touch, ending the Hoadly note, "And yet for all that, I was never in better spirits or more non-sensical in my life."[56]

Buried in his letters lie brief comments which show a sort of fever chart of his times of illness from 1742 to 1776. Once or twice at least during more than 62 months (spread through his acting career) he was ailing. Records appear of his trips to Tunbridge, Cheltenham, and Bath to take the waters for their supposed curative effects. Once he ate an ounce of bark (quinine) and stopped drinking malt liquor in the service of health. He took many powders, and was generally interested in medicines, but just as easily disillusioned with them. "Your old friend M$^r$ Cochran, the apothecary," he wrote to Peter, "has favoured us twice with his company, and hopes to have the honour of purging us; but I intend to keep his catharticks out of my guts, for I never had such health and spirits" (60).

His attacks of stomach pains, nausea, and bile came doubtless from kidney stones lodged there and in the urinary bladder. Garrick did not know it (for the evidence came only after the autopsy after his death) but he possessed only a single kidney. Ailments there were serious and painful. "Joy, joy, joy to you," he wrote to John Home, 22 February 1758, upon the success of Home's *Agis*, "My anxiety [for it] yesterday gave me a small touch of the gravel,[57] which, with a purging, weakened me prodigiously; but our success has stopped the one and cured the other." To Evan Lloyd he wrote (14 December 1769), "Tho I play'd last Night the Character of Lord Hastings & with tolerable Spirit, yet I have been very ill today, & have had a Small fit of the Stone, which has brought forth two little devils, that have much Weakened me." And so went the comments on gout (occasionally), on arthritis in his writing fingers, and all the normal human ailments from chills, to dizziness, to headaches, to sore throats, to fevers, to jaundice. Fortunately seizures were spaced over three decades so caused only temporary interference with his heavy, self-imposed working schedule.

On this two-year grand tour of France, Italy, and Bavaria he was relaxed and generally free from illness, save for chills occasionally in Paris and one *very serious* fever contracted in Munich, which nearly did him in. Two physicians attended and he finally recovered, but felt himself so close to dying that he played with writing his own epitaph,[58] noting that no crime had blackened his career, and that

> Tho' Malice through the sneering land
> Has sent her slander forth
> I never clos'd my heart or hand
> To talents of true worth (336, 337).

The fever exaggerated his lingering sense of the unfair treatment which he and Drury Lane had received from the Fitzpatrick riots, for the final line of one draft of the epitaph notes his pride that, "The good Fitzherbert was my friend / Fitz—k was my foe."

He and Eva Maria had gone for a hoped-for five weeks to the muds of Albano as curative for her painful rheumatism (345), and they hoped to spend happy days at Spaw, the most fashionable watering place in Bavaria, but he had fallen ill. Recovery immediately restored his joviality.

Only during that summer of 1764, when illness made inroads also upon the health and comfort of Mrs Garrick, did he toy with the idea of not returning to the stage. One suspects he had a bad bout of hepatitis, for he wrote from Munich to the Reverend William Arden 15 September: "I am but the Shadow of myself, that Self which at Naples,

& at Venice made no contemptible figure ev'n at Your Side, & which was always ready & willing to Second You in Every Article of the fat and fine! but . . . all the Combustibles I had been long storing up there & Elsewhere took fire at this place, & I have been confin'd more than a Month to my bed, by the most dangerous bilious Fever that Ever poor Sinner Suffer'd for the small fault of a little innocent Society." Dr. Turton was with him as fellow traveller and attended him through the seizure. "I am most truly," he continued, "yᵉ Knight of yᵉ Woeful Countenance & have lost legs arms belly cheeks &c and have scarce anything left but bones, & a pair of dark lack-lustre Eyes, that are retir'd an inch or two more in their Sockets & wonderfully set off yᵉ yellow Parchment that covers yᵉ cheekbones—thus I really am, but out of all danger, for I recover daily, have no Cough" (338). Colman and brother George had apparently written him that he must think of cutting down on his acting when he returned, and he wrote Colman, 10 November 1764, "yᵉ Doctors all have forbid me thinking of Business—I have at present lost all taste for yᵉ Stage—it was once my greatest Passion, & I labor'd for many years like a true Lover— but I am grown cold—should my desires return, I am the Town's humble Servant again—though she is a great Coquette, & I want Youth, vigorous Youth, to bear up against her occasional Capricious- ness—but more of this when I see you" (341). Ten days later he had a seizure of chills at the theatre in Paris, but from then on steadily recovered both in health and in good spirits, writing an excellent letter of encouragement to the promising, upcoming young actor William Powell, and asking others about the state of the Drury Lane compa- ny.[59] He had been collecting music for the theatre, had his eye on sev- eral dancers (331). He had asked George Colman, back in June to tell him "what People really say about me, & what you think of our affairs," maybe with a thought of abandoning management (332). But that, as comes clear from subsequent letters he simply could not do. Paris and the long vacation recovered him, and were to instigate the puckish mood in which he would draft his jocose public opinion poll in publica- tion of "The Sick Monkey."

He had always consulted the best medical advice available, jaunty though he may have been about it, as in his letter to George Colman from Nancy, 10 November 1764, "Had I been happy enough to have caught you here, my dear Friend! I should not have wanted James's Powder [a compound of antimonious oxide and calcium phosphate], l'exercise du Cheval, et beaucoup de dissipation; as all the French doctors have prescrib'd, & I have had three of 'em—wᶜʰ with three German ones, & two of my own Country makes the Number Eight—

Eight Physicians, my good friend, & still alive! & very likely to continue so."

Such a concentrated view of the subject as this tends to throw concern for his physical well-being out of proportion, but his illnesses were real, and his concern for acting in his profession during them was genuine. The saving grace of it all lies in his readily expressed sense of humor in every instance. Other persons, hoping not to be deprived of Garrick's brand of rational entertainment, took his illnesses more seriously, often, than he, notably one William Combe, author of *Sanitas, Daughter of Aesculapius to David Garrick, Esq* (1772). Therein the Muses of Tragedy and Comedy appeal to Apollo to restore the actor to health:

> But what avails our labours join'd
> With Science to enrich the mind,
> If pale and languishing disease
> Deprives him of the power to please!
>
> Bid him in Lusignan and Lear
> Call forth from every eye a tear;
> In Leon, Benedict, and Bayes
> Continual peals of laughter raise,
> And let his face, as wont, impart
> The strong conceptions of his heart.

France could and did freshen the spirit, alleviate pain, but not restore a missing kidney.

# The Literary World of Scholarship

DURING HIS VACATION from the toils of acting and theatre management, Garrick had time to ponder two areas of creativity to which he
applied himself and in which he was to continue to the end of his
career—his remarkable collection of early English drama, and his
writing of fresh pieces for the stage, including his adapting of older
plays. The latter had its impact on the general public, and would so
continue upon his return from France. The former, never heretofore
studied in any depth, had its impact on the then burgeoning world
of literary scholarship.

Arthur Murphy asserted in the final chapter of his *Life of David
Garrick* (1801) that "literature and dramatic poetry were to the last
[Garrick's] favorite topics" and pays tribute to him as "the restorer
of dramatic literature."[1] Murphy was certainly qualified by firsthand
information and judgment to make such a statement. His summation
of Garrick's ruling passion embraces both Garrick's professional life
and his association with friends of his own choosing in his private life.
Although the full and many-sided life of Garrick can hardly be sub-
divided into categories, one continuing development of his character
—his interest in the literary scholarship of his contemporaries—merits
particular examination.

Bibliographers should no longer ignore Garrick the collector of
books and stimulator of literary scholarship. He knew and cared for the
content of his remarkable dramatic library and put his books to work
with the best editors and critics of the age. His dozen or so biographers
give only passing mention to his great dramatic library, which he left
to the British Museum. Detailed and inductive bibliographical study
of its gathering and use discloses more about Garrick's taste and
values, the resources upon which he drew as a great actor, and the
influence he had upon his contemporaries, than pages of sociohistori-
cal generalizations. The friends that fame and fortune brought him
meant far less to him than the congenial intellectual associations

opened up to him through his collecting, his studies, and his patronage of the poetry of the drama.

In a word, before Garrick became a professional actor and manager, and continuing through his life he assembled and used the largest collection of English drama either written, produced, or published before 1600. With his private means he patronized the editing, writing, and publishing of a number of significant and influential books on the history of English drama. He supported his concentration in pre-Restoration plays by assembling also an exceptionally full and eclectic private library of classical and continental drama, as well as of history, biography, the fine arts, and literature—a library of 2,700 titles. It was dispersed at public auction after his death, but during his lifetime became a rich sustaining source for much in both his private and his public life.

The full significance of Garrick's involvement in dramatic poetry, other than the professional interest shared by many actors, may be grasped only in the bibliographical context of the preceding 100 years. The texts of Elizabethan and Jacobean plays in the autograph of the playwright were tentative and incomplete, hence designated as "foul papers." These foul papers were adapted for production by producers and actors, and copied out into "lengths" for roles by scribes whose secretarial habits of script and style prevailed, and were gathered into "prompt copies" owned and controlled by the theatrical companies. Subsequently the texts might often be revised (with or without the author's permission) for current or later production to accord with changes in company personnel, or with censorship, or with fluctuations in fashions and social tastes. If the company thought it advantageous to print the play, it usually submitted the prompt copy (or acting text) to a compositor-printer, who from haste, carelessness, or indecision about the hand, normalized and often further corrupted the original text. Subsequent reprintings added variants from conjectural emendations and changes made in other prompt copies, that is printed quartos with prompt additions.

Early plays were apt to be hastily and carelessly printed on cheap paper, sewn in quarto gatherings to be sold for a penny or up to one-and-six. They were not produced to be assembled in libraries. If preserved and sold second hand, the single quartos were tied in bundles, or cheaply backed with boards in gatherings of five, ten, or even 20, generally by size only and not by title, author, or date. In these nondescript bundles or volumes, quartos were listed in libraries or sales catalogues well into the eighteenth century. The gatherings sold for little, and the purchase was a gamble.

*Folger Shakespeare Library*
David Garrick.
Portrait by Sir Nathaniel Dance, 1773.

With the decline of the Elizabethan and Jacobean theatres as a source of public entertainment and the closing of the theatres in 1642, the reading of plays increased and the demand for printed plays could not be satisfied by the rare surviving quartos. A succession of printers, who first had to become collectors, turned out well-printed and bound collected editions, seldom from texts supplied by authors, but more often the more recent prompt copy from a disbanded theatrical company or the latest quarto, and hence almost invariably the most corrupted texts. These collected editions became the standard texts in the libraries of Dryden, Congreve, Swift, Pope, Johnson, Walpole, and the general run of late seventeenth- and eighteenth-century readers.

The almost notorious variations and instabilities in the texts of Elizabethan and Jacobean drama, only gradually sensed in the later seventeenth and early eighteenth century, gradually became the preoccupations of actors, producers, collectors, and scholars—an instability that was endemic in the very nature of the drama. At the outset, Sir Thomas Bodley in his plan for a public library at Oxford (1612), asserted he saw no good reason to alter his opinion "for excluding such bookes, as . . . plaies"—"baggage bookes" he called them. "Happely some plais may be worthy the keeping: but hardly one in fortie."[2] The deficiency, however, was corrected by a later librarian who given by Robert Burton the first choice of his library (1639) selected for the Bodleian the 70 and more old quartos. The revolution in bibliographical values was best recorded in 1627 by Gabriel Naudé in his *Avis pour dresser un Bibliothèque*, and translated in 1661 by John Evelyn, "to rummage and often revisite the shops of frippery *Booksellers*, and the old *Stores* and Magazines" for the ephemeral quartos of all kinds.[3] Evelyn himself assembled some of the older quartos, as did Samuel Pepys, in particular three volumes, identified as "Old Plays," 26 quartos, mostly from the 1500s and early 1600s. And inevitably George Thomason, who endeavored to acquire all the ephemeral publications of the popular presses during the Restoration, picked up 54 plays.

The extensive collecting of quartos of old plays that culminated in Garrick's collection, began with a succession of booksellers whose steadily expanding cataloguers and catalogues stimulated the recovery and market value of the old quartos, and became the first and for long the standard bibliographies of English drama. These booksellers, collectors, bibliographers, now some of the most famous names in the annals of the history of English drama, begin with William Cartwright, the actor, who endowed Dulwich College with approximately 500 old quartos in 1686;[4] also William Rogers and Charles Ley, Francis Kirkman, Nicholas Cox, and eventually the greatest of them all, Gerard

Langbaine, Jr., whose *Account of the English Dramatick Poets* (1691), abridged and continued by Charles Gildon as the *Lives and Characters of the English Dramatick Poets* (1691), became the standard dramatic bibliography well into the eighteenth century. Earlier, in 1688, in the preface to his first catalogue, called *A New Catalogue of English Plays*, Langbaine almost boasted "I have been Master of Nine Hundred and Fourscore English Plays and Masques, besides Drolls and Interludes . . . I have designed this Catalogue for their use, who may have the same relish of the Drama with my self and may possibly be desirous, . . . to make a collection" (sig. A2).[5] Undoubtedly there passed through Langbaine's hands plays out of the two very extensive libraries of Richard Smith and Humphrey Dysons, whose many old plays, as well as other books, dispersed in sales, may still be identified. Regrettably Langbaine's greatest collection of plays to date was dispersed in a sale in 1692, the copies not identifiable.

While most of the private collections formed in the seventeenth century that included dramatic literature were dispersed in sales, the individual items were not lost but purchased and preserved by other collectors. Further, these sales and the revival of the theatre in the Restoration and thereafter, stimulated the discovery of many more copies of early drama. Undoubtedly the most extensive and famous collector who harvested and preserved more from seventeenth-century libraries and sales than any other bibliophile was Edward Harley, second earl of Oxford (1680–1741). Beginning with the library formed by his famous father, the First Earl of Oxford, Harley for 40 years, 1701–41, assisted by Humfrey Wanley (1696–1761) and many others, such as William Oldys, about whom more shortly, swept the second-hand book market, ransacked private libraries, and employed agents abroad—all to assemble the magnificent Harleian Library. The Harleian Library was purchased on Harley's death in 1741 by Thomas Osborne, the bookseller, who engaged Samuel Johnson and William Oldys to prepare the monumental *Catalogus Bibliothecae Harleiana*, in four volumes, for the sale that began 14 February 1744. Prior to the cataloguing and sale, however, Robert Dodsley obtained, obviously through the mediation of Oldys, "between 6 and 700" plays out of the Harleian Library. From the plays so obtained he published 52 in his *Select Collection of Old Plays* (1744–46), in 12 volumes, the first and with later revisions the most available collection of early English drama, other than Shakespeare, until well into the twentieth century.

Garrick in turn, doubtless by the counsel of Oldys who knew more about the Harleian English books than anyone else, purchased from

Dodsley the plays, mostly in quartos, that Dodsley had obtained from the Harleian Library. Garrick then went on to purchase from Osborne all the plays listed in the *Catalogus Bibliothecae Harleiana*, Volumes III and IV, approximately 160 titles, presumably before the library went on sale on 1 February 1744. In the best bibliographical practice, Garrick thereupon obtained a copy of Langbaine's *Lives*, and marked all the plays he obtained from Dodsley with an *X* and from Osborne with an *O*. This copy of Langbaine marked by Garrick was sold with Garrick's library in 1823, and most regrettably has disappeared.[6] From bibliographical criteria that need not be cited and analyzed here, it is possible to identify almost all the titles, and with a few exceptions inevitable in perfecting and enlarging his collection, the actual copies themselves. All in all Garrick appears to have obtained from the Harleian Library through Oldys from Dodsley and Osborne approximately 550 separate quartos, and an indeterminate number of collected editions, perhaps as many as 25. He thereby embarked on his long career as a collector of English drama, with the largest and most valuable collection to date, the harvest of much of the discovery and collecting of English drama for the preceding 100 years. Garrick was not familiar with all the dramatic poetry in all the 500 quartos, nor was any one else. Yet Garrick knew what he was doing and subsequently became the most informed and extensive collector of early English drama. As already developed, back in Lichfield he had availed himself of Gilbert Walmesley's knowledge and guidance and of his exceptional library in literature in general. Johnson, the son of a bookseller and bibliophile and a scholar himself, almost from childhood, certainly imbued Garrick with a deep and abiding respect for scholarship and an exacting taste in books. As early as 1737, both men were writing plays, which implies already acquaintance with dramatic literature, and before he became an actor, as noted, he wrote two of the most popular after pieces, one from English tradition *Lethe*, and one from French, *The Lying Valet*. If Garrick did not meet Oldys, the most learned literary antiquarian when he was the librarian (and later with Johnson the cataloguer) of the Harleian Library, Garrick later supported Oldys's scholarship and made purchases from his library. Among Garrick's contemporaries in the theatre only Thomas Sheridan may have in the 1740s equalled Garrick's knowledge of English drama. Sheridan had inherited from his schoolmaster-scholar father a passion for drama, beginning with the classical. As a student for two years in the Westminster School he attended the theatre. But both before and after the purchase of the Harleian quartos Garrick brought to the theatre more knowledge of pre-Restoration drama than any actor-manager-play-wright of the century.

Unable to attend the late-afternoon book auctions because of his involvement with Drury Lane, Garrick throughout his long residence in London established close professional and even personal relationships with half a dozen prominent printer-publisher-booksellers to assist him in assembling both his collection of English drama and his separate general library. The more knowledgeable were: Somerset Draper, partner of Jacob and Richard Tonson, who held the copyright to Shakespeare's plays; Isaac and Paul Vaillant, who assisted Lord Oxford in forming the Harleian collections; J. Bedford and Andrew Millar; Dryden Leach, the expert printer; and William Griffin, who by 1749 was already doing business at the sign of Garrick's Head, Catherine Street, in the Strand near Drury Lane. All of his life Garrick was in and out of the shops of Osborne, Dodsley, and Davies, the last two specializing in dramatic literature. From 1760 on Thomas Becket became Garrick's personal bookseller-publisher-agent, and when the Adam brothers designed the Adelphi Terrace, Garrick saw to it that a bookshop was constructed for Becket (with furnishing by Chippendale) that Garrick aspired to make "as old Jacob Tonson's was formerly, y^e rendevous for y^e first people in England" (744). Later Peter Abraham DeHondt, one of the major importers of foreign books joined Becket; and all the while from 1751 on Garrick enjoyed the friendship and personal services of Jean Monnet, the versatile and tireless Paris bookseller who kept Garrick in touch with the French publications and secondhand book market. Garrick himself bought extensively when he was abroad in Paris and later in Italy; many friends were constantly buying and shipping him books from abroad. He was a great reader of catalogues, some of the more monumental that became bibliographies such as *Bibliotheca Bridgesiana, Meadiana, Rawlinsoniana Catalogus* he added to his library. Some of the additions to his quartos of plays came as gifts or through scholar friends.

In the 1740s Garrick moved into the aristocratic society whose members possessed some of the greatest libraries of the century. His first companion and tutor in bibliomania was William Windham. When Windham came into his estate in 1749 he began adding to the large collection of books he had inherited, and engaged James Raines to design a new library at Felbrigg Hall in 1753. Garrick was acquainted with Topham Beauclerk's magnificent collection. The two bought books together in Italy later. Beauclerk's library of 30,000 volumes contained bundles of plays and books in all the continental languages.

Garrick visited the library of James West in Covent Garden, who earlier had attended sales with Lord Oxford and bought at the Harleian sale among other items what are now known as the Roxburghe Ballads. Later West entertained the Garrick's at Alscott, near Stratford, during the Jubilee. Though Garrick and Horace Walpole were never congenial they were neighbors in Twickenham and Hampton. Garrick later borrowed from Walpole a copy of his *Miscellaneous Antiquities* (1772). They in general patronized the same book agents, but Walpole was almost exclusively interested in eighteenth-century rather than in early drama, assembling some 82 bound volumes with eight or ten plays in each.

By the end of the 1740 decade Garrick was welcomed into the aristocratic social circle of the Burlingtons (through his marriage with Eva Maria Veigel) the Devonshires, and the Spencers, and he was at home in the libraries at Chatsworth, Londesburgh, Chiswick, and Althorp. Eventually he was often the guest in four families into which were born four famous collectors, three in Garrick's lifetime: George John, second earl Spencer (1758–1830) who filled out the library at Althorp from 1768 on, now the John Rylands Library; Richard Colt Hoare (1758–1838) whose collection is still preserved in part at Stourhead; Charles Burney, Jr., D. D. (1758–1817), whose library is now in the British Museum; and finally William Spencer (1790–1858), the son of Georgiana Spencer, and the sixth duke of Devonshire, whose private library was perhaps the finest assembled during his lifetime.

Garrick was in touch with William Cartwright's collection and, along with Steevens and Malone, exchanged recent editions of English drama better suited for teaching, in exchange for a few of the old quartos. According to Edmund Malone,[7] Garrick as a collector directly influenced other actor-managers to assemble dramatic libraries, notably John Henderson and William Dodd whose libraries were later dispersed in sales. Most significant of all, Garrick's example inspired John Philip Kemble (1757–1823) to build up a large library of English drama, bought by the sixth Duke of Devonshire and now preserved in the Kemble-Devonshire Collection in the Henry C. Huntington Library in California.[8] All of his life Garrick associated socially and culturally with humble, academic, and aristocratic collectors. No better testimony to his liberal interest in literature in general survives than in his devotion to Thomas Beighton (1699?–1771), vicar of Egham, in Surrey, near Hampton. Garrick solicited preferments for Beighton; and they often visited each other and exchanged gifts of books, notably a gift from Beighton of 32 volumes of Greek and Latin authors published by Foulis in Glasgow, and bound in red leather, now in the Folger

Library. Presumably for many kindnesses, Beighton willed his library to Garrick and Lord Camden, who rather than divide the books, had them catalogued and offered for sale to raise more money for Beighton's estate. The catalogue, carefully prepared by Baker and Leigh, was advertised as "containing a very fine collection of miscellaneous Books, in most Languages, and in particular, a large Number of rare *Italian* and Spanish *Authors*: also a most extraordinary Collection of *Books of Emblems*, with the *finest Engravings*," the sale running from 30 March 1772 for the 12 following days and grossing £778.8.9 for the 2,695 items—a remarkable library for a country vicar. No other library in the eighteenth century so closely parallels Garrick's general library; no other collector had so liberal an influence on Garrick's general library.

Other than for Garrick's Collection of Old Plays he willed to the British Museum, a complete inventory of his general library at his death, cannot be drawn up.[9] He willed his general library to his nephew Carrington Garrick, except for books to the value of £100 to Mrs Garrick, who prevailed upon Carrington to sell her his inheritance. Mrs Garrick augmented the library after Garrick's death in 1779, and towards the end of her protracted life she "presented the greater part of the Greek and Latin Classics, together with her numerous and highly valuable books, to Christopher Philip Garrick" the only son of Carrington.[10] Finally books to the value of £150 passed to the Reverend Thomas Rackett and George Frederick Beltz, executors of Mrs Garrick's estate. Beltz entrusted the sale of the remaining books to Robert Saunders who carefully prepared the catalogue for the sale in 1823, 2,716 entries in all, running to well over 3,000 volumes. Over half the titles are of books in foreign languages with many early editions of Latin Classics and French titles. Secondly the library was distinguished by the exceptional number and quality of illustrated books from the early engravers of England and on the Continent. Of English books he had a balanced range of the recognized books in literature, history, biography, and criticism, but little post-Restoration and contemporary drama. Such plays were available in the Drury Lane theatre library, many in constant use. His English collection was exceptional in rare pre-Restoration and black-letter titles. Like most intelligent and informed collectors, he possessed the standard bibliographies, as for example the seven volumes of G. F. De Bure's *Bibliographie Instructive, ou Traité de la Connaissance des livres rares et singuliers* (1768). Although his general library was stocked with theatrical material—costumes, scenery, books on the art of acting—he as a gentleman scholar sought to cultivate knowledge and enjoyment of literature in many a wider field. His library gives point to his advice to young actors William Powell and John Henderson to "read at Your leisure other books besides the plays in which you are concerned" (345,731). The distinction between the professional and the liberal was sharply preserved by his classifying and shelving the Collection of Old Plays quite apart from his general library, yet both must be kept in mind as background for Garrick's concentration on Elizabethan drama, especially Shakespeare.

In his early determination to recover the quartos and the text of Shakespeare, Garrick inevitably made the acquaintance of Edward Capell, and he was able to discern what has only been recently accepted that Capell was one of the ablest bibliographers and restorers of the text of Shakespeare.[11] Capell was born into an established family that educated him in the Bury Grammar School, and at St Catherine's Hall, Cambridge. He was admitted to the Middle Temple where he resided all his life, save for summers later at Hastings. Through family ties, the Duke of Grafton sponsored his appointment as deputy inspector of plays in 1737, to whom Garrick thereafter had to submit the proposed acting copies of all new and revived plays, and also Capell's appointment as groom of the privy chamber in 1745; from these two sinecures Capell received approximately £300 for life. From additional inherited income and as a bachelor he was well circumstanced to become a collector and editor of drama. By 1745 Capell was already enough of a scholar to recognize the deficiencies of Thomas Hanmer's edition of Shakespeare (Oxford 1744) and thereupon "he resolved himself . . . to exert to the uttermost such abilities as he was master of to save from further ruin" the text of Shakespeare.[12] Within the next five years he obtained all the recent editions, the folios, and all the known quartos, except six, but added 12 not listed by earlier bibliographers. For the ensuing 17 years he made the most sustained and accurate collation and transcription to date of the text of Shakespeare before publishing his edition in ten volumes in 1768, printed by Dryden Leach, whom Garrick sponsored. Beginning next in 1752 he took on the assembling of a massive amount of material for his *Notes and Various Readings of Shakespeare*, the first volume not published until 1774. Discouraged by the adverse reception, he recalled the issue and bought up the printed sheets, apparently with a loan from Garrick. All the while he was collating and editing and annotating, Capell was searching for a range of illustrative material from Elizabethan sources for his third and posthumous publication, entitled *The School of Shakespeare*, 1781. The opening section that supplies the title for the volume, consists of ten pages of an "Index of Books

Extracted" and 539 pages of illustrative quotations from Elizabethan drama and literature; "the particular copies of nearly all the plays that furnish's Extracts, are now in the Musaeum, the gift of M$^r$. Garrick." Capell professed that both the *Notes* and *The School of Shakespeare* would never have been published but for Garrick's support.

Garrick's steady and very considerable patronage of Capell was in turn rewarded by Capell's guidance and major role in the perfecting and establishing (bibliographically) of Garrick's Collection during the years that Capell was in the full tide of his own collecting, editing, and publishing. Doubtless the two men associated in their book-buying pursuits, but no evidence exists that Capell was ever Garrick's agent or advisor. Shortly before 1756 (after ten years of collecting by each) Garrick engaged Capell to draw up an inventory-catalogue of his own collection to date. Capell examined every one of Garrick's quartos and collected editions, consulted the several extant bibliographies known to him and in Garrick's library, and presumably some listings that Garrick himself had already made. From this thorough examination, Capell prepared a manuscript inventory-catalogue of 54 folio pages that became the basis for further collecting, and eventually the catalogue for the transfer of the Garrick plays to the British Museum, and for its survival and utility, all in all 1,651 titles.

Checking this inventory Capell prepared two lists of wanted titles. In the first, a small, much-worn pamphlet of 14 leaves (sewn and bound) still preserved in the above catalogue, Capell listed 125 titles other than Shakespeare (except *Lear*, 1605) that were wanting, but which he had found existence of in the dramatic bibliographies he had used. Garrick consulted this listing in his further buying, and the titles ticked off with an asterisk were then later added by Capell to the catalogue (page 50 and following) then indexed. Secondly, perhaps with Garrick's help, he prepared and printed an advertisement (the most complete bibliography up to that time) of Shakespeare quartos, listing 75 quartos under 31 titles, fourteen of which were only ascribed to Shakespeare. In this advertisement Capell announced: "Two sets are collecting: with intention to deposit them hereafter, together with the earlier folios, in some public libraries. . . . To complete these sets, two copies are wanted of each edition that is without a mark, and one each that has but one: for these any price, not greatly unreasonable, will be given and for an edition, that is not in the list a consideration extraordinary."[13] He then requested communications be sent to Somerset Draper.

There is no way of identifying what copies were in either collection, but between them they had already 77 quartos. The titles with one or

no asterisks subsequently found in the Garrick Collection were catalogued and indexed by Capell in the addenda of the manuscript
catalogue. Finally Capell's services included the inserting of some
missing leaves in manuscript, in perfecting nearly 50 quartos from two
or more copies, all identified with his initials on the title pages, in
having the quartos bound up by sizes in gatherings of five to ten quartos, preparing an index for each volume, and assigning a pressmark
—the pressmark and Garrick's initials appearing on the spine of the
242 volumes. To these were added (when the collection went to the
British Museum) 11 old romances bound uniformly with the quartos,
and having the pressmarks.[14]

Percy gives some insight into the vigor with which Capell and Garrick sought to complete their collections, in a manuscript note inserted
before the title page of William Rufus Chetwood's *Theatrical Records*,
1756, now in the Bodleian: "This Author of this Book was Chetwood,
formerly Prompter to Drury Lane Play House—his list of ancient
Plays deserves Credit no farther, than it is confirmed by Langbaine,
the Author having had the Dishonesty to forge both Titles and Dates,
as I have been assured by Mr Capel and Mr. Garrick; who both con-
victed him upon the fullest Evidence, of forging the entire list of Titles
which he has given of Shakespeare's Plays. Not one of which he could
ever produce, tho' offered a large premium by these Gentlemen.
Thomas Percy, 1761."

To return to Capell and the Garrick Collection, Capell did not publicly acknowledge his bibliographical assistance to Garrick until 1781,
in his final publication, entitled *The School of Shakespeare*, in a preface entitled "Notitia Dramatica; or, Tables of Ancient Plays . . . faithfully compiled and digested in quite a new Method, by E. C." The
preface defines it as, "A Collection of what may be call'd—*The Stage's
Antiquities* having pass'd some years since through the hands of this
'Notitia's' compiler, he immediately saw in it an occasion of presenting
the Publick with what he thinks will be acceptable; namely a knowledge they may rely on of nearly every dramatic piece, of what kind
soever, which the press sent forth down to the Restoration, and to a
small period thereafter."

In short the "Notitia Dramatica" is a reworking of the inventory-
catalogue, with a few corrections and additions, a bibliography of the
Garrick Collection, so respected and used by later scholars.

Though Edward Capell's life and work are here only briefly touched
upon, he merits a place in Garrick's biography, a role that Garrick
would have gladly acknowledged. The paucity of letters is only indicative of the personal association of the two men for 30 years and more in

London in mutual respect and assistance. Mention only can be made here how the interests and talents of both men were happily combined in 1758 in the production and publication of *Antony and Cleopatra; an Historical Play, Written by William Shakespeare: Fitted for the Stage by Abridging Only; and Now Acted, at the Royal-Theatre in Drury-Lane, by His Majesty's Servants*, London: Printed for J. and R. Tonson in the Strand, MDCCLVIII, with "Conjectural Readings" and according to the colophon "From the Press of Dryden Leach" whom Garrick promoted. The following year the two men collaborated in commissioning an "Effigies William Shakespeare Britanni ad fidem tabellae unicae manu Richard Burbage depictae (circum annum, ut videtur, 1609) per R. Barret Londinensem quam exactissme expressa anno 1759, curantibus David Garrick et Edward Capell," from the inscription under the portrait now in Trinity College. Capell had borrowed the original, the now famous Chandos portrait from the Duke of Chandos; "I had intelligence of it from a very worthy and sensible man, M$^r$ Draper, partner with the late Tonsons, and brought up (as I think) under old Jacob all inquisitive people in what related to Shakespeare."[15]

The folio manuscript catalogue that passed to the British Museum was of the greatest consequence to both men: it enabled Garrick to fill out his collection; it made available to Capell the Garrick Collection; it gave Garrick the benefit of Capell's bibliographical expertise; it enabled Garrick both to use himself and to make available to others his collection; and in a very large measure collaboration resulted in the preservation for posterity of two rare collections of early English drama and literature: Capell's in Trinity College Library, and the other from Garrick as a founding benefaction in the British Museum. Although the catalogue of the latter is generally referred to as Capell's Catalogue, the focus then and now must be on the fact that it is of the Garrick Collection. There is no proof that Capell, any more than anyone of half a dozen other friends of Garrick, served as his agent in the secondhand book market, or that Garrick himself did not have a full knowledge and command of his old plays. There is no better proof of the last than Garrick's use of his library in the recovery of dramatic literature.

Garrick's first use himself of his old quartos for the preservation and reprinting of early texts, and from which others could be reproduced, was to help Chetwood. Chetwood was originally a bookseller, and then for 20 years prompter at Drury Lane, before he went over to Dublin to assist in managing the Smock Alley theatre (1741–42). His fortunes declining, he combined his experience as publisher with his considerable knowledge of the theatre to bring out in 1749 *A General History of the Stage*, addressed to the four managers Garrick, Lacy, Rich, and Sheridan. In 1750 he prepared and published in Dublin (with Garrick as a subscriber) in three installments, each containing two plays, *A Select Collection of Old Plays*. Though he does not acknowledge his sources, except for *Fair Em*, all six were in the Garrick Collection. In 1756 he announced "This Day is Published, Proposals for Printing by Subscription, Five Select, Scarce, and Valuable Plays, Printed from the Original Copies," and then listed the plays, all in the Garrick Collection.[16] Though nothing came of the proposal, Chetwood in his "State of Indigence" that resulted in his spending most of his later years in debtor's prison did not have access himself to the quartos of these old plays. The probability is that the choice of titles and texts were Garrick's, who supported the two ventures in charity for a pathetic old friend. If the conclusion is tenable, then the 11 almost unknown old plays in the two collections are some proof that Garrick was reading in depth in his collection.

On 13 May 1742, Lewis Theobald, having completed his edition of Shakespeare, announced in the *London Daily Post* that he had entered into a contract with Tonson and Draper to edit an edition of Beaumont and Fletcher, upon which he had been engaged for 15 years. He appealed for help, and Thomas Seward of Lichfield responded, along with the Reverend John Sympson.[17] The collaboration went forward by correspondence until Theobald's death on 18 September 1744, by which time only the first volume was completed but some progress had been made on the succeeding volumes. Within a month after his death Theobald's library was sold, containing 195 quartos of old plays, and several copies of poems and plays by Beaumont and Fletcher. Theobald's death left Tonson and Draper with an investment on their hands; to complete the undertaking Garrick interviewed Seward in Lichfield and recommended to Draper that "excepting some few things I believe him very capable of publishing Beaumont and Fletcher" (32). Seward took over as principal editor and to him were sent Theobald's annotated edition of 1711, which has not survived, and his valuable Collection of old Quarto's of Beaumont and Fletcher. The editing was completed by 1750 in ten volumes, Garrick reading the long preface in proof. Eventually Garrick assembled 36 quartos of Beaumont and Fletcher, some of which he may have loaned the editors or may have come to him out of the sale of Theobald's books.

Garrick's involvement in the collecting and editing of Philip Massinger was even more complex and sustained. Thomas Coxeter (1689–1747) was an early and zealous collector of old plays. He purchased

Oldys's first annotated copy of Langbaine from Oldys's landlord and refused to return it to Oldys. He proposed to prepare for publication a selection of old plays but was anticipated by Dodsley. Either directly or at the sale of Theobald's library he obtained some quartos of Massinger and was well advanced on an edition of Massinger when he died in 1747. It is impossible to identify with any certainty what books Garrick may have purchased at Theobald's sale and what may have come to him from Theobald and Coxeter at the sale of Coxeter's library in 1749. It is likely that Garrick purchased the copies and notes prepared by Theobald and Coxeter for publication and some Massinger quartos. He ultimately, if not at this time brought together one copy of each of the 18 Massinger quartos and the three plays published, presumably from manuscript, by Moseley for the first time in 1655. Seven of the Massinger quartos in the Garrick Collection are annotated, four apparently in Theobald's hand.

Both to relieve Coxeter's destitute children and to support a production of Massinger's *A New Way to Pay Old Debts*, revived at Drury Lane in 1748–49 and again in 1758–59, Garrick engaged an unsuccessful actor-dramatist-bookseller, Henry Dell, to bring out an edition of Massinger, announced in the *London Gazetteer* on 29 October 1751. The project was dropped for lack of subscribers, but only temporarily. The Coxeter-Dell edition came out in 1759 in four volumes with a fulsome dedication to Garrick and a subscription list obviously laboriously solicited by Garrick. Nevertheless Massinger did not sell well, whereupon Garrick apparently prevailed upon Davies to buy up the remainders and bring out a new issue with a new title page in 1761. For this Davies wrote a life of Massinger dedicated to Johnson, and Garrick induced George Colman to prepare as an introduction "Critical Reflections on the Old English Dramatick Writers," addressed to Garrick and first circulated by Davies as an announcement. Colman made an out-and-out appeal to Garrick to revive the old dramatists. But Garrick was not done with Massinger. Years later, Garrick's good friend Edward Tighe persuaded J. Monck Mason to re-edit Massinger. The volumes came out in 1779; Davies was the publisher; the 1759 Coxeter-Dell text with some changes was used, again with Davies's "Life" and Colman's "Critical Reflections."

Another dramatist that Garrick ardently collected, revived, and produced with himself in some of his best roles, was Ben Jonson. Garrick sponsored the publication of his works, again in support of a scholar-critic working in the spirit and after the manner of Lewis Theobald. Peter Whalley (1722–91), fellow of St. John's, Oxford, schoolman, bibliophile, editor of Pope's *Shakespeare*, a historian published in

1746 *An Essay on the Manner of Writing History* followed in 1748 by *An Enquiry into the Learning of Shakespeare*, remarkable at that time for the range covered in Elizabethan literature. Early in the same year Whalley wrote Garrick some very particular and sharp comments on his acting, to which Garrick responded modestly and gratefully (54). Also in this same year Whalley first contemplated editing Ben Jonson. By 1755 his editing had progressed to the point where he wrote Garrick in part: "When I received your old Quarto Plays, I desir'd M^r Draper w^d wait on you with my thanks & Compliments; intending, at my Leisure to make you a fuller Acknowledgement under my own hand. . . . You will the less wonder I was so solicitous for collating these 4^tos, as you know the great use they are of, in the Work I am engaged in. . . . I shall be extremely careful that your Books shall receive no sort of injury whilst in my Possession." [18]

Whalley's edition of *The Works of Ben Jonson* with an excellent life of Jonson was published in 1756 in seven volumes. [19] In the preface, Whalley acknowledges the assistance above all others of Garrick not only for the quarto of *The Case is Altered*, presumably the 1609 quarto with perhaps Theobald's annotations, but also Dekker's *Satiromastix*, 1602, marked also perhaps by Theobald, and the *Poetaster*, *The New Inn* 1631, as well as a number of Jonson's masques. Whalley concluded his preface thanking Garrick for many "personal civilities . . . his ready concurrence in furnishing whatever would adorn the work, his kindness in procuring some names, the most distinguished for quality and taste, to honour my subscription."

Garrick had assembled in his collection 11 of the 12 Jonson quartos; only the quarto of *Everyman in His Humour* is missing, certainly not because of rarity. In addition he had eight very rare masques and entertainments in quarto, and the 1610–40 folio in two volumes, but Mrs Garrick would never part with the folios and they were sold with Garrick's library in 1823. Ultimately Garrick, out of his knowledge and appreciation of Jonson, revived four of his plays, adapting the text of the first two with particular care and imagination: *Everyman in His Humour*, *The Alchemist*, *Eastward Hoe*, and *Epicoene, or The Silent Woman*.

Finally to complete the record of Garrick's support in the editing and publishing of the early English dramatists that drew upon the resources of his collection, brief mention must be made of two: Samuel Derrick's edition of Dryden and Francis Gentleman's of Shakespeare. Though of minor consequence in later Dryden scholarship, Derrick's *Miscellaneous Works of John Dryden*, 4 vols., J. & R. Tonson, 1760 (2d ed. 1767), is biographically interesting because of the collaboration that turned it out, "the solid, unpolished work of a pioneer."[20] Again as earlier, Garrick had on his hands an unsuccessful actor-playwright, for whom like Johnson he had a kindness. He doubtless persuaded Tonson to publish the collection of Dryden's writings other than his plays. Derrick and Johnson collaborated on the "Life of John Dryden, Esq." prefixed to volume I. Derrick made a special effort to assemble the various prologues and epilogues for plays and public occasions, other than Dryden's own plays, some 40 in all, "for the dates of many of them we are particularly obliged to Mr. Garrick, who with great civility gave us the use of his fine collection of old 4to plays." Further Garrick must have supplied Derrick with the list he was drawing up as a part of his intention to write a history of prologues and epilogues, a plan that regrettably he never carried out (1000).

The second acquaintance, Francis Gentleman, would-be actor and playwright, early won Garrick's friendship and patronage. Though Garrick came to reprobate the actor-writer, he charitably sought to relieve one "born & Educated a Gentleman; He has gone through great variety of distress" (213). To this end Garrick doubtless proposed and certainly gave his permission as manager of Drury Lane for the publishing of 18 of Shakespeare's plays "As they are now performed at the Theatres Royal in London," that is the promptbooks from both theatres, 24 in all, the ones from Drury Lane supplied by William Hopkins. The collection was published in 1774 in four volumes by John Bell, dedicated to Garrick "as a grateful, tho' small, return, for the infinite pleasure, and extensive information, derived from your exquisite performance and judicious remarks" on Shakespeare. The 800 and more subscriptions to the volumes are a measure of Garrick's solicitations and charity. The nature and value of the promptbook as distinct from the scholarly text was never more authoritatively and decisively stated than in the advertisement of Bell's edition, at Garrick's request if not approximately in his own words: "We hold ourselves bound in justice and gratitude to Mr. *Garrick*, to mention a delicate fear, which he suggested, when we first solicited his sanction and assistance. This fear was, lest the prunings, transpositions, and other alterations, which, in his province as a manager he had often found necessary to make, or adopt, with regard to the text, for the convenience of representation, or accommodation to the powers and capacities of his performers, might be misconstrued into a critical presumption of offering the literati a reformed and more correct edition of our author's works; this being by no means his intention, we hope it will not become liable to such an unmerited misconstruction."

The Bell-Gentleman edition of 24 promptbooks Garrick knew was to be reckoned with in theatre history as a primary source, specifically about productions. They were not to be ranked critically as were the "reformed and more correct editions" of Johnson, Steevens, Capell, and Malone for the literati.

The recovery of the quarto text was but the first essential step in the progress of literary study of plays. The next was to recover the meaning of the word in the context of the play and in the historical time and place of composition. Early editors caught up in this obligation, often glossed texts with conjectural guesses and emendations, rather than seeking to recover difficult meanings by laboriously reading in contemporary literature to catch the words in other contexts. To do so required assembling a large library of generally rare and expensive books. To meet this obligation Capell assembled what he called his Shakespeariana, to which he resorted in glossing the text of Shakespeare and preparing the formal glossary of 80 pages in volume I of his *Notes and Various Readings*.

Appropriately a measure of Garrick's impact on contemporary scholarship—not from his fame and wealth, but from the intellectual quality of his friendship—survives from a modest, all-but-forgotten scholar, Richard Warner, who when forestalled as an editor of Shakespeare labored on as a lexicographer, and endowed his college at Oxford with a library rich in early English drama and literature. A graduate of Wadham College, sometime resident in Lincoln's Inn, he retired in 1743 to his estate, Harts, at Woodford Row in Essex, where he maintained a botanical garden of note. Only a few laconic letters survive of a correspondence with Garrick, the last expressing Garrick's distress over Warner's fatal illness (539,700,885,1339). How or when the two men first met is not known, but in 1768 Warner recalled "many favours received during the course of a long uninterrupted and happy acquaintance." He was early "a great black letter critic," and before 1766 had "been long making collections for a new Edition of Shakespeare: but on Mr. Steevens' advertisement of his design . . . he desisted."[21] He projected a translation of Plautus, but in deference to Garrick he assisted Garrick's good friend Bonnel Thornton in his edition of 1766 in two volumes of the Roman dramatist. Warner corrected and revised the text for the edition of 1769, and continued with three additional volumes in 1773–74, published by Becket and DeHondt and dedicated to Garrick, "as an instance of his sense of the uninterrupted friendship with which he had long favoured him, as well as his kind advice in the prosecution of it" (xxx,xi). The advice included access to Garrick's library.

Anticipated by Steevens in editing Shakespeare, Warner turned to preparing a glossary, working through the whole Shakespeare canon. Having made some progress, he published on 1 January 1768 with a subsidy from Garrick and by Garrick's bookseller-printers Davies, Becket, and DeHondt, *A Letter to David Garrick, Esq. Concerning the Glossary to the Plays of Shakespeare.*

In the 92 pages of the *Letter*, Warner considers the deficiencies of older glossaries, supplies a succession of examples which he corrects (with a digressive defense of Shakespeare's learning in answer to Farmer). The glossary (pp. 93–110) gives a sampling under the letter A. Warner labored on with unflagging industry until his death in 1775, when he willed Garrick his manuscripts of 41 quarto volumes of notes, 20 octavo columns of glossary, an interleaved copy of Tonson's 1734 edition of Shakespeare in eight volumes, the original manuscript of the *Letter*, and an alphabetical index to words in Beaumont and Fletcher requiring explanation.[22] The glossary was for Garrick to publish at his discretion, the proceeds to go to his Fund for Decayed Actors.[23] Warner willed his library to Wadham College, where it has been preserved but neglected. The collection was especially rich in seventeenth-century folios, and collected editions of the early dramatists, more than 30 quartos of minor dramatists, some rare early editions of Plautus and Terence, as well as all the folios and later editions of Shakespeare.[24] Warner's *Letter* and load of unpublished manuscripts attest a somewhat overwhelming esteem and affection for Garrick as a collector, scholar, and textual critic of old plays.[25]

Another in the long line of scholar-editors dependent on Garrick and his materials was Thomas Hawkins, M.A. of Magdalen College Oxford, who undertook to re-edit Hanmer's edition of Shakespeare at the invitation of the Clarendon Press. He needed Garrick's quartos, and Garrick's character shines through the bibliographical details of the association. One of the features of the new edition was to be a glossary. Hawkins, finding recent eighteenth-century scholarship and editions of little help, was in his own words, "naturally thrown into a course of reading the productions of our first dramatic writers," for which he sought the quartos, and as a result set about assembling texts for another edition of early plays. Thomas Warton introduced him to Garrick, and Garrick responded (12 April 1771) that he would be pleased to assist any friend of Warton's, "if he is in town he shall with pleasure collate any plays, &c. in my collection" (627). Garrick remarked, moreover, that Dodsley's *Select Collection of Old Plays* was full of errors, and suggested it might be better to make a new selection than to reprint any of the plays in Dodsley. Hawkins accepted Garrick's advice and avoided all but two of the inaccurate Dodsley texts. Hawkins prepared most carefully for the work, and eventually Garrick sent him in Oxford a "great part of my old collection" (877). Hawkins died before the work was fully completed, and Garrick had to recover his quartos from the widow. The three volumes were, however, published in 1773 as *The Origin of the English Drama, Illustrated in Its Various Species*. Of the 14 plays therein, the first *Candlemas Day* (later called *The Massacre of the Innocents*) was from the Digby manuscript in the Bodleian. The other 13 all from printed texts, were to be found in the Garrick Collection, five directly acknowledged, four identifiable (among others *Soliman and Perseda*, with Theobald's notes). At his death Hawkins was contemplating "another selection of our old dramatic compositions" (xviii) that eventually was carried out by George Steevens in subject if not in precise plan.[26]

Sensitive all his life to the general prejudice accorded the low social status of actor, as well as to an early patronizing reference of Birch and the Wartons to "our little Garrick," Garrick must have welcomed above many of life's rewards William Warburton's acceptance of him as a close friend and equal in cultural and intellectual stature. As early as 1747 in making a gift of his eight-volume edition of Shakespeare, Warburton wrote to Garrick, "These volumes are presented by the editor to Mr. Garrick, as a mark of regard due to the merit of a true genius excelling in his profession."[27] As late as 1771 Garrick on his part asserted he had "great intimacy" with the Bishop of Gloucester (622). During a long association and correspondence of 30 years and more, they met as intellectual equals on contemporary literature and the theatre, an acceptance that Warburton accorded to few. Garrick submitted his own writings to Warburton and sought his judgment on new plays to be produced at Drury Lane. Warburton with his predilection for controversy, espoused Garrick's side in a number of confrontations. They and their wives were often guests of each other, and they shared friends that were well identified as "Warburtonians." Of Garrick's familiarity with Warburton's library, one passage in a letter from Warburton of 4 May 1756 serves better than a long summary to epitomize both their associations as bibliophiles and Warburton's respect for Garrick:

> The accommodating you with the plays you want of Shakspear, besides the trifle, is but justice to one who can make so good an use of them, and has entertained so proper and curious a design as the writing the history of our stage; which I wish you would pursue in good earnest.
>
> I suppose the Plays you want are in two 4to. vols., which Mr. Blackbourne borrowed of me for one Mr. Capel, I think his name is. Pray

take them of him, and cut out what you want. I have two more 4to. vols. in London, of Shakspear's Plays; and if there be any in those which you have not, you are very welcome to add them to your own collection. I have the First Edition of Jonson's "Every Man in his Humour," (if it be not lost,) where the names and scene are Italian: this is much at your service, if you have it not. And, I think, his Catiline, with all the imitations from the Classics quotted in the margin.[28]

Presumably Garrick availed himself of the offer of the Jonson quartos, as Whalley in his edition of Jonson acknowledged both as from the Garrick Collection.

Controversies long since dead, the bitterness of those that Warburton cut down to size, the exultation of lesser and later scholars at finding one who spoke with assurance occasionally mistaken have beclouded any evaluation of the creative influence Warburton had on Garrick, and what the long association meant to Garrick. Warburton was more to Garrick than a dominating public figure, an authority on almost every subject, the center if not the head of a circle of respected scholars, whose approval was the stamp of acceptance, a frank critic, and a trusted friend. For both men "the most agreeable subject in the world was Literary History." Although Garrick never realized his wish to be a literary historian, an ambition perhaps "entertained" from Warburton's influence, Garrick with Warburton's help as a collector-patron of letters, enabled others in various ways to accomplish his "proper and curious a design as the writing the history of our stage."[29]

A history of English drama, however, gradually involved chronology and biography as well as bibliography. Contending with the prevailing anonymity of early drama, booksellers and bibliographers had early compounded the confusion by assigning plays to authors who were little more than names. Garrick collected most extensively practically all the books to date on chronology and biography, notably those treating of actors. The culmination, the repository of over half a century of bibliographical, chronological, and biographical studies of English drama and dramatists was David Erskine Baker's *Companion to the Play-House*, 1764, in two volumes, later and better known as the *Biographia Dramatica*, fulsomely dedicated to Garrick, "unknown to Mr. *Garrick*," and published among others by Garrick's own booksellers Becket and DeHondt, with Dodsley's "A Brief View of the Rise and Progress of the English Stage" from his *Select Collection of Old Plays* and "Critical Reflections on the Old English Dramatick Writers" that Garrick had commissioned by Colman for the edition of Massinger. Of Baker's relations or indebtedness to Garrick, nothing has been discovered; he cannot be positively identified as a Baker who was a member in some capacity of the Drury Lane company. But he and his wife did play at Edinburgh, and at some provincial English theatres. The probability is that Garrick supported the project. Revised in 1774 by Isaac Reed with Malone's help, the *Biographia Dramatica* became the standard encyclopedia on dramatic writers. Steevens used an interleaved copy to index the Garrick Collection, as Kemble did later for his drama collection. As it turned out, however, Garrick's ambition for a history as such was realized in the works of several close scholar friends who accepted him as an equal in scholarship. The first of these was Thomas Percy, who made a notable contribution to the history of English drama in his "Essay on the Origins of the English Stage" (1765).

How early Percy met Garrick, his senior by 12 years, is not known, but by May 1761 he was already received into the Johnsonian circle, associated with scholars and publishers, and attending the theatre.[30] On 27 May of that year he breakfasted with Garrick and attended a rehearsal of *King Lear*. Tonson seems to have proposed the editing of George Villiers's, the Duke of Buckingham's works, and on 22 May Percy saw Garrick play Bayes in *The Rehearsal*; by 12 June Percy contracted with Tonson for the editing.[31] On 10 October Tonson wrote him: "I . . . rec^d a box containing 9 volumes of M^r Garricks which I have sent to him this morning—I have not yet got from him the plays you wrote for but I hope to send them next week."[32] A little over a year later, on 10 November 1762, Percy wrote David Dalrymple, Lord Hailes: "I had long before been employed in preparing [a new key to *The Rehearsal*] and M^r Garrick very politely gave me access to his *collection* for that purpose. I have accordingly read over every play therein, which was published between the year 1660, and 1672 when the Rehearsal was first printed: the number is a little less than 200."[33] Though not explicitly acknowledged, Percy had also at his disposal Garrick's copy of *The Rehearsal* with Theobald's notes. More at length in the "Advertisement," he added that Garrick's Collection was, "by far the compleatest ever made in those kingdoms. Here the editor found almost every dramatic piece in our language, and had thereby an advantage, which no former compiler ever had, in having all his material already collected in hand." We can only sorely regret that for various causes the edition of Villiers's works never reached the public; yet all was not lost. Percy had annotated an interleaved copy of Langbaine with around 108 references to Garrick copies, and in 1763 he included Oldys's extensive notes from Oldys's copy loaned Percy by Thomas Birch, who had purchased it at the sale of Oldys's library. In turn Thomas Warton, Edmund Malone, and John Nichols transcribed the annotations in Percy's copy, adding their own annotations in their copies of Langbaine, and thereby learned of the resources in the Garrick Collection.[34]

As mentioned earlier Garrick preserved in his collection 11 very early printed romances, as a result of their being bound in two gatherings similar to the play quartos. They were given the press numbers K IX and K X, often cited by scholars in acknowledgments. Although Percy's exacting scholarship produced only some collateral results for his generation, he accomplished one of the half dozen long-lasting scholarly books of the century in his *Reliques of Ancient English Poetry* (1765). Of the 31 pieces in the first edition, Percy included nine from the Garrick Collection, specifically acknowledging them, and in several instances citing the press numbers. He also refers to three plays in the Collection, and in the Preface makes a more general acknowledgment: "In Mr Garrick's curious Collection of old plays are many scarce pieces of ancient poetry, with the free use of which he indulged the editor, in the politest manner" (I, xv–xvi).[35]

From his collecting, study, and editing of early English literature, Percy progressed to some comprehension of literary history. He included in the *Reliques* of 1765 and in the second edition of 1767 he expanded four essays, the titles indicative of the subject matter: "An Essay on the Ancient English Minstrels," "An Essay on the Origin of the English Stage," "On the Metre of Pierce Plowman's Vision," and "On the Ancient Metrical Romances," in the last three of which he refers to books in the Garrick Collection. Garrick, on his part, wrote Percy on 3 April [1776], shortly before the triumphant close of his final season at Drury Lane, when he was looking forward to retirement: "Shall I ask a favour of You? I am hunting after the rise, progress & Establishment of Prologues and Epilogues, from their first appearance to this Moment, in all Ages, & at all times—May I not hope for a little of Your friendly assistance" (1000). Between the distractions of fame and social life and the exhaustion of a painful and fatal illness, Garrick never realized his wish, his ambition to be remembered as a historian of the theatre.[36]

One final incident, fragmentary in detail, confirms the very intimate rapport that Garrick enjoyed with Percy. Percy projected an edition of Surrey's poetry to occupy him for 45 years but never completed. On the 13 March 1763, Percy wrote Thomas Warton: "By Mr. Garrick's and D[r] Hoadley's interest, I have procured and have now in my hands, Surrey's Translation . . . of the *Aeneid*, for Tottel in 1557, from M[r] Warner, of London" who apparently had borrowed it from Garrick.[37] For in a postscript to a letter to Steevens in 1774, Garrick wrote,

"Shakespear gave y$^e$ first Ed: of Surry's Poems to one of [Brome's] Ancestors living in Warwickshire—Brome sent to Me & I lent it to D$^r$ Percy" (814). The poems in question are the *Songs and Sonnets*, printed in 1557 by Richard Tottel and since then known as *Tottel's Miscellany*. Robert Brome was proctor in the Lichfield Consistory and acquainted with Garrick as a fellow townsman. Garrick must have given the book in question to Percy as the copy in question with "Rob$^t$ Brome Lichfield" on the title page passed with some others of Percy's books eventually to A. S. W. Rosenbach, the Philadelphia bookseller.[38]

Fragmentary though the surviving records may be, so often the results when good friends met often, the evidence adds up to the conclusion that Garrick with Percy, as he did also with other scholars, passed beyond the stage of the affluent and benevolent patron, to a friendship and participation in the emerging development of English literary history.

Joseph and Thomas Warton may, early on, have spoken in patronizing fashion of "our little Garrick," but soon recognized his interests off stage in the literature which became their own interest. In company and correspondence with them Garrick became more socially and intellectually at ease than perhaps with any of his other literary friends, though it is not possible to reconstruct the duration and intimacy of their associations in London and Garrick's visits to the brothers in Winchester and Oxford. He deferred to their general literary judgment; "a play underwritten by the two Wartons would certainly merit every attention." He sent to each of the brothers his *Ode upon Dedicating a Building and Erecting a Statue to Shakespeare at Stratford-upon-Avon*, nervously hoping for their approbation more than from anyone else and wishing "from my soul that the Ode" had come from Thomas Warton (542). Early in this literary friendship, Garrick not only associated with the Wartons but was also welcomed into their literary circle that included Hurd, Hoadley, Hogarth, and Colman; on one occasion Garrick interceded in a misunderstanding between Hogarth and Joseph Warton, the details of which are outside present purposes. Garrick graciously acknowledged Joseph Warton's tribute to him in Warton's *Essay on Pope* (1756): "We therefore of Great-Britain have perhaps more reason to congratulate ourselves, on two very singular phenomena; I mean, Shakespeare's being able to portray characters so very different as FALSTAFF, and MACBETH; and Garrick's being able to personate so inimitably LEAR, or an ABLE DRUGGER. Nothing can more fully demonstrate the extent and versatility of these two original geniuses."[39]

As for Thomas Warton, Garrick from the first knew full well his poetry, his studies, his appointment as professor of poetry at Oxford, and acknowledged a presentation copy of his *Observations on the Fairy Queen of Spencer* (1754) the second edition of 1762. Encouraged by the generally favorable response to the *Observations* Warton embarked on a history of English poetry, to be interrupted and delayed for 20 years before its incomplete publication in three volumes in 1774–81. From Percy's annotated copy of Langbaine and the *Reliques*, Warton learned of the range of the Garrick Collection, and later on 23 June 1769, wrote Garrick from Trinity College: "I wish I could have had the pleasure of a longer conversation with you at Oxford. I wanted to talk to you about a work which I have now in hand. I am writing the History of English Poetry, upon a plan which I once mentioned to you; and you were so kind as to encourage me to proceed" (808).[40] He then asked to borrow the metrical romances in volumes K IX and X; Garrick responded listing the romances he sent and adding: "It gives me the greatest pleasure to hear of your intended work—it is a performance we much want" (542). Warton later acknowledged Garrick's assistance; professing that "it is no part of my plan, accurately to mark the progress of our drama";[41] nevertheless he did not pass over some early dramatic poetry. From Percy's annotations in Langbaine, he borrowed directly from Garrick, later in the *History* acknowledging his indebtedness. One passage embodies the quality of the assistance: "The only copy of Skelton's moral comedy of MAGNIFICENCE now remaining, printed by Rastell, without a date in a thin folio, has been obligingly communicated to me by Mr. Garrick; whose valuable collection of old Plays is alone a complete history of our stage."[42] To be sure Warton's acknowledged indebtedness to Garrick was very minor compared to the great range of sources cited in the three volumes of the *History*. It was the spirit and common knowledge that counted more for Warton and Garrick, and we must lament, as surely as Warton must have, that Garrick never realized an ambition expressed in a brief postscript to a letter he wrote Warton in April 1771: "I have mislaid your note you gave me, of the books I sent you from my collection —will you some time or other let me know again what they are, for I am about to print my catalogue at the end of some nonsense of mine" (627).

The hour was too late in 1771 for Garrick ever to find the time to round out his collecting with a published catalogue or to set down some of his mature thoughts on the history and merits of English drama. If it were not that "literature and dramatic poetry were to the last his favourite topics" he could not have endured a friendship with the unstable, even irascible George Steevens or have enabled Steevens to accomplish some of the better scholarship of the century. Although Garrick suffered occasionally from acts emanating from Steevens's puckish and unstable personality, he was much interested in Steevens the productive scholar. Whatever the origins or duration of their relations before 1765, the letter Steevens wrote that year, 27 December, to Garrick accompanying a presentation copy of Steevens's excellent *Twenty Plays of Shakespeare*, establishes the tone and quality of most of their subsequent creative collaboration. Only a part of the letter is here quoted: "I hope you will oblige me so far as to accept of a work which I could never have carried into execution but for the assistance you lent me, which was made more valuable by the ready manner in which you granted the favour I came to solicit. [Rejecting Capell, his library and exactness, Steeven's then continues.] I am contented with the spirit of the author you first taught me to admire, and when I found you could do so much for him, I was naturally curious to know the value of the materials he had supplied you with; and often when I have taken the pen in my hand to try to illustrate a passage, I have thrown it down again with discontent when I remembered how able you were to clear that difficulty by a single look, or particular modulation of the voice, which a long and laboured paraphrase was insufficient to explain half so well." And also in the "Preface to the Reader," Steevens publicly acknowledged his indebtedness: "Mr. GARRICK's zeal would not permit him to withhold anything that might ever so remotely tend to shew the perfections of that author who could only enable him to display his own."[43]

On 1 February 1766, only a few months after the above letter to Garrick, Steevens announced in *The London Chronicle* that he was undertaking the re-editing of Johnson's Shakespeare, and included in his public appeal for help the following paragraph: "He is happy to have Permission to enumerate Mr. Garrick among those who will take such a trouble on themselves [to receive such communications]; and is no less desirous to see him transmit Part of that Knowledge of SHAKESPEARE to POSTERITY without which, he can be his best Commentator no longer than he lives."[44] The close friendship with much communication in person and by letter, interrupted only when Garrick was briefly incensed by some witty verses of Steevens at the expense of the Jubilee, continued until the publication of the Johnson-Steevens edition in 1773. During the six to seven years of the revising, Steevens borrowed and worked through the entire collection, preparing a catalogue which he gave to Garrick by checking an interleaved copy of Baker's *Companion to the Play-House*. He even proposed revising and publishing Capell's Catalogue of Garrick's Collection but was deterred by the lack of any order. Eventually Steevens submitted to Garrick for his corrections the advertisement later included in the prefatory matter of the edition. The covering letter from Hampstead, 3 December 1772, must be read in full.

> Dear Sir
>
> The Legitimacy of an Edition of Shakespeare can no more be ascertained to Satisfaction, without the Testimony of the Poet's High Priest, than that of a Prince can be lawfully proved, unless the archbishop attends in Person. I am therefore desirous that you should glance your Eye over the enclosed Pages which are to announce the Birth, or (not to speak profanely) the Regeneration of Dr. Johnson's Edition, to the World,—I have taken the Liberty to introduce your Name, because I have found no Reason to say that the Possessors of the old Quartos were not sufficiently communicative.—You will remember the Circumstance to which I allude.[45]

Very few "circumstances" in the eighteenth century have been more often repeated and distorted. No one both understood and supported Johnson more in his deliberate and laborious editing of Shakespeare beginning in 1745 than Garrick. Familiar with the disorder in Johnson's library, his indolence in returning borrowed books, Garrick provided for Johnson, as he did for no other scholar: he made Johnson "welcome to the full use of his collection . . . he left a key with a servant to have a fire and every convenience for him," and in his absence in Italy he instructed his brother George to let Johnson have the volumes he sought. In the final stages of the editing, Johnson was sending Garrick proof, and after publication returning books he had borrowed.[46]

The "circumstances" in question were to be found in the preface of the edition, 1765, in which Johnson wrote regarding the Shakespeare quartos as sources for texts: "I collated such copies as I could procure, and wished for more, but I have not found the collectors of these rarities very communicative" (p. 105). Joseph Warton, with his flare for literary gossip, doubtless spread the word as he certainly wrote: "Garrick is entirely off from Johnson, and cannot, he says, forgive him his insinuating that he withheld his old editions, which were always open to him; nor, I suppose, his never mentioning him in all his work."[47] There is no proof to support this conjecture or supposition. Actually Johnson was on the defensive of his own indolence; if Garrick was disturbed, it was not over the neglect of public recognition for his collection, but rather that Johnson had failed to respond to his invitation and the opportunity. Later Boswell, recalling the incident, fully vindicated Garrick, and Steevens in the above letter and in the preface to the re-editing of Johnson's Shakespeare made full amends. On the other hand, Garrick's response to Steevens's repeated borrowings was "You are most welcome in Y$^r$ *own name* to any thing I can command—I have the highest regard for Y$^r$ great learning & abilities, & most Sincerely esteem You as one of the first Worthies in the literary World" (808).

Their long association for 15 years and more, socially and by correspondence, of which many letters survive,[48] ranges beyond the editing of Shakespeare. They were often together socially, notably as members of Johnson's Club, the election to which Steevens thanked Garrick on 3 March 1773, for "your sufrage and your congratulations." Garrick gave Steevens prior notice and tickets for performances of Shakespeare's plays; they borrowed and loaned books, and Steevens sent Garrick gifts of old quartos. They openly and in confidence discussed general theatrical matters such as new plays or revivals, periodical controversies, and Garrick's acting, Steevens severely criticizing the cast of Lusignan in *Zara* and praising *Antony and Cleopatra*. The ultimate example of their mutual respect and assistance developed when Garrick undertook to prepare a new acting version of *Hamlet*: he submitted it to Steevens who responded with extensive comment and approval.

Almost invariably Steevens's prickly pride or perverse sense of humor disrupted his human relations. Late in 1775, he broke with Garrick over some misunderstanding or disagreement, not identified, that was stirred up in the murky streams of the anonymous and pseudo-anonymous press. The break was aggravated by George Hardinge's defense of Capell in an adverse comparison with Steevens (1778). Although Steevens was undoubtedly indebted to Garrick for texts for his *Six Old Plays*, 1779, he made no acknowledgments. Years later after Farmer's death in 1797, Steevens commented to Percy after going through a bundle of letters to Farmer, including letters from Capell and presumably Garrick: "Garrick appears to have been as mischievous as a Monkey. He made himself a party to Y$^r$ squabbles, that he might thereby obtain an opportunity to laugh at you."[49] Though ostensibly caricaturing Garrick, Steevens ironically was only revealing his own conduct which had included concocting romances for Percy, a dogmatically perverse commentator on Shakespeare, and a list of nine quartos for Garrick "not to be found in your catalogue nor any other," to which should be added "before or since," all to propagate squabbles for his own amusement—rather pathetic in a man capable of generosity, candor, and humility.

The positive results of their association far outweighed the negative.

The apostolic succession in collecting early English literature and drama continued through Steevens to the end of the century. The mantle, Langbaine's *Lives and Characters of the English Dramatick Poets*, passed to Oldys, to Birch, to Percy, to Steevens, who transcribed Oldys's and Percy's notes into a copy of his own and then continued the accumulation of annotations often acknowledged as from the Garrick Collection; and then in turn Steevens loaned his copy to Malone before Steevens's own Langbaine ended up in the British Museum. All the while that Steevens was borrowing from the Garrick Collection and consulting it and adding to it, he was assembling a very extensive collection of old plays on his own, quite similar to the Garrick Collection in titles, sources, and bindings, now preserved intact in the Bodleian as part of the Edmund Malone bequest. In 1776 Malone went to London and by the next year was settled there and corresponding with Steevens. Drawn to the young Malone by his great promise as a scholar, Steevens by an act of unprecedented generosity gave Malone the old plays assembled to date. The benefaction was recorded by Malone in the first volume of what is now the Malone Collection: "This valuable Collection of Old Plays in 119 volumes (54 small and 65 large Quartos) was given to me by my friend George Steevens Esq$^{re}$. The volumes subsequent to the above numbers have been added by me [signed] Edmund Malone August 1778."

The similarities in two respects between the Garrick and the Steevens collections attest the close associating of the two men in collecting. First of all the *graffiti* in the Steevens quartos are often very similar to those in Garrick's, too extensive and secondary to be recorded here, but including the identification marks of Richard Smith, Langbaine, Luttrell, Harleian, Bridgewater, Thomas Rawlinson, Dulwich College, and Capell, as well as many lesser one-time owners. Interestingly enough Malone, in annotations in the Steevens quartos, refers five times to Garrick's Collection as such and one other time to the Garrick Collection in the British Museum; the distinction supports the probability that Malone actually consulted Garrick's quartos while still in his possession. Secondly Steevens had his quartos bound up in the same manner as Capell and Garrick, by size only in gatherings of five to eight titles, with a preliminary flyleaf listing the contents, and in uniform full-leather bindings with "Old Plays," "G.S.," and volume numbers on all the spines, a practice continued by Malone with his acquisitions and library.[50]

One comes away from the reading of the several hundred letters that have survived to and from Steevens with the impression that Steevens was in general remarkably generous in helping collectors, publishers, and scholars: Dodsley, Warburton, Johnson, Sir John Hawkins, Warner, Nichols, and the later generation of Isaac Reed and Malone. He was much liked as a friend, entrusted with confidences, informed, considerate, with a sense of humor, occasionally exercised at the expense of the vanity of others. His influence on Garrick was all to the good. He continued active in the third generation of eighteenth-century scholars who attained a fullness if not a perfection in the editing of Shakespeare and the history of English literature, a generation that was ever mindful of a great indebtedness to Garrick. Steevens assisted in the transferring of the Garrick Collection to the British Museum; he had printed Capell's Catalogue of his great gift to Trinity College; he enriched the Bodleian through Malone with his collection of old quartos; he contributed to the *Biographia Dramatica* scattered asperities on Garrick but on the whole an appreciative biography.

In an analytical rather than chronological biography, by categories and not synthesis, a biographer, far more than his readers, is ever aware of the dangers of an imbalance of emphasis, that in isolating and pursuing one aspect, the relation of the part to the whole may suffer, more immediately the vital and pervasive relation of Garrick as a student of the drama to the ultimate excellence as an actor. George Steevens caught in a short passage in a letter to Garrick, the unity, balance and relationship that many others implied and expressed, and must be kept in mind by readers, when he heard from Dr. Hoadly that Garrick was contemplating retirement: "Such news from you will hereafter incline me to prefer reading plays, wherein I have remembered and seen you, to the attending them at the theatre; and suffer my fancy to revive your action and manner (as far as I am able) to accompany those scenes which I must never expect to see represented again. I cannot but remember such things were—'and were most dear to me:' and yet—he hates you, 'That would upon the rack of this rough world, / Stretch you out longer,—' and I must bid King Lear farewell with the same hopes as old Kent did, of his being happier."[51]

The distinction between a life and a heritage may be illustrated in a lesser incident involving James Boswell and Garrick, "the man whom from a boy I used to adore and look upon as a heathen god,"[52] an admiration and later friendship nourished by a succession of actors in the Edinburgh theatre, later association in London, and by correspondence. The harvest of this maturing and cherished friendship are some of the memorable passages in Boswell's *Life of Johnson* that make up a chapter, as it were, in Garrick's biography. According to Boswell, Garrick somehow supported the Scottish printer Donaldson in his publication of *The Works of Shakespeare*, in which the *Beauties*

*Observed by Pope, Warburton, and Dodd Are Pointed out*, Edinburgh 1753, in eight volumes, the texts prepared by Hugh Blair and the beauties selected by the notorious William Dodd, who was later hanged for forging Chesterfield's name on a note. This apparently was the edition peddled about at the Shakespeare Jubilee. Later Boswell sponsored a reprinting, again in Edinburgh, this time dedicated to Garrick by Boswell. There is no record, however, that Boswell himself ever looked into a quarto or book in Garrick's library. Nevertheless, he wrote Garrick introducing Hugo Arnot, a fellow advocate, who was writing a history of Edinburgh and wished to consult "a little dramatic piece" that Boswell knew only from Percy's *Reliques*, "entitled Robin Hood & the Friar," in the hopes that it might clarify "a Game or Play called Robin Hood of which frequent mention is made in our acts of Parliament."[53] Garrick granted the favor, and two years later in his *History of Edinburgh* Arnot devoted several pages to the game and in his preface, dated 1779, shortly after Garrick's death he wrote: "Let me not omit to acknowledge the polite and friendly attention with which DAVID GARRICK, Esq; communicated to me some curious and valuable manuscripts—Alas! I little thought this was to be a tribute to his memory only."

As the managing producer at Drury Lane Garrick had to employ a succession of artists, that is painters, dancers, singers, musicians, and composers, and often found them temperamentally trying, but one musician composer and his family came to be very dear to Garrick. Garrick may have first met Charles Burney, the historian of music, in the 1750s in the home of Fulke Greville. Shortly thereafter Garrick and Burney collaborated on several musical and dramatic productions. Sometime early in their association Burney, influenced by Garrick's zeal for collecting and for the history of drama and with Garrick's very considerable support, projected a history of music and set about assembling a library for that purpose. While he was abroad from 1763 to 1765, Garrick sent back to Burney reports of concerts and recitals he attended and purchased books, especially in Italy, for Burney's library. Word was spread by Garrick of Burney's aspiration, and on 9 August 1771 Garrick passed on to Burney the gift from Joseph Warton from Winchester "of an old and scarce book on music"—a sixteenth-century treatise by Franchinus Gaffurius.[54]

To round out his library and reinforce his studies by experience, Burney traveled abroad in France, Italy, and Germany in 1770–72. In fact the incentive, the scope, and the success of these tours originated with Garrick, who by letter introduced Burney to many influential acquaintances. For example, Burney through Garrick met Monnet in Paris who was "of great use to me afterwards in all my enquiries concerning books and persons."[55] These carefully projected and profitable tours were fully detailed in three volumes: *The Present State of Music in France and Italy*, 1 vol., 1771; *The Present State of Music in Germany, the Netherlands*, 2 vols., 1773, published by Becket, but only after the encouragement of Holderness [Robert D'Arcy], [William] Mason, and "Mr. Garrick, my sincere and beloved friend." *The History of Music* followed in 1776, again published by Becket and promoted in the public press by Garrick. Burney's library, sold in 1814, would have been a handsome founding collection for the British Museum.

The gentlemen collector-scholars who brought to a mature fulfillment eighteenth-century collecting, editing, publishing, and the history of the drama were Isaac Reed and Edmund Malone, both of whom in their younger days saw Garrick at Drury Lane and visited him in his by then famous Collection in the elegant library designed and built by the Adam brothers in the Adelphi, and both survived him as heirs to a great tradition he helped to establish. One is much tempted to digress on Reed's attractive personality, his long friendships with most of the literary and theatrical worthies of his day, who lived and worked in unbroken amity with Steevens, a very clubable man after Johnson's tastes, who in one way or another modestly and anonymously assisted his scholarly contemporaries, and whose great library was available to all. From seeing Garrick in Drury Lane beginning in 1762, Reed progressed to dining with Garrick as his guest, and undoubtedly after Garrick's examples and with his guidance, Reed began building up a library that occupied him for forty years. The sale of *Bibliotheca Reediana*, 2 November 1807, for 38 days (Sundays excepted) was a great social event in the London season, attended by many collectors, including Malone. Two items cannot be passed over in the heritage from Garrick: No. 8875, 20 manuscript notebooks covering his attendance at the theatre from 1762–1804;[56] and No. 8833, "Notitia Dramatica," preserving "the most material facts relating to the theatres in the last fifty years." These "MSS of Mr. Reed relating to the drama, were all purchased by a gentleman, who had previously made a considerable collection upon the subject and are arranged for publication," none other than John Genest whose *Some Account of the English Stage, from the Restoration, 1660 to 1830*, Bath, 1832, has been the basic encyclopedic history of the drama until recently superseded by *The London Stage, 1660–1800*, originally undertaken simply to bring Genest up to date.

During Garrick's later years, in his library and with his assistance,

Reed first revised and enlarged to nearly twice the original size, Baker's *Companion to the Play-House* (1762) into the *Biographia Dramatica*, long the standard reference encyclopedia on the drama. He then so thoroughly revised, undoubtedly in response to Garrick's proposal, Dodsley's *Select Collection of Old Plays* that the resulting second edition, 1780, in 10 volumes, in almost every respect a new publication, continued down through the years, with revisions, the one extensive and eclectic collection of English drama, aside from Shakespeare. He replaced ten plays with 12 of more literary and historic value; he prepared all new texts, "Corrected and Collated with the Old Copies"; he gave a bibliography of all the known editions of the 60 plays. The texts for all the plays he edited were in the Garrick Collection, except Dekker's and Middleton's *Roaring Girl* (1608), available to him in Malone's library. He prepared a glossary and wrote an excellent preface with emphasis on the value of the texts of the early quartos. Finally, he recalled the original source of the Garrick Collection in the Harleian Library, and then continued in what may well be accepted as the eighteenth-century tribute to Garrick, in these words: "He should be deficient in point of gratitude, if he omitted to notice the readiness with which he was allowed the free use of whatever Mr. Garrick's Library contained for the service of this work. . . . His wish to forward any literary undertaking is too well known, and hath been too often acknowledged by those who were obligated to him, to need any eulogium on this subject at present; and his death cannot but occasion a sigh to arise in the breast of every one who had the happiness of his acquaintance."[57]

Edmund Malone was the most respected successor to Garrick as a collector of quarto texts of early English drama, restorer of the text of Shakespeare, and historian of the drama. He must have come to know Garrick both at Drury Lane and in his private life before the actor's death early in 1779. In his annotations in his quartos he carefully made a distinction between Garrick's quartos in his library and the quartos in the Garrick Collection in the British Museum. In his first publication, if he were not assisted by Garrick, certainly, the subject was one that commanded Garrick's interest and support, "An Attempt to ascertain the Order, in which the Plays attributed to Shakespeare were written," in the 1778 edition of the Johnson-Steevens edition of Shakespeare. Malone's own edition of ten volumes in 11, 1790, was the culmination and perfection of eighteenth-century Shakespearean scholarship. Finally, his introduction to volume I, "An Historical Account of the Rise and Progress of the English Stage, and of the Economy and Usages of Our Ancient Theatres," a long history of

284 pages as much on the stage itself as on the literature, was accepted as the most extensive and authoritative history of English drama until Sir E. K. Chambers's *The Mediaeval Stage* (2 vols., 1903) and *The Elizabethan Stage* (4 vols., 1923).

Malone's final paragraph in his "Historical Account" is the most authoritative and just tribute, appropriate for a conclusion to this chapter, on Garrick as an actor, collector, and tireless restorer of early English drama and of Shakespeare. "But the great theatrical event of this year was the appearance of Mr. Garrick at the theatre in Goodman's Field, Oct. 19, 1741; whose good taste led him to study the plays of Shakespeare with more assiduity than any of his predecessors. Since that time, in consequence of Mr. Garrick's admirable performance of many of his principal characters, the frequent representation of his plays in nearly their original state, and above all, the various researches which have been made for the purpose of explaining and illustrating his works, our poet's reputation has been yearly increasing, and is now fixed upon a basis, which neither the lapse of time nor the fluctuations of opinion will ever be able to shake."[58]

Thirty years before, in 1769, James Granger in his *Biographical History of England* had also emphasized Garrick's intellectual depth and breadth in the recovery of the text of Shakespeare when he remarked, "Mr Garrick who thoroughly understands Shakespeare, has exhibited a thousand of his beauties, which had before escaped the mob of actors and readers; and has carried his fame much higher than it was carried in any other period. It is hard to say whether Shakespeare owes more to Garrick, or Garrick to Shakespeare."[59]

The recovery and the restoration of the poetry of early English drama was pursued both by Garrick and his scholarly friends, not in the isolation of their libraries but in vital reciprocal relations with the current theatre, the contemporary stage. When in London they attended the theatre, Johnson only limited by his failing eyesight; their studies began, as Steevens, Reed, and Malone did, in Drury Lane and Covent Garden, in Garrick's acting; the pervasive motive in collecting, editing, and historical studies was the enriching of the repertoire and quality of dramatic productions, and all sought to bring to bear historical knowledge and perspective in their criticisms. The end, the goal with Garrick and his scholarly friends, was acting in the theatre.

In this chapter Garrick has been isolated in one area of his private life, but in his collecting, and studies, and patronage, his friendships with the leading dramatic scholars of his day, Garrick emerges as a cultivated scholar himself, with a deep understanding of dramatic poetry, an eclectic collector of early English drama, a tireless restorer of the text both on the stage and in the literature of the drama, a patron of letters with some historical perspective. As an almost anonymous benefactor he left to us a heritage of a rich and balanced Collection of Old Plays, one of the founding benefactions of the British Museum, wherein succeeding generations have been cultivating a discriminating enjoyment of the history and the poetry of the drama.

# Part Three
## The Dramatist

.

# 7

## Garrick's Own Plays

·

IT SEEMS MORE THAN POSSIBLE that young David Garrick attended
Drury Lane Theatre 17 November 1739 on an evening of unpleasant
occurrences, while he was working the wine trade with his brother
Peter. The Reverend James Miller's *An Hospital for Fools* was attempting its second performance, but no one in the audience heard a
single word of it—"The Noise of these First-Night Gentlemen was so
great." The actors plodded through with it, but "the Spectators might
see their Mouths Wag, and that was all."[1] Miller, whom Garrick was to
come to know slightly (939), had written six earlier pieces (to augment
his meager income as a clergyman), the last of which, *The Coffee
House*, performed back in 1737, had keenly satirized what the young
lawyers in town thought to be Mrs Yarrow and her daughter, the actual
proprietress of Dick's Coffee House between the Temple Gates. Miller had denied any attempt at personal satire, but unfortunately the
engraver who drew the frontispiece for his published version had
sketched the design from the very coffee house in question. The lawyer
spectators objected violently, so when Miller's name as author of *An
Hospital for Fools* was disclosed, they blanked out the performance.
The play presented a sequence of fools old and young, male and female, come to be cured of their follies by Esculapius. None is cured,
but the silliness of many human types is there paraded.

### LETHE; OR, AESOP IN THE SHADES

If Garrick did not attend the performance of *An Hospital for Fools*,
he got a copy of the play, and upon its suggestions built his very first
essay in playwriting. Miller's concept seemed worth saving. He turned
it into *Lethe*, which was performed just five months later (15 April
1748) for Giffard's benefit at Drury Lane. Garrick's beginning was

auspicious. The one-act playlet is episodic presenting a procession of types for the merriment of the audience. The setting is on a day of the year when Proserpine allows Esop (the homey, wise philosopher) to invite mortals to drink the waters of Lethe, forget their psychological troubles, and return to earth happy again. Ten characters appear, all opinionated and all critical of the system under which they live. Each is more interested in presenting his own personality than in taking the cure. The parade technique was useful, for new types could be added and old ones dropped through years of performance, to keep the skit always up to date. Since no plot is evident no character depends upon another, and the lightly satirical vignettes could change with each season, as indeed some did. Two undercurrents persist: (a) thrice as much banter is leveled at the problems of marriage of convenience as upon other affairs, and (b) jab after sly jab comes through about theatre audience behavior. Other topics such as foreign imports, landscape gardening, language, taste, the Methodist movement, and the grand tour get their comeuppances. The play is gentle enough, its effectiveness residing in sprightly dialogue and topical reference.

James Miller's fate lingered in Garrick's mind, and he was daring enough to generalize upon it as his Poet in his *Lethe* explains to Esop what manners spectators have:

*Esop*: What are your troubles, Sir?

*Poet*: I have a sort of whistling—a singing—a whizzing . . . in my head, which I cannot get rid of—

*Esop*: Our waters give no relief to bodily disorders, they only affect the memory.

*Poet*: From whence all my disorder proceeds—I'll tell you my case, Sir—You must know I wrote a Play sometime ago, presented a dedication of it to a certain young nobleman . . . but before I could taste his bounty, my piece was unfortunately damn'd—I lost my benefit, nor could I have recourse to my patron, for I was told that his lordship play'd the best cat-call the first night, and was the merriest person in the whole audience.

*Esop*: Pray what do you call damning a play?

*Poet*: You cannot possibly be ignorant, what it is to be damn'd, Mr. Esop?

*Esop*: Indeed I am, Sir,—we had no such thing among the Greeks.

*Poet*: No, Sir!—No wonder then that you Greeks were such fine writers —It is impossible to be described or truly felt, but by the author himself—If you could get leave of absence from this world for a few hours, you might perhaps have an opportunity of seeing it for your-self—There is a sort of new piece comes upon our stage this very night, and I am pretty sure it will meet with its deserts.

His focus then shifts to the pruning which the manager gave the piece (striking out all the bawdry, wit, humor) and the wretchedness of the performers. Home thoughts these were to bait Garrick for the rest of his life.

Through his Fine Gentleman character, he wings again at unruly conditions in the theatre in 1740:

*Esop*: Pray, Sir, . . . how do you pass your time, the day for instance?

*Fine Gent*: I lie in bed all day, Sir.

*Esop*: How do you spend your evenings then?

*Fine Gent*: I dress in the evening, and go generally behind the scenes of both play houses; not, you may imagine, to be diverted with the play, but to intrigue, and shew myself—I stand upon the stage, talk aloud, and stare about—which confounds the actors, and disturbs the audience; upon which the galleries who hate the appearance of one of us, begin to *hiss*, and cry *off*, *off*, while I undaunted stamp my foot so—loll with my shoulder thus—take snuff with my right hand, and smile scornfully—thus—This exasperates the savages, and they attack us with vollies of suck'd oranges, and half-eaten pippins—

*Esop*: And you retire.

*Fine Gent*: Without doubt, if I am sober—for orange will stain silk, and an apple may disfigure a feature.

A late addition (1756) to the sequence was Lord Chalkstone, a charac-ter which Garrick played himself with infinite good humor, and one whom he developed later (1766) into Lord Ogleby in his *Clandestine Marriage*. Two passages, one bantering marriage of convenience, and the other having fun with the current rage for "Capability Brown's" fashions in landscape gardening, Garrick developed with great sophis-tication: Chalkstone is bored with everything:

*Esop*: Has your Lordship no wife nor children to entertain you?

*Lord Chalk*: Children! not I, faith—My wife has, for ought that I know—I have not seen her these seven years—

*Esop*: You surprise me!

*Lord Chalk*: 'Tis the way of the world, for all that—I married for a fortune; she for a title. When we both had got what we wanted, the sooner we parted the better—we did so; and are now waiting for the happy moment, that will give to one of us the liberty of playing the same farce over again.

The English garden with serpentine streams and carefully curved walks was setting itself up against the geometric patterns of the French:

> *Lord Chalk*: None of your waters for me, damn 'em all; I never drink any but at Bath—I came merely for a little conversation with you, and to see your Elysian Fields here—[looking through his glass] which, by the bye, Mr. Esop, are laid out most detestably—no taste, no fancy in the whole world!—Your river there—what d'ye call it?
>
> *Esop*: Styx.
>
> *Lord Chalk*: Aye, Styx—why 'tis strait as *Fleet ditch*—you should have given it a serpentine sweep, and slope the banks of it—The place, indeed, has very fine *capabilities*; but you should clear the wood to the left, and clump the trees to the right: in short, the whole wants variety, extent, contrast, and inequality.

The lady writer who cannot stop talking is a riot in herself, and so the skit goes. It was a triumph at every performance—until its last one, when (after his retirement) Garrick was asked to perform Lord Chalkstone before the King at court. Northcote described the scene—"not a look or a murmur testified approbation; there was profound silence —everyone only watched to see what the King thought of it. It was like reading to a set of wax figures." [2] But the piece written so early and updating itself along the way delighted the thousands.

So utterly delightful are Garrick's farces that one is tempted to tell the story, and savor the dialogue of each, for their variety is great, and their sureness of touch (apparent in the earliest) lasts throughout the whole series. This branch of writing became more and more important in the theatre as the century progressed, for in Garrick's period, on nearly 80 percent of the evenings when performances were given, such short after pieces accompanied a full-length main piece. And because of the third-act half-price custom these were often entertainment for the many. Shops closed and working people were out at eight in the evening. They could have a seat for sixpence or a shilling.

Garrick's itch for writing satisfied itself with a piece every year save six from 1740 until he retired in 1776. Overall, he created, adapted, or had a brush hand in 67 plays, which he prepared for the stage. Of his own creations 16 were farces, two were musicals, two more were dramatic romances (or as he called them, extravaganzas), two were pantomimes, and one was, in collaboration with George Colman, one of the best comedies of the period—*The Clandestine Marriage*. Just as creative were his adaptations of 26 Shakespearean plays, and

*Harvard Theatre Collection*
Garrick as Lord Chalkstone in *Lethe*.
Engraving by Gabriel Smith.

non-Shakespearean ones; and as his letters indicate, he had a creating hand in 20 more, as manager, director, and consultant.

## THE LYING VALET

But first see the artist amidst his own creations. His second play (1741) and most enduring farce, *The Lying Valet* (brief, packed with action, conflict, surprises, in a situational plot), ran, during his time on stage, for 369 performances in all the London theatres—outstripping the *Hamlets* (195) and *Lears* (135) and *Macbeths* (134) by a factor of three.[3] By the end of the century it had been performed another 35 times. It is the first of five of his farces Englished and altered from French originals. Tight in plot, *The Lying Valet* exemplifies the *vis comica* which he really desired in stage entertainment. Hauteroche's *Le Souper mal apprêté* is the source upon which Garrick worked.

Gayless having squandered his fortune, having pawned his furniture, and standing broke, falls in love with Melissa, a wealthy but wary young lady, and she with him. At her sharp-witted maid's urging she suggests that Gayless lay out a grand supper for her and some friends to test the sincerity of his passion. Sharp, his valet, thinks him mad even to hold the thought of doing so and seeks to avoid the affair, which will show their destitution and may block the marriage with its cash value from Melissa's dowry. He meets his match (almost) in Kitty Pry (Melissa's maidservant). Ruse after unsuccessful ruse of his to escape the dinner (including threats of Melissa's losing her reputation from neighbor gossip, a cry of fire, of smallpox, of thievery, along with disguises and mistaken identities) land him and his master deeper and deeper in hot water. Amusement builds as the plotting moves on at a quickening pace. All comes round happily, when Gayless's father consents to the marriage, and forgives his spendthrift son, who, sunk with love of Melissa, thinks he will be able to reform his ways. The farce became a favorite at both theatres. Sheer fun and sprightliness, with dialogue keeping pace with action, and situations always skating on the thin ice of near breakdown! Close-knit plotting, along with a spot of a theme, came to be central in Garrick's dramaturgy, and as Garrick's own Linco said in his *Cymon*, years later (1767), "the best purifier of the blood is mirth with a grain of wisdom." The play was, also, Garrick's second contribution to Giffard (who at the time was covertly sponsoring his acting career) for it was launched at

Goodman's Fields on 30 November 1741, about a month after this unknown "gentleman" made his stage debut, and with the author in the chief role. Garrick knew when he finished writing it that it was first class, but the tone of his letter to Peter in Lichfield is modest enough: "I believe You'll find it read pretty well, & in performance tis a general roar from beginning to End; & I have got as much Reputation in y^e Character of Sharp & is any Other Character I have perform'd, tho far different from y^e others" (20).[4]

## MISS IN HER TEENS; OR, THE MEDLEY OF LOVERS

Garrick had now been sparked by an English source, and a French one in his playwriting career, and these two veins he worked up alternately, but with native material gradually overcoming in quantity the inspiration from French farceurs. However, his next play, *Miss in Her Teens* (1747), was for a Covent Garden audience, where he was appearing during the season 1746–47, and where it had a run of 18 consecutive performances, followed by 22 more ere the season was over.[5] Garrick advertised in his printed version that it was based upon Dancourt's *La Parisienne*. Its swift-moving plot, series of clear but farcical complications, presentation of types of cowards, hypocrites, effeminate as well as braggadocio males, and doting old fathers, made it another popular after piece in the theatres for the next 30 years. The shrewd manager John Rich was so sure of its drawing power that he took the chance of noting on his playbills all during that first season (and got away with it) that "nothing under full prices will be taken."

Miss Biddy (a teen-ager) loves Captain Loveit (under his assumed name of Rhodophil). His father Sir Simon had purchased a commission for him and sent him off to the army. But Loveit returns with his man Puff to pick up where he left off with Biddy, who has a tidy fortune of £15,000. His father has also fallen in love with her and with her fortune. Captains Flash and Fribble (played by Woodward and Garrick) fall in love with her. She manages 'em all, but they all converge at once for a final showdown. The Fribble character had a long and meaningful career on the stage and in Garrick's life, as will be seen,[6] and Biddy defines it: "[A Fribble] speaks like a lady, . . . and never swears, . . . wears nice white gloves, and tells me what ribbons become my complexion, where to stick my patches, who is the best milliner, where they sell the best tea, and which is the best wash for my face, and the best paste for the hands; he is always playing with my fan, and shewing his teeth, and whenever I speak he pats me—so— and cries *The Devil take me, Miss Biddy, but you'll be my perdition.* —ha, ha, ha."

She sums up the purport of the piece, "Ladies, to fops and brag- garts ne'er be kind, / No charms can warm 'em, and no virtues bind, / Each lover's merit by his conduct prove, / Who fails in honor will be false in love," and she marries the honorable soldier Bob Loveit. Father Sir Simon is reconciled since the fortune will come into the family, and the Fribble and Braggart are dismissed.

Garrick is faithful to the French original, but trims and compresses the action, showing his craftsmanlike theatrical sense, for his text allows actors ample room for stage business and interpretation. One remembers his observation (later) to Baron Grimm "that Racine, so beautiful and enchanting to read, cannot be acted because he *says everything*, and leaves the actor nothing to do."[7] Garrick knew how he would identify the "fribble" character not only by dialogue and description and action, but by the way he planned to pronounce a number of words. He made sure succeeding actors would do the same by the spellings he dictated for his printed text—"crateer" for crea- ture, "meister" for master, "serous taalk" for serious talk, and "hooman nater" for human nature. In writing he saw every page from the actor's eye.

The critics got to it after its first continuous run, for an anonymous writer for the *Gentleman's Magazine* wrote about the "Farce of Miss in her Teens Anatomized," giving a critical analysis of its thin plot, thinner characters, and lack of an obvious moral, but commenting upon the excellent acting of Garrick, Woodward, and Mrs. Pritchard, even in parts of "nonsense, stupidity, and bawdry." He deplored the taste of the town which had welcomed it for 18 nights.[8]

## THE GUARDIAN

On 3 February 1759 Garrick produced his third farcical after piece based upon a French source, *The Guardian*, taken from Fagan's *La Pupille* (1734). It had a run of 15 performances until the end of the season, and 20 more scattered ones thereafter. It drew a huge audience that first performance (box receipts £285), because Garrick gave it and the proceeds as a benefit "of Mr. Christopher Smart, an ingenious young man in poetry, but now confined in a Mad House."[9] It very gently, nay amiably, satirizes "sentimental" over-genteel comedy, in a situation of "false delicacy" (nine years before Kelly's famous play of that name). The basis of the gentle fun is lack of communication by all hands. Heartly, a very considerate man in his mid-40s, has a young ward, Harriott, who adores him—but cannot confess it for modesty and for manners' sake. His neighbor Sir Charles Clackit has a nephew (a conceited fop) who wants to marry her and persuades himself that she loves him. Heartly will give her in marriage only to one she herself chooses. Garrick changed the French text somewhat to heighten the comedy and throw gentle satire upon all the characters. In the first act, Harriott gives so many hints as to the real target of her affections that the audience quickly catches on, though Heartly fails to. Young Clackit makes a fool of himself. Sir Charles, Heartly, and the maid Lucy seem mystified. In Act II, Harriott dictates a letter which Heartly takes down (little realizing that it is really addressed to him). He passes it on to Young Clackit. But in it Harriott expresses care for a more mature lover; Sir Charles hearing of this jumps to the conclusion that *he* is the real center of her affections. Lucy, a realistic matchmaker, tries to confirm this. Gradually, Heartly realizes, falls at Harriott's feet and is accepted. Garrick played Heartly to Mrs Pritchard's Harriott, and Garrick's additions to the French text (and especially in his stage directions) make Harriott and Heartly both the objects and agents of satire upon excessive sensibility.[10]

## NECK OR NOTHING

On 18 November 1766, to lighten an evening of John Hughes's *Siege of Damascus*, Garrick produced his light farce *Neck or Nothing*, which he called an "imitation" of Le Sage's *Crispin rival de son maître* (1707). Old Harlowe contracts for the marriage of his son to Nancy Stockwell. Young Harlowe, unbeknownst to his father, has already impregnated a girl in Dorsetshire, whom he has to marry at the insistence of her strong-minded brother. Nancy is really in love with one Belford. The problem is to bring about this love marriage with family consent, for her father (Stockwell) would also like her to marry Young Harlowe. Slip, Young Harlowe's servant, has been sent from Dorsetshire to tell Stockwell the news that the contract is off. But he is waylaid by Martin, Belford's servant. Martin, in the opening line of the play, has alerted the audience that he is "sick as a dog of being a waiter." So with Slip's aid he plans to substitute himself for Young Harlowe (whom the Stockwell family has never seen) in order to marry Nancy and run off with her dowry. Slip readily agrees, "If impudence will do our business, 'tis done and the £20,000 are our own." Martin, disguised in wedding clothes is just about to get away with the swindle as he and Stockwell come from the bank with £10,000 of the dowry as a down payment, when Belford recognizes him as his own servant, and calls the constables, who carry off the culprits. Belford and Nancy marry happily.

The dialogue, as in all Garrick plays, is sprightly. Garrick knew that an early outline of the plot and of the shallow characters involved would be useful to the audience, so made Martin quickly summarize for Slip the forces they would be dealing with:

> *Martin*: I am told he [Stockwell] is a mere citizen—who thinking himself very wise, is often outwitted, and his lady has as much vanity in her way; will never be old tho' turn'd sixty, and as irresolute and capricious as a girl of fifteen. And Miss, I suppose is like all other misses, wants to be her own mistress and her husband's, and in the meantime is govern'd by her Chambermaid, who will be too hard for us, if we don't look about us.

Lucy the maid is just that, in Garrick's play, for one of his changes in the basic story involves her sharpness. To get round her, Slip has to defame her character to render valueless her information to Stockwell about the real love of his daughter for Belford. He fabricates a story of her affair with Tom, a waiter, and two fine children she had by him. Garrick was not concerned, even in so brief a piece as this, to manage mere puppets on stage. He increased obstacles, and played up motivations. The play drew medium box receipts, which gave Garrick some pause. He mused over the matter at a revival of the piece in 1774, writing to Herbert Lawrence (a friend from Lichfield days) about the degree of gullibility which an audience would accept and instancing the strain to which he put this credibility in his *Neck or Nothing* (817).

## THE IRISH WIDOW

As late as 1772, Garrick in a week's time put together his two-act *petite pièce*, *The Irish Widow*, based upon Molière's *Le Mariage*

*Forcé*, for his actress Mrs Barry in a breeches part. But the brief time of composition belies the care Garrick took to make the end of his play differ from the savage satire of the Molière original. Though this is pure farce, his Widow Brady is made into a subtly fine character. The plot moves fast and is touched up with comfortable local color—Irish brogue in the dialogue, and reference to the status of blacks (slavery had been out for a number of years).

Mrs Brady, an attractive young widow, is penniless. Her father Sir Patrick O'Neale, wishes her to marry anew, and to a good fortune. Her first marriage, forced upon her by her father, was a disaster—the husband being a drunken, profligate squanderer. Now Old Whittle's nephew falls in love with her, and she with him. By his father's will, Young Whittle must have his uncle's consent to marry, in order to come by his inheritance. But old uncle Whittle himself falls in love with the Widow Brady, whom he has seen as a quiet, lovely, retiring girl. To solve the impending problem of crabbed age's desires for tender youth, the widow changes her life-style by acting before Old Whittle the part of a romp and a hoyden. She romps and struts, and speaks broguish speech, literally wearing the 60-year-old man out. He gives up and is glad to turn her over to his nephew. In one scene she masks as her brother, challenging Whittle to a duel to save family honor, and the duel in which both are too timid to fight is made sport of.

The significant changes (largely in the denouement) which Garrick brought about from the Molière play, suggest the amiableness of Garrick as well as the temper of the times in 1772. Molière's Dorimène [Widow Brady] is a coquette willing to marry her elderly suitor not for love (for she plans that satisfaction elsewhere), but to come at his fortune, where Garrick's Widow seeks to disillusion him to save them both. Where Molière's Sganarelle is forced into a loveless marriage as a warning to the whole species of old dotards, Garrick having seen the disaster of his heroine's first forced marriage, wishes not to repeat same with Old Whittle. Sganarelle is a type. Garrick's Old Whittle is more of a person who changes his life-style under the inspiration of new love. "He's grown young again," says Thomas in the play, "he frisks and prances, and runs about, as if he had a new pair of legs . . . now, with his hat under his arm, he goes open-breasted, and he dresses, and powders, and smirks . . . —something wrong in his upper story."[11]

Elizabeth P. Stein concludes her study of Garrick's French-play group by noting that his practice seemed "to be to omit repetitious material, to transpose and combine scenes, and to introduce bits of stage business, all of which he carries through to speed up the action. Moreover, for humorous effects and also for purposes of satire, he intensifies idiosyncrasies which manifest themselves in a number of the characters in the original dramas." [12]

What indeed comes most clear in a reading of his plays in this category is his sense of stage performance for each play, and for each character—the situation, the movement, the dialogue, and the business. He worked under the limitation of time-at-disposal for an after piece. A "whole show" lasted on his stage for three hours, and *each element* in its makeup—prologue, main piece, entr'acte singing and dancing, and after piece—was important. Scripts from many a nonactor had to be rejected, or cut down, for his *not* coming to grips with this fact of theatrical life.

## LILLIPUT, THE MALE COQUETTE, BON TON

Three of Garrick's other farces, drawn from English inspiration, bracket a period from 1756 to 1775. The source for the first one was from the first book of *Gulliver's Travels*. Gulliver in Book IV, however, as one will remember, had commented savagely to his Houyhnhnm host upon the upbringing of the English nobility—"bred from their childhood to idleness and luxury, [and] as soon as years will permit they consume their vigor, and contact odious diseases among lewd females; and when their fortunes are almost ruined, they marry some woman of mean birth, disagreeable person, and unsound constitution, merely for the sake of money, whom they hate and despise." [13] But Garrick, in the heyday of his success (yet when England was warring with France and folk were thinking and writing about the quality of English life) [14] lightens the observation by centering his mockery upon upper-class adoption of French fashions and morals, and by mocking its marriages and liberties. The theme had been exploited on stage since Restoration times, but Garrick covered himself against accusation of any personal application with a bantering disclaimer in his *Prologue:*

> For giant vices may in pigmies dwell.
> Beware you lay not to the conjuror's charge,
> That these in miniature are you in large:
> To you these little folks have no relation,
> As different in their manners as their station.

He prepared the play to be acted by one large adult actor, Astley Bransby, and a corps of children, whose families he paid well for their cooperation. It was moderately popular, for it amassed 17 performances from 3 December 1756 to the end of the season. Social criticism of a sort rings from every line (as well as does allegorical jingoism)—and with a darkened stripe, which enraged a critic for the *Theatrical Examiner* (1757).

The plot builds up a proposed love affair (only rumored and without substance in Swift's story) between Lady Flimnap, wife of the Lord High Treasurer of Lilliput, and the "man-mountain" Gulliver. She becomes an eighteenth-century Lady of Quality, (the passion being entirely on her side) and propositions Gulliver:

> *Lady F*: Love is a great leveller, and I have ambition—and I think, if *I* make no objections, your lordship need not.
>
> *Gulliver*: To pretend now not to understand you, and not to speak my mind would be insincerity . . . I am unfortunately engaged.
>
> *Lady F*: Engag'd, my lord! to whom, pray?
>
> *Gulliver*: To a wife and six children.
>
> *Lady F*: Is that all! have not I, my lord, the same plea? and does it weigh any thing against my affection? have not I a husband and as many children?

Gulliver then turns against her advances with some solid middle-class sentiments:

> *Gulliver*: I allow that; but your ladyship is, most luckily and politely, regardless of 'em—I, madam, not having the good fortune to be born and bred in high life, am a slave to vulgar passions; and to expose at once my want of birth and education—with confusion I speak it—I really love my wife and children.
>
> *Lady F*: Is it possible!

Thus snubbed, after the manner of Phaedra, and Potiphar's wife of old, she seeks Gulliver's destruction, but while she is bickering with her brothers about the means, he escapes to Blefuscu.

To build up the plot and sharpen the social criticism, Garrick made Admiral Bolgolam Lady Flimnap's brother, and equipped her with a second brother (not in the source) Fripperal. Bolgolam speaks always for the solid virtues, Fripperal always for the sophisticated, bored, casual, and irresponsible point of view associated with England's casual upper class. And likewise speaks Lord Treasurer Flimnap—who is keeping a mistress on the side. Fripperal, Lady Flimnap, and Lord Flimnap close the one-act piece with four gay couplets:

*Frip*: Let love be banished—we of rank and fashion,
 Should ne'er in marriage mix one grain of passion.

*Lady F*: To care and broils we now may bid defiance;
 Give me my will, and I am all compliance.

*Lord Flimnap*: Let low-bred minds be curb'd by laws and rules,
 Our higher spirits leap the bounds of fools;
 No law or custom shall to us say nay;
 We scorn restriction. *Viva la Liberté!*

Garrick hesitates to let Swiftian ironies speak for themselves, but underscores their intent by plain speaking from Gulliver and Bolgolam. Even so, the *Theatrical Examiner* was outraged (though the audiences were not). "Lilliput is, I think," wrote he, "the most petit, trifling, indecent, immoral, stupid parcel of rubbish, I ever met with; and I can't help judging it a scandal to the public, to suffer such a *thing* to pass a second night, which at best was alone calculated to please boys and girls, and fools of fashion; it may gratify them; the manager to debauch the minds of infants, by putting sentiments and glances in their breasts and eyes, that should never be taught at any years, which are sufficiently bad when naturally imbibed." [15]

Garrick paid no attention. Colman, when he took over the Haymarket from Foote in January 1777, gave the piece a short new lease on life for seven performances, with a new *air*, a new overture, the original Garrick *Prologue*, and a new scene. It also had a new Grand Jubilee Pageant in honor of Gulliver, who, in Garrick's play, had received the honors of being elected Nardoc. The music was altered by Dr. Arnold, and Garrick himself altered this performance of the play by introducing a "procession of cards into it, with Gulliver walking as the King of Clubs." [16]

## THE MALE COQUETTE

Where *Lilliput* looks back obviously to *Gulliver*, where *Lethe* looks back to Aesop, Garrick's *Male Coquette, or Seventeen Hundred Fifty-Seven* looks back in characters, dialogue, situation and theme to numerous comedies of the Restoration period such as Etherege's *Man of Mode*, Wycherley's *Plain Dealer*, and Vanbrugh's *Constant Couple*, reviving the spirit and satire upon characters such as Dorimant—self-centered, ice-cold, hard on the surface, but defeated in the end. "We have some monsters to amuse ye," writes Garrick in his *Prologue*:

Ye slaves of fashion, dupes of chance,
Whom Fortune leads her fickle dance;
Who, as the dice shall smile or frown,
Are rich and poor, and up and down;
Whose minds eternal vigils keep;
Who, like Macbeth, have murder'd sleep,
Each modish vice this night shall rise,
Like Banquo's Ghost before your eyes.

Nor does he spare the women:

Ye ladies too, maids, widows, wives,
Now tremble for your naughty lives.

But, he consoles, with a smile of irony:

Peace, ladies, 'tis a false alarm:
To you our author means no harm;
His female failings all are fictions,
To which your lives are contradictions.
Th' unnatural fool has drawn a plan,
Where women like a worthless man,
A fault ne'er heard of since the world began.

This year he lets you steal away;
But if the next you trip or stray,
His muse, he vows, on you shall wait,
In Seventeen hundred fifty eight.[17]

He planned the play for Henry Woodward's benefit on 24 March 1757, when it appeared under its original title of *The Modern Fine Gentleman* as an after piece to *The Winter's Tale*. It was a huge success, with Woodward playing the central figure Daffodil. Sophia (played by Maria Macklin) disguises as Lord Macaroni to test the faithfulness of Daffodil, who has many hearts swooning for him in London, including those of her cousin Arabella, young Mrs Dotterel, Widow Damply, and Lady Fanny Pewit. Sophia has a serious and jealous lover Tukely, who wishes to expose Daffodil for what he is—one who tears up tradesmen's bills, loves gambling, and is a bettor on the most foolish things, who has a stable of women, none of whom he really cares for or satisfies. Daffodil says of himself:

I am for variety, and badinage without affection. Reputation is a great ornament, and ease the great happiness of life—To ruin women would be troublesome; to trifle and make love to 'em amuses me—I use my women as daintily as my Tokay, I merely sip of both, but more than half a glass palls me.

Set against him is Tukely, a Roast-Beef-of-Old-England type, one who says of himself:

> I never was so foolishly fond of my own country to think that nothing good was to be found out of it; nor so shamefully ungrateful to it to prefer the vices and fopperies of every other nation to the peculiar advantages of my own.

"Well said," comments Sophia:

> If the gentleman would put his speech into a farce, and properly lard it with roast beef and liberty, I would engage the galleries would roar and halloo at it for half an hour together.

And so they did. The balanced types of Daffodil and Tukely are matched by Sophia (the sprightly, caustic libertarian) and Mrs Dotterel—long popular as a type of stage termagant.

The plot works toward a showdown. Tukely, dressed like a woman, entices Daffodil by letter for an assignation in the park. Daffodil invites his cronies—all bettors—to attend and lay wagers about another apparent conquest. Meantime, Tukely has invited the women to be present, but concealed in the shrubbery, to listen and expose Daffodil's duplicity. The ruse works. Daffodil gets caught by both sides, having characterized each lady (in her hearing) in unpleasant terms. Daffodil runs, and all is forgiven. Garrick's dialogue is sprightly, and insinuates the kind of banter on foreigners, English upper-class fripperies, doting females, and foolish gambling that the audience relished. The parts are all good for acting—even the servants', to whom the vices of their masters descend. In the advertisement to his printed edition Garrick explained that "the following scenes were written to serve Mr. Woodward with a Benefit, and to expose a set of people [the Daffodils] whom the author thinks more prejudicial to the community, than the various characters of Bucks, Bloods, Flashes, and Fribbles, which have by turns infected the Town." The heartless and the selfish were his butts.

## BON TON; OR, HIGH LIFE ABOVE STAIRS

In about 1760, Garrick sketched out the plot for this play, another social criticism—hilarious from all points of view—of marital infidelity and marriage of convenience, by then stereotyped, but here handled with verve, with good dialogue and comic situations. He laid the sketch by for 15 years, then gave it to his brightest actor in the Drury Lane company, Thomas King, for his benefit on 18 March 1775. Its popularity carried on into the next century. The story tells that Lord

Minim and his wife Lady Minim despise one another. He is carrying on a flirtation with her cousin Miss Tittup, and she with Tittup's fiancé, Colonel Tivy. Lady Minim's uncle Sir John Trotley—the part played by King—a landowner from the country, is appalled at the goings-on he observes in London, and particularly in the Minim household. "I hate innovations," says he, "what luxury, and abomination! . . . 'Tis all deceit and delusion." His man Davy, fresh from the country, has a different view:

> Such crowding, coaching, carting and squeezing; such a power of fine sights, fine shops full of fine things; and then such fine illuminations all of a row; and such fine dainty ladies in the streets, so civil and so graceless—they talk of country girls, these here look more healthy and rosy by half!

> Sir John: Sirrah, they are prostitutes, and are civil to delude and destroy you: they are painted Jezebels, and they who harkn to 'em, like Jezebel of old, will go to the dogs.

Sir John, though old-fashioned in his values, is important to the family because he controls matters of consent and of fortune.

The first act shows the pairs in the Minim mansion squaring off about to attend a masquerade, having picked up a set of extreme manners and dress from recent travel abroad. The second act shows each pair sneaking home from the masquerade for a tête à tête. Lord Minim is about to have Miss Tittup, when noise of one approaching makes him push her into a closet. He turns, only to face his man Jeremy, but hears Lady Minim coming, so departs. She is about to be had by Colonel Tivy, when a noise makes her push him behind the fire screen. She leaves, then returns when all is quiet, as does Lord Minim. The room is darkened, and they grope about, as the others emerge and grope too. They end up with Lady Minim in Lord Minim's arms, and Tittup in Tivy's, when Sir John bursts in with a light, and in his nightcap. Accusations fly about. Colonel Tivy leaves, Lord Minim leaves, and Sir John is about to carry the ladies off to the country for a period of repentance and to cool off.

> Sir John: Thus then, with the wife of one under this arm, and the mistress of another under this, I sally forth a Knight errant, to rescue distressed damsels from those monsters *foreign vices*, and *Bon Ton*, as they call it; and I trust that every English hand and heart here will assist me in so desperate an undertaking—You'll excuse me, sir!

The timing of the action on stage kept the audience in an uproar— "receiv'd with highest applause" noted the prompter William Hopkins in his *Diary*. Restoration comedy bloomed again in this with some flashes of mordant satire, brittle speech, and a cynical view of human nature, so it was bound to have an adverse critic in the *Westminster Magazine* that month. Though summarizing the plot he seemed stunned by its conventionality and, to him, lack of wit and laughableness.[18]

Back of these plays and *Lethe* stands a Garrick manifesting some social conscience, but also fully equipped with knowledge of drama and stage tradition of England's recent past, and facility in manipulating familiar situations with a kind of newness, and verve. The grouping of the nine plays just discussed as adhering to the French and English farcical traditions, academic in a way, should not lead one to conclude that Garrick's creative genius ran only in two well-worn channels, for composition of these plays spread over a period of 35 years. Spotted between them came a wealth of experiment (11 accomplishments) in other forms—musicals, pantomimes, interludes, a burlesque, and (in collaboration with Colman) a remarkable, full-fledged comedy, not to mention his equally creative hand during the period in adaptations of major English plays.

## HARLEQUIN'S INVASION

Improving the competitive position of Drury Lane in its daily contest with Covent Garden persuaded Garrick in the 1750s, as we have noted, to have a go at pantomime as after-piece entertainment. Aided by Woodward's pen and his acting as Harlequin, Garrick was able to balance his production in this genre with that of Rich. Garrick's public position was that he was responding to popular demand in this excursion into stage bustle, music, dance, disappearance and discovery, sudden changes and quick transitions, but that he was also bringing the serious, the rude, and rustic into union with the magic wand of Harlequin. To this his oft-repeated *Prologue*, spoken at the opening of Drury Lane in 1750, bears witness:

> But if an empty House, the Actor's curse,
> Shews that our Lears and Hamlets lose their force;
> Unwilling we must change the nobler scene,
> And in our turn present you Harlequin!

*Pantomime* had enjoyed a long success on the London stage, but was accompanied with an equally long-standing attitude of scorn among serious and sophisticated critics. The pun and the pantomime shared disdain by the elegant literati—the one as the "lowest form of wit," and the other as a "grotesque" form of entertainment, ridiculous for consideration by a rational audience. Yet both forms were actually enjoyed by *all* spectators. The exclusively rational mind has never yet supported a public theatre. Garrick knew the history of the rise of pantomime from English stage beginnings in 1702 through surges of critical condemnation of theatre popularity in the teens, twenties, and thirties of the century.[19]

When Woodward, who gave Drury Lane a new pantomine yearly until 1758,[20] left to share management in the Dublin theatre at the beginning of the 1758–59 season, Garrick, always bold, daring, and impudent, always ready to meet a challenge resourcefully, ventured into the writing of a pantomime himself. As usual he sought for some novel turn which he could produce with artistry. The novelty of his *Harlequin's Invasion*, produced 31 December 1759, was a *speaking* Harlequin, his artistry lay in effective use of transparencies, and for good measure he packed social satire into the citified portion of his plot.[21] Billed as a "Christmas Gambol, after the manner of Italian comedy, with new scenes, habits and decorations," it went off with applause, and continued in the repertory for 121 performances until he retired. Tom King made such an attractive Harlequin that he requested the pantomime a number of times for his benefit nights. Garrick kept a proprietary interest in having the piece always performed *well*, writing to George from Munich, "Pray let me know if You think of yᵉ Invasion next Year—or do you keep it until I can oversee it Myself?" (337). Garrick had affection for his experiment and never considered it an ink-wasting toy.

The drift of the piece is the repelling of harlequinade as it seeks to invade Parnassus. The plot is earthy enough, but releases some imaginative sequences. Into the routines of life at Charing Cross to a tailor Snip, his proud and termagant wife, their daughter Dolly and their friends (Bounce, Forge, Taffy, Simon, Gascom, and Abraham) and to solemn Justices of the Peace (all of whom ape the manners of the upper class, operate on rumors, and enjoy fierce competitiveness among themselves) comes Mercury with a challenge:

> To Dramatica's realm, from Apollo I come.
> Whereas it is feared a French trick may be play'd ye
> Be it known Monsʳ Harlequin, means to invade ye.
> And hither importing his Legions, He floats
> On an Ocean of Canvas and flat-bottomed boats:
> With Fairies, Hags, Genii, Hobgoblins all shocking
> And many a Devil in flame colour'd Stocking.

> Let the light Troops of Comedy March to attack him,
> And Tragedy whet all her Daggers to Hack Him.
> Let all hands, and hearts, do their utmost endeavour;
> Sound Trumpet, beat Drum, King Shakespeare forever!

Mrs. Snip sees in this prophecy a chance for her milk-toast-like husband to don armor, sally forth, and save the town from an invader (probably a Jacobite since he is coming from France). Reluctant Snip goes forth and meets Harlequin in disguise, who persuades him to duck into a cave, then turns the crusaders Bounce and Gascon in after him by telling them that Snip in his armor *is* the Harlequin they too are seeking to kill. They decapitate Snip, but Harly later sews his head back on. Dolly Snip, just on the thought that her father may become a hero and thus move up in society, jilts her lover, Tailor Abraham. Bounce and Gascon, for their manslaughter, come before the Justices (who spend most of their time indulging in banalities). These pompous magistrates are decapitated by Harlequin, that is, their wigs fly off, and they are turned into old women. The culprits are reprieved when Snip turns up alive. Harlequin, masked as a Friar, after first sinking, then re-elevating the jailhouse (through the large center stage trap), is recognized and finally stripped of his power by Mercury. The forces of *Pantomime*, via the use of a huge transparency, prepare to invade Parnassus, but Mercury does them in with a storm, destroying their fleet, shouting, "Beware encroachment, and invade no more!" Attitudes are struck, and struck down, and a stirring song rouses British literary patriotism:

> To arms you brave mortals to arms . . .
> 'Tis Nature calls on you to save her,
> What Man would but nature obey
> And Fight for her Shakespear forever!

The songs throughout the piece, set by William Boyce, Michael Arne, and Thomas Aylward, came out as sheet music and were sung and played all over London. But the accent of realism turned to that of imagination, and the voice of Harlequin, as he is quizzed in the play by Farmer Simon to tell about his profession, is, one suspects, the merry voice of Garrick.

> [I am] a Fly Catcher—I was formerly altogether among the stars—I plied as a Ticket Porter in the Milky Way, and carried the Howdyes from one Planet to another; but finding that too fatiguing I got into the Service of the Rainbow, and now I wear his livery, Don't you think I Fib now, Friend Simon?

And the Lincos, the Tychos, and Farmers of Garrick's later extravaganzas speak the same language, each with characteristic variation.

Garrick the dramatist articulated nuances and thoroughly enjoyed the characters and caricatures he was creating.

One becomes certain in reading the text and imagining the performance that despite lip-service disapproval of the pantomime form therein, Garrick liked this creation. He and prompter William Hopkins worked up another one, apparently, for the performance (2 January 1775) of *Harlequin's Jacket; or, The New Year's Gift*, described as a "medley patch-up from several old pantomimes." Hopkins noted this also was well received and applauded. Since it was not printed we cannot assess its quality or prove authorship. As a "House property" it ran 20 times, and was patched up again in 1781–82 under the title "Lun's Ghost" for another 18.[22] From the way Garrick cherished his own *Invasion*, it is hard to believe that his attitude was entirely that of Lope de Vega's "Since the crowd pays for the comedies, it is fitting to talk foolishly to it to satisfy its taste."[23] Garrick saw pleasant and essential creativeness in the form he was experimenting with.

Garrick's touch of creativity also spread to the musical portion of London stage entertainment. His well-paid Drury Lane orchestra of 21 instruments performed regularly, rehearsed regularly, complemented stage action with background music at times, and for operas, ballad operas, and oratorios was basic to the whole show.[24] Garrick as manager became increasingly interested in procuring actors and actresses who were excellent singers. He had started his career in company with the tenor voice of John Beard, the jaunty, all-purpose one of Catherine Clive, the baritone and basso ones of Reinhold and Champness, and during his management he engaged 43 more. He gathered children's voices and brought on young specialist singers, such as Joseph Vernon, Michael Leoni, and Harriet Abrams. For the latter two he wrote musical plays.

The spread of his musical interests is suggested by the fact of his composing lyrics for over 106 songs for his own plays and those of others, as well as basing ten of his plays and adaptations heavily on music.[25] His songs were for solos, duets, and full choruses. Often topical, most of them, light and bantering if not satirical, paralleled the spirit of his farces. But drinking songs, love songs, pastoral pieces, solemn dirges, and epithalamia rounded out the types. Most were printed in his *Poetical Works* (1785), but without the music. The texts of dozens upon dozens appeared in the magazines and daily papers.[26] Scholars are but now gathering the scores and remnants of sheet music once so plentifully sold for sixpence. The intellectual content of many is slight, but one must bear in mind that the song quality depends on a context of music, play, and theatrical setting.[27]

The varying meters of the 106 suggest strongly that Garrick composed the lyrics for his plays with airs or tunes ringing in his ears. But Garrick also commissioned music, much music to be written for plays, adaptations, and operas. He knew Purcell's music, and he knew that of his contemporaries. From time to time he enlisted the services of John Christopher Smith, Handel's pupil, who set the music for *The Fairies*, an operatic version of *A Midsummer Night's Dream* (1755), for *The Tempest* (11 February 1756), and for Garrick's own *The Enchanter* (13 December 1760). In this piece Garrick brought young Master Leoni on the stage—a Jew who was received with great applause. At various times Charles Burney, Dr. Thomas Augustine Arne, his natural son Michael Arne, Charles Dibdin, Francis Hippolyte Barthélemon, William Boyce, Theodore Aylward, Jonathan Battishill, Samuel Howard, William Shield, and James Oswald, among others, composed at his specific request.

Garrick had opened his career by writing songs for Thomas Lowe, John Beard, and Catherine Clive in *Lethe* (1740). He closed it by bringing the attractive Jewess Harriot Abrams on stage, aged 17, and by composing for her the text of a musical after piece, *May Day*, for which he commissioned Dr. Arne to do the music. The performance, according to the tally of box receipts, and to Garrick's letter to brother George, "goes on Hummingly, & rises nightly in repute" (954). During the intervening years, thoughts of the importance of musical performances and musical accompaniment continually occupied him. His *Prologue* (1755) to *The Fairies* bespeaks his confidence in J. C. Smith's abilities:

> Struck with the wonders of his master's [Handel's] art,
> Whose sacred dramas shake and melt the heart,
> Whose heav'n-born strains the coldest breast inspire,
> Whose chorus-thunder sets the soul on fire!
> Inflam'd, astonish'd, at those magic airs,
> When Samson groans, and frantic Saul despairs,
> The pupil wrote—his work is now before ye.[28]

In August 1762 Garrick was corresponding with Dr. John Brown about two musical pieces—an opera "Armida" (which never appeared at Drury Lane), and a redoing of Jonson's *Bartholomew Fair* (which likewise never appeared) for which Brown was searching out music for songs. "I . . . am altogether of your opinion," wrote Brown, "that much will depend upon the music, and that the airs in general ought to be as light as possible. You may depend upon it I shall select them of this kind from Handel, as far as they are to be found there; but the present taste has got down so far towards the *ballad style* that I question whether the lightest of Handel's airs will quite hit the humour of the town."[29] He hoped that Garrick might enlist William Boyce's aid. Boyce was indeed in the Handel tradition, but the point for Garrick lies in the fact that popular taste in music, especially in theatre music, was in a period of change, which Garrick's commissioning may have had much to do with.

In the 1765 *Prologue at the Opening of the Theatre*, Garrick suggested the balancing power of music as arbiter when tragedy has too much *"harrow'd up the soul"*; and when the "Comic Lass has so shook your sides, / that laughter swell'd so high, burst out in tides." Music he thought "with its sweet enchanting strain / Should to its banks lure back the tide again."[30] Two years later Joseph Reed was inquiring of Garrick about a proper person to "compile" the music for his attempt to turn *Tom Jones* into an opera. He had spoken with Mr. Toms, compiler of music for *Love in a Village*, the popular musical adaptation of *Pamela*, and had learned a strange thing about theatrical composing, "Mr. Toms informed me, (which I had no conception of,) that it would be necessary to cast the characters before the songs are adapted to music, as some airs would suit one performer much better than they would another in the same character" (16 June 1767).[31] Garrick doubtless agreed in part, for he had long been composing plays with specific actors in mind.

Word has got around especially in twentieth-century books about Garrick that he did not favor musical pieces,[32] save as potboilers pandering to vulgar popular taste, but the evidence seems to show his abiding and deep interest in musical drama, and music in drama. Mr. Roger Fiske has lately sought to redress the balance of comment on this point, noting that "Garrick worked far harder in the cause of English opera than Rich in the fourteen years they were rivals, and when Beard suddenly made English operas an artistic and financial success, Garrick stepped up Drury Lane's operatic repertoire and was forever searching for successes of his own in this field. He also believed that quiet background music could heighten the emotions of such scenes as the one in *King Lear*, in which the King and Cordelia are reunited."[33] He also commissioned background music from Boyce for animating the "statue" of Hermione in *The Winter's Tale*.

Garrick, though doubtless possessing a rational outlook, an orderly mind, and a sense of pragmatic control, let his own imagination go in plotting experimental plays, and in adapting others such as *Alfred* (1751), *The Enchanter* (1760), *Cymon* (1767), *King Arthur and Emmaline* (1770), *The Institution of the Garter; or, Arthur's Round Table Restored* (1771), and *A Christmas Tale* (1773). But Garrick's creative impulse had room for satirical rationalism, for imaginative release *and* earthy realism. The whimsical result often charms. Throughout the newly created scenes and plays (distanced in time and space or set in never-never lands) runs this irresistible Garrick whimsey, for he peopled the scenes of fantasy with a good many characters of flesh and blood—the Sancho Panzas of the world.


## THE ENCHANTER


Garrick's first original musical after piece, *The Enchanter*, prepared for the Christmas season of 1760, marks his excursion into a fantasy world of the Far East (he had recently put on Murphy's *Orphan of China*), and into a musical form which downplayed recitative almost completely—the whole being carried on by the songs. The beautiful heroine Zaida (sung by Mrs Vincent) is contracted to young Zoreb (sung by Lowe). The powerful magician Moroc, lusting for Zaida, imprisons Zoreb, and carries the maiden off to his castle—hopefully to woo and win her. She resists his attempts. Unable to sleep she walks in his garden singing:

> Intruder Sleep! In vain you try
> To hush my breast, and close my eye;
> The morning dues refresh the flow'r,
> That unmolested blows;
> But ineffectual falls the shower
> Upon the cankered rose.

Moroc, on fire for love but unpersuasive, directs his attendant spirit Kaliel to try to win her over with magic spectacles and blandishments of sweet words. She remains true to Zoreb. Enraged, Moroc tells her that Zoreb is dead and that he will show her his body. A tomb thereupon arises from the ground, with Zoreb, apparently dead, lying therein. She sings:

> Back to your source weak, foolish tears,
> Away, fond love, and woman's fears;
> A nobler passion warms:
> The dove shall soar with eagle's wing,
>    From earth I spring
> And fly to Heav'n, and Zoreb's arms.

She offers to stab herself. Moroc runs to prevent her, and drops his ebon wand. Kaliel retrieves it, and finds himself free, with power now over Moroc. Challenged by the Magician, he waves the wand in the name of Virtue, strikes Moroc, and the evil magician sinks into the ground. He then awakens Zoreb to life.

Zoreb and Zaida join hands, kneel before Kaliel, thank him for deliverance, and sing a duet as the curtain falls:

> No power could divide us, no terror dismay;
> No treasure could bribe us, no falsehood betray;
> No demons could tempt us, no pleasure could move;
> No magic could bind us, but the magic of love.
>
> *Zoreb*: The spell round my heart was the image of you;
> Then how could I fail to be constant and true?
>
> *Zaida*: The spell round *my* heart was the image of you;
> Then how could *I* fail to be constant and true?

## MAY DAY

This operetta, all sung in English, enjoyed moderate success with 17 performances its first season and six more later, the last being a benefit for the actress-singer Elizabeth Young, the original Lyssa in the piece, on 15 April 1766. But Garrick finding the genre useful for introducing young singers of promise, tried his hand again on 28 October 1775, when, expressly to introduce Miss Harriet Abrams and her voice, he wrote *May Day* as an after piece. He commissioned Dr. Arne to do the rather charming music, and the piece ran for 16 performances that season.

The plot involves William's tricking his father, Old Furrow, a rich farmer, into agreeing to the young man's choice of a bride. Complication occurs because Furrow himself has fallen in love with a little Gypsy, who, unbeknownst to him, is William's beloved in disguise. To the little farm community in which the Furrows live Squire Goodwill has left a legacy from which £100 is to be given each year to the first couple married on May Day. Furrow seeks the Gypsy *and* the bounty for himself. She, coming from outside the Parish, and hence disguised lest she bring the wrath of the local girls upon herself, declares she will not marry until he first makes his son happy. Furrow agrees before witnesses to do so, asking William what he chooses. William to the old man's horror and dismay chooses the Gypsy to be his bride. Furrow cannot break his word, but can rage. The villagers dance round the Maypole laughing him out of his incipient anger, closing with a grand chorus: "When the heart is unkind, / With the frost of the mind, / Benevolence melts it like May."

Of immense interest to the audience were the Gypsy's song of the beauties of spring:

> O spread thy green mantle, sweet May, o'er the ground.
>   Drive the blasts of bleak Winter away;
> Let the birds sweetly carol, thy flow'rets smile round,
>   And let us with all nature be gay.
>
> Let spleen, spight, and envy, those clouds of the mind,
>   Be dispers'd by the sun-shine of joy;
> The pleasures of Eden had bless'd human kind,
>   Had no fiend enter'd there to destroy.
>
> As May with her sunshine can warm the cold heart,
>   Let each fair with the season improve;
> Be widows restor'd from their mourning to mirth,
>   And let hard-hearted maids yield to love.
>
> In Spring's choicest treasures the Village be dress'd,
>   Festive joy let the season impart;
> When rapture mounts high and o'erflows from each breast,
>   'Tis May, the sweet May of the heart.

and the ravishing duet between William and the Gypsy, which tells their rapture, states their fears, and advances the plot:

> Passion of the purest nature
>   Glows within this faithful breast,
> While I gaze on each lov'd feature,
>   Love will let me know no rest.
>
> Thus the ewe her lamb caressing,
>   Watches with a mother's fear,
> While she eyes her little blessing
>   Thinks the cruel wolf is near.

As the strains die away, Old Furrow's voice is heard off stage— "Where's the Gipsy?" *William*: "The wolf is near indeed!" The Gypsy soon thereafter extracts the promise from Old Furrow to make his son happy.

Such a petite charmer was obviously not written for armchair reading, but the quality of setting, lyrics, and music carried on on stage through revivals as late as 1 May 1798, which concluded with "a rural procession: Four lads bearing streamers—plough decorated with flowers—Four countrymen bearing a May Day garland—Four lasses bearing implements of husbandry—Country girls leading a lamb, decorated with flowers—Four lasses bearing a Garland—a Chorus and Finale."[34] It was then being given at Covent Garden, updated with two new songs—but Garrick would have loved it and its capability for growth.

## THE JUBILEE

The procession in the revived *May Day* would particularly have interested Garrick, who was past master of mounting processions on his stage—a funeral one for Juliet, the "procession of cards" in *Lilliput*, but particularly the pageant procession of scenes from 19 Shakespearean plays in his *Jubilee* (1769). We speak in chapter 17 about this stage version of the Stratford Jubilee event, but a word here on the text is appropriate. Garrick told Evan Lloyd that he composed it in a day and a half to meet the competition Colman was giving him at Covent Garden with his *Man and Wife* (7 October 1769), a main piece which included a pageant procession with figures from 17 Shakespearean plays.[35]

Garrick's after piece makes up in two parts and several scenes which, beside the pageant, picture a handful of shrewd, ignorant, and superstitious Stratford rustics as they experience the three days of the Jubilee (567). The first scene sketches out the enlightened conversation of two old women and the impressionable Ralph, none of whom have been able to sleep for the noise, hustle, and confusion of people who have descended upon the sleeping town upon the Avon. The gossip, as Ralph details it, is that the Pope is at the botom of all the confusion, and that though the townsfolk may rent their rooms at high profit, what with the cannon and powder imported, the town may be blown up in another gunpowder plot. He conjures up a picture of 50 devils at work in Farmer Thornton's barn, hobgoblins aplenty, burning of houses, and ravishment of women and children. A second scene shifts to the chaise in which an Irishman, come all the way from Dublin to see the affair and unable to find other shelter, sleeps in the chaise through the whole proceeding. The riotous third scene is at the White Lyon Inn yard—a scene which Garrick noted in his manuscript "is perhaps of the most regular confusion ever exhibited."[36] In it the waiters and customers and actors order, and receive, don't receive, and complain; with a Fribble being lodged in the "Love's Labours Lost"

room, with one calling for hot rolls for Julius Caesar. A waiter notes
a mixed-sex quarrel in the "Catherine and Petruchio" room. One who
wants breakfast in a hurry sees another snatch his order from a waiter's
tray *en passant*. Bedlam would prevail but for close stage management,
implied in Garrick's note about "regular" confusion. The glorious
pageant follows, with the comment on it in part 2 by Sukey and Nancy
as they saunter on a street in Stratford:

> *Sukey*: There was a sight for you! there was a Pagan!—If I had not a
> Shakespur ribbon to pin upon my heart, I could not have shewn my
> face—the dear creature is nearest my heart—I doat upon Shakespur.
>
> *Nancy*: Law, cousin Sue, how you talk to a body—I swear I know no
> more about the Jubillo, and Shakespur as you call him, than I do about
> the Pope of Rome.
>
> *Sukey*: Nancy, you have not been out of this poor hole of a Town, or
> you would not have such low vulgar fancies in your head—had you
> liv'd at Birmingham or Coventry, or any other polite Cities as I have
> done, you would have known better than to talk so, of Shakespur and
> the Jew-bill—
>
> *Nancy*: Why who is this Shakespur, that they make such a rout about'en
> —he was not a Lord?
>
> *Sukey*: Lord help you Cousin—he is worth fifty Lords. Why he could
> write—He could write finely your plays and your Tragedies; and
> make your heart leap, or sink in your bosom, as he pleas'd, 'twas
> a wonder of a man! I'm sure I cry'd for a whole night together after
> hearing his Romy and July at Birmingham, by the London Gentlemen
> and Ladies player people—I never let M^r Robin keep me company
> till I had been mov'd by that fine piece: Why he cuts Romeo into
> little stars as fine as sixpence. O, the Sweet Creature—the dear Willy
> Shakspur.

The air is filled with songs, punctuating such brave commentary. Garrick snatched the rug of criticism from under scoffers by quoting in
his piece Foote's definition of a Jubilee, and by making fun of himself
as the Steward.

> *1st Old Woman*: Have you seen, Ralph, the Mon, that is the ring leader
> of the Jubillo?—who is to fly about the Town by Conjuration?
>
> *Ralph*: Yes, I ha seen him—not much to be seen tho'—I did not care
> to come too near him—he's not so big as I, but a great deal plumper,
> —he's auld enough to be wiser too,—but he knows what he's about,
> I warrant 'en—he has brought the Pipers, and 'Ecod he'll make us
> pay for 'em—let him alone for that—he's a long yead of his own.

The finale brought the house down with song, and shouts, and the sound of cannon. It was certainly the wonder of the stage for its 91 performances that season.

## CYMON AND A CHRISTMAS TALE

John Hoadly wrote Garrick on 4 December 1766 with a note of warning: "I found your scheme of 'Cymon' was resolved to be extended to five acts. . . . The character and the scenery, &c. of the rest, may support it through two or three acts at most; but surely nothing full of Urgandas and Merlins can be drawn out longer, to keep a sensible audience pleased. Cymon, the natural Cymon, will be the hero, add what you please; and I could wish that he had none but natural things and subjects about him; but as they are, take heed of bending the bow till it loses its elasticity."[37] Hoadly was a critic whose judgment Garrick respected most, but in this case he did stretch out the Cymon "dramatic romance" to a full five acts—and saw it succeed from its first performance 2 January 1767 for some 60 performances until he retired. (It even maintained a curious stage persistence off and on, as a Christmas piece, until 1850.) It was a spectacular, embodying an obvious moral. The source seems to lie in Dryden's poetical fable *Cymon and Iphigenia*, out of the *Decameron*. As Garrick develops it, it might well have been subtitled "Good People, as *You* like it," strange mixture that it is for many, many palates. But its multiplicity of themes, and its amalgam of northern lore, Grecian pastoral, and eighteenth-century realism aligns it with such a Shakespearean mixture as *A Midsummer Night's Dream*. Somewhere in Arcadia Merlin loves Urganda, who dotes upon a simple young boy-prince, Cymon, whom she has taken over to "cure." Fatima, her confidant, urges her to give up Cymon and wed Merlin. Merlin takes matters in hand, promising that "Cymon's cure shall be Urganda's wound." Jealousies run on a wide track through the play, offering possibilities of dark interpretations. Cymon, an irresponsible simpleton, chases butterflies, and yearns to get free of Urganda's nest, to choose his own course of action. As Urganda finally frees him, Merlin causes him to fall in love with Sylvia, whose beauty has charmed a host of shepherds, her followers. Fatima (the voice of the surfeited eighteenth-century cynic) again urges Urganda to marry Merlin, and (as do the upper-class English) take Cymon along on the honeymoon, where she (Fatima) will induce him to fall in love with her. All straightens out at the close, for as Merlin remarks, "There is no magic like Virtue." The knights of the different orders of chivalry assemble to celebrate the marriage of Cymon and Sylvia. Falsehood is punished, Virtue rewarded, and all Arcadia made happy.

The contrasts in the play are great, scenically and cynically, for menace lurks in the wings. The innocent simples who triumph at last are manipulated throughout by the powerful. It seems to have become a fascinating stage piece that touched the ear, brightened the eye, and imagination of all groups in the audience. The music, composed in popular style by Charles Dibdin, made the walls of Drury Lane ring with melody. Sheet music selections, published by Longman and Broderip, carried the favorite airs into the streets and thence to the drawing rooms of London. Garrick's "If pure are the Springs of the Fountains . . ." and "Oh why will you call me again . . ." wafted who knows where.

A far cry, this, one suspects, from the farcical *Miss in Her Teens*, *Irish Widow*, or *Male Coquette*, but Garrick, now allied with the stage designer Philip de Loutherbourg, experimented in this range of extravaganza again (and successfully) with his *A Christmas Tale*, 27 December 1773. Garrick sent it on its way with a prologue based upon the metaphor of a pastry cook's shop where this is one of the dishes, then proceeds:

> Old father Christmas now in all his glory,
> Begs, with kind hearts, you'll listen to his Story: . . .
> Hear my Tale out—see all that's to be seen . . .
>
> I have no sauce to quicken listless sinners
> My food is meant for honest hearty grinners! . . .
> Open your mouths, pray swallow everything![38]

Though the tale is one told by Father Christmas at his fireside, it starts from mixed sources, echoing Chaucer's loathly Lady motif from the *Wife of Bath's Tale*, drawing upon Fletcher's *Women Pleased*, as well as from Charles Favart's *La Fée Urgèle* (1765).[39]

Magnificent and bold scenes were provided by de Loutherbourg, and showers of music came from Charles Dibdin. The play is replete with songs that now sum up and reinforce the action, and now advance it. They are thoroughly integrated with the dialogue, with the situations, the dances, the groupings, and the moral sentiments. Camilla's father on his deathbed enjoined her to marry only one who could give proof of "what the enchanted wood unfolds." Written in gold on a laurel tree appear the terms—"valor, constancy, and honour." Her lover Floridor is the son of Bonoro (a good Magician), who enjoins him never to see Nigromant (a bad magician) save to destroy him. Camilla needs protection from Nigromant. Bonoro prepares a sword and shield for Floridor to use against Nigromant, but asks Floridor to guard, for a while, the prison in which he has gathered all the evil spirits. Floridor delegates the guard duty to his squire Tycho, who falls asleep, allowing the spirits to escape and plague the isle.

Tycho's comic comments on the romance (he being a Sancho Panza type) afford levity. The evil spirits allegorically are eighteenth-century personalities—a Jesuit, an attorney, a satirical poet, a statesman (who feels himself above the law), a gamester, an actress, a glutton, and a woman of quality. When freed, they "revel, dance, and sing."

Bonoro forgives Floridor and starts him over again. The young man then displays the requisite valor, constancy, and honor (while Tycho carries on in subplot a humorous parallel romance with Robinette). Floridor goes for Nigromant in a lake of fire, and saves Camilla from Nigromant's seraglio, which burns before our eyes. All ends morally and happily, amid the flux and grandeur of de Loutherbourg's scenes —a magic garden (where leaves change color), a lake of fire, thunder effects, descents from clouds, an enchanted wood, all ending in a "beautiful, distant prospect of the sea, castles, and the rising sun."

This was not an after piece, but a full main-piece banquet. Mrs Clive wrote from retirement after a month's performance of the play, and not with her tongue in her cheek, "I hear your 'Christmas Tale' is the finest thing that ever was seen." [40] It was certainly a colorful expansion of spirit and a triumph in another dimension from his French farces. It continued on stage until 6 April 1780.

Yet Garrick's creative spirit would be ill-defined without some consideration of five pieces even shorter than his farces, but effective entertainment in his concept of the whole show. He called them variously Preludes or Interludes. Several of these he worked up as solid mementos of appreciation for fellow actors, and they were performed at their benefits. Their advertised novelty helped bring the crowds.

## THE FARMER'S RETURN FROM LONDON

*The Farmer's Return* (20 March 1762) was done for Mrs Pritchard's benefit, and was repeated some dozen times until the end of Garrick's career. The printed version was dedicated to William Hogarth, who provided an illustration for the frontispiece. This was indeed a brief interlude between the main and after piece. It lasts about 15 minutes when a farmer (Garrick) returns to his home in the country after a visit to London, and describes to his wife the sights there. Garrick returns in the piece to light social satire, featuring three London events: the Coronation of George III (1761), the Cock Lane Ghost episode, much exploited in the newspapers of the time, and a visit to the theatre.[41] In the text, essentially a monologue, Garrick misses no chance to suggest an outsider's view of the theatre. Two passages suffice to give the nature of the skit: The farmer, seated by his fire and sucking on his clay pipe, reminisces in his country dialect.

> The city's fine show—but first the Crownation?
> 'Twas thof all the world had been there with their spouses;
> There was street within street, and houses on houses!
> I thought from above (when the folk fill'd the places)
> The streets paved with heads, and the walls made of faces!
> Such justling and bustling!—'twas worth all the pother.
> —I hope, from my soul, I shall ne'er see another.
>
> What did I see at the pleays and the shows?
> Why bouncing and grinning, and a pow'r of fine cloaths:
> From top to the bottom 'twas all chanted ground!
> Gold, painting, and music, and blazing all round!
> Above 'twas like Bedlam, all roaring and rattling!
> Below, the fine folk were all curts'ying and prattling:
> Strange tumbling together—Turks, Christians, and Jews!
> —At the Temple of Folly, all croud to the pews.

He had some fun with the wife by noting that the Cock Lane Ghost knocked once on the wall to indicate a faithful wife, and twice for an unfaithful one. The wife asks if the Ghost knocked once for her. "By zounds, it was *two*," replies the farmer with a twinkle in his eye. He also took the critics lightly to task for their unfavorable remarks about William Whitehead's *School for Lovers*. The topical was obviously at center stage in this piece.

## Linco's Travels

In 1767, Goldsmith's poem *The Traveller* was marching through its nine editions, when Garrick gave to Tom King (for his benefit) his

*Harvard Theatre Collection*
Garrick as the Farmer in *The Farmer's Return from London* 1762.
Engraving by James Basire from a Hogarth drawing.

235

*Linco's Travels* (6 April 1767). Garrick's *Linco* presents in a nutshell some of the same ground traversed by Goldsmith, but frames the brief dialogue in Arcadia, where Linco, returning from visits to England, France, Germany, and Italy, regales the shepherds with his impressions. Those on Italy (they watch their purses), on France (it sings and dances its sorrows away), on Germany (even when Germans laugh they are grave) are conventional, but Garrick would never let the English off the hook scot free. He knew audiences expected a salty comment or satirical jibe before being complimented. In even humorously evaluating his countrymen, he often abandoned the easy cliché:

> *Dorcas*: Those English folks are very strange.
>
> *Linco*: In politics much given to change;
>   They are in temper like the weather;
>   Fair, storm, foul, sun—shine all together.
>   Strange contradiction, gay and sad,
>   Mop'd, merry, moody, wise and mad!
>   A strange hodge podge of good and bad.

and the spectators liked to hear that they were complex and contradictory, just so their virtues of loving liberty and being fairminded were tucked in amidst the criticism somewhere:

> Be honest and they'll kindly treat you;
> Be pert and saucy and they'll beat you.
> If you dissect an English skull,
> Of politics 'tis so brim full,
> Of papers, pamphlets, prose and verse
> The furniture can't well be worse.
>
> So furious are they to be free
> Nothing so common as to see
> Britons dead drunk for liberty . . .
>
> Their very children on the lap
> Are fed with liberty and pap.

The conclusion of the traveler's remarks are predictable—for he wonders whether Englishmen will find abroad the worth they leave at home.


## A PEEP BEHIND THE CURTAIN


In 1748 the Giordani family arrived in London and initiated a series of performances of a type that grew in popularity through the fifties and sixties—the Italian burletta. These light and satirical pieces were a counterpoise to the *opera seria* which was having a difficult time at the Opera House in the Haymarket. The burletta, based upon the Italian *burla*, or an uncomplicated practical joke, depended largely upon mimic acting, and *commedia dell'arte* approach with its dialogue in Italian (or in a broad, strange mixture of Italian and English). John Rich engaged the Giordani family and made a good thing of many, many attractive performances. It was inevitable that the form should become anglicized, and the Irish playwright Kane O'Hara performed the act by writing his *Midas* for Dublin in 1762, and doing a second version for Covent Garden in 1764.[42] He kept the hallmark of the Italian form—a simplified plot—but wrote all in English and used English tunes for the singing. It marched steadily toward a performance record of over 200 in Garrick's time.

Garrick, quick to pick up on his competition, on 23 October 1767 produced his burletta "Orpheus," cleverly seeded as the play-to-be-rehearsed within the framework of his piece called *A Peep Behind the Curtain* (23 October 1767), which turned out to be one of the most amazing burlesques of theatre activity since Buckingham's *The Rehearsal* of 1671. Significant in Garrick's production is his form, which makes the burletta not only a burlesque of opera, but the butt of satire itself in the rehearsal-genre, and, not least, an attraction—difficult for one reading the text to perceive, but apparent to the ear in any performance—namely, the use of music as a spoof upon many then current musical styles—a movement from Handelian Italian baroque to French *galante*. This was accomplished by F. H. Barthélemon the violinist-composer whom Garrick commissioned to set the music. Barthélemon had gone to London sometime after 1764 and had composed the serious opera *Pélopide*, which premiered in May 1766. Garrick was so impressed with this opera that he sought to discover whether Barthélemon could set English. The story goes that Garrick, in order to test this important requirement, wrote out a lyric for him. As he did so, Barthélemon looked over his shoulder and set it as the words flowed from the actor's pen. Garrick then handed the young Frenchman the verses, saying, "there, Sir, is my song." The Frenchman replied, "and there, Sir, is my music to it." Thereupon, Garrick picked him to compose the music for the "Orpheus." Barthélemon knew the capacities of the singers at Drury Lane, and cleverly adapted his music to them, and, by the use of the unexpected, to the satirical spirit of the playlet. For example, he introduced the rhythm of a Scotch air unexpectedly into the second movement of the overture, and closed it, not with the customary loud and brilliant finish, but by a slow, quiet, sleepy ending, calculated to suit exactly the action on stage of Orpheus sleeping and dreaming. Garrick was delighted to see how music, usually ceremonial and unrelated to any action called for in the dialogue, could be made the agent for light banter itself.[43]

In this piece, Garrick lightly satirizes the total operation of Drury Lane Theatre—its stock plays, its music, its actors, company, stage devices, and audience. Within a stock frame-story of the elopement of a young girl from her stagestruck parents with a pretended actor, the rehearsed burletta which the parents come to see marks the high point of the amusement. In the framing plot, one Wilson plans to elope with Miss Fanny Fuz, daughter of Sir Toby and Lady Fuz. Toby's brother, a lawyer, had swindled Wilson's father out of £30,000, so Wilson plans to get the daughter and bring the inheritance back into his family again. Sir Toby and his wife are attending the rehearsal of *Orpheus*. Wilson enters the theatre disguised as a player. He has a post chaise ready at the door, and while Lady Fuz is engrossed by the rehearsal and Sir Toby is snoring, the youngsters make off. Lady Fuz sees but one act of the *Orpheus*, then discovers the loss of her daughter. She wishes to go off in hot pursuit, awakens her husband, who wants to go off to dinner. The author of the burletta and the stage manager, upon learning that the runaway was not a real member of the company, wash their hands happily of the whole affair.

The burletta spoofs the classical legend of Orpheus, and, as noted, all the musical forms of current Italian opera. Orpheus subconsciously hearing and plagued by the calls of his wife in Hades to come to her rescue, decides he must "go to Hell for his wife." "I come, I go, I must, I will. Bless me, where am I, Here I am still." His problem is what to do with his mistress Rhodope, who leads him a rather hellish life above ground. Aware of his henpecked situation, he puts Rhodope to sleep, and takes off for the lower world. Passing through mountainous country en route, he leads a flock of sheep, goats, and cows in a dance, to the annoyance of the shepherds.

We learn from the author of the burletta how he planned to end the story, but we never see the outcome, because the rehearsal is interrupted by the Fuz family troubles. The author assures us, however, that his Orpheus is a mixed character whose principles melt away as he experiences the heat of the underworld. Finding his wife Eurydice is being kept by Pluto, he immediately makes up to Proserpine, and is kept by her. All four arrange matters amicably. They change partners and close with a chorus singing out the old proverb, "Exchange is no robbery." The farce was popular for a quarter of a century beyond Garrick's retirement.

## The Institution of the Garter; or, Arthur's Round Table Restored

Perhaps spurred by the success of *The Jubilee*, perhaps aware of audiences' love for pageantry and music, perhaps stimulated by genuine concern for presentation on stage of deeper roots of England's colorful heritage (deeper even than those of Shakespearean times), Garrick on 11 December 1770 mounted a spectacular musical masque, *King Arthur*. In it he adapted Dryden's opera *King Arthur*, mingling the original Purcell music with new strains and an overture by Dr. Arne. "The Masque was got up in a superb manner," wrote Hopkins, "the scenery exquisitely fine, and greatly applauded." And this was before de Loutherbourg began at Drury Lane.[44]

The following February Earl Gower was installed as a Knight of the Garter with regal ceremony, and in July the Prince of Wales was inducted. Garrick saw in these ceremonies the stuff for another dip into the British past and by August wrote to Lord Lyttleton asking the loan of a copy of Dodsley's *Miscellanies*, containing Gilbert West's dramatic poem "The Institution of the Garter" (1742), as basis for a plan he was turning over in his head for another pageant balanced by some lightly comic and subtly satiric scenes—much as he had already done in *The Jubilee*. On 4 September 1771 he wrote to Joseph Cradock (who was sizing up additional performers for him at the theatre at Leicester), "I have a thought beyond y$^e$ mere Exhibition of Procession & feasting, & if I please myself in it, You shall know it, but *Mum* I beseech You" (651).

The excitement of working up this pageant lay in Garrick's knowledge that Colman at Covent Garden (prompted by the same summer ceremonies of the Garter) was preparing a similar production, called *The Fairy Prince, with Installation of the Knights of the Garter*. Garrick presented his show on 28 October, and Colman his on 11 November. They ran for two weeks together offering Londoners a choice of splendid pageantry.[45]

Garrick's procession of Knights to St. George's Chapel at Windsor was long and bright. Garrick realized that West's poem, though in dialogue, was not dramatic. He changed it by cuts, by some expansions, and most obviously by inventing two comic scenes depicting the mob's reaction to the ceremony, with shafts of social satire tucked away in the dialogue between Sir Dingle (the Court Fool), Needle a Tailor, and Roger—who express themselves forthrightly on the way Edward III's kingdom is being run. Dingle, like Lear's Fool, has the privilege of open speech. After persuading the King to let the rabble enter and clean up the leavings of the feast, he tells the women of the crowd, "I live in a land of promises, and I'll give you a hundred more, we *give* nothing *else* here . . . Do you think I am so vulgar, or so little a courtier to remember what I promised yesterday?" Roger believes himself to be qualified for such a courtier, "for to talk much, say little, do nothing, and be paid for it, would fit me nicely." Dingle's response: "Do you know, booby, that you have crammed into a nutshell the very quintessence of Court life. Law, Physic, and Divinity keep their coaches by the same receipt. Tho' you are a booby, Roger, you was born a wit!" The comic scenes are but counterpoint for the serious lines spoken by the Genius of England in advice to Edward and coming from West's poem. With the Knights seated at the Round Table, the Genius prophesies the future glory of Edward's line, while bards, druids, and spirits join in a chorus of praise.[46]

## The Meeting of the Company; or, Bayes's Art of Acting

The prelude, *The Meeting of the Company*, opened the season of 1774–75, and contains, as we noted in chapter 2, above, Garrick's satirical strictures on all that he abhorred in bad acting, and, in addition, in bad audience behavior. The actors in the prelude enter under their own names—Parsons, Weston, Baddeley, Miss Platt, and Hurst. They are pictured just returning from activities in summer stock, and are due to hear one Bayes read them a lesson, in some 64 lines of wretched verse, on ways of acting that will ensure success, even for the most mediocre—the subtitle is "the worst equal to the best."

Drury Lane theatre and its company were so well known to the regular theatregoers, even to the names of its carpenters and sweepers, that it was amusing to see them on stage in their own persons. Instead of two interlocutors, for Bayes, as in the ancestor play Buckingham's *The Rehearsal*, the actors and the prompter, Hopkins, all comment on the lesson, and draw Bayes out, but the low comedian Tom Weston takes the lead in comment, satirical approbation, and in probing as the conceited Bayes carries on:

*Bayes reads*: "Gold is a scarce commodity—

*Weston*: So it is.

*Bayes*: Don't interrupt me—
    "Gold is a scarce commodity—but *Brass*
    "Of which no Scarcity, as well may pass.

*Weston*: There's comfort again for us, these hard times—

*Bayes*: That I may not Burden your minds too much, which may be
    overloaded already; I shall comprise the Art of Acting Tragedy &
    Comedy in a few lines—You have heard of the Iliad in a Nut Shell—
    here it is.

*Weston*: Crack away & give us the Kernel.

Since the gist of Bayes's argument has been given above, one instance of his prescription for effective stage presence will suffice here:

    "To heighten Terror—be it wrong or right,
    "Be black your Coat, your handkerchief be white.
    "Thus pull your hair to add to your distress.
    "What your face cannot, let your Wig Express.

This merry caper allowed Garrick to get some things off his chest
and to allow the audience a cutaway view (in the early part of the skit)
of how a company went into action after the summer's absence:
    Directions for the set: *"The Curtain rises & discovers the Stage full
of different people at Work. Painters, Gilders, Carpenters, etc. Singers—singing, Dancers dancing, Actors & Actresses Saluting each other,
& all seem busy."*

    *Enter Carpenter*: We shall never be ready if you don't give up the
    Stage to us! Lower the Clouds there, Rag, and bid Jack Trundle
    sweep out the Thunder Trunk, we had very slovenly Storms last Sea-
    son. M^r. Hopkins did you ever see such Litter, & hear such a Noise?

This was a one-season production, called for 11 times, and useful as
a novelty, but not for much repetition.


## THE THEATRICAL CANDIDATES


Garrick, having refurbished his theatre in the summer of 1776, opened
the season, his last, on 23 September with another prelude, instead of

a customary prologue, *The Theatrical Candidates*. It was called for on 18 occasions that year. The piece is a three-way debate about Drury Lane policy in its repertoire and about limitations in dramatic genres. Mercury descends from above to see Drury Lane, and to introduce Tragedy, Comedy, and Harlequinade to the new-furbished house. Each in turn pleads with the audience for major support of its specific type of entertainment. Mercury goes to get Apollo's judgment in the matter as they argue. Comedy wants an either-or choice, "*That* murdering Lady or *this* laughing Muse." Tragedy deplores any mixture of genres, for says she, Comedy has among the writers become "wise with stale sentiments stollen from me," and continues, "Which long cast off from my heroic verses / Have stuff'd your motley, dull sentenious farces." Harlequin enters a pragmatic note:

> For all your airs, sharp looks, and sharper nails
> Draggled you were till I held up your tails.
> She's [comedy] grown so grave, and she [tragedy] so cross and bloody,
> Without my help, your brains will all be muddy.
> Deep thoughts and politics so stir *your* gall (addressing the audience),
> When you come here, you should not think at all.

Mercury returns with Apollo's verdict which calls for a rational balance of all three in the repertory, and each in his separate genre, unless Shakespeare bring them all together. The policy was not new, for both Garrick and Rich had been carrying out a balanced series of plays for 30 years. The mixture of genres within the plays themselves seemed to need some straightening out.

## THE CLANDESTINE MARRIAGE

One of the very happy collaborations in the eighteenth century, that between Garrick and his younger friend George Colman, produced one of the most entertaining comedies of the period, *The Clandestine Marriage*. It appeared on 20 February 1766 with a brilliant cast, and has made its mark as a living stage play down to our own times. For a number of years academic controversy has flared regarding the exact proportions contributed by each collaborator. Professor F. L. Bergmann, from careful study of a manuscript discovered in the Folger Shakespeare Library (unavailable to earlier scholars) settles the matter for all practical purposes, demonstrating that Garrick actually wrote the last half of the play, "how much more we cannot know for certain, for the manuscript does not cover the whole play." It does indicate, however, that Garrick's portion includes a great deal more than previous scholarship has granted him—principally much of Mrs. Heidelberg's dialogue, "the whole character of Lord Ogleby, much of the clandestine marriage plot, and the masterful fifth act—the best writing in the entire comedy."[47]

The effect of the actor-as-dramatist shows in every scene. The plot moves with complications, with increasing tension, and with surprises that keep any audience fascinated and amused, even though the relationships and intrigues on stage present a traditional mix—the old and the young, the penniless and the rich, the social parvenus and the blameless young lovers. The title of the play itself had a certain startling, bold ring, even as late as 1766, for "consent" and "ceremony" were demanded for legal marriage by a succession of laws from the time of William III. *The General Advertiser* on 11 November 1748 reminded all readers that: "Clandestine marriages are illegal and punishable by the Statute of 7th and 8th of King William, Chap. 35 under which Law the Parson shall forfeit One Hundred Pounds; and every man married without Banns or Licence shall forfeit ten pounds, to be recovered with costs, by any Person that informs."[48] In 1754, Philip Yorke, Lord Hardwicke's *Marriage Act* spelled out clearly the seriousness and means with which marriage was to be undertaken. "From 26 March 1754, all marriages in England—save those of Quakers, Jews, and members of the Royal Family—had to be celebrated after banns, or by a special license, in the parish church, between 8:00 and noon, in the presence of two witnesses. An Anglican clergyman and the Anglican liturgy were necessary. Parliament broke sharply with the Canon Law tradition that consent, not ceremony, made the marriage. . . . Enforcement of the law was not left to the church; the government provided, and on several occasions inflicted, 14 years transportation for clergy who performed services contrary to the provisions of the act."[49] To advertise a comedy treating in bold face with the subject could both raise eyebrows and also probably breed attendance. One remembers Garrick's character Sharp, the lying valet, who glowed when he said, "Oh, the delights of impudence with a good understanding!" Garrick and Colman had a title that would draw. The clandestine marriage causes all the amusing problems in the play, which are only solved by the generosity and understanding of Lord Ogleby, and the deference to his position and wealth by Mrs. Heidelberg and merchant Sterling.

But to the story. Sterling, a parvenu whose wealth is his life, has two marriageable daughters—Miss Sterling, the elder, and young Fanny.

His household also includes his sister, the redoubtable, socially ambitious Mrs. Heidelberg (a Mrs. Malaprop before her time), who worships people of "Qualaty." Miss Sterling, her favorite of her two nieces, is about to be married to Sir John Melvil, who is coming to the house with his wealthy old uncle Lord Ogleby for the ceremony. Young Lovewell, a penniless clerk in Stockwell's counting house, has fallen in love with young Fanny (and she with him), and as the play opens he has married her clandestinely. She worries and wishes him to tell her father. Lovewell plans to wait a day to enlist the aid of Lord Ogleby whose wealth and position working in his cause might persuade both Sterling and the dominating Sister Heidelberg to consent to Fanny's marriage with one so low in the economic scale of things. He pleads for delay until Miss Sterling is safely married to Sir John Melvil. Sir John and his uncle arrive, and soon Sir John discovers that it was Fanny he wanted for wife, *not* Miss Sterling. Fanny, much perturbed, approaches Lord Ogleby hesitantly, enlisting his support of her against Sir John's advancements. Ogleby, full of self-love, mistakes the intent of her sensitive behavior and believes that he himself is the object of her affections. Preening himself, he marches forth in conquest, announcing his intent to marry her to Sterling, to Sir John Melvil and to Lovewell. Great consternation in the household! Sterling sends Lovewell to London to get some papers for Ogleby, but the young man, intending to reveal the marriage next morning, remains on the estate, hiding in Fanny's room. Mrs. Heidelberg and Miss Sterling discover that a man is there, and thinking it to be Melvil planning an elopement with the younger sister, arouse the household for a confrontation. To the group, and to the utter astonishment of everyone (Fanny having fainted at the sight), Lovewell dashes from the room.

*Miss Sterling*: Lovewell—I am easy—

*Mrs. Heidelberg*: I am Thunderstruck!

*Lord Ogleby*: I am petrify'd!

*Melvil*: And I undone!

*Sterling* (after a time) Lovewell, you are a villain!

Sterling, enraged, orders Lovewell and Fanny out of the house, but Lord Ogleby generously interposes, whereupon Sterling and the nobility-worshipping Mrs. Heidelberg, forgive them. Poor Miss Sterling stands by in an angered daze.

The confluence of characters in the last scene makes excellent drama, for not only the main ones, but the servants arrive, each with an attitude or comment that adds to the merry excitement—all with perfect timing.

Garrick and Colman topped themselves in this piece, which works with the essence of comic dramaturgy. For herein are the manners comedy of the Restoration (plot and situations) blending with the older humors comedy of Ben Jonson (characters Ogleby and Heidelberg); clever servants from Roman tradition (Brush and Canton); amusing types and local color in speech; sentimental lovers, but treated with a touch of whimsy (Lovewell and Fanny); a pound-minded merchant (Sterling), "the very abstract of Change Alley"; and a sour-maid who has missed her market, material for the termagants of Restoration plays (Miss Sterling). Contemporary spectators not only enjoyed the ridicule of landscape gardening, as practiced by the tasteless Sterling crowd, but saw the lineage of Lord Ogleby direct from Garrick's Lord Chalkstone, coming from his Fine Gentleman in *Lethe*, and cousin germane to his Sir Charles Clackit in *The Guardian* and Sir Simon Loveit in *Miss in Her Teens*. And not the least attractive feature of that opening night (and of several succeeding ones) was the Garrick *Epilogue*, in the form of a playlet. Four Ladies and three Lords are playing cards, and discussing (in between bids) new plays and the values of song and opera. They await Miss Crochet, who is at Drury Lane planning to damn *The Clandestine Marriage*. She returns to report that the damnation failed to materialize, but maybe the next night they could bring it off.

*Col. Trill*: But tell us, Miss, the subject of the play.

*Miss Crochet*: Why, 'twas a marriage—yes, a marriage—Stay!
    A Lord, an Aunt, two sisters, and a Merchant—
    A Baronet, ten lawyers, a fat serjeant,
    Are all produc'd—to talk with one another;
    And about something make a mighty pother;
    They all go in, and out, and to, and fro,
    And talk and quarrel—as they come and go.
    Then go to bed, and then get up—and then
    Scream, faint, scold, kiss—and go to bed again.
    Such is the play—your judgment! never sham it.

*Col. Trill*: O damn it!

*Mrs. Quaver*: Damn it!

*1st Lady*: Damn it!

*Miss Crochet*: Damn it!

*Lord Minum*: Damn it!

Garrick, the psychologist of crowds, enjoyed no end complimenting his audience in general by setting up extreme imaginary freaks in it to criticize his plays. It made everyone watching hug himself and feel superior. Colman may have polished up the character of Mrs Heidelberg, so capably portrayed on stage by Mrs Clive, but to Garrick's sense of comic creativity went Lord Ogleby—the superannuated juvenile in spirit, but the no-fool in his observations on the persons, decor, habits, taste, and motives of the Sterling family. Garrick made him a character and a caricature. The scene where he winds himself up to face the day—with a sip of surfeit water, a sniff of cephalic snuff, a splash of peppermint water, some oil for gouty joints, and some rouge for his complexion, lasts long in the memory and offers the actor great chance for humorous interpretation. His scenes with Mr Sterling, polite in speech, but cruel in meaning, as his parenthetical remarks undercut civilities, characterize him on first appearance as the brittle hard-nosed lord of a Congreve or Etherege play, but Garrick gives him a subtle warmth and genuine sense, which makes plausible his willingness to extricate Fanny from the clutches of her father and incredible aunt. Garrick's comic creativity at its best!

# 8

# Garrick's Adaptations of Older Plays

NOTABLE IN THE Garrick canon of plays is the complete lack of attempt at a tragedy—comedy, farces aplenty, pantomime, musicals, burlesques, preludes, interludes, and skits, many with serious veins (semi-exposed, for satire has a serious as well as a merry bent), but no formal tragic piece. He found God's plenty in the tragic vein in the great plays of England's past, largely (but not exclusively) in Shakespeare. His genius lay not in imitating those plays (as a number of writers had tried to do), but in making their texts live anew on stage by restoring them in many ways to their authors.

Twenty-nine of Shakespeare's corpus of plays (tragedy, comedy, and history) had enjoyed some sort of life on the Restoration and early eighteenth-century stages, but *few* appeared in full Shakespearean dress. Of the 29, ten were early failures (*A Midsummer Night's Dream*, *Coriolanus* (rewritten by Tate as *The Ingratitude of the Commonwealth*); *Richard II* (as Tate's *Sicilian Usurper*); *2 Henry VI* (as Crowne's *Misery of Civil War*); and *1 Henry VI* (Crowne's *Henry VI*, *with the Murder of the Duke of Gloucester*); *The Merry Wives of Windsor* (as John Dennis's *Comical Gallant*); *Twelfth Night* (as Charles Burnaby's *Love Betrayed*); *Measure for Measure* (as Davenant's *Law Against Lovers*); *Pericles*; and *A Midsummer Night's Dream* (made into an opera *The Fairies* by Elkanah Settle).

Three more were made into operas, or near operas, *Macbeth*, *The Tempest*, and *Timon of Athens* (done by Shadwell with Purcell's music, and giving Timon a new mistress, and a lady whom he would marry). Nine more remained in drastically altered condition—suitable, to be sure, to the times, but not long-lasting in their altered forms. Four of these had new titles—*The Jew of Venice* by Lansdowne; *Sauny The Scot* (Lacy's *Taming of the Shrew*); *The Injured Princess* (altered from *Cymbeline*); *Caius Marius* (Otway's version of *Romeo and Juliet*)—*Titus Andronicus* (altered by Ravenscroft); *Lear* (altered by Tate); *Troilus and Cressida* (altered by Dryden); *Measure*

*for Measure* (Gildon's version); *Richard III* (Colley Cibber's alteration). Six certainly remained close to the Shakespearean versions, the
only alterations being made by cuts—*Hamlet, Othello, Julius Caesar,
1 Henry IV, The Merry Wives* (after the failure of *The Comical Gallant*), and *2 Henry IV*. One other remained, *Henry VIII*, but with an
emphasis placed heavily upon a spectacle of the coronation scene.[1]

It has been fashionable to downgrade the adaptations and altered
versions, but while a Betterton, or a Wilkes, or a Barton Booth played
in them, they moved audiences to merriment or to deep emotion. "I
must not omit praises due to Mr. Betterton," writes Colley Cibber,
"He like an old stately spreading oak stands fixt, environ'd round with
brave young flourishing plants; there needs nothing to speak his fame,
more than the following parts . . . , and he lists sixteen of which eight
were Shakespearean—Pericles, Lear, Hamlet, Macbeth, Timon,
Othello, Henry VIII, and Falstaff."[2]

Garrick had read of Betterton's fame, and had talked with actors who
had seen him. Garrick knew of the 11 Shakespearean plays still in the
theatre repertories—a cut version of *Hamlet*, Tate's version of *Lear*,
Colley Cibber's *Richard III* (in which he had made his own debut), an
infrequent performance, or two of Theobald's version of *Richard II*,
*Julius Caesar, Henry VIII*, and *Othello*, Davenant's *Macbeth*, Theophilus Cibber's revival of *Romeo and Juliet*, Shadwell's *Timon*, and
*The Tempest*, made operatic by Dryden, Davenant, and Shadwell.
When he came to London a mini-revival of interest in *Twelfth Night,
As You Like It, Cymbeline, The Winter's Tale*, and *King John* appeared, perhaps under sponsorship of the Shakespeare Ladies' Club,
and aided by a reaction against new plays attendant upon passage of
the Stage Licensing Act of 1737.[3] In tragic drama, Garrick very early
began to *read* Shakespeare, and to see tremendous possibilities, not
only for acting parts in the plays, but for fresh approaches to the texts
of most of them—especially of *Hamlet, King Lear, Richard III, Macbeth, Othello*, and *Romeo and Juliet*—in all of which he shone, and to
all of which he put his creative hand for heavy restorations and some
adjustments of the original text. Close examination of a number of
them shows the way Garrick the skillful adapter worked. The principles therein established carried over to his adaptations of non-Shakespearean tragedies as well—to Southerne's *Isabella* and Voltaire's
*Zaire*.

## MACBETH

Throughout, Garrick showed intellectual and aesthetic concern for Shakespeare's sheer magic weight of wording and a reverence for Shakespeare's poetry, seen dramatically in his rescue of the text of *Macbeth* from the bland verbiage of Davenant who, for example, had flattened Lady Macbeth's reaction to her lord's news about his early honors, the witches' hints, and the impending visit of Duncan:

> Glamis thou art, and Cawdor, and shalt be
> What thou art promis'd; Yet I fear thy nature
> Has too much of the milk of human kindness
> To take the nearest way: Thou would'st be great
> Thou dost not want ambition, but the ill
> Which should attend it: what thou highly covet'st
> Thou covet'st holily: Alas! thou art
> Loth to play false, and yet would'st wrongly win
> O how irregular are thy desires!
> Thou willingly, great Glamis, would'st enjoy
> The end without the means! Oh haste thee hither
> That I may pour my spirits in thy ear:
> And chastize with the valor of my tongue
> Thy too effeminate desires of that
> Which supernatural assistance seems
> To crown thee with.

Davenant's meanings are clear, but Shakespeare's stirring and quickened imaginings for lady Macbeth in moving verse are absent. Garrick restored them here, and in the text throughout the play:

> Glamis thou art and Cawdor—and shalt be
> What thou art promis'd. Yet do I fear thy nature:
> It is too full of the milk of human kindness
> To catch the nearest way. Thou would'st be great,
> Art not without ambition, but without
> The illness should attend it. What thou would'st highly
> That would'st thou holily; would'st not play false,
> And yet would'st *strongly* win. Thou'd have, great Glamis
> That which cries, thus must thou do, if thou have *me*
> And that which rather thou dost fear to do,
> Than wishes should be undone. Hie thee hither
> That I may pour my spirits in thine ear,
> And chastize with the valour of my tongue,
> All that impedes thee from the golden round
> Which fate and metaphysic aid doth seem
> To have thee crown'd withal.

The words in italics clue us to Garrick's source, which was the most recent issue of the text by Lewis Theobald (London, 1740).

Garrick the actor-dramatist saw need for having a text that would show the psychological strain and appealing imagination of Macbeth, hence restored the following lines to his soliloquy before Duncan's murder, "If it were done, when 'tis done . . . ," omitted in the Davenant version:

> And Pity like a new-born babe,
> Striding the blast, or heavn's cherubim hors'd
> Upon the sightless courses of the air,
> Shall blow the horrid deed in every eye,
> That tears shall drown the wind. I have no spur
> To prick the sides of my intent, but only
> Vaulting ambition, which o'er leaps itself
> And falls on th'other.

Likewise he restores four lines (indicated by italics) in Macbeth's reaction to news that Fleance has escaped:

> Then comes my fit again: *I had else been perfect.*
> *Whole as marble, founded as the rock;*
> *As broad and gen'ral as the casing air,*
> *But now I am cabin'd, cribb'd, confin'd bound in*
> *To saucy doubts and fears.* But Banquo's safe?

Davenant, with a passion for balance, had added many lines for Lady Macduff to make her a better foil for his Lady Macbeth. These Garrick eliminated, and kept to the original text. In the Shakespeare play the last we see of Macbeth is as he exits fighting with Macduff, crying, "Lay on, Macduff, And damn'd be he that first cries, hold, enough," only to have his head brought in a moment later by the victorious Macduff. Garrick wanted his Macbeth to die on stage, so created a dying scene that was enthusiastically received by his audiences. His lines follow, with no attempt to imitate Shakespeare, only to provide vehicle for his demise as acting the part, picking up, however, on the 'life as a stage' image, his 'vaulting ambition,' and the trail of blood he has left:

> 'Tis done! the scene of life will quickly close—
> Ambition's vain, delusive, dreams are fled,
> And now I wake to darkness, guilt, and horror.
> I cannot bear it, let me shake it off—
> 'Two' not be; my soul is clogg'd with blood—
> I cannot rise! I dare not ask for mercy—
> It is too late, hell drags me down. I sink,
> I sink—Oh!—my soul is lost forever! (Dies)

Garrick's first performance, 7 January 1744, advertised "the Tragedy Reviv'd as Shakespeare Wrote it," which called forth some surprise from Quin, who asked, "What does he mean? Don't I play Macbeth as written by Shakespeare?"[4]

## ROMEO AND JULIET

During the early months of the 1748–49 season Garrick prepared *Romeo and Juliet* for its first performance ever at Drury Lane theatre, instructing Spranger Barry and Mrs Cibber in the title roles. It first appeared on 19 November 1748, ran 19 times during the season, and grossed the managers some £3,000.[5] In adapting the text he worked with a freer hand than some of his subsequent admirers wished,[6] for aside from cuts in the basic text, he transposed some scenes, made some emendations, and provided additions to the death scene, allowing Juliet to awaken just before Romeo expires, as Otway had done. Davies thought it "written with a spirit not unworthy of Shakespeare himself," and Frances Gentleman agreed. He wished that Garrick had both retrenched more and added more of his own, but who can account for tastes! Readers seemed to like it as well as theatregoers. Demand for the version was so steady that a new printing appeared on the average of every three years from 1748 to 1787.[7] Garrick tells in the "advertisements" of the first three editions just what changes in outline he had made.

In the first place he made certain structural changes concerned almost entirely with the excision of Rosaline in Act I (as had T. Cibber) and with the addition of a death scene to Act V. In the second place he sought throughout the play to reduce "quibble," the endless puns and plays upon words that crop up in the speeches of the main as well as the subordinate characters—deference to eighteenth-century "taste." In the third place he made some, though not extensive, effort to reduce the "jingle" in the play. This term refers to the use of rhyme in certain passages instead of blank verse. The motive seems to have been to obtain a piece in which the dialogue should be as natural as possible. Injury done to the play on this score is not great, inasmuch as Garrick's emendations of rhyming words amount to less than 28 throughout the whole play. The usual process may be exemplified:

*Friar Lawrence:* Young son, it argues a distemper'd head
So soon to bid good morrow to thy *bed*:

> Care keeps his watch in every old man's eye,
> And where care lodges, sleep will never *lie*;
> But where unbruised youth with unstuff'd brain
> Doth couch his limbs, there golden sleep *doth reign*. (II. ii. 32–38)

Garrick substituted the words *pillow* and *hide* for *bed* and *lie*, and rearranged the last two lines to read:

> But where with unstuff'd brain unbruised youth
> Doth couch his limbs, there golden sleep *resides*.

Later, when Benvolio speaks:

> O noble Prince! I can discover all
> The unlucky manage of this fatal *brawl*
> That slew thy kinsman, brave Mercutio.

> *Lady Cap.*: Tybalt, my cousin! O my brother's child!
> O Prince! O cousin! husband! O the blood is spill'd
> Of my dear kinsman. Prince as thou art *true*,
> For blood of ours shed blood of Montague. (III. i. 148–55)

Garrick changes *brawl* to *quarrel*, and rearranges Lady Capulet's speech, which he gives to Capulet, as follows:

> *Cap*: Unhappy sight alas! the blood is spill'd
> Of my dear kinsman. Now as thou are *Prince*
> For blood of ours shed blood of Montague.

The "jingle" has been removed but not much poetry that would feed the waters of the spirit has been sacrificed. Garrick did not comb through the play to break up all the rhymes. He altered enough to satisfy the average playgoer of the century. When, however, he came upon such a speech as Friar Lawrence's at the opening of Act II, scene iii, "The grey-eyed morn smiles on the frowning night, Chequering the eastern clouds with streaks of light . . . etc.," he made no attempt to regulate it: he merely cut the eight lines referring to a drunkard and to the "womb" of nature, and left the remaining 20 intact. It was contemporary Francis Gentleman who wanted to dignify this speech by turning it into blank verse, and did so in his *Dramatic Censor*.

To compete with the performance at Covent Garden (after 1750) with its solemn dirge at Juliet's funeral, Garrick wrote such a dirge for his version, and commissioned William Boyce to set it to music.[8] Lady Capulet lost much by Garrick's cuts; Lady Montagu lost all. But in the acting text Romeo still loves, Mercutio cracks wise, Tybalt is hasty and ill-tempered, Capulet and Montagu remain typical Italian fathers. Benvolio is as pleasant a companion, and the servants are still louts. The Nurse is still garrulous and risquée (if not bawdy) in her reminiscences. The beauty of Juliet still "hangs upon the cheek of night Like a rich jewel in an Ethiop's ear." The play gains speed and movement. The serious loss to the lover of words is, perhaps, found only in the shortening of the delightful verbiage in the love scenes between Romeo and Juliet at the ball. In reducing the "quibble" Garrick lost some pretty word-play concerned with *saint, pilgrim, lips* and *sin.* Juliet falls rather swiftly in love with Romeo—too much so at the ball to suit Francis Gentleman, and some others.

Just after Romeo drinks the poison Garrick added his new 75-line death scene which so thrilled eighteenth-century audiences.

*Rom:* . . . *seal with a righteous kiss.*
   Soft—soft—she breathes, and stirs (Juliet wakes)

*Jul:* Where am I? defend me powers!

*Rom:* She speaks, she lives; and we shall still be bless'd!
   My kind propitious stars o'erpay me now
   For all my sorrows past—rise, rise my *Juliet,*
   And from this cave of death, this house of horror,
   Quick let me snatch thee to thy Romeo's arms,
   There breathe a vital spirit in thy lips,
   And call thee back to live and love! (Takes her hand.)

*Jul:* Bless me! how cold it is! Who's there!

*Rom:* Thy husband.
   It is thy *Romeo,* Love, rais'd from despair
   To joys unutterable! quit, quit this place
   And let us fly together—(Brings her from the tomb.)

*Jul:* Why do you force me so—I'll ne'er consent
   I'll not wed *Paris—Romeo* is my husband—

*Rom:* Her senses are unsettled—Restore 'em Heav'n!
   Romeo is thy husband; I am that Romeo,
   Nor all th' opposing pow'rs of earth or man
   Can break our bonds, or tear thee from my heart.

*Jul:* I know that voice—Its magic sweetness wakes
   My tranced soul—I now remember well
   Each circumstance—O my lord, my *Romeo!*
   Had'st thou not come, sure I had slept forever;
   But there's a sovereign charm in thy embraces
   That can revive the dead—O honest *Friar!*
   Dost thou avoid me *Romeo?* let me touch
   Thy hand and taste the cordial of thy lips—
   You fright me—Speak—O let me hear some voice
   Besides my own in this drear vault of death,
   Or I shall faint—support me—

*Rom*: O I cannot,
    I have no strength, but want thy feeble aid,
    Cruel poison!

*Jul*: Poison! What means my lord; thy trembling voice!
    Pale lips! and swimming eyes! death's in thy face!

*Rom*: It is indeed—I struggle with him now—
    The transports that I felt, to hear thee speak,
    His impetuous course, and all my mind
    Was happiness and thee: but now the poison
    Rushes thro' my veins—I've not time to tell—
    Fate brought me to this place—to take a last,
    Last farewell of my love and with thee die.

*Jul*: Die! was the Friar false!

*Rom*: I know not that,
    I thought thee dead! distracted at the sight
    (Fatal speed) drank poison, kiss'd thy cold lips
    And found within thy arms a precious grave—
    But in that moment—O—

*Jul*: And did I wake for this!

*Rom*: My powers are blasted,
    Twixt death and love I'm torn—I am distracted!
    But death's strongest—And I must leave thee, Juliet!
    O cruel, cursed fate!—in sight of heav'n—

*Jul*: Thou rav'st—lean on my breast—

*Rom*: Fathers have flinty hearts, no tears can melt 'em
    Nature pleads in vain—children must be wretched

*Jul*: O my breaking heart—

*Rom*: She is my wife—our hearts are twin'd together
    Capulet forbear—Paris loose your hold—
    Pull not our heartstrings thus—they crack—they break—
    O Juliet! Juliet

*Jul*: Stay, stay for me Romeo—a moment stay; fate marries us in death
    And we are one—no pow'r shall part us. (Faints on Romeo's body)

Hereupon the text returns to Shakespeare where Friar Lawrence
enters and speaks:

Saint Francis be my speed! How oft tonight
Have my old feet stumbled at graves! Who's there?
Alack! what blood is this which stains [21 lines cut]
The stony entrance of this sepulchre?
*Ah Juliet awake, and Romeo dead.* What Paris too
*Oh* what an unkind hour
Is guilty of this lamentable chance!

Then follows the remainder of Garrick's addition:

*Jul*: Here he is still, and I will hold him fast,
    They shall not tear him from me—

*Friar*: Patience Lady—

*Jul*: Who is that! O thou cursed Friar! Patience!
    Talk'st thou of patience to a wretch like me!

*Friar*: O fatal error! rise thou fair distrest
    And fly this scene of death!

*Jul*: Come thou not near me
    Or this dagger shall quit my Romeo's death. (Draws dagger.)

*Friar*: I wonder not thy griefs have made thee desp'rate.
    What noise without? sweet Juliet, let us fly—

At this point the text returns again to the Shakespearean one, where the Friar offers to dispose of her "amongst a sisterhood of happy nuns," but leaves upon hearing the approach of others, and Juliet stabs herself. The final scene is short in Garrick's version. The explanation of everything is briefly carried out. Montague and Capulet become reconciled, and the Prince closes in six of Garrick's lines:

> Let Romeo's man, and let the boy attend us:
> We'll hence, and further scan this sad disaster.
> Well may you mourn, my lords (now wise too late)
> These tragic issues of your mortal hate:
> From private feuds, what dire misfortunes flow,
> Whate'er the cause, the sure effect is WOE.

## OTHELLO and RICHARD III

On 7 March 1745 Garrick first appeared as Othello, and we know for certain that he sought for novelty in the text he was to act in, and that the novelty was his restoration of the "trance scene" early in Act IV. This argues for Garrick's close reading of the Shakespearean text, his pondering the way to suit motion to the words, and broken speech of his response to Iago's hints of concupiscence between Desdemona and Cassio:

*Iago*: I know not what he did.

*Othello*: What? What?

*Iago*: Lie—

*Othello*: With her?

*Iago*: With her, on her, what you will.

Othello's speech becomes disordered by the shock, as his imagination runs before and after, as he repeats "Handkerchief" "Confess" "instruction," "Noses, ears, and lips" "O devil." The stage direction reads that he falls into a trance. He must freeze or fall in order to give meaning to Iago's immediate gloating: "Work on, my Medicine, work! Thus credulous fools are caught," and after a few more observations calls out, "What ho, my lord! My Lord, I say, Othello." And Cassio entering tries to help break the spell under which Othello is laboring, "Have you not hurt your head?" As Othello comes to, he gropes still for full consciousness, "Dost thou mock me?" and runs on about the theme of cuckoldry for a moment or two. Garrick's interpretation here regards text, but actually innovates wordless action.

Existing prompt copies and the Bell edition "regulated from the prompt book, with the permission of the managers by Mr. Hopkins" (1773) have been studied in search of the Garrick contribution. Nothing definitive has been found, save for the usual cuts and emendations to comply with religious reverence, and numerous small grammatical changes. Iago never exclaims "Zounds," or "Diablo," even his "I'faith" is changed to "trust me." Cassio needs must say "fore Heav'n," instead of "'fore God," and Othello and Desdemona are not even allowed a "by Heaven," or a "Heav'n bless us." "With *who*, Emelia," becomes "With *whom*, Emelia." Iago calls Othello a "lustful Moor" instead of a "Lusty Moor;" "her motion blush'd at herself," becomes "blush'd at itself," and so go 17 or 18 tightenings of the text with rather meticulous care. By the time of the Bell edition the trance scene had again been omitted, as well as the ocular evidence of the Handkerchief in Cassio's hands, the musicians and clown scene at the beginning of Act III, and Desdemona's preparing for bed with her "Willow Song" at the close of Act IV. One feels Garrick had no hand in such cuts. He had long ceased to play either role, Othello or Iago.[9]

## RICHARD III

Garrick's performance as Richard III is usually dismissed with the comment that he played the Colley Cibber text, which he certainly did on the night of 19 October 1741. Cibber had made his alteration in

1694, when William III was nearing the end of his reign, and when uncertainties about the succession were in the air. Cibber had taken scenes liberally from Shakespeare's 3 *Henry VI* to start his version, and the Master of the Revels, when reading it for production, struck out the whole first act on the ground that "the distresses of King Henry VI, who is killed by Richard in that act, would put weak people too much in mind of King James then living in France." Cibber had to stretch the four remaining acts to five, until the first one was much later recovered.

It now becomes apparent, however, that Garrick gradually made the text his own, and in it emphasized the bloody, cold, and complex nature of Richard (as he understood him to be). A careful collation of three texts—a 1734 duodecimo printed for W. Feales, "As it is now acted at the Theatre Royal in Drury Lane," with Cibber cast as Richard, a duodecimo printed in Dublin, 1756, for Brice Edmond, "As it is now acted at the Theatre Royal in Drury Lane, Covent Garden and Smock Alley," with Garrick cast as Richard, Bell's edition, 1774 (regulated from the promptbook with permission of the managers), also with Garrick cast as Richard—shows that Garrick did not use the Cibber exclusively.

The Shakespearean play in the Globe edition is 3,621 lines in length. Cibber's play is 1,500 lines shorter, and Garrick's version is 75 lines shorter than Cibber's.

The more notable additions and subtractions are as follows: In Act I when Richard makes his first entrance, Cibber has him describe himself briefly in 28 lines. Apparently Garrick did the same until sometime after 1756, when he restored five of Shakespeare's lines to the speech—lines which emphasize the tyrant's physical deformity and his lack of interest in love and the follies of peacetime:

> Nor made to court the Am'rous looking glass
> I, that am rudely stamp'd, and want love's majesty
> To strut before a wanton, ambling nymph.
> (I, that am curtail'd of man's fair proportion)
> Cheated of features by dissembling nature.

The restoration of this gives more point to the effrontery of his courting Lady Anne. And in the acting, Garrick allowed him recurrent changes of pace between the moody, the calculating, the splenetic, as he constantly assesses himself, his motives and his person, throughout the play. The rest of Garrick's significant changes were in the nature of cuts in order to speed up the play. The result was, according to Francis Gentleman, "a very peculiar merit . . . that each act rises above the other, and the whole piece is alive with increasing spirit to the end." [10]

Lady Anne's curse, in Act II, upon the head of the man who killed Henry VI, the same length in the 1734 and 1756 versions, is shortened in the 1774 version. But Garrick did not curtail the speeches of his supporting cast only. He cut lines from his own part with as much rigor as from the parts of others. In the same act five lines of his love-making to Anne are marked for excision as early as 1756, and are absent in the 1774 version as well.

> I ask but leave to indulge my cold Despair:
> By Heav'n there's joy in this Extravagance
> O! Woe—'tis melting, soft, 'tis pleasing Ruin.
> Oh! 'tis too much, too much for Life to bear
> This aching tenderness of thought.

But enough was retained that he might exult,

> Was ever Woman in this humour woo'd?
> Was ever Woman in this humour won?
> I'll have her but I will not keep her long.

Perhaps it was for the sake of the mid-eighteenth-century standard of delicacy that in Act III he, as Richard, only hinted in his advice to Buckingham, "But above all infer the bastardy of Edward's children," and left out the following nine lines (present in Cibber's text, which cut ten more from Shakespeare's and so changed the meaning as to render it absurd), which elaborate upon that advice:

> Nay for a need, thus far come near my person.
> Tell 'em, when my mother went with child of me
> My princely father then had wars in France
> And by true computation of the time.
> Found that the issue was not his true begot
> Which in his lineaments too plain appear'd.
> Being nothing like the noble York my father;
> Yet touch this sparingly, as 'twere far off.
> Because you know, my Lord, my mother lives.

Also in the third act, according to the Cibber version, Lady Anne, just before she is told by Richard that she has outlived his liking, soliloquizes on her sleepless nights. The soliloquy,

> How many labouring wretches take their rest
> While I, night after night, with cares lie waking.

is a rude mixture of Cibber's invention and King Henry IV's observations of the beginning of Act III of 2 Henry IV. This melding Garrick cut after 1756 and came to the point more swiftly. In the Prayer-book

Scene in that act Garrick cut six lines in 1756 from Buckingham's speech reprimanding Richard for not taking the crown offered, but restored them before 1774.

In the fourth act, a whole speech of Richard's in which he professes to the Queen his love for her daughter Elizabeth was cut by Garrick as early as 1756. The omission speeded up the action and gave the actors a chance to display their talents in making the situation convincing. The cutting by seven lines of the last speech of Richard's in that act gave Garrick the opportunity, by looks and motions, to interpret his state of mind to the audience instead of expressing it in a simile.

> And as a wretch whose fever-weaken'd joints,
> Like strengthless hinges, buckle under life
> Impatient.

which Cibber borrowed from 2 *Henry IV*.

In the last act Richard reads an invention, as he calls it, of the enemy's to scare him:

> Jockey of Norfolk, be not too bold
> For Dickon, thy master, is bought and sold.

He then calms himself and orders his men out to battle, warning them that they are to fight

> A scum of Britons. Rascals, Runaways,
> Whom their o'ercloyed Country vomits forth.
> To desperate adventures, and assured Destruction.

Cibber and Shakespeare continue this strain of vituperation:

> If we be conquer'd let men conquer us.
> And not these Bastard Britons.

But Garrick omitted them, and cut also in his 1756 version two spurious lines of Cibber's which he restored to the 1774 text.

Each time Garrick performed this character, from his gradually changing text, audiences enjoyed the pleasures of recognizing what had in a way become familiar, but also enjoyed supplemental novelties of interpretation which the actor constantly created. The character thus came through, upon repetition, like a palimpsest. Not only did gesture and tone reveal new depths, but textual changes administered to them and to qualities of character perhaps not fully fathomed at a first viewing. Richard's character is cued for the actor by the statement in the Cibber text (from 3 *Henry VI*) "I that, have neither pity, love, nor fear." and Garrick worked from that.[11] The Cibber-Garrick version held the stage through the nineteenth century.

## KING LEAR

Richard Cross, the Drury Lane prompter, noted in his *Diary* for the night of 28 October 1756: "KING LEAR with Restorations from Shakespeare." Box receipts which had averaged £140 per night shot up to £200.

As with the Davenant *Macbeth* and its development, Garrick started *Lear* with Tate, but ended with a play much closer to Shakespeare. Thoroughly apprised of the mainsprings of tragic appeal as pity and fear, he alternately dissolved his audience in tears and froze them with horror (if we can credit the hyperbole of mid-century comment). But pity won, for Garrick saw in *King Lear* a Shakespearean play which could surpass competition from all writers of pathetic tragedy and could command the emotional pleasure of tears more successfully than sentimental comedy. Tapping the strong vogue for the pathetic and sentimental, Garrick skillfully met public desire for these dramatic types in his production of *King Lear*, and without much sacrificing the sacredness of Shakespeare's text. In 1753–54 a flurry of controversy arose in several London journals—Hawkesworth's *The Adventurer* and Murphy's *Gray's Inn Journal*—about causes for Lear's madness. One school felt it was caused by loss of the sceptre, the other that it stemmed from an emotional cause, namely his reaction to the ingratitude of his daughters.

Close scrutiny of Murphy's papers reveals the slant Garrick was giving to his performance. Although the pathetic doubtless had a particular appeal for Murphy, his response is rather typical of the London audience. "In every speech in Lear's mouth," he wrote, "there is such an artful mixture of thwarting passions that the *heart-strings* of an audience are torn on every side . . . His sudden apostrophe to his daughters must *draw tears* from every eye—'O Regan, Goneril, Your old kind father whose frank heart gave all!' He still continues to dwell in imagination upon the crime of ingratitude, which appears to him so shocking that he exclaims, 'Let 'em anatomize Regan;—see what breeds about her heart . . . Is there any cause in Nature for these hard hearts?' this last stroke *cannot fail to draw tears from every eye*." [12]

Murphy comments that the close of the tragedy "is full of terror and commiseration, and our great poet has here given us a death . . . without the dagger and the bowl. But perhaps after all the heart piercing sensations which we have before endured through the whole piece it would be too much to see this actually performed on the stage; from the actor . . . already named I am sure it would, though I should be glad to see the experiment made, convinced at the same time that the play, as it is altered will always be most agreeable to an audience, as the circumstances of Lear's restoration, and the virtuous Edgar's alliance with the amiable Cordelia, must always *call forth those gushing tears which are swelled and ennobled by a virtuous joy.*"[13]

Tate in his adaptation, back in the very politically dominated year 1681, had rendered the text clear, if somewhat flat, had reverted to the original story and restored Lear to his throne, had made Edgar and Cordelia lovers, and had given her a confidante Arante, had omitted the Fool, and in overall effect had shifted focus from King Lear, to Lear's kingdom, and the changes (when well performed) eminently satisfied the spectators.

The critical flurry in the 1750s focused attention again upon Lear himself, and was stimulated by Garrick's acting. The critical controversies, in turn, doubtless stimulated him to make the extended revision of the acting text, which he performed on 28 October 1756. Barry's success in Lear at Covent Garden during the season 1755–56, together with Theophilus Cibber's thrusts in his *Two Dissertations upon the Theatres*,[14] also added impetus to the project.

The first printed text of Garrick's revised version seems to be that published by Bell in 1773, "regulated from the prompt books with permission of the managers." The Bell editors used as bases for their texts sometimes old prompt copies, sometimes the latest ones. The text of *King Lear*, identical in Bell's 1773 and 1774 printings, may well represent an accurate transcription of Garrick's 1756 play. But Garrick apparently did not leave his 1756 revision without further restorations from Shakespeare. A duodecimo printed for C. Bathurst in 1786, after Garrick's death, bears the title *KING LEAR, Altered from Shakespeare by David Garrick, Esq., Marked with the Variations in the Manager's Book at the Theatre Royal in Drury Lane*. This edition differs from the Bell text by including more lines from Shakespeare and excluding more lines from Tate. The cast listed places Garrick and Miss Younge in the leading roles. Miss Elizabeth Younge played Cordelia to his Lear during the last years of his performing.

Collation of three texts—Tate 1681, Bell 1774, and Garrick 1786— shows how far Garrick went in restoring Shakespeare and banishing Tate. The text of *Lear* in the new Variorum edition runs to 3,201 lines. Tate cut the play by one third. The Bell edition, though cutting sweepingly from Tate, restored sufficient from Shakespeare's text to exceed the Tate count by 255 lines. The Garrick version cut 18 more Tate lines and restored 50 additional Shakespearean ones. Garrick's version, whether viewed from the 1774 or 1786 text, is far from Tate's in title, scene, and act division; in language, character emphasis, and in pointed moral. But Garrick retained the happy ending, a shortened version of the love between Edgar and Cordelia, Cordelia's confidante Arante, and omitted the Fool.

In retaining these structural features, he continued, as a manager, to sacrifice to the altar of poetic justice, to bow to the shrine of neoclassical dramatic theory which allowed no comic element to enter the province of tragedy, and to cater to public taste for tears and pathos.[15] Yet, what a refreshing play his is compared with Tate's! The triumph of Shakespeare in scene after scene in all his plays often lies in the magic of wording. When Tate altered Shakespeare's phraseology, time and again he took the lustre from the jewels he was restringing. In the restoration of Shakespeare's wording Garrick was able to pay best honor to the god of his idolatry, though as manager he left offerings at other shrines.

Witness the effect. Edmund's soliloquy upon bastardy opens Tate's play, and this villain speaks with the tongue of the "fuddling" laureate:

> Thou Nature art my Goddess, to thy law
> My services are bound; why am I then
> Depriv'd of a son's right, because I came not
> In the dull road that custom has prescribed?
> Why bastard, wherefore base, when I can boast
> A mind as gen'rous, and a shape as true
> As honest madam's issue? Why are we
> Held base, who in the lusty stealth of nature
> Take fiercer qualities than what compound
> The scented births of the stale marriage bed;
> Well then, legitimate Edgar, to thy right
> Of law I will oppose a Bastard's cunning.
> Our father's love is to the bastard Edmund
> As to legitimate Edgar; with success
> I've practis'd on both their easie natures;
> Here comes the old man chaf'd with th' information
> Which last I forg'd against my brother Edgar,
> A tale so plausible, so boldly utter'd
> And heighten'd by such lucky accidents
> That now the slightest circumstance confirms him
> And base born Edmund spite of law inherits.

Upon the heels of this Lear divides the kingdom and Tate gives first inkling of Edgar's love for Cordelia.

Garrick restored Shakespeare's opening scene in which Kent and Gloucester discuss the probable division of the kingdom. In 1774 Garrick still retained Tate's lines of love-making between Edgar and Cordelia. They are marked for excision, however, in the 1786 text. When in Garrick's versions at the opening of the second scene Edmund soliloquizes, he does so in Shakespeare's rich idiom:

> Thou Nature art my Goddess, to thy law
> My services are bound. Wherefore should I
> Stand in the plague of custom, and permit
> The curiosity of Nations to deprive me
> For that I am some twelve or fourteen moonshines
> Lag of a brother? Why bastard? Wherefore base!
> When my dimensions are as well compact
> My mind as generous, and my shape as true
> As honest madam's issue? Why brand they us
> With base? with baseness? bastardy! base, base?
> Who in the lusty stealth of nature take
> More composition and fierce quality
> Than doth, within a dull, stale, tired bed,
> Go to the creating a whole tribe of fops
> Got 'tween sleep and wake! Well then,
> Legitimate Edgar, I must have your land:
> Our father's love is to the bastard Edmund
> As to the legitimate. Fine word "legitimate"
> Well my legitimate, if this letter speed,
> And my invention thrive, Edmund the base
> Shall top the legitimate:—I grow, I prosper;
> Now Gods stand up for bastards!

The restoration is complete and exact, giving the actor of Edmund's part more of a characterization than did the meagre lines of Tate. Edmund was again presented, after 70 years, not merely as a treacherous, scheming villain, but as a man possessing certain intellectual curiosity, who saw not only the injustices of custom toward natural sons, but observed also the tyranny of words which in themselves create attitudes and shape prejudices. He played with the words *bastard*, *base*, and *legitimate*, repeating them until they lost all significance. Garrick understood the difference between the charged effect of Shakespeare's speech which made for drama, and the briefed utterance of Tate which produced merely the introduction to a story.

When Tate's Lear asks an expression of love from Goneril, she replies:

> Sir, I do love you more than words can utter
> Beyond what can be valu'd rich or rare,
> Nor liberty, nor sight, health, fame or beauty
> Are half so dear; my life for you were vile;
> As much as child can love the best of fathers.

In the 1774 text Garrick had restored some Shakespearean lines:

> I do love you, Sir,
> Dearer than eyesight, space and liberty,
> Beyond what can be valued rich or rare
> No less than life with grace, health, beauty, honor,
> As much as child are loved or father found,
> A love that makes breath poor, and speech unable,
> Beyond all manner of so much I love you.

In the 1786 text appears the exact and complete restoration:

> Sir, I do love you more than words can wield the matter
> Dearer than eyesight, space, . . .

Similar care is to be noted in the restoration of Lear's ensuing words:

> *Tate's Lear:*
> Of all these bounds, ev'n from this line to this
> With shady forests and wide skirted meads
> We make thee Lady, to thine and Albany's issue
> Be this perpetual—what says our second daughter?

> *Garrick's Lear (1774,1786) and Shakespeare's:*
> Of all these bounds ev'n from this line to this,
> With shadowy forests and with champains rich'd
> With plenteous rivers, and wide skirted meads
> We make thee Lady—to thine and Albany's issue
> Be this perpetual, what says our second daughter?
> Our dearest Regan, wife of Cornwall, speak.

Such careful restorations even in places of no great dramatic significance and in words, which traveling swiftly across the footlights mean little in the sum total of impression, show the respect which Garrick held for Shakespeare's text. His faithfulness in text extended to cut passages as well as to expanded ones. Shakespeare's Kent belabors Lear's treatment of Cordelia in an earnest speech of 11 lines, which Tate cut to three. Garrick left the speech at three lines but made sure the wording was Shakespeare's.

A final example, from the heath scene, points the difference between Tate and Garrick as text-makers. Lears from Betterton to Garrick attuned themselves to the brewing storm in Tate's phraseology:

> Blow winds and burst your cheeks, rage louder yet,
> Fantastic light'ning singe, singe my white head:
> Spout cataracts, and hurricanoes fall,
> 'Till you have drown'd the towns and palaces
> Of proud ingrateful man.

But Garrick restored the pounding words of Shakespeare:

> Blow winds and crack your cheeks! Rage! Blow;
> Ye cataracts and hurricanoes, spout

'Till you have drench'd the steeples, drown'd the cocks!
You sulphurous and thought-executing fires,
Vaunt couriers of oak-cleaving thunderbolts,
Singe my white head! and thou all-shaking thunder
Strike flat the thick rotundity o' the world!
Crack Nature's mold, all germens spill at once
That make ingrateful man.

Garrick's play, however, is not all pure Shakespeare with cuts. It retains Arante, the female companion whom Tate provided for Cordelia. Her appearance is brief and she fades out completely during the storm scene. Only once is a Shakespearean character which remains, changed. Shakespeare's Regan, cruelest of the sisters, reaches the climax of her cruelty in her command to the servants who have gouged out Gloucester's eyes:

Go, thrust him out at th' gates, and let
Him smell his way to Dover.

Garrick retained the Tate version at this point, wherein Regan taunts Gloucester, "if those eyes fail thee call for spectacles," leaving it to the dying Cornwall to say:

Turn out the eyeless villain; let him smell
His way to Cambray.

Garrick eliminated entirely Tate's scene at the beginning of the fourth act where Regan and Edmund are "amorously seated in a grotto listening to music." Though Garrick retained the happy ending he cut the moral curtain speech which Tate devised for Edgar:

Our drooping country now erects her head,
Peace spreads his balmy wings, and plenty blooms.
Divine Cordelia all the gods can witness
How much thy love to empire I prefer!
Thy bright example shall convince the world
(whatever storms of Fortune are decreed)
That Truth and Virtue shall at last succeed.

Differences between the Tate version and the 1774 text are too numerous for further listing. Their quality has been accurately suggested by the foregoing examples. Differences between the 1774 and 1786 texts are marked not in outline but in the further restorations of Shakespeare which appear in the latter. Just when Garrick made these restorations we have no way of telling. What we do know is that from 1747 until the close of his stage career he was giving the play more and more of a Shakespearean flavor. Tate's play was the tragedy of Lear's kingdom. Garrick's and Shakespeare's the tragedy of King Lear.

## Isabella; or, The Fatal Marriage

Garrick wrote constantly in an atmosphere of theatre competition which thrived on variety as well as artistry. In providing variety for London audiences from his own pen he sometimes led and sometimes followed directions his competing managers were taking. In March 1757 John Home's *Douglas*, already popular on the stage at Edinburgh, had moved to continued popularity at Covent Garden—calling forth the allegiances of Scots patriotism and English sportsmanship. Heroine Matilda's extended melancholy, even of weeping for seven years after marrying Lord Randolph, helped set the atmosphere of "celestial melancholy" underscored in the *Epilogue* to the tragedy and nurtured outside the theatre by the "graveyard school of poets." On the second of December following that opening at Covent Garden, Garrick brought on his adaptation of Thomas Southerne's *Isabella; or, The Fatal Marriage* (1680). Was it a coincidence, or a competitive ploy, that Isabella laments her husband Biron with seven years of tears, a Biron whom she had married against her father's consent? Biron, away at the wars, is thought to have died. Her villainous brother Carlos keeps his letters from her. She is driven to marry the tender Villeroy. Biron turns up, is waylaid and stabbed by Carlos, and after a pitiful recognition scene dies, as Isabella goes mad. *Douglas*, with Barry and Mrs Woffington in the leading roles, had an initial year's run in London of nine nights. *Isabella*, with Garrick and Mrs Cibber in the leading roles, had an initial year's run of 12 nights; and brought the managers nearly £2,500. Box receipts are not extant for *Douglas*. *Isabella* remained in the Drury Lane repertory for two more years. *Douglas* outlasted it temporarily on stage, running 128 times from 1757 to the end of the century, but by an odd coincidence *Isabella* returned and amassed a total of 128 performances from its inception to the end of the century. The differences: Garrick's talent adjusted to the obvious taste of the town, looked back, perhaps, to the school of Otway; Home's talent, though capitalizing on the long build-up of the melancholy "graveyard" poets, seemed more in tune with the emerging romanticism. Both plays are packed with emotion, jealousy, villainy, and madness.

Garrick thought enough of the play to cast himself as Biron; Mrs Cibber, as Isabella—a part suited to her who had played distraught women so well—Jane Shore, Monimia, Belvidera. In his advertisement to the printed version, which came out within two weeks of its stage premiere, he explains his general policy of alteration—to remove indecorous passages, to shorten some speeches, and to add only for the sake of unity. Many of Isabella's speeches seemed overly long for presentation on the mid-century stage, so he cut many lines which seem to any reader to be elaborations of points already made. He concentrated the action, by eliminating comic parts. Cross noted succinctly in his *Diary*, "This play is alter'd, that is all the comedy is cut out, and is still five short acts, went off well—but heavy." [16] Garrick seems to have cut about 226 lines and to have filtered in about 193, mostly in the third act in the form of a masque and songs celebrating the marriage of Isabella with Villeroy. The scene brims with subtensions and irony:

*Isabella*: I could have wished, if you had thought it fit,
Our marriage had not been so public.

*Villeroy*: Do not you grudge me my excess of love,
That was the cause it could not be concealed . . .

*Isabella*: I have no more to say.

But the occasion builds with an epithalamium, a concert of music, recitative, and a duet:

*Man*: O the raptures of possessing,
Taking beauty to thy arms

*Woman*: O the joy, the lasting blessing
When with virtue, beauty charms.

The emendations are few, such as substituting "matrimony" for Southerne's "bed together." Count Baldwin has a serious twinge of conscience at the close, warning other parents with "flinty hearts" to have compassion and forgive before tragedy strikes. The villain Carlos is led off by the constables for due punishment. The play was popular enough to appear in Bell's *British Theatre* (1776) with a Thornthwaite print of Mrs Yates as Isabella, and Master Pullen as her son in a moment of theatrical wretchedness. [17]

## ZARA

Garrick's long and successful *performing* of Old Lusignan (once Jerusalem's Christian king) is described in chapter 16, below. For a dozen years he shared with Mrs Cibber (Zara) the emotional scenes of fatherly recognition succeeded by feminine tragedy. Her love for the Sultan Osman, her discovery that her friend Nerestan was actually her broth-

er, and her desperate conflict of religious faith had in the performing
as far back as 1736 established Mrs Cibber as a leading tragic actress,
in the translation of Voltaire's *Zaire* made by Aaron Hill in 1732. In
1766 she lay dying, and Mrs Yates succeeded to her role. In 1766
Rousseau was visiting London. In 1766 Garrick provided a fresh acting
piece by adapting the Aaron Hill version, by shortening the rant, making Osman a more single-minded pagan, and by restoring, in English
translation, a good many lines from the original Voltaire text. Garrick's
acting copy was a working copy for Drury Lane, but became the basic
text for performances throughout the rest of the century. Professor
F. L. Bergmann's close study of the copy now in the Folger Shakespeare Library demonstrates the consistency with which Garrick, as
adapter, followed his three major guidelines; of altering words that
might offend religious moralists, of restoring original texts, and of
improving actability of the piece by cutting long speeches, wherein
seeming repetition of a point clogged action.[18]

In this text, based upon a 1763 edition of Hill's play, Garrick cut
some 306 lines (not a great many) mostly by shortening speeches
throughout, trimming a line here and there, not by removing any
scenes. Hill's introduction of Osman in Act I seemed meant manifestly
for a reader. Garrick had his eye upon performance, and therefore
eliminated the following four lines:

*Selima*: Hark! the wish'd music sounds!—'Tis he—
he Comes— (exit Selima)

*Zara*: My heart prevented him, and found him near:
Absent two whole long days, the slow pac'd hour
At last is come—and gives him to my wishes!

Garrick substituted a flourish off stage and the entrance of Osman
without the help of the women (who on stage can express in their faces
their anticipation and joy).

Rant always worried Garrick. He omitted or reduced excess of it, for
example 11 lines between the Sultan and his minister Orasmin on the
apparent defection of Zara. Osman had made his point, but Hill allowed him to strike some attitudes and carry on:

Orasmin, Prophet! Reason! Truth! and Love!
After such length of benefits to wrong me!
How have I over-rated, how mistaken,
The merit of her beauty!—Did I not
Forget I was a monarch? Did I remember
That Zara was a slave?—I gave up all
Gave up tranquility, Distinction, Pride,
And fell, the shameful victim of my love!

*Orasmin*: Sir! Sovereign! Sultan! my Imperial Master!
   Reflect on your own greatness, and disdain
   The distant provocation—

The play deals, of course, with religious conflicts and personal faith in the minds of Lusignan, Osman, and Zara particularly. But Garrick for the sake of English decorum omits Osman's calling upon Heaven "to blast that unbelieving race," the Christians, and Chatillon's calling Nerestan "a Christian Saviour, by a Saviour sent," and Zara's swearing by "the dread presence" of "Heaven's Living Author." And along the way Garrick tends to ennoble the character of Zara, and subtract somewhat from the statesmanlike tolerance of Sultan Osman.

Close scrutiny of Garrick's emendations of words or phrases shows his careful reading of Voltaire's original. When Lusignan first appears led from his dungeon and groping for light, he cries in Hill's text, "Where am I! What forgiven Angel's voice has called me to revisit long-lost day?" Garrick changes Hill to read from the original, "from the dungeon's depth what voice," eliminating Hill's "forgiven Angel." Professor Bergmann discusses all such restorations in full. The point is that, as so often with a Shakespearean text, Garrick has a care for the original, even where again in the swiftness with which words cross the footlights the change of correct but single words would seem to amount to little. A sense of authenticity went hand in hand with him in his renewals on stage of older plays. Garrick's influence continued, for the Bell editions of 1776, and later of 1791, and Mrs Inchbald's of 1808 remain basically Garrick's, from his acting copy of 1766.

## HAMLET

Garrick's most controversial alteration down through the years was *Hamlet* (made in 1772), though few of those who cried out against it had ever seen Garrick play in it, and *none* had seen his text. Davies who had seen him act it thought he was "injudicious" in cutting out the gravediggers, Osric, and the fencing match, of leaving the audience in some suspense about the ultimate fate of Ophelia, and of adding a new, quickened ending.[19] Murphy, who had seen it performed (but at the time suffering from Garrick's rejection of his play *Alzuma*), wrote a parody on its first act in which Shakespeare's Ghost berates Garrick for altering it: "On my scenes by ages sanctified, in evil hour thy restless spirit stole, with juice of cursed nonsense in an inkhorn, and o'er my fair applauded page did pour a Manager's distillment . . . ," to which he makes Garrick reply: "His plays are out of joint—O cursed spirit, that ever I was born to set them right."[20] James Boaden in 1831 (without having seen it) wrote of Garrick's "rash violation of the whole scheme . . . an actor's mutilation of all parts but his own" and "written in a trashy commonplace manner sullying the page of Shakespeare and disgracing the taste and judgment of Garrick."[21] Isaac Reed thought Garrick was working in the spirit of Bottom the weaver.[22] Biographer Percy Fitzgerald called it a Gothic mutilation (1868),[23] and others have somewhat recklessly mounted the same bandwagon. Tate Wilkinson wanted the Drury Lane acting copy to play in the York circuit, but Benjamin Victor (treasurer) answered, "It is not in my power to send you the corrections lately made in *Hamlet*. No such favor can be granted to anyone. I presume the play will never be printed with alterations, as they are far from being universally liked."[24]

Garrick never printed the alteration, but rather liked it and wrote to Mme Necker in 1776 just what he had done to the shape of it: "The Copy of the play You have got from the Bookseller will mislead You without some direction from Me—the *first Act* which is very long in the original, is by me divided into *two Acts*—the 3$^d$ Act, as I Act it is the 2$^d$ of the Original—the 3$^d$ of the original is the 4$^{th}$ in Mine, and ends with the famous scene between *Hamlet* and his *Mother*—and the 5$^{th}$ Act in my Alteration consists of the 4th & 5th of the original, with some small alterations, and the omission of some Scenes, particularly the Grave diggers" (1008). Earlier he had written to Morellet (4 January 1773): "I have play'd the Devil this Winter, I have dar'd to alter *Hamlet*, I have thrown away the gravediggers, & all y$^e$ 5$^{th}$ Act, & notwithstanding the Galleries were fond of them, I have met with more applause than I did at five & twenty—this is a great revolution in our theatrical history, & for w$^{ch}$ 20 years ago instead of Shouts of approbation, I should have had y$^e$ benches thrown at my head" (730).

Both John Hoadly and George Steevens had encouraged Garrick in his plan, and the play, contrary to the critics, was popular. It held the stage for eight years and was played 37 times. In the previous eight years, Shakespeare's *Hamlet* had been played 26 times. Garrick during his four remaining years on stage received £3,426 in box receipts for this alteration alone. An average house at the time ran to £160 per night. Garrick's first three performances of the altered version brought £284, £272, and £264, respectively. Why publish, when Drury Lane had in this piece a gold mine?

But in 1934 Garrick's acting copy came to light in the Folger Shakespeare Library, and can now be studied in all of its remarkable vigor,

in its mighty restorations of over 600 lines in the forepart of the play
never before seen on the eighteenth-century stage, its minimal additions of only 11 lines from Garrick's own pen, and its multiple restorations of Shakespearean wording and phrasing for accuracy—*metals* for
metal, *Seas* for sea, *the Wind at help,* for the Wind sits fair, *repast
them with my blood,* for "relieve them with my blood" of the earlier
stage texts. He used for his sources the scholarly apparatus that had
been built up by that time, and principally Dr. Johnson's edition. With
the exception of Osric and the gravediggers (who are out), every character in the play is made richer by the restorations. The controversial
fifth act has now been printed in full.[25]

To get the feel for Garrick's decision to alter, for he had been making
subtle changes ever since he began playing the part, brief review of the
status of the text on the eighteenth-century stage is pertinent.

The *Hamlet* that Garrick used as a foundation for his alteration is a
duodecimo, one of the many reprintings of the text of "the accurate
Mr. Hughs." The nature and the history of this text are important for
an understanding of Garrick's version.

At the beginning of the eighteenth century Betterton was the only
Hamlet the London audience wished to see, despite the fact that he
was an old man. He acted an altered version of *Hamlet* prepared by
Sir William Davenant in 1676 from a 1637 quarto. The first eighteenth-
century issue of Betterton's version is a quarto printed in 1703 for
Richard Wellington, with the stage cuts indicated by inverted quotation marks. Betterton died in 1710, having played Hamlet for the last
time at the Haymarket on September 20, 1709, when he was well over
70 years of age. Robert Wilks succeeded to the title role, which he had
first played as early as January 15, 1708, at Drury Lane. Until his death
in 1732 he was the accepted Hamlet of the London stage, although
Booth and Powell occasionally played the part. Each great Hamlet,
wishing to be distinctive in the character, tried to improve or to change
the method of his predecessor sufficiently to make his an individualized performance. Wilks changed the Betterton performance by restoring two notable passages that the earlier player had cut from the
stage presentation; namely, the whole of the "Angels and Ministers
of Grace defend us" speech, and Hamlet's advice to the players,
"Speak the speech, I pray you." He also was interested in a version
of the play which was closer to the Shakespeare text than the Davenant
alteration.

Accordingly he sought the help of his friend Mr. John Hughs, and the
result was an edition of the play printed in 1718 which may be called
the Hughs-Wilks' *Hamlet*. The presumption is that Wilks dictated the

cuts and that Hughs restored the text, for although some blots remain, yet in very many cases Hughs with a copy of Rowe's edition before him restored the old readings where Betterton and D'Avenant had unnecessarily departed therefrom. From Rowe he inserted part of the folio text which did not occur in the quartos. It cannot claim to be a good text judged by present-day standards, but for 1718 compared with what was then available it was no doubt an excellent work. Hughs edited this again, and it was finally printed in 1723 after his death. It is to this latter edition that Theobald refers in his *Shakespeare Restored* when he mentions the text of "the accurate Mr. Hughs." It ran into nineteen editions before 1761, and the subsequent ones developed a mass of printer's errors.[26]

After Wilks's death a number of Hamlets performed at the different theatres; but neither Ryan at Covent Garden, nor Giffard at Goodman's Fields, nor Mills, and subsequently Milward at Drury Lane, equaled their predecessors in the role of the Danish prince. Although many generalizations have been written about their performances there is no evidence that they played any other than the Hughs-Wilks text. The year 1741 found Denis Delane as a rising young star in *Hamlet* at Drury Lane; but his presentation was quickly eclipsed by that of Garrick, who almost immediately after his first appearance in the part in Ireland, August 12, 1742, became the accepted Hamlet of the English theatre.

Garrick received many letters from friends and anonymous correspondents advising him of possible improvements in his performance of the part. He began with the Hughs-Wilks text, its cuts and its stage directions, then gradually revised his presentation and created his own text. He seldom allowed his texts and revisions to be printed. The close of the season of 1763, however, found him in poor health, suffering from a temporary period of unpopularity, and severely attacked by Fitzpatrick. He sought escape and rest in a journey to France, from which, as we know, he did not return for two years. The theatre was left in charge of George Colman. Inasmuch as Garrick might not play again, Colman allowed Garrick's acting text of *Hamlet* to be printed. This edition, issued by Haws and Company in 1763, materially differs from the Hughs-Wilks text. The cuts, instead of being marked for excision, are omitted, thus making a very short play. Some lines cut by Wilks are restored, others retained by him are eliminated by Garrick.

Garrick returned from France in 1765 in fine spirits, and resumed acting. In 1772 he gave the altered version of *Hamlet* we are now discussing; but instead of using as a foundation for this alteration a copy of his own 1763 edition, he employed the 1747 edition of the Hughs-Wilks text. A glance at this text makes clear his reason: he was not interested in merely leaving out the gravediggers and Osric, as the critics suppose; having cut the greater part of the fifth act he had to restore almost as much in the preceding part of the play, some 629 lines in fact.

Betterton's acting version had cut entirely the characters Voltimand and Cornelius; the King's address to the Court in the first act; the advice of Polonius to Laertes, and a large portion of Laertes's advice to Ophelia; most of the "Angels and Ministers of Grace" speech; 11 lines of the Ghost's speech; the entire scene between Polonius and Reynaldo; 38 lines of the first conversation with the players; Hamlet's advice to the players; 23 lines of the Mouse Trap; 47 lines of the scene between Hamlet and his mother after the death of Polonius; and Fortinbras's army, Hamlet's converse with the captain, and the soliloquy so important in the development of Hamlet's character, "How all occasions do inform against me." These are but the major cuts. Many of the King's lines, as well as many of Rosencrantz and Guildenstern, Marcellus, and Horatio, were also omitted.

This made for a much more swiftly-moving play, and in the words of Hazelton Spencer, substantiates "the historical critic's view of Hamlet as the beau ideal of active young manhood."[27]

Wilks cut out the Dumb Show and the Fortinbras ending; and in other respects, except for small changes, followed the Betterton version. And so the acting text remained (with the exception of the minor changes noted in Garrick's 1763 edition) for 50 years.

The theatergoers who had been accustomed to this interpretation saw from the stage of Drury Lane, on December 18, 1772, a radically different play.

Inasmuch as Garrick's first act ended when Horatio and Marcellus plan to meet on the parapet the following night, all the speeches cut in the Betterton version had to be restored to give substance to an otherwise short and thin act. The act thereby gained numerous descriptive passages, and some purple patches, notably Horatio's lines on Rome:

> A little ere the mightiest Julius fell
> The graves stood tenantless and the sheeted dead
> Did squeak and gibber in the Roman streets . . .

With this restoration the subordinate characters become something more than mere puppets to start the show going. Ninety-four lines were restored, including the scene in which Cornelius and Voltimand are sent as ambassadors to Norway. It was necessary to return those men to the play because Garrick wished later to restore the soliloquy,

"How all occasions do inform against me," which refers to the Fortinbras episode, and to the very material about which these men give us knowledge.

In Garrick's second act Laertes is allowed to speak 28 more lines of advice to Ophelia, and Polonius is allowed 15 lines of admonishment to his son for the first time in the century. Garrick's brain furnished him with two more. The description of Danish drunkenness is cut as usual. The whole of the Ghost's speech is restored, and the exclamation, "O horrible, most horrible," is given to Hamlet in order to break the length of the speech. The Ghost only once urges Horatio and Marcellus to swear as Hamlet presents the hilt of his sword. Seventeen lines are here cut from the Hughs-Wilks version.

Garrick was deeply interested in the character of Polonius. One of the indications that the old courtier is part of the rotten morass which forms the Danish court is his sending Reynaldo to spy upon Laertes. This scene is here for the first time restored, as is also the material relating to the Fortinbras subplot. As usual there is much excision in the conversation between Hamlet, Rosencrantz, and Guildenstern. The description of the players is cut considerably, that part being omitted which in Shakespeare's time referred to the boy actors ("an Aery of children, little Eyases"), and the sole reason for the players' traveling is the change for the worse in the administration of Denmark under Claudius. In the earlier version the players' speech concerning Pyrrhus and Priam had been cut almost entirely. Garrick restored 20 lines in order to give some point to Polonius's "This is too long." The earlier actors, perhaps, had taken the hint literally and applied the shears with vigor. Garrick gave the soliloquy, "O what a rogue and peasant slave am I," as Betterton gave it, except that he supplied *wretch* for *rogue*, as had Wilks.

Inasmuch as the conspiracy between the King and Laertes was to be cut, Garrick was careful to restore each aside and speech in which the King displayed his character and the workings of his conscience.[28]

Garrick omitted the Dumb Show, but for the first time included the whole of the Mouse Trap play. This, especially the restoring of lines to the Player Queen, gives point to the line, "The lady doth protest too much, methinks." The conversation between the King, Rosencrantz, and Guildenstern, when the plot is first made to send Hamlet to England, is restored. The king's whole prayer, and Hamlet's meditation are retained, though they had been cut from Garrick's 1763 text. An appreciable number of lines is restored to the scene between Hamlet and his mother, especially such lines as show the state of Hamlet's emotional conflict.

Nor does one find the fifth act "trashy" or "commonplace," unless one so feels about the following 30 lines with which Garrick closes the play, as Hamlet sweeps to his revenge. The rest of the lines in the act (and those here in italics) are Shakespeare's:

*Queen.* O Hamlet—Hamlet—
   *For Love of Heav'n forbear him!*—(To Laertes)

*King.* We will not bear this Insult to our Presence,
   Hamlet, I did command you hence to England,
   Affection hitherto has curb'd my Pow'r,
   But you have trampled on Allegiance,
   And now shall feel my Wrath—Guards!

*Hamlet.* First feel mine—(Stabs him)
   *Here thou Incestuous, Murd'rous, damned Dane*
   There's for thy treachery, Lust and Usurpation!

*King.* *O yet defend me, friends, I am but hurt—*
      (Falls and dies)

*Queen.* O Mercy Heav'n!—Save me from my Son—
      (Runs out)

*Laertes.* What Treason ho! Thus then do I revenge
   My Father, Sister, and my King—
      (Hamlet runs upon Laertes's sword and falls)

*Horatio.* And I my prince, and Friend—(Draws)

*Hamlet.* Hold good Horatio—'tis the Hand of Heav'n,
   Administers by him this precious balm
   For all my Wounds. Where is the wretched Queen?
      Enter Messenger

*Messen:* Struck with the Horror of the Scene, she fled—
   But 'ere she reach'd her Chamber door, she fell
   Intranc'd and Motionless—unable to sustain the Load
   Of Agony and Sorrow—

*Hamlet.* O my Horatio—watch the wretched Queen,
   When from this Trance she wakes—O may she breathe
   An hour of Penitance, 'ere Madness ends her.
   *Exchange forgiveness with me brave Laertes,*
   Thy Sister's, Father's Death, come not on me,
   Nor Mine on thee!—

*Laertes.* Heav'n make us free of 'Em!

*Hamlet.* O I die Horatio—but one thing more,
   O take this hand from me—unite your Virtues—
      (joins Horatio's hand to Laertes')
   To calm this troubled Land—I can no more
   Nor have I more to ask but Mercy Heav'n. (dies. —)

*Horatio. Now cracks a Noble heart—Good Night sweet Prince,*
*And Flights of Angels sing thee to thy rest:*
*Take up the Body such a Sight as this*
*Becomes the Field, but here shews much Amiss.*

END

What now of the character of Hamlet? There is ample testimony from contemporary writers of the powerful effect of Garrick's Hamlet upon his audience. Lichtenberg saw him play the prince in 1775, and remarked on the power of the conception. Garrick's Hamlet was no "sick weakling pining for the ministrations of Freud," nor was he the "beautiful flower" about which Goethe speaks. He was vital, he was active; and the inner workings of his mind, and the conflicts that faced the thinker driven on by deep and active emotions were apparently presented in an unforgettable manner. Such psychological delineation was Garrick's stronghold. It was what made him stand head and shoulders above his contemporaries in the characters of Richard III and Macbeth. And all the passages which he restored to the Danish prince were those which showed the conflicts within Hamlet's being.

Garrick's major hand in the alteration of tragedies is also seen in three more tragedies—in *The Roman Father*, *Antony and Cleopatra*, and *Mahomet*.

In William Whitehead's *The Roman Father*, staged 24 February 1750, Garrick prunes away nearly one-fifth of the whole in order to make a play out of Whitehead's exercise in declamation. He did not interfere with Whitehead's development of plot, rather he thought the laureate's wordiness interfered with the active execution of that development.[29]

Also on 3 January 1759 Garrick produced his carefully thought-out alteration of Shakespeare's *Antony and Cleopatra*—the first performance within man's memory of that magnificent and complex play. He asked Edward Capell to help with it, and the acting copy in Capell's hand is now in the Folger Shakespeare Library. He played Antony himself, and new-dressed the scenes greatly anticipating success, but as Cross remarked in his *Diary*, "This play tho' all new dress'd and had fine scenes did not seem to give the audience any great pleasure or draw any applause."[30] Garrick extended it to six performances. The text has baffled nearly every producer, because of the range of the play —in time and place—from Rome to Athens, to Alexandria—indoors, outdoors, in street, fortress, bedroom, and banquet barge over a course of many years—five acts and 27 scenes. The Garrick-Capell text marches more swiftly than the original through the first three acts. Some scenes are cut, others telescoped—with the general view of concentrating on the tragedy of love, and of minimizing the political background. Two scenes go from the fourth act, but there is no cutting in the fifth, save five lines from the Clown, who brings a fig and asps, which comment upon the proportion of women that the devil mars. In the excision of 657 lines, how fared the characters and the poetry? Two characters, Pompey and Octavia, have dwindled from individuals with lives of their own to rather insignificant background puppets. The first no longer parleys politically with Caesar, and the latter makes no show in either a betrothal scene nor a parting scene with Antony. Caesar's character suffers not at all despite cuts, nor does Antony's materially. Cleopatra's inner conflicts still contribute to her "infinite variety." Contemporaries, however, deemed that Garrick was too short for the towering Antony, that the whole company failed to carry all the parts well, that a group of hostile critics was targeting it, and that Dryden's *All for Love*, with its easy choices and lack of character complexity, was still popular.[31]

Finally, on 25 November 1765, Garrick fitted the Reverend James Miller's *Mahomet the Impostor* for the stage, another translation from Voltaire. It had been first performed 20 years earlier. Garrick's alterations were slight, and the play was popular. Garrick followed his principle of shortening (by some 230 lines), to cut lengthy rhetoric to compassable stage dialogue, and to subordinate emphasis on the incest theme. No novel touches of adaptation were taken in these changes.[32]

Garrick's adaptings were, of course, a lifelong occupation in his professional connection with Drury Lane, and were by no means limited to renewals of tragedy. Ben Jonson's *Every Man in His Humour* caught his particular interest in 1751. But in sequence he had a major hand in acting copies of *The Rehearsal* from 1742 on, *The Alchemist* from 1743, and *The Provoked Wife* from 1744. When manager he worked on Buckingham's *The Chances* in 1754 and again in 1773; *The Taming of the Shrew* in 1754 (reduced to three acts and titled *Catherine and Petruchio*); *A Midsummer Night's Dream* (an opera in 1755, and the play in 1763); *The Winter's Tale* in 1756 (also cut to three acts, and often played on the same evening with *Catherine and Petruchio*); *The Tempest* from 1756; Shirley's *The Gamester* (a dark comedy as he made it in 1757); *Cymbeline* with a record of fine performances from 1761; Wycherley's *The Country Wife*, which in 1766 he altered into a bland, ~~bland~~ obviously moral and popular comedy, *The Country Girl* (during the period of the amiable humorists); Dryden's *Masque King Arthur and*

277

*Emmeline* in 1770; *Love's Labour's Lost* in 1773, and in that same year Mallet's *Alfred, a Masque*, and Tomkis's humour comedy *Albumazar*, which he brought forward from 1668.[33]

In each of these the principles already discussed in the dramaturgy of his own comedy and farces, and of his tragic adaptations prevail. He experimented, he sought in selecting each for a broad range of interest, he prepared each text (some of which he even printed) from an acting point of view, considering where quickened pace was necessary, where character depth could be demonstrated, where dialogue could be made sprightly, or where it could be usefully returned to its original. He did not shy away from amusing risqué scenes and situations, but was careful not to offend religious sentiments, and was constantly aware of basic morality, as well as a merry obligation in stage performance.

## EVERY MAN IN HIS HUMOUR

Garrick's first full comedy adapted from native sources, Jonson's *Every Man in His Humour* (1751), provides a key to his comic theory, wherein he gave (as Jonson had suggested) "deeds and language such as men do use . . . when one would show the image of the times," to ridicule popular errors by bringing laughter upon them. Kitely in Jonson's *Every Man In*, frustrated by events that pass him by, capitulates towards the end of the play, "I thought so," says he, mistaking his wife's situation as in a bawdy house. "I'll die." (IV. iii. 51). Garrick's adaptation picks up the hint, and sets forth a marvelous speech-*cum*-action for his Kitely in the same circumstance. He apparently brought the house down in a gale of laughter.

> So, so; 'tis too plain—I shall go mad
> With my misfortunes; now they pour in torrents;
> I am bruted by my wife, betrayed by my servant
> Mock'd at by my relations, pointed at by my neighbors,
> Despised by myself—there is nothing left now
> But to avenge myself first, next hang myself,
> And then—all my cares are over![34]

The play had been revived for three performances back in 1725 at Lincoln's Inn Fields, with seven characters omitted—Matthew, Cash, Cob, Formal, Bridgit, Tib, and a servant. Also, three new ones had been added: Lucinda, Clara, and Marwit.[35] But Garrick was so interested in the possibilities of the whole play that he just trimmed lines

*Harvard Theatre Collection*
Garrick as Don John in *The Chances*.
Engraving by J. Hall from E. Edwards's version of a painting by
de Loutherbourg.

from the characters and kept the cast list as Jonson had it. He made a scene for the fourth act comprised of Jonson's lines by rearrangement, and did such further telescoping that the plot-line came clear, and actability improved. He actually reduced Jonson's 33 scenes to 16 by rearrangements and speeded progress by eliminating about 665 lines. No criticism fell upon him for this handling. The character suffering most was Cob, the water carrier, who lost three scenes of low comedy, but remained functional in the play.

Garrick's principal motive for excisions and rearrangements was his desire to facilitate scene changes. As Professor Bergmann has noticed; "In the first eight scenes of Jonson's fourth act, four different sets and five scene changes occur. By reducing the scenes to three, and shifting scene 5 from Windmill Tavern to Moorfields, and playing the succeeding two scenes there (rather than to Jonson's "A Street"), Garrick needed only 2 stage sets and three scene changes in the act." [36]

The most important change was Garrick's reorganizing Jonson's Act IV, scene viii (which became his IV. iii), in order to focus the play on Kitely's jealousy, and eliminate much low comedy. Garrick had clarified some words, and broken up some long speeches with a line or two of his own earlier, but here he added 26 lines of dialogue at the most dramatic point in the play. Kitely is attempting to conceal jealous agitation over the supposed conduct of his wife.:

> Dame K: But sure, my dear,
>   A wife may more moderately use these pleasures,
>   Which numbers and the time give sanction to,
>   Without the smallest blemish on her name.
>
> Kitely: And so she may, and I'll go with thee, child,
>   I will indeed—I'll lead thee there myself.
>   And be the foremost reveller—I'll silence
>   The sneers of envy, stop the tongue of slander;
>   Nor will I more be pointed at as one
>   Disturbed by jealousy—
>
> Dame K: Why, were you ever so?
>
> Kitely: What! Ha! never—ha, ha, ha!
>   She stabs me home (aside) Jealous of thee!
>   No, do not believe it—speak low, my love,
>   Thy brother will o'er hear us—No, no, my dear,
>   It could not be, it could not be for—for—
>   What is the time now?—I shall be too late—
>   No, no, thou mayst be satisfy'd
>   There's not the smallest spark remaining—
>   Remaining! What do I say? There never was,
>   Nor can, nor ever shall be—so be satisfied—

*Royal Collection*
Garrick as Kitely in *Every Man in His Humour*.
Painting by Sir Joshua Reynolds.

281

Is Cob within there? Give me a kiss,
My dear, there, there, now we are reconciled—
I'll be back immediately—good bye, good bye—
Ha! Ha! jealous! I shall burst my sides with laughing.
Ha! Ha! Cob, where are you, Cob? Ha ha—(exit)

And Garrick, of course, was professionally even busier than this list of adaptations suggests, for we know from his letters that his creative hand played a role in Murphy's *The Orphan of China* and *The Way to Keep Him*; in Cumberland's *The West Indian* (for which the author thanked him profusely) and *The Note of Hand*; in John Brown's alterations of *Bartholomew Fair*; in John Delap's *The Royal Shepherd*; in Hugh Kelly's *False Delicacy*; in Alexander Dow's *Zingis*; in Thomas Francklin's *Earl of Warwick*; in Robert Jephson's *Braganza*; even in William Kenrick's *The Widowed Wife*; in Benjamin Victor's *Timon*; in Mrs Centlivre's *The Wonder*; and in George Colman's *The Jealous Wife*.[37]


## COMMON DENOMINATORS IN GARRICK'S DRAMATURGY

From Garrick's own plays, from his adaptations both in comedy and tragedy, and from his statements in correspondence with playwrights one sees developing a handful of common denominators which reveal his guiding principles in playwriting. His cardinal one (and doubtless the basis for the success of his plays and adaptations) derives from the inextricable combination in him of playwright *and* actor. Aesthetic effectiveness of drama for him (as distinct from the novel, say) flowered only when it was acted on stage before audiences. Excellent acting he thought could bring words to life, and present events to thrill in tragedy, amuse in comedy, or throw the house into an uproar with farce. He wanted, as he wrote to Baron Grimm, to leave actors something to do. Grimm, in turn, thought Garrick "perfected his great talents by a profound study of human nature, and by researches full of shrewdness and broadness of thought."[38] Observation from mingling with London's crowd, was reinforced often by note taking of details at various ceremonies, where he gained copy bound to come out after passing through the alembic of his imagination into a piece for the stage. "Mr. Garrick was on Monday morning last in the Chapel to see the Installation, and at night at the opera house at the ball, in both which places he seemed very attentive to what was going forward, particularly in the former, as he took notes. So that from the indefatigible attention of that manager to lay before the public everything that is curious, we may expect to be presented . . . with a full and true account of the Installation of the Knights of the Bath."[39] To alertness for copy, Garrick in writing also kept in mind the capacities of his fellow actors to carry off the unique qualities of the characters he sketched. Evidence comes occasionally from manuscripts submitted to the Lord Chamberlain for licensing, where at times actor's names appear instead of character names appearing in the later printed texts.[40]

All studies of his plays have taken care to point out the sources from which he worked, often with elation over discovery of the seed plot in a continental piece, and accounting him heavily derivative. What he did with the materials at hand, however, was not only what counted, but what marks his creativity in refashioning, the distant and the old. His friend Thomas Warton reminds us of the sort of "malicious triumph one feels in detecting the latent and obscure source from whence an original author has drawn some celebrated descriptions; yet this," he continues, "soon gives way to the rapture that results from contemplating the Chymical energy of true genius which can produce so noble a transmutation."[41]

All in all, however, Garrick showed major concern for an actively moving plot (clear enough for audiences to follow), for sparkling dialogue, for hints in the dialogue for potential characterization (which the actor's art could make effective), for a confluence of people and events at the close to bring about exciting curtain, for a healthy self-spoofing again and again (tucked away almost as a signature in his farces), for touches of contemporary relevance (topical and cheering), and for basic morality.

Ample evidence relating to the first four of his guidelines: plot, character, topical reference, and dialogue has appeared in the discussion of his several plays. A word more about curtain effectiveness in his merging of characters and events, about his self-spoofing signature, and about his principles of basic morality.

Garrick the player, the reader of many plays, the writer of many others, and the manager interested in exciting curtain scenes which would entice the return of audiences repeatedly, saw to it that his farces, entertainments, and adaptations showed a confluence of all threads of action, and a convergence of all parties for the final curtain. The convention was, to be sure, time honored. His French sources did this sort of thing brilliantly. But no characters of Garrick's casts left the theatre for lodgings or the tavern early. He constructed his plays so that everyone counted, and counted in a finale. They were not only there for the country dance and the bow at the close, but nearly always had a speaking part in the finish. Sharp, Kitty, Melissa, Gayless, Justice Guttle, Mrs Gadabout, Beau and Mrs Trippet, daughters and servants cry out in chorus at the end of *The Lying Valet*, "A dance!" "By all means," agrees the hungry Justice Guttle—"but after supper!" Fourteen characters make up the cast of *The Clandestine Marriage*, including a maid and a chambermaid. Twelve of them have speaking parts right up to the drop of the curtain, and so it goes with *May Day*, *Bon Ton*, *The Guardian* and Garrick's others. No use to labor the point, but Garrick the writer was Garrick the actor, *and* Garrick the manager all in one. If as manager he was forcing rehearsals (as indeed he did) and doing all he could to emphasize ensemble performance with full and interested participation by all hands throughout each piece (as indeed he did), he was writing to give opportunity for each actor to stay with the ensemble till the end.

A personal signature (runes for Cynewulf, a tail and bob rhyme for the Townly Dramatist, a self-portrait of the artist among the angels, Hitchcock's appearance somewhere in a crowd in all his motion pictures) has been traditional in all branches of art. Garrick's hidden signature in his own plays (so many of which were published anonymously) turns up in a line or comment which anticipates and disarms criticism of the author by tossing a shaft of silvery laughter at David Garrick the manager or the actor—small in stature. He had used the device in forms other than dramatic, as we know—as early as 1744 poking fun at himself in *An Essay upon Acting*, and again in 1765 in his fable of *The Sick Monkey*—but there "testing, just testing," as a microphone operator might say.

Examples: In Garrick's *Peep Behind the Curtain* (1767) lover Wilson devises a ruse to enter the theatre in order to snatch Miss Fuz from her stage-struck mother, who is watching a rehearsal.

*Marvin*: But how will you gain entrance to Drury Lane?

*Wilson*: I was near being disappointed there, for unluckily the acting manager, *who scarce reached my third button*, cocked up his head in my face and said I was too small for a hero . . .

In *The Jubilee* (1769) one asks—"The Steward—have you seen him, Ralph?"

*Ralph*: Yes I ha' seen him—not much to be seen tho' . . . . He's not so big as I, but a great deal plumper—he's old enough to be wiser too.

In *The Meeting of the Company* (1774) Bayes tells Weston that by use of his "equalizing" formula he shall be both hero and fine gentleman, "and you won't be the first 'little man' who has tried to be both."

Possibly this iteration was a defense of sorts, subconsciously marking an insecurity in the extrovert, but it appears generally in such professional and sophisticated form that one is inclined not to attribute a substratum of despair to it. The custom of "puffing" a play, a performance, or an actor was common. Garrick followed this practice, but occasionally used this device of what one might call the "anti-puff" with amusing effectiveness.

A final common denominator, which indeed says something about Garrick the man as well as the professional dramatist is a constant turn of phrase in his plays about moral action. He knew how to titillate, understood the pleasures of mild shock in the risqué and the ribald, from the wealth of Restoration plays handed down to him, but found a new theatrical value in supporting the change in moral practices of his time. His plays as a whole and in their several parts emphasize moral improvement in men and manners. Considerable initiative seems to be present in his treatment. Perhaps he was but following a similar trend in all the arts of the late eighteenth century, yet many commended him for walking arm in arm with a movement for uplifting the tone of the community. Some even felt he was breaking ground and taking the lead as a creative dramatist, as a producer, and as a person whose private life seemed exemplary.[42]

Garrick corresponded with 41 clergymen during his professional years, including the archbishops of Canterbury and York, eight bishops and two deans. The Anglican clergy were deeply interested in the cultural movements of the period, and Garrick sensed the value of their approval of his writings. Staunch polemicists such as William Warburton credited Garrick with more than a modicum of leadership in the movement: "I honour you for your repeated endeavours in stemming the torrent of vice and folly. You do it in a station where most men, I suppose, would think you might fairly be dispensed with from bearing your part in the duty of a good citizen on such a necessary occasion; but it is for this very thing I chiefly honour you."[43]

The situations Garrick sets up in his plots, and the dialogue by which he communicates them are racy, occasionally risqué, but not licentious or obscene. Generally so sprightly is his dialogue that what might become vapid and preachily insipid escapes such clogs. The movement to improve men and morals began long before Garrick appeared. General identification of aesthetics with moral behavior, stemming from the

285

Greeks, was freshened by Addision in the *Spectator* papers (1711). Moralism in drama moved into the obvious utilitarian category in somewhat heavy-footed fashion with George Lillo, while Garrick was still a schoolboy in Lichfield. "The more extensively useful the moral of a tragedy," wrote Lillo, "the more excellent that piece must be of its kind."[44] Garrick, probably by conviction, certainly by business instinct, and flattered by the comments of the clergy, bestrode this horse and rode it consistently.

In his "Advertisements" to editions to *The Country Girl* (1766) and *The Chances* (1772) Garrick spoke to the point, reflecting the social atmosphere within which he worked. Of *The Chances*, "Should the play in its present state be thought a more decent entertainment, it is all the merit claimed from these necessary though slight additions and alterations." The play as he adapted it looks back through the Duke of Buckingham's text to the original base in Fletcher's play. It clears the text of some "exceptionable passages" from Buckingham, omits lines directly referring to the Deity (perhaps as a bow to his clerical friends), and underscores the change in character wrought in Don John by tagging on some final lines: "My former vanities are past and gone / Now I change the wild wanton for the sober plan / And like my friend become a moral man."

For *The Country Girl* (his adaptation of Wycherley's *The Country Wife*) Garrick explained, "Though nearly half . . . is new written, the Alterer claims no merit but his endeavour to clear one of our most celebrated comedies from immorality and obscenity." By excising Horner, the Fidgets, and Squeamishes he unloaded most of what was perceived at the time as the super-charged immorality of Wycherley. Margery Pinchwife became Garrick's Peggy Thrift, whose guardian Jack Moody gives out that they are married to prevent assaults upon her virtue. Pace picks up in the streamlining of Wycherley's movement and the reduction of his cast of 14 to Garrick's of seven. Attitude changes as the old central "cuckold" theme shifts to a traditional triangle one. At the play's end Moody becomes an about-to-be husband, so instead of provoking a guffaw at Pinchwife's new-cut horns the conclusion brings off a romantic climax in which two young lovers are united at the expense of a jealous old man. Garrick rewrote the play (his fullest alteration of an older one) to bring out a new young actress Miss Ann Reynolds (Peggy), and to advance the fortunes of young Samuel Cautherly (Belville). It had a season's success, running 13 times, including a "Command," and a "Benefit" performance. Public reaction showed not only in the box office, but in the pages of *The Critical Review* (November, 1766). "It must . . . be allow'd that the writer of

*The Country Girl* has considerably improved on his original in the concentration of the fable; not only converting the libidinous Horner into the modest Mr. Belville, but by dissolving the marriage between Margery Pinchwife, and representing his heroine as a simple spinster." Garrick in no sense pandered to public taste. From his position of power, and from good conscience he subtly molded it.

But Garrick's professional approach, even where morality and theological overtones were involved, always considered three elements—the probability of stage success for the *text* (either a fresh-created one, or an old one to revive), *capabilities* of his actors, and the pulse of probable *audience response*. On the very point under discussion—the moral impact of plays—comparison of *The Country Girl* (revived for particular circumstances prevailing in his company in 1766) with Garrick's adaptation a decade earlier of James Shirley's *The Gamester* is apposite. The blandness of the former, suiting the young performers of the main roles and agreeable to the audience, differs considerably from the dark ironies of the latter, in which Garrick himself played Wilding. He knew that he in his acting could control the results of performing the old "bed trick," and could handle the psychological revenge which his stage wife sets up for him (the cuckold theme not minimized but made imaginary). At the same time he could ridicule in the brittle "comedy of manners" style the contemporary 1757 scene in the tavern sequences of the Old Barnacle subplot. Barnacle wants his sheepish nephew to gain the reputation of a contemporary "blade" of gentlemanly distinction, hence pays to have him beaten in a brawl. "Blades" he believes "roar in brothels, break windows, swear dammes to pay their debts, and march like walking armaries, with poiniards, pistols, rapiers and batons, as though they would murder all the King's people, and blow down the streets." The play as Garrick adapted it, remains tough, a farcical piece of social satire. All comes clean in the end when Wilding reforms:

> The Syren's voice shall charm my ear no more,
> With joy I quit that treacherous or fatal shore
> Where a friend's ruin is by friends enjoyed,
> And every virtue is by turns destroyed!

Garrick had sought in his prologue to remind the audience that the piece came straight from the English, not the French, tradition, painting "English manners, Englishmen." But some hissing had occurred on the first night. Somewhat disturbed Garrick sent the play to Warburton for comment. Warburton seeing a tough morality in it approved the piece. He accounted for the hissing: "It was not the virtue of the audience which took offense at a supposed adultery; it was not their vice which was disappointed when they saw none committed; it was their vanity which was shocked, in finding themselves outwitted by the poet. They had sat long enough in their suspense to be secure in their sagacity, that Wilding had been really cuckolded; and to find themselves mistaken at the last, was enough to put them out of humour."[45]

Garrick in these matters was professional but not a prude. He experimented both with his own texts and with his adaptations, thus testing the limits of public taste. His *Lilliput* (1756) received a bad review, as noted above in chapter 7, seeming to put into the mouths of children (who played the parts) "immoral sentiments and sophisticated frippery." That petite after piece is more subtle than the critic for the *Theatrical Examiner* (1757) found it.[46] Garrick tweaked lots of noses therein, and its run was well-accepted. Garrick likewise saw the "brawniness" of Wycherley, so revived *The Plain Dealer* (7 December 1765), having asked Isaac Bickerstaff to trim it for the stage. Even with Bickerstaff's excisions of speeches and reduction of the obvious sensuality of the Olivia-Manly-Fidelia triangle, the strict moralists in London protested. But the public at the box office paid scant attention to the protesters.[47]

"If the Wantons of Charles's days," wrote Garrick in his advertisement to *The Country Girl*, "is now so reclaimed as to become innocent without being insipid, the present editor will not think his time ill employed" in adding variety to the entertainment of the public. The heart of the matter, Garrick was then convinced, lay in the "absolute necessity for *reforming* many plays of our most eminent writers; for no kind of wit ought to be received as an excuse for immorality, nay it becomes still more dangerous in proportion as it is more witty. Without such reformation our English comedies must be reduced to a very small number and would pall by too frequent repetition or what is worse continue shameless in spite of public disapprobation." And such sentiments were just what the public wanted to hear and read.

Moral influence comes through so patently in flashes of Garrick dialogue, in prologue, epilogue, and advertisement, that one may wonder a bit whether a certain ambivalence might not be present in the seeming iterative overkill. Many a remark is capable of being benignly spoofed by a look, a wink, an intonation in the acting. But as Garrick was a man of his times, not of ours, no call appears to re-create him in the image of another age. Yet one recalls Sharp's line, "Oh the delights of impudence and a good understanding!" as basic to Garrick's own character. The temptation is great to grant Garrick, the professional

Garrick, the possibility, which sophisticated men of all times have seized upon, of playing both sides of the street, occasionally, to please composite audiences. The thought has its appeal, but the evidences for moral action are indeed deeply embedded in his texts. Garrick the actor saw, as he wrote or adapted, the effective way of turning seeds and sketches into agreeable interpretations.

# Part Four
## The Producer
.

# David Garrick Abroad:
# An Heir to the Classical Traditions

THE RENAISSANCE of the study and influence of the Greek and Roman inheritance in the eighteenth century, of neoclassicism, was both sustained and pursued first in the grammar schools and universities. Although Garrick was unable to continue in the university discipline, he had a sound foundation in Greek and Latin as attested by no less an authority than Samuel Johnson and by Garrick's later assembling an extensive collection of classical books. Secondly, academic classicism was rounded out (given a substantiality) by the grand tour embarked on in search of classical remains, the "phantoms of Greece and Rome," and progressing to the living realities of Italy and France, first the architecture, sculpture, and painting and only gradually to the languages and the resources of Italian and French life. While the renaissance was Italian in origins, neoclassicism was stimulated and fostered by France, and although most educated English in the eighteenth century read and, to a lesser degree, wrote Latin and French, very few English and French understood and spoke other than their native languages. Hence the English consorted abroad with the English, (often with more ease than they did in England), and only belatedly progressed to intercommunication, to the cultural enrichment of English life in the fine arts, literature, science, political theory, and social refinement. Not until the middle years of the century did the grand tour become a diversified and conventional cultural and intellectual institution that created for more than a select few a cosmopolitan maturity founded on classical antiquity.

Although English biographers and French friends made much of Garrick's paternal Huguenot ancestry—the family name, an Anglicization of *garrigues*, the French term for the semibarren areas of scrub oak, broom, cistus, and fragrant herbs east of Bordeaux stretching into the Provence, Garrick himself, as far as can be discovered, never made an allusion to French origins, much less exploited them at home or abroad. On his return from his first visit to France in 1751, he wrote

John Hoadly in July, "I am return'd . . . safe & sound from Paris & as true an Englishman as ever" (105).

He did keep in touch with his father's family in and about London, the Cazalets and Fermignacs, but there is no evidence they spoke French in their homes or kept up Huguenot ties in France. Late in life, Garrick all but ignored a French lady, Mme Wity (née Garrick), who sought to establish genealogical ties with him (1116). He learned to read French in the Lichfield Grammar School well enough to be able, at the age of 15, to annotate, in Latin, a French grammar, *Le Jardin des Racines Grecques*, in his learning of Greek, and later, as we know, Walmesley hoped Garrick might perfect his French and Italian in Johnson's school at Edial. In 1751 and later in 1763–65 he attended the theatre and communed with French friends in Paris apparently with no limiting linguistic handicap. Suard recalled, however, that "Garrick deeply regretted that he could not assume the accent and learn the language of the country. He would have liked to mingle with the actors of Paris, and, without other reward than the pleasure he would have given and the success he might have had, to act with them in French comedy and tragedy."[1] As a matter of fact, few Frenchmen attending the mixed social gatherings in Paris and Italy, which included Garrick, understood spoken English; hence Garrick selected and emphasized in recitation in their salons the episodes from Shakespeare wherein the meaning was easily interpreted by pantomime.

As for the several hundred letters addressed to Garrick by his French friends, all but three—Claude-Pierre Patu, the Baron d'Holbach, and L'Abbé Bonnet—wrote Garrick in French.[2] Garrick in turn, presumably wrote them in English, yet 12 of his letters to them survive in French from such diverse sources as drafts, copies, editorial translations, and in autograph—though his autograph does not necessarily prove that he alone composed the text. In his earliest letter in French, to the actor La Noue (7 August 1751), written with the acknowledged assistance of Charles Denis, Garrick remarks, "J'espere si fort me perfectioner par votre agreable commerce et amitié, que dans peu, Je serai en Etat de Marcher Sans Secours"—a wish or ambition he never actually realized (107). In the last of five letters he wrote to the actor Henri-Louis LeKain he noted: "Si la Connoissance de la Langue françoise voudroit me permettre de vous dire . . . Je ne serai pas reduit a vous Ecrire seulement quatre lignes comme Je fait" (442).[3] To the one Frenchman whom Garrick wrote more often than to any other, the manager Jean Monnet, one letter only survives (presumably in translation). In it, speaking of "notre cher ami Favart," Garrick wrote, "j'ae honte de lui écrire en française. . . . plût à Dieu que vous et notre ami Favart vous entendissiez notre langue!" (417).[4] It is hardly surprising that Garrick lacked confidence in his command of French to write Voltaire in his native language (340,564). As late as 1775 Garrick wrote to Préville from England, "Excusez je vous prie que j'aye envoyé mes regards [et] services dans le plus mauvais françois" (880).

Garrick's earliest association with a Frenchman was with Jean Monnet (1703–85), Garrick's senior by 15 years, who like Garrick had come up in the theatrical world by energy, ambition, and ability. Among other attainments (employment), as director he restored the Opéra-Comique until it rivaled the Comédie-Française and the Comédie-Italienne, both eventually seeing to it that his license was canceled. He thereupon sought to negotiate a contract in London for a French company, but failing to obtain a contract with Rich at Covent Garden, on Garrick's advice, he engaged the Little Theatre in the Haymarket. Supported by a subscription of £400, he opened in November 1748 with a company of French comedians he had assembled in Paris. Anti-Gallican riots forced him to close after two nights, much in debt but rescued by Garrick, among others, who gave for him a benefit performance on 27 May 1750. Though Garrick does not mention Monnet in his Paris *Diary* of 1751, references in Monnet's later letters support the probability that the two had been together in Paris in the summer of 1751. Monnet introduced Garrick to Charles Simon Favart (1710–92), whom Monnet had engaged as author, reader of plays, and stage manager of the Opéra-Comique. The friendships were fully established when Garrick was in Paris in 1764–65.

Not until the summer of 1751 did the Garricks for the first time "Journey to Paris," about the only record of which lies in Garrick's cryptic and fragmentary *Diary*.[5] They would have been almost unnoticed tourists outside the English colony there, were it not for Charles Denis (1705?–72), son of a Hugenot refugee clergyman, the brother of Peter Denis, who in 1750 had married the natural daughter of John Jacob Heidigger, manager in London of the Queen's Opera House, with which Charles was later to be associated. Charles had previously studied medicine in Paris for nine years before abandoning the profession for literature and translating. He guided the Garricks in their sightseeing and introduced Garrick to literary French friends, among others Charles Collé, on one social occasion Garrick acting a scene from *Macbeth*.[6]

Second only to his attending the theatres, Garrick devoted his time in Paris to viewing the array of monuments and *objets d'art* singled out by most guide books, such as the cathedrals, religious foundations, palaces, libraries, "les hôtels" and gardens. He enjoyed both Gothic and baroque architecture, his standard of comparison being Burlington House and Chatsworth. Further the pictures and statuary he mentions were much in the style of the Burlington's collections. "No Hotel has so good a Collection of Pictures as there is at Chiswick, in general Rubbish to 'em."[7] Not by foreknowledge, but accident, he visited the gallery of M Julienne, who had assembled furniture, china, curiosities, and pictures, such as the Garricks were assembling in the villa in Hampton. As was then the current fashion in the English colony, Garrick visited (13 June) the studio of Jean Etienne Liotard (1702–90) and engaged him to paint his pastel portrait for which he sat five times and later dined with Liotard. On the same visit to Paris Liotard may have been commissioned for a companion pastel of Mrs Garrick, both gifts to Lady Burlington, and now at Chatsworth.[8] Other than for royal spectacles, Garrick took little notice of contemporary French life, except to condemn the disorderliness of the French audience in the theatre and the overpainting of French women: "In our walk [May 31] we saw two *very pretty French women* unpainted, w$^{ch}$ was a greater curiosity than any I have yet seen in Paris."[9]

As for rounds of visits and dinners with English residents, these may be epitomized in Garrick's words: "Monday, June 10th: Made twenty visits of English Gentlemen in y$^e$ morning & at night saw the *Femmes sçavantes* of *Moliere* with y$^e$ *Zeneide* after which sup'd with Lord Huntington, L$^d$ Stormont, Mr. Stanley, etc."[10] Garrick welcomed introductions to Alexis Piron, the poet, and Jean Sauvé ("dit de la Noué"), the actor. Garrick's letter to his brother Peter might best sum up the brief summer visit to Paris in 1751: "I had much honour done Me both by French & English, & Every body & thing contributed to make me happy—The great fault of our Countrymen is, y$^t$ when they go to Paris, they keep too much among themselves; but if they would Mix w$^{th}$ y$^e$ French as I did, it is a most agreeable Jaunt" (106).

Although Garrick was only a month in Paris, the visit aroused in him an interest in French life that was to become a developing influence in the succeeding years. For the immediately ensuing 12, however, he depended on his Paris banker, Charles Selwin, and on Jean Monnet for news, books, commissions—such as negotiating a contract with Jean Georges Noverre, the premiere ballet master of the century. Garrick's sponsorship at Drury Lane of Noverre and his ballet company was frustrated, as earlier with Monnet, by the current anti-Gallicism of the English mob in the pit; nevertheless Noverre and Garrick continued good friends. On the other hand, Garrick became personally cognizant of the gathering Anglomania, in which he was a focus, in the visit and correspondence of a gifted young Frenchman, Claude-Pierre Patu, who came over to London in November 1755, purposely to attend Garrick's acting at Drury Lane. Forced to return to Paris by the London fogs and his failing health, Patu thereafter until his death in August 1757, at Saint Jean de Maurienne, wrote Garrick nine long letters, acknowledging eight from Garrick, saved and endorsed by Garrick "Letters of the poor Patu." Much in the manner of Monnet and Garrick's later correspondence, Patu ordered books, welcomed Garrick's friends, advised Garrick on current French journalism, announced his publication of translations of English plays in two volumes, and above all else praised Shakespeare, while enjoying the respect of Voltaire.[11]

The 12 years between Garrick's return from Paris and the signing of the Peace of Paris, following the Seven Years' War, opening France again to English visitors, were the most exhausting for Garrick as actor, manager, and in his private life. His successes aroused much envy, made public in the press; he was harassed by ambitious playwrights, actors, and actresses, and many of his early friends were in ill health, retired, or dead. He himself had about satiated the London theatregoers with too-frequent appearances. By the summer of 1763 he wisely but reluctantly, "advis'd by several Physicians . . . to give Myself a Winter's respite" (315), decided to go abroad. Meanwhile, his fame had been spreading in France; earlier, on 10 April 1762, Sterne, with a £20 loan from Garrick in his pocket, wrote Garrick from Paris, "You are much talked of here, and much expected, as soon as the peace will let you—These last two days you have happened to engross the whole conversation of two great houses where I was at dinner."[12]

In anticipation of his visit, the company, 11 in all, of the Comédie-Italienne, prepared and signed 18 July 1763, a pass, or freedom of the house, presented in a gold snuffbox to Garrick, "le Premièr Des comédiens De londre," on his arrival in Paris, by M Labbat, their controller.[13]

On 15 September 1763, the opening day of Drury Lane, he and Mrs Garrick sailed for France. He had the means to travel as an aristocrat in his own carriage, and to engage the most elegant apartments where he wished to sojourn for a month or more. For both his countrymen and foreign society he became one of the heroes of the current Anglomania.

The projected tour of a winter abroad, however, eventually dragged out for nearly two years, during which time Garrick as an individual had to surmount three crises: the crippling almost chronic rheumatic fever of Mrs Garrick; next his own serious illness, in which he had to face the third and terrifying crisis of possibly terminating his career as manager-actor by death. In the psychological progression and resolution of these challenges lie insights into the quality of the man. The tour began auspiciously, however, almost triumphantly in a succession of recognitions and receptions both by the English communities abroad and by the distinguished personages of France and Italy. In conformity with the conventions of the grand tour, Garrick set about keeping a journal, "I shall write down immediately as I am struck with different Objects, Customs, & Manners without the least attention to what has been said by y$^e$ many Writers of great or little reputation who have publish'd their Sentiments upon the same things,"[14] but Garrick was not temperamentally one to commune with himself; he thought mostly in personal relationships. Hence the *Journal* soon languished, and the narration of the tour is better found in his letters home to friends.

The reception of the Garricks by the English colony in Paris was repeated (though not on the same scale) in most of the cities they later visited. Richard Aldworth Neville, the minister-plenipotentiary, who early had associated with Garrick's friends, Rochford, Rigby, and Windham, introduced the Garricks to Paris society with an elegant supper party to which were invited, besides the members of the English colony, the leading figures in the theatre and in current French literature, such as Mme Clairon, d'Alembert, Marmontel, and presumably Diderot, Grimm, and d'Holbach, though the last three are not mentioned as present by Garrick. Inevitably the conversation progressed to a comparison of French and English drama. In Garrick's own words: "I was in Spirits & so was the *Clairon*, who sup'd with us at M$^r$ Neville's—She got up to set me a going & spoke something in Racine's Athalie most charmingly—upon which I gave them the Dagger Scene in Macbeth, y$^e$ Curse in Lear, & the falling asleep in S$^r$ John Brute, the consequence of which is, that I am now star'd at y$^e$ Playhouse, & talk'd of by Gentle & Simple. . . . the Nobles & the Litterati have made so much of Me that I am quite asham'd of opening my heart Ev'n to You," that is George Colman, to whom he was writing (317). Their original plan, however, was not to linger in Paris but to winter in Italy. They set out for Lyon on 28 September. Passing through Savoy, Garrick "had a most warm invitation from *Voltaire*, whom I shall take in my return" (318). They found the countryside and mountains "the most Enchanting Scene that fancy can paint . . . like one great Garden" and approaching Chambery, "We walk'd a great part of y$^e$ way"[15]; they even enjoyed the transit over Mt. Cenis. In the passage from France to Italy, however, Mrs Garrick was crippled by rheumatic arthritis that was to plague her for months to come.

In Turin "M$^r$ Pitt, & all y$^e$ English here, are most particularly kind to Us" (319). Delayed a week by repairs to their carriage, the Garricks began sight-seeing, but after all, as Garrick observed, "*Turin* is a good Place for two Days but for a Week 'tis not sufficient." [16]

Passing on to Milan, they were welcomed and entertained by Count Karl Joseph von Firmian, governor of Lombardy and a patron of arts, who was their guide and for whom Garrick ordered from England "all y$^e$ Prints of myself that have any Character." [17] At this point the *Journal* lapses. They passed on through Genoa, then two days at sea in a felucca, to Leghorn and on to Florence where they feasted "upon Virtù in the Gallery & in the Pallaces. . . . The English here are all agreeable, & hold their Conversations in our Appartment (& we have a most magnificent one upon the banks of y$^e$ Arno) almost Every Night" (320). In Florence Garrick was received by Count Francesco Algarotti, the poet, well known in England, who in turn wrote letters introducing Garrick to Italian friends in Bologna and Venice. [18]

They stayed on in Rome for a fortnight, but Garrick's spirits were so sunk by his first impressions that with reluctance he was dragged to see the Pantheon. "But my God, w$^t$ was my Pleasure & Surprize!—I never felt so much in my life as when I Entered that glorious Structure; I gap'd, but could not speak for 5 Minutes—It is so very noble, that it has not been in y$^e$ Power of Modern Frippery, or Popery (for it is a Church you know) to extinguish Its grandeur & Elegance—Here I began to think myself in *Old* Rome, & when I saw the ruins of that famous amphitheatre . . . I then felt my own littleness." As for the Tiber, "it is very strange that so much good poetry sh$^d$ be thrown away upon such a pitiful River; it is no more Comparable to our Thames, than our modern Poets are to their Virgils & Horaces."

Not until 17 December did they reach Naples—"our Journey's End" —to reside there for two months and more. They much enjoyed the theatre, Garrick being invited to see the Italian actors perform in the palace before the king and later to prepare a dramatic fable for them to perform extempore (321). As for the English colony, "We dine & sup with Lord Spencer, Lord Exeter, the Minister [probably Philip Changuin, whom Garrick was later to introduce to Mme Riccoboni], the Consul [Isaac Jamineau], &c &c &c almost Every day & Night, we have balls more than twice a Week & parties innumerable" (322). They were also often with Lady Orford, Lady Spencer, and Lord Palmerston, later one of the pallbearers at Garrick's funeral. And it was in the winter of 1763–64 in Naples, Rome, and elsewhere that the acquaintance with the Spencers ripened into a close friendship later in England. As for the Neapolitans "they are a new race of beings, & I have the highest Entertainment in going amongst them, & observing their Characters from y$^e$ highest to y$^e$ lowest" (321). As for "The Nobility

of y$^e$ Country, [they] . . . have descended from their great pride &
Magnificence to honour Us with their Smiles—in Short we are in great
fashion & I have forgot England & all my trumpery at Drury Lane"
(323). While in Naples Garrick prepared and sent to Dr Burney a report on the present state of music in Italy (324). Also in Naples Garrick
engaged Antonio Carara of Padua as a valet who, in addition to Italian,
spoke and wrote excellent French and English. Carara continued with
the Garricks to London and later on Garrick's recommendation accompanied English parties abroad and for years thereafter carried out
abroad all sorts of commissions for Garrick (587).

The Garricks' plan was to return through Rome for a month, then to
Bologna, Venice, and through Germany to England. Their final days in
Naples were depressing. Thousands were dying of famine, and Mrs
Garrick was severely crippled by persistent rheumatism in her right
hip, brought on by having been caught in a storm when the carriage
broke down on the journey south to Naples.

Back in Rome, they settled into an apartment formerly occupied by
Devonshire. Although Garrick had looked forward to the return, his
thoughts now were all on England and Drury Lane; he was dispirited
at the possibility of not being able to return for the opening in the
autumn. He wrote Devonshire, "I have lost all relish for the Stage both
as Manager and Actor" (326), and as a distraction offered to buy some
pictures and statues for Devonshire, who, in response, professed a
lack of funds, but continued: "I should, however, be obliged to you if
you would get me all the prints that Bartolozzi has engraved; as you
are such a connoisseur, you must know him."[19]

So far the Garricks had followed the beaten paths of the grand tour,
and had been pleasantly diverted and praised. Had they been able to
adhere to their original intention to be back in London for the 1764–65
season, Garrick might have accomplished little more than to restore his
energetic domination of Drury Lane—inexhaustible in his appetite,
on and off the stage, for continuing recognition in his profession. But
illness had taken much out of the pair, and more was to follow. Garrick
wisely contemplated the recreations and preoccupations of his wealthy
and aristocratic friends—diversions of leisured gentlemen. The image
of actor-manager, famous theatrical public figure—sought out, applauded, and entertained as a celebrity—faded as he thought of his
interests as a private individual. In Rome he made a beginning in his
patronage of artists, of portraiture that was private and not dramatic.
Shortly he was to begin collecting pictures and books.

On the first visit to Rome, Garrick carried letters of introduction
from James (Dance) Love of the Drury Lane company to his two broth-

*Ashmolean Museum, Oxford*
David Garrick, Esq.
Portrait by Pompeo Girolamo Batoni, 1764.

301

*Earl Spencer Collection, Althorp Park*
Marble Bust of Garrick.
By Joseph Nollekens.

ers, Nathaniel, a painter, and George the younger, an architect, then studying in Rome, who cordially received the Garricks. Of Nathaniel Dance Garrick wrote (2 January 1764) "the Painter is a great Genius, & will do w$^t$ he pleases when he goes to London." Either on first meeting or later when the Garricks returned to Rome, Garrick commissioned a portrait by Nathaniel.[20] Later in England he did a well-known "Garrick as Richard III," and a splendid private likeness which he gave to John Taylor, a fellow painter.[21] Also while in Rome, Garrick commissioned a portrait by the fashionable artist, Pompeo Batoni, who painted at approximately the same time, the portrait of Georgiana, countess Spencer. Earlier, in a letter of 24 December 1763, Garrick had inquired of George Colman, "What is become of your Terence?" (321) to be published as the *Comedies of Terence* in April 1765, with the *Phormio* dedicated to Garrick. In the portrait by Batoni, Garrick is holding before him, open to the masks for the *Andria*, the edition of Urbano 1736, the text from an early Vatican source, the translation by Nicolas Fortguerra, and the illustrations by Batista Sintes. Garrick gave the portrait to the Reverend Richard Kaye, whom he presumably met in Florence.[22]

One day in Rome Garrick recognized, passing in the street, Joseph Nollekens, "the little fellow to whom we gave the prizes at the Society of Artists,"[23] and commissioned from him an excellent bust, given later to the Reverend William Arden, Lord Spencer's tutor. Arden's widow, in turn gave the bust to Spencer, and it now resides at Althorp. Earlier while the Garricks were in Naples, Angelica Kauffman, much courted for awhile by Dance, painted yet another portrait of Garrick, given by him to Lord Exeter, with whom Garrick associated in Naples.[24] While Garrick was in Florence, Thomas Patch, a popular caricaturist in the Italian manner, is generally credited with an elaborate and finished caricature of Garrick, Sir Horace Mann, and three other figures.[25] The much debated conversation piece, "Garrick in the Green Room," long attributed to Hogarth, was actually produced by Allessandro Longhi, the subject, Garrick reading a scene from *Macbeth* for the Duke of Parma and guests.[26] The Duc d'Orléans, to add to his collection of portraits of notables, commissioned Caramontelle for two pencil and water-color figures of Garrick—one the tragic, the other the comic Garrick, which are still extant.[27] Finally Lemoyne executed a bust of Garrick in terra cotta, a copy of which he sent Garrick in London. Acclaimed at the time, it seems not to have survived.[28]

From Rome, in May, on their progress to Venice, the Garrick's detoured to Parma to dine as guests with the Duke of Parma, the Duke of York, Lord Spencer, and other notables. On the occasion Garrick performed the dagger scene from *Macbeth*; the Duke was so impressed that he praised Shakespeare and Garrick in good English and presented Garrick with a "very handsome gold box, with some of the finest enamelled paintings upon all sides" (335). In Venice in particular They enjoyed the spectacular *régate* staged for the Duke of York. Garrick had apparently all along been purchasing some pictures and books, but in Venice he assembled some 180 books in Italian with the advice of Joseph Baretti who was his guide, intending to sell them to Topham Beauclerk. Only a few of the titles were later in the sales catalogue of Garrick's library.[29]

But a month's residence in Venice became a disillusioning experience: Mrs Garrick's crippling illness was not alleviated by the damps of the canals, and the Garricks in mid-June moved to the hot mud baths at Abano, near Parma. Garrick still hoped to be back in London in time for the opening of the autumn season. "I fret to be at home, I dread the Italian Suns, & I am affraid that my presence is necessary to make a Plan for y$^e$ next Winter. . . . I have no Joy now in thinking on y$^e$ Stage, & shall return (if I must) like a Bear to a Stake—and this baiting, my good friend, is no joke after forty" (332). All the while they were attending on Mrs Garrick's recovery, Garrick continued buying pictures and books; while resident in Abano he was "in treaty for no less than two Pictures by Tempesto, two Bassans, a Vandyke, a Rubens, a Paul Veronese, &c. I have a little money to throw away, & I don't see why I should not be a little ridiculous as well as my betters" (334).[30]

The return to London was contingent on Mrs Garrick's recovery; for five weeks they lingered in Padua that Mrs Garrick might undergo the treatment of the hot mud baths, before setting out for Spa by way of Munich. They enjoyed the Tyrolian scenery, and with a saving sense of humor the cloaca in Germany, as earlier in France and Italy—recorded for the scatological obsession of his friend Townley (336).

On 2 August in Munich, Garrick was seized with a violent fever, and later an attack of the stone, and for five weeks was seriously ill, surviving only through Mrs Garrick's care and "Eight Physicians, my good friend, & still alive" (341), and by a saving grace of humor, never more effectively pursued on the stage than in pain and uncertainty and disability and slow recuperation. As he wrote his good friend William Arden, "all the Combustibles I had been long storing up [at Naples, & at Venice] & Elsewhere took fire at this place, & I have been confin'd more than a Month to my bed, by the most dangerous bilious Fever, that Ever poor Sinner Suffer'd for the small fault of a little innocent society" (338). Believing, at one point, his illness might be

*Marquess of Exeter Collection, Burghley House*
David Garrick.
Portrait by Angelica Kauffmann, Naples, 1764.

fatal he composed his own epitaph,[31] but good spirits prevailed and he wrote George: "I have often made Myself happy that *You* could Enjoy *Hampton* tho I could not. I hope You have had y$^r$ family there, sent for the Cows, had the old Mare, rid about, Eat y$^e$ best fruit, & got y$^r$self stout as a Lion" (337).

All thoughts of returning in the autumn were given up, and the Garricks passed through Augsburg, Frankfort, and Nancy to Paris, with no other thought in mind than the long recuperation that lay ahead of Garrick. From Nancy he wrote Voltaire his regrets in not having been able to visit him at Ferney.[32] His first letter from Paris to George Colman was a long appeal for "News, news, news, my dear Friend," and although he could not then return to London his thoughts were all upon Drury Lane, and his own somewhat uncertain future: "y$^e$ Doctors all have forbid me thinking of Business—I have at present lost all taste for y$^e$ Stage—it was once my greatest Passion, & I labor'd for many years like a true Lover—but I am grown cold—should my desires return, I am the Town's humble Servant again" (341).

Hampered by protracted convalescence, the Garricks did not return to Paris, which was not included in their original plans, until 10 November. By 25 December they were settled in the "expensive lodgings," in the Hôtel de Malthe, Rue Nicaise, recently occupied by John Wilkes, where they were to reside, being further delayed by recuperation, before returning to London 25 April 1765 (344,356). Of the Garricks' reception and activities during the six months in Paris, almost nothing is to be learned from Garrick's letters to England. For all his London friends knew, Garrick was preoccupied only with the fortunes of Drury Lane and the response that might await him on a return to acting. From subsequent memorabilia and correspondence, however, with French friends whose letters (more than 300) he carefully preserved, and approximately 50 of his own that survived haphazardly, it is possible to reconstruct much that was engrossing Garrick in Paris.[33]

It is a commonplace in Western history that for several decades in the middle years of the eighteenth century, France took the lead in intellectual, artistic, and political creativity. All the brilliant thinking and talking and writing there were not centered in a church or university, but rather in the private salons in Paris and in the provinces, the participants and guests often associating in more than one salon. Although Garrick undoubtedly was an occasional guest in a number of these salons, such as that of Mme Geoffrin, who made a point of inviting artists as well as Englishmen such as Hume, Adam Smith, Wilkes, and Walpole, Garrick himself in his letters mentions frequenting only two of the famous salons.

Towards the end of the Paris sojourn, he wrote (17 March) Charles Denis, now resident in London, that with all his "complaints I have had spirits enough at times to Enjoy the Conversation of Your old Friends at M^r Pelletier's [*fermier-général*]—their old Society is kept up—and they meet at his house Every Wed^y. . . . Crebillon, Collé, Saurin [all playwrights], & the Master of the house in particular ever and Ever talking of You. . . . I don't know a more agreeable Company, & where Wit & true Social liberty reign so triumphantly" (354). Regarding the far more renowned and influential salon of the Baron d'Holbach, Garrick wrote Colman, 16 February, "We had a fine laugh at Baron D'Albach's (where you din'd once) about the *Wicked Comp^y* I keep; I am always with that Set" (350). For 35 years d'Holbach, the "maître d'Hôtel de la Philosophie," held his dinners and salon in his elegant mansion in Rue Royale, butte Saint-Roche, the salon on Thursdays and Sundays. Most public figures of any consequence were sooner or later his guests, but over the years, approximately 15 of the more prominent formed the d'Holbach coterie.[34] D'Holbach had studied at Leydon (1744–48) and throughout his life wrote voluminously and anonymously; his greatest contribution, however, was his lavish hospitality and the encouragement and support he gave his contemporaries. Ten years later, Garrick writing Suard, recalled, as he often did earlier, d'Holbach's hospitality: "Let my most dear and worthy Baron d'Holback know that his kindness and attentions to us, when at Paris, are never out of our hearts and minds: pray remember that Madame La Baronne is always included in our grateful remembrances" (989).

In the years following the return to London and to Drury Lane, Garrick sent greetings to and corresponded with several members of the d'Holbach coteries, among others, Diderot, Grimm, Marmontel, Chastellux, and Suard. For example only, Denis Diderot, the editor, with D'Alembert, of the great *Encyclopédie*, sent (1773) Garrick his essay, *Le Paradoxe sur le Comédien* for his confidential commentary before passing it along to Suard, "j'en aurois besoin pour un ouvrage auquel je travaille."[35] The Baron Friedrich-Melchior Grimm, diplomat and author, ordered and sent Garrick the *Encyclopédie* at Diderot's request to whom Garrick had addressed his order. Later Grimm in 1771 accompanied the Prince of Hesse-Darmstadt on his tour of England, attending several performances at Drury Lane and being received by Garrick (652). Marmontel, a most versatile and admired writer, first praised by letter to Garrick his acting following his performance at Neville's dinner party. But it was Grimm who published perhaps the finest account of the moving impression that Garrick's salon acting made on his French friends.[36] On the other hand there was the glamorous François-Jean, Chevalier de Chastellux, officer, man of letters, amateur actor, friend of Wilkes, much liked by Garrick though their correspondence was hampered by Garrick's later illness and Chastellux's undecipherable handwriting. In admiration of Garrick, Chastellux undertook to translate Shakespeare, progressing no further than a lamentable adaptation of *Romeo and Juliet*. He visited Garrick in England in 1771 and later with Suard accompanied Madame Necker when she came over to London in 1776 to attend Garrick's final performances at Drury, and later all were entertained by the Garricks at Hampton (519,730,872,989,1026).[37]

Garrick's most sustained and valued friendship, however, was with the journalist Jean-Baptiste-Antoine Suard (1733–1817), whom, longer than any other, d'Holbach cherished as a brother. Overly apprehensive, perhaps, about the impact of current English journalism on the box office receipts at Drury Lane, Garrick followed with great interest the French journalism of Grimm, Marmontel, the restless and tireless de la Place, and later the notorious pamphleteer Nicholas Henry Linguet whose *Journal* "Entertains and instructs me much—his Mistakes, of which there are plenty, afford me pleasure" (1110).[38] In Suard, however, Garrick found an informed, responsible, and superior journalist with a sense of style; the two later exchanging full and cordial letters. Suard had a better command of English than most French writers; he was the Garricks' guide and companion in Paris. They later exchanged books, literary news, and with generous tolerance discussed the merits of Shakespeare versus French drama, Suard frankly supporting his countrymen. Suard generally addressed Garrick as "mon cher Roscius," and few in France or England wrote more discriminating appreciation of Garrick's acting. He married the charming daughter of Panckouke, the publisher, whose shop Garrick frequented. Twice Suard visited Garrick in England, in the spring of 1768 and again in 1773, later recalling "des momens délicieux que j'ai passés à Hampton, dans Southampton-street, et surtout à Drury-lane."[39]

To the French actors that sought his acquaintance, Garrick responded with unaffected candor and warmth. From observing and commending Mme Clairon and LeKain as actors in 1751, Garrick progressed in 1764–65 to a personal acquaintance with both, professionally tempered, however, by the current conflict in which all were caught up, between the traditional rhetorical style of Clairon and LeKain and Garrick's espousal of a natural style. Yet Garrick generously supported Clairon in her strike against the arbitrary royal control of the Paris theatre; later from England he wrote Mme Riccoboni, "my thoughts of Clairon cannot be exceeded—I am as constant to my Sentiments of her, as she is inimitable" (361). The friendship between Garrick and LeKain, each head of his profession in his own land, was more varied and affectionate.[40] But Garrick had most admiration for Préville, the outstanding comedian. As late as 7 January 1775, writing Préville, Garrick recalled, "Ne m'avez vous pas oublié mon cher Compagnon in ivresse? n'avez vous pas oublié nos expeditions romanesques sur les boulevars, quand les tailleurs de pierre devenoint plus pierre que leurs ouvrages En admiration de nos folies," the first recalling an incident when "à cheval, du bois de Boulogne, [Garrick] lui dit: 'Je m'en vais faire l'homme ivre; faites-en autant.' Ils traversèrent ainsi le village de Passy,'" the villages persuaded that Garrick was more drunk than Préville (880).

For Garrick, the attraction, even fascination and the influence of French culture did not wane on his return to London, though never to return to France. The occasional letters of many French friends; the visits of French friends to England, such as Morellet; the literary exchanges, such as with Mme Riccoboni; the expansion of his library of French literature were all a part of a growth in knowledge and appreciation of French life. The variety of all the subjects, events, and attitudes converged in Jean Monnet, who in admiration and affection for Garrick became his professional and personal agent, intermediary. Monnet more than anyone else both sustained and amplified the French ties and influence. Garrick in turn shared his friends and English heritage with Monnet.

On 27 January 1765, Garrick wrote George Colman, whom Garrick had earlier introduced to Monnet, "our old Friend Monet . . . is y$^e$ gayest man in Paris—He has got Enough by his Operas to live happily, he has honorably paid all his debts that his unfortunate expedition to London brought upon him. He is greatly belov'd by the Men of Wit & Pleasure who have assisted him in collecting materials for three Vol$^s$ of the most chosen Songs in the french language—it will be a compleet history of their Lyrick poetry—He has great taste himself & he began his Collection, when he was y$^e$ Manager of Operas—His Engravings for y$^e$ Musick, his elegant designs exquisitely executed, with the happy choice of the poetry, will make a very great addition to y$^e$ Musical Library—the songs are all new set by y$^e$ best Masters here" (347). The book in question, *Anthologie françoise ou chansons choisies, depuis le XIII$^e$ siècle jusqu'a present* (Paris, 1765) Garrick undertook to promote through Becket with notices in *St. James's Chronicle* and the *Public Advertiser*, prepared and sent Garrick by Monnet and altered by Colman.[41] Following a visit by Monnet to London in 1766, presumably at Garrick's invitation when Garrick placed at his disposal his house in Southampton Street, entertained him at Hampton, carried him to Bath, and sent him home delighted,[42] the two men launched and continued an extensive correspondence of which Garrick preserved at least 65 letters from Monnet in French. On the other hand only one of Garrick's letters survives, in a French translation, from what must have been an equal number to Monnet, judging by Monnet's frequent acknowledgments.[43] Professionally he kept Garrick up to date on the current French theatre. Of a more personal nature, he arranged for the education of Garrick's nieces, Arabella and Kate, with Mme Descombes in Paris and shortly rescued Bell from the attentions of a M de Molière; he supplied Mrs Garrick with dress materials and style books notably on the dressing of the hair. He purchased for Garrick quantities of books, engravings, and furnishings; he received and entertained members of the Drury Lane company on visits to Paris, and exchanged news and greetings from mutual friends. He opened his final letter to Garrick of 4 December 1778, less than two months before Garrick's death: "Pendant quelque temps j'ai cessé de vous écrire, mais je n'ai pas cessé de vous aimer et de me rapeler souvent avec plaisir les preuves de votre amitié."[44]

As remarked earlier, the grand tour, undertaken by the Garricks as a diversion and for recuperation lapsed into a crisis both professionally and personally for him. Garrick gained in Paris only a partial recovery in health, and not until a year after his return to Drury Lane for the 1765–66 season was he fully reassured that he might be able to continue acting. Threatened thus with forced retirement Garrick had to grapple tentatively with his resources to create a private and a social identity other than that of an actor.

For all of his life to date, except for a few intimate friends, Garrick was first and last to himself and to his countrymen an actor-manager. Furthermore, he was ever aware of the traditional English low opinion of actors, more often than not well-founded, as being little more than mimics. The almost, at time, malevolent prejudice was not limited to the moralist, academic, and gentry. A fortnight before Garrick visited Florence, Walpole wrote Sir Horace Mann, the English envoy who in title and personality was the head of the English community in Florence, warning him soon to expect "The famous Garrick and his once famous wife. He will make you laugh, as a mimic, and as he knows we are great friends, will affect great partiality for me; but be a little on your guard, remember he is *an actor*."[45]

On the other hand, Paris, at one of its more brilliant periods, seems to have awakened in Garrick, to have supported Garrick in a conviction that there was something more in acting than dominance and popularity, something more in society and friendship than repartee, gossip, reminiscences, and display. The French philosophers, critics, and writers, dignified acting as a fine art, not just a trade or a passing entertainment. They sought a philosophical basis for their criticism of the theatre; they treated acting as a cultural and refining influence, on a footing with the other fine arts. Where the ancients honored the dramatist, the French esteemed the actor. In this open-minded respect for the actor, the French turned to Garrick, the greatest English actor, for his ideas, judgments, and insights—his interpretation of the literary qualities of a play. Challenged by this respect for his profession, Garrick, without losing any of his astuteness as a manger, developed into a more confident artist. Tom Davies, Garrick's contemporary biographer, summarized the change in Garrick's style of acting on his return to London: "It was remarked by the most discerning judges, that our Roscius had, by visiting foreign theatres, greatly profited in his mode of representation; they observed, that his action, though always spirited and proper, was become easy and unrestrained; that his deportment was more graceful, and his manner more elegant; that he did not now appear so solicitous for applause as to disturb his own feelings, and lessen the pleasure of the audience."[46]

At the risk of an arbitrary oversimplification, a distinction might be drawn between the professional impact, on the one hand, of Continental travel on the artist, writer, and actor, such as Garrick and many of his contemporaries, and, on the other hand, the enlightening, the cultivating of the amateur, the liberal arts traveler, the audience, the individual addressed by the artists. The first sought mastery; the second sought and often gained an intellectual and emotional refinement. Further, there was for both, a primary gain in viewing the passing scene, the heritage of antiquity, from the vantage point of two distinctive cultural patterns. There was more than variety and multiplicity, a defensive chauvinism, rather a gain in catholicity in taste and an assessing, a sorting out of values. The grand tour drew England back into the humanistic, the classical fold.

Garrick enjoyed an additional opportunity, granted very few of his contemporaries, of being welcomed into the inner circles of French life, and of having the resulting insight sustained and expanded by friendships and correspondence for the remainder of his life. As a result of a greater rationalism, he gained a controlled emotionalism in his private life. He resolved the paradox of the comedian; on the one hand he objectively controlled his mimicry, his acting—as Johnson remarked, Punch does not feel. On the other hand he assimilated into his own living the emotions he commanded and stimulated.

311

He first of all survived almost disastrous illness by a personal sense of comedy. He rehabilitated himself by responding to human values in friendships, in literature, in his home life, in the fine arts. He experienced more than the satisfaction of the market value and fashion of paintings. It is pertinent to recall that in Garrick's library of 2,700 titles, more than half of the books were in French. He continued, indeed, his idolatry of Shakespeare, such as the Stratford-on-Avon Festival to come, which some thought more a promotion of the actor than of the plays. Further, Johnson to the contrary, Garrick became more clubbable, more inclined to companionship rather than self-promotion in social gatherings, with more sympathy and compassion. Outside the theatre his life became even less defensive and aggressive. The changes may, of course, have been in part a maturing.

To rephrase the influence of the grand tour and France on Garrick, he became through it part of the "enlightenment"; he attained some of the objectives and values of European neoclassicism; he responded personally to the impact of his art, his acting; and in a larger and equally commendable sense he attained a cosmopolitanism.

# 10

# Garrick's Theatrical Innovations

THE FIRST FIVE YEARS OF Garrick's final decade in the theatre showed a remarkably creative burst of energy, despite his qualms about his health. The continental sojourn had rejuvenated him, even finally in health, but especially in the French experience with the Parisian theatres, the actors, and the playwrights. His own professionalism received assurance and it expanded in spirit, as he compared the two stages in his mind. And the associations made in Paris were to continue for the years to come. He thought about the meaning of it all as he prepared in April 1765 for the homeward journey, and his conclusions were later confirmed time and time again.

In his earlier visit in 1751 he had followed a brisk schedule of sightseeing, had dined with a few persons in both the English community and the French, but mostly with an actor or two, for his weather eye had been turned toward possibilities of recruiting dancers. Despite disappointments in many French performers at that time, he had found a grace in French stage dancing that prompted him to keep informed about any newly planned spectacles combining music and dance with proven audience appeal. In the interim between journeys he had himself taken 45 dancing lessons from M Frederick, just to improve his own skills, and possibly upon advice from his exquisite ballerina wife.[1]

He had not been exactly unknown on his first trip, for he had been generous in giving a benefit for the beleaguered troup of French comedians who with their manager, Jean Monnet, had come to London in 1749. Its performers had seen him act, and Monnet had kept up a steady correspondence thereafter. But this time (1763–65) the trip especially to Paris rewarded him not only personally but professionally, for there he had picked up ideas and devices for staging plays—lighting, scenery, props—which revolutionized his stage productions in London. He also developed some friendships of lasting use to him in his profession, as well as an abundance of acquaintances, authors, journalists, actors who wrote about theatre matters, and later were to

313

send plays for possible translation to the English stage, who were to
visit London, and who were to indicate how profound his influence had
been upon changes in French acting, ballet performance, and comic
theory. Salted into this correspondence are vivid descriptions of internal warfare between the French actors, between actors and authors,
and between authors and audiences. Reading their comments through
the coming years Garrick was to see that theatrical troubles as well as
theatrical triumphs bear certain international similarities. Comparisons were to be reassuring.

His most constant informant, factotum, and Parisian liaison man was,
of course, Jean Monnet, whom he had helped in 1749.[2] Monnet honored Garrick and was to carry out all sorts of commissions for the Garricks, from notes on Parisian hair styling and fashions to sending to the
manager talented people. A regular central intelligence agent he was.
The bright and able son of a baker, he had begun his career by putting
on plays at the Paris fairs, where he proved to be so successful that the
major houses forced him to close, an event which dampened but did
not stop his theatrical enterprises.[3] He had an uncanny ability for
sighting theatre talent. He had brought Préville into acting prominence in Paris. He had put Garrick in touch with Noverre. Through
him Garrick met M Torré, master of pyrotechnics and firework displays, who fabricated for him the licopodium torch which on stage
could give spectacular flashing and lightninglike effects.[4] He was to
send him F. H. Barthélemon, the violinist-composer, who prepared
the delightful and satirical music for Garrick's burletta "Orpheus" in his
playlet A Peep Behind the Curtain (1767). Monnet's services continued
for he later sent Garrick John Philip de Loutherbourg, who revolutionized stage settings at Drury Lane in the 1770s.[5] As Garrick's friend in
Paris, Monnet accepted visitors whom Garrick recommended, put
them up, and guided them around town. Later when Monnet lost
monies heavily Garrick offered to come to his aid again, but the French
friend would not take from him a second financial lift. He published
his Memoirs instead and recouped his fortune.[6]

From the French actors Garrick could discover little that was new or
touched him deeply. He admired the stately performances of Mme
Clairon and Louis LeKain, whom he perceived as actors keyed to an
older style than his, one appropriate, perhaps, for declaiming the
sonorous lines of tragedies by Corneille and Racine, Crébillon and
Voltaire.[7] To them he was kind and cordial, for later he invited them
both to England, offering Clairon financial support after she and other
members of the company had been jailed (for a theatre boycott) by

the Marechal de Richelieu on whom depended the direction of the Comédie Française.[8] She was to pour out her proud and sad story to Garrick in letters. Avoiding England, however, she repaired to Switzerland, visited Voltaire, and (her career ended) went into the protection of the Margrave of Anspach.[9] She had some vituperative things to say about LeKain, so Garrick decided not to become embroiled in her argument with the company and with the ministry. LeKain did come to England in 1766, but Garrick was away at Bath taking the waters for an attack of gout. They did not meet, but Garrick had brother George take care of LeKain in London.

Garrick did not act on stage in France. He gave a few extempore characterizations at private parties in Parisian *salons*—the falling asleep of Sir John Brute, Lear's curse, the air-drawn daggers in *Macbeth*. Such exhibitions were not his concept of dramatic performance, only solo diversions for special occasions, yet the mobility of his face, the appropriateness of his gestures, the mimesis that he displayed in an arialike technique drew applause in the *salons* and prompted reports in the press. F. M. Grimm wrote in his *Correspondance littéraire*, "one must have seen him to be able to form an idea of his superiority . . . when one has not seen him, one has not seen acting . . . Garrick indulges neither in grimaces nor in caricature; all the changes which take place in his features come from the manner in which his deepest feelings work."[10] He did pause, he did give a start, now and again, but all with underplaying, rather than overdoing the interpretation. Yet a younger actor Molé thought he had caught the spirit of Garrick's different style, and therefore in his own acting opposed the formal ways of tragic performance of the older members of the Comédie Française. Unsuccessful at first in Paris he had gone to the provinces to mature. Upon return he was cast mostly in comic roles, but when LeKain felt it was undignified to repeat the prose lines of the newer plays by Diderot and Beaumarchais, Molé was allowed to play tragedy. Under the impression that he was bringing a Garrick-like tone to the stage he seems to have raved, started, stopped suddenly before picking up the part again in Ducis's adaptation of *Hamlet*, at which the pit, writes Hedgcock, "applauded frantically, while ladies in the boxes literally swooned with enthusiasm."[11] All seemed to think this was the fresh "English style" of acting. Garrick offered financial aid to Molé at one time, but the actor refused it. Later he reconsidered and applied for 200 louis. Garrick left word with his banker to provide the sum on demand, but Molé never went to take advantage of it. If Molé's shouts, even in the "dumb show" in *Hamlet* were, as he thought, in the style of Garrick, the realistic performing of the English actor had fallen upon second-rate shoulders.[12] For this was not Garrick's way. He noted in his *Journal* his disappointment with Mme Dumesnil in *La Gouvernante*, a comedy by La Chaussée, "she has certainly expression in her face, & some other requisites, but she is made up of trick; looks too much upon y^e ground and makes use of little startings and twitchings which are visibly artificial & the mere mimickry of the free, simple noble workings of y^e Passions."[13]

Another sort of performer was A.-A. LeTexier, who had developed a one-man-show repertoire on the side, for his position at Lyons was cashier in the tax office. The solo performances appealed in Paris for a time, but the performer lost face in an exhibition before the King and thereupon found his leaving the tax office without permission had led to an investigation and charge of mismanagement of funds. He left for England with an introduction to Garrick by La Place, translator of Shakespeare's plays. Garrick breakfasted with him in 1775, and gave him freedom of the house at Drury Lane, for he appreciated his talents. LeTexier in turn enthusiastically watched Garrick perform. He hoped Garrick, through his friendship with Mme Necker, would ask M Jacques Necker, Louis XVI's minister of finance, to intercede in his favor in the Lyons affair. Garrick had accepted him as a man of probity, but gracefully bowed out of being drawn into "the exile's quarrels" even though he thought his acting abilities exceptional.[14]

Half a dozen French playwrights whom Garrick met in Paris were to seek by letter his advice and action in framing their works for his London theatre. Pierre Augustin Caron de Beaumarchais while in London called upon Garrick to show his manuscript of *The Barber of Seville*. His gracious note of thanks speaks of Mrs Garrick's appreciative review of the text, and that Garrick's suggestion for improving a scene in the fourth act was immediately accepted.[15]

Diderot introduced the playwright Fenouïllot de Falbaire to him who pressed his play *L'honnête criminel* upon the manager, but Garrick rejected it.[16] Despite this denial of young Fenouïllot's play Diderot maintained strong interest in Garrick's acting and as we know developed his *Paradoxe sur le comédien* on what he had learned. The playwright De Belloy found Paris antithetic to his *Pierre le cruel*, and hoped that its tone and content would appeal to Londoners, who if they applauded would shame the French. He was to negotiate with Garrick to have it translated and performed.[17] Garrick asked Murphy, with whom he was on good terms at the time, about this strange request. Murphy advised him to read the play, judge its probability of success, and if it seemed promising offered to translate it for him. The possibility of a "revenge" piece executed by British applause intrigued him. "Such an event would be unparalleled in the history of the drama!"[18] De Belloy noted he wished no profit, merely the justice of a reprimand to Parisians. Garrick read and rejected the play. In gallant French fashion the author thanked him for considering it.[19]

Garrick was to turn down two tragedies of M de Rozoi, and to engage for a while in letter discussions about Shakespeare with Jean François Ducis, translator and adapter of some Shakespeare for the French stage. Ducis several times stated that he wished to come to England, and learn the language so he could do better in purveying the great Shakespeare to his countrymen. Garrick noted that he would be glad to see him, and offered him the freedom of the house at Drury Lane. But Ducis never arrived.[20]

The prolific writer of comedies, Charles Simon Favart, whose *La Fee Urgèle* became a source for Garrick's popular *A Christmas Tale* (1773), a man whom Garrick respected both as a writer and as a gentle person, asked nothing of him in Paris but noted, "You will write to me when the whim takes you, and I will answer you in the same fashion."[21] And he composed two very charming and flattering verses to the actor:

> *Many in One*
> Several men in him we see;
> And he alone the sketch can paint
> Of all that's odd and all that's quaint,
> A past and present gallery.
>
> . . . . . . . . . . . .
>
> Is this thy portrait, Garrick? 'Tis not strange
> That, painting thee, the artist's hand should falter,
> For at thy will, both form and features change;
> Thy heart alone, dear friend, thou canst not alter.
> But could the painter on the canvas place
> Thy frankness, wit, and generosity,
> Thy taste and feeling, genius and grace,
> At once, dear friend, I should exclaim: 'Tis he![22]

Who would not be flattered by such eulogies two years after Favart had seen him? Garrick replied demurring graciously as to the accuracy of the compliments, and matching the style with a verse in response:

> I feel the danger of thy syren art,
> Struck with a pride till now I never knew,
> Soothe not the folly of a mind and heart
> Which boast no merit but the love of you (444),

and adding, "I am no less flattered by the account you gave me of the state of your country's letters and the theatres; and if you will take the trouble to continue this correspondence two or three times a year . . . I should consider it the greatest of favors."[23]

The prominent playwright Cailhava d'Estandoux, devotee of Molière, who was to ask Garrick for advice and information in writing his *L'Art de la comédie* (1770) read Garrick's plays with the thought of translating them for the French stage. He found, as did Mme Riccoboni, that many being based on French originals would provide nothing new for French audiences. But he was to enjoy Garrick's friendly correspondence, and keep him abreast of happenings at the Comédie Française. Garrick already knew of the infighting there among actors, but must have been appalled by the behavior existing now and again between certain actors and authors. Cailhava wrote of the fate of his play *Le Tuteur dupé*, "No sooner had the actors accepted my [play] with acclamation, than I called on Molé. I begged him to be good enough to take upon himself a part which was not worthy of him, but which he would adorn by his talent. On that point I said all the most flattering things one can say. He took my rôle with disdain, came to the first rehearsal, made fun of every sentence in the first act, ran after a cat during the second, asked me in the third if he was the lover of the young or of the old lady, declaring that there was nothing in the piece that could make it clear, went to sleep in the fourth, woke up in the fifth only to read the asides instead of his part, ending by saying that he would not act in a bad play and exhorted his comrades not to produce it." The company deliberated, and decided to play it since they had accepted it. "They gave the piece without taking the trouble to study it. No one knew his part save Préville, who acted divinely."[24]

The play made a successful run, however, to Molé's dismay, but Garrick eyed his own company in comparison—organized and well-disciplined—with satisfaction.

Among the French dramatists Garrick found interests for further acquaintance and correspondence. As for the French actors, he recognized a gulf in taste and method separating their styles and interests from his own, except for Préville, whose acting he thought might be held up as an example for members of his own company. During the last months in Paris he drafted a fascinating account and appraisal of the French comedian Pierre Louis du Bos (Préville), who had impressed him most preparing it as an "Extract of a letter from an English Gentleman at Paris to his Friend in London." He had it copied out and submitted to the *St. James's Chronicle* where it appeared 22–24 June 1765 (362 n.4).[25] The skill and diversity he found in Préville's acting (quite similar to his own) he longed to see in *all* English actors. Anonymous publication, he thought, would alert them to some things which they could emulate.

He found Préville (independent of the stage) to be a man of parts yet one who understood his profession thoroughly. Part of his skill lay in the control of his features to express ideas and character: "His eyes are rather of the sleepy kind, and very happily express, with the raising of his brow and opening of his mouth, folly, confusion, and amazement." His anger could "throw such ridiculous vivacity into his eyes, that you see a weak, cowardly mind, bustling up a resolution which he can never attain; and his anger subsides as ridiculously as it was raised." When the part required he could "throw such an archness, spirit and intrigue into his countenance, that he appeared the very Davus of Terence." In one play he acted five parts—in the first a half-starved, sneaking compound of flattery and absurdity. It came across. Then he was a shrewd, sly, suspicious Compagnard, and next a Swiss soldier importantly drunk *without grimace*, then a figure swelled into the full-blown pride, pomp, and passionate arrogance of a Sargeant of Law, and ended with the "soft, smirking, self-conceited, familiar insignificance of a scribbling Abbé." He could be natural, and he could have finesse. For Garrick the key to Préville's whole excellence lay in his creativeness, bred from ability, schooled by practice, and polished by observation. He could make the dullest *petite pièce* shine with humor, and give "high colouring and finished strength to the slightest outline. . . . His genius never appears more to advantage than when an author leaves him to shift for himself" and show his "comic power and excellencies of pantomime." Then, wrote Garrick, "Préville supplies the poet's deficiencies and will throw a truth and brilliancy into his character, which the author never imagined."

Herein lay the art of acting—the creativeness of it. Garrick knew he himself could match and even surpass a Préville performance. As they both once imitated a drunken peasant, Garrick topped the Frenchman because he added a drunkenness in the legs which his friend omitted.

The ideas in the forefront of Garrick's mind were how (as manager) to provide the conditions on stage fertile enough to stimulate such acting not by one or two new actors, but by a company. The plans came. That January he was brim full of projects for improved stage effects, acting technique, novelty, variety, and artistry. Lighting was a key factor, but scenery, costuming, and stage props, all that go into the grand illusion that the theatre can create (without seeming calculated) he thought about, and about.

Yet mingled with plans came a thin strain of hesitation—about his relations with an occasionally hostile English press, and about the burdens of the daily routines of management. He faced the question that lay at the back of his mind: Did London audiences want him as much as he wanted to return to the stage? How satisfied were they with the newly rising actors? How strong was the Drury Lane company? How long could he count on the services of Hannah Pritchard, Catherine Clive, Susanna Cibber, William Havard, and other stalwarts who had with him weathered the vicissitudes of theatre fortunes? How effective would they be as they aged? He had few doubts about his own endurance, yet knew, after the Munich illness, that he must cut down and assume new roles advisedly.

His concern about the oncoming young was only that they be competent at the outset and have the chance to train and excel. He knew he had become less suited in middle age for some roles, that a fine young actor could more effectively portray an aged king than a fine old one could carry off the role of a young lover. He was prepared to yield to others many of his parts. He only wanted his young performers to be professional in their goals. His letters of advice to young William Powell, and younger John Henderson, on the quality of acting amply demonstrate that he feared no rivals, but had no expectancy of lasting forever himself (345,731). A clause in his letter to Powell, however, though advising him to balance the disappointments of the profession with its pleasures and triumphs betrays an awareness about things he himself had to face up to again, should he return to *full* participation in theatrical matters, "I have not always Met with gratitude in a play House." And by the term *playhouse* he meant the actors, the supporting company of servants, and the audiences.

As he turned these matters over in his mind he had written to his actor friend James Love back on 27 January 1965, "I hear your houses are full—you will send me all kind of News—theatrical, political, musical, and nonsensical—Give me an Acc$^t$ I beseech You (an impartial one) of any Youngsters of Either Sex who promise something—I have my reasons for this desire, so pray be particular and distinguish their Marits, if you can perceive any" (348). His reasons were linked to designs for new recruitment. He wished, of course to be wanted again, but his hopes were also great for fresh faces.

Garrick had kept in touch, and rejoiced that Drury Lane had maintained its status vis-à-vis Covent Garden during his absence. The seasons had been relatively calm after the riots of the 1762–63 season, and both theatres experimented fitfully with musicals. Covent Garden came out with a major box-office success the second year with Isaac

Bickerstaff's *The Maid of the Mill* adapted from Richardson's *Pamela*. During Garrick's first year of absence Colman put on two new main pieces—Frances Sheridan's *The Dupe*, and Richard Rolt's English opera *The Royal Shepherd*, plus five new after pieces: Thomas King's *Love at First Sight*, Colman's own *The Deuce Is in Him*, James Love's pantomime *The Rites of Hecate*, Allen's interlude *Hymen*, and a farce *The Counterfeiters* taken from Moore's *Gil Blas*. He did an ill-fated *Midsummer Night's Dream* (for a single performance, but recouped with *The Fairies* taken from it).

Beard at Covent Garden put on Murphy's *No One's Enemy but His Own*, and his after piece *What We Must All Come to*, Kane O'Hara's burletta *Midas*, James Townley's *False Concord*, Hull's *The Absent Man*, and Charles Dibdin's *Shepherd's Artifice*. His staple depended upon some revived pantomimes.

Garrick's chief roles had been taken over by William Powell and Charles Holland, both initially trained by Garrick. The second season was less successful for both theatres—two operas at Drury Lane (Rolt's *Almena*, and Hull's *Pharnaces*) also Lloyd's *Capricious Lovers* (cut to a two-act farce) and Mrs Griffith's *The Platonic Wife* (which made it for six nights). Of the new after pieces none lasted more than two nights—Mrs Clive's *Faithful Irish Woman*, Murphy's *The Choice*, and Townley's *The Tutor*. Beard's season just about matched Colman's with Arne's *Guardian Outwitted*, Hull's *The Spanish Lady*—neither long standing, and *The Maid of the Mill*, already noted. Hum drum! Mozart and his sister (aged seven and 12) played concerts in town each season.

That Garrick was needed must have been fairly evident to the Drury Lane company, and to thoughtful theatregoers.

A broadside chart of actor ratings appeared for the season 1765.[26] Garrick's name was not among those rated, for he was in France, but 41 others, all familiar to the public, were listed, evaluated on a scale of 20 for outstanding qualities under a dozen headings, such as figure, grace, spirit and ease, sensibility, dignity, humor, elocution, voice, dress, dumb show, noise. The best-played roles of each were specified, with Holland rating high in six; Havard doing well as Mad Tom in figure, sensibility, elocution, and dress; with Bransby and four others rating 20 points each in the category of "noise"; with Mrs Cibber and Mrs Clive topping out in many other categories. Garrick had this in hand as he returned, but hardly needed it, for he knew the capabilities of each of them. The chart served merely to fix some stereotype values in the minds of the paying public. Today we would call it a mechanical, computerized *Rosciad*. It lacked the subtle understanding of Garrick's "Letter on Préville." What did occupy him fully when he returned to full management was, as we shall see, recruiting and training the young in major roles.

Garrick hoped, but had no way of knowing, that Drury Lane would yield increased annual income (which it did) for the profit of the whole company.[27] He knew that success lay in an appealing repertory, good management, and excellent acting. He remembered the former onslaught of the Grub Street press, from which he had enjoyed a sweet vacation, as doubtless the press had from him. Both remained to face-off again. Without new leadership and fresh prformance his theatre might exist, but would fail to shine.

Curious by nature, somewhat cautious by experience he sought to test public opinion by a characteristic ruse—the anonymous flyer in the press in a Fable in the manner of La Fontaine's. Hence he drafted "The Sick Monkey, Addressed to Mr Garrick Upon His Arrival," and had it planted by Colman in London as an anonymous pamphlet. A hundred introductory lines recalled the supercritical press of 1763:

> Whether you fled for health, or quiet
> Harass'd with rule, or sick with riot,
> Or whether you have kept us lean,
> As slander says
> With Lenten plays
> To make our appetites more keen

you are now come home, and (Garrick hoped) "we greet you kindly." Perhaps today we find the "Fable" somewhat belabored, about a monkey whose case of depression is diagnosed by a doctor as resulting from frustrated pride—the loss of curl in his tail. The advice: Take a vacation, do not fret and bite your thumbs. To what the critics write shut your eyes, buy up the heap and burn it, but keep the poison from your head and clap it to your tail.

Garrick's letter to Jean Baptiste Suard (7 May 1765) reports the fortune of the piece: "*The Sick Monkey* is publish'd, & makes a noise—It was thought at first to be a terrible satire . . . but at present they begin to find out the joke, & the Sale will be a great one. . . . I have not yet answered the general question from all sorts of people—*Whether I shall act again*. Our stage is at present in a declining state, and must have some assistance from me either as actor, manager, or both" (358).

Demands of management had in no way become less exacting during Garrick's absence. Perennial grievances of some actors and some authors combined again to make public relations delicate. To these problems, which Garrick expected and felt confident of solving with his former aplomb, was added for a period of several months a new one—battle with his partner Lacy. Details are obscure. Only three letters between Garrick, James Clutterbuck (his financial adviser), and John Paterson (his lawyer) allude to the affair, but suggest the seriousness if not the full extent of the imminent break.

The managers' agreement of 1750 had provided that if either was dissatisfied with the alignment of duties, proposals should be made for selling the patent at auction. Apparently Lacy, perhaps during the administration of stage affairs by Colman, had encroached more than usual on matters of accepting and scheduling plays, developing scenes, and possibly casting. These were Garrick's provinces, management of which he had delegated to Colman. Possibly with the actor's return Lacy persisted in "intervening" in these areas. Perhaps he operated scenery, properties, wardrobe in too close and conventional a fashion. Whatever he did, the disagreement seemed to Garrick for a time past reconciling. He asked Clutterbuck to estimate the worth of his share in the patent before confronting Lacy with a proposal for dissolving the partnership. The situation in view of his plans and expectations was depressing.

Clutterbuck's reply was calm, businesslike, kindly, and astute. He pointed out that Garrick's share was then worth about £27,500, but that (*a*) no man in his right mind would buy it up unless the purchase brought with it guarantee of Garrick's remaining in the company as an actor, and (*b*) that should Lacy purchase it, he would within three months of management return the company to the chaos from which the partnership had rescued it. Should that happen, whence would come the payments for the Garrick share, which must indeed be spread over a period of years with interest attached? Payments must come from the profits of a well-run company.

These sound arguments set forth clearly for Garrick the leading position he occupied in the world of theatre management. Coupled with his basic enthusiasm for carrying out innovations to improve production the arguments were very persuasive. He brooded, and the matter smouldered for a time when Paterson, the envoy between the two managers' offices, reported his own talks with Lacy. Their conferences had been long and detailed. Peterson told Garrick that Lacy was most sincere in his desire to continue the partnership, as well as his former friendship. He "says that, in the eighteen years you have been together, he does not recollect having interrupted you in the management of the stage more than twice, and as to the last time, seems to think himself to blame for the manner of doing it, and I really believe is sorry for it. He says, he desires you may go on upon the old footing, and has given me his word of honor that in such case he will never object to your management but in a private and friendly manner."[28]

Garrick replied quickly, for he had been busying himself with changes (as we shall see): "I should have quitted Drury Lane Theatre with reluctance. . . . I fully subscribe to Your proposals in y$^r$ letter & an ready to meet M$^r$ Lacy as my Partner & friend without having the least remembrance that we Ever disagreed" (390). Thus they continued until Lacy's death eight years later, but with Garrick's hand in management immensely strengthened—a fortunate circumstance in view of the forthcoming (but yet unforseen) activities of the Stratford Jubilee.

The rewards of management were actually no longer calculated by Garrick in increased profits, which, over and above his salaries for acting and managing (which remained fixed for years and years), had been steady and sufficient. Personal rewards must come to Garrick not so much in pounds and pence, or power, as in leadership, a kind of appreciated creativeness in all fields of theatrical responsibility.

Tucked away in Garrick's memory was his experience in Turin, where he found rapprochement between actors and audience intolerable—"the People in y$^e$ Pitt & Boxes talk all y$^e$ while as in a Coffee house, & y$^e$ Performers are Even with 'Em, for they are very little attentive, laugh & talk to one another, pick their Noses, & while they are unengag'd in Singing, they walk up to y$^e$ Stage Boxes . . . turn their backs, & join in y$^e$ laugh & Conversation of their Brethren, without y$^e$ least decency or regard for y$^e$ Audience; I never was more astonished in my life" (319). Decorum of behavior on stage had long been a matter of pride for Garrick, but decorum could shift. The greatest assistance to good acting was, in his view, the providing of stage conditions which by their artistic effectiveness could both hold audiences spellbound and stimulate actors to their best individual and collective efforts. He put his finger upon lighting and scenic effects as two areas for experimentation and improvement. He had already cleared his stage of loungers and extra seating which detracted from grace of performance.

Garrick had early introduced oil lamps in his footlights, for his first trip to France convinced him of the folly of tallow-candle lighting. Of the Comédie Française then, he wrote, "y$^e$ glass branches [light holders] give it a rich look, but y$^e$ candles instead of lamps at y$^e$ front of y$^e$ stage are very mean."[29] Things had improved by 1763 but still the French theatre had been dark. The Opera was better.[30] Theatre auditoriums in those days were semilighted throughout a performance, for to darken them and reillumine between the acts would have meant snuffing out and relighting hundreds of candles, smoke from which would blur vision and cause coughing. Besides audiences liked to see themselves and view their neighbors during the performance. Stage lighting, however, should maintain a brighter contrast. His Drury Lane stage had been lighted from above by several huge girandels of candles, which on pulleys could be raised and lowered for certain effects, just as the footlights could be sunken into a trough at the prompter's command. Movement of these two sources had to be coordinated to maintain a flat light, lest shadows from below or above distort facial expressions. Under these conditions actors had to perform down stage in order to communicate subtle gesture or expression change. Garrick, aware of his own mobile face and piercing eyes, was seeking ways to improve their use in genuine ensemble acting. New lighting was the key.

Even before he left Paris he arranged with Jean Monnet to supply him with designs and materials for innovations in lighting like those he found operating there in 1765. Monnet wrote on 15 June 1765 "I have completed your errands and I shall transmit with M. Boquet's drawings a reflector and two different models of the lamp which you want for the footlights of your theatre." A month later he sent the actual models with Benjamin Van der Gucht, the painter. Doubtless with Lacy's concurrence (or maybe this was a cause for their rupture) Garrick abolished the overhanging girandels, used sparkling candles (perhaps in glass chimneys) among the footlights against bright reflectors, and added reflecting lights in the wings. A miracle of sorts seemed to have been wrought. Reporters commented in the press. One for the *Annual Register*, September 1765, noted "on the opening of Drury Lane playhouse . . . the audience was agreeably surprised to see the stage illuminated in a clear and strong manner without the assistance of the rings hitherto used for that purpose. This is done by the disposition of lights behind the scenes, which cast a reflection forwards exactly resembling sunshine, greatly to the advantage of the performers, but more to that of the spectators, who have now no longer the air they breathe tainted by the noxious smoke of between two or three hundred candles, nor their sight blurred by them and the rings supporting them. The French theatre has long been illuminated without these offensive rings, though not to that perfection attained by Mr. Garrick, who however is supposed to have taken the hint from it."[31]

The *Public Advertiser* was more particular (25 September 1765), "The Drury Lane Managers have absolutely created an Artificial Day, or to vary my expression and sentiment they have given us a perfect meridian of wax." The wing lights "consisted of a series of perpendicular lamps, either oil or candle, backed by reflectors, all mounted on turnable iron posts or frames. Masked by the wings, this device could be turned away from the stage to diminish the light."[32] By one additional inventive step Garrick made the upright forms into a sort of pyramid with boxlike tiered sections, some of which could be fronted with colored glass, so that the turning could not only soften or brighten, but also color the scene. Depending upon the number and location of such devices actors could retreat up stage more often and still communicate nuances of expression revealing complexities of characterization. Range of actions was increased. Look and gesture were enhanced. Six years later Jean Phillipe de Loutherbourg was to come to Drury Lane and bring these effects begun by Garrick to perfection.

Garrick was as delighted as his audiences were. The experiment worked, catching not only the fun of novelty in light and color, but providing conditions for subtle characterization. The gas lights of the nineteenth century and the electricity of the twentieth could but intensify the effects. Lines could now be altered in texts for which motion and gesture could compensate, and the art of acting could step a pace forward from heavy reliance upon the sound of words alone. The possibilities for new scenic effects abounded.

Bright lighting with its contrasts and new angles of focus called for new scenes. Scenes (i.e., pictured background on flats) were "property," as was the wardrobe. They had fallen probably under the main responsibility of Lacy. He was concerned with the economy of operating the house, hence with the multiple use of sets and painted backdrops, especially since the public had raised no constant cry for change. Authors in isolated instances, from the time of Aaron Hill's *The Prompter* (1734–36), had mentioned the importance of proper scenic effects, but as scenic effect was at the foot of the priority list among Aristotle's categories for drama and for his neoclassical adherents, innovations had been made mainly to accompany performances of no intellectual content—shows where all was spectacle as exemplified in pantomimes. Garrick was dissatisfied with this state of affairs, for under his concept of management total performance of the evening required attention, and the effects of each part should strengthen each other part where support could be given.

He had observed the eye appeal got by a tiered stage and color when Noverre put on his *Chinese Festival* back in 1755. In that year also Roger Pickering had published a long and precise pamphlet, *Reflections upon Theatrical Expression in Tragedy*, an appendix of which is relevant. In it Pickering elaborated his ideas about costuming and scenery as material aids to convincing acting. Applause, he thought, would fill the house "if the streets, buildings, rooms and furniture, gardens, views of the country were executed in the taste of the country where the scene of the action lay." Verisimilitude was his cry, but he did not argue for *new* sets for *every* tragedy. "I mean only," he wrote, "that there should never be such a scarcity of scenes in the theatre, but that whether the seat of the action be Greek, Roman, Asiatic, African, Italian, Spanish, &c. there be one set at least adapted to each country, and that we may not be put upon to believe ourselves abroad, when we have no local imagery before us but of our own country."

Garrick, of course, had often recited with vigor the Prologue to *King Henry V*, wishing for a "Muse of fire" to help his spectators, even as Shakespeare had, to imagine the stage as "the vasty fields of France." And Lacy had seemed satisfied with sort of stock scenes (suggested by Sheridan for his Irish stage) as the minimum number for multiple use. Sheridan had noted, "some temples, tombs, city walls and gates, outsides and insides of palaces, streets, chambers, prisons, gardens, forests and desarts." All should be prepared by a master, but "otherwise they should be as simple and unaffected as possible to avoid offending the judicious eye." [33]

Garrick himself had never been satisfied with down playing this aspect of performance. He had paid special attention to appropriate scene painting for Johnson's *Irene* and Hill's *Merope*, both in 1749, for the *Chinese Festival* in 1755, for Murphy's *Desert Island* and *The Way to Keep Him* in 1760, for *Antony and Cleopatra*, and the *Orphan of China* in 1759, and for *Cymbeline* in 1761, among others. John French was the chief Drury Lane designer before Garrick went on his continental tour. When he returned his *Treasurer's Books* indicate that his carpentry and painting staff increased, and the imaginative services of James Messink from Dublin, and Pierre Royer were added. [34]

A manuscript in Garrick's hand, mysterious because we cannot identify the play for which it was planned, appears in the Forster Collection of Garrick papers as a memorandum to Lacy. It suggests four scenes: "a wild prospect terminated by a waterfall. On one side a ridge of rocks, rising above each other, on the opposite side a cave, the mouth of which is incrusted with shells, pebbles, and other marine productions. Near the cave a rush [rushes] . . . Scene 5 changes to the coast with an extensive view of the sea, which is afterwards agitated by degrees into a violent storm . . . Scene VI: during the storm, which is accompanied by an expressive symphony . . . a numerous band of Indians men and women arrive in their canoes . . . The sky gradually clears, A beautiful rainbow appears . . . Scene the last the ship comes on, at first with but two sails, but in the end she appears crowded with them." [35] Here scenes, machines, and music blend with the possibilities of new lighting effects, in Garrick's imagination at least to make for a startling stage vision.

Another manuscript, endorsed in Garrick's hand, refers to two sets of drawings and descriptions in French and English of the Palace of Armida, perhaps of Sacchini's opera.[36] If so it refers to the opera put on at the King's Opera House 8 November 1774, with "new scenes by Colombo." The details explain a mock-up from which carpenters could work. It notes how the traps and flats were used, how a mock stone wall could be made to crumble on stage, how beams made of wicker frames covered with cloth could come burning down, "as Medea's car crosses the stage." The rich use of colors, gilt, red, green and white, is detailed.[37] Both manuscripts, though undated and apparently never implemented, afford a glimpse of Garrick's new and persistent interest in "dressing the scene." The first may well have come before he engaged de Loutherbourg, the latter certainly after.

Persistent is indeed the adjective to use, for the newspapers, more frequent in their comments on theatrical performances after 1765 than before, nearly always make some mention of "new scenes." *The London Evening Post* (24–27 November 1770) carried a long account of Bickerstaff's new play at Drury Lane, *'Tis Well It's No Worse*, concluding, "the managers took all imaginable pains to add to the play by a variety of new scenery, dresses, and decorations." Garrick was making constant use of knowledge he had gained in France.

In the 1771–72 season, furthermore, his encouragement of scenic change was to have lasting impact on the English theatre, when he engaged Jean Phillipe de Loutherbourg, the Alsatian landscape painter. At age 22 (eight years under the acceptable age for candidacy) de Loutherbourg had been elected to the French Academy, and was impressing all Paris with his paintings of landscapes, rural scenes, and domestic animals. Monnet introduced him by letter to Garrick. Garrick saw in the work of the young man novel concepts and first-rate artistic ability. He took him on at the high salary of £500—equal to that of his topmost actors—with the understanding that he would "take care of all decorations, the machines dependent on them, the way of lighting and manipulating them, would devise scenes, produce every winter a beautiful play with grandiose new effects mutually agreed upon, suggest appropriate costume, and prepare all novelties in the summer season so ample time would be had for executing them." His scenes revolutionized stage settings by bringing on different levels, broken arch lines, lush backgrounds, distant perspectives, transparencies with startling color changes, and instant scene-changing effects.[38]

Fifteen plays received his magic touch in the four remaining years of Garrick's management.[39] Baroque was out, and the picturesque marched pleasantly in. The timing was most appropriate. Garrick, the imaginative producer, seized the chance to carry much further than he could have alone the directions which he had envisioned when he returned from Paris. Apparently with his own new lighting he had tended to overemphasize color, at least in the opinion of Thomas Gainsborough, with whom he discussed these matters. Gainsborough suggested that he modulate color, soften his music, and "steal back into the mild evening gloom." "Now I'll tell you my sprightly genius how this is to be done—maintain all your light, but spare the poor abused colors, till the eye rests and recovers—Keep up your music by supplying the place of *noise* by more sound, more harmony, and more tune, and split that cursed fife and drum."[40] Garrick responded, not by putting on the brakes, but by releasing the inventiveness of de Loutherbourg. Consequently for play after play, (especially the Christmas entertainments) magic gardens where the colors of leaves changed, lakes of fire, descents from clouds, waterfalls, and distant prospects of the sea, castles, and the rising sun appeared and were applauded. Imagination luxuriated. Journalists commented on the combination in such settings of the tender stillness and lush rocky asymmetrical sublimity.[41] A whole age was left behind. The fulfillment of a second stroke of leadership in Garrick's management came to pass.

Lighting which brought the Milky Way on stage must, Garrick knew, affect costuming. Novelties in color and sets must be accompanied by improvement of dresses. To the two-volume *Dresses of Different Nations . . . and of the Principal Characters of the English Stage* (1757) already in his library, he now added the three-volume French work *Desseins de Differens Habits de Costume du Théâtre Français* (1765). Hundreds of color plates adorned each, and he continued to increase ownership of these books about costume until his retirement. He was ready to respond favorably to the postscript of a "*Letter to David Garrick, Esq.*," written soon after his arrival in England, published in the *London Magazine* (November 1765), signed D. L. P. [Drury Lane Playhouse?] which read: "My clothes are some of them worn out, and others a little dirty; beg therefore that you will, order me a new gown for the winter."

His first priority in costuming was style, elegance of dress—*not* as many writers have attempted to show (or have damned him for not showing) costumes historically and geographically accurate according to the historical sensitivities of nineteenth- and twentieth-century historians.[42] London society was aglow with changing fashions in dress.

*The Westminster Magazine* in the 1770s published each month a description of the "Dress of the Month as established at St James's and in Tavistock Street." The rapid turnover in men's fashions provided the master of theatrical wardrobes opportunity to purchase elegant clothing worn but once or twice by dukes and earls. Garrick set up for his leading ladies—Mrs Cibber, Mrs Yates, Mrs Abington—amounts of from £50 to £60 annually to find [provide] their own fashionable dresses for the stage, and the ladies were trend-setters in their apparel. The budget for the wardrobe department—keepers, cleaners, feather specialists—increased. Yet Garrick, whose eye was always upon ensemble performance, was careful about the effect of ensemble clothing. The author of the *Collection of the Dresses of Different Nations* had remarked in 1757: "As to stage dresses . . . they are at once elegant and characteristic, and among many other regulations of more importance, of which the public is oblig'd to the genius and judgment of the present manager of our principal theatre, is that of dresses, which are no longer heterogeneous and absurd mixtures of foreign and ancient modes, which formerly debased our tragedies, by representing a Roman General in a full-bottomed peruke, and a sovereign of an Eastern empire in trunk hose."

Garrick had ordered up new Roman "shapes" for his production of *Antony and Cleopatra* (1759). He had spent large sums in carrying out the proper motif, specified by Noverre and Boquet, in *The Chinese Festival* (1755). He approximated "early English dress" in his own costume for Richard III, as the Hogarth painting shows. He had long indicated on handbills (and continued to do so) "Characters new dress'd in the manner of the times." He evidently pored over the illustrative plates of the costume books for models and suggestions. What he found there is available for us all to see, namely not much differentiation for the ages past. Furs and skins had been adopted by the French actor LeKain to distinguish barbarous personages—a convention speedily imitated by Garrick in England.

But, as Hogarth's print also shows, elegance and comfort prevailed over what we now would call historical authenticity. The theatres (both stage and auditorium) were unheated. Macklin, be it remembered, in testimony at his trial for killing actor Hallam, noted that he had come into the greenroom to get warm. Even Roman togas and Egyptian dress could not be scant in winter seasons.[43] "Old English" costume as understood by Garrick and most of his generation was a vague term. "Any becoming dress of that Age, or like that Age, will be proper, & you may please Yourselves," he wrote to Luke Gardiner, who had inquired about proper costuming for Macbeth, "The Ancient dresses are certainly preferable to any Modern ones" (1147). Precise description is wanting, but the costume books were also imprecise.

Four or five styles emerged, and their traditional appearance stimulated the imaginations of the audience sufficiently to waft them abroad or into the past as the text intended—Turkish or Eastern (for oriental or exotic characters, with turbans and full trousers gathered at the shoe-top); Spanish (with feathered hat and full ruff); old English (with ruff, trunk hose, slashed pants); Roman shapes (with toga and pleated short skirt); and the Iachimo suit (with vertical striped knee trousers and jacket) for Italian and Renaissance figures.[44] Harlequin, of course, wore a particolored, tight-fitting suit, a sort of leotard with diamond-shaped designs. Ermine-edged robes for royalty, armor plate for some soldiers (red coats for others), a remarkable variety of hats and head coverings for men and women modified the conventional costume, and caught the eyes of the spectators. Our best authorities are still the many, many extant pictures of Garrick in his parts, along with his fellow actors and actresses. But after his return from France elegance and contrast on stage (between the liveried and the gentlemen) counted, and Garrick brought to bear on this aspect of performance constant reference to books on costume, plus financial support for style.[45]

Drury Lane opened its 1765–66 season with the customary plays with large casts, which would bring back all company members from their summer activities. And so went the offerings until the first of November when the theatres were shut for 11 days while the country (some of it at least) mourned the death of William, duke of Cumberland. No swelling crowds had appeared since September, but on 14 November "By Command" Garrick reappeared on the stage as Benedict. The King was present, and gentlemen had been asked to send servants by three o'clock to save places. The house was full. Garrick worked the audience up in four ways by his carefully prepared Prologue. He shared reminiscences, "'Tis twice twelve years since first the stage I trod / Enjoy'd your smiles, and felt the critics' rod." To this excited and friendly audience he presented the image of the actor cut down by troublesome pamphleteers:

> A very nine-pin I, my stage life through,
> Knock'd down by wits, set up again by you.
> In four and twenty years the spirits cool
> Is it not long enough to play the fool?

He commented jocularly on his loss of suppleness and gain of weight, "He's much too fat for battles, rape, and murder!" And he closed with a patriotic (and self-serving) flourish, calculated to capture the affections of box, pit, and gallery:

> Should the drum beat to arms, at first he'll grieve
>
> . . . . . . . . . . . . . . . . . .
>
> Then cock his hat, look fierce, and swell his chest,
> 'Tis for my King, and zounds I'll do my best!

Applause, and yet, and yet, and yet despite his triumph (for here the actor and manager blend inevitably) Garrick must have had a gloomy moment at the close of the evening when a "disturbance" began breeding. "Those not in black," it seemed insulted the rest. "One young gentleman from Bond Street had a sword run into his eye."[45] But the disturbance was soon at an end. It had to do with only a section of the audience against another, not against the theatre, the management, or the player.[46] He played Benedict a week later to a quiet and attentive house that grew gayer as the evening progressed.

Garrick liked the older plays and found his company qualified in the roles. With a change here and there, with stylish new costumes and new sets those plays appeared as new performances. He revived *Mahomet*, not played for 20 years (with some slight alterations of his own) giving the lead to young Powell. He revived *The Plain Dealer*, with Holland in the lead, which ran for 15 performances and put the extreme moralists a bit on edge. It likewise had not been played for 20 years, but was freshened by some additions by Isaac Bickerstaff. He worked up the hit of the season (20 February) with the new *Clandestine Marriage*, jointly created by Colman and himself. With King and Mrs Clive in the leading roles it succeeded tremendously, running 20 times and remaining in the repertory. In January he himself played Lusignan in *Zara*, again "By Command." His earlier Prologue was called for. He "went on directly to speak it," noted Hopkins, "as soon as he appeared, a general clap, and a loud huzza,—and there was such a noise from the House being so crowded, very few heard anything of the Prologue."

All seemed worthwhile again, no doubt. But, "As soon as the play began there was a great disturbance in the Gallery, and some called out, Guards! Guards! that they could not go on.—Mr Lacy went on the Stage, and looked up in the gallery, and came off again without saying anything.—They soon grew quiet, and the play went on.—Monsieur Rousseau sat in Mr Garrick's box."[47] Lacy was known to be stern, careful of the property, willing to call the constabulary, and just might have spotted and identified a perpetrator. Garrick was again in the thick of theatrical hurly-burly. He appeared several times more in succeeding weeks, then rested only to appear again on 22 May in a benefit for a cause which he had long thought about, and which he fostered each year thereafter, "towards raising a Fund the relief of those who from their infirmities shall be oblig'd to retire from the stage." More about this fund later, but its creation was one of Garrick's great and lasting managerial achievements.

On 12 April he permitted James Love to have a new play for his benefit—*Falstaff's Wedding*—written by William Kenrick "as a sequal to 2 *Henry IV*, and in imitation of Shakespeare." The benefit was successful but marked the sole performance of the play, as was likely to happen with a new play not launched by mid-season. Garrick had long ago rejected the piece, for he had had no capable Falstaff in his company. Now that he had one in Love, and his friend Berenger was sponsoring the play for Kenrick, he produced it. One supposes that Garrick was accommodating Love and Berenger, not the irascible Kenrick. In fact, by scheduling it late, Garrick may have been burying the piece to keep the insistent Kenrick off his back for a while. If so the ceremony was complete, for the author was reduced thereafter to reading *Falstaff's Wedding* an act at a time in his series of lectures entitled "The School of Shakespeare." Kenrick's enmity was to explode again in 1772,[48] but was of little moment to Garrick in his triumphal season of return.

Full houses demanded extra attention, so Garrick eased their crowded circumstances outside (as well as inside the theatre) by regulating the traffic flow. He arranged with the city fathers that the "passage way from the Strand up Catherine Street to Drury Lane be clear for carriages," an announcement that appeared on play notices at the opening of the 1766–67 season. A refreshed Garrick, assured of audience backing, settled again into enjoyable sessions of reading new plays submitted to him, as he had enjoyed this activity earlier. John Hoadly sensed the return of this spirit in his letter of 9 October 1768, "I do remember well the circumstances of setting upon *The Jealous Wife* [1761] at Hampton and particularly of your getting up and acting the character of the Major [Oakly] in jovial terms across the room, before you spoke a word of introducing it instead of Mr. Mack; and we immediately saw the propriety of it."[49] Playreading is an art, and Garrick demonstrated in the Hampton drawing room that he acted as he read every part, saw the limitations and possibilities, and ways to improve any play sent to him.

Mrs Garrick and chosen friends also reacted at these sessions. And she contributed suggestions for bettering any script or score which caught her imagination. Even Charles Dibdin, whose relations with Garrick were often tense and sometimes thorny, was prompted to note Mrs Garrick's fine ear and discriminating hand on a similar occasion when she offered improvements in his music for *The Padlock*. His published dedicatory letter to her (1768) reveals the human warmth and serious attention given in the bosom of the Garrick family to the artistic efforts placed before them: "I cannot reflect without pride, Madam, that a lady of Mrs Garrick's taste approved this music before it had received the sanction of public applause. And permit me to boast that some part of its success is owing to the judicious changes in consequence of your observations upon first hearing it."[50]

The comment is apt, for Garrick among his other innovations was increasing the number of musical performances at Drury Lane. He himself continued to write songs for plays, and was commissioning, in addition to Dr Thomas and Michael Arne and William Boyce, other composers such as Theodore Aylward, F. H. Barthélemon, and Charles Dibdin to write the music for delightful pieces, such as the dramatic opera *Cymon* (1767), *Linco's Travels* (1767), the burletta "Orpheus" (1767), the *Jubilee* (1769), and *King Arthur* (1770). The movement of this music from standard baroque toward romantic gallante is again in our own time being restudied by musicologists and theatre historians as an example of changing tastes in the century.[51] Garrick's earlier songs for *Lethe, Isabella, The Way to Keep Him, Miss in Her Teens* continued to be set and sold to the sheet-music trade. He viewed with satisfaction the number of settings being made by different composers to his popular *To Sylvia*; "If truth can fix thy wav'ring heart." They were being sold at the music publishers from the Strand to Oxford Street, and "To Sylvia" had even appeared in the series of songs (with their music) running monthly in the *London Magazine*.[52] Garrick supported his 21-piece theatre orchestra (twice the size of the one in the Comédie Française) well, demanded rehearsals from musicians on the same basis of monetary forfeits (stoppages) as for actors,[53] worked in background and mood music appropriate for plays, and presumably modulated noise to increase harmony—as Gainsborough had suggested.

The swirl of traffic outside and the burgeoning audiences inside the theatre were soon matched by a swirl of discussion emanating from the pamphlet publishing houses, debated in the coffee houses, and magnified in the taverns. A new edition of *Thespis* downgraded, in the *Rosciad* manner, a number of Drury Lane performers, soon to be followed by *Anti-Thespis; or, A Vindication of the Principal Performers at Drury Lane Theatre*. Garrick personally fared well in these. The bite of satire was made for some upcoming actors, such as Miss Pope.[54] One wonders what response Garrick made when as manager he faced groups of his company in the greenroom after these notices got bruited about town. Doubtless he was masterful, shouldering with them the woeful comments, winking at and deprecating the aspersions, emphasizing that comment good or bad kept the theatre and its personalities in constant view, as indeed did another sort of pamphlet and contra-pamphlet flurry. *The Stage the Highroad to Hell* (1767) came forth with a fundamentalist 43 pages, advising its readers of the pitfalls of attending the theatre. Closely following came, *Theatrical Entertainments Consistent with Society, Morality, and Religion; or, A Letter to the Author of 'The Stage the Highroad to Hell', shewing the Writer's Arguments to be Fallacious, his Principles Enthusiastic, and his Authorities (particularly from the Ancients) Misconstrued and Perverted*. The titles tell all. But the diarist Sylas Neville, a man about town, liberal politician, and frequent theatregoer, writing not for the public confirms an interest which some members of the audience had in the opinions of both the moralists and the writers of *Thespiads*.

Garrick the manager seemed to be getting more daring in his revivals, for on 3 February 1767 Neville saw *The Provoked Wife*. "Brute inimitably played by Garrick," but "*The Provok'd Wife* is very immoral, as it presents an intention to commit adultery in too agreeable a light." On 7 March he saw *Rule a Wife and Have a Wife*, with "Estifania by Mrs Pritchard excellently, tho she is too old for the first part of the character. Leon inimitably by Garrick." The house was so full he was squeezed and could not read his paper before the play started. He saw it again on 23 May, "Garrick played Leon. By having seen him in the character before, and having read the play, I enjoyed the excellency of his acting more than I ever did." Garrick spaced plays in the repertory so that they carried freshness, and so that critics could discern excellencies comparatively. Neville saw Garrick in *Lethe* and in *Hamlet* before the season ended, finding the corner of the orchestra the best place to stand in, and the gallery the worst, if one wanted to get the full effect of facial expressions on the actors. He thought Garrick looked very healthy, and should perform more often. To see him in *Hamlet* he went from door to door at the theatre from half past four to half past six before being able to get into the crowded theatre: "Dreadfully squeezed, but rewarded by seeing Garrick play Hamlet. The expression in his features, his eyes particularly, surpasses anything I ever saw. He is a little man, but handsome and full of that fire which marks the stronger, and of the softness natural to the tender passions."[55] Management was humming. Stage lights, stage scenery, brilliant costumes, pleasing music, and fine acting were drawing crowds.

Having moved once more into the current of the theatre, Garrick dominated it. New challenges to follow up his innovations in production occupied him increasingly. Critics, save for two pamphlets, had not delivered any serious blows. One of these responded (in January 1767) to the challenge thrown out two years before by Garrick in his "Sick Monkey" pamphlet. Entitled a *Letter from the Rope Dancing Monkey in the Haymarket to the Acting Monkey of Drury Lane*, its 48 pages dealt largely with the plagiarism of Dr Francklin's *Earl of Warwick* from La Harpe's play of the same name, which Garrick had accepted as a new play. It also blasted Colman's Prologue as "scrawl-work and tediously prolix," and Garrick's Epilogue as unseemly in the mouth of Margaret, who had died as the curtain fell. The calumny, "Davy who (obliging mortal) never failed in nonsense and stupidity," may have caused the manager to wince, but since the play was succeeding, and since he was occupied with new theatrical interests, he doubtless consigned the pamphlet to his file of diverting oddments. The problem was more Francklin's than his.

The second attack appeared as a weekly publication from October 1767 through April 1768, titled *The Theatrical Monitor; or, The Green Room Laid Open*. Its self-justification was predictable. The editor complained that other papers impeded publication of true criticism, hence a new one was needed. The Folger Library owns a dozen issues containing marginal comments in ink plainly in Garrick's hand from which we may gauge his attitude toward a series of scurrilous remarks therein. "I deal in facts," states the paper. "Conscious virtue . . . with its own natural unborrowed merit holds off arts of slander. I have no pay." Garrick's accompanying comment: "You don't deserve any. Poor man! Poor man!" "I am independant," continues the paper, "My motive . . . to take my pen now and then (bad as you say it is) arises from public spirit." Garrick's pen comment, "Bad enough indeed!" *Monitor IV* (14 November 1767) contends that modern players have fallen below the esteem the Greeks once held all actors in. It sees the cause in the fact that the public identifies the players with the evil characters they perform, hence the Congreves and Wycherleys are basically at fault. The author quotes from Pope:

> Vice is a monster of so frightful mien
> As to be hated needs but to be seen,

But seen too oft, familiar with her face
We first endure, then pity, then embrace.

"Man becomes base enough to wear the mask of morality to decry human nature, and secure his private interest." This observation in context nominates Garrick as a hypocrite. The pen comment runs, "This is Mr. Monitor himself indeed!" *Monitor XIV* comments on Garrick's "vulgar and abominable method of hiring," scorns him as an actor, playwright and manager. Pen comment, "What vulgar trash is this!" *Monitor X* (30 January 1768) appeared after a long cessation, apparently caused by a long illness of the editor. A nonscurrilous issue, it deals with the five well-known elements of a play—fable, character, sentiment, dialogue, setting. Pen comment, "This number cannot be the production of Monitor as it has something of common sense in it!" Other pen comments follow but their purport is that the writer [Garrick] though interested is no longer wounded by the Monitor's drift of thought, and rather dismisses him.

Garrick might well dismiss such papers, except that the publications form part of the underground press that kept alive an irritant, at least, for the public image that Garrick would have himself and Drury Lane maintain. Yet the editorial slant became so personal, vitriolic, and hackneyed, that Garrick must have believed that rational Englishmen would cease to read the paper. The Monitor complains in essence of bad casting at Drury Lane, unhistorical costuming, Billingsgate squabbles in its farces, harlequinade too often, the use of fake advertisements of "By Desire," miserable morality (as applied to Garrick's play *Neck or Nothing*), mean plagiarism and a mangled product in his *Country Girl*, and multiple stupidity in his *Cymon*. As to his acting, Monitor deplores "a little Ascanius in high heels doing Sir John Brute." The editor approves of Smith at Covent Garden, feels Garrick is not treating the Yates family (of actors) well, revives the ten-year-old Murphy gripe about the delayed performance of *The Orphan of China*, and rehearses at great length (unfavorable for Garrick) the Garrick-Macklin "case" of 1744, now nearly a quarter of a century past. The Monitor saw perpetuation of the earlier cartel now that Colman was managing Covent Garden. His high praise for *The Widowed Wife* (no. VIII) suggests collusion with William Kenrick, who just may have been on the editorial board. Despite the light touch of the penned comments, it could not have been pleasant for Garrick to encounter a new onslaught from Grub Street after a few pleasant years free of such attacks and after he had brought so much of theatrical value to Drury Lane from France.

But by actual count Garrick had been fairly exempt from pamphlet warfare, and would be allowed another breather as the press focused on the problems of management at Covent Garden. John Rich who died in 1761, had stipulated in his will that when Covent Garden should be worth £60,000 it might be sold. John Beard, his son-in-law and successor, had decided after 40 years of singing, acting, and managing to retire and found that he could sell the patent for that amount. He did so on 1 July 1767 to the foursome George Colman, actor William Powell, and young businessmen James Harris and John Rutherford.

Garrick was upset that Colman was buying into the management, and for a time their friendship was strained. When he met Colman at Bath he wrote to brother George "We pull'd off our hats, but did not smile—our Friends here will stir heaven & Earth to bring Us together" (450). When the next season opened Garrick watched with amazement and astonishment, and the Town watched with him, the progress of the trouble which the four-way management of the rival theatre got itself into—a lockout, a take-over of the wardrobe, a searching examination of the books, public controversy, and actor despair. The house nearly went under, but managed to survive. The story is of interest here only as accounting for a shift in press attention from former target Garrick.[56]

A serious matter to be examined in Garrick's public relations with the press is the degree of truth in charges hinted at in *The Monitor* of Garrick's control and influence on a wide segment of the press, and mentioned by Fitzpatrick and the X.Y.Z. group before Garrick went to the Continent.[57]

It may never be possible to document exactly the extent to which Garrick himself was involved with the dailies, weeklies, and monthlies from 1747 to 1776—involvement, that is, which enabled him in any way to censor articles unfavorable to the theatre and to himself. Accusations were made by William Kenrick again in 1772 in his prefatory "Letter to Garrick" to the 4th edition of his *Love in the Suds*: that the actor quashed notification in the newspapers. "I was inform'd of your having used your estensive influence over the press to prevent its being advertised. . . . By what right or privilege do you, Sir, set up for a licenser of the Press?" Such accusations, easy to make and calculated for inflammatory effect, seem upon examination difficult to substantiate. A Garrick supporter had asked how, if Fitzpatrick's earlier contention were true, he and his X.Y.Z. writers managed so easily to publish their derogatory critiques in *The Craftsman*, *The London Chronicle*, and the *St James's Evening Post*.

What range of daily, weekly, monthly periodicals must one examine, and what facts do we know either to substantiate or dispel the dark hints of the opposition? Of the six morning and eight evening papers, concern must be with four of the former—the *Public Advertiser*, *Gazetteer*, *Morning Chronicle*, and *Morning Post*—and four of the latter—the *London Chronicle*, *St James's Chronicle*, *London Packet*, and *Lloyd's Evening Post*. Of the 16 weekly and monthly periodicals, concern must rest with about ten.[58] The 18 thus mentioned were what might be called the opinion-makers of the time. The others were chronicles of business, shipping, politics, and other specialties without much concern for the theatres.[59]

Involvement with the press did come at the outset of Garrick's career as patentee. Influence over the press can hardly be said to have been undue—obviously he and the managers of the other theatre, the opera house, the Gardens, and the book publishers sent as many favorable accounts ("puffs") as possible about their activities. No discernible edge was given to Garrick in these. He exercised no power over the press, nor could he influence it by censorship, but nevertheless suspicion of his power became rampant. Let us examine in turn the three avenues of possible participation—involvement, influence, censorship—and finally this unfounded but recurrent suspicion of undefined power.

*Involvement*: The nerve center of successful theatre operation lies in advertising. The principal modes were those which had proved successful earlier—playbill, newspaper notice, and oral announcement from the stage of the next night's play. Until the spring of 1763 managers instructed the prompter to prepare notices for the daily papers. Historians of journalism tell us that "The newspapers had messengers whose duty it was to wait about the theatre to get the earliest possible copy of each new bill of the next day's performance," and run with it to the composing rooms of their respective offices. Each received a shilling for his labor. Both theatres followed this procedure.[60]

The disgruntled Drury Lane subtreasurer John Powel, however, in his "Tit for Tat" manuscript (1749), noted that Lacy and Garrick had not for two years paid for playbill advertising in the *General* [later *Public*] *Advertiser*, a fact which he attributed to the managers' having a share in the paper. The share was one (or two) for the theatre, not a personal investment for either of the managers. Newspaper shares were investments of varying value, because the estimated life expectancy of the papers varied considerably. In 1772 one share for the *Morning Post* had a book value of £350, but could not be purchased for under £800.[61] But by that time the essential "advertising group" of London dailies had been equalled in number and circulation by a group whose staple was "scandal and West End gossip."[62] As circulation increased, the properties became more and more valuable. A large section of each paper in both groups focused upon political affairs. The ministry sought a controlling hand in this coverage, but its only control lay in its ability to increase the government tax from time to time. Such an increase, passed on to purchasers, sometimes wiped out the paper. In 1763 a battle, which was contesting the political endeavors of John Wilkes, demonstrated the independence of the press. This was followed early in 1770 by the publication of the "Junius Letters" with an effectual triumph of a free press.

On 14 March 1763 Garrick, as a stroke of good management, consolidated regular notice of performances in the *Public Advertiser*, and for this monopoly the paper paid Drury Lane £100 annually. The managers at Covent Garden adopted the same policy, and were paid the same. Evidently Woodfall, the publisher, thought these were valuable monopolies to hold, even though they had to do *only* with the insertion of play notices. Other papers, such as the *Gazetteer*, continued to carry them occasionally, but theatregoers depended upon the *Public Advertiser* and upon posted bills for regular and exact information. Puffs, paragraphs, cards, and other insertions, even in the *Public Advertiser*, had to be paid for by the managers concerned at costs of from 2s. 6d. to 6s. per reasonable length insertion (about 2½ inches of column space). Theatrical account books reveal such payments. Involvement to this extent was normal business practice, and the columns were open to *all* comers.[63] They were in no way limited to Garrick.

*Influence*: No instance seems to occur whereby any stockholder could hold over 50 percent of the stock and thus perhaps be able to dictate policy. In fact, Professor Robert L. Haig, in his study of the *Gazetteer* prints Proprietors' and Printers' Contracts, showing that the paper was initially financed, and its policy supported by 20 stockholders, each holding a *single* share, and he suggests that other papers had similar arrangements. *None* of the stockholders of the *Gazetteer* could hold more than that single share. And to avoid conflict of interest none could hold shares in *another* newspaper. Regular meetings were held in which financial reports were examined. The printer, not the publisher, was to bear one-half of the legal and court costs resulting from any claims against a paragraph inserted without counter signature by two proprietors. A share lapsing (by death or departure of the holder) went into a common fund, until its disposition could be determined by the proprietors at a regular meeting.[64] If the *Public Advertiser* was similar in regard to its conflict of interest clause, Garrick must have purchased as an outsider, for its financial support only, and for some dividend return. He could have had no policy voice since he had shares at times in the *Morning Chronicle*, in the *St James's Chronicle*, and the *London Packet*.

The papers doubtless exerted some influence on the widening reading public, but were open to all comers for the purchase of advertising or news-column space. The public had long recognized a "puff" for what it was—an attempt on the part of some concerned party to display his book, play, or performance in the best light possible. Puffs ran in length from three lines in a news column, "Last night the new Comedy such and such was performed at Drury Lane before a polite and distinguished audience, and met with universal applause," to three columns telling a story from Roman history to inform the public of the background of a forthcoming tragedy, to a 53-page pamphlet in its own print, such as MacNamara Morgan's *Letter to Miss Nossiter on Her Performing the Character of Juliet* (1753), at Covent Garden building up the reputation of a new actress. Murphy, irked by Morgan's imputation therein that he was in Garrick's pay, and therefore editorially controlled by the actor, struck back in his *Gray's Inn Journal* (No 16) by praising Mrs Gregory, another new actress appearing at Covent Garden—with no mention of Drury Lane. The sophisticated recognized the puffs and probably were amused by them.[65]

When Garrick really wanted to influence London's reading public his method was not to pressure a news publisher (either positively or negatively) but to float an anonymous pamphlet in which he, with the subtle irony of which he was master, could direct attention to the very emphasis he wished to make, and not submerge his point in columns of political news, advertisements for lost horses, patent medicines, sermons, books, and sailings of the merchant fleet. His *Essay on Acting* (1744), *Fribbleriad* (1761), *Fitzgig, or the Modern Quixote* (1763) and his various advertisements of adapted plays (before acknowledging himself as adapter) and his "Sick Monkey" (to test public reaction in 1765 to his return) all attest individual pamphlet entrepreneurship, hardly a part of the daily newspress.

*Censorship power*: Garrick held a share in Henry S. Woodfall's *Public Advertiser*, and one in Henry Baldwin's *St James Chronicle* (begun in 1761). He seems to have had one in Henry Bate's *Morning Post* (1772) and one for a short time in the *London Packet* (1770). As far as is known he held no shares in the monthlies. He was on congenial terms with many editors, had correspondence with some, and met others socially.[66] But Henry S. Woodfall, his brother William Woodfall (*Morning Chronicle*), Henry Baldwin, Henry Bate, Francis Newbery (*Public Ledger*), the editors of the *Gazetteer*, and those of the monthlies to which Garrick contributed verses, Christopher Smart and Richard Rolt of the *Universal Visitor* (1756), E. Cave (*Gentleman's Magazine*), Robert Dodsley (*Museum*), John Hawkesworth (*Adventurer*), and Ralph Griffiths of the *Monthly Review* were not dupes for anyone or any group, and their journals embraced wider fields than drama and theatre alone. That Garrick could have influenced or had any censoring hand in their papers, or in Smollett's *Critical Review*, or in Dr Johnson's *Idler* or *Rambler*, or Murphy's *Gray's Inn Journal* is unthinkable. Survey of the pages of these papers and magazines reveals criticism both beneficial and prejudicial to Drury Lane and to Garrick in particular. No editor would have gained anything by having the genial and engaging actor-manager dictate policy, or censor submissions. The newspaper editors became increasingly jealous of maintaining independence, especially at the time when Garrick's so-called "power" might have been felt (i.e. from 1761 on) in light of the journalists' contest with the ministry and the popular attitudes toward troubles with the American Colonies. Their independence was not to be jeopardized by a favoritism in any field.

Several specific examples of journalistic independence are instructive. Perhaps the most prestigious impartial critical review was the *Monthly*, edited by Ralph Griffiths from 1749 on. In his statement of editorial policy he noted that he had a stable of experts in the many fields which he covered, *none* of whom was allowed to review his own works. Colman and Murphy often reviewed items in the drama for him, but he did not allow them to "puff" their friends. Benjamin C. Nangle's invaluable *Index of Contributors to the Monthly Review, First Series (1749–89)* shows that Garrick was asked for *four* contributions. But his archenemy William Kenrick, who reviewed from 1759–65, contributed over 152, and Murphy, certainly no Garrick partisan, during those years, more than 300.[67]

In the dailies, even in the hands of his friends, objectivity ruled. While in Naples (31 January 1764) Garrick read a copy of the *St James's Chronicle* (for 22 December 1763) and was appalled at the sport Henry Baldwin made of him and the Duke of Devonshire and the Peace Treaty of Paris. The letter, political satire, was by "Bettsey Schemewell" (323 n.7). A proprietor with a "controlling" interest would hardly have been treated so.

A Card [brief pronouncement] and some unpleasant comment appearing in William Woodfall's *Morning Chronicle* (5 February 1776) set the stage, Garrick thought, for the damnation of Bate's *The Blackamoor Washed White*. Garrick chided Woodfall, "I may differ w$^{th}$ you in what is call'd y$^e$ impartial publication of letters which are brought to You—if any tend by falsehood to prejudice even a Stranger to You, I think you would not be justifyd in publishing them" (983). The reprimand did no good. Woodfall replied, "I acted against you, not as Mr. Woodfall, who honours and respects you, but as the printer of *The Morning Chronicle*, who ought to know, to hear, to see—not through his own organs, but those of his correspondents."[68] No influence, arbitrary power, or ability to censor here.

On 20 March 1773 Garrick had gone so far as to sell out his share in the *Public Advertiser*, writing to Henry S. Woodfall: "I imagine that I am but a poor caput Mortuum among my Brethren of y$^e$ Publick Advertiser—& what is worse I have a property the very reverse of that of a Boy's top, for the more I am whip'd the less I spin. I must therefore desire you to dispose of *my* share. . . . I shall have no objection to give up the Dividend too which I have receiv'd" (754).

*Suspicion of Power and Influence*: A reputation for having power and influence with the press was easy to come by for many reasons. It worked both for and against Garrick. His holding a share in the *Public Advertiser* was commonly known, and his daily involvement with play-notices argued an easygoing relationship with the editor. Also in the 1780s an alert reading public could sense the forming up of camps of contributors to the daily, weekly, and monthly journals. The first, the theatre group, as it was called by a modern biographer of Colman,[69] was a covey of young writers becoming Garrick admirers—Bonnell Thornton, Robert Lloyd, Charles Churchill, and George Colman. The group was opposed by what Garrick called "the Pottinger Gang"—Isreal Pottinger (printer) Thomas Vaughan, writer for the *Morning Post*, occasionally joined by Arthur Murphy, and other frustrated authors who valued drama as it appeared on the page rather than as it would go on the stage.[70] They had, of course, their organs of communication—*The Busy Body*, *The Morning Post*, *Gray's Inn Journal*, *The Theatrical Review*, and the like. In the swirl of attack and counterattack associated with publication of *The Rosciad*, the triumvirate Churchill, Colman, and Lloyd were busy. Garrick did not "openly participate in their activities, but his influence was of particular importance in the establishment of a newspaper wherein the men of the theatre could express their points of view.[71] Of this newspaper,

*The St James's Chronicle*, E. R. Page attests that "Garrick, Thornton, and Colman were shareholders . . . and made it most successful as a retailer of literary contests, anecdotes, and humorous and witty articles."[72] It won its points initially, at least—theatrical, literary, political —by lightness of touch and satirical banter. To this Robert Lloyd added in 1762 his *St James's Magazine*, a monthly which lasted only two years until his death in 1764. Neither paper, however, carried its reverence for Garrick very far. Witness his displeasure with Baldwin, mentioned above. The triumvirate dissolved with the deaths of Lloyd and Churchill (1764), but *The St James's Chronicle* carried on with considerable impartiality in its columns. It defended Garrick, quite properly, in 1773 against accusations by Macklin that the manager conspired with two Drury Lane actors to destroy his performance of *Macbeth* at Covent Garden.[73]

Garrick enjoyed turning out bits of sprightly verse, of which he contributed over 101 pieces to the *St James's Chronicle* (a few only on theatrical matters), and when Colman was planning his *London Packet* Garrick wrote to him on 15 February 1767 full of good spirits, "I will prepare some comicality for it; I have a hundred thoughts about it & will always be doing something" (447). Mary E. Knapp has traced Garrick's contributions of *vers de société*—occasional verse, prologues, songs—through the pages of the *St James's Chronicle*.[74] Most of them appear simultaneously in a dozen other papers and magazines, too. His *reputation* as a contributor was well established. We can, through his letters trace other contributions to the paper. When Moody learned of a pirated edition of *The Jubilee*, about to be played in Dublin, Garrick asked for details and promised to insert a piece about it in the papers. In 1763, angered with Davies, but wishing in no way to hinder his free expression, he wrote asking for specifics in regard to his accusations, "Or if you like it better—you have leave to publish your [*illegible*] in the *St James's Chronicle*" (314). While in Paris, as we have noted, Garrick asked Colman to insert an advertisement for Monnet's *Anthologie française ou chansons choisies depuis le XIII^e siècle jusqu'a present*, which was done. In January 1765 he asked Colman to insert a "Letter from Paris" for which he suggested details, saying that if Colman were to mention him he should only comment, "our little Stage Hero looks better than he did" (347), which everyone since has thought a little cheap. The rest of the letter would be newsy enough— about a hermaphrodite's marriage, the *Philosophical Dictionary* thought to be Voltaire's, opera performances, and engravings.

Garrick got the *St James's* to insert his "Character of Preville" in its 22–24 June 1765 issue. He was mildly upset to have Derrick's verses on Gainsborough's portrait of him with the statue of Shakespeare inserted in the paper "to be abus'd." In February 1767 he Englished Favart's story of Mr B—, and had Colman insert it in the *St James's*. In 1769, a bit touchy about the mass of satiric pieces about the Stratford Jubilee appearing in the papers, he was especially exasperated that Keate [or Stevens] had "bragged to the partners of the 'St. James's Chronicle' that he had written them all, thirty-five or forty in number" (570). One mentions the close association Garrick had with this paper because his reputation as a shareholder was well known, as were his contributions, and as were a number of attacks in it upon him. But what one sees in Garrick's contributions to the press is positive, occasionally self-serving to his vanity, but seldom malicious. Of his 459 titles of verse, which Professor Knapp has organized under the headings of Occasional, Prologues, Theatrical Skits, and Songs, over 200 found their way into 19 dailies, seven weeklies, and 14 monthlies. All in all the 200 pieces were printed in 1,007 places in these periodicals—the largest group in the *St James's Chronicle*, but closely upon its heels (in numbers) in the *London Chronicle*, whose editor William Strahan, was anything but a Garrick idolater. Soon after arriving in France Garrick had written to Colman, "A Gentleman shew'd me two London Chronicles in which they have abus'd Me most clumsily; I read their Malignity with as much sang froid as Plato himself would have done" (319).

Analysis of Professor Knapp's *Checklist* reveals that only 22 percent of Garrick's verse contributions to the press, though they began in 1740, came before 1765. The bulk came after his return from France— much what he called nonsensical, but many, such as his indignant verses answering heartless people making fun of Foote's accident neither nonsense nor comical. He had a reputation for being *in* with newspaper proprietors, and he demonstrated, at least by his contributions, that he was a constant creative writer. He "puffed" a few things for the interests of his theatre. D. Nicholl Smith suggested that a "long letter about Johnson's *Irene*," which appeared in the *General Advertiser* (18 February 1749) though purporting to be by one living a long distance from London who had come to see the play, may well have been a "puff" by Garrick to stretch out the performance of the tragedy.[75] And Garrick would continue to speak favorably of the theatre and the actors when he could.

Garrick twisted no arms of editors or printers to work in his causes. In 1771 he learned from Henry S. Woodfall in some conversation that Junius would be writing no more letters for publication. The "Junius Letters" against the ministry provided a *cause célèbre* in London for some time, and although Garrick was friendly with John Wilkes and other opposition figures, he was also friendly with people at court. After all he was managing a royal theatre. When he heard the news from Woodfall, he passed it along in a letter to someone at court, as well as to others, thinking it a piece of very interesting information. Word of this got to Junius (whoever he was) and a month later brought on Garrick a very blunt threat, transmitted by Woodfall: "Now mark me vagabond. Keep to your pantomimes, or be assured you shall hear of it. Meddle no more thou busy informer!—It is in *my* power to make you curse the day in which you dared to interfere with JUNIUS" (661 n.3).

Garrick, flabbergasted, replied in a long letter sent through Woodfall, accusing Junius of extremely bad manners, and wishing to drop the subject. Woodfall transmitted it, and replied to Garrick later that probably an enemy was seeking to stir up baseless resentment. There the matter dropped. Garrick though a shareholder, seems not to have acted as though he could have power over that paper, or censure it.[76]

A craving for power finds all avenues of approach. Aside from shares held in four daily papers, the question then arises about what if any extraordinary privileges or favors Garrick may have given to any of the proprietors, possibly to influence them in his favor. One thinks straightway of Henry Bate, because Garrick did write James Townley, hearing he had a curacy open, recommending Bate. This was in June 1774. Bate got the curacy. A year later he wrote to the Duke of Cumberland recommending Bate for a commissionership of the peace in Middlesex, but the place had already been filled. But Garrick was a sociable, outgoing person who recommended many, many people for places suitable for them. He was certainly not seeking to curry favor from the admirable but unknown Thomas Beighton when he helped him gain a curacy from Lord Camden, and his humanitarianism alone prompted him to write to the Marquis of Rockingham to save Turbutt's son from death for stealing a silver goblet.[77] Garrick and Bate were for long on the best of terms. Bate worked for Garrick, not in terms of the *Morning Post*, but as an occasional reader of plays and as a talent scout to have, for instance, a look at the acting of young Sarah Siddons. Their friendship was not venal. Bate's only journalistic favor to Garrick seems to have been inspired by his own fury at reading Captain Thompson's slur on the actor in the *London Packet* (29 February 1776), reproaching him for allegedly conspiring to damn his play *The Syrens* at Covent Garden. Garrick had not done so, and Bate proceeded to flay Thompson for ingratitude, noting in his article in the *Morning Post*

(1 March 1776) that, after all, Garrick had been responsible for Thompson's promotion in the Navy.

Garrick's correspondence reveals no special favors, or even urgings from the actor to Ralph Griffiths, or to Henry or William Woodfall. When in 1773 William was editing the *London Packet* he had printed a piece of false information about Garrick's being unwilling to play *The West Indian* as a command performance. Garrick chided him for this. Six months after retiring from the stage he asked William to have his brother Henry insert a corrective statement about Garrick's coming to town to pay Mrs Barry a visit of condolence on the death of her husband. Actually he came up to do business for the King. He thought the court might take the *Public Advertiser* notice ill—for the King "always sees y$^e$ *Publick Ad$^r$*" (1079).

As for Henry Baldwin and the *St James's Chronicle*—the state of Garrick's power and influence in 1775 may be judged from his letter to Colman on 25 July that year, "I have been insulted greatly—first to have a Paper, in which I have a property, abuse me for puffing myself, & then I am suppos'd the Author of a paragraph, or a letter in y$^e$ *Morn$^g$ Chronicle* [23 June and 12 July], which the Printer himself almost avows, & which by my honor, I never heard of till you mention'd it to me:

"I have done my Share to y$^e$ paper, nay I have told that worthy Gentleman M$^r$ Baldwin, that I would look out things whenever he was in want of Nonsense—but I give y$^e$ matter up now, & as he may be assur'd I will trouble myself no more about it, he may abuse me as fast as he pleases" (925).

Garrick appeared continually in the newspapers in his clever, offhand squibs which delighted readers and were reprinted for decades. For example his well-known epigram on Quin. Davies attests the convivial friendship which developed between Garrick and Quin, after the latter's retiring from the stage, and tells of the many times Quin visited the Garrick's at Hampton, their gourmet tastes, and Quin's delight in good food. Garrick was happy to contribute to a newspaper the mutual spoofing and comical lines he sent to the *Public Advertiser*, and nine other papers, in September 1765. He was just back from France and eager to enjoy the social rounds not only with dukes and duchesses, printers and publishers, but with respected actors. A topic of conversation in the papers centered upon mummies, so Garrick dashed off "Quin's Soliloquy on Seeing Duke Humphrey at St Albans:"

> A plague on Egypt's arts, I say;
> Embalm the dead! on senseless clay

Rich wines and spices waste!
Like sturgeon, or like brawn, shall I,
Bound in a precious pickle, lie,
Which I can never taste!

Let me embalm this flesh of mine
With turtle fat and Bourdeaux wine,
And spoil th' Egyptian trade!
Than good Duke Humphry happier I,
Embalm'd alive; old Quin shall die
A mummy ready made.[78]

It can be shown over and over again that Garrick's contributions to
the newspapers were not for aggrandizement or for self-service but for
such entertainment in idle minutes. Some appeared over his own signature, and some were anonymous, and some came over pseudonymous and strange initials—a W.H?, a Lady, a G, or a Q. This game was
played by all in the eighteenth century, especially by Christopher
Smart.

Garrick was *involved* with the press—as a playhouse advertiser, and
as a public contributor of verse. His involvement was well known.
Accusation of power and undue influence was easily attached by the
frustrated, but revelation about the conditions of stock holdings, observation of the sturdy independence of managing editors (with whom
he dealt, and from whom he took abuse) leaves no factual basis for the
accusation. *Accusation of any sinister influence*, though sometimes
made, simply cannot be substantiated. His *reputation*, therefore, for
power far outran his performance or actual attempt. At all events in
1765 as the season opened Garrick's chief interest was not for the
newspapers. He was concerned, as he had written to James Love,
about available new talent which he might bring to strengthen Drury
Lane. The concern intensified in the late 1760s with the passing of his
old guard.[79]

Recruitment of new actors is perhaps more pertinent to stage history
than to Garrick biography, yet so consistent was his drive in the late
1760s and 1770s that mention of his interest, methods, and policies
helps delineate the man. His method started with a network of friends
knowledgeable in acting and the ways of the theatre. Many such
friends were actors whom he had trained and who were now managing
outlying theatres of their own in Bristol, Bath, Edinburgh, the York
circuit, Liverpool, Dublin, and Cheltenham. The theatre at Richmond
became a special observing ground for upcoming talent.[80] Walpole
back in 1748 had written to George Montagu just coming from a play
there, "Garrick, Barry and some more of the players were there to see

the new comedians; it is to be their seminary."[81] George Colman the younger recalled in his *Random Records* how Garrick in the late 1760s rode over to Richmond for similar purposes.[82] Thomas Sheridan, Mossop, and Barry brought or sent news from Dublin. King, Palmer, and Parsons from managing summer theatres in Bristol reported from there. Ross, Love, and West Digges kept Garrick in touch with the theatre in Edinburgh, and Tate Wilkinson sent word now and again from northeast England. Jean Monnet and Anthony Carara, along with members of the English community in Paris, notified him of dancers and singers who would grace the stage at Drury Lane.

Love had told him while he was still in Paris about a 25-year-old prospect, James W. Dodd. "Your account of *Dodd* pleases Me," Garrick wrote (3 March 1765) to Love, who had recounted something of Dodd's life as a strolling player, "I dread a Stroler. . . . I never could account for the Country Actors being so very wide of y$^e$ mark. Pray Enquire, & let me know more about that *Dodd*—We want a second Obrien most dreadfully—what a loss to Us that young man is" (351).[83] He had been back in England but a month when Hoadly wrote from Bath giving another and full account of the acting of Dodd, Mrs Dodd, and a Miss Reynolds. Hoadly's assurance satisfied Garrick, so by September Dodd was engaged, especially for coxcomb parts, and continued many, many years at Drury Lane.

Garrick had also heard about 23-year-old Robert Bensley, and liked what he heard, engaging him the same season. Garrick advised him to study hard and to gain continuing experience in the summer theatres as well. After several seasons Bensley moved to Covent Garden, but returned in 1775 a seasoned actor. Garrick's way of interviewing, as well as his relationship with actors, appears in correspondence with this young man on the eve of his second tour at Drury Lane (12 August 1775). Always accentuating the positive, and supposedly to let applicants show themselves to best advantage, he would ask them what parts they would like to act (as well as what ones they wished to play if engaged) to give a sample of their powers. Bensley wrote, "You puzzle me in giving me the choice of what character I shall play first. I had rather be guided by your judgment than my own," but Garrick's way allowed actors to lead from strength, or fail in pieces of their own choice.[84]

He had, as we know, long developed the potential of Samuel Cautherly, first employed as a child actor 28 April 1755. The seasons 1765–67 were almost "Cautherly years," for Garrick deemed that though young, he was then ready for a number of major roles—George Barnwell, Zaphna in *Mahomet*, Dorilas in *Merope*, the Dauphin in

*King John*, Hamlet, and Romeo. His opportunities were unbelievable. Although Cautherly never lived up to Garrick's hopes, he remained in the company until 1775.[85] In the 1766–67 season Garrick brought forward Miss Reynolds as recommended by Hoadly. In fact he adapted Wycherley's *Country Wife* into quite a different play devising the part of Peggy (formerly Margery Pinchwife) for her, taking pains to train her in the part in which she pleased the public on 25 October 1766.[86] One recalls Garrick's spotting and nourishing acting-singing talent when he brought the young Jewish boy Master Michael Leoni to play in his extravanganza *The Enchanter* (13 December 1760). He made a parallel recruitment of the young Jewish girl singer, 15-year-old Harriet Abrams, a pupil of Arne's, later in his *May Day*, 28 October 1775.

People have speculated why Garrick, after hearing about John Henderson in 1773, and after a pleasant and helpful correspondence with him, failed to bring him immediately to Drury Lane. Henderson was 26 at the time, and pleased audiences at Bath immensely, and in major roles. Richard Cumberland suggested that Garrick see him in London in two parts of his choice then negotiate employment. Garrick, knowing the differences between Bath and London audiences, wished Henderson to choose any three parts (to show talents in tragedy and comedy) and to perform ten or 12 times, after which the "Publick voice will be known" (889). Henderson demurred, asking for a three-year contract and assurance that he alone should choose his roles—four the first, four (new ones?) the second, and four the third year. Garrick never having seen him act, yet having got him his engagement with Palmer in Bath, sensing here a wish to return to the "star" system, thought the stipulation a bit high-handed, and at that time quite out of the question. He turned him down and was in no very agreeable mood to judge him even when he saw him in April 1775. Garrick wrote to Colman—"I have seen y$^e$ great Henderson, who has Something, & is Nothing—he might be made to figure among the puppets of these times . . . however . . . I . . . see sparks of fire which might be blown to warm even a London Audience at Xmas. He is a dramatic Phenomenon, & his Friends, but particularly Cumberland has ruined him—he has a manner of [r]aving, when he w$^d$ be Emphatical that is ridiculous, & must be chang'd, or he would not be suffer'd at y$^e$ Bedford Coffeehouse" (903).[87]

Garrick in retrospect seems to have missed on this opportunity. But did he? Henderson's biographer John Ireland attributed the non-engagement to Garrick's hurt vanity when Henderson "a country actor" gave an imitation of him. Garrick once, indeed, watched Henderson imitate Barry, Woodward, and James Love. He asked him to do one of himself. Henderson obliged by doing Garrick as he had seen him in Benedict. Two auditors present thought the imitation excellent. Garrick noted—"if, if, if that was his voice, he had never known it himself, for upon his soul it was entirely dissimilar to everything he conceived it to be, and totally unlike any sound that had struck upon his ear until that moment."[88] The quality of voice, of course was what startled Garrick, even as a tape recording of our own voices now startles and seems unfamiliar to us, though frequent repetitions do yield the likeness which others sense immediately.

A reading of the Henderson correspondence, however, indicates clearly the reason for Garrick's demurrer in the early 1770s. Henderson therein, with the applause of Bath audiences ringing in his ears, wanted the power to dictate his own roles, rather than fit into ensemble performance. Garrick was building the company anew, not collecting stars. Henderson feared having to take his turn with secondary roles even occasionally. He had, he wrote Ireland, "only six parts, and they would not sustain him for a whole season. I must then be forced upon others in which I have no merit, or none that will support the name I have got. . . . I am not ripe enough for London . . . the only dread I have is that of being put upon inferior characters as—'till Garrick leaves the stage, I must be at his theatre."[89] Henderson, Garrick thought, would not accommodate himself to functioning in a large company. His action of recommending Henderson elsewhere was a triumph of judgment, not of a defect of vision, character, or theatrical acumen.

When recruiting Garrick consistently thought of the "whole show." He had brought from Paris his Italian valet, Antonio Carara, whom he set up later as a travel guide to friends and parties going to the Continent. Carara, with Monnet, kept an eye on prospective dancers for Drury Lane. He negotiated the engagement of Signora Paccini, having written from Venice: "I have already found out the woman, and have almost settled the affair. . . . Her name is Paccini. . . . With regard to the men, we have here at present two very good." He thought Paccini superior to Mlle Hidoux, and urged action on the contract before the carnival in Venice, in which they were working, closed.[90] Garrick replied favorably, and Carara was able to get one of the group, spelling out the details of the agreement for the Paccini—a salary of £325, but with a listing in the bills as "First Dancer." She would stand her own travel expenses, but must have a benefit at the best season of the year. The managers countered that she must dance whenever called upon "to the best of her power and abilities," and wrote into the articles a £500 forfeit should they not fulfill any part of their bargain.

Garrick tried out many more, as indicated in *The London Stage* (4, III)—Miss Priscilla Hopkins, Mr Wilde, Miss Sharp, Mr Budel. Basically he wanted youth with some acceptable experience who despite talents for special roles could be trained to act well with the rest, and in various other parts. His richest prize, of course, was Sarah Siddons, although she still needed seasoning in the provinces. During July preceding his final season he wrote to Henry Bate, "If You pass by Cheltenham . . . I wish you would see an Actress there, a M^rs Siddons, She has a desire I hear to try her Fortune with Us; if she seems in Your Eyes worthy of being transplanted, pray desire to know upon what conditions She would make y^e Tryal" (926). The words "transplant" and "tryal" are keys to his principle of recruitment—a trial period for new growth amid the circumstances provided by a London audience was important. The timing for the Siddons's appointment was right—Brereton seemed about to depart from Drury Lane, and Miss Pope had left. It also seemed possible that the Yateses would leave, but Garrick was cautious. He asked a second opinion from John Moody, and a third from Thomas King, who could observe her in *The Fair Penitent* at the summer theatre. Reports were all favorable, especially from Bate, so Garrick negotiated, but discouraged her husband William Siddons, from ever dreaming of acting at Drury Lane.

Mrs Siddons was at the time seven months pregnant, and was delivered of a child on 15 November 1775. She first appeared at Drury Lane in Portia on 29 December 1775. "A good figure rather handsome —wants Spirit and ease, her Voice a little coarse very well receiv'd," wrote Hopkins in his *Diary*. That same day, after rebuilding the company for a decade, Garrick decided to retire.[91] Mrs Siddons's *Reminiscences*, written down 56 years later, may not be accurate in detail, but yield the impression abroad at the time about some savagery in the playhouse, as actresses vied with each other, the awe the actors felt for Garrick, and the fortunes of an innocent newcomer.

She thought (in 1831) that Garrick made much of her to counteract the difficulties he was having with Mrs Yates and Miss Younge, whose airs were, she confessed, "enough to try his patience." "The fulsome adulation that courted him in the Theatre," she added, "cannot be imagined, and whosoever was the luckless wight who should be honored with his distinguished and envyd smiles of course became the subject of spite and malevolence. Little did I guess that I myself was now that wretched victim; for some times He would hand me from my own seat in the Green-room to place me next to his own. He also selected me to personate Venus at the revival of The Jubilee. This gained me the malicious appellation of *Garrick's Venus* and the ladies who so kindly bestowed it upon me, so determinedly rushed before me in the last scene, that had he not broken through them all, and brought us forward with his own hand, my little Cupid and myself, whose appointed situations were in the very front of the stage, might as well have been in the Island of Paphos at that moment."[92]

The several companies that Garrick brought together from 1765 to 1775 were well rounded, and their performance pleased London spectators mightily. Little wonder that actors aspired to Drury Lane, for in the *Account Books* and *Treasurer's Books* where figures are comparable between it and Covent Garden it is clear that Garrick's payroll outdid that of his competitor by £17,884 over the decade, and his expenditures for house repair and refurbishing were consistently higher than those at Covent Garden. Yet the overall comparable profits were about equal.[93] Garrick cared for his people and for the elegance of his theatre as one of England's great cultural institutions. The thrust of Garrick's renewed energy had lasted long, and accomplished much not only for the period itself, but for theatrical art to come. Management deals with hard circumstances and routines, but mainly, as at Garrick's top level, with the unusual problems and their solutions. Garrick's extroversion, jubilancy, and vivacity, tempered by occasional defensiveness, long thought, diplomacy, and wit, his firm and businesslike sense of management balanced by humane treatment of his fellows and by subtle generosities had a course still to run of six more years before retirement would open up a new and relaxed life.

# Part Five
## The Private Man

.

# London Social Life

THE FIRST THREAT or temptation of diffusion in friendships and exploitation of popularity almost overwhelmed Garrick in his opening season as a professional actor in 1741–42. In Goodman's Fields Theatre, Garrick justified and defended his choice both financially and socially. "As to Company y^e Best in Town are desirous of Mine, & I have rec'd more Civilities & favours from Such Since my playing than I ever did in all my Life before" (17). "M^r Pit, who is reckon'd y^e Greatest Orator in the House of Commons . . . Sent a Gentleman to let Me know he & y^e Other Gentlemen would be glad to See Me" (18). Towards the close of the first season, he again wrote Peter, "I have sup'd Twice w^th y^e Great M^r Murray Councell^r & Shall with M^r Pope by his Introduction. . . . I din'd with L^d Hallifax & L^d Sandwich Two very ingenious Noblemen Yesterday & am to dine at L^d Hallifax's next Sunday with L^d Chesterfield . . . in short I believe nobody (as an Actor) was ever more caress'd & My Character as a private Man makes ['em] more desirous of my Company—(all this Entre nous as one Broth^r to Another)" (23). Thus Garrick particularized the liabilities of this expanding fame.

Garrick had the wisdom and the control, however, not to be distracted by all the adulation of celebrities. The blaze of the notoriety of the first season died down, and Garrick for the five following years pursued his ambition shrewdly and patiently in Dublin and London and offstage in the company of his private friends.

Two enduring friendships, however, with the aristocracy and current political figures, originated and were sustained by genuine interest in the theatre as such. The first, as already developed was with William Windham. The second, initially perhaps in association with Windham, was with William Henry Zuylestein, the fourth earl of Rochford (1717–81), of which only less fragmentary records survive. Rochford was familiar enough with Garrick's career at Drury Lane to write Garrick as early as 17 October 1745: "how agreeably you surprise me in telling me, we shall see you and Mrs. Cibber together; but how will Woff relish that? or, to speak more properly, how will you relish it? for to tell you my mind, I believe the other party can wean them-selves much easier than you can, or I have no skill in woman's flesh."[1] Years later in 1766, on Mrs Cibber's death, Rochford could confidently assert, "I have never heard it surmised that there was ever any im-proper intimacy between Garrick and Mrs Cibber."[2] As for Garrick's and Rochford's private or personal relations, as early as the summer of 1744 Garrick accepted an invitation to visit (with Windham) the Rochfords at their country home, St Osyth, near Easton in Essex, for Rochford's birthday, 13 September.[3] Rochford by his marriage to Lucy Young, maid of honor to Queen Caroline, moved in court circles, but he, the same age as Garrick, doubtless sought out the friendship. In anticipation of the birthday celebrations Lady Rochford wrote Garrick, "I wish it was as much in my power to hinder your attendance on Mr Fleetwood and settle you in a pretty farm, agreeable to your wishes, in Suffolk at £200 a year."[4] Garrick presented her with Edward Moore's *Fables for the Female Sex* (1744) inscribed with verses.[5] In turn she presented Garrick with Ariosto's *Orlando Furioso*, translated by Sir John Harrington, with plates (1607).[6] Several years later Garrick com-posed some inscriptions for a monument in Rochford's garden in Eas-ton in memory of Lady Rochford's goldfinch.[7] In the same early letter, quoted above on the actresses, Rochford, in a reflective mood con-tinued: "believe me, David, it is a hard task to conceal our thoughts from those we love" and continues "describing . . . a sort of men that I have met with in my lifetime, that are my utter aversion; and such are they who are not melancholy enough to hate society (for then one should at least be rid of them), but when they are in it, become ob-servers of one's words and actions, and never communicate any thing they know themselves, not even to those they call their dearest friends. . . ; but to describe more strongly to you the sort of man I hate, I must without flattery tell you he is the reverse of you."

In 1745, on the initial success of the Scottish rebellion Garrick pro-posed volunteering in a regiment reportedly being raised by Rochford, to which Rochford responded, "I know nobody I should be so proud of commanding as yourself, but, thank God, we have now old regi-ments enow at Home to quell the sad remains of those rash traitors" (34,34 n.5).[8] Near the close of this letter Rochford adds "I am obliged to you for the songs: they are very pretty, but they are set in a wrong key, and I was obliged to transpose them before I could play them."

Beginning in 1748 Rochford, a Whig, embarked on one of the most active, influential, and respected careers in the armed services, the court, the state, the ministry. He was in England, however, at the very

8

distinguished party, the first of the Garricks' guests at Hampton, in August 1755, that included the "Duke of Grafton, Lady Holderness Lord & Lady Rochford, Marquis D'Abreu [with whom the Rochfords had become acquainted in Spain] & M^r Walpole" (155). By then Garrick and Rochford had been friends for ten years and more; in the ensuing 23, of which no records survive, they certainly were occasionally together, though Garrick must have regretted that he was not in Paris when Rochford was in residence as the ambassador. Less than a year before his death Garrick wrote Rochford (12 April 1778): "My good Lord As you are well known to smile upon Me, I am address'd on all quarters to befriend some petition or Other—let me assure y^r Lord^p this is at least as disagreeable to me, as it can be to You—but what can I do?—not to continue the delusion, that I have some interest w^th Lord Rochford would be such a loss of importance, that I cannot readily give it up" (1171),[9] on this occasion petitioning successfully William Frederick Glover, occasionally an actor, to be appointed surgeon in the Essex Militia, having only the week before solicited Rochford for the appointment of his nephew to the West Essex Militia of which Rochford was the colonel (1169). Although in the later years they may not have been often together, each certainly followed the career of the other, and both were members of an expanding community of public and private life. Inexorably, as a public figure, Garrick further had to cope with the rising tide of the transient socially ambitious who sought identification with the actor and not the man.

It will be recalled that Eva Maria, until she departed for England from Vienna at the age of 21 or 22, had grown up a member of the most cultured and aristocratic court in Europe, with a cosmopolitan education, with a command of French and Italian language and literature, and accepted as an artist disciplined both in mind and in body. With introductions from Viennese aristocracy to the Burlingtons, she traveled to England to accept a contract as a ballet dancer in the Italian Opera Company in the Haymarket. On invitation from the Burlingtons she shortly became resident in Burlington House, "in my little Yellow bed" and later at her marriage gave Piccadilly as her legal residence. Her debut performance at Drury Lane was attended by the King and Queen and many of the English aristocracy, and she was universally accepted socially not as an actor-dancer to be exploited and demeaned.

Lady Burlington rejected Garrick as a possible suitor and ultimately accepted him only out of consideration for the wishes of Eva Maria. Although the Garricks by invitation from the Burlingtons began their honeymoon in Chiswick, Garrick rented an Elizabethan manor house in Merton in order to preserve his identity or dignity—to be free from subordinating dominance of the Burlingtons. In her patronage and bounty Lady Burlington was not so much interested in the ballet or theatre as in the public notoriety as well as the private flattering attention of two popular figures. But what may have been originally a benefaction before the marriage became an increasing burden in the ensuing eight years as Lady Burlington, although not yet 50 (13 September 1749) at the time of the Garricks' marriage, declined into paranoic senility. When together in Burlington House, or Chiswick, or Londesburgh, the Garricks were tirelessly attentive to Lady Burlington's wishes and whims, and when separate they endeavored to satisfy Lady Burlington's insistent demand to carry out errands but most of all her insistence on receiving letters. Garrick opened his first letter to Lord Burlington, 18 July 1749, with the remark, "Next to receiving Complim$^{ts}$ & thanks, I know Your Lord$^P$ has an aversion to writing Letters," but not so Lady Burlington (57). The burden of the correspondence fell on Garrick, the intruder and outsider, simply because of Mrs Garrick's as yet limited command of spoken and written English. The upshot was that in the two and a half months the Garricks were summering at Merton with free access to Chiswick and Burlington House, immediately after their wedding 22 June, Garrick wrote 25, if not more, generally long letters to Lady Burlington in Londesburgh, not in the role of an actor-manager but in his private character. More often than not Garrick was responding directly to letters from her ladyship.[10] Writing both for himself and Mrs Garrick, he became thoroughly domesticated in the routine of acknowledgments, protests of appreciation and gratitude, thanks for the gifts of chickens, ale, pies, current social gossips, accidents, pets, the visits of neighbors, such as John Shackleton who had succeeded Lord Burlington's friend William Kent as court painter to George II, progress in the restoration of the new home in Southampton Street, to which Lady Burlington contributed the gift of a picture for the dining room, and calls at Burlington House and Chiswick to see that all was in order. Of a more personal nature, Garrick responded to Lady Burlington's request that he look over and comment on the manuscript of two essays by Lady Burlington's grandfather, George Savile, marquis of Halifax, that she was preparing for publication (58,64,67,77); made some comments on a portrait of Mrs Garrick by Lady Burlington, and reported in two final letters on the opening of Drury Lane in the autumn of 1749 (80,81).

Although in the earlier letters Garrick was much too self-conscious in his protestations of gratitude to Lady Burlington and love for Mrs Garrick, he more and more wrote with patience and good humor, subordinating himself with more objectivity, treating Lady Burlington as an individual without alluding to her aristocratic origins and position. Mrs Garrick injected a saving grace of blunt good humor in postscripts or brief notes Garrick set down at her dictation. By late October or early November, the Garricks moved into their Southampton Street house and the Burlingtons were in London; thereafter the Garricks were often in their company and attending the social gatherings of the titled and socially prominent in Burlington House.

During the summer of 1750 the intimacy of the Garricks and Burlingtons expanded from occasional social visits and correspondence to traveling together from London to Londesburgh, setting out in late May with stopover visits of a few days or more with the Hartingtons at Harwick Hall, then to Chatsworth, a brief visit with Charles Watson-Wentworth, Lord Rockingham, at Wentworth Woodhouse in West Riding, and on to Londesburgh by June 9 for a summer visit until August 6. The dependence of the Burlingtons on the Garricks for companionship and managerial assistance at Burlington House and Chiswick became more insistent and varied. On 18 April 1751, Garrick reported to Lord Burlington he had been at Chiswick for two days overseeing some bricklayers and plasterers; presumably in return for this and other favors, Lord Burlington gave him "a fine Horse" (101).

Following their short visit to Paris, the Garricks joined the Burlingtons at Chiswick to accompany them to Londesburgh for the summer until late August in 1751: "I have had great kindness shew'd Me by y^e whole Family" (106). The following summer Garrick reported, "I am oblig'd on account of Lord Burlington's late Indisposition to attend him this Latter part of y^e summer into Yorkshire" (117), not to return alone with Mrs Garrick to London until around the first of September. The Burlingtons followed in November calling in Southampton Street on the Garricks who in turn dined with them in Burlington House (121, 123,129). Once again early in July 1753 the Garricks were with the Burlingtons in Londesburgh, for the last time, however, as Lord Burlington's increasing illness resulted in his death in December (137 n.4).

Lady Burlington lived on at Chiswick until 1758 in declining health, confused, suspicious, lonely, unable to manage the household. Garrick, at her request became the correspondent, the intermediary in imaginary offenses, disaffection of staff, persecutions, "for the State of affairs at Chis^k are much to be dreaded—all kind of discontent, quarrels, heart burnings & Suspicians are going forward: Much Mischief is at work" (153). Mrs Garrick had to be in constant attendance, days on end, to comfort Lady Burlington and preserve some order. Through it all, in all the pettiness and frustration and deterioration of what was once a magnificent household, Garrick was patient, compassionate, sympathetic with the individuals who were suffering, loyal to the family that had meant so much in his life. After all, what an extraordinary opportunity and experience the friendship with the Burlingtons had been; to have been guests and lived in three of the most magnificent establishments of eighteenth-century art, music, libraries, gardens, the full range of country community social life; to have not only observed but learned to assimilate aristocratic culture at its best; to be recognized in and out of London as companions of the Burlingtons in their later years. For the Garricks, in particular, who may have been first sought out as popular actors, but who were soon cultivated as individuals, the friendship of the Burlingtons enabled them to become a part of a highly cultured, artistic way of life, to be at ease with and accepted by the aristocracy.

Garrick's long friendship with the Burlingtons and especially Lord Hartington undoubtedly prepared and stimulated Garrick to look about for a country home of his own. On 4 July 1753, he instructed Peter to look over an estate in Derbyshire, near Chatsworth, and on 16 July Peter was to inquire into one in Leicestshire: "I own I love a good Situation prodigiously, & I think the four great Requisites to make one are, Wood, Water, Extent, & inequality of Ground" (126). Balked in the purchase of several properties in the shires, he concluded "I shall content Myself with y$^e$ Bank of y$^e$ Thames" (134), shortly in January 1754 first renting and then purchasing what was known as the Fuller House in Hampton (137 n.4). He and Mrs Garrick immediately launched upon a restoration, expansion, and furnishing of what became their famous villa in Hampton, inspired and guided by all they had observed and enjoyed in Burlington House, Chiswick, Chatsworth, and Londesburgh in style and quality, though not to be sure on the same scale. Within one year the Garricks established themselves in the social register, the aristocracy of accomplished hosts.

Garrick's first welcome into the Burlington household was through William Cavendish (1720–64), marquis of Hartington, later (1755) fourth duke of Devonshire, who became one of Garrick's closest noble friends. On 28 March 1748 he had married Lady Charlotte Elizabeth Boyle (1731–54), baroness Clifford of Londesburgh, only surviving child of the Burlingtons, after a courtship of three years, she being 17. That summer Garrick visited Chatsworth for the first time, the magnificent country home in which he was to know four generations of Cavendishes. Earlier, however, doubtless prompted by the Burlingtons, Lord Hartington had used his influence to forestall a demonstration in Drury Lane against the Violette, who through a misunderstanding had on one evening performed only one and not three dances as scheduled.[11] On coming of age he had been elected an M.P. from Derbyshire, in which Chatsworth was located; later in 1755 he was appointed lieutenant-governor of Ireland, where he accomplished a political reconciliation.

In the Burlington household, Eva Maria and Lady Charlotte must have formed the friendship they pursued after their respective marriages, in visits at Burlington House, perhaps Chiswick, certainly at Chatsworth. On 15 August 1749, from Merton, Garrick wrote Lady Hartington: "I am deputed by a Lady, (whose Commands your Lad$^p$ may imagine I cannot but obey) to inform You, that a Small Burn on y$^e$ right hand, got by a strong zeal in cooking some roast beef, hinders her from acknowledging the Pleasure of your last letter" (66). Much to be regretted, none of their correspondence seems to have survived. Between, however, Lady Hartington's involvement in the maternity of three children, and Mrs Garrick's early inexperience with English, the two men took over a correspondence, beginning in the summer of 1750 when the Garricks first were guests at Londesburgh, of which more letters survive, exclusive of those on theatrical business, and those with Lady Spencer, than to any other correspondent.[12]

Extensive though the surviving correspondence may be, most of the earlier letters are given over to Garrick's reporting to Hartington the routine, the disintegration of the Burlington household, the vagaries, suspicions, and resentments of "her almost unintelligible Ladyship" and no longer are of much biographical or historical interest, except for occasional insights into Garrick's capacity for personal friendships. For example, on 13 July of Garrick's first summer at Londesburgh, he wrote Lord Hartington: "I have vex'd myself all this Day for being disappointed of sending my Londesburgh *Diary*, as I propos'd—I had taken my Notes & made my Observations for that purpose, but my Lady Burlington who always sticks in my Skirts, told me (somewhat maliciously) this Morning, y$^t$ *she* had sent an Account of y$^e$ Company to Lady Hartington, & consequently y$^e$ best Part of my Performance was of no value," a remark that did not deter Garrick from writing a most entertaining letter, recounting how "I murder a Rabbit now & then, & have been fatal to y$^e$ woodpeckers, but from a five Years cessation of Arms, I really cannot distinguish between tame & Wild Pigeons" (90). He accepted Lady Burlington's eccentricity in good humor and much enjoyed the banquets with the neighboring gentry. "I must beg leave to inform Y$^r$ Lord$^p$ [Lord Hartington to whom he was writing] that I have at this present writing such a Mixture of Ale Champaign, florence, claret & Cowslip Wine within Me, that My head may be in my Pocket for any use I have of it. . . . My Lord Langdale who had Eaten three plates of Soup, two of Salmon, one of Carp besides yᵉ head, two Dozen of Gudgeons, some Eels, with Macaroni, Omlett & Rasberry tart, & adding to these, Strawberries & cream, Pineapple &c &c &c, grew a little sick after yᵉ third bottle of Burgundy, & I believe had left the Maigre Compound [Sciaenoid fish] upon yᵉ table he took it from, had not a handsome dram of brandy come to his & Our Relief. . . . My Lord recover'd his Spirits again, & told us very seriously, that *fasting* Days never agreed with him" (91).

One of the most charmingly spirited letters Garrick ever wrote was to Lady Hartington in anticipation and welcome to Londesburgh (110, 111). With Lady Hartington's death in December 1754 at the age of 23, and Hartington's departure for Ireland in 1755, leaving his three children with Lady Burlington, Garrick reported more and more on the "Sweet-ones . . . with whom I play'd a long time Yesterday. . . . Lᵈ C[avendish, later fifth duke of Devonshire] rides like a Man, & in Every thing will answer & fulfill yʳ Lordship's Wishes—He grows greatly & tho not without his merriment his disposition seems to be reserv'd & Sedate: *Master Richᵈ* is most surprizingly alter'd, & from yᵉ Silent, sour *Dapimibomenos* [one who only answers questions], he turns out yᵉ liveliest drollest, most Engaging Child, that ever was seen. . . . Lady Dorothy, is Every thing Yʳ Lordᵖ can Wish" (150). Hartington with all his distractions and duties in Ireland, often, as Garrick acknowledged "return[ed] Me Letter for Letter" (149). Garrick congratulated Hartington on his successful administration in Ireland, and reported on 26 February 1756 (now to Devonshire): "I din'd Some time ago with Several Gentlemen, among wᶜʰ were no less than Six Members of Parliament, chiefly of yᵉ Minority [of which Devonshire, a Whig was the leader], & by yᵉ turn of their discourse I could gather, that they have warm Expectations of Yʳ Grace's Sanction" (159), that is to be appointed 10 May first lord of the treasury and prime minister, which took place 16 November 1756 when Devonshire returned to London. On Peter's insistence Garrick obtained for him through Devonshire the sinecure as collector of customs at Whitehaven (173, 307,308). But even after Devonshire returned to London, the Garricks continued very much in attendance on Lady Burlington until her death on 14 September 1758, and the dispersal of the staff (211). Devonshire, failing as prime minister (27 March 1757), was appointed lord chamberlain, in turn to be dismissed in 1762, when he retired to Chatsworth, where the Garricks were his guests and together at the Ascot races in July before the Garricks sailed for France on 15 September, Garrick lamenting that the Duke ("the best & most honourable of men") had been brought into the scurrilous comments in the public press (310,319,323).

In response to Devonshire's "very flattering Commands to give You some Account of our proceedings when we got into Italy" where the Duke himself had traveled earlier, Garrick wrote three full and excellent biographical letters. The first from Florence, 30 November 1763: "The English here are all agreeable, & hold their Conversations in our Appartment (& we have a most magnificent one upon the banks of y$^e$ Arno) almost Every Night; there is one M$^r$ Kaye [from near Londesburgh] among them, who is known to y$^r$ Grace, & is beat constantly by M$^{rs}$ Garrick at Chess" (320).[13] A second from Rome, 24 March 1764, he wrote from the room in an apartment which was once the Duke's, and opened his heart to a melancholic thought which crossed his mind but did not linger: "I have lost all relish for the Stage both as Manager and Actor. I am almost tempted to repent of my Follies, & be a Merry Andrew no longer" (326). He proposed that he purchase for the Duke pictures and statues, should Devonshire approve his taste. The Duke responded at the thought of Garrick's becoming a dilettante in art, noted that they would have many battles on that subject, declared he had no money for pictures, but asked Garrick to get for him all "the prints that Bartolozzi has engraved: as you are such a connoisseur, you must know him."[14]

When Devonshire died at Spa, in Germany, on 3 October at the age of 44, Garrick was recovering from his most debilitating illness. "They kept his Death from Me," he wrote Colman, "by the manag$^t$ of the best of Women & Wives, Till I was better able to struggle with such a Heart breaking loss—He lov'd Me to the greatest Confidence, & I deserv'd it by my gratitude, tho not by my Merits" (341).[15]

Neither social status, public careers, a mutuality of friends, nor ambition and vanity—no record survives of Garrick boasting of his recognition by the Burlingtons and Devonshires—launched and sustained the friendship. Circumstances only offered the opportunities for the cultivation of private, humane values. Devonshire may well have introduced Garrick to Whig politicians and thereby stimulated Garrick's more than superficial knowledge of the contemporary political drama; the two also shared the enjoyment of the great art collections assembled by the Burlingtons and they had conversed on artistic good taste with the candor to differ. Yet the disparities were more manifest. Devonshire, one of the wealthiest and best established hereditary aristocrats, "a fashionable model of goodness whose composition and virtues must have endeared him at any time," appointed to the highest political offices was subjected to reversals, all but ignored by his contemporaries, remained faithful to the memory of one he loved from her girlhood and lost early.[16] In contrast Garrick, from an obscure, often hard-pressed, provincial family, was to become the most successful and famous member of his profession, solely dependent on himself in all the competitive and transitory fashions of the theatre, blessed in his marriage, socially ambitious, secure in many devoted friends. What had the two as a common ground of friendship? Both had shared in the disintegration of the great Burlington family, the early death of Lady Hartington, an affection for the motherless children, the transitoriness of popularity, the envy of rivals, a compassion for human sorrow. Devonshire found in Garrick one in whom he could confide. He could trust his integrity and Garrick responded in gratitude to one who accepted him as an individual, for himself alone and who trusted him.

A series of incidents, minor in the sequence of life's major affairs, reveals the intimacy of their friendship. On the tenth of November each year all members of the royal household attended His Majesty on his birthday in new and elegant suits. The choice and design of these was a personal matter for each. In 1753, 1757, and 1758 the Duke asked Garrick to select materials, engage the tailoring, and supervise the decoration of such suits for him. In 1758 Garrick wrote to him on the subject, and used the occasion to solicit a loan for funds to complete his renovation of Hampton. Garrick had some patterns drawn up, and some rich materials procured (210). The Duke expressed his pleasure in his letter of 10 September 1758, preferred velvet with a lace or brocade waistcoat, and wished to play down much trimming—though such trim was fashionable and elegant at the time. He enclosed in his letter a note for £500 for Garrick's work on the Hampton estate, specifically requested no security for it, and concluded "if you wanted as much more, it is at your service, and I am very glad it is in my power to be of any convenience to you."[17]

Except for casual, general social encounters, Garrick did not associate with the aristocracy or landed gentry other than in the company and in the mansions of Windham, Rochford, and the Burlingtons and Devonshires in London and in the country until after 1765. Abroad, however, he was cordially received in the English communities by the aristocracy who were less class-conscious than they were at home. The Garricks, therefore, on their return from France were sought out and entertained as cultivated and companiable individuals, and in the renewed tide of popularity, Garrick was as selective and discriminating as he was in the many roles he was again playing at Drury Lane. All the while he was renewing old friendships, he was responding to the cordiality of more public figures and a younger generation. He was not always able to resist the distractions and applause of his public social life and restrain himself to the enduring private companionship with a few accomplished and distinguished individuals.

Among the older acquaintances who now sought the company of the Garricks, was George Lyttleton (1709–73) first baron Lyttleton, 18 years Garrick's senior, at one time or another pursuing a public role as a politician, author and patron of authors, social celebrity, critic, lavish host in a country mansion he had rebuilt, an almost Hogarthian caricature in appearance and manners, who lived in great elegance, was deserted by his wife and rejected by a profligate son, the darling of the very refined coterie of the Blue Stockings, and who died in heavy affliction, known to his generation as the "Good Lord Lyttleton" in contrast to his son. He was the first public celebrity cited by Garrick to his brother Peter as "The Great nay incredible Success & approbation I have met with from $y^e$ Greatest Persons in England" (18); and a week later: "$M^r$ Littleton was $w^{th}$ Me last Night & took Me by $y^e$ hand & Said he never saw Such playing upon $y^e$ English Stage before" (19). The intimacy included Lyttleton's nicknaming Mrs Garrick "Pidpad," presumably an allusion to her pronunciation of English. They exchanged books and occasional letters; Lyttleton prevailed on Garrick not to reply to an attack on Mrs Garrick's Catholicism by Archibald Bower, whom Lyttleton patronized. They shared a friendship with Joseph Warton, whom Lyttleton had appointed his domestic chaplain. In June 1770 the Garricks entertained Mrs Montagu and Lord Lyttleton at Hampton, and thereafter the three were often together in the gatherings of the *bas bleu*. By 1770 Hagley had been restored and Lyttleton eagerly sought to show it off to the Garricks on a long visit with Mrs Montagu and Mrs Carter in the summer of 1771. The quality of their long friendship was best memorialized by Lyttleton in a letter to Garrick, from Hagley, reflecting on their late long visit together, "I think I love you more than one of my age ought to do; for at a certain time of life the heart should lose something of its sensibility; but you have called back all mine, and I feel for you as I did for the dearest of my friends in the first warmth of my youth."[18] To which Garrick responded in part, "It is my utmost pride and ambition to deserve the kind thoughts of the great and good, and my wishes are completely fulfilled in your letter . . . and I flatter myself, though you will find greater qualities in your other friends, you will never experience more sincerety, warmth, and true attachment than in your humble servant" (655).

The temper only, and not the onset and duration of Garrick's ties with Henry Herbert, tenth earl of Pembroke (1734–94), Garrick's junior by 17 years, can be sensed from the fragmentary records.[19] Married in 1755 to Elizabeth, daughter of Charles Spencer, third duke of Marlborough, with a country home in Wilton House in Wiltshire, he became lord of the bedchamber to the Prince of Wales, 1756; aide-de-camp to George II, 1758. He was an exceptionally able cavalry officer, publishing in 1762 *The Method of Breaking Horses*, the basic handbook in the British cavalry. Garrick may have met him in Paris in the early sixties through the Rochfords, who were close friends. By 1768 Garrick and Pembroke enjoyed many mutual French friends and were on easy and familiar terms regarding the French and English theatres, Pembroke undertaking to obtain a copy of Fenouïllot de Falbaire's *Honnête Criminel*, which Garrick rejected for production in an English translation (976).[20] Less than a month later, 24 March, Pembroke made an appointment with some mutual French acquaintances to visit Hampton, and at the same time, on Garrick's solicitations, he subscribed to Hawkesworth's *Telemachus*. On 20 March 1771 Garrick purchased a commission for his nephew David in the First Royal Dragoons, of which Pembroke was the commander, from which for reasons of health he later resigned to Pembroke's regret (1067,1169). About 1773 Garrick was elected to Almack's, a fashionable club in Pall Mall, later known as Brooks's, about which Pembroke wrote Garrick: "The Almackists, my Dear Sir, have, in one respect, done a foolish thing in choosing you of their club, as it will often bring me there, who have no other employment amongst them, but that of watching the cheats of the nobility, gentry, & others, who compose it" (954 n.1).[21] In the later years the Garricks and Pembrokes were occasionally together at the Stratford Jubilee, at Hampton, and Wilton House.

An even younger man, The Honorable Thomas Fitzmaurice (1742–93), Garrick's junior by 25 years, shared with Garrick both French and English friends. He was the brother of Lord Shelburne, about whom more at length shortly. Fitzmaurice had extensive estates in Ireland and a county seat, Knighton, on the Isle of Wight, for which he was M.P. when Garrick visited him late in July 1772. In 1773 he exchanged his parliamentary seat of Calne, Wiltshire, for Wycombe, Buckinghamshire, but resided in London in Pall Mall, near the Garricks, hence only glimpses of the friendship survive in brief notes setting up visits (702,702 n.3,787,787 n.6). Before the year of 1772 was out, Garrick had written Fitzmaurice on November 28 (in a letter that has not survived) on familiar terms regarding the production of his comedy *The Irish Widow*, performed at Drury Lane 25 October, and that he was perusing and correcting a composition, perhaps a revision by Fitzmaurice of *The Irish Widow* for production in Dublin. Fitzmaurice replied on 9 December from Dublin that he was leaving shortly for London.[22] On 21 December he wrote Garrick from Pall Mall hoping for a place in "Her Majesty's box," that is Mrs Garrick's in Drury Lane. On 19 January 1773, Fitzmaurice invited Garrick and Mrs Garrick to attend a "sitting at Mr Dance's" presumably for a portrait, and inquiring when "you sit next to Sir Joshua" Reynolds, an invitation that Garrick was unable to accept as he was going in quarter of an hour to Sir Joshua (739). On 19 April Garrick sent Fitzmaurice for his criticisms and observations an advertisement Garrick had prepared to announce his revision and production of Beaumont and Fletcher's *The Chances*, to be performed 20 April, to which Garrick replied he had accepted all observations but one and procured two seats for Fitzmaurice for the opening performance (758).[23] In three more brief notes later in 1773, Garrick thanked Fitzmaurice for a gift of strawberries from the Dowager Countess of Shelburne, Richmond House in Twickenham, inviting him for dinner at Hampton and congratulating him on the honorary degree of doctor of civil laws conferred on Fitzmaurice for his writing (760,782,801). More and more Mrs Garrick was included. Fitzmaurice married May, countess of Orkney *sua jure*; around 1775 he purchased Llewenny Hall, Derbyshire.

We have elaborated on Garrick's relations with Fitzmaurice to illustrate Garrick's capacity for establishing friendships in his later years, this time with a much younger man. The friendship was based not on name or fame, but on a literary content, the promotion of a publication, the revision of a play, social gatherings, and personal attachments, historically perhaps of secondary importance and interest, but a primary example of the qualities in Garrick's private life, not distorted by adulation, but pervaded with a liberal intellectualism as vital and fresh as in his early years.

To isolate in narrative and to concentrate on the episodes and communications in Garrick's personal friendships with the Rochfords, Burlingtons, Devonshires, with Pembroke, Lyttelton, and Fitzmaurice, is not to ignore the many other social occasions when the Garricks were guests. Even from the haphazard survival of mid-eighteenth century correspondence, the number and distinction of Garrick's acquaintances and friends among the landed gentry, the aristocracy, and court circles are overwhelming. Aside from the hundred and more letters to the Burlingtons, Devonshires, and Spencers and their correspondence, Garrick addressed on an average every twelfth letter to someone with a title, and he saved letters from 25 additional aristocratic correspondents to whom his own letters are missing. The names and titles are most impressive until the occasion of most acquaintances is inspected: either they sought Garrick or he addressed them for patronage, assistance in amateur dramatics, the favor of seats for a performance, acknowledgments—none of which we need to pursue here: for example Sir Grey Cooper, secretary to the treasury; John Montagu, fourth earl of Sandwich, lord of the admiralty; and Sir William Young, lieutenant-governor of the Island of Dominica.

Apart from the visits to Chatsworth, Londesburgh, and Althorp, not until the summer of 1771 were the Garricks generally invited to the luxurious summer parties that were the feature of country life among the aristocracy. In July and August of that year, the Garricks were successively the guests of General Conway and Lady Ailsbury at Park Place, Berkshire; Lord and Lady Edgecumbe at Mount-Edgecumbe in Devonshire; and Lord Lyttelton at Hagley. In the summer of 1772 the Garricks declined an invitation from Lord and Lady Hyde at The Grove in Hertford, but instead visited the Honourable Thomas Fitzmaurice on the Isle of Wight. In June 1773 they visited the Earl Temple at Stowe in Buckinghamshire; in August they were with the Earl of Shelburne at Bowood House in Wiltshire; and during that summer and the following they stayed with Lord and Lady Camden at Camden Place, Kent. The summer invitations of 1775 were from the Duke of Newcastle at Oatlands, Surrey; the Devonshires at Chatsworth, Derbyshire; and from Lord and Lady Ossory of Ampthill, Bedfordshire. They again visited the Ossorys in 1776, and were with Lord Palmerston at Broadlands in Hampshire in 1778. This accounting is by no means the complete record of all the Garricks' rounds of visits to mansions of the landed aristocracy. Often these invitations and acceptances were the result of but slight acquaintance, and there was little more in the association than the prestige of the title and the fame of the actor.

With all the dates and mansions and roster of guests gathered in animated social discourse, in conversations, rarely was a Boswell present, rarely has any record survived of the "discourse that trilled round." Of one memorable English weekend for all who were present a record survives, of a host, his guests, and some echoes of the dialogue.

William Petty (1737–1805), the first marquis of Lansdowne, better known as the second Lord Shelburne, the brother of Fitzmaurice, was one of England's more prominent statesmen, though very unpopular and much reprobated, and a great patron of literature and the fine arts. He was often at Mrs Montagu's parties; he assembled a magnificent library; Lansdowne House in London was the center of the most liberal and cultivated society of the day; Bowood, the Earl's country seat in Wiltshire, partly designed by the Adam brothers, in the Italian style with Doric columns, was set in a magnificent garden with a lake and mausoleum, laid out by "Capability" Brown. The Garricks had been his guests both in London and at Bowood, and in turn later entertained him and their mutual friend Morellet at Hampton.

In July 1772, Shelburne, who with his close political supporter Colonel Isaac Barré, had become acquainted with the Abbé André Morellet in Paris, prepared to welcome Morellet on his arrival for an extended visit of six months to England, by inviting to his country seat "High Wycombe" on the Isle of Wight a number of distinguished public and political figures. Shelburne, however, was unable to welcome Morellet on his arrival in London and act as host to Morellet and to the guests invited to High Wycombe, whereupon his brother, the Honourable Thomas Fitzmaurice took over the "long promised party" on the Isle of Wight in late July.

Shortly after Garrick reached High Wycombe, he sent to Dr John Hawkesworth, before his arrival, for his approval before publishing "them to y^e loving Company here," the following verses in tribute to Fitzmaurice:

> *The Golden Pen*
> To Me, the veriest Coxcomb then,
> *Fitzmaurice* gave a golden Pen;
> As long by him, It had been us'd.
> And Thro' it's point much good transfus'd,
> I thought, it would retain It's force,
> Let it but move, and wit of course:
> Tho in my hand so bright it shines,
> I wish in vain for golden Lines:
> Apollo sure my folly curses,
> And Midas' Fate in me reverses;
> His Ears indeed adorn my head,
> But at my touch, Gold turn to Lead:
> Give me again my Goose's quill,
> What's Pheobus' Lyre, without his Skill. (702)

Others who joined the company were Dr John Hawkesworth and Hans Stanley, M.P. (1720?–80), an active political figure, governor of the Isle of Wight, residing nearby at Paultons, where the Garricks were later his guests. For the weekend Stanley offered to make a "yatch" available to the party for excursions on the water. He was a good classical scholar, and in 1778 wrote Garrick as follows: "According to the Permission you were pleased to give me, I send you the Odes of Pindar, and shall be much obliged to you if in perusing them, you will mark any Place that you think wants Correction, or any Amendment; that occurs to you on a separate Piece of Paper; I can sincerely assure you, that there are very few Persons whose Criticisms or Emendations, I shall think so likely to improve that Work."[24] Later the same year the Garricks were guests at Paultons when Garrick was seriously ill; Stanley was one of Garrick's pallbearers.

To return, however, to the High Wycombe estate, July 1772. Other guests were Colonel Isaac Barré, after long service in the army, notably with Wolfe at the fall of Quebec, by Shelburne's patronage M.P. for Chipping Wycombe (1761–74). Finally of the party was Benjamin Franklin, "qu'il suffit de nommer," as Morellet concluded.

Morellet kept a full journal of the dialogues and debates, mostly on politics, economics, trade, American affairs, and tolerance. Garrick inevitably continued the debate, pursued earlier in Paris on the French evaluation of the merits of Shakespeare and had Morellet read *Richard III* and *Othello*.[25]

Franklin demonstrated his experiments on electricity and oil on water. Morellet understood spoken English with difficulty, but Garrick understood Morellet's French fully. He recalled the Garricks' visit to Paris when Garrick "avait pris quelque goute pour moi . . . pour la manière . . . sur celle dont je disputais, qu'il trouvait remarquable, me disait-il, par la véhémence et le naturel de mes mouvemens. Chez le baron d'Holbach, lorsqu'il me voyait aux prises avec Diderot ou Marmontel, il s'asseyait le bras croises, et nous regardait comme un dessinateur une figure qu'il veut saisir."[26] Further Morellet makes it clear that at the gathering at High Wycombe, Garrick was more interested in the various manners of communication than in the subjects, and later in London when Garrick invited Morellet to attend the production of *Othello* he insisted that Morellet watch Garrick's acting only, "tant il avait de confiance dans la vérité de son jeu. Je contrevenais de temps en temps à la défense, en ouvrant le livre que j'avais porté avec moi presque malgré lui. Il me faisait alors des yeux terribles. Je me déterminai à ne plus regarder que lui, et veritablement, quoiqu'un grand nombre de mots fussent perdus pour moi, si je n'entendais pas tout, il ne s'en fallait guère."[27]

The gathering at High Wycombe has been selected as illustrating Garrick's continuing, ceaseless attention to the diversity of human characters, especially in social intercourse, to grasp what qualities in gestures and dialogue enhanced communication. He was both a participant and a very acute observer of dramatic dialogue, in society and on the stage. And what an extraordinary cast he could observe at High

Wycombe: Benjamin Franklin, the most histrionic contemporary American figure; Wilkes by the power of his oratory, in 1772, sheriff of London and lord mayor, twice rejected by the aldermen; Colonel Isaac Barré, a massive, swarthy soldier, his face disfigured by a bullet still lodging in his face from the fall of Quebec, the most feared and effective parliamentary antagonist; John Hawkesworth, an aggressive journalist and self-made man; Fitzmaurice, the litterateur; Shelbourne, the established, cultured aristocrat; and the Abbé Morellet, a learned and aggressive controversialist.

The social diversity of the dramatis personae assembled at High Wycombe stands as a reminder, a tribute to the eighteenth century, that class distinctions did not always dominate social discourse, that an established society granted a margin of security to recognize and honor talent as well as birth. The guests at High Wycombe, the host also, were all brought together because of their demonstrated abilities, all were in some measure already known to each other. With two of the Englishmen, Garrick had been long acquainted: John Wilkes and John Hawkesworth.

## JOHN WILKES (1727–1797)

Garrick's first acquaintance and later friendship with John Wilkes grew out of the association of the Reverend Charles Churchill, George Colman, and Robert Lloyd at Westminster School—all three in various ways later cooperating with Wilkes and Garrick in diverse journalistic ventures. Churchill in 1760–61 had abandoned the church and teaching, deserted his wife to consort with prostitutes, from whom he contracted a fatal infection of syphillis, and was turning to writing for a living. Garrick had not yet met Churchill when on 16 March 1761 he published *The Rosciad*, which grew out of a close study of the theatre, satirizing most actors but praising Garrick. Garrick's offhand remark that Churchill was thereby seeking free admission to Drury Lane was communicated to Churchill, who responded in May with *The Apology*, warning Garrick of his displeasure. Churchill was immediately praised as a superior satirist, and Garrick well-advised or in apprehension wrote at some length to Lloyd, who could be counted on to pass on the letter to Churchill, what might seem rather a nervous commendation, to the effect: "At the first reading of his 'Apology,' I was so charmed and raised with the power of his writing, that I really forgot that I was delighted when I ought to have been alarmed" (267). Some months later, on 17 December, Garrick wrote Colman from Bath, "I have this moment seen our Friend Churchill" (280), and in half a dozen letters to Colman from late 1763 from abroad he asked especially to be remembered to Churchill, to be kept abreast with his writings. From Paris, 10 November 1764, he wrote Colman: "Churchill I hear, is at y$^e$ point of death at Boulogn . . . what a lust of publishing has possess'd him for some time past . . . I am sorry, very sorry for him— such Talents w$^{th}$ prudence had commanded the Nation" (341).

In the meantime, Wilkes in the 1750s had married and separated from a respectable heiress and had been accepted by the Beefsteak Club and the profane and profligate Medmenham Abbey crowd that included Churchill and Robert Lloyd, but his ambitions were literary and political. He had offended and made amends to Johnson, and was launched on a political career as a member of Parliament, only to be frustrated in his ambitions by Lord Bute, the prime minister. Whereupon, recognizing Churchill's satiric talents, Wilkes enlisted his collaboration in publishing *The North Briton* (1 June 1762) in opposition to Smollett's support of Bute in his *The Briton*. In this affair Wilkes and Churchill became embroiled with Garrick's good friend Hogarth.

In April 1763 Wilkes was prosecuted and under indictment by Parliament charged with seditious libel following the publication of *North Briton* No. 45. He fled to France in December, and on 19 January 1764 was expelled from the House. Later Garrick in Rome was much pleased that Devonshire had spoken often in Wilkes's defense. On his European tour Garrick followed with interest the affairs of Churchill and Wilkes, and wrote to George, after Churchill's death, about a bond Churchill had given him for a loan—"I ask'd him for nothing—he was in distress, & I assisted him" (343). When Wilkes left Paris for an Italian tour in December 1764 he turned over to the Garricks his "expensive lodgings in the Rue Nicaise" (344).

When Wilkes returned to Paris in the autumn of 1765, the Garricks had already returned to London. During the months their visits overlapped, and their separate year or so of residence in Paris, they were welcomed in the famous salons and shared many acquaintances and friends. Both men were much cultivated by the French intellectual aristocracy of the day, Garrick as the actor-critic and Wilkes as the political radical. The Paris encounters became a common ground of interests and communications for the later ten years and more they were together in London, each to his own profession—Garrick to new attainments in acting, and Wilkes as the great champion of personal freedom, as sheriff, and lord mayor of London, and M.P. from the county of Middlesex.

What drew these two men together? That Garrick sought the good-will of Churchill and Wilkes in the early sixties was normal, but not extraordinary, for Churchill had begun the relationship by praising Garrick, without Garrick's ever knowing him. He certainly loaned Churchill money out of compassion, not as any bribe. Why, one wonders should Garrick seek the company of men whose licentious manner of living he deplored, and whose reputations could only compromise him in the politer and more moral society he sought. Save for *The Rosciad* neither had much to contribute to Drury Lane theatre, though both often attended. Both Garrick and Wilkes had capacities within to create friendship. And friendship, Johnson notwithstanding, was not limited to an "unbosoming" capacity or process. Garrick understandably did not afford Wilkes the opening to unbosom his moral lapses pursued both for pleasure and self-confidence, such as his traveling in France and Italy not only with his daughter, to whom he was devoted, but trailing the notorious Italian mistress Carradini. The men had in common a devotion to French and Italian literature, some command of the classics, mutual friends, a capacity for sympathy and devotion, a candor, a professional competence, and above all else, gracious manners and wit. These last were to win over Johnson on a famous occasion when Boswell maneuvered an introduction of Wilkes to Johnson at Dilly's in May 1776: "Two men more different could perhaps not be selected out of all mankind. They had even attacked one another with some asperity in their writings," yet Wilkes won over Johnson, they, "had so many things in common—classical learning, modern literature, wit and humour, and ready repartee."[28]

The paradox had been divined years before when Garrick and Wilkes were first becoming acquainted in 1762, by Edward Gibbon. "I scarcely ever met with a better companion [than Wilkes]: he has inexhaustable spirits, infinite wit, and humour, and a great knowledge; but a thorough profligate in principle as in practice; his character is infamous, his life stained with every vice, and his conversation full of blasphemy and bawdy."[29] But the finer side shows in his letter to Garrick from Paris 17 January 1767:

> I keep a steady and a longing eye on dear England, but I do not know when I am likely to see its white cliffs again. Perhaps I may be doomed, like all my predecessors in Plutarch, to pass the rest of my life in exile: so dangerous is it to do great services to any country. If that should

be the case, I will alleviate the evil by philosophy, by the amiable philosophers you know this country [France] produces, by a good conscience, and the *superbiam*. I believe you will let me say *quaesitam meritis*. My place of banishment, at least, is left me, and the pursuit of those studies, which in every place and every age are the duty and ornament of life.

I am less dissipated than ever here, and my *history*, &c. advance very fast. If I had an amanuensis, I should send you some parts, but that is almost the only convenience I cannot have here. I enclose you a few trifles. The others of that kind I dare not venture, and they are too numerous.

I hear that you are collecting your works for publication. I rejoice at it. Do not be content with charming the present age, but command posterity to admire you, and give me the happiness of reading, when I cannot have that of seeing you. [30]

Garrick replied on 17 March sending Wilkes copies of the two plays he had written and produced that winter "as a small tribute of Gratitude for y^e great pleasure you have given Me" (449). The remaining fragmentary records and correspondence, following the High Wycombe gathering, cover invitations to Wilkes and his daughter Mary ("Polly") to Hampton, or to join Mrs Garrick in her box; congratulations to Wilkes on his election as sheriff, regrets that Garrick cannot accept an invitation, a wish "that a time may be appointed when we may *laugh & play & sing & tell old Tales*," and solicitation for help to have a lottery approved for the architects the Adam brothers' sale of the Adelphi (638,495,502,812,813).

## JOHN HAWKESWORTH (1715?–1773)

John Hawkesworth had probably been invited to the High Wycombe because of his current editing and publishing (1771–73) of *An Account of the Voyages Undertaken for Making Discoveries in the Southern Hemisphere*, by Banks and other explorers, the material for which Garrick or Dr Burney had obtained for Hawkesworth from their friend Lord Sandwich. Morellet solicited Garrick to negotiate with Hawkesworth that he and Suard translate the work into French.[31] Hawkesworth had been intimate with Johnson back in 1744, succeeding him as compiler of the "Parliamentary Debates" for the *Gentleman's Magazine*, and Johnson may have introduced him to Garrick. Johnson thought so well of him that he included him in the Ivy Lane Club about

1750 and invited him to collaborate with him and Bathurst and Warton in the *Rambler Essays*. With Johnson's advice and support Hawkesworth published a 12-volume edition of Swift's *Works* and a *Life*. In 1756 Garrick produced Hawkesworth's adaptation of Dryden's *Amphitryon*, made under his guidance and at his request, and he thought well enough of Hawkesworth's knowledge of the theatre to seek his support in rejecting Home's *Douglas* in 1757 (157,167,169,176,177).[32]

The Garricks and the Hawkesworths were on pleasant social terms, often being together at Hampton, and at Bromley, Kent, where Mrs Hawkesworth established an excellent boarding school. Garrick called upon him again to adapt Southerne's *Oroonoko* and Mrs Arne's *Edgar and Emeline*. The two were close collaborators, for Garrick sent him for advice and corrections an advertisement for his own adaptation of Southerne's *Isabella*, and for defense against the accusations of Dr John Hill, published by Hawkesworth in the *Gentleman's Magazine*. Garrick in turn assisted Hawkesworth in his review of Goldsmith's *An Enquiry into the Present State of Polite Learning in Europe*, in 1759, in the *Gentleman's Magazine* (198,222,226,228,236,238).

While supervising the schooling and upbringing of Samuel Cautherley Garrick asked Hawkesworth to engage a tutor and enroll him in Mrs Hawkesworth's school. Finally, which may in part account for Hawkesworth's being invited to join the gathering at High Wycombe, Hawkesworth had translated and dedicated to Lord Shelburne, Fenélon's *Adventures of Telemachus*, 1768 (228,229,236).

Garrick apparently did not join in the controversy, often very adverse, over Hawkesworth's handling of the *Voyages*, which brought on Hawkesworth's death, perhaps suicide, in 1773, but their long association and collaboration was almost terminated by a misunderstanding. Garrick had urged Hawkesworth to engage Becket as the publisher; instead he chose Strahan who offered him three times as much for the copyright, thereby guilty of what Garrick considered a "breach of promise" (762). To two of Garrick's very sharp notes all but terminating further communication, Hawkesworth wrote two admirable letters justifying his decision,[33] to which Garrick responded in candor, if not unbosoming himself, in a letter worth quoting in full, the draft being endorsed by Garrick "A very disagreeable mistake between us":

Dear Sir
It may be the fault of my temper but I am so form'd, that when my Mind receives a Wound particularly from the hand of a friend, I cannot get it heal'd, so readily, as I could wish—as I have always been thought, & by yourself too, very Sincere, Zealous & Active in my Friendships, I hope my being agitated (for any real or suppos'd Neglect of a Friend)

in proportion to that Zeal & Activity may meet with indulgence—the moment I am at peace with myself, I will answer your letter in the Spirit in which it is written, in y^e mean time give me leave to assure You that I am Your sincere Well Wisher & humble Serv^t (763).

## CHARLES BURNEY (1726–1814)

The weekend party at High Wycombe was in many respects typical of Garrick's social life in London and in the country houses, with commoners, the fashionable, and the aristocracy. All the while that individuality was respected and cultivated, there was always a pervasive presence of the outer world, the title, the position, the profession, the ambitions and attainments, more particularly patronage, a new book, current politics, critical evaluations, courtesies, and acknowledgments. Like so much of the drama, Classical, French, and English, the dialogues went forward in a public area, the drawing room, the dining room, the library, the garden, the hunt, the club—not in the privacy of two or three sitting down together, such as Johnson sought. Private social life depends much on propinquity, which Garrick enjoyed with Charles Burney, like himself at home in London. For their friendship we hopefully turn to the mass of diaries, journals, and letters recorded and preserved by the Burney family—a hope doomed to disappointment. The wealth of family papers passed to Fanny Burney, the daughter, who, we now know destroyed her father's journals of 1745–66 and many of his letters. In her *Memoirs* of her father, "hardly a single quotation from Burney's papers . . . escaped her interference," and her *Early Diary 1769–1778*, though more reliable was much cut and "edited" by her in her later years.[34]

As early as 1745 Garrick and Burney were together as members of the Drury Lane company, Burney his first year in London as a member of the orchestra under Arne and with Garrick as an actor, and after 1747, when Garrick became the manager, they participated in a number of productions. Garrick immediately extended to Burney the backstage privileges of the music room and of observing productions from the wings, all enlarging Burney's experience and understanding of dramatic technique[35] as well as of Garrick's ambitions and capacities as an actor-producer. Having won Garrick's favorable notice for his compositions for Moses Mendez's *Robin Hood*, a musical after piece at Drury Lane 13 December 1750 (and performances thereafter) Burney was commissioned to compose music for Woodward's *Queen Mab* 26 December 1750, which ran many, many times thereafter into the 1775–76 season. Burney continued almost immediately with music for the masque, *Alfred* (Thomson and Mallet), first performed at Drury Lane, 23 February 1751, when his most promising career in music was frustrated by a serious illness that forced him to settle in King's Lynn until 1760, when the family moved back to London to Portland Street.

At this juncture Burney vacillated between pursuing a history of music projected as early as 1753 or continuing as a composer for the theatre. When Garrick crossed over to the Continent in 1763, he left an adaptation of *A Midsummer Night's Dream*, with his deputy, George Colman, Burney being in charge of the music. Failing on the first production, 23 November 1763, Colman cut and redacted it into a two-act musical pantomime, *The Fairies*. On his return from abroad, Garrick engaged Burney to prepare a translation and adaptation of Rousseau's *Le Devin du Village*, eventually produced as *The Cunning Man*, with mixed success, 21 November 1766. The text was published by Becket and DeHondt, the second edition adding on the title page, "Imitated, and Adapted to his original music, by Charles Burney." Burney's career as a composer of theatrical music came to an end in 1767, however, when Garrick offered him the commission "to set to music an English opera call Orpheus."[36] When Burney, however, learned that François Barthélemon had also been invited to provide a setting for the piece, he was deeply hurt and returned his copy to Johnson, on the staff at Drury Lane, to whom Garrick immediately wrote (in part), "Pray tell M$^r$ Burney that I will sooner give up Every line that I Ever wrote than he sh$^d$ have the least reason to be suspicious of my regard & Friendship for him—the affair of *Orpheus* was done in a hurry & without thought, but as I have not a greater opinion of Anybody than of him I will pay M$^r$ Barthélemon immediately for what he has done & be happy that he (M$^r$ Burney) will take it under his Care & protection—I will have no Uneasiness about such a trifle" (475). Burney accepted the apology, but declined to carry out the commission for "Orpheus" and thereby ended his ambitions and career in the theatre.

As early as 1753 Burney had been contemplating and collecting a library for a history of music, from the inception encouraged and supported by Garrick. A fresh and decisive impetus came in 1763 when Burney gave Garrick a list of books to purchase for him in Italy and requested that Garrick send back to him reports on concerts and recitals he might attend—"the present state of music in Italy."[37] Burney's long-cherished wish to visit France was not realized until June 1764 when he went over to Paris to place two daughters, Esther and Susan, in a boarding school, returning the following summer to bring them home. On both occasions he bought books and visited libraries; according to Fanny, years later, from the sojourn in Paris "may be traced the opening of his passion for literary pursuits."[38] To gain academic accreditation, Burney matriculated and took the degree of Mus.D. on 23 June 1769 at Oxford, and thereupon determined to go ahead with his long projected history of music. He put his library in order and drew up a plan for the history. On 5 June 1770 he left England for his first tour. The incentive, the scope, and much of the success of this and later tours originated with Garrick and other friends, who by letter introduced Burney to many influential acquaintances. Through Garrick, Burney met Monnet in Paris who was "of great use to me afterwards in all my enquiries concerning books and persons."[39]

Before Burney departed on 7 June, Garrick on 3 June wrote his very knowledgeable and experienced Italian valet, Antonio Carara, introducing Burney, "my Particular Friend, & I must desire You to do him all the Service in Your Power" (587), and on the same day to "My Dear Suard. I shall make no apology to You for recommending my friend Doctor Burney to Your Acquaintance & friendship, because he is a most amiable, honest & ingenious Man. . . . [I]n this Gentleman, (my worthy friend) the honour and Genius of his profession, are happily united—You need but to know him to Esteem, & Love him" (588). From Naples on 17 October 1770, Burney wrote Garrick acknowledging the effectiveness of recommendations of him to friends in Paris, and reporting at some length on his Italian encounters and researches.[40] Burney recorded these carefully projected and profitable tours in journals from which he prepared and published in full detail three volumes. The first volume, *The Present State of Music in France and Italy*, was published 3 May 1771. "My father," Fanny wrote, "prints this book for himself. He has sent a multitude of them to his particular friends as presents: among others, to the famous Dr. Hawkesworth, to that charming poet Mr. Mason, to Mr. Garrick, and Mr. Crisp, who all four were consulted about it when in manuscript, and interested themselves much with it."[41] Volumes 2 and 3, *The Present State of Music in Germany, the Netherlands, and the United Provinces*, 1773, like volume 1, was brought out by Garrick's publisher Becket, on the encouragement of Holderness, Mason, and "Mr. Garrick my sincere and beloved friend." On the appearance of the latter volumes, Garrick wrote Burney: "Ten thousand thanks to You for your most kind & agreeable Present—I have . . . read a great deal of y$^r$ book—'tis clear, interesting, and instructive & delightful—Nothing can be more pleasing to y$^r$ friends nor more agreeable to y$^e$ Public" (759).

Through all the half dozen very laborious and trying years for Burney, from 1770–76, Garrick encouraged him directly and spread the word of his projected volumes. On one occasion Garrick passed on to Burney from Warton at Winchester the gift of a sixteenth-century treatise on music by Franchinus Gaffurius (645). Further he persuaded Goldsmith to invite Burney, along with Johnson and himself, to contribute to Goldsmith's projected "English Dictionary of Arts and Sciences," incomplete at Goldsmith's death, Garrick adding to his letter to Burney (11 June 1773), "The 2 Vol$^s$ of Tables in Musick are bought for y$^o$ & I will send them soon" (772). Early one morning in March 1775, Garrick calling on the Burneys in St. Martin's Street, while entertaining the whole family with some pantomimes and chatting with Dr Burney, inquired: "But pray, Doctor, when shall we have the History out? Do let me know in time, that I may prepare to blow the trumpet of Fame? 'He then put his stick to his mouth, and in Raree-show-mans' voice, cried', "Here is the only true History, Gentlemen please to buy, please to buy.'"[42]

Garrick and Burney associated with each other as professional and social equals. "Burney not only transcended his profession but simultaneously elevated it, in the same way as Garrick and Reynolds had won respect for the exponents of their arts by their own achievements and social demeanour."[43] Except for the eight years (1752–60) when Burney was almost exiled to King's Lynn to recover his health, and even in this period he was often in London, the two men for 30 years and more were neighbors in London, in each others company season in and season out, exchanging few letters generally only to set appointments.

Fanny Burney's earliest record, in her *Memoirs* of her father, of the private relations of the two men dates from shortly after the death of Burney's first wife on 27 September 1762, when the Garricks in sympathy for his grief invited him often into their home. She prefaced the passage: "The ensuing paragraph on his [Burney's] warm sentiments of this talented and bewitching pair, is copied from one of his manuscript memorandums."

> My acquaintance, at this time, with Mrs. as well as Mr. Garrick, was improved into real friendship; and consequently, on the Saturday night, when Mr. Garrick did not act, he carried me to his villa at Hampton, whence he brought me to my home early on Monday morning. I seldom

was more happy than in these visits. His wit, humour, and constant gaity at home; and Mrs Garrick's good sense, good breeding, and obliging desire to please, rendered their Hampton villa, on these occasions, a terrestrial paradise.

Mrs Garrick had every faculty of social judgement, good taste, and steadiness of character, which he wanted. She was an excellent appreciator of the fine arts; and attended all the last rehearsals of new or revived plays, to give her opinion of effects, dresses, scenery, and machinery. She seemed to be his real other half; and he, by his intelligence and accomplishments, seemed to complete the Hydroggnus.[44]

By 1766, Garrick had become acquainted with Burney's household; in a letter of 27 June, mostly on theatrical business, Garrick closed: "Mr$^s$ Garrick joins with me in our best Wishes to y$^r$ self and amiable Daughter—love to all y$^e$ Brats" (412), presumably the daughter he had in mind being Fanny. Her first reference to the Garricks in her *Early Diary* was in May 1771 when the Garricks with their nieces called on the Burneys in Queen Square. Thereafter, Fanny recorded several visits of which there were many more, to the Burney household, generally in the morning, when he greeted the children with pet names, entertained them with pantomimes and short teasing dialogues, and take-offs of acquaintances, his two favorite children being Charlotte whom he identified as "Comedy" in Reynold's portrait of Garrick between comedy and tragedy, and Charles. After one of the visits, Fanny remarked: "How many pities that he has no children; for he is extremely, nay passionately fond of them."[45] In turn the Burney children were often Garrick's or Mrs Garrick's guests in his box at Drury Lane, when they thrilled at Garrick in Bayes, Richard III, and Lear, and Dr Burney once remarked that they would like to attend a performance of Abel Drugger in Jonson's *Alchemist*.[46] Garrick responded, "I would rather have your family in my box, than all the Lords and Commons" (804).[47] Elsewhere she remarks, "he seems indeed to love all that belongs to my father, of whom he is really very fond."[48]

During the visits in the home and public encounters Fanny was more the observer than a participant, with one exception, as may be gathered from an excerpt of one of her letters to Samuel Crisp, included as a fragment in the addenda to the *Early Diary*. Following Garrick's retirement, he and the Burneys by chance attended the same performance at the Haymarket of *Hamlet* and *Piety in Pattens*, with Henderson as the Spanish prince. Garrick recognizing the Burneys came over to greet them. In the next day or so he called at Queen Square, wishing to borrow Simon Linguet's *Annales politique* (1110, 1111).[49] He then turned to Fanny: "But *Piety* in *pattens* blushed at shaking hands with me in 'public'. Didn't you? didn't you? then the folks all stared, and we (I admire his saying *we*) looked so handsome!" He then took off on Johnson, repeating Johnson's oft-repeated remark: "Yes, yes, Davy has some convivial pleasantries in him; but 'tis a futile Fellow." [50]

Expanding episodes from the *Early Diary*, plus additional material from hers and her father's diaries and journals, Fanny Burney took over in the *Memoirs* the biography of Garrick as well as of her father, with very little insight into the relations of the two men, except in one vignette. In the *Early Diary*, in 1775, she recounts a visit of Garrick, one morning, to Burney in his study—"Chaos" as Garrick dubbed it. "My father was beginning a laughing sort of an apology for his litter, and so forth, when Mr. Garrick interrupted him with—'Aye now; do be in a little confusion; it will make things comfortable.'" The men talked of loaning books; Garrick confused the wig-dresser with some pantomime; Garrick professed he was ready to "blow the trumpet of Fame" for the *History of Music* (a passage already quoted); he teased the children and the maid a bit; took off Johnson in the oft-repeated occasion when he wished to borrow Garrick's copy of Petrarch; and Fanny concluded: "In truth, I desire no better entertainment, than his company affords," [51] and that is about all she ever perceived. From about two pages of text, she later in the *Memoirs* expanded the episode, the visit to eleven pages. To this she added a second episode in conclusion recalling and accepting Goldsmith's "retaliation" for Garrick's distich on him: "Attend, passer by, for here lies old Noll; / Who wrote like an angel—but talked like poor Poll." The following was both Goldsmith's and Fanny's final word on Garrick: "He cast off his friends, as a huntsman his pack, / For he knew when he would he could whistle them back." [52]

Although Burney was hard-driven between his recitals, music lessons, and writing to support his family and did not win recognition or any financial appointments much before the publication of the *History* in 1776, and was often absent when Garrick called, yet the two men moved in the same general community of acquaintances, shared in memories and correspondence with Morellet, d'Holbach, Diderot, and Suard (1110,1111). [53] They were often together in the company of Boswell, Burke, and Reynolds, though infrequently in the Thrale household; both were members of The Club, Garrick in 1773 and Burney not until 1784. Both assembled extraordinary libraries in their respective professions; Burney once remarked: "Garrick, long since, said I had stript ev'ry stall in Moorfields." [54]

Although Burney's family did not continue their father's tradition in music, his son Charles became a classical scholar and a bibliophile. Garrick took particular interest in the boy, and on one occasion, calling to borrow some journals from Burney's library, Charles was at home and pleased to help (1231). When he was a "school-boy, Garrick spoke of him as '*Cherry Nose*'; . . . So (Fanny explains) Garrick has named poor Charles, on account of his skin being rather the brightest. Charles was a stripling when Garrick called him 'Cherry Derry,' keeping up the jest by changing the words in 'Hurry Durry'—a common expression."[55] In fact Charles's life was almost wrecked by "a Mad rage for possessing a library" that led him to purloin some classical books from the library of Caius College, where he was an undergraduate, for which he was expelled in 1777, and after a long and distressing recovery of himself, the penalty was rescinded. He assembled an extraordinary classical library, eventually purchased by an act of Parliament for the British Museum. Almost alien to his classical studies, his ministry in the Church, and his years as a schoolmaster, Charles, in memory and gratitude for Garrick's introducing him to the theatre and his kindness, assembled some 300 to 400 volumes of material for a history of the stage, now known as the Burney Collection.[56]

Although Fanny Burney's destruction of her father's papers has limited, even compromised the biography of her father, and for present purposes, his long and intimate friendship with Garrick, far more to be regretted is Burney's failure to carry out what he wrote his son Charles on 23 April 1806: "Much, obliged for your Garrickiana—but I shall not pillage the memoranda w$^{ch}$ you have been making of his Public character & characters—His private life & character is all I shall meddle with —& that I will venture to say no one knows better, if so well as myself—nor has anyone that I know of, among his biographers attempted to do him justice in that particular—Davies was never allowed to sit down in his house—Murphy never sat at his table—& Cumberland was his aversion—and he must have hated Garrick cordially—though for fear posterity sh$^d$ know that such Men as Garrick and Sheridan were his Enemies, he praised them highly."[57] From surviving fragments, it is not clear if Burney ever carried out his intention of writing a biography, or if he did, his daughter preserved only a few fragments perhaps incorporated in the *Memoirs*. No one was better qualified from long association, affection, and exacting standards of judgment; yet the wish to do Garrick justice was a tribute to Garrick's private life.

Two days before Garrick's death, Burney called at the Adelphi and though admitted to his chamber, was disappointed in finding him already in a coma. In the funeral procession, Burney was with White-

head, the poet laureate, Beauclerk, and Wallis, and in his doggerel
chronology memorialized Garrick, in part:

> Such dignified beauties he threw in each part,
> Such resources of humour, of passion, and art;—
> Hilarity missed him, each Muse dropped a tear,
> And Genius and Feeling attended his bier.[58]

# 12

# Garrick the Occasional Poet

·

Dr Johnson thought Garrick a sprightly conversationalist and one, despite his driving and busy life, who had written "more good prologues than Dryden."[1] Of his volubility—in company, in correspondence, in prologues and epilogues, in composing or adapting 67 plays—the evidence is ovewhelming. But his versifying, not much spoken of now, which showed all sides of his character—some superficialities, some profundities, much comical nonsense balanced by serious comment and feeling, by sensitive understanding, and complemented by bubbling gaiety—was great in quantity, and widespread in accessibility to his fellow men. Two admirers—a contemporary publisher and a modern scholar—enable us to assess the quality and the popularity of much of what he, with the resurgence of a sort of affected Renaissance *sprezzatúra*, would have called his ink-wasting toys. Actually he referred to his verse as some "comicality," but we must not be fooled (447).

In 1785 the publisher George Kearsley searched files of newspapers and periodicals collecting enough of Garrick's verse to fill two volumes, amazed that none of his friends and admirers had set themselves to the task earlier. "The Author," he wrote in his preface, "careless and indifferent about his smaller productions, dispersed them in such a variety of publications, that, were he now living, he would probably have found some difficulty in assembling them together, or even, without assistance, to recollect them." In 1955 Mary E. Knapp, having labored many years in locating not only the sources of the published verse, but also of an equal abundance still in manuscript—most of which passed around among friends in the Garrick circle—published her *David Garrick: A Checklist of His Verse*. She gives us 459 titles, about half of which were printed in over 1,000 places among contemporary periodicals and newspapers.[2] Professor Knapp notes that Garrick was "acclaimed by his contemporaries not only as the greatest actor . . . but as a successful and prolific minor poet," turning to verse over a life-long career to "ridicule his enemies, compliment his friends, comment on daily happenings." Having examined his existing manuscripts she notes that he wrote with "aptitude and point," but worked hard and painfully on revising his epitaphs, and often his prologues.[3]

Alexander Pope, we remember, "lisped in numbers" (as he wrote) "for the numbers came," and his instinctive but very polished outpouring produced thousands upon thousands of lines. Yet almost any articulate and educated man (or woman) in the mid-eighteenth century tried a hand at versification for an epistle, an epigram, a parody, a compressed and pointed comment. The succession of laureates did it all the time. The air was conducive to such expression. Ours not to make comparisons, however, but to look into Garrick's verse for traits which reveal the man, his interests, and the artist.

The "occasional verse" of the time lacks rigid definition as a genre, but yields paradigms a plenty. Its sheer quantity in English prosody down to Garrick's time makes it a force in the fashions of the age to contend with. Earlier it appeared largely in the "poetical miscellanies" (dating from 1521), but was on the increase until 1750 when, as Garrick found, outlets for its publication widened still with the proliferation of newspapers and periodicals. Sometime ago, Arthur E. Case produced *A Bibliography of English Poetical Miscellanies, 1521–1750,*[4] in which he listed 481 for the whole period, but more important for our purpose 74, which appeared from 1737 when Garrick went up to London to 1750 when he himself was turning out verses and publishing them. These 74 included such florilegia as *The Beauties of the English Stage*, consisting of the "most celebrated passages, soliloquies, similes, descriptions, and other poetical beauties in the English plays ancient and modern"—two volumes, which Garrick knew—and a large group of other titles, with content not so much selected from gems of the past as from new-written verse rejoicing in the titles of "The Delights of the Muses," "Miscellaneous Poems Never Before Printed," "The Muse's Library," several "Quintessences of English Poetry," collections of "Syrens," and "Larks," "Thrushes," "Robins," and "Garlands," "Poems on Several Occasions," "New Foundling Hospitals of Wit," and "Banquets of English Poetry." The rising reading public had an insatiable appetite. Nor did it lack instruction of how-to-do books to fashion occasional verse of all sorts. Witness not only Edward Bysshe's *Art of English Poetry* (with nine editions from 1702 to 1762), but John Newbery's *The Art of Poetry on a New Plan*, in two volumes, 1762, with chapters working up ways of writing (giving both precepts for genres and examples) from the epigram, epitaph, elegy, pastoral, and epistle (on subjects from health, exercise, and the passions) to fables, allegory, satire, and on to the summits of achievement—drama and epic poetry.

The verse of the "occasional" poem is, throughout, rather flush with the page, skillful at its best in its meters and attitudes, but engaged in "no metaphor swelled high," even as Dryden had characterized the verses of his "excellent friend Sir Robert Howard," back in 1660. The dominance of the couplet was marked in the vast quantity of the miscellany verses—with juxtapositions, antitheses, parallelisms, compression, pith, precision, and logic. "The triumphant quality, if such quality may be said to exist in this light artillery," writes a modern student of the genre, "lies in the fluid conversational mode. . . . It illuminates the habits, tastes, prejudices, and activities of people, most of them ordinary in the 18th century."[5] By Garrick's time its humor, by and large, is amiable, its raillery not very cutting (at least those qualities characterize Garrick's contributions), many in couplets, many in ballad quatrains, many in the rambling ode form, and some in a variety of other forms, including rhymed dialogue. Garrick knew the wealth of possibilities which English prosody offered in practice, but as a performer to whom lines were important (and couplets are the lines most easily memorized) he used that form heavily. Couplets also carry a loaded cargo which in recitation can be enriched by look, voice, or gesture. It is hard to think of Garrick's writing verse without thinking of its spoken rhythms and sounds.

Kearsley organized his edition under the accepted headings of the day for such verse—prologues and epilogues, songs, epigrams, epitaphs, and miscellaneous odes and sonnets. Garrick's 114 songs for his plays suit the music composed for them by expert musicians or sing themselves, now in iambics, now in anapests, now in dactyls. The allusions in many are stock-in-trade—the Sylvias and Damons of Roman pastoral legend:

> IF truth can fix thy wav'ring heart,
>   Let Damon urge his claim;
> He feels the passion void of art,
>   The pure, the constant flame.
>
> Though sighing swains their torments tell,
>   Their sensual love contemn;
> They only prize the beauteous shell
>   But slight the inward gem. . . .
>
> May Heav'n and Sylvia grant my suit,
>   And bless the future hour,
> That Damon, who can taste the fruit,
>   May gather ev'ry flower![6]

His earliest *songs* (1740) for Beard and Mrs Clive in *Lethe* differ appropriately for the characters they played.[7] Beard, as Mercury, becomes the "barker" for the waters of Lethe:

> Ye mortals whom fancies and troubles perplex,
> Whom folly misguides, and infirmities vex,
> Whose lives hardly know what it is to be blest,
> Who rise without joy, and lie down without rest
> Obey the glad summons, to Lethe repair,
> Drink deep of the stream, and forget all your care.

Mrs Clive, in a song which became popular in the sheet-music trade, sings as a Fine Lady going to a rout:

> The card invites, in crowds we fly
> To join the jovial rout, full cry;
> What joy from cares and plagues all day,
> To hie to the Midnight Hark-away![8]

The swing of a marching song, also wildly popular, which he wrote in 1756, after war was engaged in with France, sings itself:

> THE lilies of *France*, and the fair *English* rose,
> Cou'd never agree, as old history shows,
> But our *Edwards* and *Henrys*, those lilies have torn,
> And in their gay standards such ensigns have borne
> To shew that *Old England*, beneath her strong lance
> Has humbled the pride and the glory of *France*.[9]

On the other hand some airs in his *The Enchanter* (1760) have a beguiling simplicity:

> The birds in spring,
> Will sport and sing,
> And revel thro' the grove;
> And shall not we,
> As blith and free,
> With them rejoice and love?[10]

But the songs in his plays are not there as fillers, but to reveal character or advance the plot. The musical accompaniment by the Barthélemons, Arnes, and Oswalds of the time helps mightily to tune the solos, many duets, and some choruses. All are apposite to stage action. The joy of Miss Abrams's song in his last playlet, *May Day* (1775), though nothing startling, is romantic before its time.

> O spread thy rich mantle, sweet May, o'er the ground
> Drive the blasts of keen winter away;
> Let the birds sweetly carol, thy flow'rets smile round
> And let us with all nature be gay.[11]

Through such songs Garrick added in Johnson's phrase to "the gaiety
of nations," and increased "the public stock of harmless pleasure."
Garrick was also successful in writing epitaphs, many of them revealing a genuine sense of loss and regret for friends. He revised his epitaph for Hogarth many times, even submitting it to Johnson, as noted
in chapter 4, before he reached the form in which it now appears on
Hogarth's tomb in the Chiswick churchyard. In Bath Abbey, on the
tomb of James Quin, is inscribed Garrick's tribute to the century's
greatest Falstaff:

> THAT tongue, which set the table on a roar,
> And charm'd the public ear, is heard no more!
> Clos'd are those eyes, the harbingers of wit,
> Which spoke, before the tongue, what Shakespeare writ.[12]

His lines commemorating Sterne are a touching expression of admiration and fine friendship:

> Shall Pride a heap of sculptur'd marble raise,
> Some worthless, unmourn'd titled fool to praise;
> And shall we not by one poor grave-stone learn
> Where genius, wit, and humour sleep with Sterne![13]

The epitaphs on Beighton, Havard, and Paul Whitehead speak sincere
and gentle sentiments; in fact, his ten lines on the Reverend Thomas
Beighton have caught the elegiac flavor and gentleness of Thomas
Gray:

> NEAR half an age, with every good man's praise,
> Among his flock the shepherd pass'd his days;
> The friend, the comfort of the sick and poor,
> Want never knock'd unheeded at his door;
> Oft when his duty call'd, disease and pain
> Strove to confine him, but they strove in vain:
> All moan his death, his virtues long they try'd,
> They knew not how they lov'd him 'till he dy'd;
> Peculiar blessings did his life attend,
> He had no foe, but CAMDEN was his friend.[14]

In 1765 the son of old actor Robert Turbutt was charged with having stolen a silver goblet—an offense punishable at the time by death,
unless a nobleman interceded with the King. Garrick interceded with
Charles Watson-Wentworth, second marquis of Rockingham, in the
youth's behalf, and he was spared. In appreciation Garrick wrote his
nine stanzas of "Advice to the Marquis of Rockingham on a late occasion," which was printed in three magazines, and in two later collections:

WELL may they, Wentworth, call thee young:
What hear and feel! sift right from wrong,
   And to a wretch be kind!
Old statesmen would reverse your plan,
Sink, in the minister, the man,
   And be both deaf and blind . . .
You should have sent, the other day,
Garrick, the player, with frowns away;
   Your smiles but made him bolder:
Why would you hear his strange appeal,
Which dar'd to make a statesman feel?
   I would that you were older.
You should be proud, and seem displeased,
Or you forever will be teas'd,
   Your house with beggars haunted. . . .

Garrick then carries on with light irony about what an old statesman would have been like under the same circumstances, (Rockingham was but 27 at the time) and turns the advice in the final stanza into a compliment:

Indeed, young statesman, 'twill not do—
Some other ways and means pursue,
   More fitted to your station:
What from your boyish freaks can spring,
Mere toys!—the favor of your king
   And love of all the nation![15]

In 1757 Thomas Gray had broken new ground in eighteenth-century English poetry, both in tone and manner by publishing his Pindaric ode, *The Bard*, founded on a Welsh tradition that King Edward I, when completing the conquest of Wales, had ordered all the Bards that fell into his hands to be put to death—a stirring piece of narrative, dialogue, and prophecy about the enduring nature of poetry and the ephemeral nature of politics. Garrick was one of the few Londoners at the time of publication who understood the poem and relished the new style. Even Horace Walpole, Gray's great friend and Garrick's disparager, wrote Garrick in appreciation of his verses "To Mr. Gray on the Publication of his Odes in 1757." With Garrick's permission he printed at his Strawberry Hill press five dozen copies (195 n.1). Garrick was never zealous about having any of his verses acknowledged and (characteristically one must say) wrote Walpole, "As My Name will be of little Consequence to M$^r$ Gray or the Sonnet, I would not chuse to have it printed w$^{th}$ it" (195). Some whimsy, some banter on public taste, some sensitivity, and some feeling for English tradition breathe in the lines:

REPINE not, Gray, that our weak dazzled eyes
    Thy daring heights and brightness shun;
How few can track the eagle to the skies,
    Or like him gaze upon the sun!

The gentle reader loves the gentle muse
    That little dares, and little means,
Who humbly sips her learning from Reviews,
    Or flutters in the Magazines.

No longer now from learning's sacred store
    Our minds their health and vigour draw;
Homer and Pindar are rever'd no more,
    No more the Stagyrite is law.

Tho' nurst by these, in vain thy muse appears
    To breathe her ardours in our souls;
In vain to sightless eyes, and deadn'd ears,
    The lightning gleams, and thunder rolls!

Yet droop not, Gray, nor quit thy heav'n-born art,
    Again thy wond'rous powers reveal;
Wake slumb'ring virtue in the Briton's heart,
    And rouse us to reflect and feel!

With antient deeds our long chill'd bosoms fire,
    Those deeds which mark'd Eliza's reign!
Make Britons Greeks again—then strike the lyre,
    And Pindar shall not sing in vain.[16]

Garrick's poetic *Epistles* of which a good many exist, are much in the tradition common since Chaucer. They were not in general for publication, but for a cheerful novelty to his correspondents. Seven such letters appear in the published *Letters*, to Richard Rigby (friend, unscrupulous politician, and paymaster of the forces), to Samuel Foote, Henry Wilmot (a solicitor of Gray's Inn, who often entertained the Garricks), Richard Owen Cambridge (a Twickenham gentleman of leisure and letters), Sir William Browne, M.D. (of the College of Physicians), Henry William Burnaby (amateur artist and caricaturist), and to Richard Cox (banker) (363,581,593,600,662,866,1250). For the most part they are bread-and-butter letters thanking the recipients for visits they made possible, or are suggestions which Garrick followed up. The flavor appears in the few lines to Sir William Browne, who in some bantering lines had warned Garrick about moving to the Adelphi Terrace, which might sink in the Thames. Garrick exercising his light-verse touch banteringly replied:

In vain, wise S$^r$ William, with horrors You'll fill me,
And foretell if I move to th' Adelphi t'will kill me:

Some friends somewhat Foolish have rung in my Ears
The same Silly doubts, and possess'd me with fears,
But Now I'll pack up & away in a trice,
For there can be no doubt, when *You* give advice. (662)

Garrick duelled lightly with Dr John Hill, antiquarian, botanist, critic, dabbler in medicine, playwright, in *jeux d'esprit*, some published in his lifetime, some not. When Hill criticized his pronunciation of the vowel *i*, Garrick replied:

If 'tis true, as you say, that I've injur'd a letter,
I'll change my note soon, and I hope for the better;
May the right use of letters, as well as of men,
Hereafter be fix'd by the tongue and the pen;
Most devoutly *I* wish that they both have their due,
And that *I* may be never mistaken for *U*.[17]

But his sharpest epigram on Hill concerned his play *The Rout*:

For physic and farces
His equal there scarce is;
His farces are physic
His physic a farce is.[18]

Although much of Garrick's verse is local and minutely topical in interest, he like other Britons was caught up with the fast flow of current political events as England became "Great Britain" in a very real way. "Never had England played so great a part in the history of mankind as in the year 1759," writes John Richard Green in his *A Short History of the English People*. "It was a year of triumphs in every quarter of the world. In September came the news of Minden [where six English regiments had routed the French drive into Germany]. In October came the tidings of the capture of Quebec. November brought word of the French defeat at Quiberon Bay." These battles stopped a French invasion (Quiberon) of England, laid foundations (Minden and the earlier [1757] battle of Rossbach) for the emergence of modern Germany, and stopped the encirclement by France of the American colonies (Quebec), incidentally moving forward the ultimate development of the United States. These piled on the conquests of Clive in India, at the battle of Plassey bred a psychology of comfort and the excitement of power in the English people, especially in London.[19] "We are forced to ask every morning what victory there is," wrote Horace Walpole, "for fear of missing one." No wonder that all Englishmen sang with fervor and joy Garrick's "Hearts of Oak" in 1759, and long after:

Come cheer up, my lads, 'tis to glory we steer,
To add something new to this wonderful year,
'Tis to honour we call you, not press you like slaves,
For who are so free as the Sons of the Waves?
    Heart of oak are our ships,
    Jolly tars are our men,
    We always are ready,
    Steady, boys, steady!
    We'll fight and we'll conquer
    Again and again.

The burden of the message came in the final stanza:

Great Britain shall triumph, her ships plough the sea;
Her standard is Justice, her watchword 'Be free!'
Then cheer up, my lads, with one heart let us sing,
Our soldiers, our sailors, our statesmen, our King.[20]

Nearly ten years later Garrick wrote to Boswell (8 March 1768), "I never was more flatter'd . . . that You should chuse my hurly burly Song of *Hearts of Oak*, to spirit up the Corsicans . . . tho I have heard it sung from North to South & East to West in England, yet I never dreamt that it would reach Corsica" (493). A major embroilment had been going on with the French, of course, since 1755, with consequences to Drury Lane theatre in the Noverre riots, as we have noted. Many poems of the day, and many of Garrick's Prologues rang with British jingoism and ridicule of the enemy that his audiences liked to hear. And his derision rings even in his epigram, which appeared in three magazines in 1755, on Dr Johnson's *Dictionary*:

TALK of war with a Briton, he'll boldly advance,
That one English soldier will beat ten of France;
Would we alter the boast from the sword to the pen,
Our odds are still greater, still greater our men:
In the deep mines of science, tho' Frenchmen may toil,
Can their strength be compar'd to Locke, Newton, and Boyle?
Let them rally their heroes, send forth all their pow'rs,
Their verse-men and prose-men; then match them with ours!
First Shakespeare and Milton, like gods in the fight,
Have put their whole drama and epic to flight;
In satires, epistles, and odes would they cope,
Their numbers retreat before Dryden and Pope;
And Johnson, well arm'd like a hero of yore,
Has beat forty French, and will beat forty more![21]

The "forty French" refer, of course, to the membership of the French Academy which did much to stabilize and make precise the French language.

Again in the area of the tilting of lances among friends of the Club, Garrick's "Jupiter and Mercury, a Fable," done in late 1773, seems to have led up to Goldsmith's famous "Retaliation." Jove asks Hermes to fetch clay so he can mold "an odd fellow." "Right and wrong shall be jumbled—much gold and some dross; / Without cause he be pleas'd, without cause be he cross." The portrait of the Quixotic Goldsmith turns into a left-handed compliment to his versatility, for Jove and Garrick grant him learning, ability, and fine taste:

> For the joy of each sex, on the world I'll bestow it:
> This Scholar, Rake, Christian, Dupe, Gamester, and Poet,
> Thro' a mixture so odd, he shall merit great fame,
> And among other mortals—be GOLDSMITH his name![22]

Goldsmith's "Retaliation" is familiar to all, where he likewise mixed praise with sharp banter, and describes Garrick,

> As an actor, confess'd without rival to shine;
> As a wit, if not first, in the very first line,
> Yet, with talents like these, and an excellent heart,
> The man had his failings, a dupe to his art.
> .  .  .  .  .  .  .  .  .  .  .  .  .  .  .  .  .
> On the stage he was natural, simple, affecting;
> 'Twas only that when he was off he was acting.[23]

The Goldsmith characterization, catchy and simple as it is, has plagued the image of the real Garrick through the works of his 13 succeeding biographers. Garrick's thumbnail sketch in a mock epitaph had preceded it. "Here lies Nolly Goldsmith, for shortness call'd Noll / Who wrote like an angel but talk'd like poor Poll."[24]

The badinage did not stop with one round, and he later dashed off a *jeu d'esprit* "On Dr. Goldsmith's Characteristical Cookery":

> ARE these the choice dishes the Doctor has sent us?
> Is this the great Poet whose works so content us?
> This Goldsmith's fine feast, who has written fine books?
> Heaven sends us good *meat*, but the *Devil sends cooks*.[25]

In a later letter Garrick alluded (playfully enough) to himself as "my Vinegarship," and to William Burke, a relative of Edmund's as "Your Peppership" (640).

Garrick's other turns of wit and epigram—"A Riddle," "Upon a Lady's Embroidry," "Lines on the Back of His Picture," "Upon a Lord's Giving a Thousand Pounds for a House," "An Old Prophecy in Gothic Characters"—all found their way rather promptly into print,[26] and amused readers then as similar bits amused the Augustans before him and amuse us now. We have taken notice of his longer poems pitched to more serious matters—his *Fribbleriad* (1761) against the snarlers of the X.Y.Z. papers; his *Sick Monkey* (1765) testing the climate for his return to acting; and his *Ode* on the occasion of the Shakespeare Jubilee (1769). Earlier, in the 1750s, Garrick had through attachment to the Marquis of Hartington increased his acquaintance with the Pelham ministry through acquaintance with Henry Pelham, the prime minister, and had gained a favor from him of a pension granted to James Ralph, writer and largely unsuccessful playwright (473). The line to the government was potentially useful to the manager and actor, but over and above utilitarian cares, Garrick seemed in the mid 1750s genuinely fond of Minister Henry Pelham. When he died in 1754 Garrick wrote an elegiac *Ode* to his memory, no more startling in poetic quality than most elegies for public figures, but seemingly the only one for Pelham. The death was unsettling, for he was a "peace" minister in the wake of Walpole. "See," wrote Garrick,

> as you pass the crowded street,
> Despondence clouds each face you meet,
> All their lost friend deplore:
> You read in ev'ry pensive eye,
> You hear in ev'ry broken sigh,
> That Pelham is no more!

He hopes, of course, that Providence will guide a new ministry, but laments the passing of the old, and as for him,

> No bounty past provokes my praise,
> No future prospects prompt my lays,
> From real grief they flow;
> I catch th' alarm from *Britain's* fears,
> My sorrows fall with *Britain's* tears,
> And join a nation's woe.[27]

But life went on, and his Drury Lane was engaged in a decade-long sprightly competition with Rich's forces at Covent Garden. To his repertory he added John Brown's new tragedy *Barbarossa* (with a long run), Woodward's new pantomime *Proteus, or Harlequin in China* (for a long run), *A Midsummer Night's Dream* turned into an opera, and a new masque by Mallet, *Britannia*. His prologue to *Barbarossa* cleverly concealed the playwright whose first attempt it was, and, his epilogue was more pensive—written for Woodward to speak, and minding the audience of its power to create "taste" in the theatre:

> In us reflection breeds a sober sadness,
> Which always ends in politics or madness:
> I therefore now propose, by your command,

> That tragedies no more shall cloud this land;
> Send o'er your Shakespeare's to the sons of France,
> Let *them* grow grave—let *us* begin to dance!
> Banish your gloomy scenes to foreign climes,
> Reserve alone to bless these golden times
> A farce or two—and Woodward's pantomimes![28]

His prologue to the opera *The Fairies* pointed its reliance on Shakespeare, and praised well and highly the music of Handel's pupil, John Christopher Smith. "They're sparks he caught from his great master's blaze!"[29] His prologue to *Britannia*, spoken in the character of a sailor, rang changes again on the English superiority complex, even as the clouds of war with France were gathering. Like many of his prologues this was a whipper-up of patriotism, in language and style calculated to stir his very mixed audience.

> What! shall we sons of beef and freedom stoop,
> Or lower our flag to slavery and soup?
> What! shall these *parly-vous* make such a racket,
> And shall not we, my boys, well trim their jacket![30]

As Professor Mary E. Knapp has noted in her study of all eighteenth-century prologues, their success as verse and as dramatic pointers "depended on the promptness with which they seized on the ephemeral and on the timeliness of their observations."[31]

Garrick was a master at both seizing upon timeliness and often in creating a timeliness in these barometers of audience taste. He started early (aged 24) by writing a prologue for *Pamela*, an adaptation for the stage of Richardson's very popular novel. Such occasional pieces had, above all to be clear, and move with quickened pace. He divides his 32 lines about equally to serve three purposes: to raise an image to catch attention, to move into the subject of the play, and to apply the moral.

> AS in the airy regions of Romance,
> The advent'rous Knight sets out with shield and lance,
> Straight his disinterested valour flies
> To helpless Damsels, and to Beauty's cries;
> This only motive rising in his breast,
> The god-like plea—of innocence distress'd.
> Thus dares our Author Errant of tonight
> In Virtue's aid romantically fight.
> . . . . . . . . . . . . .
> To-night his honest labour means to prove,
> A low-born virtue worth a great man's love;
> An honest pride, where conscious honour glows;
> An artless innocence—whence truth still flows.
> . . . . . . . . . . . . .

A merit greatly poor, that far outshines
The glare of titles, or the wealth of mines.
· · · · · · · · · · · ·

Yet some there are less liable to blame,
Who only want reflection to reclaim,
· · · · · · · · · · · ·

To such our Author offers this address,
Not certain nor despairing of success;
Amongst this cast of men he hopes to find
Some converts—for the honour of mankind;
On minds like these his morals may prevail,
And who escap'd a Sermon, feel this Tale.[32]

The prologue suited the preachy tale. Quite otherwise was the epilogue to his *Lying Valet* (November 1741), where Garrick spoke in the character Sharp, the lying valet he had just played. 'Tis a spoofing poetical essay on "lying" as a successful and universal habit, and for its closing lines one must imagine impish young Garrick laying his hand upon his heart, looking mockingly toward heaven.

Mine, tho' a fibbing, was an honest art;
I serv'd my master, play'd a faithful part:
Rank me not, therefore, 'mongst the lying crew,
For though my tongue was false, my heart was true.[33]

The wheel turned full circle with his epilogue to Havard's tragedy *Regulus*, which he wrote for Mrs Woffington to speak, and she could do it convincingly.

May ev'ry Matron *Marcia's* truth approve,
May ev'ry Maid like constant *Clelia* love!
May ev'ry *Decius* find a faithful friend,
And ev'ry *Corvus* meet the villain's end!
· · · · · · · · · · · ·

May ev'ry virtue be transplanted home,
And Britain boast the worth of Ancient Rome![34]

And so he goes through a hundred more such acting pieces, now talking straight to the point, now creating a delightfully brief beast fable with which to pink the customary inhabitants of box, pit, gallery, and upper gallery, now using fashions in food, in clothes, in gardens, in architecture as a base for introducing or commenting on a play, now working the strain of patriotism, almost always stressing a moral, breaking up a sort of ritual sameness by moving from narrative to dialogue, and even to singing prologues. "Happy that player, whose skill can chase the spleen," wrote he in his epilogue to *The Foundling* (1748), "And leave no worse inhabitant within." Such seemed to be his

ideal function for plays, but *also* for the reciting of prologues. Both he
and his actors lived up to the aim. He could sway an audience in the
space of 30 lines to dream his dream of seeing Shakespeare performed
movingly, and of grasping their own responsibility in the theatrical
partnership between text, actor, and spectator, in the face of the blunt
reality of an actor's needing to eat, as in his prologue at the opening
of the theatre in 1750:

> Sacred to SHAKESPEARE was this spot design'd,
>   To pierce the heart, and humanize the mind.
> But if an empty house, the actor's curse,
>   Shews us our Lears and Hamlets lose their force;
> Unwilling we must change the nobler scene,
>   And in our turn present you Harlequin;
> Quit Poets, and set Carpenter's to work,
>   Shew gaudy scenes, or mount the vaulting Turk:
> For tho' we Actors, one and all, agree
>   Boldly to struggle for our—vanity,
> If want comes on, importance must retreat;
>   Our first great ruling passion is—to eat
> To keep the field all methods we'll pursue;
>   The conflict glorious! for we fight for you:
> And should we fail to gain the wish'd applause,
>   At least we're vanquish'd in a noble cause.[35]

The compactness, the turn, the play, the switch from tone to tone,
shows Garrick at his best. But he was there again and again, showing
remarkable dexterity in saying over and over again the same thing, but
always with a new and refreshing turn of phrase. Audience taste, and
its shifts, was the bone and marrow upon which the theatre throve.
Garrick reminded spectators again, and again in his various para-
phrases of Johnson's words "The drama's laws the drama's patrons
give," but he peppered and played upon the audience time after time
in cleverly devised reminders of what they were, and banteringly what
they could be. "What can provoke these wits their time to waste," he
wrote in his epilogue to *Athelstan* (1756):

> To please that fickle, fleeting thing, call'd taste?
> It mocks all search, for substance it has none;
> Like Hamlet's ghost—'Tis here—'Tis there—'Tis gone.
> How very few about the stage agree!
> As men with different eyes a beauty see,
> So judge they of that stately dame—Queen Tragedy;

whereupon in liveliest fashion he plays out in a dozen couplets the
reactions (and hence desires) of critics, tender ladies, belles, and how
they and the horsey crowd perceive the genre.

> Her ladyship, who vaults the courser's back,
> Leaps the barr'd gate, and calls you Tom and Jack;
> Detests these whinings, like a true virago;
> She's all for daggers! blood! blood! blood! Iago!

Having scored several identifiable types to our infinite amusement, he brings all round happily again—but his point has been made.

> If taste evaporates by too high breeding,
> And eke is overlaid, by too deep reading;
> Lest, then, in search of this, you lose your feeling,
> And barter native sense for foreign dealing;
> Be this neglected truth to Britons known,
> No tastes, no modes become you, but your own,[36]

and everyone is anxious to return to the theatre the next night.

Garrick's subtle tribute to John Rich (Lun), the master of body language in his harlequinades, combines with his announcement of an innovation in the field of pantomime, for audience taste demanded it and Garrick wanted pantomime to go well in his theatre. Thus his prologue to his *Harlequin's Invasion* (1759):

> BUT why a speaking Harlequin?—'tis wrong,
> The wits will say, to give the fool a tongue:
> When Lun appear'd, with matchless art and whim,
> He gave the pow'r of speech to ev'ry limb;
> Tho' mask'd and mute, convey'd his quick intent,
> And told in frolic gestures all he meant.
> But now the motley coat, and sword of wood,
> Requires a tongue to make them understood.[37]

Garrick could banter his audience, and he could apologize, not abjectly but with engaging whimsy, as he did in an "Address to the Town" in the character of Busy Body just after the half-price riots of Fitzpatrick had been resolved (1763):

> SINCE my good friends, tho' late, are pleas'd at last,
> I bear with patience all my suff'rings past;
> To you who saw my suffrings, it is clear,
> I bought my secrets most confounded dear.
> To any gentleman not over nice,
> I'll sell 'em all again, and at half price.
> Would I had been among you! for no doubt,
> You all have secrets, could I find them out.
> .   .   .   .   .   .   .   .   .   .   .   .   .   .
> There is one secret still remains behind,
> Which ever did, and will distract my mind—
> I'd give up all for that—nay, fix for ever,
> To find the secret—to deserve your favour![38]

On the last night of the season (4 June 1761) the proceeds of Drury Lane went to the benefit "for Decayed actors belonging to the theatres," which Garrick later was to turn into the permanent Theatrical Fund. The day also marked the declaration of peace, as French and English hostilities, long drawn out, subsided. Like most of his fellowmen Garrick was as eloquent for this peace as he had been enthusiastic for the drumbeats of conquest in 1759, so his prologue that evening was serious but suggestive of many meanings (national peace, theatrical peace, peace with the critics, and peace of mind among spectators). He assumed the style of straight talk.

> WHILE all is Feasting, Mirth, Illumination,
> And but one wish goes thro' this happy nation;
> While songs of triumph mark the golden time,
> Accept, for once, our grateful thanks in rhime,
> In plain, but honest language, void of art;
> Simplicity's the rhet'ric of the heart.

He was thanking them, of course, for attending in large numbers the benefit for old actors.

> What can we ask, blest with such favours past?
> This only—that those favours still may last.
> May this day's joy return with many a year,
> And, when it comes, with added joy appear!
> May Art and Science reach the topmost heights,
> May ev'ry muse prepare for nobler flights!
> May every blessing every hour encrease,
> And all be crown'd with that chief blessing, PEACE![39]

So effective was Garrick, in the eyes, minds, and ears of the people in this particular form of occasional verse that he was called upon, long after he quit the stage to provide such openers for managers, playwrights, and actors. He had handled most wittily a resurgence of genteel and overly sentimental comedy in his prologue to *Albumazar* (1773), to *False Delicacy* (1768), to *She Stoops to Conquer* (1773), where again the action by the speaker adds infinitely to spoofing the content of the text.

> EXCUSE me Sirs, I pray—I can't yet speak—
> I'm crying now—and have been all the week!
> *'Tis not alone this mourning suit,* good masters,
> *I've that within*—for which there are no plaistes.
> Pray wou'd you know the reason why I'm crying—
> The Comic Muse long sick is now a-dying.[40]

Garrick the prologue-smith of the century was a force not to be lost, therefore, he composed a prologue for the opening of the theatre under Sheridan's management in 1776, which was asked for repeatedly. Among other images he played upon the metaphor of the theatre as a stagecoach.

> Your late old coachman, tho' oft splash'd by dirt,
> And out in many a storm, retires unhurt;
> Enjoys your kind reward for all his pains,
> And now to other hands resigns the reins.
> But the new partners of the old Machine,
> Hoping you'll find it snug, and tight, and clean,
> Vow that with much civility they'll treat you,
> Will drive you well, and pleasantly will seat you:
> The road is not all turnpike—and what worse is,
> They can't insure your watches or your purses;
> But they'll insure you, that their best endeavour
> Shall not be wanting to obtain your favour;
> Which gain'd—gee up! the old stage will run for ever. [41]

In a period when Churchill slashed with the savagery of old Augustan satire, and when Foote mocked or corroded the objects of his verse and criticism, Garrick laughed gently and wittily in a silver stream of banter, piquant at times, but balanced with compliment. When serious he was straightforward and clear. He was as Johnson said "no common man, and the cheerfulest man of his age," so in his versifying he was alert to what was serious and witty in London life but happy to take his place among that mob of gentlemen of his time who wrote with ease, for his light social verse was graceful, his epigrams cleverly turned, his prologues and epilogues splendid.

# 13

# Garrick's Friendships with
# Women of Distinction

UNTIL Garrick left Lichfield at the age of 20, he had been rather surrounded by the women of his family and the wives of the officers and the clergy of the town. With his father away at Gibraltar and his brother Peter away at sea, he early assumed responsibilities for the household of his agreeable, but ailing mother, his ineffectual sisters, and a debilitated aunt. He responded with kindly tolerance at home, and was welcomed in the community as a lively, good natured, and spirited young fellow. Through his life he was concerned for the welfare of the Lichfield family. He patiently subsidized a sister and her husband, and later looked after the two daughters of his brother George, both socially and financially. In his associations and friendships with men in London and abroad he included the wives and daughters in all social relations and correspondence. All these women responded with gratitude and affection.

Young Frances Cadogan, daughter of Garrick's physician and good friend, William Cadogan, typifies such a relationship. From handling her father's social correspondence she began writing Garrick on her own about life in the Cadogan household and about her reading. Garrick replied in some 16 letters in the pleasant spirit in which she wrote. She was given the special privilege, along with Hannah More, of attending Garrick's funeral in Westminster Abbey. The same spirit of unaffected confidence graces his letters to his nieces Arabella and Catherine Garrick, and his wife's niece Elizabeth Fürst.

Professionally Garrick employed a succession of actresses, dancers, and singers, and female members of the Drury Lane staff. Only a few became friends—his leading lady Hannah Pritchard; her good friend Catherine Clive, with whom he corresponded at great length; and with Susannah Maria Cibber, toward whom he was always gracious. With one more, he was in love, Margaret Woffington. The tone of his letters to these few as well as to the many more with whom he corresponded, was gentle, businesslike, often patient, occasionally exasperated, but manifestly thoughtful of the recipient. Some few correspon-

403

dents, rejected authors and temperamental actresses, as we have seen, were explosive and unreasonable. They generally received well-tempered replies. Only occasionally do his letters go beyond the usual business negotiations to the social formality of invitations and notes of thanks.

In correspondence outside of the theatre circle, before his first more personal letter to Lady Spencer (1 June 1764), he wrote to only eight women: after his return from France and Italy until his death he wrote about 140 letters to 41 female correspondents, and with the passing of years he mingled more and more socially with a wide and delightful circle of women. The sources of this increase lay as much in external conditions as in Garrick. The salon, under the patronage of women, was spreading in England, and salons were attended by writers, painters, musicians, rarely actors; and public figures in the fine arts and literature were invited into the homes of the patronesses. More and more women aspired to write. On the other hand, Garrick temperamentally sought the company of women, less because of their flattery than for their sensitive refinement. He was as robust and masculine, as direct, as any of his male friends, a match at any time for such men as Cadogan, Richard Rigby, Samuel Foote, John Wilkes, and Johnson, and he played his low-character roles with the same gusto and imagination that he sensed and portrayed in his full range of male roles. He began, however, to understand and enjoy the distinctive psychology and individual personalities of women, no better example being his concurrent cultivation of the friendships of such diverse individuals as Frances Cadogan, Mme Riccoboni, Mrs Montagu, Hannah More, and Lady Spencer. While Garrick had the gift to win their confidence and draw out their personalities in ways that helped them cultivate their own separate identities, several women in like manner encouraged or enabled Garrick to reveal himself. Their importance lay not in their social position or literary reputation, but rather in the ways they influenced and brought out the personality of the actor in his private life.

## Eva Maria Violette, Mrs Garrick

Garrick's affair with Mrs Woffington had cooled and ended with the season of 1745. His acting and negotiations for management occupied his major thoughts for the succeeding year and a half until on 11 March

1746 occurred an event which was to influence his life and career until he died. On that day the play bills for the King's Opera House in the Haymarket announced in large letters: "Madem. VIOLETTE, a New Dancer from Vienna will perform this day for the first time."[1] She continued dancing in London, and although Garrick did not meet her at once, three years later she was to become his wife. He saw her dance and joined in the enthusiastic praise of her elegance and artistry shared by the public at large and by such connoisseurs as Horace Walpole.

Eva Maria Veigel (1724–1822) was born in Vienna on 29 February 1724, of Catholic parents, Eva Maria Rosina and Johann Veigel (Faigel). She was baptized in the Cathedral of Saint Stephen. Her father, formerly a valet to the Graf von Parr, was at the time of her birth a resident burgher of Vienna. Early she became a pupil of the imperial ballet dancer, Franz Anton Hilverding (1710–68), a pioneer in developing the ballet as an independent art, basing his compositions on a scenario and interpreting the action by natural movements. His reforms were later perfected by Jean Georges Noverre. Eva Maria Veigel was Hilverding's most successful pupil. As was the general practice, she assumed a stage name, Violette, the French translation of her family name. At the age of ten she danced publicly in the Imperial Company as Psyche in Hilverding's ballet *Amour und Psyche* (1734) at the *Karntnertortheatre*, when her talents were immediately recognized. She won entree to court circles. Prince Eugene of Savoy invited her as the solo dancer at his parties, and the Countess Rabutin became her patroness.

Court gossip circulated that she left Vienna at the wish of the Empress Maria Theresa to remove her from the attentions of the Emperor. Whatever the reason in 1746 she went to London, accepted a contract with the Italian Opera there, certainly with letters of introduction from the Stahrembergs to the Earl and Countess of Burlington, who upon her arrival became her ardent patrons. She had traveled thither in the company of her brother Ferdinand Charles, and an unidentified person by the name of Rossiter. She was in men's clothing and was seasick, along with most of the passengers, on the way from Holland to Harwich. In the company was Alexander Carlyle, later a famous Scottish divine, who discovered her sex from her voice and protected her from the rudeness of English inn servants on her journey to London.[2] Her early success was recognized in a note in Horace Walpole's letter of 5 June, "The fame of the Violetta increases daily,"[3] and by the fact that she was contracted by James Lacy for appearances at Drury Lane the following season.

The great actors had congregated at Covent Garden during the

*Devonshire Collection, Chatsworth*
Eva Maria Garrick.
Pastel by Jean Étienne Liotard, France, 1751.

1746–47 season, leaving Drury Lane with only Spranger Barry and Mrs Woffington, and a corps of dancers, under Mlle Mechel, Signor Soloman, and the new Italian dancer Signora Padouana. Eva Maria Violette joined this group. She first appeared there on 3 December in a grand comic dance, *The German Camp* and one called *The Vintage*, in both she was paired with Soloman, the premier dancer.[4] More grand dances followed—*The Turkish Pirate; or Descent on the Grecian Coast* (a grand dance involved the whole troupe), and another popular comic one called the *Laundress's Visiting Day*. "The comic entertainment," wrote a reviewer for the *London Courant*, "is a fine piece of low humour . . . and afforded a great deal of Mirth."[5] In both la Violette starred. On 14 January her absence from the dance caused "Noise at the Playhouse," for which she apologized two days later in a notice in the *General Advertiser*.[6] She was not hissed, therefore, when next she appeared. Remarkably she, a newcomer, was given a benefit performance early in the season (11 February) before the ballet master Soloman and his première danseuse, la Padouana, and even before the leading actors Barry, Mrs Woffington, and Mrs Clive. Her standing was no doubt aided by His Majesty's commanding her benefit performance.[7] Walpole continued his praise.[8] When Garrick became manager of Drury Lane in 1747, she had moved to Covent Garden. Actually when the two met socially is unknown.

Lady Burlington, flattered and stimulated by having so popular a person as la Violette in her patronage, set elaborate maneuvers afoot to provide a suitable marriage for her, with a coach and a coat of arms. But the young dancer was quietly responding to the attentions being paid her by Garrick. Both he and she, as the most popular theatrical figures of the current season, were invited to many social gatherings, such as the Duke of Richmond's riverside garden party for the Duke of Modena, where Horace Walpole observed Garrick "ogling and sighing the whole time." Although love between the two was mutual from the outset, the courtship was opposed by Lady Burlington, and Garrick sensed her doubts about him. After the wedding he wrote to the Earl, for transmittal to the Countess: "Your . . . Doubts proceeded from Your Esteem for her, & from a very just Opinion you had conceiv'd of y$^e$ People in my Profession" (57), and Mlle Violette, in turn aware of the Countess's social and material ambitions for her, had told Garrick, who passed the word along to the Countess, "that tho' She lik'd me very well, & was determin'd not to marry any body else, yet she was *as* determin'd not to Marry *Me* if Your Ladyship had put a Negative upon Me" (58). During the courtship the Countess was won over, but she demanded all the ceremonies, and a marriage contract including a dowry.[9]

On 6 June 1749, William Hogarth wrote his wife, "I dont know whether or no you knew that Garrick was going to be married to the Violette when you went away. I supt with him last night and had a deal of talk about her."[10] They were married on 22 June 1749, first in the chapel in Russell Street, Bloomsbury, by the Reverend Thomas Francklin, and later on the same day by the rites of the Roman Catholic Church in the chapel of the Portuguese Embassy. Mrs Garrick received the annual interest on £5,000 from Lady Burlington's Lincolnshire estates, and Garrick agreed to settle upon her £10,000, with £70 a year for pin money. They passed the first summer of their marriage in the residence of the Burlington's at Merton, outside of London, until October, when they moved into the house they had been renovating in Southampton Street.

Two months after the wedding (3 August 1749) Garrick wrote to the Countess, "I will likewise take care that our Mother at Vienna (for whom I have the greatest tenderness) shall be made happy with regard to her Daughter; did she know my thoughts, she would be very Easy; but as it is very natural for her to have apprehensions, so I shall look upon it as my Duty to quiet 'em, as soon as possible: I love & regard Every Body that belongs to her, & I flatter Myself that they will have Nothing to be sorry for, but the Loss of her, which (I can feel) must be no small Matter of Concern to 'Em" (63).[11]

Their marriage was indeed a remarkable one; testimony as to their mutual fidelity and affection abound, both from comments by acquaintances and from their own statements and actions. Near the end of his life Garrick asserted, "I have not left M$^{rs}$ Garrick one day since we were Married, Near 28 years." And Mrs Garrick's constancy continued in a widowhood of 43 years sustained and honored in the traditions and life-style of their years together. Their harmonious life together was founded and sustained by positive qualities of intelligence, character, mutual interests, and affection. A poem addressed to Garrick shortly after the marriage, ended with the couplet, "Who is the paragon, the marvelous she, / Has fixed a weathercock like thee?" He replied, in what was both a profession of his love and a prophecy of their lives together:

> 'Tis not, my friend, her speaking face,
> Her shape, her youth, her winning grace,
> Have reach'd my heart; the fair one's mind,
> Quick as her eyes yet soft and kind.
> A gaiety with innocence;

A soft address, with manly sense.
Ravishing manners, void of art,
A cheerful, firm, yet feeling heart.
Beauty that charms all public gaze,
And humble amid pomp and praise.[12]

Though much in the vein of love verses and poetic diction of the period, the qualities of his devotion to Eva Maria and the virtues he sensed in her were borne out in their lives.

Both were energetic and at the top of their professions; both were at home not only in the theatre but in aristocratic society. She charmed and continued to do so, all whom she met. Tucked away in almost every extant letter to him from hosts of correspondents is some compliment or best wishes to his wife. Sooner or later in addition to her native German, she had a command of French and Italian. Although she always spoke English with a German accent, she gradually, at first with Garrick's help, not only read English, but wrote her letters in fluent, though somewhat mannered, English. She collected Italian literature and continued to add to their large library long after Garrick's death. Both had experienced the rowdyism that occasionally occurred in the London theatres; she agreed with David's wish that she no longer be exposed to clamorous rivalries before and behind the curtain and gave up her career to support his. She read the plays he was contemplating producing; she attended rehearsals and productions and, in the evenings after a production, he turned to her for understanding, criticism, and support in evaluating his successes and failures. She was notably competent in matters of costuming, in music, and in every aspect of the theatrical dance. She was, indeed, the most informed, experienced, acute, and dependable advisor that Garrick consulted. Above all else she seems never to have lost a balanced sense of reality; "humble amid pomp and praise," often expressed in a wry sense of humor. If ever a man needed this saving grace, Garrick did; and she began administering it when they had been married less than a month. On July 18, she wrote the Countess of Burlington in a letter obviously with Garrick's help, that "his Swell'd Face began to be more troublesome than Ever it was, I thought by telling him a fat face is very becoming, I might perhaps bring him to compose his fancies, but then the nasty Looking-glasses to whom he flew every minute, destroy'd all my project—the next Day it was wars and wars, the pain was greater than before: I recollected a remedy, which was, Tobacco and a Large Bason of punch, that made him drunk and consequently Easy for helf a night, but then began again to complaind how much his Beauty Suffer'd—I try'd another thing which is compos'd of warm flower, wich entierly reduc'd the Swelling of his Cheek. in Short in three days hi was a beautifull as before" (58 n.3).

With shrewd observance and "quickness of eye", she remarked on the long contested rivalry between Covent Garden and Drury Lane in the production of *Romeo and Juliet* (1750): "I was at the Play Les't Saturday at Coven-garden, all what *I* can Say of it is, that M^r Barry is too jung (in his ha'd) for Romeo, and Mrs. Cibber to old for a garle of 18: the house was praty foul, but hafe Paf[y]s [i.e., came in after the third act for half price]. I wish thie woold finish both, for it is to much for my Little Dear Spouse to Play Every day" (app. A, p. 1344).[13]

Second only to their professional concentration and success in the theatre, the Garricks established three residences, the centers of their private and social life. A whole chapter [14] must be given to the magnificent art collections with which they furnished these homes to their own great satisfaction in a common interest in the fine arts and to the enjoyment of their widening circles of friends. The first, a house, no. 27 Southampton Street was within earshot of the Strand and a five-minute walk from Drury Lane. The building still stands with some survival of the old elegance in the paneling. Here they resided during the season at Drury Lane from October 1749 until March 1772, when they moved to the Adelphi Terrace, but it was in Southampton Street their many acquaintances and friends in London and foreign visitors to the city called by, often for a late and ceremonial breakfast.

Wishing not only for more room they purchased in 1754 and restored, over a period of 20 years, a villa on the banks of the Thames in Hampton, adjoining Bushy Park. In addition to gardens, a grotto, a Temple to Shakespeare, an elegant orangerie, there flourished in the gardens a mulberry tree planted from a slip of the famous mulberry tree in Shakespeare's garden in Stratford. To Hampton, the Garricks invited many intimate friends as well as famous guests from England and abroad; and exchanged calls with many landed and aristocratic neighbors, not the least being Horace Walpole.[14]

After the villa at Hampton, the Adelphi Terrace was the Garricks' third residence. When the Adam brothers in 1768 leased Durham Yard to build a block of fine houses, the Garricks had known them for some years and, in support of the undertaking, contracted to rent one of the units. Nothing quite like the Adelphi Terrace had been projected before: the brothers demolished all the buildings on the property and constructed great causeway arches along the Thames embankment; on the top of this masonry they laid out a handsome terrace overlooking the Thames, and overlooking the terrace a series of elegant residences designed and decorated in what was by then the most admired contemporary adoption of the classical style.

Although Eva Maria Garrick's marriage embraced fully both the theatre and the home, her companionship and influence reached out into English life. In the ten years she danced in Vienna, she was often a guest in the social assemblies of the titled and the court whereby she gained some insight into aristocratic society and cultivated refined manners herself. In England, received and patronized by the Burlingtons, she must have lived as a guest in Burlington House in Piccadilly, in "my little yellow room," for perhaps as many as three years and was introduced to the most fashionable titled society, and it was through Eva Maria that Garrick was welcomed into the Burlington household. On his own, he did not fully attain an entrée into the same level of society until in the 1770s, when as the greatest of English actors he was entertained in a succession of the great country estates. The general individual consequence for Garrick himself, however, was far greater than the social and cultural.

Eva Maria's subtle influence on Garrick in his tastes, in his standards of exemplary action, in providing a life at once agreeable and graciously social can hardly be overestimated. His cheerfulness as well as patience, his shrewdness as well as genuine compassion, his ego as well as his sense of obligation all found quiet and continuing support in her. She seemed to be universally beloved. Sterne wrote of her to Garrick from Paris (19 March 1762), "I see nothing like her here, and yet I have been introduced to one half of their best Goddesses."[15] Two years later Baretti wrote from Venice (14 July 1764) that he had "really a great value, and even affection, for your lady ever since she poured me a dish of tea the first time I saw her in London. I shall never forget that adventure, though she may. She did it in so graceful a manner, I could still paint her in that pretty attitude, had I Reynolds's or Guido's powers."[16] Fanny Burney and Hannah More praised her often, but it remained for Mrs Mary Delany to summarize all the tributes when she wrote, "As to Mrs Garrick, the more one sees her the better one must like her; she seems *never* to depart from a perfect propriety of behavior, accompanied with good sense and gentleness of manners, and I cannot help looking on her as a *wonderful creature*, considering all circumstances relating to her."[17]

More recently sociological and historical studies have been concerned with the probability that Garrick was acquainted with more women, professionally and socially, than his male contemporaries and thereby he participated in the general emergence of women as individuals in the third quarter of the century. Biographically, however, of more significance, he pursued and enjoyed friendships with four distinguished women, shared fully with Mrs Garrick socially and individually. Three of the four were virtually on their own and childless when Garrick knew them; the same three were writers and critically widely read; all four were quite distinct and diverse individuals. In their company and with their distinctive personalities, Garrick was stimulated and enabled to expand his own complex personality and to attain a commendably sophisticated intimacy of mutual interests, values, and warm personal affections. The superiority of their lives, their loyalty to the man as well as the actor are a measure of his intelligence, social graces, and abilities, a recognition, a tribute to an extraordinary personality.

## MARIE JEANNE RICCOBONI (1713–1792)

Garrick's earliest and most enduring literary friendship with a woman had its inception during the Garricks' residence in Paris from November 1764 to 25 April 1765, when he became acquainted with the actress-novelist Marie Jeanne Riccoboni (Laboras de Mézières). Their mutual devotion "cannot have grown out of occasional meetings at the *salon* of the Baron d'Holbach and it is reasonable to suppose that the actor and his wife were often the guests of Mme Riccoboni,"[18] then at the height of her fame and well established in fashionable Parisian society. They never were again together; during the 12 ensuing years, until Garrick's death, their friendship was pursued in correspondence in the spirit of the dominating theme of her epistolary fiction, of "sense and sensibility" in the affections of mature men and women, "une liaison sentimentale laquelle, pour avoir été réellement vécue, n'en a pas moins la beauté d'une création artistique."[19] Of the Garrick-Riccoboni correspondence that began in 1765, only nine of Garrick's letters survive of the 24, and perhaps more, that Mme Riccoboni acknowledged, while Garrick carefully preserved 38 of hers.

Marie Jeanne de Heurles was born in Paris in 1713 to parents of some means and education. Her mother's marriage was annulled when it was discovered the father was already married. Marie Jeanne was exposed to all the bitterness of the deserted mother, Marie Dujac, who early placed her daughter in a convent, where she was wretched. At 14 she returned to her mother, to escape from whom she married the first

Marie Jeanne Riccoboni.
Engraving by Bovinet.

413

man who came along, the Italian actor Antoine François Riccoboni, the son of Luigi, the director of the Comédie Italienne.[20] Six weeks after her marriage she joined the Comédie Italienne and for 27 years, until 1761, was cast in comic roles that were not congenial to her abilities or disposition. She retired with the usual crown pension of a thousand livres, on which with her later prose-fiction she had to support her "graceless" mother and her despicable husband until their deaths in 1769 and 1772. She briefly found an outlet for her affectionate nature in a liaison with young Comte de Maillebois, who deserted her in 1745 to marry the daughter of the Marquise d'Argenson. In 1772 when Garrick sought material from her for a short life he wished to prefix to the translation of *Sophie de Vallière* she responded: "J'ai mis dans un de mes ouvrages [*Les lettres de Fanni Butlerd*, 1757] l'événement qui a changé les premières disposition du sort à mon égard et sans le sçavoir, le public s'est vivement intéressé à des malheures qu'il a regardés comme une fiction," and then briefly and almost bitterly summarized her life until 1751, when she turned to writing fiction.[21] In 1755 she moved into an apartment on the Rue Poissonnière, which she was to share with an actress companion, Marie Thérèse Biancolelli, for 35 years. Before meeting Garrick in 1764–65, she had published five novels modeled on those of Marivaux and Samuel Richardson, and including a free translation of Fielding's *Amelia*, four in epistolary form; three professed to be translation from English with English characters. By 1765, her novels had gone through 26 editions; and in 1766 she dedicated to Garrick *Les Lettres de la Comtesse de Sancerre*, published by Becket and DeHondt. Many were translated into English, and were it not for the piracy and dishonesty of publishers she would have realized a small fortune from her writings.[22] The Revolution deprived her of her pensions, and she died in misery in 1792.

Although the prototype and settings of her prose-fiction were English, Mme Riccoboni never visited England, though often invited by the Garricks; instead she endeavored to cultivate English and Scottish visitors in Paris, among whom were David Hume and Robert Liston, who became the "father of the diplomatic body throughout Europe" and who taught her and her companion English.[23] She later by letter introduced Liston and Adam Smith to Garrick, who in turn introduced her to Isaac Bickerstaff, the playwright, Sir Richard Burke, and Philip Changuion the diplomat, with all of whom Mme Riccoboni later corresponded.[24]

Under the pressure of his manifold obligations, Garrick often wrote briefly and belatedly; Madame Riccoboni wrote far more at leisure and at length, full of affection for the Garricks. The casual reader must not be thrown off by the opening badinage, the disorder, the hyperbole, the flattery that was more witty than serious; she quickly turned to intellectual matters and business. Garrick responded in like manner: "How could a Lady of Y$^r$ wit & delicacy, make so good a creature as M$^{rs}$ Garrick (whom you pretend to love, & admire too) so jealous by writing such a flattering Love-letter to her husband? . . . you have a great deal to answer for, & what will put even your own Wit to difficulties to justify . . . I don't doubt but you well understand the difference between a *tinder* & a *tender* heart—I should imagine (if I have any knowledge in Character) that you, like me, have a *tinder* one and . . . M$^{rs}$ Garrick, has a *tender* one" (361). Both parties knew what they were about, and as Garrick remarked later in the correspondence, he reverenced "her too Much, to be always saying, Petit-Maitre-like, a Million of Nothings, at the Expence of his hearer." He founded his regard for her, he said, on "the best basis, that of a good Mind, & a better heart" (474). Often wittily imitating her opening elaborations, like her he turned quickly to the matter at hand, remarking once "now, my dear friend, I will finish this Love part of my letter . . . and proceed to business" (616).

The business generally consisted in finding translators and promoting the publication in England of her novels, by Becket and DeHondt. For example, when he found Arthur Murphy too involved legally to undertake a translation of her *Lettres d' Elisabeth Sophie de Vallière,* he found a translator in Macuen (about whom nothing else has been discovered) and saw the novel through the press. It was announced and favorably reviewed in the *Monthly* and *Critical Review* in July 1772, undoubtedly through Garrick's influence.

Although Garrick first became acquainted with Mme Riccoboni as a novelist and served her interests well with translators and an English publisher, they certainly soon discovered they shared as actors a far more common interest in the literature of the drama. They agreed that Mme Riccoboni might prepare some translations of English drama, to which end Garrick was to make a selection from Becket's stock. She preferred, she wrote, comedies to tragedies, modern rather than older but left the choice to Garrick. She in turn made her own selection: "J'essayerai de traduire tout ce qui me paroîtra pouvoir ne rien perdre de son agrément dans notre langue. . . . Notre bien aimé baron [d'Holbach] sera assez complaisant pour me revoir et me corriger."[25] She contemplated preparing a brief history of English drama as an introduction to the translation of a number of modern English comedies, but shortly abandoned the project. She continued, however, to build up her library of English dramatic pieces, and Garrick offered to send her "every Play, or dramatic piece as they are Acted, & before they are publish'd" (519). Progressing in her selecting and translation, she wrote Garrick a careful analysis of the differences between English and French tastes, as follows: "Mon ami, le goût de toutes les nations se réunit sur de certains points. Le naturel, la vérité, le sentiment inté-ressent également l'Anglois, le François, le Russe, et le Turc. Mais l'esprit, le badinage, la saillie, le ton de la bonne plaisanterie, chan-gent de nom en changeant de climat. Ce qui est vif, léger, gracieux dans une langue, devient froid, lourd, insipide, ou grossier dans une autre: la précision, la justesse, sources de l'agrément, ne s'y trouvent plus. Ce qui élèveroit un éclat de rire en France pourroit attirer une huée à Londres ou à Vienne. Partout la plaisanterie dépend d'un rien et souvent de rien est local. En général ceux qui se font un métier de traduire, ont peu d'idée de ces nuances délicates. Aussi n'ai-je jamais vu une traduction supportable."[26]

Garrick responded immediately: "You have really given so true & ingenious Account of national taste with regard to the Drama, that it would make a great figure in y$^e$ best Collection of letters that Ever were written. . . . Your Scheme of translation is a very right one, & Our Authors ought to thank you for making them palatable to french taste; Your Ideas upon that subject are so very exact & Striking, that I would advise you, nay Entreat you, to enlarge what you have said to Me upon that head, & publish it, before your translation, by way of Preface" (519). This she did in a four-page *Advertissement* for her first volume of translations, later called *Le Nouveau Théâtre Anglais* (2 vols, 1769). On publication, she immediately sent Garrick a copy of volume 1; he immediately took exception, however, to some of her observations on Shakespeare and Elizabethan drama,[27] communicat-ing his criticisms to the Chevalier François Jean Chastellux, who in turn passed them on to Mme Riccoboni. She immediately made a most spirited, informed, and dignified defense. She regretted she had upset him and wished no breach in friendship.[28] She removed the offending *Advertissement* from other copies, but it was reprinted in her *Oeuvres Complètes*, Paris, 1818. For a while she considered a third volume of some earlier English drama, such as Beaumont and Fletcher and Jon-son, but found, "Tout cela est si confus, si loin des moeurs; tant d'esprit, si peu de conduite, de raison, de décence, de natural, qu'en vérité cette lecture est un tems perdue."[29]

With all her devotion to Garrick, Mme Riccoboni did not, however, include any of his dramatic pieces in the *Nouveau Théâtre Anglais*, but responded to his gift of all his pieces with several flattering criticisms: Of *Cymon*, she wrote Garrick: "Vous avez ce qui manque à la plupart de vos auteurs, du naturel et de goût. Ce que vous appellez *humour* n'est pas rendu par le mot goût; Fielding, Swift ont ce *humour*, mais raremont du goût. Mettre tout à sa place, dire ce qu'il faut, ne jamais s'éscarter de la vérité, suivre la nature et ne pas l'outrer, viola la goût et votre pièce en est rempli."[30] Garrick made a special point of sending her *The Clandestine Marriage*, written in collaboration with Colman, which pleased her very much. Her translation was published in Amsterdam in 1768.[31] As for Garrick's other dramatic pieces, she wrote: "J'ai relu toutes vos jolies pieces, vous ave embelis beaucoup de nos sujects, mais il sont trop connus pour les présenter à des lecteurs avides de nouveautés. C'est dommage! Car sans vouloir vous flater, ce que vous appellez vos *farces*, sont les plus charmantes comédies du monde."[32]

While Garrick, on his part, promoted Mme Riccoboni's literary reputation in England and enlarged her knowledge of English drama, she in turn, more than any of his French correspondents, kept him informed on all the literary developments in Paris, books, plays, literary gossip, the shifting political scene, on friends and acquaintances: Fenouïllot, Diderot, Marmontel, Préville, Molé, Morellet, d'Holbach, Grimm, Suard, Favart, LeKain, Madame Necker, and Mlle Clairon. The Hume-Rousseau quarrel stirred her to a long and eloquent passage on the perversities and distortions of academicians and philosophers in all their egotisms and rivalries.[33] On Garrick's involvement in the current Shakespeare-Voltaire controversy, she remarked: "Il faut respecter les opinions générale, même celles qu'on désapprove, quand elles ne blessent ni la morale ni l'honneur."[34] With the passing of the years she commented more and more in almost every letter on the many contemporary English books she was reading, once annotating 47 titles in her library. The popularity of Young's *Night Thoughts*, she considered as marking a change in French tastes,[35] and as for sentimentalism, "le sentiment est la folie du jour, on se l'est mis si fort en tête qu'il rest peu dans le coeur."[36] Few had the temerity to write Garrick, as she did: "Occupé de l'apothéose de Shakespeare, sacrifacteur et favori du dieu dont vous consacrez le temple, daignerez-vous écouter la voix d'une simple mortelle?"[37] The calm and pervasive voice of this "mortelle" was not lost on Garrick, but on us who have not the time or patience to explore the contents and nuances of her letters on her private life. One can not but become thoughtful and compassionate, as Garrick did, in a friendship with a woman who could write of herself: "En cessant d'être jeune une femme n'est plus rien; j'existe encore et quand je ne devrois à ma petite réputation que votre connoissance et votre amitié je me sçaurois très bon gré de m'être fait auteur."[38]

For Garrick, she was a woman who lived intellectually, not content with the fashionable persiflage on current intellectual fads; one who like himself won and held her position in his and society's esteem by ability and accomplishment. In no other correspondence between Garrick and a woman (and with very few men) was there so sustained a professional content, an exchange of ideas and values about the theatre, writing, criticism, literature, and personal philosophy. In July 1772 he gave her a medallion portrait of himself, the artistry of which she praised, even more the "character" it portrayed. Again in 1777 he sent her a piece of jewelry, this time set with portraits of Mrs Garrick as well as of himself.[39]

The friendship between Marie Jeanne Riccoboni and Garrick was like an episode in the current epistolary fiction wherein women for the first time became vocal and emancipated, the medium of the refining of the affections between men and women. In her private life she was the recurring protagonist in the genre, the sensitive, intelligent, affectionate, and accomplished mature woman who attained and maintained an integrity and emotional balance in the face of all the inhumanity that contemporary society inflicted on the Clarrisa Harlowes, and she carried over in her letters to Garrick all the skills she perfected in her fiction. Her letters are long, personal, candid, reflective, an "evocation of the mysterious genesis of love in the sensitive woman."[40] First and last, to be sure, she constantly by example and precept made Garrick aware of the graces of the French enlightenment, the rationality, the objectivity, the espousal of tolerance and range of human values, the classical sense of tragedy, the cultivated manner that counts above all else. She discerned the distinction between Garrick the fabulous public figure and Garrick the private man, and sensed how the first often corrupted the second. If she had any conscious, or even unconscious motive in her novels and correspondence, it was that she wished to sustain the individual. In her next to last letter to Garrick, of 17 April 1777, she wrote: "Je ne sçaurois vous exprimer, mon très aimable et très cher ami, combien je suis touchée de sçavoir votre bonheur troublé par de cruelles maladies. Quel mauvais génie mêle l'amertume à tous les biens dont l'humanité pourroit jouir? Dans l'immensité des créatures qui habitent ce *meilleur* des mondes possibles, peut-être n'en existe-t-il pas une seule parfaitement heureuse. La plaisir et la peine sont momentanés, il est vrai; mail l'instant où la joie anime notre être fuit rapidement, au contraire celui de la douleur semble rallentir la march du tems; il laisse une profonde trace de son passage et livre l'âme à la crainte de le voir renaître. . . . Il vaudroit mieux chercher à la détruire que découvrir son origine. On ne lui connoît encore de remède que le plus impatientant de tous, la patience." [41]

The paucity of Garrick's surviving letters, the wealth of hers, hampers a balanced evaluation of what the friendship meant to Garrick. Limited though the records may be, yet supported by his correspondence with other friends, Garrick was motivated more than by her genuine and informed interest in the drama, or his benevolence of which there are many examples, or his love of fame, for she had little to contribute, by flattery, which poured in on him in and out of the theatre, or by a community of French and English friends in Paris. Rather he seemed to be responding as he did as a great actor, to the challenges of tensions and resolutions that were creative. He welcomed all her reporting of Parisian life, not simply as gossip, but as a reflective discrimination in human values. In the flux, the distractions of his public life, here was one who challenged him again and again to pause and reflect, and to this challenge he responded intellectually and humanely.

In almost a complete contrast in every way to Mme Riccoboni, Mrs Elizabeth Montagu dominated the cultivated life in London; she lived not in isolation as a recluse but always as a conscious protagonist of current cultural values in fashionable social gatherings. She was discriminating, detached and tolerant, and positive as regards human motivation and conduct; she and Garrick met, one might say, as socially sophisticated equals.

### MRS ELIZABETH MONTAGU (1720–1800)

With the growth of Garrick's fame and accumulation of wealth that enabled him to develop his villa at Hampton and later his town house in the Adelphi, and to entertain the expanding community of friends, the Garricks participated more and more in the mixed assemblies, or salons, of culturally ambitious London hostesses. The assemblies of these ladies with elegant town houses, few or no children, and more than ample inheritances and incomes, paralleled in a way the famous salons of Mme du Deffand, M and Mme Helvétius, the d'Holbachs, Mme Geoffrin, and others in Paris, where the Garricks had been warmly welcomed. Their professed purpose was to encourage informed and witty conversation on current subjects, to patronize learning and literature, to entertain distinguished friends and visitors to London. More often than not the hostesses sought to satisfy vanity, often in rivalries, and accepted, as did their guests, the conviction that the ultimate attainment of intellectual activity for cultivated men and women was social intercourse. Dr Johnson gradually abandoned the isolation of the creative writer to expend his powers in conversation, not limited to male company in club or tavern, but in the drawing rooms of a succession of hostesses who triumphed in his presence.

Flattery became competitive and prolix, in Boswell's words, "a commerce of reciprocal compliments."[42] The personal letter became a projection of conversations much taken up with enumerating assemblies, guests, and allusive flourishes, often attempting the sort of stenographic reporting of Boswell, Fanny Burney, or Mrs Thrale. The accomplished hostess maneuvered her guests to perform before an impressible coterie. The triumph, not to be denigrated by the uninvited, was achieved when each guest returned to his privacy pleased with his hostess, the refreshments, and himself. The sheer mass of such correspondence still defies organization by the modern scholarly toiler.

Mrs Garrick's diaries preserve something of a calendar of the many invitations they both extended and accepted.[43] From them one might make a long list of social goings and comings, but the quantity seems less important than the quality and tone of relationships made in them. The perfections in conversational talents, the emotional involvements and satisfactions, the sustaining capacities of the assemblies, were of the day that was at once ephemeral, contextual, personal, and hard to grasp by a later generation short of tireless study in depth of the personalities of all participants, of the range of the allusions, of the passing significance of the many diverse subjects brought up and, one might say, agitated. The round of assemblies presented a spectacle as if a company of actors in the same character roles, day after day, improvised an entertainment much on the same themes, with no audience, but for their own pleasure only—a comedy of manners from the stage of life. Garrick not only flourished in this refined social atmosphere, he contributed his talents and applauded those of others. The stimulation of his intelligence and his humanity, as well as his natural vanity, was all a part of the sustaining reward.

In the wide range and diversity of the aspiring and emerging hostesses, authoresses, critics, and intellectuals, Garrick cultivated and enjoyed a personal friendship with only a few. The most sustained was with the most energetic and successful hostess of them all, Mrs Elizabeth (Robinson) Montagu. She excelled others in the numbers of her assemblies and guests, in the elegance of the entertainment, in her skill of maneuvering, in her own extensive literary knowledge, and in her highly perfected graciousness.

Born into wealth herself, encouraged to develop her precocity in literature by Dr Conyers Middleton in Cambridge, she had the foresight to marry in 1752 a wealthy landed aristocrat, Edward Montagu, 29 years her senior. She found herself at an early age the wealthiest commoner (and after 1775 a widow) in London, with an elegant house in Sandleford and one in Hill Street, Mayfair. She also possessed almost limitless energy. By inviting to her parties men and women with a taste for literature and conversation—as she wrote Garrick, "I never invite idiots to my house"—[44] she rescued cultured society from whist and quadrille. Sooner or later she entertained everyone of any literary reputation. She had first seen Garrick as Richard III in 1742, when he was playing in Goodman's Fields. She and the Garricks began exchanging visits as early as 1752, and continued to do so until Garrick's death. They were often together at Bath, as guests of Lord Lyttleton at Hagley, in the houses of their friends, in Mrs Montagu's country home at Sandleford, and in London in Hill Street.

Much of their correspondence is taken up with extending, accepting, regretting invitations, thanks for hospitality, the occupancy of Garrick's or Mrs Montagu's box at Drury Lane, along with a quantity of mutual adulation. Later in their friendship Garrick wrote Lord Lyttleton, "Mrs Vesey [also a London hostess] is a most agreeable woman, Mrs Montagu is *herself alone*. Were they eighteen and I an Adonis of twenty-one, I should love one and adore the other—I would kiss the hands of the Sylph, but fall at the feet of the Minerva" (655). When Lyttleton passed this word along to Mrs Montagu she replied: "Even at that age I prefer'd adoration to love, not, perhaps, that I thought it the sweeter homage, but I was told, it was more perseveringly loyal."[45] But two episodes in their long acquaintance had a more personal literary content.

On 24 July 1770 Mrs Montagu sent Garrick the manuscript of a comedy with a covering letter in which she asserted the play was by a male acquaintance, and though "you may perhaps suspect me of having a hand . . . I do assure you, by all that is most serious, I have not therein either art or part; I have not either invented or corrected, nor knew anything of it till it was almost finished."[46] The labored tone is suspect. Garrick accepted the letter at face value, and three weeks later wrote her in all innocence and confidence about the play, called tentatively "Bon Ton": "I read over the Comedy with a most uncommon prejudice in It's favour, & Sorry, very sorry I am to say, that with all the influence M^rs Montagu has, & Ever shall have upon Me, I could not turn, or twist my Mind to approve of the Performance: The Scenes are merely dialogues without the least interest in the fable, or indeed Enough of a Story to carry on y^r Attention—I likewise think that the Characters are not well mark'd, & that the vis comica is wanting through the Whole—Lady Ethrington bids the fairest for a dramatic personage; but she is not new—the follies of her Ladyship have been so highly & exquisitely expos'd in one of the last Dialogues in Lord Littleton's Collection, that I should be afraid of It's Success upon the Stage" (604).[47]

The comic irony in the situation was that Garrick did not know then nor later that the dialogue in question, xxvii in Lyttleton's *Dialogues with the Dead* (1760) had been written by Mrs Montagu, and she, in turn, perhaps flattered by the impersonal praise, gracefully accepted the rejection of the play without once intimating then or later that she was the author: "I acquiesce in your sentiments of the comedy, as they are just, and I glory in your sentiments of me, because they are partial. . . . I wish I had powers for writing a comedy, because I know it would produce an excellent prologue" by Garrick.[48]

That same year, although Mrs Montagu had published her *Essay on the Writings and Genius of Shakespeare* (1769) anonymously, she took "the liberty to send [to the Garricks] . . . a book [the *Essay*], no otherwise worthy of their acceptance than as it is written by one who is proud of being known as their admirer and their friend."[49] Like the studies of many abler scholars, recalled now only in the history of Shakespeare criticism, Mrs Montagu's *Essay* in its day was informed, well-written and spirited, not to be dismissed as Johnson dismissed it because it was written by a woman, or because of the excessive praise of her friends. Clearly her sources were both from the stage and the study, and she continued a devotee of Garrick's productions of Shakespeare. She further won Garrick's gratitude when she had supported him in his defense of Shakespeare and the English stage in the controversy in progress in Paris, when he was resident there in 1765, as to the superiority of French or English drama.

In 1776 she attended the meeting of the French Academy and heard D'Alembert read Voltaire's attack and a defense.[50] Following D'Alembert's presentation, she was asked (she wrote), "by an Academician if I would answer this piece of Voltaire's, and [he] did not doubt but I could do it well."[51] Garrick welcomed her return to London in a letter of 26 October 1776: "I heard w^th pleasure of y^r being at the french Academy when Voltaire exhibited his malevolent Nonsense (for

*Huntington Library and Art Gallery*
Elizabeth Robinson Montagu.
Engraving by E. Bartolozzi from a portrait by Reynolds.

which too among other Obligations I thank You) upon our belov'd
& immortal Shakespeare: could any thing possibly add to my Admiration of M$^{rs}$ Montagu, it was the Expression of contempt & astonishm$^t$
which, I hear You put on, at hearing the Weak and impotent ravings
of Age, Envy, hatred & Malice" (1055). Later she regaled him with
the full report of the occasion.

As was true of so many of their mutual friends, the relations of Garrick and Mrs Montagu were predominantly social and not personal;
they almost invariably met in company that sooner or later included
Johnson, Reynolds, Lord Lyttleton, Walpole, Burke, the Spencers,
Mrs Thrale, Fanny Burney, Mrs Elizabeth Carter, and Hannah More,
and many more memorialized in the social, political, and literary histories of the period. Furthermore, Mrs Garrick, second only to her
long friendship with Hannah More, cherished her friendship with Mrs
Montagu, long after Garrick's death.

What did the friendship with Elizabeth Montagu mean to Garrick,
what does it reveal of his character? Mrs Thrale recorded in September 1778 that she remarked to Johnson: "Mrs Montagu is the first
woman for literary knowledge in England, and I hope I may say in the
world." Dr Johnson: "I believe you may madam. She diffuses more
knowledge in her conversation than any woman I know, or, indeed,
almost any man."[52] And on a later occasion he observed: "Mrs. Montagu does not make a trade of her wit; . . . but Mrs Montagu is a very
extraordinary woman; she has a constant stream of conversation, and it
is always impregnated; it has always meaning."[53] Johnson would not
have said the same of Garrick's literary knowledge in general, but
certainly no one had a greater command than he of the literature of
the theatre. Such was, nevertheless, both the source and sustaining
element in the long friendship wherein they met as individuals and as
equals. As for wit, neither labored to turn a phrase, to have their conversation recorded.

On the other hand both had no hesitation in exercising their special
skills: Mrs Montagu as a presiding hostess, Garrick as an actor who
animated what he had to communicate by voice and gesture, and each
respected and relished such skills. Further, both were very able in
handling their private financial affairs; they each knew the value of
money, spent it wisely, and enjoyed without ostentation the luxuries
that wealth afforded. Above all else, as Garrick imaginatively and effectively interpreted a wide range of characters on the stage, they
both sought, understood, tolerated, and enjoyed a wide variety of
characters in social life, including, of all eccentric wits, Dr Messenger
Monsey; and they were seldom fooled in their evaluations.[54] Yet such

an eclecticism, while it was discriminating lacked, as was often observed
by contemporaries, an obvious element of warmth or affection; that is
neither party had "particular" and intimate friends. Such passionate
human relations may well be a mixed blessing, and the less confident
too often seek an intimacy to support their ineffectiveness and loneliness, as Johnson did in his later years in the company of Mrs Thrale,
Fanny Burney, and Hannah More. Garrick's tensions year in and year
out originated and were resolved in his handling of himself and in turn
his company at Drury Lane, and Mrs Montagu in the management of
her household, the choice of guests, the redecorating of her houses;
but socially both functioned with confidence, both were sustaining
others. To gather socially with the Garricks and Mrs Montagu was to
be challenged, demanding though this may have been. Such gifts or
talents inevitably aroused resentments in rivals or the less accomplished, but in not one more sorely in being dropped or neglected
than Johnson. When he was forced by pending engagements to decline
an invitation, he wrote her (17 December 1775): "All that the esteem
and reverence of mankind can give you, has been long in your possession, and the little that I can add to the voice of Nations, will not
much exalt you; of that little however you are, I hope, very certain."[55]
When she replied kindly requesting he set a date, Johnson responded
(21 December): "I know not when any letter has given me so much
pleasure or vexation, as that which I had yesterday the honour of receiving. That you, Madam, should wish for my company, is surely a
sufficient reason for being pleased; that I should delay twice, what I
had so little right to expect even once, has so bad an appearance, that
I can only hope to have it thought, that I am ashamed."[56] Johnson so
wrote not out of gratitude that Mrs Montagu gave Miss Williams, long
his dependent and companion, an annuity from 1775 until her death,
but in respect for Mrs Montagu herself. "The greatest fault [according
to her biographer, Reginald Blunt] in her character was neither her
vanity nor her ostentatiousness nor her affectations, though of all these
she was and could be justly accused, but . . . her lack of that *don
d'aimer* which so transfigures life. . . . It is this passionless level of un-
swerving common sense, this steadfastness to the middle of the road,
this subnormal temperature of the mind which has made finer characters unsympathetic."[57] Not that she was unsympathetic herself, however; like Garrick she was most generous and never failed to share in
the sorrows of friends. Understandably, Garrick at times seemed overcome by the flattery of all sorts of acquaintances, most of all by the
aristocracy who sought his fame to distinguish their social gatherings,
and he in turn satisfied his own vanity by entertaining famous guests

at Hampton or in the Adelphi, no less than Mrs Montagu did in her two mansions, yet all the evidence supports the conclusion that these two sought each other's personalities,[58] not just the actor but the man, not primarily the fashionable hostess, but a woman with knowledge, taste, and judgment. Such a friendship is a measure of the intellectual and cultural stature of both Mrs Montagu and David Garrick. Of Garrick's regard for Mrs Montagu, there is his endorsement to one of her letters: "Mrs Montagu, first of women."[59]

## HANNAH MORE (1745–1833)

Garrick's friendship with Hannah More, as with Mrs Montagu, although generated and sustained by a common interest in the literature of the drama and the theatre and participation in the social ramifications of the Blue Stocking coterie, soon took on a distinctly personal meaning to each of them. Although they did not meet until 27 May 1774, they became intimately acquainted during the 1775–76 season, Garrick's final one at Drury Lane, the Garricks inviting her in the spring to be their guest at the Adelphi and at Hampton for several months, an invitation repeated in 1777 and 1778 during Garrick's retirement of two years before his death early in 1779. In the few months each year of their association in London and their limited correspondence, Garrick found in Hannah More the personality and affection he might have welcomed in a daughter. Always in the background and in the context of their friendship, were their frequent foregathering in the company of the Reynolds, Mrs Montagu, Johnson, Burke, and all the learned ladies whom Hannah More memorialized in her long poem the *Bas Bleu* (1782). Neither the extent nor quality of the friendship is to be found in their fragmentary surviving correspondence, Garrick's 15 letters generally, written in haste and on immediate business, with only two of any length and personal insight, while he preserved but 20 of what must have been more he received from her. What she professes as her criteria in correspondence also dominated her immediate social and personal relations. "What I want in a letter is a picture of my friend's mind, and the common sense of his life. I want to know what he is saying and doing; I want him to turn out the inside of his heart to me, without disguise, without appearing better than he is, without writing for a character. I have the same feeling in writing to him. My letter is, therefore, worth nothing to an indifferent person, but it is of value to the friend who cares for me."[60] The progress and the significance of the friendship are more objectively and reliably to be sensed, not so much in the correspondence as in a biographical narrative.

Hannah More was the precocious fourth of five daughters, who accepted and supported her recognizably superior capacities and with whom she lived in affectionate harmony all her life. She cultivated, pretty much on her own, a command of the language and literature of Latin, French, Spanish, and Italian as well as English, under her schoolmaster father, the tutors in the girls' school she and her sisters founded in her native Bristol, and through her now industrious wide reading. The Mores established themselves through industry, foresight, a social sophistication and hardihood, a hardheaded sense of values of a sound private school, so successfully that they accrued enough profit to have constructed an excellent schoolhouse in Park Street, the new and fashionable district in Bristol, to prosper there until 1790, when they retired in very comfortable circumstances.

Hannah was absorbed in the drama, notably in the productions of the Bristol Royal Theatre, built in 1766 from the contributions of 50 Bristol benefactors, according to Garrick who wrote the prologue and epilogue[61] for the opening performance, "the most complete of its dimensions in Europe." William Powell, from Garrick's company at Drury Lane, was the first actor-manager; Hannah assisted him in productions and sought the acquaintances of actors both in Bristol and later in London. Sooner or later many of the Drury Lane company, all except Garrick, appeared in the Royal Theatre or the nearby theatre in Bath, and Hannah's later letters to Garrick are much taken up with the current productions in Bristol.

In her twenty-third year she became betrothed to a neighboring squire, William Turner, 20 years her senior, who having postponed three times and at the last moment the wedding day, settled upon her an annuity of £200 in compensation for the humiliation he had brought upon her, whereby she became financially independent. She thereupon withdrew her full-time assistance to her sisters in the school and concentrated on literature and the drama. To enliven instruction in the Bible, she composed for the school *Sacred Dramas*, often produced before publication in 1782. She continued with the play, *The Search after Happiness*, produced from manuscript copies in many schools before being published in 1772 and going through nine editions by 1787. She acquired quite a local reputation as an occasional versifier, notably of epitaphs. She much enjoyed the acquaintance and the proposal of the Somerset poet, John Langhorne, who encouraged her with

427

*City of Bristol Museum and Art Gallery*
Hannah More.
Portrait by Frances Reynolds, 1780.

extravagant praise. The wealthy and established parents of students and other socially prominent in Bristol, such as Mrs Edward Lovell Gwatkin, who long continued her correspondent and friend, sought her company. Above all else, the sisters in their school, and Hannah in particular profited from the long friendship and guidance of their next-door neighbor in Park Street, James Stonhouse, physician, divine, later a baronet. With four degrees from Oxford, clinical studies abroad, he was, nevertheless, caught up in the evangelical ferment that later became dominant in Hannah's life, sought preferment, was appointed to several livings; he became an eloquent preacher and writer, residing after 1764 most of the year in Bristol, where he was active in Bristol society.

In the winter season of 1773–74, Hannah, age 28, intelligent, widely read, able, and socially mature, with her sisters Sarah and Martha, paid the first of their annual visits to London, carrying a letter of introduction from Mrs Gwatkin to Sir Joshua Reynolds's sister, Frances, who undertook to introduce them to her acquaintances, among others Baretti, Burke, Percy, and Johnson.[62] The sisters engaged a flat in Henrietta Street near Covent Garden, set out on extensive sight-seeing tours, including a visit to Hampton and Garrick's villa. Hannah's report to Mrs Gwatkin gives some sense of Hannah's range and vitality: "We went to see Mr. Garrick's [villa]: his house is repairing, and is not worth seeing, but the situation of his garden pleases me infinitely. It is on the banks of the Thames; the temple about thirty or forty yards from it. Here is the famous chair, curiously wrought out of a cherry tree [mulberry] which really grew in the garden of Shakespeare at Stratford. I sat in it, but caught no ray of inspiration. But what drew, and deserved, my attention was a most noble statue [by Roubillac] of this most original man, in an attitude strikingly pensive—his limbs strongly muscular, his countenance strongly expressive of some vast conception, and his whole form seeming the bigger from some immense idea which you suppose his great imagination pregnant. The statue cost five hundred pounds."[63] Most of all, the sisters attended the theatre, but were disappointed in Garrick's not appearing because of illness. They returned in May and saw him as Lusignan in *Zara* and in *King Lear*. Hannah forthwith wrote to Stonhouse an ecstatic account of the performance and her reactions; Stonhouse in turn on May 21 sent Garrick a copy of the parts of Hannah's letter relating to him, with a covering letter, which reads in part: "She is a young Woman of an amazing Genius, & remarkable Humility. . . . *The inflexible Captive*, (or Regulus) which I put into your Hands last year, & w^ch, as *Havard's* was on that Subject, you declind, has

passd two Editions, & is much admird.⁶⁴—And it will be the *Interest*
of yᵉ Players to *act* it at Bristol. . . . She ordered *Cadell* the Bookseller to present you with her Tragedy which I presume He did, & as
she is now in Town & Lodges at Mʳˢ H[*tear*]'s in Southampton Street
just by you, I could wish you wᵈ call on her to acknowledge the Receipt
of it.—You would not be displeased with the Interview, & I know she
would take it very kindly, as she has a great Desire to see you.

"I have heard *accidentally* you think the Death of Count Patkule
wᵈ be a fine Subject for a Tragedy. If this be a Fact, & you shᵈ think
proper of giving any Hints of a plan of that Kind to her, She would
probably do justice to it—if properly encouragd—but She is so very
humble in her own Nature, & so indifferent to Applause, that she is
easily discouraged. I don't *know*, that she *would* undertake it. She has
wrote another Tragedy taken from Metastasio's Olympiade I think the
Title is, much more full of Business, than the other, but she does not
care to bring it into public View. I have read it, & there are some
pathetic & interesting Scenes in it; but I have not Judgement enough
to know whether it would be likely to succeed *in Representation*.—
She has wrote some little Farces—which I have not seen—but I am
told she has a good comic Genius" (App. D, p. 1356).

Both the content and the tone of Stonhouse's letter indicate that he
and Garrick were acquainted, if not intimately, at least for several
years, most likely in Bath where Stonhouse often preached and Garrick vacationed for his health. Appended to his letter introducing Hannah to Garrick, Stonhouse repeated several passages from her personal
letter to him on Garrick's acting. Only her emotional exuberance on
Garrick as Lear is short enough to quote here: "How shall I convey to
you the remotest, the most glimmering Idea of what were my Feelings
at seeing Garrick in King Lear! Surely He is above Mortality.—Is
it possible He can be Subject to Pain, Disease, & Death, like *other*
Men?—And must those refulgent Eyes be ever clos'd in Night? Must
those exquisite Powers be suspended, & that Silver Tongue be
Stopp'd? His Talents are capacious beyond human credibility. I felt
myself annihilated before Him, & every Faculty of my Soul was
Swallowed up in Attention. The Part of *Lusignan* had only given me a
slight *Ebauche* of his Superlative Abilities: It was but the *Dawning*
of the intolerable Lustre, with which He shone in Lear. I thought I
should have been suffocated with Grief: It was not the superficial Sorrow one feels at a well-acted Play, but the deep, substantial Grief of
real Trouble. His Madness was the Madness of Nature, of Shakespear,
of Lear, of Garrick. In the Midst of the Play I whisperd my Sister
Patty—'I could never be angry with Him, if He refusd ten of my

Tragedies.'—In short I am quite ridiculous about Him.—Whether I eat, stand still, or walk—Still I can nothing but of *Garrick* talk. . . . Yet *my Heart ach'd* for the Depredations Time is beginning to make in his Face, which was not visible, till He appear'd in his own Form in the Epilogue; & of which He affectingly reminded us in these Words 'I was young Hamlet once'" (app. D, p. 1358).

Garrick, on his part, between his obligations to Stonhouse and his need or gratitude for comfort in his illness and the reassurance he had not waned as an actor, wrote Hannah More as follows: "M$^r$ Garrick presents his best Comp$^{ts}$ to Miss More, & her Sisters & as he is un-luckily Subpoened to Attend Westminster Hall to morrow Morning, he must desire them to give M$^{rs}$ Garrick & him the Pleasure of their Company on Fryday—the Coach will be with them between Nine & ten—what can M$^r$ Garrick say for the most flattering Compliment which he *Ever* receiv'd—? he must be Silent" (839).

What took place at this first meeting, Friday, May 27, and the im-mediate outcome is not known. Roberts, the editor of Hannah's and her sisters' correspondence, was either indifferent as to dates or the sisters supplied none, with the result that it is impossible to establish how much longer they continued in London.

In February 1775, the sisters returned to lodgings in London and in the ensuing six weeks they renewed ties with the Reynolds and Burke; they were often in Johnson's company, and almost immediately the Garricks called on them and Garrick entertained them by reading passages from Pope's *Essay on Man*. Hannah was introduced to Mrs Montagu in mid-February at one of her parties consisting of "Mrs Carter, Dr. Johnson, Solander, and Matty, Mrs Boscawen, Miss Rey-nolds, Sir Joshua." "Mrs Montagu received me with the most en-couraging kindness; she is not only the finest genius, but the finest lady I ever Saw."[65] Shortly after she could write one of her sisters, "I have been at Mrs Boscawen's. Mrs Montagu, Mrs Carter, Mrs Chapone, and myself only were admitted. We spent the time, not as wits, but as reasonable creatures: better characters, I trow. The con-versation was sprightly, but serious."[66] She attended the opera once with the Garricks who left London on April 1 for Bath from which place they visited the More sisters in Bristol, Hannah presumably re-turning to Bath with them to collaborate with Garrick in the produc-tion of her *Inflexible Captive*, which he had turned down earlier, on April 18 at the Theatre Royal. Garrick wrote the epilogue for the first production and made some alterations in the text. The production was a gala occasion in Bath attended by all the fashionable society.

Garrick's professional career was drawing to a close the first six

431

months of 1776, and Hannah's social and dramatic aspirations were on the rise. She came up to London in January where on the eighteenth she was with the Garricks in the afternoon, and with Dr Johnson in the evening. Shortly thereafter she and sister Martha passed three days at Hampton—"the temple of taste, nature, Shakespeare, and Garrick; where everything that could please the ear, charm the eye, and gratify the understanding passed in quick succession. From dinner to midnight he entertained us in a manner infinitely agreeable. He read to us all the whimsical correspondence, in prose and verse, which, for many years, he had carried on with the first geniuses of this age. I have now seen him in his mellower light, when the world has been shaken off. . . . The next time we go, Hannah is to carry some of her writing; she is to have a little table to herself, and to continue her studies; and he is to do the same." [67] In February Hannah dined at the Adelphi. "It was a particular occasion—an annual meeting where nothing but men are usually asked. I was, however, of the party, and an agreeable day it was to me. I have seldom heard so much wit, under the banner of so much decorum . . . Colman and Dr. Schomberg were of the party." She followed up with a party for Mrs Boscawen, Mrs Garrick, Miss Reynolds, Dr Johnson, Dean Tucker, and Garrick. "Garrick was the very soul of the company, and I never saw Johnson in such perfect good humor. Sally knows we have often heard that one can never properly enjoy the company of these two unless they are together. . . . Johnson and Garrick began a close encounter telling old stories 'e'en of from their boyhood days' in Lichfield." [68] In March Hannah, by invitation, moved into Adelphi with the Garricks, and accompanied them as they went back and forth to Hampton, attended parties with them, and assisted in giving parties in return. Of her residence in the Adelphi she wrote: "It is not possible for anything on earth to be more agreeable to my taste than my present manner of living. I am so much at my ease; have a great many hours at my own disposal, to read my own books, and see my own friends; and, whenever I please, may join the most polished and delightful society in the world! Our breakfasts are little literary societies; there is generally company at meals, as they think it saves time, by avoiding the necessity of seeing people at other seasons. Mr. Garrick sets the highest value upon his *time* of anybody I ever knew. From dinner to tea we laugh, chat, and talk nonsense; the rest of his time is generally devoted to study." [69]

On 19 March she met Boswell for the first time, the day before Johnson and he set out for Oxford. On 15 April she attended with the Garricks the trial of the Duchess of Kingston (Elizabeth Chudleigh); on Wednesday, 24 April she assisted the Garricks in giving a very elegant dinner for Madame Necker and her party who had come over from Paris especially to see Garrick in his final performance of *Hamlet* on Saturday the 27th: "We had beaux esprits, femmes sçavantes, academicians, &c., and no English persons except Mr. Gibbon, the Garricks, and myself; we had not one English sentence the whole day."[70]

All the while Hannah was attending Covent Garden and Drury Lane, the latter with Mrs Garrick during the season that included 27 performances of Garrick, seven in his final appearance in major roles. No more eloquent and discriminating appreciation of Garrick in *Hamlet* has come down to us than the several paragraphs that Hannah wrote Stonhouse, too long to be quoted in full, only the final lines: "So naturally, indeed, do the ideas of the poet seem to mix with his own, that he himself seemed to be engaged in a succession of affecting situations, not giving utterance to a speech, but to the instantaneous expression of his feelings, delivered in the most affecting tones of voice, and with gestures that belong only to nature. It was a fiction as delightful as fancy, and as touching as truth. . . . I found myself not only in the best place but with the best company in the house, for I sat next the orchestra, in which were a number of my acquaintances (and those no vulgar names), Edmund and Richard Burke, Dr Warton, and Sheridan."[71]

She saw Garrick once again in *Lear* on 21 May but returned to Bristol before 4 June when Garrick wrote her in acknowledgment and appreciation of her letter to Mrs Garrick, with an unidentified enclosure, concluding: "We have wanted You at some of our private hours —Where's yᵉ Nine? We want yᵉ Nine![72]—Silent was Every Muse— I can ⟨Say no more, but in plain English we love & esteem You—Yours my dear Miss More most affectʸ⟩" (1022; arrow brackets indicate conjecture by editors of *Letters*). She responded on the tenth day of Garrick's final appearance in a letter free from flattery and affectation that must have consoled Garrick as much as any he received: "I think by the time this reaches you I may congratulate you on the end of your labours, and the completion of your fame—a fame which has had no parallel, and will have no end. Yet, whatever reputation the world may ascribe to you, I, who have had the happy privilege of knowing you intimately, shall always think you derived your greatest glory from the temperance with which you enjoyed it, and the true greatness of mind with which you lay it down."[73] On June 12, Garrick acknowledged her letter, with a postscript in his own hand dictated by Mrs Garrick, concluding: "I have sav'd his Buckles for you, which he wore in that last moment, and which was the only thing that They could not take from him" (1024); "My Buckles my Wife gave me" (1112).

For the 12 months following Hannah More's return to Bristol and Garrick's final performance on 10 June 1776, and retirement, their friendship was continued by letters only. Hannah was occupied with writing her play *Percy*, and the Garricks were enjoying the new freedom in winding up the sale of the patent, convalescence, especially at Bath for Garrick in his now serious illness, and in visiting friends in the country. They were disappointed, by illness, in their hopes of visiting in July 1776, and again in the spring of 1777, the More sisters in Bristol. Hannah on her part made an extended tour and visit in April, May, and June, passing through London on the way to Bungay and into Norwich. Nearing the completion of *Percy*, she came up to confer with Garrick: "As soon as I got to London, I drove straight to the Adelphi, where to my astonishment I found a coach awaiting for me to carry me to Hampton. Upon my arrival here I was immediately put in possession of my old chamber." She continues: "Last Saturday we had a very agreeable day. Our party consisted of about twelve; for these dear people understand society too well ever to have very large parties. The Norfolk Wyndhams, Sheridan and Lord Palmerston said the most lively things. But Roscius surpassed himself, and literally kept the table in a roar for hours. He [?] his famous story 'Jack Pocklington' in a manner so entirely new, and so infinitly witty, that the company have done nothing but talk of it ever since. I have often heard this story; it is of a person who came to offer himself for the stage, with an impediment in his speech. He gives the character, too, in as strong a manner as Fielding could have done.

"After supper, on Sunday, Garrick read to us, out of Paradise lost, that fine part on disease and old age." [74]

During all the 12 months, from June 1776 to June 1777, when Hannah and the Garricks were not together, the writing and revisions of her play, *Percy*, were going forward in all candor and confidence by correspondence. She asked Garrick to check her sources in Percy's *Reliques*. [75] Mrs Garrick, and presumably Garrick also, read these first two acts, though their comments have not survived. Of the third act, Garrick wrote on August 20: "I don't think You were in y$^r$ most Acute & best feeling when You wrote y$^e$ 3$^d$ act—I am not satisfy'd with it, it is the Weakest of the four, & raises such Expectation from the Circumstances, that a great deal more must be done, to content y$^e$ Spectators & Readers" (1043). The criticism was repeated and continued in a letter of December 17: "I have read & Studied y$^e$ four—the 3 will do & well do—but y$^e$ 4$^{th}$ will not stand Muster—that must be chang'd greatly but how, I cannot yet Say. . . . I was very cold before about y$^e$ 4$^{th}$ Act" (1072). In the mid-summer of 1777 he admonished her: "Let your fifth act be worthy of you, and tear the heart to pieces, or wo betide you! I shall not pass over any scenes or parts of scenes that are merely written to make up a certain number of lines. Such doings, Madame Nine, will neither do for you nor for me" (1104). To this challenge she replied, "I tremble for my Fifth Act, but I am afraid I shall never make others tremble at it."[76] On 1 September she sent Garrick the full play; "I was very desirous to convey it to Mr. Harris through your hands, as you kindly offered to take that trouble. I have made great alterations."[77] She continued, however, to revise and on 2 November sent Harris through Garrick "an entire new copy."[78]

The production by Harris at Covent Garden was announced for 10 December 1777. Shortly after 2 November she came up to London to assist in the greenroom with rehearsals, staying in Garrard Street. "Pray what is the meaning of a hundred Miss Moors coming purring about you with their poems and plays and romances?" wrote Kitty Clive to Garrick, "Send them to Bristol with a flea in their ears."[79] Garrick provided the prologue and epilogue though both Johnson and Sheridan were considered. Garrick took command with all his stagecraft, with the result that the play was very successful, running 21 nights in December and January. On 11 December Garrick wrote Lady Spencer: "Our Tragedy has succeeded beyond our warmest expectations. It was receiv'd with the most cordial applause, & there was not a dry Eye in the house, so I have done my duty & shall now think of my Pleasure."[80] Hannah had a copy made for Garrick to read to Lady Spencer (1148). The praise was almost universal, the profits £600, plus £150 from Cadell the publisher, the total sum most carefully invested by Garrick for Hannah. On 22 March 1778, Catherine Clive wrote Garrick: "I must needs say I admire you (with the rest of the world) for your goodness to Miss More; the protection you gave her play, I dare say, she was sensible was of the greatest service to her; she was sure every thing you touched would turn into gold; and though she had great merit in the writing, still your affection for tragedy children was a very great happiness to *her*, for you dandled it, and fondled it, and then carried in your arms to the *town* to nurse; who behaved so kindly to it, that it run alone in the month."[81]

All the exertions and parties became so exhausting that Hannah fell ill and in January Mrs Garrick insisted that she move into the Adelphi, later accompanying the Garricks to Hampton until in April, when she returned to Bristol. During the two months and more that Hannah was their guest, the Garricks cared for her in her illness, extended to her the thoughtful courtesy of allowing her to come and go as she wished, entertain her friends, as well as participate in their social life. For example, "I dined with the Garricks on Thursday [April 9]. He went with me in the evening, only intending to set me down at Sir Joshua's, where I was engaged to pass the evening. I was not a little proud to be the means of bringing such a beau into such a party. We found Gibbon, Johnson, Hermes Harris, Burney, Chambers, Ramsay, the Bishop of St. Asaph, Boswell, Langton &c.; scarcely an expletive man or woman among them. Garrick put Johnson in such good spirits that I never knew him so entertaining or more instructive. He was as brilliant as himself, and as good-humoured as anyone else,"[82] an evening sensitively recorded by Boswell.

After Garrick's death in early 1779, Hannah, who had sent him some acts of another tragedy *The Fatal Falsehood*, which was not successful, turned from drama to evangelical journalism.[83] But aside from mutual interests in drama, Hannah, and Garrick, and their circle indulged in another fashionable exercise of the day, namely the passing round in manuscript (and sometimes publishing) pieces of occasional verse. She was considered the poet of the Blue Stockings; Johnson even flattered her as "the most powerful versificatrix in the English language."[84] Early in their acquaintance Hannah presented Garrick with her two ballads, printed by Cadell, *Sir Edward of the Bower* and *The Bleeding Rock*, gracefully dedicated to him. Garrick acknowledged the present by sending in return a printed copy of his *May Day; or, The Little Gipsy*. At one of Hannah's parties in February 1776, Garrick read aloud *Sir Edward* "with all his pathos and all his graces" so effectively that Hannah and Mrs Garrick wept.[85] Hannah sent other short pieces, and in mid-June 1777 Garrick sent her a draft of his prologue to *Lethe*, entitled "The Blackbird and the Nightingale," a fable accounting for his fated acceptance of an invitation to read a revision of *Lethe* at court. He asked her to mark what she thought was amiss, and to speak frankly, which she did (1104). Finally, the occasion of Garrick's being allowed to remain in the Gallery at Westminster Hall, through Burke's efforts, when it was cleared on motion from Charles Baldwin, M.P. from Shropshire, prompted him to send Hannah a spirited account, enclosing a copy of his "Verses on Mr B—Moving to clear the Gallery of the House of Commons when Mr Garrick Was Present, 1777," adding "you shall have y$^e$ first copy, tho' you must take care Not to suffer them to go from y$^r$ hands—I have, upon my word, given them to nobody" (1184).[86] At its best, occasional verse aspired to wit, satire, comedy, eulogy in human affairs. If some of the content and pleasures of Garrick's friendships is to be understood, the phenomenon, if not the occasional verse itself, must be recalled; and though limited, there is no better example than Garrick's exchanges with Hannah More.

What might appear to be a disproportionate attention has been given to the friendship of Garrick and Hannah More because she serves as a touchstone to Garrick in the private life of his home and in his association with the *bas bleu*. He was neither singular nor unique in responding to an attractive, vivacious, and intelligent young woman 20 years his junior. Hannah More, other than in the company of her sisters, had grown up in association with men and women her seniors, and in the Blue Stocking coterie all were older than she by at least one generation and to all, among others Johnson, her rather mature attentiveness was regenerating. More than perhaps any other individual, excepting his brother George and Mrs Garrick, Garrick welcomed her into his private life, not in a stereotyped liaison and not because of her aggressive piety and morality, which he honored, but out of respect for her as a talented and effective personality; in private life he valued her as he did others as an individual. After all what might a schoolmistress and evangelical moralist, the daughter of an obscure schoolmaster and his wife (a farmer's daughter), add to Garrick's fame or social position, or how might her flattery sustain his ego? Be it recalled that during the years of his friendship, from 1775 until his death in 1779, Garrick was cultivated by the establishment and the aristocracy, that his social life was a round of days and weeks in elegant homes and country mansions, that all the while he was involved in what for Garrick was a very exciting friendship with Lady Georgiana Spencer. And yet Hannah More was the only one ever invited into the Garrick household for not weeks but months at a time, who was welcomed as an almost daily companion in private as well as public social life.

First of all Garrick found in Hannah More a person like himself, who had risen in the world by merit only, who sought social life with a cultural content—a common devotion to literature, the theatre, history, poetry, both outgoing and yet responsive to others. He neither patronized nor sought to dominate her; he never burdened her with his age or illness or reluctance to retire. He held her to the highest standards in the theatre. In all the frustration of many irritations from the outside and of illness, there was always the saving grace of wit. When she was ill in her lodging in London in the spring of 1778: "The Garrick's have been to see me every morning. The other day he told me he was in a violent hurry—that he had been to order his own and Mrs Garrick's mourning—had just settled everything with the undertaker, and called for a moment to take a few hints for my epitaph.

437

I told him he was too late, as I had disposed of the employment, a few days before, to Dr. Johnson; but that I thought that *he* (Garrick) would praise me most, I should be glad to change."[87]

Above all else they consciously cultivated literature and supported the drama in the moral conviction that imaginative writing and the theatre were the most effective means for creating moral values in the individual and in social life. Actually Hannah More was a moralist both in Garrick's manner and also in Johnson's, hence her devotion to both men.

Finally perhaps the most extraordinary quality in Garrick's relations with Hannah More was his great kindness to her, thereby fulfilling what he and Johnson and Hannah held as the greatest of all human virtues, that is altruism, generosity, sympathetic comfort such as only a friend can give.

Garrick's later letters to her, after his retirement, are some of the best he ever wrote, and she in turn after her first nervous and rather effusive letters, wrote with information, with wit, concerned with ideas, with literary values, with a sense of gracious human relations. Their correspondence, surviving only in part, preserves some of the qualities of their conversations in the hours and weeks and months they were together.

On receiving word of Garrick's death on 20 January 1779, Hannah hastened to London to comfort Mrs Garrick "who was prepared for meeting me; she ran into my arms, and we both remained silent for some minutes; at last she whispered, 'I have this moment embraced his coffin, and you come next.' She soon recovered herself" to accept gracefully her widowhood.[88] Mrs Garrick did not attend the magnificent funeral ceremonies, but Hannah More, accompanied by Frances Cadogan, was granted in recognition of the friendship, the privilege, by the Dean, to attend the ceremonies in Westminster Abbey concealed in a small gallery in the Poets' Corner and immediately above the open grave. Her account of Garrick's final illness and burial is the most moving that has come down to us. It is some measure of the qualities in Garrick's character, above all else in his relations to his wife and to Hannah More, that for the 30 years after his death, each year Hannah More was welcomed by Mrs Garrick for a visit either at the Adelphi or at Hampton, in memory and tribute.

"I shall never cease to remember with affection and gratitude so warm, steady, and disinterested a friend; and can most truly bear this testimony to his memory, that I never witnessed, in any family, more decorum, propriety, and regularity than in his: where I never saw a card, or even met (except in one instance) a person of his own profession at his table; of which Mrs. Garrick, by her elegance of taste, her correctness of manners, and very original turn of humour, was the brightest ornament. All his pursuits and tastes were so decidedly intellectual, that it made his society, and the conversation which was to be found in his circle, interesting and delightful."[89]

## LADY GEORGIANA (POYNTZ) SPENCER (1737–1814)

Garrick, Madam Riccoboni, Mrs Montagu, and Hannah More, like most of Garrick's individual friends, had come forward professionally and socially each on his or her own merits. All were in one way or another strangers in Paris or London without the benefit, the background of an established family in a country seat. Except with the Burlingtons and Devonshires Garrick had never been able to enjoy to the full the leisured life of a country aristocrat, the mansions, the gardens, libraries, and galleries, the hunts, the dinners, the long afternoon and evening conversations with family and neighbors, until he was welcomed by Lady Georgiana Spencer. As perhaps the ultimate test of Garrick's capacity for social sophistication, he progressed from being a guest to becoming culturally a member of and at home in the country with an established aristocratic family.

By the terms of his inheritance from his ancestress, Sarah, duchess of Marlborough, John Spencer, in 1761 Baron Spencer of Althorp, in 1765 first Earl Spencer, was precluded from accepting any public office. The old Duchess stipulated: "This I think ought to please every body, for it will secure my heirs in being very considerable men. None of them can put on a fool's coat and take posts from soldiers of experience and service, who never did anything but kill pheasants and partridges."[90] Had she added foxes she would have anticipated the preoccupation of John Spencer, who lived to the full the private and much sought-after life of a wealthy aristocrat—traveling abroad; residing in London; hunting on his estate, Althorp, and elsewhere; entertaining many acquaintances and friends. Lady Spencer was the daughter of the Right Honourable Stephen Poyntz, who by his own abilities was a much respected official in court circles, honored (among other distinctions) by having King George II the godfather of his daughter, who was named Georgiana after the King. She and John Spencer were married privately the day after he came of age, and when she was 17. They enjoyed a very happy married life for 28 years. She occupied herself with her two daughters—one becoming the Duchess of Devonshire, often mentioned in Garrick's letters; the other, the Countess of Bessborough—and with her son, George John, viscount Althorp. Lady Spencer was a much admired and beloved hostess of an extensive social life at Wimbleton Park House and at Althorp, moving about on the Continent, in London, and among the fashionable country estates. She described her life in an extensive correspondence, much in part later published, and "each day wrote an account of the sport in the 'Chace Books,'" which still survive at Althorp.[91]

The Garricks met the Spencers sometime before 1759, possibly through the Devonshires, but more likely through courtesy visits as neighbors in Hampton and Wimbleton Park. On 13 June of that year Garrick wrote Mr Spencer soliciting his charity for a John Moody, who happened to be a guest, "When I had the honor of Seeing You & Mrs Spencer at Hampton. . . . Mrs Garrick & I should have paid our Duties at Wimbleton this morning had not we heard from poor Mrs Mostyn that you were in town."[92]

The acquaintance expanded into a friendship when the Garricks and Spencers were often together in Italy in 1763–65. In 1763 in Naples Garrick on Christmas day "attend[ed] Lord & Lady Spencer . . . to *Herculaneum*" (321). A month later, still in Naples, the Garricks were "continually with Lady Orford, Lady Spencer, Lord Exeter Lord Palmerstn & the Nobility of yᵉ Country" (323). They were together again in Rome, and later Garrick from Albano, near Padua, in a letter to the Duke of Devonshire (offering to purchase pictures for him) mentions Lord Spencer as being "in treaty" for some pictures. But "Lord & Lady Spencer left us more than a fortnight ago, & my Pleasures & Spirits are gone wᵗʰ them" (334). Back in London in the autumn of 1765 Garrick wrote Lady Spencer: "I must declare a truth, that since the death [October 3] of my great Friend the Duke of Devonshire, I never have had so great a desire of being taken Notice of by any body as by Lord & Lady Spencer."[93] In 1768 Garrick learned from Ambrose Isted that the Spencers had received a "bust" of him (possibly the one made by Nollekens in Rome). He wrote Cradock that he "could not wish it in more agreeable hands. . . . I am greatly honourd that they think my head worth the having" (527). In December 1770 Garrick asked Lady Spencer's aid in obtaining a living for his friend Evan Lloyd, the Welsh poet, to which Lady Spencer replied cordially on 30 December that such a living in Wales was beyond their influence, and continued: "It is an age since I have seen you or Mrs Garrick. I hope I shall have the pleasure when I come to town; and remember that you have long promised me a dinner, and a Paoli at

*Earl Spencer Collection, Althorp House*
Georgiana Poyntz, Countess Spencer.
Portrait by Pompeo Girolamo Batoni, 1764.

Hampton, of which I expect you should acquit yourself some fine day next summer." [94]

Sometime during the ensuing four years, Garrick sorely offended Lady Spencer, with a resulting hiatus in their friendship and correspondence. Exactly when or how the cordial relations were restored has not been recorded, though Garrick continued for some years to apologize for his offense. Pleasant relations were restored, however, in the spring of 1776, when Lady Spencer, along with many others, sought the special favor of seats to attend several of Garrick's final performances. With this opening Garrick solicited the Spencers as subscribers to his friend Benjamin Victor's *Original Letters, Dramatic Pieces, and Poems* (1776), dedicated to Garrick.

Lady Spencer and her friends exchanged charades and rebuses, some of which she sent to Garrick. He in turn sent one containing the word *Rayskill* which she misinterpreted as "raise hell" and which did not please her. Further she did not approve of a possible double meaning of Garrick's prologue to the revival of Congreve's *Old Bachelor* (19 November 1776). Garrick, thereupon, elaborated a much too long and self-conscious clarification of the misunderstandings, concluding: "Lady Spencer may be assure'd, that my Devotion can never be designedly sullied by impure gifts." [95] To which she responded: "Never send me such a Jeremiade again, as long as you live. I doat upon all your nonsense, but I shall never dare make any more saucy observations upon it, if you take what I say in such sober sadness. I was in hopes that you would either have acknowledged the truth of my lesson, and have kissed the rod, or that you would have been as pert as I was, and have called me a prude." [96] Her good humored response restored the former witty objectivity, and he continued to send her occasional verse and prologues in draft for her comments and approval.

Pleasant social relations were renewed on Garrick's retirement, and in July the Spencers and Garricks once again exchanged visits to Hampton, the Adelphi, and Wimbleton. In October the Garricks made a two-day journey to Althorp for a longer visit, when he must have been welcomed as a member of the hunt and wore the enviable red coat; in November he wrote, "I have been out at Hampton & riding my Althorp poney to get rid of the gout." Immediately Lady Spencer invited the Garricks to return for the Christmas season. When they replied they were unable to accept, she wrote: "And so you will not come, after all the pains I have been taking to make room for you. I am sorry for it; there are ten to twelve red-coats here already, and yours would have looked very smart among them." [97] The Garricks were again, however, guests at Althorp in December–January 1777–

78, and finally after several postponements, because of Garrick's serious illness, for a week or ten days in January 1779.[98] Garrick himself, in all good humor, entered into the spirit of the social acceptance and triumph of having his name entered in the Althorp Hunt, the most imposing roster of 46 sportsmen, gentry, officers, lords, and ladies.[99]

With a margin of leisure after his retirement in June 1776, Garrick formally solicited, as was the courtesy of the day, a correspondence with Lady Spencer, welcomed by her but with the understanding "that you would never expect me to be punctual [in replying], but write on from time to time, whether I answered your letters or not."[100] Whereupon, from the summer of 1776 until his death Garrick wrote Lady Spencer 51 letters, still preserved at Althorp, while but 14 of her letters to Garrick survived in the Forster Collection, 13 published by Boaden.[101] Consciously aspiring to excell or practice the epistolary art, as he did with others such as Boswell, Garrick wrote more at length than Lady Spencer and with animation and great pleasure, quite different in content and tone from those to Mme Riccoboni, Mrs Montagu, and Hannah More. Further, he expanded his letters to include a range of topics: the latest reports on the American war, a new style in head dress, electric eels, benefit performances for the Theatrical Fund, the comings and goings of the Duchess of Devonshire, anecdotes about servants, the perils of a journey into Wales, on his retirement, mutual acquaintances, anecdotes, charades, Benjamin Franklin and lightning rods, and his own comings and goings. The effusive and mannered style was not entirely conventional; an undercurrent of a slightly nervous or self-conscious desire to be ever agreeable and animated is redeemed by occasional flashes of wit and a sense of humor. Certainly he was pleased, even flattered, as were most of his prominent contemporaries to be so cordially noticed by Lady Spencer, to be a month-long guest at Althorp, riding out in the red coat of the hunt. When some rumor appeared in the newspapers about baronetcy for him, he wrote Lady Spencer: "I am so satisfy'd with the troubles I have undergone already, & the Honour I have of being smil'd upon by a certain Lady Huntress, that I would not, if I could, accept of honours which I don't deserve, & which cannot add a mite to my happiness, or keep my ancles from swelling, after a fortnight's rectification at Althorp."[102]

Garrick often endorsed the letters he received with a personal tribute. On several from Lady Spencer he noted: "Nature for ever!" or "Lady Spencer, always natural!", "Lady Spencer, delightful and natural."[103] The term "natural" Garrick clarified in a letter to Lady Spencer after visits to the Earl and Countess of Upper Ossory and Althorp:

"I thought in her presence, that I was return'd to the Stage again; she perform'd the character of Hospitality, & benevolence, not in that manner which captivates by natural true feeling, but as it is assum'd & put on, with various decorations, in order to cover the want of simplicity, & heart-felt kindness; O my Lady Spencer, one genuine smile of unaffected benevolence sent from the top of a table with these plain words—*Mr Garrick will you have any fish?*—is worth all that Counterfeit Art can say, has said, or will say to the End of the world."[104] He found in Lady Spencer as a hostess the ease and simplicity born of control and long experience, the naturalness he sought in his acting and recognized in the graceful performance of a musician or hunter. By exercising a most exacting control of herself, except when gambling at whist, she set the standards in her social relations and challenged all who came into her presence to respond from the better elements in their own personality. Garrick honored one of these standards when he wrote her (19 March 1778): "It is not in our Power very good Lady to attend you to night. Mrs Garrick has promised to take some Ladies to our box to see the *School for Scandal* and I am drinking with such spirit that I am not fit, for the Company of Lady Spencer."[105]

Even more directly and ironically, Garrick paid his tribute of admiration for Lady Spencer's unaffected, natural qualities in her manners and letters when he wrote her enclosing two letters to him from Mrs Montagu and Mme Necker, as follows: "Le Buryère says (who had it not himself) that Natural Simplicity in writing, & every thing, will ever be an over-match for finery & affectation. By my honour, (if I have any) I know no letters superior to Lady Spencer's—and whoever sticks the pen in the heart, instead of the head, & writes not for fame, is sure to get it. The inclos'd letters may amuse you—the top of the tree in England & France. Nobody but myself has seen Mrs M's—& Mrs Necker's is pronounc'd by the Beaux Exprits, to be unpayable."[106]

As for Lady Spencer she was pleased, even flattered, to have the company and the letters of the greatest of actors. "You know we are all your toad-eaters, at least I answer for myself."[107] Twenty years her senior, he would not have been welcomed by Lady Spencer were it not for his engaging personality. In her home he was not urged to perform the dagger scene from *Macbeth* or the madness of Lear. At Althorp he was not featured as a public figure, as so often he was applauded by the Blue Stockings; but rather he was included as one of a gathering of guests, to converse at the table, join in charades, pursue the conversation on general topics, participate in the hunt. In Lady Spencer's conversation as in her letters, there was no intellectual content, liter-

ary gossip, or allusions. Garrick once read her Hannah More's play
*Percy*, and announced enthusiastically its triumph on the stage, but
she did not encourage further readings or theatrical news. Rather she
wished to have "all of your new productions," that is prologues, epilogues, and occasional verse. At Hampton and Adelphi she sought the
graciousness of her hosts, the good taste in literature and the arts, the
genteel living in a well-appointed home, and at Hampton a spacious
garden. In turn, the friendship was no isolated private affair; it embraced guests at Wimbleton House, the splendors of Althorp, the
gatherings of the Spencer family and guests, long conversations,
games, the hunt, elegant dinners, the cultivated amenities of English
country life at its best. She attained in her self and awakened in Garrick a sense of the art of living, of coping gracefully with the day that
is overhead, the passing hour with friends, a sympathetic insight into
the joys, the perils, the disasters of living. For all this he called her
"the first of Women" (1041).

As 1778 drew to a close, Garrick's health became more precarious,
and following a visit to the Spencers at Wimbleton, he became seriously ill. Cheered by Lady Spencer's insistence and preparations for a
further visit by the Garricks to Althorp (to which he brought a quantity
of red silk to dress the ladies for the hunt) the Garricks accepted, but
were delayed by his illness until 3 January 1779. Garrick had recently
drafted a prologue for a production of Fielding's *The Fathers* (his last
contribution to the stage) which he sent to Lady Spencer for comments
and suggestions. She complied, with a number of practical and tasteful suggestions.[108] He had thought that *Tom Jones* would be diverting
to her, as to everyone, as well as himself. To her he had written several
months before: "I have been diverting myself with Tom Jones (I hope
your Ladyship has the best Edition of Fielding's Works at Althorp)
& I have been much entertain'd. I intend to take a peep into all his
Works, for as Tragedies & Comedies are now too much for an Old
Gentleman, he must be gently & gradually set down to rest, with
Novels, Tales, Fables, & lighter food of the mind. A Good sermon on
a good day will assist the digestion of the week's vainer amusements.
In short, if I live, for I am not yet quite safe on Shore, the poor re-
mains of my foolish Life shall be devoted to your Ladyship's commands
—tho', now and then, I obey a certain look of your Eyes, which my
Spirit is scarce able to execute; & pray let me assure (once for all) the
Goddess of my Idolatry, that I never dare to be conceited with her,
that if I seem somewhat disinclin'd to do my duty, it proceeds from
a fear & feeling of not answering expectation. Stone, Bile, & Gout are

so fond of living with me & making my little tenement their house of revelling, that when they please to dance about me, my tongue is useless, & the rest of my faculties are watching their motions."[109]

After a little less than two weeks at Althorp with the Spencers, Garrick was brought home to the Adelphi, after a most painful journey, to die on 20 January 1779. The last letter he ever wrote was to Lady Spencer, 15 January: "I . . . found my Doctor reading in my little library, & most affecly, waiting for my coming. . . . He jok'd and I look'd the more Miserable. By the bye His College Jokes are not the best in this world. Mrs Garrick is very happy to have got me once again in her *Glutches*—she calls here and there, rings the bell, like Mrs Oakly [in Colman's *The Jealous Wife*], while I sit wrapt up in a suit of flannels, like the very figure of Peter Grievous. My pain is still lingering, as loth to quit so desirable a Mansion, but Dr Cadogan has rais'd the College Militia against the foe, and the battle has began already."[110]

In sympathy and tribute to Lady Spencer's affection for Garrick, Richard Rigby wrote Lady Spencer 28 January, three days before the state funeral, offering her a room in the Pay Office, past which the procession would move down Whitehall to Westminster Abbey: "for her Ladyship to see the last of poor Garrick's remains."[111] The ostentatious pageantry of the funeral procession was conceived theatrically by the chief mourner, Richard Brinsley Sheridan, as a tribute to Garrick the actor, but four women wept in privacy—Eva Maria Garrick, Hannah More, Frances Cadogan, and Georgiana, Lady Spencer, for Garrick the husband, the companion, the friend.

# 14

# Patron of the Arts

.

THE EXHIBITIONS IN London museums and the furnishings of England's many stately houses give the impression that every Englishman of means in the eighteenth century was an art collector. Many were virtuosi, caught up in the vogue for acquisitions of oddities and antiques. Many were, in their appreciation of fine arts, fine books, fine architecture, fine gardens, and fine furniture, sensitive to the excellence of their possessions and tasteful in the use and display of their *objets d'art*.[1] The Garricks had the means to collect and thoroughly enjoyed the art and artifacts with which they surrounded themselves in their three homes. In 30 years of a happy marriage each shared with the other the joy of purchasing and the pleasure of living with their collections of furnishings, books, engravings, and pictures.

Both were exceptionally endowed for the patronage and enjoyment of the fine arts. Both had been reared in surroundings conducive to the cultivation of taste in paintings, music, and architecture. The church, second only to royalty, was the most munificent patron of artists of all kinds; hence to grow up a few doors from the Lichfield Cathedral and close, as David did, was to absorb in the full tide of daily living almost unconsciously a sense of architecture, sculpture, painting, music, pageantry, as well as the drama of the liturgy. Years later this ecclesiastical art (Christian and classical) became a point of focal interest in the Garricks' grand tour (as it did for so many others who traveled the Continent in the century). Eva Maria Veigel was no less qualified in her early upbringing. Baptized and worshiping in the Cathedral of St. Stephen's in Vienna, growing up as she did in the most artistically cultured court circles in Europe—one that honored the dance, not to be exploited and demeaned, as in England, but as a respected art in which those who excelled were disciplined and enriched in mind and body—she came into London's circle of art patrons with a background of sensitivity and sureness of cultural maturity that was not the least part of her appeal to the rising young actor. Both were artists on stage in their own media, and Garrick as theatre manager chose and employed painters, engravers, designers, architects, musicians, composers, and singers as well as actors. In each artistic category he looked for excellence.

While yet in his twenties Garrick sought the company of artists and at the same time was guest in country mansions with art galleries —such as that of Windham's at Felbrigg Hall. Almost from their first meeting in London the Garricks were guests of the Burlingtons, first in Burlington House, and for the first month after their wedding in Chiswick Manor; thereafter, they spent their first four summers at Londesburgh, and were often at Chatsworth. In these four residences they were in immediate association with perhaps, taken as a whole, the greatest assemblage of classical and contemporary art in England.[2] Their knowledge of early continental art, "Italian light on English walls," was broadened by their grand tour, during which they concentrated on both ecclesiastical and Renaissance art and mingled with contemporary artists, notably English artists who were completing their studies and training by residence abroad.

Before going abroad in 1763, however, Garrick had associated with many of the leading artists of London. Sooner or later he knew more about contemporary art in England and was more involved with patronage of the arts than any of his contemporaries, save for Burlington and Horace Walpole. Like all their compatriots, the artists clubbed together in taverns, the most prestigious meeting at Old Slaughter's Coffee House, and later the coterie known as the Saint Martin's Lane Academy, so named after the location of the tavern. As a member Garrick began in the 1740s associating with the most productive contemporary artists, Hogarth, Hayman, Gravelot, Reynolds, and Roubillac.[3] Without pursuing here the complexity of proposals, maneuvers, and acts that led to the establishing of the Royal Academy of Arts in 1768, it is to be recalled that in 1754 the Society for the Encouragement of Art, Manufacture, and Commerce was founded, Hayman being chairman, and Garrick a subscribing member. In 1759 Garrick was one of the speakers at a dinner of the artist members of the society at the Turk's Head Tavern,[4] and by 1760 his influence was such that Goldsmith solicited him (to no avail) to be appointed the secretary.[5] Over the years proposals were made for public exhibitions, and eventually (26 February 1760) in a letter written for him by Dr Johnson, Hayman appealed in the press for such an exhibition. In response a committee of 30, of which Garrick was a member, was set up to carry out the project. Sixty-nine artists exhibited, and 20,000 persons attended, each paying a shilling for admission and for a catalogue. But the members of the society, other than artists, objecting to the qualifications for admission and the use of the funds, the artists as such seceded and formed a Society of Artists destined to flourish under Reynolds's leadership until 1768, when it became by act of George III the Royal Academy of Arts. In 1770, wishing a new building, the academy projected an exhibition hall, designed and built by the Adam brothers near the Adelphi, Garrick and Lacy deeding to James Paine, for the Society of Artists, a parcel of land on the south side of Exeter Street on 4 June 1771.[6] The corner stone was laid with a great ceremony at the Adelphi Tavern: the membership books, listing Garrick and many of his friends, also bore the name of Samuel Johnson, each to pay a membership fee of £2 a year.

Because Garrick's participation in all the meetings, proposals, and developments in creating and operating the Society of Artists was direct and personal and undocumented, his influence in the society may be estimated only by conjecture. Two brief anecdotes give some insights into his attitude and participation. When passing along a street in Rome in 1764 he recognized Nollekens as a "little fellow to whom we gave the prizes at the Society of Artists." At the exhibition of Benjamin West's *Death of Wolfe*, R.A., 1771, which attracted attention without precedent, Garrick, supposedly, reenacted the scene on the floor immediately in front of it, characteristically to improve on West by choosing the moment of rapture when the dying general heard the cry "They run, they run!".[7] During his lifetime Garrick (along with Mrs Garrick) was the subject of 26 portraitures exhibited at the Society of Arts, and later Artists (second in number only to George III), in oil, engraving, mezzotint, marble, metal, wax, crayon, and wood—inspired by his fame as an actor.[8] For 25 years Garrick was welcomed into the community of artists in England. Out of his friendship and patronage of that community he attained both knowledge and far-reaching influence in the fine arts—above all else in dramatic portraiture.

Garrick and Maria were avid readers about art, assembling in their general library the earlier as well as later standard histories, encyclopedias, catalogues, and criticisms of archeology, architecture, sculpture, painting, engraving emblems, gems, medals, and coins—some 50 in all, beginning with André Félibien's 15 monumental volumes (1676–1725) on architecture, sculpture, and painting with the lives of artists.[9]

Passing over the many illustrated books on history, biography, literature, drama, and travel, of which there are many, we have selected a few examples in the several categories of the volumes assembled by the Garricks on the fine arts, among others: Roger de Piles, *Disserta-*

*tion sur les ouvrages de plus fameux Peintres*, Paris 1681 [613]; Charles Patin, *Histoire des Medailles* (1665), Paris, 1695 [1750]; Andrea Palladio, *I quattro Libri dell' Architettura* (1570) Venice, 1581 [1875]; Aenea Vico, *Ex gemmis et cameis antiquorum*, Rome, 1750? [1022]; Mathew Pilkington, *The Gentleman's and Connoisseur's Dictionary of Painters*, 1770—long the first and standard work in English [1851]; Robert Adam and James Adam, *Works in Architecture*, 1773 [262]. The primary medium, then and now, in the pursuit and history of the fine arts consisted of illustrations by engraving, collected both as reproductions in separate prints, assembled and bound up in volumes, and as illustrations in books on art. Garrick doubtless began his study of the fine arts with a collection of 92 etchings by Arthur Pond, "From Drawings and Sketches by eminent Masters, viz, Raphael, Claude Lorraine, Guercino, Carracci, Carlo Maratti, Watteau, Ghezzi, And. Montegna, Polid. da Caravaggio, Permeggiani, N. Poussin, Rembrandt, &c. gilt 1742" [2135] and "45 Landscapes, after Claude Lorraine, Gasp. Poussin, Salv. Rosa, &c. engraved by Vivarès and others, very fine, early Impression, half bound, gilt . . . 1744–6" [2136]; Anthony Van Dyck, "A Collection of 103 Portraits, Scripture Subjects, &c. from his Paintings by Bolswert, Diepenbeek, Pontius, Galle, Hollar, Gunst, &c, fine impressions" [2651]; and Peter Paul Rubens, "Works consisting of 413 Engravings, by Eminent Artists after his paintings; the whole systematically arranged in subjects, forming 8 Large Vols." [2402]. He also added to his library the catalogues of famous collections of art, such as *Galeria Giustiniana*, "consisting of above 300 engravings of Statues, Busts, Bas-Reliefs, &c. 2 vols, fine set, Roma 1631" [1072; see also 532, 1073]; Bernard de Montfaucon, *Antiquité expliquée et rprésentée en figures* (French and Latin), Paris, 1719, 1724, ten volumes, folio [1866]; Joseph-Antoine Crozat, *Cabinet de Crozat, ou recueil d'estampes d'après les plus beaux Tableaux*, two volumes; folio, Paris, 1763 [532]; David Terniers (le Jeune), *Le Grand cabinet de tableaux, du archiduc Leopold-Guillaume*, "246 plates, fine copy," Amsterdam, 1755 [1073].

The fine arts for the Garricks were incorporated in their daily living, where their interests were absorbed more than in attendance at exhibitions or galleries. They created and furnished three residences that embodied their shared interests in the arts and their good taste, which together with their cultivation of a social life became a great satisfaction to them and their many friends through the years.

In the first summer of their marriage, Mrs Garrick was much occupied in redecorating and furnishing their first home. On 25 July 1749, she wrote Lady Burlington, "Mr. Garrick has bought the house on

Southampton Street for five hundred guineas, Dirt and all; 'tis reckoned a great bargain."[10] The house, no. 27, was within earshot of the Strand, and five minutes' walk from Drury Lane. Here was their town house from October 1749 until March 1772. In a few years, wishing for more room for entertaining, and for his increasing works of art but most of all to enjoy the life of a country gentleman, Garrick in January 1754 first rented, then on 30 August, contracted to buy what was known as the Fuller House in Hampton.

The property is described in part in the deed, as "All that Garden, or parcel of ground as the same is enclosed by a brick wall . . . abutting upon the House and Garden late of Ric^d Caswell on the West, and Bushy Park on the East."[11] The house faced on the Thames, and was separated from an additional parcel of land along the shore by the London-Hampton road, under which Garrick constructed a grotto tunnel. In the succeeding 20 years, more or less, he had the house altered and enlarged by the architect Robert Adam, including a front portico with four Corinthian columns. The gardens were laid out with the help of "Capability" Brown. In August 1755, with Adam's help, he had constructed on the bank of the Thames an octagonal brick "temple of Shakespeare," with a dome and an Ionic pillared portico. Inside the temple he placed a life-sized statue of Shakespeare made for him by Roubillac.[12] Finally, with the architect's help he constructed a handsome orangerie to the rear of the house. Through the years Garrick continued to add to these land holdings until the property held by Mrs Garrick after his death was the fifth largest in Hampton. Gradually the Garricks assembled there a magnificent collection of furniture, china, contemporary paintings, and his large library.[13]

Within a year of purchase the Garricks were prepared to entertain "the Duke of Grafton, Lady Holderness, Lord and Lady Rochford, the Marquis D'Abreu and Mr. Horace Walpole," among the first of a long succession of family, friends, distinguished public figures, foreign visitors, and aristocrats, many of whom have left descriptions of the elegant home and grounds, and the cordiality of their reception. Mrs Delany caught the general tenor of most reactions when she wrote in 1770 "the house is singular [distinguished] . . . and seems to owe its prettiness and elegance to [Mrs Garrick's] good taste."[14] "Well, doctor," said the actor to Johnson, "When, having taken him the rounds of his newly-acquired possessions, he finally planted him in front the summer house, 'and how do you like the spot?' The answer was: Ah, David, it is the leaving of such places as these that makes a death-bed terrible."[15]

Finally, as for the Garricks' third residence, no. 5 (later no. 4) Adel-

Garrick's house at Hampton, with Temple of Shakespeare in the foreground.
Engraving by William Bernard Cooke from a drawing by Peter Dewint.

phi Terrace, the plans are to be found in the Soane Museum and the furnishings in the Inventory of 1779.[16] No record or catalogue has turned up of an auction of the contents, except for the pictures, about which more at length shortly. The furnishings were of the best. So much were they works of fine art that the Victoria and Albert Museum published in 1920 from the manuscripts (20 folio pages) in their possession: the *Accounts of Chippendale, Haig & Co. for Furnishing David Garrick's House in the Adelphi, 1771–72*, a record not only of the labor, but of individual pieces of furnishing, the decorations of rooms, and the draperies. The selection of the prevailing colors of japanned white and green seem to have been Mrs Garrick's choice. Some of the furnishings were removed, repaired, re-upholstered from the residence in Southampton Street, which was sold when the Garricks moved to the Adelphi. Chippendale was a skilled artisan, a member of the Society for the Encouragement of Art, Manufacture, and Commerce, and customarily carried out the wishes of his clients in the plans and style of the Adam Brothers. One gathers from the records that the Adelphi residence was tastefully, not ostentatiously, furnished, 24 rooms in all, one containing the finest furnishings and the oil paintings.

The quality and elegance of the furnishings at Hampton and Adelphi were matched by the porcelain and silver service—all in all nearly 500 entries in the sale catalogue.[17] Of the 56 entries for Seve, Chelsea, and oriental porcelain, the highest price was paid for "A very superb cafe set of the rare old Seve porcelaine, beautifully painted and richly gilt, in cafe pot, 6 ditto cups and saucers, sugar basin and cover, milk pot, cream ewer, basin, 4 large and 4 small spoons, in handsome inlaid case, lined with green silk" [54]. The service of plate, 80 separate pieces, was sold by the ounce. As for jewels, £147 was paid for "A pair of very beautiful brilliant top and drop ear-rings, large stones of the finest water" [100]. On display also were many smaller art objects, classified by Christie under the heading of "Trinkets, medallions, cameos, intaglio, marble busts and statuary" [156–A], "a gold snuff box of scalloped shape, of very fine French chasing."[18]

Even the briefest summary of Garrick's memorabilia must include at least three creations out of the Shakespeare mulberry tree. The most famous, though not to modern taste, was the mahogany chair, designed by Hogarth, "richly carved, on the back of which hangs a medal of the poet carved by Hogarth," originally in the Shakespeare Temple, now exhibited in the hall of the Folger Library. Secondly a cup carved from Shakespeare's mulberry tree, which was presented to David Garrick, by the mayor and corporation, at the time of the Jubilee, at Stratford on Avon, "lined with silver, gilt, with a cover surmounted by a branch of mulberry leaves and fruit, also of silver gilt." Garrick also prized an enamel portrait on gold, after a design by Giovanni Battista Cipriani and executed by John Howes, presented to Garrick by the actors of Drury Lane in appreciation of his establishing the Theatrical Fund [77], now in the Folger Library. Most tasteful of all was the mulberry box carved by T. Davis of Birmingham with scenes from Shakespeare, also presented by the Stratford Corporation of Stratford, 1769, now on exhibition in the British Museum.[19] All such artifacts were precious in meaning and personal associations for the Garricks; the auction catalogues for which are a dirge of what was once alive and harmonious with all the furnishings and decor.

While in a large measure the domestic furnishings as such were selected and arranged by Mrs Garrick, David concentrated on the collecting of richly illustrated books and of engravings. The sales catalogue of his library, 1823, featured in large type the distinctive qualities of the *Splendid Books of Prints*, and two years later Christie issued *A Catalogue of a Valuable and Highly Interesting Collection of Engravings, Consisting of English and Foreign Portraits . . . The Property of the Late David Garrick, Esq.*, May 5th 1825. First regarding the books, 300 of them are richly illustrated by prints, over half by artists before 1700. The nearly 60 artists and engravers whose works appeared therein include the great names in the history of the genre, as a mere sampling will show. Along with his contemporaries Garrick was much interested in books and plates on classical ruins, such as *Vestigi delle Antichita di Roma*, with 50 plates by Marcus Christoph Sadeler, 1606 [2654]; Giuseppi Vasi, *Delle Màgnificenze di Roma Antica e Moderna*, numerous plates, five volumes, 1747–59 [2653]. He had two early editions of Ovid's *Metamorphoses*, with woodcuts and plates, 1584 [1829], 1524 [1827], and a third (n.d.) with 132 plates by Simon de Passe [1828], and a later one, 1732, with numerous plates by Bernard Picar [1874]. His works of Virgil, translated by John Ogilby, had a portrait by William Faithorne and numerous plates by Hollar, 1654 [2656].

Equally popular with artists in all media were Biblical and ecclesiastical subjects, such as Albrecht Dürer's 20 wood engravings of the *Life of the Virgin Mary*, 1518 [811]; *Histoire des Ordres Monastiques, Religieux et Militaires*, eight volumes, 1714–19, "with an immense number of plates" [1288].

Garrick seems to have taken an especial interest in emblemata. The earliest of his half dozen books on this genre was Janus Jacobus Boissardus, *Emblematum Liber Ipsa Emblemata, ab auctore delineata; a*

*Theodoro de Bry, sculpta*, 1593 [241]; Jan Muller, *Emblemata Sacra*, 1610 [1666]; as well as Marcus Zuerius Boxhorn, *Emblemata Politica et Orationes* 1635 [190]; Andrea Alciatus, *Emblemata* (1547, many eds.) 1691 [17]: the very rare *Moral Emblems* of Robert Farley, translated from Jacob Cats, 1627 [864]; and Heinrich Ulrich's *Emblems* with 30 plates bearing on its elegant binding the arms of Charles I [2393].

From all that can be learned of Garrick's policies in assembling his private library, he did not buy for provenance, rarity, speculation, or status. Rather, all of his life, he sought a wide variety of books, rare or monumental, as well as some of the major publications of the current press, out of a liberal personal taste for literature and the pictorial arts. Of contemporary books, some of which came out in his later years, were Robert Wood's *The Ruins of Palmyra* with excellent plates, 1753, [2662], much praised by Walpole, and Gavin Hamilton's *Schola Italica Pictura; sive selectae quaedum summorum e Schola Italica Pictorum Tabulae*, 1773 [2408]. Of personal interest for Garrick was Horace Walpole's *Anecdotes of Painting in England*, two volumes with portraits and plates, Strawberry Hill, 1762 [2612]; Lord Baltimore's *Gaudia Poetica*, composed in Latin, English, and French, 1769, with plates, "Given to me by Lord Baltimore, who dy'd at Naples, 1771" [1021], and *Shakespeare's Works*, by Sir Thomas Hanmer, in six volumes, with Hayman's plates, second edition, 1771 [2357], Hayman having consulted Garrick about the illustrations (33).

His curiosity extended, of course, to illustrations of literary works: *Les Cent Nouvelles*, black letter, with woodcuts, ca. 1515 [497]; woodcuts of the *Romant de la Roza*, 1526 [2152]; Holbein's plates for Erasmus's *Praise of Folly*, 1668, and 1676 [836, 833], Thomas Coryate's *Crudities*, 1611 [516], "all the plates except the frontispiece," and many Elizabethan broadsides, some seventeenth- and eighteenth-century French and English classics, such as Voltaire's works with engravings by Gravelot; J. Urry's edition of *Chaucer*, with portraits by Nicolas Pigne and Vertue, 1721 [798]. Some of the more monumental volumes, Garrick must have bought for the plates alone, such as: Johann Jacob Scheuchzer, *Physica Sacra*, Latin and German "with 750 plates, fine impression, 4 vols, large paper [the Harleian copy] russia gilt leaves, Aug. Vind." 1731 [2407]—actually selections from the Bible dealing with natural history. Also in the same category was August Johann Roesell Von Rosenhof's *Natural History of Insects* in German, "with an immense number of coloured plates, 7 vols, elegant" [2119]; Philip Miller's "Figures of the Plants describ'd in his *Gardener's Dictionary*, 300 coloured plates, 2 vols, calf extra, 1771"

[1617]; and J. Miller's *Illustrations of the Sexual System of Linnaeus* "with a double set of plates, plain and coloured, before the writing, 2 vols, elegant, 1777—Garrick's subscription copy" [1615]. The largest collection of plates was to be found, of course, in Diderot's and d'Alembert's 12 volumes of plates for their great *Encyclopédie*, 1751 [1062].[20]

One searching for clues to Garrick's relish for the engravings listed in the hundreds of items in the Christie *Catalogue of Engravings* (1825) is blocked by the brevity of the entries for the gatherings and parcels (some 90 of them), the frequent use of *etc.* and the uncertain distinctions between *after* and *by*. The mass is as impressive as the widespread subject matter, however, and the names of the artists and engravers suggest the excellence of the prints: plates by Rembrandt, Rosa, Castiglione, Dürer, Hollar, Goltzius, Monteuill, along with the Frenchman Gerard Edelinck, and William Faithorne the greatest of English portrait engravers. Eighty-five plates were by Rembrandt; 122 by Dürer; 65 of costumes, by Hollar; 89 by Goltzius; and 80 by Callot. A total of 1,018 by 18 engravers were portraits. Among the drawings were 50 designs of scenery, generally in black lead, a parcel of designs for theatrical dresses, and various pen and pencil sketches by de Loutherbourg. Art historians can check the prices paid at the auction, and judge thereby something of the value of the individual pieces in the collection, but the monetary value can tell us little about the delight Garrick and Eva Maria had in poring over the prints in their possession. Landscapes, as well as portraits abounded, especially 15 by the English artist William Woollett, two of which won first and second prizes at the annual exhibition of the Society of Artists [1220]. A parcel of caricatures by Charles Bunbury, Garrick's good friend, whom Walpole considered a second Hogarth, pencil sketches by de Loutherbourg, landscapes by Gainsborough, bound volumes of Canaletto's views of Venice, Piranesi's of Rome, de Buffon's birds, and Alexander Cozens's *Principles of Beauty Relative to the Human Head*, 1778 [148], valued for its plates, were included. Of professional interest in Garrick's library were Hollar's *Female Dresses*, 1613 [1139], and his plates for Elias Ashmole's *Institution, Laws, and Ceremonies of the Most Noble Order of the Garter*, 1672 [268], and *Desseins de Différence Habits de Costume du Théâtre Français* in colors drawn by J. L. Faesch, in three volumes, 1765 [660]. Above all Garrick collected the engravings of Hogarth, notably in a gathering entered in the catalogue of Garrick's library: "1330 HOGARTH'S (W.) WORKS, consisting of 106 plates . . . brilliant impressions." In recognition of Garrick's patronage of engravers and print sellers, Matthew Darly dedicated his comic prints of *Macaronies, Characters, Caricatures*, 1772, to Garrick [804]. Devonshire, respecting Garrick's knowledge and taste, commissioned him to purchase prints for him in Italy. Many of the rarer and more striking engravings and mezzotints were glazed, framed, and hung throughout the two mansions.

The harvest, however, of the Garricks' travels abroad, knowledge of art history, gifts of collector friends, association with artists, and patronage of the Society of Artists, was roughly 225 works of art by around 50 artists listed in the inventories of Hampton and the Adelphi at Garrick's death, and in *A Catalogue of the Small, but Valuable Collection, of Italian, French, Flemish, Dutch, and English Pictures . . . to Be Sold by Auction, By Mr. Christie, in His Great Room, in Pall Mall, on Monday, June the 23rd, 1823*.[21] The Garricks, however, seem to have had no particular plan or policy for displaying their *objets d'art*, nearly three fourths of which were at Hampton, where there was more wall space, especially for drawings in the Green Dressing Room. The larger and more select oil paintings were hung in the parlors and dining rooms of the two houses. In addition to the artistic qualities, almost all the works of art were displayed and enjoyed by the Garricks and their friends for the personal associations. Postponing for the moment the half dozen major artists who were personal friends, another sampling of the Garrick collections will further serve to substantiate their discriminating taste.

From abroad there were first of all interiors, landscapes, portraits, and religious paintings by continental artists and their English followers, not infrequently in copies. Of the following the Garricks owned generally only one or a pair, at Hampton by Telleman, van der Does, Zuccarelli, Bruegel, Watteau, van Dyck, Farata, Monomy, Mieris, Le Nain, Rosalba, Mario Ricci, Poussin, and Goupy; at the Adelphi by Pietro Peregino, Frans Hals, Tintero Zuchero, Rembrandt; also Salvator Rosa [Christie I, 41], Gonzalo's *A Painter's Gallery* [Inventory I, 84; Christie I, 18]. Andrea del Sarto's *The Holy Family* [Inventory I, 87; Christie I, 70] a gift of Lord Baltimore in Rome, and Guido's *Pinabel and Brandmante*, a gift of Lord Burlington [Inventory II, 93; Christie I, 67]. Pietro Fabris, whom Garrick first met in Naples through Sir William Hamilton, and who was later in England, was represented by eight pictures of Vesuvius, Naples, and Italian landscapes;[22] and the Garricks had eight pictures by Jean Pillemont. Of English artists, generally members of the Society of Artists, they had pictures by Forest Marlow, Richard Wilson, Lambert, Andrews, Barralet, Wootton, Bunbury's *Billiard Players* [Inventory I, 74], and John Taylor, with whom Garrick became acquainted at Bath and who in response to some complimentary verses by Garrick gave him an oval *Landscape and Waterfall* [Inventory I, 18; Christie I, 3]. Of Philip James de Loutherbourg, whom Garrick engaged at Drury Lane as a scene painter and who gained early fame for landscapes, the Garricks had the good taste to display five pictures.

In accord with their interest in characters on and off the stage, the Garricks collected many portraits, often in copies, of the Earl of Essex by Zucchero, Shakespeare, Jonson, Milton, Betterton by Kneller, [Inventory I, 63], Raleigh, Molière, as well as of friends, such as Hoadly, Berenger by Liotard, Colman, Sir George Hay, the Countess of Burlington, a whole-length portrait of Windham in military dress, and Mme Clairon by Rosalba [Inventory I, 84]. Sir Peter Lely's *Portrait of the Duke of Monmouth*, presented by Lely to Mrs Bracegirdle, in turn by her to Congreve, by him to Wilks the actor, was given to Garrick by Thomas Wilkes, Garrick's good friend in Dublin. In turn Garrick sent Wilkes a small signed copy of Van der Gucht's Jubilee portrait, copied from *Garrick as Steward of the Shakespeare Jubilee*, 1772, commissioned by Garrick.[23] Benjamin Van der Gucht, painter and dealer (the thirty-second child of engraver Bernard Van der Gucht), made something of a reputation as a painter of landscapes, of which the Garricks owned several. His greatest skill was in portraiture. For the Garricks he did the portraits of Mrs Flasby [Inventory I, 22; Christie, I, 7], Mrs Garrick's companion; George Garrick; the nieces Mrs Schaw and Mrs Payne [Inventory I, 50; II, 100]; perhaps also of Carrington Garrick; Captain David Garrick [Burrell, 21]; and several drawings of the Garricks—all of these family portraits passed to heirs, presumably among others, a "Portrait of Mrs Garrick, in black silk cloak and hat" by Liotard [Inventory I, 18; Burrell, no. 8]. There were also medallions in metal, plaster, and wax; Nolleken's *Wounded Infant Borne on a Dolphin* [Inventory I, 41; Christie I, 76] and the *Dying Gladiator* in marble at Hampton [Christie I, 89]. There were many busts, of Shakespeare [Inventory I, room 35], Halifax [Inventory I, p. 2, no. 24], Voltaire [Inventory I, p. 10, no. 127], of Pope and Sterne by Roubillac [Christie I, 72, 73], Newton [Inventory II, p. 9, no. 113], Van Nost of George III [Inventory II, p. 9, no. 114], and terra cotta of Garrick by Flaxman [Christie I, 72–75].

Garrick's relations with many artists themselves were marked by that easy familiarity and frank approach habitual in his relations with his men friends in general. The iconography of Garrick as an actor is the most extensive of any actor because he was the most successful and the most popular. As a rule artists and engravers took the initiative in the selection of scenes they wished to depict from popular plays.

If one was of Garrick, it became a conversation piece including other actors. Portraits of Garrick alone in a role were almost invariably copied from the original full conversation piece. Such conversation pieces were (and are) to be understood in the context of an arresting dramatic point in a play. They were known and collected by contemporaries through the extensive production of engravings by Gravelot, Pond, Hall, Dixon, Boydel, MacArdell and others. Careful study of each dramatic conversation piece featuring Garrick establishes that the initiative was more often the artist's and the engraver's. In a recent (1977) Zoffany exhibition in the National Portrait Gallery in London only six portraitures of Garrick with other actors appeared, but ten were shown without Garrick, out of 115 paintings, prints, and drawings. On the other hand conversation pieces of Garrick's historic first and later stage appearance in *Richard III* were sooner or later turned out by Bardell, Nathaniel Dance, Fuseli, Hayman, and de Loutherbourgh as well as by Hogarth.

As for the portrayal of Garrick the man rather than the public figure of an actor in various media, enumeration and examination add little biographical insight, save for evidence of the gradual onslaught of age, as may be seen from the series of illustrations in this book. Associations made abroad in 1763 were continued in England, with, for example, Faesch, Nollekens, and Angelica Kauffman, whose studio Garrick visited in London, and with George and Nathaniel Dance. As for foreign and English artists resident in London, little has turned up covering Garrick's possible personal relations with Roubillac and Soldi, Hodges, James, Roberts, Edwards, Worlidge, Flaxman, Sir Thomas Hudson, Sherwin, Brompton, Van Nost, Van Loo, Victor Vispré, and perhaps most regrettable of all with Robert Edge Pine and Benjamin Van der Gucht, all of whom either painted Garrick or some of whose works he owned.

Garrick's personal rapport with individual artists whose works he collected bears on the understanding of Garrick the man and his effectiveness as an artist-actor. Almost every private portrait has a complex history of copies, often by the artist himself, of engravings, or successive sales and exhibitions, all of which fall within the province of the history of art. He sought the company of many accomplished artists, however, frequented their studios, and supported their Society of Artists. Both the artists and Garrick the actor had a mutual interest in the variety and artistic qualities of the human face, and in each portrait Garrick's marvelous and expressive eyes became focal for the painter, as they were for members of every audience that saw him play. Garrick liked these, but collected the other paintings of contemporary artists as a gentleman connoisseur of private means and a culti-vated taste.

In 1762 Hogarth gave Garrick a pen drawing of Garrick in Garrick's interlude *The Farmer's Return*, which drawing Garrick had glazed, framed, and hung in the gallery at Hampton [77; Inventory I, p. 10, no. 29]. The oil portrait of Mr and Mrs Garrick, Garrick seated at a table, pen in hand, for which Mrs Garrick is reaching, composing the prologue to Foote's *Taste*, in which Garrick had taken the part of Peter Puff satirizing the affectations of art dealers and virtuosi, was still in Hogarth's studio at his death in 1764 [Christie, I, 64]. The portrait passed from Mrs Hogarth to Mrs Garrick at Garrick's death in 1779, and was hung by Mrs Garrick over the chimney in the dining room at the Adelphi. The four great oil paintings, *The Election*, which Gar-rick bought in 1762 outright from Hogarth, were on display at Hamp-ton [Christie I, 63]. Later in 1823 they were auctioned to Sir John Soane and are now in his museum. Garrick also had in his collection Hogarth's picture of *Falstaff Enlisting His Recruits* [Christie I, 20], a small portrait of a lapdog, and a sketch of *The Happy Marriage* [Christie I, 37].

The relationship of the two was a close and understanding one, though no two men were more unlike in personality than Hogarth and Garrick. Yet their kinship progressed to deep affection and admiration. Elaboration of their influence on each other (more accurately, parallels between them) might be spun out for pages. What really counted cre-atively, was the trained eye for action both possessed, the intuition for comedy and tragedy, and the extraordinary range and vitality of their restless creative activity.

When Garrick in the mid-1740s began associating with Francis Hay-man, Hayman was generally recognized as the most versatile and lead-ing English artist. He had been a scene painter at Drury Lane; an illustrator of Congreve, Cervantes, and Pope, cooperating with Ho-garth in the decorative paintings at Vauxhall; a leader in the artists' gathering at Old Slaughter's Coffee House and later of St Martin's Lane Academy; chairman of the Committee in 1755 to found an academy; and finally president of the Society of Artists (1766–68), which he deserted to become a member of the Royal Academy under Reynolds' presidency. He started as a decorative painter, and ended as a historical painter. In all these roles Garrick became acquainted with the man and his works. The two lengthy surviving letters from Garrick to him, while written with care and deference, imply Hay-man's thorough familiarity with Garrick's theatrical affairs. While visit-ing in Lichfield Garrick wrote commending illustrations Hayman was

revising for the Thomas Hanmer *Shakespeare* [*Post* 10 October 1745].
A year later (18 August 1746), Garrick wrote from Cheltenham "I was
very sorry I could not have Y$^r$ Company y$^e$ Night before I left London;
as Hogarth had disengag'd himself from Y$^r$ Pall Mall appointment, I
was in hopes of Seeing you, but I am affraid I sent to late; however for
the future, if You can fancy Me as much as I do You, we will be merry
togeather & Make up for past Deficiencies" (47). In this same letter
Garrick detailed his concept of a fine possibility for a dramatic illustration for *Othello*. He chose the moment of revelation when Emelia
cries out "O thou dull Moor!"[24]

Garrick was in the full tide of current fashion when he was painted
with William Windham (in 1745) by Hayman—a picture which hung in
Felbrigg Hall until Windham's death in 1761, when it passed to Garrick (as one of Windham's executors) and remained with Mrs Garrick
until her death (28).[25] As for Hayman's three dramatic conversation
pieces that included Garrick, one was doubtless commissioned by
the actor around 1747 to promote Hoadly's *The Suspicious Husband*,
with Garrick as Ranger. It was first owned by Hoadly, but after a long
subsequent history, hangs now in the Mellon Collection at Yale. Hayman also did a version of Garrick as *Richard III*, first exhibited at the
Society of Artists in 1760, now in the National Portrait Gallery. The
third dramatic conversation piece was of *Garrick as Hamlet with the
Queen and Ghost*, which survives only in an engraving by Grignion.
At Hampton Garrick hung Hayman's *The Finding of Moses*, in crayons
[Burrell, p. 8, no. 14]; a portrait of *Quin in the Character of Falstaff
and Prince Henry, from Shakespeare*, and *A Study of Two Boys* [In-
ventory I, p. 37; Christie I, 25].

In Benjamin Wilson, a less able painter, the intermediary between
Hogarth and Zoffany, Garrick found a most congenial friend, whom he
patronized out of affection for the man rather than for his attainments.
Following a sojourn in Dublin, Wilson took residence in London in
1750, and doubtless through Lords Orrery and Burlington first met
Garrick. Garrick did not collect Benjamin Wilson's works. He was essentially a portrait painter. One portrait of Garrick is generally attributed to him, with Garrick holding a folio copy of Shakespeare, open
at *Hamlet*, long in possession of the Lords Kenyon. A glimpse of Garrick's being consulted as an art critic survives in an early letter to
Wilson (20 May 1759): "I forgot to call at Your house Yesterday Morning, as I promis'd Lord Newnham, to see his Picture—could You possibly defer sending it home till next Fryday (when I will most certainly
See You about y$^e$ hour of twelve) I shall be really oblig'd to You if you
can" (231).

Wilson was entrusted with fitting up, painting the scenes, and in general preparing the Duke of York's playhouse in St James Street, Westminster, in 1767. Garrick and Mrs Garrick by invitation attended a rehearsal and two plays there, after which he wrote to Sir Francis Blake Delaval (22 April 1767) soliciting his patronage of Wilson. "I wish it was in my power to relieve [our friend Wilson] for I think so good a heart, & so ingenious a Mind have deserv'd more favour from the Great, than he has yet experienc'd" (453). Garrick did engage him to assist at the Shakespeare Jubilee in Stratford, read to him (for approval) his *Ode* on the occasion, and they returned to London together in the same coach.

Of far more consequence, however, was Wilson's employment of Johann Zoffany on his arrival in England in 1761, as a painter of accessories. In Wilson's studio Garrick met Zoffany and immediately recognized his exceptional talents as a painter of dramatic conversation pieces. When he invited Zoffany to reside at Hampton, Wilson protested; without disrupting their friendship, Garrick replied in a sharp letter on 21 August of the next year, in part: Zoffany "will be now at Liberty to begin the Conversation Piece he mentions, I rely on his fancy to make it *a most Excelent Picture*, & I shall Endeavour in my way but at humble distance to prepare a proper Companion for it" (292). The resulting picture was *Garrick in His Interlude "The Farmer's Return,"* for which Zoffany used Hogarth's pen drawing. The picture was exhibited at the Society of Artists the same year. Garrick possessed the original, and Zoffany made three autograph copies—one now in the Mellon Collection [Inventory II, 127; Christie I, 43]. The companion piece was *Garrick as Jaffier with Mrs. Cibber as Belvidera in Otway's "Venice Preserved," Act 4, Scene ii,* in turn exhibited at the Society of Artists, 1763. One of the three autograph copies is easier seen now in the Garrick Club. These first two conversation pieces, the Garricks eventually hung opposite the fireplace in the elegant dining room in the Adelphi [Inventory II, 42, 43; Christie I, 125, 126]. These two conversation pieces established Zoffany's reputation. He continued painting *Garrick as Sir John Brute in Vanbrugh's "The Provoked Wife"* for the Society of Artists, 1765, of which he prepared two autograph versions, one of which he retained, the other Garrick bequeathed to his brother George.[26] Zoffany followed with *Garrick as Lord Chalkstone,* an autograph single figure of Garrick (Society of Artists, 1766) was owned by the Garricks [Inventory I, 14; Christie I, 50]; *Garrick with Mrs. Pritchard in "Macbeth,"* which passed to Garrick's good friend George Keate;[27] and finally *Garrick as Abel Drugger in Ben Jonson's "The Alchemist,"* which was exhibited at the Royal

Academy in 1770. Reynolds offered 100 guineas for it and immediately sold it to the Earl of Carlisle for £125.

Zoffany at the time he was working in the dramatic conversation genre, was in a measure inventing (certainly perfecting) a second type of conversation piece—that is of a social group, as distinct from the current family group portraits. His earliest, and one of the most famous was of *Garrick and His Wife Outside the Shakespeare Temple at Hampton* (ca. 1762). Ten years later he completed the companion piece—*The Garricks Taking Tea on the Lawn by the Thames at Hampton* (1773). Neither was engraved, for they belonged to the Garricks' private life, and both were hung in the dining parlor at the Adelphi [Inventory II, p. 27, nos. 121, 122; Christie I, 54, 53]. Also listed in the inventory (p. 27) as hanging over the parlor door were two more dramatic pieces by Zoffany: "A View of part of Hampton House and Garden and David Garrick sitting in the Lawn reading," and "View in the Garden & two Miss Garricks at Play, whole length." Perhaps these may be the same as Christie I, no. 52: "A pair of small views of the Villa and Grounds of Mr. Garrick at Hampton," the first displayed by the National Portrait Gallery exhibition of Zoffany in 1977, as *A View of Hampton Garden with Garrick Writing*.

Two portraits of Garrick by Zoffany have survived; one, a copy of which was willed by Mrs Garrick "to my nephew, Nathan Egerton Garrick, the portrait of my late husband without a wig, by Zoffany, which I bought after his death of Mrs. Bradshaw, to whom it had been given as a present."[28] It is now in the National Portrait Gallery. The second, an unfinished portrait, and now in the Garrick Club is attributed, rather convincingly, to Zoffany. Finally in the Christie sale [I, 44] there was a *Portrait of Mrs. Garrick with a Mask*.

Although both Garrick and Zoffany were indebted to each other for much of their fame while alive (and ever since in dramatic and art history), yet far more meaningful and significant is the fact that each recognized the artistic abilities of the other; that Garrick collected more of Zoffany than of other painters, not solely as his patron, but in recognition of superiority of his portraiture, and displayed Zoffany, certainly with pride, in the more elegant rooms in his mansions.

In more literary and learned circles Garrick associated more with Sir Joshua Reynolds than with any other artist. Both sought to raise the dignity of their professions, both were widely influential, but not on each other. Though temperamentally not very congenial, each nevertheless respected the talents and attainment of the other. Only in later years did Reynolds compose, with some asperity, his *Portrait* (in words) of Garrick, with the thesis "when this passion [for fame] is

*The Garrick Club*
David Garrick.
Unfinished oil painting by Johann Zoffany, ca. 1770.

carried to excess, it becomes a vice."[29] One reading it gets the feeling, however, that Reynolds was "bringing out" Johnson in it as an advocate for Garrick. Reynolds, however, turned Garrick's fame to his own advantage.

Following three years of study of the old masters in Italy, to learn from the past, Sir Joshua settled in London about 1752, where he had many opportunities to meet Garrick, perhaps first through Benjamin West, but not until 1762, at the Society of Artists did he exhibit his first picture of Garrick—*Garrick Between Tragedy and Comedy*, which he immediately sold for £300 to the Earl of Halifax. Four surviving copies are attributed to Reynolds, and the picture was frequently reproduced in engravings and mezzotints. Reynolds' interpretation of Garrick's being drawn toward Comedy was true of both Garrick and the spirit of the age. Reynolds' only dramatic conversation piece featuring Garrick was *Garrick as Kitely in Every Man in His Humour* (1768), five copies of which by Reynolds survive. He gave the original to Edmund Burke.

Not until 1772–73 did the Garricks sit for a portrait by Reynolds. It was completed in 1776 and exhibited at the Royal Academy as *Portrait of Garrick and His Wife* (739). Of this Reynolds produced two versions—one for Mrs Thrale, that later was bought by Dr Charles Burney. A second version was bought by the Duke of Dorset. Four copies of each of these survive. Edmund Burke owned one of the latter. There is no evidence that Garrick, with all his "passion for fame" purchased the original, or any copies of Reynolds' portrait of himself and Mrs Garrick, nor any of Reynolds' paintings. Almost as an afterthought in Christie *Catalogue* I, under "further Addenda" occurs the ambiguous entry—"Infant St. John with a Lamb, an elegant fancy picture, *formerly presented* by Sir Joshua." It has not been identified in the inventories of 1779, of the furnishings at Hampton and the Adelphi.

With the younger artist Thomas Gainsborough, Garrick was more congenial, partly perhaps because of Gainsborough's support of the Bath theatre, and certainly because of his unaffected candor. Born in Ipswich, later steward of the theatre there in which Garrick had done apprentice acting, he came to London in 1740 to serve an apprenticeship of ten years under Hayman, Gravelot, and others. He studied Van Dyck and the Dutch painters and painted one of his early successes for the Court Room of the Foundling Hospital. He settled in Bath from 1757 to 1774, but returned to London to reside with Dr Isaac Schomberg, Garrick's friend, in Pall Mall.

Garrick knew him first in Bath, where he commissioned him to do

*Collection of Major General E. H. Goulburn, D.S.O.*
Garrick Reading to Mrs Garrick.
Painting by Sir Joshua Reynolds, 1773.

his portrait with his arm around the bust of Shakespeare. The background of the portrait was Prior Park, in which Garrick's friend Bishop Warburton was residing. The picture appeared in an exhibition of the Incorporated Society of Artists (April 1766) under the title *A Gentleman Whole Length*. Patrons immediately identified Garrick, and the picture was adversely criticized in the *Public Advertiser* (398). Two years later when the Corporation of Stratford invited Garrick to contribute a picture for the New Town Hall, Garrick engaged Gainsborough to rework the 1766 picture. To Garrick's offer of compensation, Gainsborough responded 27 July 1768: "I am already overpaid for the shabby performance; and if you have a mind to make me happier than all the presents London can afford, you must do it by never thinking yourself at all in my debt. I wish for many years for the happiness of Mr. Garrick's acquaintance, and pray, dear Sir, let me enjoy it quietly" (26,27).[30]

Presumably shortly thereafter, in response to a letter from Garrick, Gainsborough wrote, "I intend with your approbation my dear friend, to take the form from [Shakespeare's] pictures and statue [the latter by Peter Scheemaker after Kent, Stratford Church] just enough to preserve his likeness *past the doubt of all blockheads* at first sight, and supply a soul from his works; it is impossible that such a mind and ray of heaven could shine with such a face and pair of eyes as that picture has it [Martin Droeshout's in the First Folio, 1623]" (28,29).[31] Gainsborough even proposed visiting Stratford for a look at the statue, but the weather frustrated him. He gave as his price 60 guineas, and was so paid by the Stratford Corporation for the finished picture (of which there were four copies) which hung in the Town Hall until destroyed by fire in 1946. Shortly after the picture was accepted, and in reply to Garrick's expression of gratitude, Gainsborough sent him a "Chalk scratch," a "pair of landscapes, with Cattle and Figures."

Sometime before 22 June 1772 Gainsborough completed for Mrs Garrick a portrait of her husband. He wrote Garrick, "I ask pardon for having kept your picture so long from Mrs. Garrick . . . my chief reason for detaining it so long was the hopes of getting one copy *like* to hang in my own parlour, not as a show picture, but for my own enjoyment, to look when I please at a great man, who has thought me worthy of some little notice" (32,33,34).[32] He also made copies for James Clutterbuck, and Dr Schomberg. Garrick left the original to Albany Wallis.

The Garricks' ties with Gainsborough were not limited to the theatre. They hung in their home his *Shepherd Boy and the Magpie*, also a *Drawing of the Parade at Bath* [Inventory I, 70] and a *Rustic Land-*

467

*scape* [Christie I, 84]. The mutual confidence of the two was so well founded that Gainsborough wrote Garrick in 1772 condemning the perennial bad taste in the theatre for glare and color, continuing, "when the streets are paved with Brilliants, and the Skies made of Rainbows I suppose you'l be contented, and satisfied with Red, blue & yellow . . . Now I'll tell you my sprightly Genius how this is to be done—maintain all your Lights, but spare the poor abused Colors, til' the Eye rests, and recovers." In turn Garrick's greatest support for Gainsborough came around 1777 when he introduced him to his energetic journalist friend, Sir Henry Bate Dudley, who became Gainsborough's most ardent and successful defender and art critic in his *Morning Post*, and later *Morning Herald*, and to whom biographers are indebted for much now known about the artist.[33]

Gainsborough saw in Garrick a fellow artist (both in his professional and private life) and advised the young Bath actor John Henderson in the strongest terms (18 July 1773): "Stick to Garrick as close as you can, for your life, you should follow his heels like his shadow in sunshine . . . Garrick is the greatest creature living, in every respect; he is worth studying in every action. Every view and every idea of him, is worthy of being stored up for imitation; and I have ever found him a generous and sincere friend . . . never mind the fools who talk of imitating and copying; all is imitation . . . What, Sir, makes the difference between man and man, is real performance, and not genius or conception. There are a thousand Garricks . . . Why only one Garrick with Garrick's eyes, voice, etc?"[34]

Artists can on canvas crystallize a moment in still life and we are thankful to be heirs to a reasonably full series of Garrick portraits, dramatic and personal. Close study of the dramatic ones reveals arresting moments, not of Garrick, but of his bringing to life a Hamlet, a Macbeth under strain, a bold or frightened Richard, a sly and cunning Drugger. Close study of the personal ones reveals not a moment rekindled from a play, but a composite of attitudes of a restive, vivacious, vigorous, sensitive, and complex man. Each genre complements the other, but for the full picture of the mobile actor we turn to the many voices of contemporary observation seen in press and pamphlet where friend and foe alike joined in admiration of his impressive comic and tragic performance on stage.

Although the pursuit and the collecting of the fine arts were basic, essential to Garrick as an artist himself, as an actor, the end of his acting was not more acting, productivity at the expense of creativity, but a quality in private life. Garrick as a man of his age enjoyed portraiture; the human face and form fascinated him, but he did not dis-

*From Joseph Knight's* David Garrick
David Garrick.
Detail engraving by W. Boucher after Reynolds.

play theatrical conversation pieces that included himself, except those painted by good friends. Most of the personal portraits he gave to friends. In Johnson's words, "everyman is always present to himself, and has, therefore little need of his own resemblance; nor can desire it, but for the sake of those he loves . . . in diffusing friendship, in reviving tenderness, in quickening the affection of the absent, and continuing the presence of the dead."[35] To interpret Garrick's patronage of the fine arts as an overweening desire for publicity, the enhancement of his own image, is to neglect Garrick's perceptions of the artistic qualities in portraiture as well as acting, to ignore the arts as a medium for the Garricks of social discourse, to pervert what is the end of all art, the cultivation of human values, without becoming caught up in all the more recent obfuscated theorizing as to the psychological, even pathological aberrations of aesthetics. The eighteenth century agreed that the impact of a work of art was a moment of impersonal stability in the midst of chaos, of insight into some of the universal human values of order, and control. Surrounded daily by all the arts of their own choosing in their homes, the Garricks acquired an objectivity in observation and taste, the deepening of emotions, a refinement of manners, a capacity for generous and sincere friendships.

# Part Six
## The Actor

.

# 15

# Garrick's Great Comic Roles

Young David Garrick came to the stage with a sense of impish fun. He seemed to know that he could communicate this sense and create merriment among spectators by playing up the idiosyncrasies he had observed in the actions of his fellow men in their daily living. But he carried all off without exaggeration, leading his spectators to cry up from the start his "naturalness" and realism. Apt and important mimesis was at the heart of his acting. Unspoiled by adulation, he listened to critical voices and improved in finesse. The more mature Garrick spoke out on the subject of acting theory—for he was more than a mimic, bringing intelligent calculation to his performing, bent as he was on the artistic goal of dramatic effect—which for him lay in showing individualized characteristics of those whose roles he played. He schooled and disciplined himself until he attained a professional carriage that made all his actions seem effortless—as though he did everything with his right hand. He was aware, however, at every juncture that in the art sometimes moments of unexpected vision, power, and unschooled effects occurred at the point of action on stage, fleeting moments of achievement which electrified audiences and crowned the satisfactions of the player. He knew also that success came from excellent ensemble performance. Excellence of one amid a field of dross would not keep the profession afloat. The high quality of every player's performance contributed to the aesthetic pleasure of all in the theatre, including the actors themselves (528).[1]

During his career he performed 46 different comic roles 1,331 times,[2] and each time, according to contemporary comment, he played with just sufficient difference to give a pleasing freshness to his interpretations—a freshness required in repertory theatres. Though he expressed no theory of laughter and its psychological values, his whole presence on stage bespoke his understanding of the health-giving qualities of merriment. He knew as Ben Jonson knew before him and George Meredith knew in the century following him that men's lives

473

were often shapeless, and that volleys of silvery laughter directed at the distortions could, on stage, seem to set the characters back in well-rounded balance. Experience of such healthy activity might indeed have a subtle valuable carry-over to the spectators themselves. But like Farquhar Garrick was interested in a "tale handsomely told" and wished in carrying out his action on stage to absorb the attention of every beau and lady, servant and sober citizen in the audience. The man David Garrick, turned artist and actor, made real his vision of giving new insights into the personalities of those he presented.

Mention of new insights posits that audiences came with concepts about fictional characters long stereotyped. And so they had been. The critics, at least those whose names we know, all possessed a basic set of standards, a topical list of points of importance, a scale, a line upon which to hang their comments, and by which to keep them somewhat consistent. Schooled by the classics, in the head of each lingered the concept of the "rules" (shades of Aristotle) relating to the art and artifice of playmaking, and the importance of text and structure. The crossover was short from this to a sense of "proper" interpretation of text by actors. Schooled by the moralists, in the head of each lingered a concept of "right" didactic aims for plays (shades of Jeremy Collier and Arthur Bedford) and the moral emphases actors should provide. Schooled by the rhetoricians from Quintillian to Gildon, in the heads of these lingered a concept of the "passions" as universal phenomena, and of proper ways formally to communicate them by bodily motion, facial expression, voice, and gesture. Yet all such critics, as well as the nameless in the audiences, were human beings who enjoyed no end witnessing a grace seemingly beyond the reach of art, the 'je ne sais quoi' of the French, an effect so recognizable within their personal experiences that the actor seemed to convey it without the intervention of studied art. Garrick achieved this "grace" by a studied art to conceal art. Its effect was to open doors of new and fresh possibilities for viewing the characters he played. Francis Gentleman sensed what Garrick was doing—portraying "something critical and new" which gave a meaning, perhaps, "beyond the author's view."[3] Gentleman found this immediately convincing, and somewhat frightening. But for Garrick to work toward such a concept was to be creative; accomplishment of the goal was supreme art. The Garrick influence in this approach worked by way of continuing practice not through a manifesto of a new criticism.

One prominent school of criticiam flourishing up to the middle of the century practiced a judicial weighing and balancing of the "beauties" versus the "blemishes" of a play, or a performance. Such an aesthetic led to a mechanical summation of the one or the other—the more "beauties" discovered the better the piece, or performance. This balance for measuring aesthetic effects gave way as the century progressed to an increasingly profound critical concern with the characters of both comedy and tragedy as individuals with lives of their own, working out their destinies, adjusting their life-styles, mocking their elders and contemporaries, or sinking under the course of stern events beyond their control—acts, attitudes, and reactions which have defined the human condition from the beginning. This shift from the "judicial" to "interpretive" criticism becomes marked towards the end of the century. One can see its motion in contemporary reactions to Garrick's portrayals of characters.[4]

Description of this change has most to do with stage and intellectual history, but becomes pertinent to biography in that the new *dramatic* criticism developed from *theatre* criticism, which in turn centered upon the *actors* (in an age of great acting) and in particular upon Garrick's new acting insights, which indeed were a manifestation of the man and his artistic vision. George Steevens recognized the contribution Garrick was making when in 1765 he was editing Shakespeare. "Often when I have taken the pen in my hand to try to illustrate a passage, I have thrown it down again with discontent when I remembered how able you were to clear that difficulty by a single look, or particular modulation of voice, which a long and laboured paraphrase was insufficient to explain half so well."[5] Elizabeth Montagu sensed what Garrick was doing, writing to him in May 1770, "All the labours of the critics can do nothing by the dead letter of criticism against the living force of Mr. Garrick's representation."[6]

The genres—comedy, tragedy, farce—were in no sense monolithic types for Garrick, nor were the three basic types of comedy itself— situation (farce), comedy of character, and comedy of dialogue. The keynote to each was variability. To borrow a set of distinctions from Macbeth's urging on the murderers of Banquo, and apply it to the distinctions of comedy:

> Ay, in the catalogue ye go for men;
> As hounds and greyhounds, mongrels, spaniels, curs,
> Shoughs, water-rugs and demi-wolves, are clept
> All by the name of dogs: the valued file
> Distinguishes the swift, the slow, the subtle,
> The housekeeper, the hunter, every one
> According to the gift which bounteous nature
> Hath in him closed, whereby he doth receive
> Particular addition, from the bill
> That writes them all alike, and so of man. (III, i)

475

And so of comedy in Garrick's eyes. The gay but gentle rake Ranger; the witty, self-centered but to-be-overcome Benedict; the drunken but arrogant Sir John Brute; the opportunistic, commanding, intelligent Archer; the conceited, self-revealing Bayes; the uxoriously jealous Kitely—all are as different from the explosive juvenile and pride-ridden Don Felix as they all are from each other, and from the clever servant Sharp; the poseur Fribble; and the sly, terrified, but shrewd Abel Drugger. The essential personality of each, not any comic similarity (i.e., latent potential in all to make one laugh) appealed to Garrick, and made these characters his favorites for performing.

Garrick the *manager*, as we have seen, underwent at times heavy bombardment. Garrick the *actor* was praised even by opponents almost to a man. Real and petty grievances faded in the presence of his art. The impact made by the actor comes clear in descriptions by his viewers, and the descriptions often reveal the special qualities of the actor in his artistry. He triumphed in eight comic roles.

## BAYES IN 'THE REHEARSAL'

Buckingham's *The Rehearsal* (1671), we remember, pokes merciless fun at a would-be playwright, Bayes, who drafts a herioc play which in search of excessive novelty turns all conventions of dramatic communication topsy-turvy—whispers, or nonspeech (for exposition), barnyard similies (for flights of poetry), two kings (of Brentford of all places) as heroes, intrigues among courtiers (who turn out to be an usher and a physician), unheroic heroines (two for good measure), the Goddess Pallas, who turns the contents of a coffin into a freak banquet. All are put into rehearsal for the benefit of two interlocutors (Smith and Johnson) who stand amazed, then bored. Then these two sidemen string Bayes along to bring him out in his absurdities. The actors who are to rehearse can make nothing of their lines, movements, or business, even when coached by Bayes, who believes his text to be the greatest. The original performance struck, of course, at Dryden, then wearing the bayes of England's poet laureate. The text interwove in the dialogue of the "play within the play" lines from some 17 heroic plays of Dryden's era. Its universal satire, however, levels at the follies of dramatic craftsmanship itself, in the "new way" of writing.

Aged 23, and during his first season of acting, Garrick took on the role of Bayes. He was amazed, as were others, at his success, for he wrote to his brother Peter, "I have y$^e$ Greatest Success imaginable in y$^e$ Part of Bayes, & instead of clapping Me they huzza w$^{ch}$ is very uncommon approbation" (22). In the repertory he played it, over the years, 91 times. People were eager to compare his performance with those of recent memory by other actors who had in their day triumphed in the part. Eastcourt (1671) was a mimic, Colley Cibber a coxcomb in the part, Theophilus Cibber inventive but, according to Davies, acted with too much grimace. All former comedians brought laughter on Bayes's extravagances rather than upon the man himself. In Davies's words they by their actions told the spectators that they felt all the ridicule of the part, but Garrick appeared quite ignorant of the joke made against him. They seemed to sneer at the folly of Bayes *with* the audience; the audience laughed loudly *at* him. By seeming to understand the satire they caught at the approbation of the pit; he gained their loudest plaudits without letting them know that he deserved it. They [the Cibbers] were in jest; he was in earnest.[7] Garrick became the character and deadpanned it throughout.

But he was the character with a difference from the beginning, and gave it constant freshness as he continued to play it over the years. To the double satire in the play (upon heroic plays, and upon the craft of playwriting) Garrick added in performance satire upon pompous acting, stressing much Bayes's instructions to the players. Murphy is explicit, "The actors had lost all judgment . . . the best performers of the day had recourse to strutting, mouthing, and bellowing. . . . He seized the opportunity to make the *Rehearsal* a keen and powerful criticism on the absurd style of acting that prevailed on the stage."[8] What brought the huzzas at first, no doubt, was Garrick's skillful mimicking of three prominent actors, exaggerating their style with enthusiasm, and apparent approbation, in order to demolish it. Denis Delane, for example, a ranting declaimer at Drury Lane, and Hale and Ryan at Covent Garden exhibited the mannered acting which Garrick felt was false. On three occasions in the play he as Bayes became them, as he instructed them in their parts (in the absurd rehearsed play). The deadpan and earnest instruction began with Delane, in Murphy's words: "Bayes retired to the upper part of the stage, and drawing his left arm across his breast, rested his right elbow on it, raising a finger to his nose, and then came forward in a stately gait, nodding his head as he advanced, and, in the exact tones of Delane, spoke the lines, 'So boar and sow, when any storm is nigh, / Snuff up and smell it gath'ring in the sky.'" Delane, of course was the instru-

477

ment, false acting the target of the satire. Then he imitated the plaintive voice of Hale in another ridiculous speech in the text, and the "tremulous raven-tone" of Ryan in a third.[9]

Garrick soon abandoned the personal mimickry in order clearly to attack the concept he was driving at. To this end he changed voice and costume. Davies notes that "when he first exhibited Bayes he could not be distinguished from any other well-dressed man; but he soon altered it to a dress he thought more suited to the conceit and solemnity of the dramatic coxcomb. He wore a shabby, old-fashioned coat, that had formerly been very fine, a little hat, a large flowing brown wig, high topt shoes with red heels, a mourning sword, scarlet stockings, and cut-fingered gloves."[10]

Thomas Wilkes documents the change in 1759, when after watching Garrick he noted, "Mr. Garrick's satire is levelled at no particular person, but a whimsical unfashionable compound, extremely laughable, and still more so, when one compares it with the importance, and consequence, which he effects to maintain. His contempt for Mr. Smith's judgment; his astonishment and uneasiness at the players' being gone to dinner."[11]

A writer for the *Universal Museum* in March 1762 preferred Garrick in Bayes to any of his other comic parts for his "infinite fund of original humour." Was there "ever anything better spoke," wrote he, "than Bayes' telling the plot of his play; he amplifies himself into a full stop of confusion, and unable to go a step further, cries—'In fine you'll understand it better when you see it,'—and runs out to call the players. Never was any humour so striking as his manner of speaking this —when he turns about and finds Smith asleep, the contempt that is marked in his face is admirable. When Smith expresses his surprise at an army's being concealed at Knightsbridge, Johnson says, "No, not if the Innkeepers be his friends,'—'His friends!' replies Bayes, 'aye Sir, his intimate acquaintance; or else indeed I grant it could not be.' Here the natural humour of the poet is equalled by that of the actor . . . The moment the coffin changes to a banquet, Garrick cries out, 'Where's your Shakespeare now, Smith!' This [line] is not in the original, but is humorous and characteristical . . . Every syllable is spoke in such an admirable manner that the audience have hardly the power to clap, they are so engag'd with laughing."[12]

Garrick at this time had his whole company cooperating with him, and bantered them caressingly by updating the names of the characters in the play. "When Yates speaks a little Latin falsely, he says— 'and you Mr. Yates, you that was bred an attorney, not to speak it right!' Blakes, who acts Prince Prettyman, comes on with his usual

*Harvard Theatre Collection*
Garrick as Bayes in *The Rehearsal*.
Engraving by Pollard.

*gait*, and Bayes mimicks him, saying 'Now enter Mr. Blakes—not Prince Prettyman!' Garrick adopted Cibber's innovative use of "new rais'd troops" but also continued to insert contemporary and amusing topical references to the delight of the audiences. One such was reported when Garrick took up the part again in 1766, performing it at royal command. When Bayes is informed by one of the actors that the players have left and all gone to dinner, Garrick's Bayes exclaimed against them, "I'll *Rosciad*, I'll *Thespis* ye, I'll make ye tremble," at which a burst of applause ran through the whole house.[13]

People even found topical references where none existed, for Garrick was once accused of mimicking the voice of King George II in speaking the line *"Here are fine troops M$^r$ Johnson!"* The audience tittered and none of the actors knew why until the report spread. Garrick denied that he had ever heard the King speak, or had ever been at one of his military reviews (1347).

To get away with satirizing contemporary acting, Garrick obviously developed a marvelous characterization (or was it caricature) for Bayes. Principally he individualized him, and stayed with the serious characterization all the way, seeming to be the part—the object *and* the agent of the satire—and in doing so touched upon contemporary relevancies, yet he slightly distanced the character from accusations of personal animus toward fellow actors by new and appropriate costume.

That the subject, and the turn he gave to it, was dear to him appears not only in his keeping the part until 1772, but in his writing his own playlet (he called it a *Prelude*) *The Meeting of the Company* for performance 12 November 1774. He had toyed with the idea of reinforcing his strictures on bad acting for several years, thinking at one time to introduce a new scene about it into *The Rehearsal* (671). But he saved the skit for the *Prelude* subtitled "Bayes's Art of Acting, or the Worst equal to the Best," with its formula for upsetting values and equalizing all performance. He was serious throughout his career in mocking poor acting.[14]

## ARCHER IN 'THE BEAUX STRATAGEM'

Farquhar's play *The Beaux Stratagem* (1707) bantering romance, satirizing the system which perpetuated incompatible marriages, and having fun with two young adventurers seeking marriages of convenience to restore their financial credit was one of the most popular comedies of the century.[15] The plot centers at an inn and at the house of Lady Bountiful in Lichfield. Romantic love in the end succeeds, while the harsh bonds of a mis-marriage are displayed (with irony and humor) and are about to be broken as the curtain falls. An innkeeper, Boniface (fence for highwaymen), his saucy daughter Cherry, and Lady Bountiful's servant Scrub amuse and complicate the proceedings.

Garrick performed early (1742) the character of Archer, one of the beaux, which he later alternated with that of Scrub, to demonstrate to members of his company that any part well done was a credit to the profession. This play, to be sure, has more "good" parts than any comedy in the period. Archer and Aimwell his friend alternate roles in their expeditions to the countryside—one day in that of master, the next in that of his serving man. During the period of the play Archer has the role of Aimwell's serving man. The actor playing the role has the chance not only to play the part assigned, but in doing so subtly to reveal his basic character and station. The part seemed made for Garrick, who, as Thomas Wilkes tells us was "the footman, the gallant, and the gentleman by turns. His addresses to Cherry were easy and jocular. With Mrs Sullen [the charming and distressed wife of a country, drunken boor] he was polite and unaffected, particularly in the gallery scene, where the gentleman's education ought to shine upon the manners of the footman, where he talks of pictures and mythology."[16]

Garrick played the part 100 times, performing it at least once during every year save four of his acting career. He brought it to a refreshing new high for John Hill, who (though no friend of Garrick the man or manager) commented at length in *The Actor* (1750) emphasizing what he saw in Garrick's skillful "turns." "Till this excellent performer played this piece we never knew what beauties it was capable of in the sudden transition from passion to passion in the last act, when he alternately rejoices in the success of the scheme he was upon, and becomes the surly accuser of the friend who had partnership in it, and whom an instant before he was hugging in his arms; then he conceives new hopes from promising circumstances, which fail his expectation and return him to despair. In fine his mixture of the passions at the same instant in the dread of discovery from an old acquaintance, his transport in immediately afterwards finding this very person the messenger of better news than could have been expected; his passion for Mrs Sullen and his dear Cherry at the same time; his concern at the suppos'd loss of that good natur'd creature, and his joy at receiving news both of her and his money at once, all this, notwithstanding all that has been said of Mr. Wilks [the Archer idol of the early century]

481

Mr. WESTON & Mr. GARRICK *in y*ͤ *Characters of* SCRUB & ARCHER,
in the STRATAGEM.

Printed for J. Smith Nº. 35, Cheapfide & R. Sayer, Nº. 53 Fleet Street, Decʳ. 20, 1771.

*Harvard Theatre Collection*
Weston and Garrick as Scrub and Archer in *The Beaux Stratagem*.
Engraver unknown.

never was so expressed as to interest the audience in every one of the
several passions together . . . till we saw Mr Garrick in the character."[17] Hill was to be sure foreshortening the action taken in a number
of scenes to illustrate his point. Garrick was supreme in the climaxes
of plays—in timing, expression, attitude, and gesture. But his climaxes
were entertaining because of the gradual and effective buildup to them
throughout the play. Those trained upon principles of ancient rhetoric
saw Garrick as making "turns." Those not so schooled were pleased
with what they recognized as subtly exaggerated realism. Gentleman
wrote of him in 1770 "The attributes for supporting this part are vivacity of deportment, significancy of look, and pert volubility of expression; every one of which Mr. Garrick possessing it is no wonder his
performance should be capital; the scenes in which he particularly
outstrips competition are those with Cherry [early in the play], where
he delivers Lady Howd'ye's message, and the picture scene with Mrs
Sullen."[18]

The detail, however, marking Garrick's interpretation, rather than
generalization about his ability to portray a gay rake and opportunistic
fellow comes from the verbal close-up which Lichtenberg so often supplies. He wrote of Garrick and Weston playing Archer and Scrub to
his friend E. G. Baldinger on 10 January 1775: "Garrick appears in all
the insignia of His Majesty the lackey, fine suit, red feather, white silk
stockings, and a pair of quite unexceptionable calves and buckles.
Weston [who, Lichtenberg felt, surpassed Garrick in this scene], on
the other hand, poor devil, had a miserable hempen wig spoilt by the
rain, a grey jacket which he might be able to fill out if he got more
to eat, and a green apron and red stockings. He is filled with pious
astonishment when he catches sight of the gentleman's gentleman,
. . . though imagining him to belong to the same class of beings as
himself. . . . Archer, who is making use of him for his own purposes,
is particularly gracious, and Scrub, being sensible of this, does his
best, when he sits down, to cross his legs negligently like Archer; but
when the latter stretches out his silken calves as he talks, the poor
devil tries to cover his red woollen ones as far as possible with his
apron."[19]

Several months later Lichtenberg having seen the play again prepared a longer statement for H. C. Boie for insertion in the *Deutsches
Museum.* "It is impossible to describe a scene such as this, in which the
two favourites of an enlightened people strive to add to a fame established long ago; yet without overacting, since they are kept in check
by a most practiced judgment. . . . Garrick wears a sky-blue livery,
richly trimmed with sparkling silver, a dazzling beribboned hat with a

red feather, displays a pair of calves gleaming with white silk, and a pair of quite incomparable buckles, and is, indeed, a charming fellow. And Weston, poor devil, oppressed by the burden of greasy tasks, which call him in ten different directions at once, forms an absolute contrast. . . . He is all pious astonishment when this gentleman's gentleman (as the Göttingen girl said) appears. Garrick, sprightly, roguish, and handsome as an angel, his pretty little hat perched at a rakish angle over his bright face, walks on with firm and vigorous step, gaily and agreeably conscious of his fine calves and new suit, feeling himself head and shoulders taller beside the miserable Scrub. And Scrub, at the best of times a poor creature, seems to lose even such powers as he had and quakes in his shoes, being deeply sensible of the marked contrast between the tapster and the valet; with dropped jaw and eyes fixed in a kind of adoration, he follows all of Garrick's movements. Archer, who wishes to make use of Scrub for his own purposes, soon becomes gracious, and they sit down together. . . . This scene should be witnessed by any one who wishes to observe the irresistable power of contrast on the stage, when it is brought about by the perfect collaboration on the part of author and player, so that the whole fabric, whose beauty depends entirely on correct balance, be not upset, as usually happens. Garrick throws himself into a chair with his usual ease of demeanour, places his right arm on the back of Weston's chair, and leans towards him for a confidential talk; his magnificent livery is thrown back, and coat and man form one line of perfect beauty. Weston sits, as is fitting, in the middle of his chair, though rather far forward, and with a hand on either knee, as motionless as a statue, with his roguish eyes fixed on Garrick. If his face expresses anything, it is an assumption of dignity, at odds with a paralysing sense of the terrible contrast. . . . While Garrick sits there at his ease with an agreeable carelessness of demeanour, Weston attempts, with back stiff as a poker, to draw himself up to the other's height, partly for the sake of decorum, and partly in order to steal a glance now and then, when Garrick is looking the other way, so as to improve on his imitation of the latter's manner. When Archer at last with an easy gesture crosses his legs, Scrub tries to do the same, in which he eventually succeeds, though not without some help from his hands, and with eyes all the time either gaping or making furtive comparisons. And when Archer begins to stroke his magnificent silken calves, Weston tries to do the same with his miserable red woollen ones, but, thinking better of it, slowly pulls his green apron over them with an abjectness of demeanor, arousing pity in every breast. In this scene Weston almost excels Garrick by means of the foolish expression natural to him."[20]

Garrick, of course, was delighted. This was exactly the sort of complementary performing that he had striven for during his whole career. Weston through financial carelessness and love of the bottle was often a grievance to Garrick the manager, but Garrick tolerated his weaknesses and encouraged his acting every step of the way. About this time he wrote to George, "Weston is dying, & with him goes a good Actor, & a very bad Man" (954). Lichtenberg shows, more than any contemporary commentator, in his picking up of Garrick's detailed action, what surprising and delightful character revelations came across the footlights the evenings when Garrick played.

## ABEL DRUGGER IN 'THE ALCHEMIST'

*The Alchemist* (1610), one of Ben Jonson's many plays satirizing man's overweening desire for gold, displays a scheme foisted upon a set of gulls by the resourceful Face (servant of one Lovewit) and his colleague Subtle (a fake alchemist). Lovewit, out of town for a time, leaves his house in charge of his servant, his crony Subtle, and their paramour, Doll Common. A confidence game is set up, and the gulls who come trooping in (and finally get too crowded to be kept in their separate rooms, closets, and hallways) include a lawyer (Dapper), a tobacconist (Abel Drugger), a Knight (Sir Epicure Mammon) a gamester (Surly), two hypocritical puritans, an angry boy, and a widow. The close-knit plot builds suspense, for its breaking point will come at any of four points: when Lovewit returns to his house (an imminent possibility); when one of the gulls, Surly, who is not gulled reveals the fraud; when the comings and goings of the gulls (who bring their treasures to be turned to gold) overcrowd the accommodations, and begin comparing notes; and when the three tricksters fight among themselves for greed and for possession of Doll Common.

"Abel Drugger," wrote Thomas Wilkes, "is certainly the standard of low comedy, and Mr. Garrick's playing it the standard of acting in this species."[21] Drugger's time on stage is relatively short and his opportunities for speaking are considerably limited. His presence begets some moments of comedy of sheer situation which had been exploited (long before Garrick's appearance) by the accidental dropping of a glass urinal by Colley Cibber as he played the part. The sequence he made of it became incorporated in subsequent acting.

Garrick assumed the role early (1743) and performed it at least once

Mr GARRICK *in the Character of* ABEL-DRUGGER *in the Alchymist.*

*London, Printed for R. Sayer at N.º 53 Fleet Street & J. Smith at N.º 35 Cheapside. A*

*Harvard Theatre Collection*
Garrick as Abel Drugger in *The Alchemist*.
Engraver unknown.

a year (save for five scattered ones) until the very end—80 performances in all. On 12 April 1776 he wrote to George, "Last Night I played Drugger for yᵉ last time. . . . I thought yᵉ Audience were Mad, & they almost turn'd my brain" (1005). Such applause he had had from the beginning. Davies tells us in three sentences how his acting differed essentially from the performing to which audiences had become used in the 1740s. "Mr. Garrick freed the stage from the false spirit, ridiculous squinting, and vile grimace which, in Theophilus Cibber, had captivated the public, by introducing a more natural manner of displaying the absurdities of a foolish tobacconist."[22] The moment he came upon the stage "he discovered such awkward simplicity, and his looks so happily bespoke the ignorant, selfish, and absurd merchant, that it was a contest not easily to be decided, whether the burst of laughter or applause were loudest."[23] Through the whole Garrick underplayed the part, and strictly preserved a "modesty" of action which was new and effective.

Lichtenberg is again most perceptive regarding what Garrick was up to in his performance of the grotesque. He compared the appearance of Weston and Garrick in the role. "Scarcely has [Weston] appeared on the stage than a large part of the audience becomes oblivious of the play and heeds nothing but him and his antics. . . . People have eyes but for him alone. With Garrick it is quite otherwise, for one perpetually sees him as an effective part of the whole and a faithful mirror of nature. Therefore he could play his part badly in the eyes of his England, while Weston could scarce do so. Now Ben Jonson has indicated only a few points in Abel Drugger's character; and if a player can once get his line from this, he can proceed more or less *à son aise* with no fear of overstepping the mark. Weston has an excellent opportunity of ridding himself of his own personality, especially in the long intervals when Abel Drugger is dumb and in the room. . . . But when Garrick plays Abel Drugger it is the critic who leads the applause. Here we have a vastly different creature, an epitome of the author's purpose, heightened by a comprehensive knowledge of his characteristic traits, and interpreted so that he may be clearly understood from the top gallery downwards. . . . Every moment poor Abel is giving fresh indications of his character; superstition, and simplicity. . . . When the astrologers spell out from the stars the name, Abel Drugger, henceforth to be great, the poor gullible creature says with heartfelt delight: 'That is my name.' Garrick makes him keep his joy to himself, for to blurt it out before every one would be lacking in decency. So Garrick turns aside, hugging his delight to himself for a few moments so that he actually gets those red rings round his eyes which often accompany great joy, at least when violently suppressed, and says to himself, 'That is my name!' The effect of this judicious restraint is indescribable, for one did not see him merely as a simpleton being gulled, but as a much more ridiculous creature, with an air of secret triumph, thinking himself the slyest of rogues."[24] One suspects that Garrick was not merely trying for an obvious contrast in approach to that of T. Cibber, but was pursuing the course, so evident in his acting of all parts, of giving the unique humor and distinguishing detail of characterization that continued to astound his public. A remarkable, but nameless critic for the *London Chronicle* wrote of his performance on 5 March 1757, "how admirably does he exhibit the minutest circumstances with the exactest precision, without buffoonery, or grimace."

But one wishing more details of the whole performance should read the three long columns of the *London Chronicle* for 9 October 1759 under the rubric *The Theatre*. The author there briefed the plot, and sought to lure the public to the theatre by describing the acting not only of Garrick, but of Burton (Subtle), Palmer (Face), Mrs Pritchard (Doll), as indeed he should have done, for the remarkably tight plot, which Garrick maintained in its inexorable closing in on the con artists and the multiplicity of gulls in this get-rich-quick scheme, is what the play is all about. But the reviewer could not refrain from giving up one of the three columns to Garrick's performance of the amazing tobacconist.

Drugger cries out in the wings off stage that he "will see the Doctor." But his "first appearance would disconcert the muscular economy of the wisest mouth in London or Westminster. His attitude, his dread of offending the Doctor, his saying nothing, his gradual stealing in farther and farther, his impatience to be introduced, his joy to his friend Face, are imitable by none. Mr Garrick has taken that walk to himself, and is the ridiculous above all conception. He is Abel Drugger himself; we cannot believe that it can be Garrick. . . . When he first opens his mouth the features of his face seem as it were to drop upon his tongue—it is all caution—it is timorous, stammering a-a-a-nd and-and so-so-so something inexplicable, that words would but wrong the actor, and all colouring must be faint to express the action or expression of Garrick. When he stands under the conjuror to have his features examined, his teeth, his beard, his little finger, and the nail of his little finger, his awkward simplicity, and his concern mixed with hope, and fear, and joy, and avarice, and good nature, are above painting."

The business is brief, but the character shows forth, as Face urges Abel to give the Doctor a fee. Abel responds with a generous offer of *a* crown. Face repeats incredulously '*a* crown?' Abel misunderstanding

Bell's British Theatre, 1777
Garrick as Abel Drugger in *The Alchemist*.
Engraving by Thornthwaite.

Face and thinking his comment a reprimand for liberality, sticks by his meagre offer as though it were the wealth of the Indies. "He loudly opposes him," continues the Chronicler, "crying out importunately and repeatedly, 'I'll *give* him a crown; I'll *give* him a *crown*.'" The routine is repeated with the offer of tobacco, Abel suggesting gift of a pound of it. Face urges a hogshead. Abel is incredulous, but finding Face in earnest, Garrick shakes his head muttering "a hogshead! I'll bring him *two* pound." All this seemed admirably done. When Abel defends the confidence group and buffets Surly, the reviewer thought it so realistic that Garrick must have "stood several hours to see Broughton, Slack and other celebrated buffers of their time in order to make this picture so very striking." Abel does not know "friend from foe in this perambulation, and is going to strike all opposers, even his friend Face, whom he forgets in his fury, saying to the very scenes 'Will you, by G–d!'"[25]

Fortunately we have Garrick's own discussion of the difference between a "passion" for tragedy, and a "humour" for comedy, illustrated by his description of how Drugger should present (and how he himself actually did present) the by-play attendant on the breaking of the urinal—which so delighted audiences. There he not only described his stage business, but gave his reasons for performing each gesture and look.[26]

Garrick's suggestions for preparing for the presentation of a grotesque simpleton fearing to be caught in the act, and the Chronicler's and Lichtenberg's and Davies's descriptions of the effect produced upon themselves and the audiences in which they sat bespeak with marvelous clarity that Garrick lays down no rules for acting abstract universals, but is creating the character of Drugger. Ample leeway is granted in the Jonson text for the inclusion of interpretive business.[27] Garrick did not play Scrub in the same fashion. No patterning, but abundant understanding of the advantages of particularization. Result: great joy in box, pit, and gallery. And great challenge to the critics to define and describe the effects. Garrick sets his precepts and his examples forth not as *the* right way, but as a way—which worked.


## SIR JOHN BRUTE IN 'THE PROVOKED WIFE'

Vanbrugh's *The Provoked Wife* (1697) deals severely but comically with another marriage of convenience of an incompatible couple, Sir

*Harvard Theatre Collection*
Garrick as Abel Drugger, with Burton and Palmer, in *The Alchemist*.
Engraving by J. Dixon, 1771, from a painting by Zoffany.

*Harvard Theatre Collection*
Garrick as Sir John Brute in *The Provoked Wife*.
Engraving by Isaac Taylor for *The New English Theatre*, 1776.

John and young Lady Brute. His opening statement sets the tone of the play, which is a five-act tug-o-war between the two. *Brute:* "What cloying meat is love—when matrimony's the sauce to it. Everything I see, everything I hear, everything I feel, everything I smell, and everything I taste—methinks has wife in it. No boy was ever so weary of his tutor as I am of being married. My lady is a young lady, a fine lady, a vertuous lady—yet I hate her. There is but one thing on earth I loath beyond her: that's fighting." *Lady Brute:* "The Devil's in the fellow I think . . . , I thought I had charms enough to govern him . . . I think I have a right to alarm this surly brute of mine—but if I know my heart—it will never let me go so far as to injure him." His debaucheries and bravado, mixed with cowardice, are matched with her insinuations that he is being cuckolded for his brutishness. Quite a tussle. The closing lines suggest that no one has got really hurt: *Brute:* "Surly I may be, stubborn I am not / For I have both forgiven and forgot." And he ends claiming possession of great good nature.

Working under the initial drive for expanding his own repertoire, and for creating novelty in playing stage favorites, Garrick in 1744–45 worked up five new ones—Scrub, Othello, King John, Tancred, and Sir John Brute. The first four he gradually dropped, playing one of them, Othello, only three times, but Brute he played every single season of his career for a total of 105 performances. Novel it was as he created it, and famous it became from the start. The critics gave it close scrutiny because it differed markedly from the Brute they were used to (and had enjoyed) in Quin's performance, and in Colley Cibber's. Cibber had made Brute a soured and overbearing man retaining faint remembrance that he had been a gentleman. Quin "made him a Brute indeed, an ill mannered, surly swine of a fellow."[28]

Garrick conceived him as a more vigorous and dashing a dog than Cibber's, and a more subtle and complex figure than Quin's extreme. After all Vanbrugh the originator was ridiculing a total situation and everyone in it, but with sophistication, not with obvious bludgeoning. Even after Garrick had been performing it for over a decade the critic in the *London Chronicle* was amazed that he attempted it at all, for the play was still rather strong meat for the moral appetite of some Londoners in the 1750s.

Quin's rendering bred instant detestation among the ladies, "but with Mr. Garrick it is quite a different case: the knight is the greatest favorite in the play; such a joyous agreeable wicked dog, that we never think we can have enough of his company, and when he drinks confusion to all order there is scarce a man in the house who is not for that moment a reprobate at heart."[29] Lines were early drawn, and even as late as 1761 Churchill could give the palm in the *Rosciad* to Quin's smashing vigor.

But packed houses for 30 years and 105 performances tell a story of growing satisfaction, authenticated by an interesting change in the perceptions of a number of contemporaries.

The paragraph in a London paper for 9 January 1753 sounds like a "puff" calculated to attract the public to the theatre, but highlights elements to look for in the performance: "On Tuesday last the Comedy of *The Provok'd Wife* was presented when the part of Sir John Brute was performed by Mr. Garrick. The different habits of a man palled with matrimony and tired of women, surly to the ladies and joyous among men, cowardly and blunt, yet sensible and witty were all blended together by the performer, and marked with so much delicacy and humour that we are tempted to enlarge upon this head."[30] But the author chose to be silent "rather than bedaub him with the coarse awkward touches practised by some writers."

Murphy thought Garrick swept all before him in the part. "He was in fact another proteus, in the celerity with which he transformed into different shapes. The moment he entered, Sir John Brute was seen in his face, his gait, and his whole deportment. His voice which was naturally clear and agreeable to the ear, was changed to a rough and sullen tone."[31] Another writer for the *London Chronicle* (3 March 1757) gives some details of Brute's return from an evening's revelry: "Whoever has seen Garrick sit down in his chair, must acknowledge that Sleep comes upon him by the most natural gradations: Not the minutest circumstance about a man in that situation escapes him: the struggle between sleep and his unwillingness to give way to it is perfectly just. The lid depressed, yet faintly raised; the change of his voice from distinct articulation to a confused murmuring; the sudden oppression of his senses and the recovery from it; his then beginning his broken chain of thoughts, and the malicious smile that unexpectedly gleams from him till he is at length totally overpowered, are all such acknowledged strokes of art that they keep the whole house agitated at once with laughter and admiration." The governing word here is *art*, the author's recognizing in Garrick the professional who observed, studied, practiced, and represented with truth and seeming artlessness the individualized yet recognizably familiar experiences to all.[32]

The play which Garrick performed is another of those in whose text he took a major hand. His prompt copy in the Folger Shakespeare Library shows that Garrick kept his attention on cutting those passages which might offend good taste and religious convictions, made a much more sympathetic character out of Lady Brute, improved (by worsen-

Mr GARRICK in the Character of Sr JNo BRUTE

Printed for J. Smith No 35 Cheapside & R. Sayer No 53 Fleet Street. Act V. Scene II.

*Harvard Theatre Collection*
Garrick as Sir John Brute, Act v, sc. ii, of *The Provoked Wife*.
Engraver unknown.

495

ing) the character of Brute and Razor, tightened the pace of the play, and eliminated ideas no longer clear to the audience.[33] Presumably he marked out this book early on, either in 1744 when he first took the part, or in 1747 when he became manager. The point to be kept in mind is that Garrick envisioned the flow of the whole play, not just his own part in it; for his role, though outstanding, depends upon the harmonious performance of all.[34]

Although a number felt Brute's riotous revelry, or his street brawl as he impersonated a fine lady the most amusing, pictured, indeed, as they were by Zoffany, Lichtenberg again reinforces (very late in Garrick's career) the return home and falling asleep as the high point. "In all playhouses there is generally one or another of the actors who can represent a drunken man very tolerably. . . . Mr. Garrick plays the drunken Sir John in such a way that I should certainly have known him to be a most remarkable man, even if I had never heard anything of him and had seen him in one scene only in this play. At the beginning his wig is quite straight, so that his face is full and round. Then he comes home excessively drunk, and looks like the moon a few days before its last quarter, almost half his face being covered by his wig; the part that is still visible is indeed somewhat bloody and shining with perspiration, but has so extremely amiable an air as to compensate for the loss of the other part. His waistcoat is open from top to bottom, his stockings full of wrinkles, with garters hanging down, and, more-over—which is very strange—two kinds of garters; one would hardly be surprised, indeed, if he had picked up odd shoes. In this lamentable condition he enters the room where his wife is, and in answer to her anxious inquiries as to what is the matter with him (and she has good reason for inquiring), he, collecting his wits answers: 'Wife, as well as a fish in water'; he does not, however, move away from the doorpost, against which he leans as closely as if he wanted to rub his back. Then he again breaks into coarse talk, and suddenly becomes so wise and merry in his cups that the whole audience bursts into a tumult of applause. I was filled with amazement at the scene where he falls asleep. The way in which, with shut eyes, swimming head, and pallid cheeks, he quarrels with his wife, and, uttering a sound where 'r' and 'l' are blended, now appears to abuse her, and then to enunciate in thick tones moral precepts, to which he himself forms the most horrible contradiction; his manner, also, of moving his lips, so that one cannot tell whether he is chewing, tasting, or speaking: all this, in truth, as far exceeded my expectations as anything I have seen of this man. . . . Garrick possesses a talent for giving individuality to everything in so high a degree that it contributes not a little to his superiority."[35] Thus Garrick's new type of acting made its impression.

He kept the text fresh by subtle changes over the years, and he kept the interpretation fresh by obvious innovations in costume. Lichtenberg found this Brute "not merely a dissolute fellow, but Garrick makes him an old fop also, this being apparent from his costume. On top of a wig, which is more or less suitable for one of his years, he has perched a small, beribboned modish hat so jauntily that it covers no more of his forehead than was already hidden by his wig. In his hand he holds one of those hooked oaken sticks, with which every young poltroon makes himself look like a devil of a fellow in the Park in the morning. . . . Sir John makes use of this stick to emphasize his words with bluster, especially when only females are present, or in his passion to rain blows where no one is standing who might take them amiss."[36] Later, of course, he introduced a topical caricature of the headdresses of ladies of fashion (October 1775) in the lady-in-disguise scene. Hopkins noted in his *Diary,* "Mr G.—— never play'd better, & when he was in Woman's Cloaths he had a head drest with Feathers, Fruit etc. as extravagant as possible to Burlesque the present Mode of Dressing—it had a Monstrous Effect."[37]

Bayes, Archer, Drugger, and Brute, all humorous, all satirical, each so different from the other, had lives of their own on stage immediately before Garrick's first appearance. He re-moulded each to the delight and increased understanding of his spectators, and gave each a new and vibrant life for the 30 years of his performing. He reached for the distinctive humor the uniqueness of each, and found it.

### RANGER IN 'THE SUSPICIOUS HUSBAND'

In February 1747 *The Suspicious Husband* came on stage, the first good new comedy in England in 20 years, according to Murphy.[38] The author, Benjamin Hoadly, was the eldest son of the Bishop of Winchester, and doctor to George II. The play follows the tradition of comedy of manners, but tinged (as all eighteenth-century plays were) by a touch of the philosophy of "benevolence," which saw some goodness in the heart of every man. Even the salty Samuel Foote found the "characters real, the incidents interesting, the catastrophe pleasing, and the language pure, spirited and natural."[39] Hoadly wrote the

Mr GARRICK *in the Character of* Sr John Brute *in the* Provok'd Wife *Done from an Original Picture of the same size, in the Possession of Her Grace the Dutchess of Northumberland.*

*Printed for R. Sayer Nº 53 in Fleet Street, & J. Smith, Nº 35 Cheapside. 1769.*

*Harvard Theatre Collection*
Garrick as Sir John Brute in *The Provoked Wife*.
Engraver unknown.

498

*Act*     PROVOKED WIFE.     *Scene*

*Mr GARRICK in the Character of Sr JOHN BRUTE.*
*— So, how d'ye like my Shapes now?*

Bell's British Theatre, *1776*
Garrick as Sir John Brute in *The Provoked Wife*.
Engraver unknown.

499

play largely with Garrick in mind for the role of Ranger. Both were discussing it in August 1756, and it appeared six months later. Suited for Garrick in every way, the play brims with the *vis comica* which marked his standard for comic writing. A month after its debut a long article appeared in the *Gentleman's Magazine* [40] detailing its complicated plot and evaluating the effect. "Instead of long dialogues full of quaint repartees, common-place wit, forc'd conceit, and double entendres, some unexpected event arises every moment," wrote the reviewer. And so it does. Mr. Strictland is a jealous, old London householder, jealous of his honor and standing as a responsible citizen, suspicious of his ward Jacinta's actions with her lover Bellamy, suspicious of his wife, and so suspicious of his wife's friend Clarinda that he banishes her from his household. In seeking other quarters she is followed by her lover Frankly, to avoid whom she turns back to the Strictland house, where Frankly follows, enters, and doubles the suspicions of Strictland. Jacinta, determined to elope with Bellamy, prepares a rope-ladder drop on a moonlit evening when the coast is clear. Strictland's activities that evening upset the timing, and the genial rake Ranger passing by seeing the ladder and the casement above open, climbs in only to find Mrs Strictland sitting alone in Jacinta's room. As he begins his routine philandering approach, Strictland is heard coming. The wife hurries Ranger off through another room hoping he will escape unnoticed—for explanations would just complicate matters. He leaves his hat, which Strictland finds. The maid avows it belongs to Jacinta, who has dressed in boy's clothes to elope. And so the complications pile one upon another. The comedy of intrigue to by-pass bull-headed Strictland leads to the use of nearly every comic device the stage had known since the days of Aristophanes—mistaken identities, ladders for escape and entrance, letters passed to the wrong persons, an identifiable object (the hat) found in a compromising place, duels proposed in defense of "honor" (supposedly smirched), eternal comings and goings, clever servants to mix up then help unravel pyramiding complications. All becomes sorted out and ends happily enough—truly a merry play unburdened by any discernible moral. The reviewer longed for Ranger's reform so as not to downgrade a moral which the play might have shown.

But the rake struck Foote as a lively portrait of that real character in life. His errors arose from a want of reflection rather than from basic licentiousness. "A lively imagination with a great flow of spirits hurries him into all the follies of the town, but there is not the least shadow of wickedness or dishonour in any of his actions. . . . We are blind to

Garrick and Mrs Pritchard as Ranger and Clarinda in *The Suspicious Husband*.
Painting by Francis Hayman, 1747.

501

Bell's British Theatre, *1776*
Garrick and Mrs Abington as Ranger and Clarinda in *The Suspicious Husband*.
Engraving by Thornthwaite.

his foibles, entertained by his adventures, and wish to see the rogue reclaimed." Davies also stressed the nature of this rake (as Garrick played him) so acceptable to the mid-century, "A young fellow vicious by custom, and irregular through fashion; but honest, benevolent, and humane from temper and inclination."[41]

This much of Ranger's character was prescribed by the text, and Garrick immediately brought it to life, making it a favorite piece for him as well as for the public. In fact Ranger was his *most often* performed character in his whole repertoire of over 90 roles. He gave 121 performances of it from 1747 to 1776, acting it each year, save three, of his stage life. Murphy generalizes on the bland but pleasant character—"Ranger, as Garrick presented him, was the most sprightly, gay, frolicsome, young rake that had ever been seen on the stage."[42] Ten years after its debut *The London Chronicle* (1757) rehearsed the details afresh and commented (what critics were discovering, and knew not quite how to accept, save with excitement) "More is meant than meets the ear from this actor [Garrick] in general."

Garrick, firm in his popularity and anticipating solid backing for playing the role, wrote a sprightly Epilogue for it in the form of a beast fable. It turns out to be one of his earliest documents analysing the makeup of his audience, and what he might expect from each section of it. Bantering in tone, to be sure, and pleasantly taunting the spectators, it displays Garrick's cool appraisal, and the challenge he knew he had to meet by his performances. It might have been "iffy" as a Prologue to the first performance, but as an Epilogue coming just after his brilliant performance of Ranger, he knew it would score. An Ass, he wrote, felt need for writing a play and did so:

> The parts were cast to various beasts and fowl:
> The stage a barn—the Manager an Owl.
> The house was cramm'd at six, with friends and foes;
> Rakes, Wits, and Criticks, Citizens, and Beaux.
> These characters appear'd in different shapes
> Of Tigers, Foxes, Horses, Bulls and Apes. . . .
> Each, as he felt, mark'd out the Author's faults,
> And thus the *Connoisseurs* express'd their thoughts.
> The Critick-Curs first snarl'd—the rules are broke!
> Time, Place, and Action sacrific'd to joke!
> The Goats cry'd out, 'twas formal, dull, and chaste—
> Not writ for beasts of gallantry and taste!
> The Horned-Cattle were in piteous taking,
> At Fornication, Rapes and Cuckold-making!
> The Tigers swore, he wanted fire and passion.
> The Apes condemn'd, because it was the fashion![43]

Stentor Telltruth (the pseudonymous William Shirley), one of the "curs" who later snapped at Garrick's heels, produced a run of articles called *The Herald; or, Patriot Proclaimer* in 1758, several papers of which attacked the theatre management, and occasionally the actors. Shirley was candid in his stated purpose, "to break if possible the magic infatuation to which he [Garrick] has subdued the public mind, and aims to rule it by." Even Telltruth, he admits, must accord Garrick superiority over others in acting, but the Stentor tends to concentrate usually on what he finds to be failures in Garrick rather than points of merit. Ranger, however, stopped him: "There is indeed a middle character that he is truly excellent in, which is Ranger, to which his sprightliness gives an uncommon grace; and it is perhaps from that single circumstance that he shows more genuine humour in that part than in any other character he performs."[44]

Lichtenberg did not see Garrick play the part, or he would have sent a perceptive close-up about it to the Göttingen papers, but Francis Gentleman saw Garrick perform it many times. His labored encomium turns out to be general, however, rather than specific: "Mr. Garrick was [the author's] faithful representative; the volatile humour of the inconsiderate Templar was admirably described by the most metamorphosable actor; insomuch that we remember several young fellows, who, having more spirit than sense, attempted to imitate his Ranger in real life, for which both their bones and pockets suffer'd smartly."[45]

Obviously Garrick performed Ranger with a pleasingness agreeable to all—friend and foe, moralist and libertine.[46] By it he kept alive the tradition in eighteenth-century comedy of (slightly modified) the comedy of manners—the slash of satire yielding a bit to amiable humor. This he preferred to what has long been termed "sentimental comedy." His own *Clandestine Marriage* was to follow in this vein, as he and Colman planned and wrote it together, and his company performed it with great success in 1766.

## BENEDICT IN 'MUCH ADO ABOUT NOTHING'

Shakespeare's comedy *Much Ado* is, of course, filled with various kinds of merriment from the amusing problems of the basic plot, where the suspicions of Claudio for the purity of his beloved Hero are happily resolved, to the blundering incompetence of the constabulary with Dogberry and his crew, to Shakespeare's fresh additions to the original Sicilian story in the matchmaking of the confirmed antagonists Benedict and Beatrice. It had been played at sporadic intervals only eight times in the whole century before Garrick virtually revived it. He sensed in it the closeness of the bipolarity-of-sex theme to what had amused audiences since the time of the Restoration. He sensed the appositeness of that to a particular episode in his own life, and saw in the play another fine example of Shakespearian comedy. "Sacred to Shakespeare was this spot design'd," wrote he about Drury Lane and its repertory, "To pierce the heart, and humanize the mind."[47] And to be sure during his reign as manager, Shakespearean plays provided 27 percent of all performances of tragedy and 16 percent of all performances of comedy at his theatre.[48] Of the three comic Shakespearean roles he played himself[49] Benedict was his favorite, was the third most frequently performed of all his comic parts (113 times), and was done by him at least once each year from 1749 until the end, a 28-year span, and the audiences kept asking for more.

The noun most frequently used by contemporaries to describe Garrick's comic performances is *vivacity*—a suggestive term, but worn thin by repetition. Yet one can hardly escape using it for the quality of his performing Benedict. Wilkes noted his Benedict as "an agreeable display of wit and humour giving us a most lively picture of the gaiety and sprightliness of the poet's age."[50] Garrick chose the part just after he became manager and during the time he was courting Eva Maria Violette, about to be his wife. His first appearance during the 1748–49 season opened with Benedict on purpose to allow the bachelor jokes in it to break upon him as citizen Garrick. Cross noted in his *Diary*, "It being the first time of Mr Garrick's playing since his Marriage, the Jests in Benedict were receiv'd with uncommon applause."[51] Wilkes noted that same year, "Beatrice and he are very good counterparts. The eager solicitude of his look, while he is attending to a conversation on himself, is perfectly comic; so it is in his soliloquy, wherein he so gravely reasons himself into a resolution of falling in love, and the self-flattering air he assumes on her speech to him, 'If I don't pity her I am a villain, etc.' let these be compared with his spirited raillery against matrimony, and we shall see the different beauties of each in their true light."[52]

Theophilus Cibber, of course, sour on Garrick from belief that he had blocked his attempt to gain license for a third theatre, leveled a blast at his acting, "pert vivacity," "caricature of gesture," "pantomimical manner of acting every word of a sentence." He wrote specifically in dispraise of Garrick's action accompanying Benedict's sentence, "If I do, hang me in a bottle like a cat, and shoot at me." This short sentence "requires not such a variety of action as minutely to describe the cat being clapped into the bottle, then being hung up, and the farther painting of the man shooting at it."[53] A piece of comic business this, and a particularization of the vivacious Benedict that seemed to disturb no one else in the theatre. Whether Garrick often repeated it none can tell. Since he was apt to invent fresh business for each performance, one doubts that any of it became routine.

Practiced and professional though Garrick was by the time he undertook Benedict, he refused to venture on the part in any surefooted, offhand manner. Any play was to be well rehearsed, or its performance was an insult to the audience, but he was apt to prepare a Shakespearean one with particular care. In fact he wrote to John Henderson that "he was up to two months rehearsing Benedict before he could satisfy himself that he had modelled his action and recital to his own idea of the part."[54] The pains he took paid off, for he and Mrs Pritchard turned out to be an unbeatable pair in the play as long as she acted.[55]

When he returned from France he managed, as we have seen, to get this play requested as a command performance to return him to acting. The success which attended it confirmed his desire and willingness to resume. Davies comments on the resounding applause he received for the performance and for the patriotic prologue which he wrote and spoke at the time—called for on ten succeeding nights. But more importantly Davies further writes, "It was remarked by the most discerning judges, that our Roscius had, by visiting foreign theatres, greatly profited in his mode of representation; they observed, that his action, though always spirited and proper, was become easy and unrestrained; that his deportment was more graceful, and his manner more elegant; that he did not now appear so solicitous for applause, as to disturb his own feelings."[56]

Though he could not go so far himself, Francis Gentleman wrote in 1770, many leading critics thought Benedict to be "hist best comic character, notwithstanding, we *are* willing to allow the pre-eminence of his significant features, the distinct volubility of his expression, and his stage manoeuvres. In the scenes of repartee with Beatrice his distinct vivacity gives uncommon satisfaction."[57] He felt Garrick was getting too old for the part, but could think of no youngster who could equal him. A writer for the *Morning Chronicle* two years later was not

*Mr. Garrick, in the Character of Benedick.*

*Ha! the Prince & Monsieur Beu! I will hide me in the Arbour.*

Act II. Sc. 3.

Publish'd by J. Wenman 1 July 1778.

*Folger Shakespeare Library*
Garrick as Benedict in *Much Ado about Nothing*.
Engraver unknown. Published by Wenman, 1778.

disturbed by Garrick's age, because of his professional competence. "Mr Garrick yesterday played Benedict with a degree of excellence and propriety which sets both description and applause at defiance. Words cannot express the ease, the humour, the feeling and the gentleman-like carriage of this great actor in his scenes with Beatrice and Count Claudio." The author was concerned, however, about the future of the stage, for "how much it is to be lamented that a single man, verging upon sixty, should as a general actor throw at an insurmountable distance every youthful competitor for the wreath of superior excellence." [58]

The memory of Garrick's unique interpretations and their suitableness to the total play lasted long. Frederick Reynolds, the playwright, had as a Westminster schoolboy seen Garrick as Benedict. Harris, the Covent Garden manager, asked him next morning what scene he liked best. He replied that it was where Garrick challenged Claudio, and explained that, "He there made me laugh more heartily than I ever did before, particularly on his exit, when sticking on his hat, and tossing up his head, he seemed to say as he strutted away. 'Now Beatrice, have I not cut a figure?'" "You are right my boy," rejoined Harris, "Whilst other actors by playing this scene seriously produce little or no effect, Garrick by acting it as if Beatrice were watching him, delights instead of fatiguing the audience." [59]

In 1775 he still impressed Lichtenberg with his grace, youthfulness, and power to communicate the feelings of a stage character to an audience: "In the dance in *Much Ado about Nothing*, he excels all the rest by the agility of his springs; when I saw him in this dance, the audience was so much delighted with it that they had the impudence to cry *encore* to their Roscius. In his face all can observe, without any refinement of feature, the happy intellect in his unruffled brow, and the alert observer and wit in the lively eye, often bright with roguishness. His gestures are so clear and vivacious as to arouse in one similar emotions. With him one looks serious, with him one wrinkles one's forehead, and with him one smiles; in his intimate joy and the friendly manner in which he appears in an aside to take the audience into his confidence, there is something so insinuating that one's heart goes out to this charming man." [60] To create individual characters and instant empathy for them marked the quality of Garrick's professionalism. Wilkes felt this power in his Lord Chalkstone, his Schoolboy, and even in his Fribble, for "he gives us not resemblances, but realities; he does not exhibit, but creates." [61]

KITELY IN 'EVERYMAN IN HIS HUMOUR'
AND
DON FELIX IN 'THE WONDER'

In the 1750s within five years of one another Garrick revived *Every Man in His Humour*, and Susannah Centlivre's *The Wonder; or, A Woman Keeps a Secret*. The characters he acted—Kitely, the jealous merchant in Jonson's play, and Don Felix, the spoiled and immature young Portuguese nobleman—offer contrasts in Garrick's performance of quite different comic parts dealing with essential jealousy. They were the eighth and twelfth (respectively) most often performed roles in Garrick's repertoire—Kitely for 81, and Felix for 70. The one offered dialogue in plentiful supply, but in language somewhat unfamiliar to Garrick's actors, so he was challenged to make it entirely understandable while preserving its flavor, as discussed in chapter 5, above. The other, everyone seemed to agree, moved with undistinguished dialogue, leaving much for actors to animate.[62] The plots were entertaining in both—probable, well-paced, full of movement where characters just miss each other at points of suspense—thus adding to the amusing complications.

*Every Man in His Humour* was Jonson's earliest (1598) attempt in the "comedy of humours" to show

> deeds and language such as men do use,
> And persons such as Comedy would choose
> When she would show the image of the times,
> And sport with human follies not with crimes.

It succeeded in its own day, and with Garrick's revival in 1751 became a main staple in the Drury Lane repertory. It seeks to laugh back into shape half a dozen gulls and persons pulled all one way by a particular obsession—a braggart soldier, Captain Bobadil; an over-possessive father, Knowell; an explosive squire, Downright; town and country gulls, Stephen and Matthew; but particularly a London merchant, Kitely, recently married to a young and beautiful wife whom he suspects (unjustly and without foundation) of cuckolding him. The comic treatment of his reelings and writhings of jealousy emerges prominently. Jonson develops Kitely's character (not caricature) in the merchant's care for his business, his reputation amongst the citizenry, his timidity in offending anyone, especially his brother-in-law, Wellbred (whom he wishes to eject from his house because of his companions, whom he suspects have an eye on his wife). Wellbred brings these to the house, and Kitely tries to get his brother, Downright, to eject him. Wellbred is only seeking a match between his friend young Knowell and his sister, Bridgit. The catalytic agent is Brainworm, the clever servant who manages to set all parties at loggerheads, and to cause a meeting of all at Cob the waterman's house. There come Dame Kitely (who has been led to think that Kitely is there visiting Bridgit) and Kitely (who suspects Cob's house to be the rendezvous for his wife and some lovers). The group is brought finally before Justice Clement, in whose presence a rational explanation for all actions emerges, and makes each party look foolish and become cured of his "humour."

Kitely's humor of unfounded jealousy begets laughter to drive it back into balance. "The anxiety and the fears here natural to the part, and the awkward endeavour at disguising the ruling passion, are capital," wrote Wilkes, "both in the poet and the player, particularly where the husband unawares drops it that he has been pointed at as one disturbed with jealousy:

> *Dame Kitely*: Why, were you ever jealous?
>
> *Kitely*: What?—ha! never! Ha, ha, ha (she stabs me home)—jealous of thee! No, do not believe it—speak low my love.

Garrick's laugh here is, as his wife afterwards express'd it, 'seemingly without mirth, constrained, and affected to the utmost.' His supposed detection of old Knowell, in an intrigue with his wife, at Cob's house, is a scene that would make an exceeding good picture. In a few words here before the Justice and indeed, through the whole part [Garrick] shows a deep knowledge of the human heart; and it is equal to anything that ever was seen."[63] "To disguise his suspicions, writes Murphy, "Garrick assumed an air of gaiety, but under the mask the corrosions of jealousy were seen in every feature. Such was the expression of that various face that the mixed emotions of the heart were strongly marked by his looks and the tone of his voice."[64]

Jonson's skillful plotting, during which the several sets of characters have moved in their various byways ending up at the close of the fourth act in a crisis, whose solution cannot be foreseen, hinges on Wellbred's account of Cob's house—supposedly one of ill fame. When they all meet before Justice Clement, Dame Kitely tells him the reputation of the house, and that she went thither to find her husband. "Did you find him there?" asks the Justice. "In that instant," writes Murphy, "Kitely interposes, saying in a sharp eager tone, 'I found *her* there.' He who remembers how Garrick uttered these words, slapping his hand on the table, as if he made an important discovery, must acknowledge, trifling as it may now be thought, that it was a genuine stroke of nature."[65]

Garrick put this play into longer rehearsal than for any other play, working with each actor in his part. Sensibly, however, he recognized, says Davies, that "all that can be expected from genius is to take the outline and observe a few hints towards the coloring of a character; the heightening, or finishing, must be left to the performer."[66] Garrick suggested an outline to Woodward for playing Bobadil, but Woodward went his own way, and Garrick applauded the result; for Garrick had gone his own way too in part after part, and he recognized Woodward as particularly competent. The play was frequently commanded, and Garrick redoubled the rehearsals before each such request, uneasy that otherwise perfection might not come about. But he always carried through well.

Wilkes's comment above notes basic differences between the jealousies of Kitely and Felix. Distinctions were constantly on Garrick's mind, as he wrote to H. P. Sturz (1769): French politeness "has reduced their Characters to such a sameness . . . that when you have seen half a dozen French Men and Women you have seen the whole: in England . . . every Man is a distinct Being, and requires a distinct Study to Investigate him. . . . Since you have left us, I have played the character of a young (fye, for shame!) jealous *amoreux*, in the Comedy *The Wonder*; and it has been followed in a most extraordinary manner" (528).

In Mrs Centlivre's comedy *The Wonder; or, A Woman Keeps a Secret* (1714) Don Felix, a headstrong, super-proud son of a Portuguese Grandee, Don Lopez, escaping from a forced marriage, and having seriously wounded a fellow Portuguese, fears for his life should the wounded Antonio die. He returns, however, from flight because of his passion for Violante, Don Pedro's daughter. Felix's sister, Isabella, under similar pressure from Don Lopez to marry for convenience, not for love, escapes her locked room, is picked up by a Scot, Colonel Briton, and taken for refuge to her friend Violante's house. Briton, visiting there the next day, is caught sight of fleetingly (as he escapes over the fence, for no man is supposed to visit Violante) by Felix, who flies into a rage, thinking that Violante has taken a lover. Isabella beseeches Violante not to disclose to anyone her hiding place, lest her firey tempered brother think family honor smirched, and complicate matters with his sword. This secret Violante keeps at her own near peril as events unfold. A game of dodging and disguise follow, complicated by Felix's jealousy until all problems are solved happily at the close.

The unknown reviewer for *The London Chronicle* in October 1758, noted that "The writing of [*The Wonder*] is below censure, and the acting of it above praise." Specifics are wanting describing Garrick's acting and stage business, his improvisations, gestures, attitudes, and looks. But that it was different and impressive comes across again and again in the general appraisals of the time. A writer for *The Annual Register* (8 June 1776) commented on Garrick's final performance in the play: "His performance was inimitable, never were the passions of love, jealousy, rage etc. so highly coloured, or admirably set off [How long critical adherence to universals hung on!], in short he finished his comic course with as high a theatrical climax, as he had done the Saturday before his tragic one."

Garrick chose the play for its Plautean *vis comica*—intrigue relying on mistaken identities, disguise, coincidence, quick comings and goings into closets (for concealment) wrong bedrooms, and exact timing, together with its attractive "downstairs" subplot. Felix's beloved Violante dominates the play in its parade of mistakes and recoveries, or near misses, and final conquest *by the women* of the piece.

Extrication of Felix from Violante's house, right under Don Pedro's nose, disguised as maid Flora's mother, gave possibilities for comedy of situation. For a duplicate escape Garrick rewrote a scene (very comically) to give the actors a chance that Mrs Centlivre had missed.[67] But the fine scene in Act v was the sort Garrick excelled in. After his thundering about and crying infidelity to Violante's face, she bids him begone, sits, and looks away. He sits and gradually draws his chair nearer, "looking at her sometimes without speaking, then he draws a little closer." "Give me your hand at parting, Violante, won't you!" He lays his hand upon her knee several times. "Won't you—won't you —won't you." *Violante*: "Won't I what!" *Felix*: "You know what I would have, Oh my heart." Just an echo here from Garrick and Mrs Pritchard in Benedict and Beatrice, but only a faint memory, for the characters and the acting differ.

By 1772 even the unco guid were coming round to see a fine effort in Garrick's comic treatments, if not always the positive moral results they devoutly wished for. One such wrote, "Garrick not only with all the united powers requisite to expose deformity of every kind, but with a bright example in his own person (the severest satire on indecorum) gains it is true the applause of the town as a debt to his merit, but scarce one proselyte from his scourge on folly. . . . He lashes the ridiculous characters of every stamp, age and complection. Although in his Fribble, Ranger, Mr. Oakly, Benedict, Bayes, Chalkstone, Brute etc., he strikes home, and places such beings in a disadvantageous

Mrs BARRY and Mr GARRICK.
in the Characters of Donna Violante and Don Felix in the Wonder.
Done from an Original Picture in the Posseſsion of Her Grace
the Dutcheſs of Northumberland.
Printed for J. Smith Nº 35 in Cheapside & R. Sayer, Nº 53 Fleet Street, 1769.

Garrick and Mrs Barry as Don Felix and Violante in *The Wonder*.
Printed for J. Smith, 1769.

point of view, yet we find the real characters in life still existing."[68] A far cry this, from the diatribes of Jeremy Collier and Arthur Bedford 60 years earlier! But the real effect of the actor came in the aesthetics of comic performance, and the therapeutic results of laughter.

A single long sentence from George Meredith's "Essay on Comedy and the Uses of the Comic Spirit," though made a century later, seems to express well Garrick's understanding of the function of comedy,

> Men's future upon the earth does not attract it; their honesty and shapliness in the present does; and whenever they wax out of proportion, are overblown, affected, pretensious, bombastic, hypocritical, pedantic, fantastically delicate; whenever it sees them self-deceived or hoodwinked, given to run riot in idolatries, drifting into vanities, congregating in absurdities, planning shortsightedly, plotting dementedly; whenever they are at variance with their professions, and violate the unwritten but perceptible laws binding them in consideration one with another; whenever they offend sound reason, fair justice: are false in humility or mined in conceit, individually or in bulk; the spirit overhead will look humanely malign, and cast an oblique light upon them, followed by volleys of silvery laughter.

Garrick set the stage for this, chose the medium, acted the part, became the great instrument in his individualizing and compelling art—professional, but easy; attractive and creative to the end.

# 16

# Garrick's Great Tragic Roles

Joshua Reynolds, late in life, sketched out a "Dialogue" which might have been held between Edward Gibbon and Dr Johnson in which the historian attacks Garrick in order to bring out Johnson's defense that, "Garrick was no common man." Gibbon insists in it that surely Garrick in acting "feels the passion at the moment he is representing it." *Johnson*: "About as much as Punch feels. . . . Garrick's trade was to *represent* passion not to feel it." [1] Audiences, however, as noted, thought Garrick felt, that in becoming the persons he personated he involved himself totally—intellectually, imaginatively, emotionally. "I feel," wrote Edward Taylor (1774) watching Garrick in Lear, "because he seems to feel, and that I do involuntarily and instantaneously." [2] How else, one would think, could the realistic details spectators saw have entered into his acting? They noted again and again his "inexhaustible fire," "imagination warm and alive," "just sense of every passage."

Johnson, however, was right, for he understood the *art* of acting. Garrick's letters speak of the extreme difficulty of some roles, and of the energy expended in carrying off to his own satisfaction, say, the death scene in *Macbeth*. One must distinguish between the nervous (and physical) energy released in preparing a characterization (along with that in working out on stage some of its movements) and the supposed psychological and emotional involvement in acting it. Death falls on stage must seem realistic and may hurt. Certain tensions and their maintenance must seem to crack the sinews of the character undergoing them, but Garrick disciplined his action, knew and developed the art to conceal art. He conceived each character, delineated it so that the public thought he was the very person, but he distanced himself from enervating total psychological involvement. A gentleman remarked to Tom King that no one roused feelings in a spectator as did Garrick, and "none suffered more than he from these exertions." "Pooh," said King, "he suffer those feelings! Why, Sir, I was playing with him one night in *Lear*, when in the middle of the most passionate and affecting part, and when the whole house was drown'd in tears, he turn'd his head around to me and whisper'd 'D—mn me Tom, it'll do.'"[3]

The letters are in no way hypocritical about the difficulty entailed in acting some parts, for the "fatigue" often noted relates not to "core" involvement, but to nervous and physical energy expended as displayed (under control) on stage, and related to the delicacy of his physical condition. After all he perfected himself in just over 90 different roles, and performed them over the years just over 2,500 times on stage.[4] He was careful of his health, but often spoke in correspondence of the drain which preparation and acting of parts caused. Behind his expressions of concern about the physical consequences of overexerting himself in the heavy roles one detects no hypochondria, or self-serving complaining, but rather desire to measure up to the greatness of the dramatic heritage which his England enjoyed. From the dimmer side of the footlights he always seemed spry, agile, and dynamic. Greatness, he had been told a hundred times, as he began playing, lay in remarkable performance of great *tragic* roles.

An early example suggests his vision, preparation, and accomplishment—his performing King John in Shakespeare's play, one of the roles which broke his health in 1745. Death scenes in such plays had to be done with extreme care lest their elongation appear contrived, artificial, and excessive. If done without balance the aesthetic effect of the play became endangered. Davies recorded the action for posterity: "In the battle excursion John and Hubert prepare the reader by the sickness of the King for the close of the tragedy. These short scenes are of real importance, though often neglected by actors of some merit, because not attended with expected applause. It was the great excellence of Garrick to hold in remembrance the character he played through all its various stages. No situation of it whatever was neglected by him. By his extreme earnestness to appear always what he ought to be, he roused the audience to a correspondent approbation of his action. In this dialogue with Hubert, Garrick's look, walk, and speech confessed the man broken with incessant anxiety, and defeated both in body and in mind. Despair and death seemed to hover round him. . . . In the dying scene the agonies of a man expiring in a delirium were delineated with such wonderful expression in his countenance that he impressed uncommon sensations marked with terror, on the admiring spectators, who could not refuse the loudest tribute of applause to his inimitable action. Every word of the melancholy news uttered by Faulconbridge seemed to touch the tender strings of life, till they were quite broken, and he expired before the unwelcome tale was finished."⁵ *Admiration* in the century connoted awe and surprise and wonder at the opening up of insights hitherto unknown.

The ten *tragic roles* most often acted by Garrick, and most written about by spectators delineate sufficiently his vision of responsibility to entertain London audiences.⁶ The ten most called for tell us more about the man and actor (for their range is great) than comment upon his total of 43 such roles. Since Garrick's acting powers continued to grow toward perfection it is meet to view his impact in the parts as they appeared, yet to try to sense the essence of each as he played it from initial to final performance. To avoid vain speculation we tend to let contemporary voices be heard in descriptions of the roles.

A recurring word in all the commentary is *new* or *novel*, recording the surprise felt at Garrick's fresh ways of communicating insights into characters often familiar. At first this impressive novelty was commented on as it seemed to reside in his conversational tone instead of tragic rant; in under rather than overplayed gesture; in facial expression revealing inner thought and incipient imaginings; in the command that lay in his piercing eyes; and in the range and modulation of his voice, which could send a distinct whisper to the top of the upper gallery. Later the same commentators became enchanted with Garrick's finesse in performing, and in the depth of characterization revealed by a comparison of his individualized interpretations with the "turns" upon the nine "universal passions" familiar to them from the school of actors Quin, Cibber, Bridgwater, and Delane. Words save for *inimitable* often failed the critics.

## RICHARD III

It took but a single night's performance of *King Richard III* on 19 October 1741 at Goodman's Fields theatre for word to spread through London that something new was commencing in the world of the theatre. Next day Garrick wrote excitedly to his brother Peter, "Last Night I play'd Richard yᵉ Third to yᵉ Surprise of Every Body" (15). A week later he wrote again, "I have not yet had my Name in yᵉ Bills & have play'd only yᵉ Part of Richard yᵉ 3ᵈ wᶜʰ brings crowded Audiences every Night & Mʳ Giffard returns yᵉ Service I have done him very amply" (17). The 24-year-old actor was on his way.

Springs of aesthetic enjoyment run equally from "recognition" and from "discovery." The oldest in Garrick's audience could remember many a performance of *Richard III*, for it had been played some 88 times in London since 1700, rather consistently each season, and by a succession of competent actors—Colley Cibber (whose adaptation of the play held the stage), Lacy Ryan, Dennis Delane, and James Quin, among others. Garrick in taking on this particular role was challenging comparison with the best and in a favorite play. Recognition would be baffled and discovery, if it developed as he hoped, would make the eyes open and the breath come quick in the throats of spectators.

Davies relates what Garrick's audiences saw and felt: his "easy and familiar, yet forcible style in speaking and acting, at first threw the critics into some hesitation concerning the novelty as well as the propriety of his manner. They had been long accustomed to an elevation of the voice, with a sudden mechanical depression of its tones, calculated to excite admiration and intrap applause. To the just modulation of the words, and concurring expression of the features from the genuine workings of nature, they had been strangers, at least for some time. But after he had gone through a variety of scenes, in which he gave evident proofs of consummate art, and perfect knowledge of character, their doubts were turned into surprise and astonishment, from which they relieved themselves by loud and reiterated applause. They were more especially charmed when the actor, after having thrown aside the hypocrite and politician, assumed the warrior and the hero. When news was brought to Richard, that the Duke of Buckingham was taken, Garrick's look and action, when he pronounced the words, "Off with his head! / So much for Buckingham!" were so significant and important, from his visible enjoyment of the incident, that several loud shouts of approbation proclaimed the triumph of the actor and satisfaction of the audience. . . . Mr. Garrick shone forth like a theatrical Newton; he threw new light on elocution and action."[7]

Even the crusty Macklin was impressed, who wrote to William Cooke: "It was amazing how without any example, but on the contrary with great prejudice against him, he could throw such spirit and novelty into the part as to convince every impartial person on the very first impression that he was right. In short, Sir, he at once decided the public taste; and though the players formed a cabal against him with Quin at their head, it was a puff to thunder."[8] Both these comments were written somewhat after the event itself, but convey what occurred and what the outcome was. The public imagination was released. Among the articulate in due course the new interpretive brand of dramatic criticism of tragedy came about.

In that first season many letters of advice came to Garrick. The Reverend Thomas Newton, who had come down from Lichfield to see him, reacted on 16 December, "I endeavoured to find all the fault I could; but with all my criticisms there are two or three things only, and those hardly worth insisting upon, which I could wish otherwise." He thought Garrick arose too quickly from his couch in the fifth act, that he was not peevish enough in tone when he told Lady Anne that she had committed the worst of crimes, "outlived [his] liking"; that he should have suited action to words when comparing the young princes to spiders, and, when saying "I would have some friend tread upon them," should have made not only a motion with his hand but with his foot also.[9]

The Cibber version which Garrick acted and interpreted takes its cue from Richard's long and revealing soliloquy from Act III, sc ii, of Shakespeare's *3 Henry VI*, where his villainy is clear, calculated, intellectual, and dispassionate. Richard likes to observe the effect of a cold brutal statement upon a sensitive mind, as well as of a passionately acted and imploring statement upon a prejudiced mind. His relations with Anne are at first imploring, and afterwards harsh, yet his success in both is what pleases him. Garrick carried this impression over which at first, as Davies said, baffled the critics. But Richard possesses a distinctive character, and a complex makeup. He is not merely the stereotyped villain. And Garrick conveyed this distinctiveness to his interpretation. Until the episode at Bosworth field Richard is in full possession of a cool, calculating brain, whatever his outward actions are—a conscious hypocrite. Garrick conveyed this in his manner of speaking the line in question to upset Lady Anne, "not peevishly, but with the last part in the same tone as the first, only exalted a little." Newton bespoke a box seat for the next performance so he could see more of Garrick's facial expression as he looked at Lady Anne, and also when he arose from his couch in Act v. His next letter expressed complete satisfaction. "Our Ladies are almost in love with Richard as much as Lady Anne. And for us men, we like him better the second time than even the first: your voice was more in tune and order."[10]

Garrick thoughtfully considered even the minutest criticism from his early well-wishers. By 1759, however, a soured Theophilus Cibber published his satirical anti-Garrick blast. Cibber's contention was that Garrick's style was *not* natural but full of "extravagant attitudes, frequent affected starts, convulsive twitchings, jerking of the body, sprawling of the fingers . . . the caricature of gesture by pert vivacity."[11] He thought Garrick too variable in his mood in Richard. Although the directions in the text are clear for Richard to comment frequently on his own deformity, when Garrick spoke the lines

> Why, I, in this weak piping time of peace,
> Have no delight to pass away the time
> Unless to spy my shadow in the sun
> And descant on mine own deformity,

while pointing to the ground and seeming to fix his attention for sometime on the misshapen shadow, Cibber felt he was out of character. Theophilus, apparently, in playing the part would have shrunk from the sight of his shadow. Garrick going haltingly off stage all the way looking at but in a way not admiring his supposed shadow, Cibber laid to "mummery."[12]

Cibber was by then a minority of one, and Garrick shrugged off the diatribe. That same year Thomas Wilkes, in his *General View of the Stage*, saw in Richard a character composed of wickedness, perfidiousness, spleen, and ambition—attitudes matched by his deformity of person. "All these marks of character are preserved by Garrick in the part." Wilkes reveals ways in which Garrick's action conveyed this characterization. In the first act he had all the "settled malice of the murderer, and after he kills the king the unrelenting irony with which he views the blood upon his sword is perfectly preserved. . . . Whenever he speaks of his own imperfection he shows himself galled . . . in one passage his drawing a parallel between himself and the rest of humankind, to all of whom he finds himself unequal, determines him in villainy. . . . Garrick . . . shows by his acting the cross-grained splenetic turn of Richard. He shows you that the survey hurts him, whereas I have seen some actors here smile upon themselves as if well-pleased with their own appearance. That they were wrong the performance of this masterly actor confirms."[13]

So compelling was Garrick's representation of fictional characters that they became real and familiar human beings to viewers who themselves turned analysts and wrote about the drives which animated a Richard, a Jaffier, a Macbeth, and how their compulsions should be conveyed. Wilkes comments in detail on Garrick's dissimulation in the courtship of Lady Anne, on the hypocrisy he displays before the mayor and aldermen, on the glow of satisfaction that lights up his countenance as he speaks the lines:

> The golden dream is out,
> Ambition like an early friend throws back
> My curtain with an eager hand, o'erjoyed
> To tell me what I dreamt is true,

*Folger Shakespeare Library*
Garrick as Richard III.
Painting by Sir Nathaniel Dance, ca. 1769.

and on the intrepidity he displays amid the discouraging tidings and repeated disappointments he receives in the fifth act. The contrast between calmness and terror in the tent scene, followed by his regaining command of himself and the field deeply impressed Wilkes, who echoed comments of many another.[14]

Arthur Murphy was moved also. "The moment he entered the scene the character he assumed was visible in his countenance; the power of his imagination was such that he transformed himself into the very man; the passions rose in rapid succession, and before he uttered a word, were legible in every feature of that various face. . . . The rage and rapidity, with which he spoke, 'The North!—what do they in the north, / When they should serve their sovereign in the West!' made a most astonishing impression on the audience. His soliloquy in the tent scene discovered the inward man. Everything he described was almost reality; the spectator thought he heard the hum of either army from camp to camp, and steed threatening steed. When he started from his dream he was a spectacle of horror. He called out in a manly voice 'Give me another horse,' he paused, and with a countenance of dismay, advanced crying out in a tone of distress, 'Bind up my wounds,' and then, falling on his knees, said in a most piteous accent, 'Have mercy heaven!' In all this the audience saw an exact imitation of nature. . . . He was then on the eve of battle, and in spite of all the terrors of conscience, his courage mounted to a blaze. When in Bosworth field, he roared out 'A horse, a horse, my kingdom for a horse!' all was rage and fury, and almost reality."[15]

In 1770 Francis Gentleman opened his *Dramatic Censor* with an essay on Cibber's text of *Richard III*, commenting upon interpretations by various actors, preeminent among which stood Garrick. Close reading of the essay indicates three ways by which Garrick in speaking significant lines suggested (at that date) an element of loneliness in the makeup of Richard as counterpoint to his various moods of exultation. Gentleman's touchstones were the way Garrick spoke the lines "I am myself alone" (with heartfelt discontent); "Henry the Sixth / Did prophesy that Richmond should be king / When Richmond was a peevish little boy. / 'Tis odd—a king—perhaps" (the *perhaps*, meditatively and with a tone of continuation); and "*Conscience avaunt*— Richard's himself again" (with the italicized words uttered in a low tone expressive of mental agony). Gentleman found this subtle line of characterization in no other actor.

An anonymous author in the *Morning Chronicle* (1 June 1772) commented on "Mr Garrick's acting King Richard the Third," noting the laboriousness of the character, and finding it hard to determine "whether that transcending actor excelled most in the deliberating subtle calm and protean veriability of political ambition, or in the explosive impetuousity and fire-eyed execution of intrepid heroism."[16]

Early commentators found in Garrick's Richard a bloody, cold, and calculating villain. Later ones found these elements but also (by Garrick's reading of the lines) evidence of an inner struggle between ambitious exultation and conscience, and between anxious hope and guilt. Hypocrisy was there, impatience was there, contempt for others was there too, yet underneath was loneliness, and bleak wretchedness. Yet in the fourth and fifth acts Richard broke out (in Gentleman's words) "like a flame long smothered" and became a different man. Garrick conceived a way without rant and roar of creating this complex character as a living individual. Audience expectancy continued to build up, as Gentleman's notes for the Bell edition of the acting copy indicate, "a general murmur which the meeting of Richmond and Richard always occasioned," arose, followed by the eager applause that attended the tyrant's fall. The murmur meant that mighty forces were about to clash, that small and deformed Richard had acquired a stature worthy of great defeat. He was an adversary who commanded the horizon, if he did not quite touch the sky.[17]

Richard, daring, bold, wicked, gleeful, splenetic, perfidious, ambitious, lonely, characterized by rage, rapidity, and intrepidity—how to convey a sense of tragedy from this unlikeable complexity? Garrick did so by indicating depths of personality in the King, remembrance, twinges that allied him to mankind, though he felt himself divorced from it. But the strain! The professionalism of an actor carried him through, but the physical strain reached him, as his late letters indicate: to Joseph Cradock (spring of 1776) "I can play Richard; but I dread the fight and the fall. I am afterwards in agonies" (1012 n.3); to Colman (27 May 1776) "If I am confus'd or unintelligible impute it to Richard what an Operation!" (1019); to Hannah More (4 June 1776) "My wife has y$^r$ letter. . . . I am not to read it, till I have got over y$^e$ fright of having the King's Command to morrow for Richard, tho' I play'd it last Night better than Ever—it will absolutely kill me—What a Trial of breast, lungs, ribs, & What not" (1022). Comments these in private, for the eyes of friends. But professionally? for the audience? The Hopkins *Diary* reveals what happened in the theatre; 27 May 1776 Richard, Garrick, first time in five years. The ladies were asked to send servants to hold places at 5:00 o'clock, the doors of Drury Lane would open at 5:30 the play to begin at 6:30. Hopkins noted: "Mr G. voice and Spirits was never finer he never wanted Spirit or Voice thro' the whole part and convinced the Audience that those Amazing powers he has always possess'd are now as brilliant as ever. Never was a part play'd with greater Propriety nor an Audience more lavish of their Applause."[18] The following week he played it twice, once by command. Hopkins: "It is Vanity to endeavor to describe Mr G. Merits they beggar all Description, suffice it to Say that he was what he represented," and finally "I cannot say enough of Mr Garrick's performance tonight."[19]

Garrick was in no way jealous of the role, but yielded it willingly again and again to members of his company—to Mossop, Holland, Reddish, King. The play became popular at the other theatres too. In fact during the Garrick years audiences throughout London saw thrice as many performances of Richard III as they had during the 40-year period before Garrick came on stage. And when Garrick himself played the King, box receipts always mounted. The 25 extant account records for his 83 performances show income of £5,368 for only one third of his appearances in the part. The role was profitable. But it was much more. It had opened to him the great possibilities for creating anew other Shakespearean roles.

## CHAMONT IN 'THE ORPHAN'; LOTHARIO IN 'THE FAIR PENITENT,' AND PIERRE IN 'VENICE PRESERVED'

Focus in the past upon Garrick's playing major roles has tended to obscure his performing in an area of importance to him—the roles of supporting characters. He was superb in Richard, Lear, Hamlet, Macbeth, and Romeo, but he cared for blended excellence in the presentation of all roles. The central figure in Otway's The Orphan is Monimia—a part written originally for the great Restoration actress Elizabeth Barry. Traditionally the figures of central male importance were Castalio and Polydore. Chamont, Monimia's brother is a Laertes-sort of figure—the soldier home from the wars looking after the welfare of his sister, and bungling things at that.

Otway wrote his The Orphan; or, The Unhappy Marriage in 1680, and it was popular on stage from its premiere. The popularity continued at least until October 1799, bringing fame to a long succession of actresses. It tells the story of two brothers, Castalio and Polydore both in love with their father Acasto's ward Monimia, of the pride and sense of honor of her brother Chamont, and of his love for their sister Serina. Monimia loves Castalio and secretly marries him. They cannot announce until a day passes. She retires to her quarters in the Acasto household telling Castalio to knock thrice lightly at her door late that night, come to her and make no sound of voice lest the family be awakened. Polydore, boiling with passion, ignorant of the marriage, overhears the direction to Castalio, has his page delay Castalio, and substitutes himself in the marriage bed. Castalio, knocking later is refused as an imposter, after which the catastrophic plot unravels. Chamont, jealous of his sister's honor, had precipitated the action by hastening the marriage. Only he and Serina survive. Throbbing through the play are great passion, high honor, family pride and brotherly friendship all brought to catastrophe by mistaken identities, bad timing, searing strokes of conscience ending in the self-inflicted deaths of two loving brothers, and the self-poisoning of the beautiful Monimia.

Davies thought Garrick saw in Chamont chance for interpreting the different motives and actions that make an individual not the stereotype—the roughness of the soldier, the tenderheartedness of a brother, the jealousy for family honor, and the spirited young man.[20] Young when he took on the role (scarcely a month after playing Richard) and carrying on with it until 1759, Garrick was well suited to it. It had dash. But as Wilkes noted he gave it a unique depth especially in Chamont's scenes with the aged Acasto. Francis Gentleman thought the character a real oddity, but one "calculated to show an able actor advantageously." The advantage would never have occurred to him had Garrick not acted in it. "The quickness and fire of look, as well as expression and gesture which so eminently distinguish Mr. Garrick from all his contemporaries, nowhere operates more happily than in Chamont; passions which are really absurd and laughable, as the author has drawn them, are by him rendered respectable and striking; the calmer passages he delivers with unequalled sensibility, and his transitions to impetuous ones are so masterly, that all attempts to describe his excellence must injure it."[21] Details which we would now like to have are missing. Contemporaries thought Garrick in performance leavened the acting of the whole cast.

## LOTHARIO IN 'THE FAIR PENITENT'

Lothario is not the main part in Nicholas Rowe's *The Fair Penitent* (1703). He is the undoer—cynical and gay—of the strong, bitter, unfortunate heroine Calista, amid her honor-bound family and family friends. The play of passions lasted out a century of performing, at least until November 1799. In it two Genoese factions, led by the noble Sciolto and his opponents, the hard-driving family of the elder Lothario, clash. Sciolto gives surety due his friend the dead Altamont, and rescues young Altamont, his son, from degrading servitude with the Lotharios. Thus he restores the family name and gives his daughter Calista in marriage to young Altamont. She, however, has fallen in love with Lothario, has on one night yielded to him, and as she accepts her father's dictum that she marry Altamont has been forsaken by the rake Lothario. She seeks to lure him back by a letter which he drops, and which falls into the hands of Horatio, Altamont's good friend. Horatio, horrrified that his friend has married a fallen woman, hoping the letter is a false contrivance of an enemy, confronts Calista with it, who tears it up and shouts defiance at the accusation—though the writing be hers. She laments every moment she is on stage the subjugation of woman to man in the ways and customs of the world. Honor besmirched, duels arise. Lothario braving it out and seeking to gall Altamont is slain in the Sciolto household. His man Rossano calls up the opposing faction. Sciolto gives his daughter a dagger, urging her to quit the scene in the high Roman fashion. She does and dies. Sciolto dies exhausted from wounds received in fighting the Lothario faction. Horatio and Altamont survive contemplating the fate of an "injured bridegroom and his guilty bride," concluding, "If you would have a nuptial union last / Let vertue be the bond that ties it fast." Lothario's sprightly lines of a despoiler contrast with the honey-rolling sentiments of Altamont and Horatio, but separate him miles from such an innocuous rake as Ranger in Hoadly's comedy *The Suspicious-Husband*.

Lothario dies a villain's death in Act IV. Gentleman thought him "the most reproachable character our moral author ever drew . . . a snake with a beauteous variagated skin, which lures the unguarded hand to a poisonous touch." This malevolent, self-centered, superficial, inconstant Garrick portrayed effectively. But such was Gentleman's moral revulsion to the man that he dismissed even Garrick's performance in a single sentence, "Mr Garrick's execution of this part displayed very emphatic vivacity, and placed him as much above competition, as the extent of the character would admit." [22]

The play has taken on significance in theatre history because Richard Cumberland claimed to have seen it when a boy, with Quin as Horatio, and Garrick as Lothario—the one heavy and sawing the air in declamation; the other light, active, firey—and thought a whole century of acting technique had passed in a single scene. [23] Garrick himself enjoyed the role. It was different. He performed it 80 times, dropping it in 1760, but returning for one benefit performance in 1766. Wilkes felt that other actors played Lothario as a modern buck, infatuated with women and far gone with wine. "This is only a part of his character; he is moreover a man of noble blood, large fortune, and bears 'as great a name as the proud city boasts of,' which Mr Garrick takes care to mark by a spirit and deportment peculiar to nobility."[24] Garrick wrote the Countess of Burlington of his great satisfaction with the role, but relinquished it when he considered himself overage to present it convincingly (80).[25]

## PIERRE IN 'VENICE PRESERVED'

Pierre shares, of course, a three-way lead in Otway's *Venice Preserved* (1682), a play which has lasted on stage well into the twentieth century. Central to its plot is the strained friendship between the liberal but cynical conspirator Pierre and the displaced son-in-law of Venetian Senator Priuli, one Jaffier. Pierre draws Jaffier into his plot to overthrow the Venetian government. Jaffier places his lovely wife, Belvidera, in the custody of a conspirator, Renault, as temporary hostage for his performing in the secret plot. Renault tries to seduce her, and Jaffier in despair and anger reveals the plot to her, who persuades him to alert her father and save the Senate. Idealistically hoping for amnesty for his friend Pierre if he tells, he does so, only to discover that all conspirators, save himself, are doomed—Pierre to be hanged. As he ascends the scaffold Jaffier gets leave to mount with him for a final word. In hasty mutual agreement Jaffier stabs Pierre (to save him from torture) then stabs himself with the same dagger. Belvidera goes poetically mad, seeing in her distracted mind's eye the ghosts of Pierre and Jaffier, and dies as the curtain falls.

Garrick in the spring of his first season worked up the part of Pierre, a character scorning the establishment, long in statements about current Venetian abridgments of individual liberty, shocking to audiences in his frank statement that he was a villain, but soon endearing himself to many by his provisos of that statement. Pierre is perhaps a political Lothario. Garrick played the role nine times before he became manager, dropped it 15 years, coming back to it only for benefit performances for Mrs Cibber and Charles Holland in the 1759–60 season. The night he played for Mrs Cibber he must have been horrified at her breaking out of character by bowing to the audience in acknowledging applause before the act was over, when he had so long schooled his company to give complete attention at all times to the flow of action in the play at hand. So unusual was the break that the author of an article in Goldsmith's *The Bee*, probably referring to this performance, wrote, "I can never pardon a lady on the stage who, when she draws the admiration of the whole audience, turns about to make a low curtsey for their applause—such a figure no longer continues Belvidera, but at once drops into Mrs Cibber." Of course it was Mrs Cibber's benefit, and perhaps excusable, but not so in Garrick's eyes.[26] He played once more for Holland, to Davies's surprise that he returned to the part which he had abandoned earlier "for Pierre's fire and spirit were not equally supported by grandeur and dignity of person."[27] Pierre was single-purposed, Jaffier, however, did offer more possibilities for interpreting changes of mind, decisions upon decisions, and manifold relationships with the other characters of the play.

## JAFFIER IN 'VENICE PRESERVED'

In his first season as manager Garrick undertook the new role of Jaffier. Murphy thought this character "the fittest for the stage in the whole of the drama."[28] Jaffier's "frame of mind," he wrote, "is composed of moral qualities and the most sensible dispositions; the mild affections (public as well as private) are planted in his nature; love and friendship are his ruling passions; he doats on Belvidera and is sincerely attached to Pierre; he feels the public good, and has a high sense of honour. But those affections are not upon an even balance; they take their turn and his virtues counteract one another. The consequence is that by his own conduct, he brings himself to highest misery. This is the mixed imperfect character which Aristotle, with good reason, prefers to all others and particularly to those of perfect virtue, as the former comes more home to the feelings of the spectators, and is therefore more sure to excite compassion, and answer the true end of tragedy."[29]

Murphy analyzed the character of Jaffier for five full pages concluding: "Such is the character in which Garrick called forth all his powers. The greatest passions, expressed by Otway with the greatest energy, were perfectly suited to the genius of Garrick."[30] Most of his contemporaries agreed, but now, as manager, he entered upon the role under the gun of criticism even of some admirers. An anonymous correspondent ten days after his first appearance took him to task for his end-stopped lines in the passage, "When in your brigantine you call'd to *see* / The Adriatic wedded by our Duke," where by stopping, even momentarily, at *see* the listening spectators could not tell whether he meant *to see*, or to the waters of the *sea*. Also the correspondent felt that in sequences of nouns—truth, honor, justice, etc.—he spoke with a rapidity that obscured meaning, and dropped his voice at the end, so that a valuable word or two were lost.[31] Garrick's success had prompted such close observation, especially of plays in which he took new parts, and the criticism genuinely disturbed him—not as reflection upon him, but as indication of failure in communicating, which struck at the heart of the art of acting. He took pains, therefore to answer the letter, which he found came from the Reverend Peter Whalley: "Your Remark from Venice Preserved is likewise true— *When in your Brigantine, &c.* but I am in Hopes the other Slips you speak of in the same Play, were owing to my Illness on Mrs. Cibber's Benefit Night; I could scarce bring my Words out, and all the Time did not know whether I stood on my Head or Heels—the Part of Jaffier is a most difficult, laborious Character, and will take me up much Time, before I have attain'd what I imagine may be done with it." As extenuation of his seeming errors of judgment he continued, "I am often troubled with Pains in my Breast, arising from Colds; and at such Times I have it not in my Power to speak as I would; my Breath often fails me, and I am oblig'd to stop in a wrong Places, to enable me to finish a Sentence" (54).

He soon attained, however, in the eye of the public, what he imagined could be done with the role of Jaffier. In 1751 Samuel Derrick dedicated to Garrick his first *Dramatic Censor*, devoted entirely to *Venice Preserved*. Derrick saw (what all have seen in Otway) pathos at the center of the impression the dramatist wished to make. Degrees of it, to be sure, varied for Pierre, Jaffier, Belvidera, and for the city on the Adriatic. Derrick quoted a line from Sheffield to set the tone. "The dull are forced to feel; the wise to weep." Any defects he found in Otway's text were for him overcome by the plausible acting of Garrick. Quoting Jaffier's speech, 'Yes, if my heart would let me / This proud, this swelling heart, home would I go / But that my doors are hateful to my eyes," he tries to tell the effectiveness of Garrick's speaking: "He who has not seen, never can conceive what additional beauties Mr Garrick gives to the speaking of this soliloquy; the different passions which agitate the soul of Jaffier are, by turns, to be traced in his countenance; despair and dejection are so visible in his face, that the benevolent heart pants to relieve him, and he pronounces that line beginning 'O Belvidera . . .' in a manner so pathetic and so strongly affecting that to hear him, and at the same time stop the bursting tear is impossible."[32]

Derrick objected to Garrick's costume, wishing him to wear a suit of solemn black, instead of a pompous Venetian dress. But this he soon forgot in the action taking place on stage. Garrick's appearance among the conspirators, because of his complete portrayal of a displaced person, "throws a lustre over the scene which would alleviate defects. For he expresses the passions suited to Jaffier's character in a manner as lively and affecting as possible." At Belvidera's protest in being left alone with the conspirators, crying "Look on me, tell me, speak, thou dear deceiver," Garrick's behavior displayed "so fully love and despair struggling in his soul, that, notwithstanding our being angry with Jaffier for his ungenerous severity to his wife, we are oblig'd to pity sufferings so finely presented."[33]

Garrick took the bribe from Priuli "with all the seeming horror and detestation which a man of honour must have for such an offer." In the scene with Belvidera in Act IV, "both Mr. Garrick's looks and acting are so admirably adapted that, from this only, we might judge how Belvidera gained on him, and in what manner her arguments impress him without his speaking; an addition which never can fail of filling the eye with tears and making the heart sympathize." Derrick praised equally Jaffier's conveying to the audience his final decision, as rendered by Garrick, to die with friend Pierre.

Many such sentiments, almost in the same wording were given by Thomas Wilkes,[34] and 20 years later by Francis Gentleman. A number of the scenes impressed themselves indelibly on the minds of sympathetic audiences, and all involve not memory of a single character, but of the ensemble. "After the court breaks up," writes Gentleman, "Jaffier and Pierre are left judiciously to a conference wherein we find them contrasted in a masterly manner; conscious guilt clothes one with contrite submission, deeply provok'd resentment warms the other to violent disdain; each is sustained with the genius of ability, and we are alternately prejudiced in favour of both. . . . Every spectator . . . who can see and forgive the failings of a fellow creature . . . must here sympathize with the perturbation of Jaffier, who is now wrought up to look upon his beloved and loving wife as the great source of his most pungent misery. The conflict between love, honour, and injured friendship rises to the borders of distraction, when Belvidera appears . . . conscious of the dagger she has planted in her husband's heart, fears to see him, yet has no other guardian. . . . Mr Garrick steps forward and beggars description, by an amazing variety of transitions, tones, and picturesque attitudes; the distracted confusion which flames

Garrick and Mrs Cibber as Jaffier and Belvidera in *Venice Preserved*.
Engraving by J. McArdell, 1764, from painting by Zoffany.

in his countenance, and the gleams of love which shed momentary softness on the stern glow of rage, exhibit more complicated beauties than any other piece of theatrical execution we have seen." [35]

Inevitable comparisons were made between the actors who played Jaffier. Barry performed exceedingly well, but comment about him seems to have been limited to his graceful and commanding figure and soft, pathetic tones. Garrick's revelation of innermost character by particularization of voice, look, gesture (what Gentleman lamely calls 'picturesque attitudes') moved the hearts of contemporaries as nothing else did. His genius here seized upon what made him such a marvelous professional elsewhere—the art of acting so subtly at times, but so affectingly as to draw the spectator on to participate creatively himself. A writer for *The Craftsman* (December 1752) in a mock 'Court of Censorial Inquiry' re Barry's and Garrick's acting of Jaffier, stated this, Garrick's contribution, precisely: "Mr. Garrick seems to speak out but half his mind, as if there was more working in his breast, while Mr. Barry by throwing out his voice seems to vent all his grief, and so leaves nothing for the imagination of his audience to supply." [36]

## KING LEAR

Actually the fifth major tragic role Garrick assumed his first important year of acting was the aged, brisk, hard-bitten, proud, cantankerous King Lear, spoiled by power which he gave away, reduced to a bare forked animal on the heath, turned mad by exhaustion, age, and the psychological hurt of the ingratitude of his daughters. Shakespeare had set himself a severe artistic problem of making this crusty, ancient King a tragic figure before the play was done. He succeeded magnificently, but the following generations could not take the play as it stood. The gasp was too great as the King died. Nahum Tate altered the structure, made bland the text, and provided an ending wherein Lear was restored to his throne (as in the original story upon which it was based). Tate's shift in emphasis (in 1681) reflected political concerns of his time, for it changed the play from King Lear to Lear's Kingdom. His ending lasted until 25 January 1838, when McCready reverted to the tragic ending.

Garrick, challenged by the part, and phenomenally successful in it after an initial settling-in period in which Macklin's coaching improved his acting, performed over the years the subtle art of cutting out the

Tate scenes and phraseology, and restoring Shakespearean lines, so that at the close of his career, and 85 performances later, the text (save for the happier ending) had drawn closer and closer to Shakespeare's original.[37]

Notable earlier actors had performed it, from Betterton to Quin, and oncoming ones—Barry, Powell, Mossop, Henderson, Kean, McCready, the Kembles—would continue to do so. A slogan from Garrick's time read that in the play "Barry was every inch a king, but Garrick was every inch King Lear." Contemporaries recognized again the individualizing detail which Garrick brought to the part. He was not representing by "aria technique" madness, rage, fatherly affection, despair, anger, pathos as abstract essences, but a King of ancient, ancient British history through his own character and his faults, coming to an understanding of man in his bare essentials, bereft of power, ceremony, followers, facing the thunder and lightning from above in a poor hut on a storm battered heath, and coming round in the recognition scene with Cordelia through love and understanding to a reaffirmation of life. The concept even in the Garrick-Tate-Shakespearean acting text was tremendous.

Garrick had been center stage with Richard, had moved to supporting roles in the characters of Chamont, Lothario, and Pierre, and now returned to the leading and dominant role in England's greatest tragedy. The ambition of the 24-year old was boundless, but he knew his capacities, and sensed his ability to leave an indelible mark here of his new concept of acting. His makeup as an aged man was satisfactory, his costume was conventional—a furred gown (with ermine for a king) and flowing white wig. His body, face, voice, and gesture did the rest. Londoners were amazed at the infirm but irascible old monarch who took the stage where Garrick had lately acted the firey soldier Chamont and the young rake Lothario. Garrick recognized the heath scene as the high point of the play, and its sequel (the reconciliation with Cordelia) as the turning point. Very early the artist Francis Hayman asked his advice about painting a startling scene from *Lear*. A significant factor in Garrick's reply 10 October 1745 was the arrangement of characters on the heath: Lear on the ground with Edgar by him—his attitude leaning upon one hand and pointing wildly towards the heavens—Kent and the Fool attending—Edgar in frantic affectation—Kent solicitous on one knee. The significance lies in the inclusion of the Fool, who was omitted from the acting text, indicating that Garrick read carefully the Shakespearean text (as he did for representing *all* Shakespearean plays—deriving his concept of layout and of characterization from the original.

In 1747 Samuel Foote published *Treatise on the Passions* in which he gave liberal quantities of advice to Garrick about Lear, one of which was to record profounder irony in the speech to Regan beginning, "Dear daughter I confess that I am old." The speech was not in the Tate text. Garrick had restored it to the stage. An anonymous writer that same year published his *Examen of the New Comedy Called The Suspicious Husband*, in ten pages of which he replied to Foote's strictures, vindicating Garrick's interpretation of Lear. The writer found Foote ignorant of Shakespeare's text, hence unable to realize that Garrick's actions, though accompanied by many of Tate's lines, were instigated by the authentic play. "He condemns you greatly for your manner of uttering the curse against Goneril, but had he looked into Shakespeare, he would not have been so severe upon your *tears shed at the conclusion*, or have said that the strange mixture of grief and passion was highly unnatural; for the speech immediately following the curse is your direction and authority."

This writer fairly puts us back into the pit of Drury Lane that year: "I shall recollect your manner of executing a part of the play, and then let the judges pronounce their sentence. You fall precipitately upon your knees, extend your arms—clench your hands—set your teeth—and with a savage distraction in your look—trembling in all your limbs—and your eyes pointed to Heaven (the whole expressing the fullness of rage and revenge) you begin 'Hear Nature! Dear Goddess!' with a broken, inward, eager utterance; from thence rising, every line in loudness and rapidity of voice, till you come to 'and feel / How sharper than a serpent's tooth it is / To have a thankless child.' Then you are struck at once with your daughter's ingratitude and bursting into tears with a most sorrowful heartbreaking tone of voice you say . . . 'Go, go my people.' This in my opinion is the strongest climax of Rage; and the break from it at the end of the speech, gives a natural necessary variety, and was visibly designed so by the author."[38]

Yet another clue lies in Thomas Warton's discussion of *King Lear* in *The Adventurer*, wherein Warton tells explicitly of Garrick's influence upon his own appreciation of Lear, "I should be guilty of insensibility and injustice, if I did not take this occasion to acknowledge that I have been more moved and delighted by hearing this single line—'O me, my heart! my rising heart—but down,' spoken by the only actor of the age who understands and relishes these little touches of nature, and therefore the only one qualified to personate this most difficult character of Lear, than by the most pompous declaimer of the most pompous speeches in *Cato* or *Tammerlane*."[39] We note that the single line that so impressed Warton he heard from Garrick on stage, but it comes from the Shakespearean, not the Tate text. Garrick's Lear was instigating a flurry of essay discussions of the king and his madness in *The Adventurer*, and by Murphy in *Gray's Inn Journal*.[40] Garrick knew that plays were not books, but prompt books to be adapted to respond to changing tastes. He was both changing taste by restoring the older text, and responding to taste by the slant he was giving the play in the acting.

The "pathetic" and the "sentimental" were in the air. Plays of Otway, Cibber, and Steele playing to these tastes were current. Murphy, in *Gray's Inn Journal*, no. 65, shows the way in which Garrick was playing to the public desire for the pathetic even in the older plays: "In every speech in Lear's mouth," he wrote, "there is such an artful mixture of thwarting passions that the *heart strings* of an audience are torn on every side. . . . His sudden apostrophe to his daughters must *draw tears* from every eye—'O Regan, Goneril, Your Old kind Father whose frank heart gave all!' He still continues to dwell in imagination upon the crime of ingratitude, which appears to him so shocking that he exclaims, 'Let 'em anatomize Reagan;—see what breeds about her heart. . . . Is there any cause in Nature for these hard hearts?' This last stroke cannot fail to draw tears from every eye." Edgar's alliance with Cordelia, he concludes, "must always *call forth those gushing tears which are swelled and ennobled by virtuous joy*."[41] Garrick played to this attitude, of the pathetic and found it worked.

The effect of the Garrick performances was astounding. It took Joshua Reynolds three days to recover from the effects of seeing Garrick's last performance of the character. But Dr Fordyce spells out more fully than anyone, perhaps, what effects Garrick did produce. Writing to Garrick 15 May 1763 he couches his praise in the third person: "He has seen Mr. Garrick in his other characters with delight always. . . . But in King Lear he saw him with rapture and astonishment. . . . And I am much mistaken if, in the representation, he [Garrick] does not feel his soul expand with a freedom and fulness of satisfaction, beyond what he experiences in any other part.

"Such violent starts of amazement, of horror, of indignation, of paternal rage, excited by filial ingratitude the most prodigious; such a perceptable, yet rapid gradation, from these dreadful feelings to the deepest frenzy; such a striking correspondence between the tempest in his mind, and that of the surrounding elements. In the very whirlwind of passion and of madness, such an exact attention to propriety, that it is still the passion and the madness of a king. Those exquisite touches of self-reproach for a most foolish and ill-requited fondness to two worthless daughters, and for the greatest injustice and cruelty to one transcendently excellent. Those resistless complaints of aged and royal wretchedness, with all the mingled workings of a warm and hasty, but well-meaning and generous soul, just recovering from the convulsion of its faculties, through the pious care of a worthy, but injured child and follower; till at length the parent, the sovereign, and the friend, shine out in the mildest majesty of fervent virtue, like the sun after a fearful storm, breaking forth delightfully in all the soft splendor of a summer evening. These, Sir, are some of the great circumstances which so eminently distinguished your action two nights ago." [42] Fordyce noted the applause of the audience, and the fact that a French lady in his party, used to the frigidity of French drama "was moved and melted in the most sensible manner." But, he continued, "what struck me most . . . was the sustaining with full power, to the last, a character marked with the most diversified and vehement sensations, without departing once . . . from the simplicity of nature, the grace of attitude, or the beauty of expression." [43]

The transition from madness and exhaustion to recovery through love impressed writer after writer, some of whom suggest in their descriptions of the effect upon them of Garrick's detailed acting, but mostly he touched their hearts and released springs of emotion within themselves they scarcely knew they had. Thomas Wilkes wrote, "I never see him coming down from one corner of the stage with his old gray hair standing, as it were, erect upon his head, his face filled with horror and attention, his hands expanded, and his whole frame actuated by a dredful solemnity, but I am astounded, and share in all his distresses; nay as Shakespeare in some different place, with elegance observes upon another subject, *one might interpret from the dumbness of his gesture*. Methinks I share in his calamities, I feel the dark drifting rain, and the sharp tempest with his, 'Blow winds—'till you have burst your cheeks! Here the power of his eye, corresponding with an attitude peculiar to his own judgment, and proper to the function, is of force sufficient enough to thrill through the veins and pierce the hardest bosom. What superlative tenderness does he discover in speaking these words—'Pray do not mock me; for as I am a man, / I take that lady to be my child Cordelia.'

"His whole performance in the fifth act is inimitably graceful. The spirit which he exerts, the endeavouring to collect all his strength to preserve his dear daughter from the hands of the assassin, are not to be described. His leaning against the side of the scene, panting for want of breath, as if exhausted, and his recollecting the feat, and replying to the fellow who observes, that the good old King has slain two of them, 'Did I not, fellow?' have more force, more strength, and more propriety of character than I ever saw in any other actor."[44]

The vignettes that these contemporaries give almost return us to the "aria perfection" concept of acting, yet Garrick was insisting that his whole company act up to his level of interpretation. Most came close, and the commentators usually got round to them, but had the habit of taking each one up in turn. In this scene of reconciliation Lichtenberg tells us twice of the superb supporting action of Mrs Barry (playing Cordelia to Garrick many years later), "Raising her large eyes, gleaming with tears, to heaven and silently wringing her hands, she hastens towards her forlorn old father and embraces him with great propriety of demeanour and, so it seemed to me, the radiant countenance of one transfigured."[45]

Murphy was particularly impressed by the madness of Lear, developing a controversy as to its cause in articles in his *Gray's Inn Journal* in 1754.[46] Later in his *Life of David Garrick* he noted the actor's distinguishing genius here. "He had no sudden starts, no violent gesticulation; his movements were slow and feeble; misery was depicted in his countenance; he moved his head in the most deliberate manner; his eyes were fixed, or if they turned to any one near him, he made a pause, and fixed his look on the person after much delay; his features at the same time telling what he was going to say, before he uttered a word. During the whole time he presented a sight of woe and misery, and a total alienation of mind from every idea but that of his unkind daughters."[47]

Murphy's detailed observations are corroborated by John Hill, the antiquarian, dramatist, and self-termed "Inspector" general of plays sent to the *Daily Advertiser*. Of Lear's madness wrote he, as Garrick played it: "'Tis an odd Effect of a Laugh to produce Tears; but I believe there was hardly a dry Eye in the House on his executing that first absolute Act of Madness in the Character. While I admired the Action, I was almost at a Loss to comprehend in what Manner it was performed: 'Twas not anything like the Laugh of Mirth or Pleasantry, the Triumph of a happy Imagination; but seemed merely the Exertion of the Organs of the body, without any Connection with the Soul; an involuntary Emotion of the Muscles, while the Mind was fixed on something else. Upon the whole, other Lears I have seen . . . Must pardon me, if I declare, that the frantic Part of the Character seems never to have been rightly understood till this Gentleman studied it."[48]

This was, of course, but one action and presentation of the results

*Harvard Theatre Collection*
Garrick as King Lear.
Engraving by J. McArdell, 1761, from a painting by Benjamin Wilson,
ca. 1760.

of conflicting passions in the king. Davies concentrates on the opposite pole: "We should reflect that Lear is not agitated by one passion only, that he is not moved by rage, by grief, and indignation, singly, but by a tumultuous combination of them altogether, where all claim to be heard at once, and where one naturally interrupts the progress of the other. Besides the lines are so full of rich and distinct matter, that few men can roll them off with any degree of swiftness. . . . Garrick rendered the curse so terribly affecting to the audience, that during his utterance of it they seemed to shrink from it, as from a blast of lightning."[49]

Garrick's penetration of the character of Lear comes through in his reply to a now lost letter from Edward Tighe which commented, apparently on Garrick's performance of 21 February 1770: "*Lear*," writes Garrick, "is certainly a *Weak* man, it is part of his Character—violent, old & *weakly* fond of his Daughters—Here we agree, but I cannot possibly agree with You & M$^r$ Ranby that the Effect of his distress is diminished by his being an *Old Fool*—his Weakness proceeds from his Age (fourscore & upwards) & such an Old Man full of affection, Generosity, Passion, & what not meeting with what he thought an ungrateful return from his best belov'd Cordelia, & afterwards real ingratitude from his other Daughters, an audience must feel his distresses & Madness which is y$^e$ Consequence of them—nay I think I might go further, & venture to say that had not y$^e$ source of his unhappiness proceeded from good qualities carry'd to excess of folly, but from vices, I really think y$^e$ bad part of him would be forgotten in y$^e$ space of an Act, & *his distresses at his Years* would become Objects of Pity to an Audience" (574). Garrick accepted Shakespeare's challenge of making tragic one who at the start is brusque, foolish, and unsympathetic. The actor's demeanor throughout the play, portraying weakness accompanied by a deepening understanding as the woes pile up, aimed at evoking pity from the spectators.

His success in this is told again and again. One identified by Boaden as G. Tighe wrote on 27 May 1773: "Instead of laboured thanks, accept a simple fact. Miss Montgomerys sat just before us, and (in spite of your admirable performance) it was impossible not to watch their countenances. The expression of the eldest was wonderful, and such as the *mighty master would have smiled to see.* She gazed, she panted, she grew pale, then again the blood rose in her cheeks, she was elevated, she almost started out of her seat, and *tears began to flow.* . . . Mr. B. is infinitely obliged to you for the most exquisite entertainment he has received these eleven years. He saw 'Lear,' Anno 1762."[50]

Garrick at 60 closed his acting career by a series of performances of his great parts. People came from as far as the Continent to see him. For his performance of Lear on 13 May 1776 Hopkins noted, "The people flock'd about the doors by Two o'clock. there never was a greater Overflow—Mr G. was never happier in Lear—the Applause was beyond description 3 or 4 loud Claps Succeeding one another at all his exits and many Cry'd out Garrick for Ever &c." Hannah More wrote at the time to Mrs Gwatkin: "The eagerness of the people to see Garrick is beyond anything you can have an idea of. You will see half a dozen duchesses and countesses a night in the upper boxes: for the fear of not seeing him at all, has humbled those who used to go, not for the purpose of seeing, but of being seen; and they now courtsy to the ground for the worst places in the house."[51] For his final performance of the character a writer for *The London Chronicle* reported: "The curse at the close of the first act, his frenetic appeal to heaven at the end of the second on Regan's ingratitude, were two such enthusiastic scenes of human exertion, that they caused a momentary petrifaction thro' the house, which he soon dissolved universally into tears. Even the unfeeling Regan and Goneril forgetful of their characteristic cruelty, played through the whole of their parts with aching bosoms and streaming eyes."[52]

Mme Susanne Necker, wife of Louis XVI's finance minister, and mother of Mme de Staël, came from Paris to see Garrick's last performance on stage. Her comment makes fitting close to this great part: "Quelle superbe et touchante leçon vous nous avez donnée! quelle horreur pour l'ingratitude! quelle amour! quelle respect pour la vieilesse! même injuste, même égarée."[53] High spots remembered—yet a sequence which made the whole play impressive. But the prompter has the last word: "Human nature cannot arrive at greater Excellence in Acting than Mr Garrick was possess'd of this Night All words must fall far short of what he did and none but his Spectators can have an Idea how great he was—The Applause was unbounded."[54]

## HAMLET

A long career on stage with the King of the ancient Britons was matched by one that slightly out did it with the Prince of Denmark. Hamlet was Garrick's first new tragic role in the London season of 1742–43, and it carried on for 90 performances, until 1776. Garrick also amassed with it the largest quantity of commentary of any of his plays. He had a running start, so to speak, in his Hamlet because he made his actual debut in it in August 1742, while acting at the Smock Alley theatre in Dublin. Two days later he received a letter from a spectator, symptomatic of many he was to receive throughout his career.

The writer approved a number of actions, was surprised at others, and pointed out what he deemed specific errors in the pronunciation of single words—mostly having to do with the vowels *a* and *e*. To his ear Garrick spoke *metron* for matron, *Isrel* for Israel, *villin* for villain, *Horetio* for Horatio, and gave a short *i* to the wind that blows. The writer thought he paused too long before uttering his surprised "Angels and Ministers of Grace" phrase at seeing the Ghost, that he should not bow to the Ghost when it identified itself, and that he should reinstate the directions to the players. However, he approved dropping the musical accompaniment when Hamlet first enters, and his concluding remarks were favorable, "The scene between Hamlet and Ophelia, and likewise that with the Queen, you played so inimitably well and with such a strict justice, that I never saw any thing equal to it in my life; and indeed I can almost say the same for the whole character." [55]

And so he launched the role that every man and every actor, even now, believes he himself can play. The pattern of early criticism, desiring perfection in minutest detail repeated itself for Garrick in this role, as one "Ignoto" (in January) thought that Garrick reacted overenthusiastically to the appearance of the Ghost, where he should have pronounced *Tropically* with a short *o* rather than a long, and where his conversation with the Gravediggers was too serious. [56] Garrick had cut his teeth in this play by playing Hamlet's Ghost at Goodman's Fields long before he went to Ireland. Doing it with customary dedication, he knew what strong motivation should animate Hamlet. He knew from the Hamlet (Giffard) opposite whom he then played how he wanted to differentiate the part.

As with his performance of Lear, Garrick developed no conceit from the praise he received, willingly listened to early and sound advice, and modified stage business when it seemed best for the pleasure of the audience. He restored at some period the advice to the players; he dropped the bow to the Ghost. We have no way of knowing what all of his response to vowel pronunciation was. But "Ignoto" thanked him for responding favorably to his short for a long *o*, and for being somewhat easier in conversation with the Gravediggers. Each one who wrote the actor returned to the theatre to see how his advice had fared, and followed up with more correspondence. Peter Whalley suggested that he should split the Ghost's speech by giving the line, "Oh horrible, Oh horrible, most horrible," to Hamlet.[57] Garrick did so. Whalley wrote again suggesting that he pause twice in surprise in the line, "My father's spirit! / in arms! / all is not well."[58] Garrick's response to such advice was always gracious, for he felt a sort of participatory relationship to exist between actor and audience. But he did not just take the advice of the latest speaker on the subject. His correspondence with Whalley is illustrative, for Whalley had also criticized him for breaking, by his pauses, the meanings of a sentence occasionally. Garrick's reply: "My Ears are always open to Conviction; I willingly kiss the Rod, and would shake the Hand that administers such wholesome Correction as yours has done. The Faults you mention I am afraid I have been guilty of; because the Bye-stander will always be a better Judge of the Game than the Party concerned—but I am surpris'd that I should be thought to regard the Measure of Verses so injudiciously as to disjoin the Members of the Sentence, when at my first setting out in the Business of an Actor, I endeavour'd to shake off the Fetters of Numbers, and have been often accus'd of neglecting the Harmony of Versification, from a too close Regard to the Passion, and the Meaning of the Author" (54), and he argues his practice and policy at some length. Each argument gives some insight into his concept of performing.

Four persons watched Hamlet, conferred, and concluded Garrick had not got into the spirit of the Prince. He was too bustling, insufficiently melancholy and languid. "But a gentleman present assuring us you mended greatly every time, and that you then acted the part incomparably better than you had done at first, we all agreed to go the next night."[59] They went and were delighted with the improvement, but still longed for a more melancholy Dane. Letters flowed on, but the tide was turning. "The acting of Hamlet has convinced every one they never saw it performed before," wrote another "ingoto," questioning only Garrick's makeup. "How does the additional colour in the countenance suit with one supposed to be of a very melancholy cast of mind?"[60] Obviously people from reading or seeing other actors perform built up stereotypes against which to measure Garrick. He was individualizing the Dane in a different way, making him not so hesitant, but active, driving on to the revenge with all the intelligent action that the circumstances of the text allowed. He recognized the morass of the Danish court that might engulf him. He assumed the madness that he needed for protection, but moved inexorably towards the revenge his father's Ghost demanded.

But the play had become so familiar to many a spectator, and English ears had become so attuned to its rhythms that comment continued about Garrick's interpretation for 20 years. A writer objected, hesitantly to be sure, that Garrick's pause on *grown* in his comment about Gertrude, "Then she would hang upon him / As if increase of appetite had grown / By what it fed on," was misplaced and should have been on *appetite*.[61] Garrick explained to one H. H. (24 January 1762) the difference between his concept of a stop (or pause) and a suspension of voice. He had been accused, he said, of "injudiciously" stopping in the line, "*I think it was to See—My Mother's Wedding*." "I certainly never *stop* there, (that is close y$^e$ Sense) but I as certainly *Suspend* my Voice, by which Your Ear must know, that y$^e$ Sense is suspended too—for Hamlet's Grief causes y$^e$ break & with a Sigh he finishes y$^e$ Sentence—*my Mother's Wedding*—I really could not from my feelings act it otherwise" (281). Garrick could never fall into a stereotype under this flood of comment. Each of his 96 performing roles became a distinct challenge, and each was delivered with a slightly changing piece of acting.

For Murphy his countenance and gesture led the onlooker into the character: "When Garrick entered the scene, the character he assumed, was legible in his countenance; by the force of deep meditation he transformed himself into the very man. He remained fixed in pensive attitude, and the sentiments that possessed his mind could be discovered by the attentive spectator. When he spoke the tone of his voice was in unison with the workings of his mind, and as soon as he said 'I have that within which surpasses show,' his every feature confirmed and proved the truth. The soliloquy which begins with, 'O that this too, too solid flesh would melt' brings to light, as it were by accident, the character of Hamlet. His grief, his anxiety, and irresolute temper are strongly marked. He does not yet know that his father was poisoned, but his mother's marriage excites resentment and abhorrence of her conduct. He begins with it, but as Smith observes in his excellent notes on *Longinus*, he stops for want of words. Reflections crowd upon him, and he runs off in commendation of his deceased father. His thoughts soon turn again to his mother; in an instant he flies off again, and continues in a strain of sudden transitions, taking no less than 18 lines to tell us, that in less than two months, his mother married his father's brother. . . . In all these shiftings of the passions his voice and attitude changed with wonderful celerity, and, at every pause, his face was an index to his mind. On the first appearance of the Ghost, such a figure of consternation was never seen. He stood fixed in mute astonishment, and the audience saw him growing paler and paler. After an interval of suspense he spoke in a low trembling accent, and uttered his questions with great difficulty."[62]

The intimacy of Drury Lane theatre offered continuing possibilities for these close-up views, as we might call them today. Murphy applauded the way in which Garrick gave the advice to the players, thought him powerful in the soliloquies, warm, interesting and pathetic in the closet scene with Gertrude, and convincing in his assumed madness. Davies was also impressed along with the rest of the audiences with Garrick's confrontation with the Ghost, but was even more so with Garrick's propriety and vigor in the soliloquies, which "unfold the springs of action in the persons of the drama," and which "were delivered by Garrick with singular exertion. The strong intelligence of his eye, the animated expression of his whole countenance, the flexibility of his voice, and his spirited action, riveted the attention of an admiring audience."[63] He most appreciated the one beginning "O what a wretch and peasant slave am I." In his *Dramatic Miscellanies* Davies gives a full-dress account of Garrick's Hamlet, including the supporting action of Woodward, Mrs Pritchard, and Mrs Cibber. He praised Garrick's consistency of characterization, marked here by filial piety, as in Lear it was marked by filial ingratitude. He comments on Garrick's expression of glee when the Mousetrap play catches the King, by whirling a white handkerchief, and of Garrick's desire to have Woodward play Polonius in a serious manner. The play moved spectators in an eerie way when Mrs Pritchard as Gertrude in the closet scene responded to Hamlet's query, "Do you see nothing there," by turning her head slowly around, "and with a certain glare in her eyes, which looked everywhere and saw nothing, said "Nothing at all, yet all that's here I see."[64] Garrick's best effects came in such an ensemble situation, not as single exercises. Lichtenberg commented on Mrs Maria Smith, who was Ophelia at Drury Lane in 1775, as a young woman and a good singer, whose "long flaxen hair hung partly down her back, and partly over her shoulders; in her left hand a bunch of loose straw . . . her whole demeanour in her madness . . . gentle as the passion which caused it. The songs . . . she sang charmingly . . . fraught with plaintive, tender melancholy." He thought he could hear them far into the night when he was alone.[65]

The intelligent bystanders who have left us the most detailed descriptions of Garrick in Hamlet are two Germans—Friederich Gunderode, who saw him in 1773, and Lichtenberg in 1775. Gunderode, a decided Francophile, disliked English acting, but counted himself fortunate to see Garrick's Hamlet: "I was all eyes and ears," he wrote, "during the performance and was amazed at the extraordinary acting of this man. He was then over 60 years of age [actually 57] yet he played the part of a young man of twenty with all the verve and sensibility of youth. The melancholy which marked every feature of his face when he made his first appearance, the bold answer which he gives in reply to the King's inquiry into the cause of his sadness, all this won me over to him completely. But later when the scene with the Ghost came, when his soul was stirred to its depths, when he drew his sword and bravely followed the spectre whilst his hair stood on end with horror, I could perceive more plainly than ever that the man had absolute control over his features, and that he was completely absorbed in the impressions of the situation. His scenes with the courtier, with the Queen, and with Ophelia were equally masterly. He spoke the famous monologue in the first scene of the third act with the greatest concentration of his whole being. His soul felt at the moment the full import of these words, otherwise he could never have uttered them as he did. I do not hesitate to call Garrick the greatest and most excellent actor of the century."[66]

The ghostly motivation scene and the "to be or not to be" soliloquy impressed Lichtenberg as it did Gunderode, but the former describes the acting, whereas the latter comments on the impression it made. "Hamlet," writes Lichtenberg, "appears in a black dress, the only one in the whole court, alas! still worn for his poor father. . . . Horatio and Marcellus, in uniform, are with him. . . . Hamlet has folded his arms under his cloak and pulled his hat down over his eyes; it is a cold night and just twelve o'clock; the theatre is darkened, and . . . quiet. . . . Suddenly, as Hamlet moves towards the back of the stage slightly to the left and turns his back on the audience, Horatio starts, and saying: 'Look, My Lord, it comes,' points to the right, where the ghost has already appeared and stands motionless, before anyone is aware of him. At these words Garrick turns sharply and at the same moment staggers back two or three paces with his knees giving way under him; his hat falls to the ground and both his arms, especially the left, are stretched out nearly full length, with the hands as high as his head, the right arm more bent and the hand lower, the fingers apart; his mouth is open: thus he stands rooted to the spot, with legs apart, but no loss of dignity, supported by his friends, who are better acquainted with the apparition and fear lest he should collapse. His whole demeanour is so expressive of terror that it made my flesh creep even before he began to speak. The almost terror-struck silence of the audience, which preceded this appearance and filled one with a sense of insecurity, probably did much to enhance this effect. At last he speaks, not at the beginning, but the end of a breath, with a trembling voice: 'Angels

*Folger Shakespeare Library*
Garrick as Hamlet.
Engraving by J. McArdell, 1754, from a painting by Benjamin Wilson.

and ministers of Grace defend us!' words which supply anything this scene may lack and make it one of the greatest and most terrible which will ever be played on any stage. The ghost beckons him; I wish you could see him, with eyes fixed on the ghost, though he is speaking to his companions, freeing himself from their restraining hands. . . . He stands with his sword on guard against the spectre, saying: 'Go on, I'll follow thee,' and the ghost goes on off stage. Hamlet still remains motionless . . . and at length when the spectator can no longer see the ghost, he begins slowly to follow him, now standing still and then going on, with sword still upon guard, eyes fixed on the ghost, hair disordered, and out of breath, until he too is lost to sight. . . . What an amazing triumph."[67]

He then describes Garrick's delivery of the "O that this too, too solid flesh would melt" soliloquy, marking his manner of shedding tears, and thus piercing the heart. "The famous soliloquy: 'To be or not to be,'" he notes, "does not naturally make the same impression. . . . But it produces an infinitely greater effect than could be expected of an argument on suicide and death in a tragedy; and this is because a large part of the audience not only knows it by heart as well as they do the Lord's prayer, but listens to it . . . as if it were the Lord's Prayer . . . with a sense of solemnity and awe, of which someone who does not know England can have no conception. In this Island Shakespeare is not only famous, but Holy; his moral maxims are heard everywhere . . . [even] in Parliament."[68]

Two facts come clear from such descriptions. First, that Garrick did not discard completely the ways and means of gaining theatrical effects suggested by the rhetoricians—the stance, the gesture, position of hands, arms, direction of gaze, and opening of mouth were those pretty much set forth by Le Brun and the early theoreticians. When Garrick used them, he used them well, and appropriately, and they never became hackneyed usages called forth on every occasion. Such was part of his sure-footed professionalism. Second, he played to the pleasures of "recognition" in his audience, as well as to "discovery" and surprise.[69]

The longer Garrick played Hamlet the more it became a classic to which commentators genuflected in words of general appreciation, as did Gentleman in his *Dramatic Censor*: "In this character we must place Garrick far above any other competitor; his reception of, and address to the Ghost; his natural picturesque attitude, terror struck features, low, tremulous expression, rising in harmonious gradation, with the climax of his speech and feelings, all give us the most pleasing,

I had almost said astonishing sensibility; in all the pointed parts of the dialogue his matchless eyes anticipate his tongue, and impress the meaning upon us with double force; no man ever did, nor possibly ever will speak hemistichs, broken sentences, and make transitions with such penetrating effect . . . where other good performers often pass unnoticed, he is frequently great; where the author is languid he gives him spirit; where powerful, due support." Gentleman instances the Ghost scene, and the closet scene.[70]

The German visitors were seeing Garrick in his own late adaptation of the play, which he put on in December 1772, and played thereafter. He cut the Gravediggers, rewrote the fifth act, and introduced over 600 lines of Shakespeare's text to the forepart of the play that had never been performed on the eighteenth-century stage. For this he was both praised and damned. But the adaptation provided novelty, pace, and active performance. It remained in manuscript, lost to the world until 1934, but is now available and can be consulted by the curious.[71]

As he closed his career Garrick gave a last performance of Hamlet on 30 May 1776. "Pit and Boxes put together, most of the tickets were sold for a Guinea apiece [normal price three to five shillings] and the whole quantity Sold in about Two hours."[72] The tremendous proceeds went to the support of the Theatrical Fund. Hannah More saw it, and wrote to Dr Stonehouse, "I have at last had the entire satisfaction to see Garrick in 'Hamlet.' . . . I pity those who have not. Posterity will never be able to form the slightest idea of his perfections. The more I see him, the more I wonder and admire."[73]

Garrick began Hamlet experimentally and on his own, far off in Dublin. He worked with it constantly, absorbing significant input from contemporary comment, got the Londoners so involved that they discussed it in coffeehouses, taverns, and homes, closed it with a drastic, but theoretically legitimate, experiment in a ninetieth performance and a blaze of glory. Towards the last the acting, though consummately professional, was not always easy. He wrote to Thomas Rackett, Jr, in December 1775, "I play'd Hamlet last Wednesday & after the play yr. Father & Mother went home with us to take part of my Chicken. the moment I got into my great chair, I was as lifeless as the Brawn's head you have sent me, but very unlike that I was tasteless too, and no mustard could quicken me—dead—dead—dead—however I recover'd the next day & played Archer" (960). Professional to the last! He knew this was his final season, some sentimental attachment, therefore, clung to his taking leave of his best parts, and throwing every effort into them.

## MACBETH

With Lear and Hamlet especially, Garrick's acting was interlocked with texts which he constantly adapted. Most of his adaptations remained as prompt-copies until 1774 when John Bell, with the aid and permission of the prompters at both theatres, published many volumes of texts of plays (Shakespeare's and others) "as acted at the theatres." Along the way, however, Garrick had advertised his performance of *King Lear* (1756) "with Restorations from Shakespeare," and in 1763 had allowed his then acting copy of *Hamlet* to be printed. From this copy, from the Bell editions, from suggestions made in letters and in critical pamphlets, although we have no full record, we observe an ongoing process of constant freshening in train, both with the texts and with the performing.

The constant changes in word, accent, and attitude well-impressed upon spectators, especially in the *Hamlet* text, carried far beyond the walls of Drury Lane theatre into the homes and private conversations of those to whom drama counted for more than a night's entertainment. Garrick contributed and participated in such discussions. An instance: One evening he had been talking with Daniel Wray (trustee of the British Museum), Charles Yorke (attorney general), and others about the meaning of the phrase "the mobled queen" in *Hamlet*. Antiquarian Wray wished Garrick's opinion, which Garrick gave, then next day wrote his afterthoughts about it to Yorke. "He asked me what was Mobled? I answered *Clouted*—but something running in my head, & the Demon of Criticism, (slipping down with $y^e$ Burgandy), possessing me at $y^e$ Instant; I said, is it not Mob-led?—When I return'd home, & was looking into a Memorandum book, where I had collected Every Scrap about Shakespeare, I found that I had met with this interpretation of Mobled, in some pamphlet, or Other, and that I had written under it—absurd and ridiculous—and most certainly it is so—$D^r$ Warburton says—Mobled, or Mabled signifies veiled—Johnson—huddled or grosly cover'd—Capel has it—Ennobled Queen—$w^{ch}$ I don't understand—Shakespear certainly means, wretchedly clad: '—a Clout upon that head / Where late the diadem stood &c.' I have taken the liberty to say thus much, lest I $sh^d$ be thought too ignorant by those I had the honour of conversing with Yesterday" (525). Garrick's memoranda, his search into old editions, and his discussions with contemporary scholars meant much to him in his acting and interpretations. Such discussions deriving from Garrick's acting frequently attached themselves to his Macbeth over the years.

549

Macbeth, Davies tells us, before Garrick's performing it was not considered by the actors a character of the first rate. "All the pith of it was exhausted, they said, in the first and second act of the play." And audiences believed them, forming "their judgments from the drowsy and ineffectual manner of Garrick's predecessors who could not force attention or applause for the three last acts. When Roscius was informed what judgment the players had conceived of *Macbeth*, he smiled and said he should be very unhappy if he were not able to keep alive the attention of the spectators to the last syllable of so animated a character."[74]

Whether Garrick smiled, just what he said, or when, may be fiction, but the facts are clear about a most daring move he made with the play when he first took the part of the Scots King on 7 January 1744. With the successes of Lear and Hamlet established—rather new plays as he presented them—his *Macbeth* was advertised as presenting the text "As Shakespeare wrote it." The announcement brought from Quin the surprised but revealing remark, as far as knowledge of Shakespeare among leading actors was concerned, "What does he mean? Don't I play Macbeth as written by Shakespeare?" He did not, of course, for he was playing the Davenant version, which had held the stage since the late seventeenth century.

Garrick "broke through the fetters of foolish custom and arbitrary imposition" in Davies's words, "and restored *Macbeth* to the public almost in the same dress it was left us in by the author." Davies's thumbnail sketch of the Garrick text will do for purposes here. "A scene or two, which were not conducive to the action, he threw out in representation; others that were too long he judiciously pruned; very few additions were made, except in some passages of the play necessary to the better explanation of the writer's intention. He composed, indeed, a pretty long speech for Macbeth when dying, which though suitable perhaps to the character, was unlike Shakespeare's manner. . . . But Garrick excelled in the expression of convulsive throes and dying agonies."[75]

Garrick, thoroughly familiar with audience and critic response by 1744, to forestall criticism of the novelty and to advertise the new departure in Shakespearean productions, published a six-penny pamphlet with a mocking attack upon himself—"*An Essay on Acting, in Which Will Be Considered the Mimical Behaviour of a Certain Fashionable, Faulty Actor . . . to Which Is Added a Short Criticism on His Acting Macbeth.*" The title page contained two mottoes of mock seriousness—"'O Macbeth has murder'd G—k,' Shakespeare," and "'So have I seen a Pygmie strut, mouth and rant, in a Giant's robe,' Tom

Thumb." Small in stature, Garrick had mocked his own ability to assume the role of the powerful, probably six-foot-tall Scots General and King, then criticized the use of contemporary costumes (tie wogs and red coats). He criticized his eye movement in the dagger scene, and satirized Quin's clutching gestures in the same. He suggested a preposterous way of handling Banquo's Ghost at the banquet, and concluded with a mock diatribe against himself as a mimic. He managed to include in all this spoofing, sound praise of Shakespeare and deftly to draw the attention of readers to a number of scenes which he intended to act with a difference. He meant his audience to come with eyes open to change and with critical minds. He was sure of his text. It had been prepared with the aid of Dr Johnson's *Miscellaneous Observations on the Tragedy of Macbeth.*[76]

This *Essay on Acting* in a way may be said to be Garrick's manifesto of a different concept of performing from that spelled out by the rhetoricians. He compares the fright and introspection of Drugger's breaking a urinal and Macbeth's fright and introspection in murdering Duncan. We learn from his minute description of Macbeth's reaction, exactly how he acted the scene. "When the *Murder* of *Duncan* is committed, from an immediate *Consciousness* of the Fact, his *Ambition* is ingulph'd at that Instant by the Horror of the Deed; his *Faculties* are instantly riveted to the *Murder* alone, without having the least Consolation of the *consequential Advantages*, to comfort him in that Exigency. He should at that Time, be a *moving Statue*, or indeed a *petrify'd Man*; his Eyes must *Speak*, and his *Tongue* be *metaphorically Silent*; his *Ears* must be *sensible* of *imaginary* Noises, and *deaf* to the *present* and *audible* Voice of his Wife; his *Attitude* must be *quick* and *permanent*; his Voice *articulately trembling*, and *confusedly intelligible*; the Murderer should be seen in *every* Limb, and yet every *Member*, at that Instant, should seem *separated* from his *Body*, and his *Body* from his *Soul*: This is the Picture of a compleat *Regicide*, and as at that Time the *Orb below should be hush as death*; I hope I shall not be thought *minutely circumstantial*, if I should advise a *real* Genius to wear *Cork Heels* to his Shoes, as in this Scene he should seem to *tread on Air*" (p. 9).

This advice is serious. Following hard on, one reads the mocking description of Quin's clutchingg the air-drawn dagger and bobbling his eyes. His is the verso of the coin: Garrick's was the very opposite to Quin's performance. "In this visionary Horror," preparatory to the murder, "he should not rivet his Eyes to the *imaginary* Object [which, of course Garrick was going to do], as if it *really* was there, but should show an *unsettled Motion* in his Eye, like one not quite awakened from some disordering Dream; his *Hands* and *Fingers* should not be *immoveable* [as Garrick's were to be], but *restless* and endeavouring to disperse the Cloud that over shadows his optic ray, and bedims his intellects; here would be Confusion, Disorder, and agony! *Come let me clutch thee!* is not to be done with *one* motion only, but by several *successive* catches at it, first with one Hand and then with the other, preserving the same Motion at the same Time, with his Feet, like a Man, who out of his Depth, and half drowned in his Struggles, *catches* at *Air* for *Substance*: this would make the Spectator's blood run cold, and he would almost feel the Agonies of the Murderer himself " (p. 18).

All spectators after reading this watched Garrick's next performance with a fixed gaze and new sensations. The pamphlet had its effect; and indeed Garrick's art may by then have improved to such an extent that only a few quibbling comments, such as those attendant on early performances of Lear and Hamlet, appeared. Garrick triumphed again!

First Garrick sought the essence of the character as he deemed Shakespeare revealed it. Holding that in mind he bent all his faculties to communicate that in the changing actions of the play. "What is the *Character* of *Macbeth?*" he asked, "He is an experienc'd General, crown'd with Conquest, *innately Ambitions*, and religiously Humane, spurr'd on by *metaphysical* Prophecies, and the *unconquerable Pride* of his *Wife*, to a deed, *horrid* in *itself*, and *repugnant* to his Nature; but as it is the *Ladder* to the *swelling Act of the Imperial Theme*, his *milk* soon becomes *Gall*, imbitters his whole Disposition, and the Consequence is the *Murder* of *Duncan*, the *taking off* of *Banquo*, and his own *Coronation.*"

Garrick knew he could not do this part alone. He needed above all else an excellent Lady Macbeth. Mrs Pritchard teamed with him for years. He played the character but a single time (22 September 1768) with Mrs Barry after Mrs Pritchard's departure from the stage in 1768. A reviewer for the performance 6 March 1755 showed the effective actions of both, especially in the scene following the murder of Duncan: "It was universally acknowledged that the involved countenance, preserved throughout all the scenes, previous to the murder; the astonishing expression of horror after the commission of that execrable deed, the masterly dissimulation in the subsequent scene, through which a consciousness of guilt was suffered to betray itself; with the several delicate touches marking the agonies of a tortured mind; particularly the fixed stare, and total inattention in that passage when Macbeth, after enlarging on the happiness of Duncan, in being removed from all sublunary ills, concludes, 'nothing can touch him further'—were equal to anything that even Mr Garrick has exhibited on the stage. It has

Harvard Theatre Collection
Garrick as Macbeth.
Printed for R. Sayer, 1769.

*Folger Shakespeare Library*
Garrick and Mrs Pritchard as Macbeth and Lady Macbeth.
Engraving by V. Green from a painting by Zoffany, 1776.

been long admitted that the prize of acting hangs between this character and King Lear. . . . Mrs Pritchard displays great judgment and a surprising power of countenance in all the capital scenes of her part."[77]

Davies was more detailed in his account of Mrs Pritchard, especially of her support in the banquet scene: "This admirable scene was greatly supported by the speaking terrors of Garrick's look and action. Mrs Pritchard showed admirable art in endeavouring to hide Macbeth's frenzy from the observation of the guests by drawing their attention to conviviality. She smiled at one, whispered to another, and distantly saluted a third; in short she practised every possible artifice to hide the transaction that passed between her husband and the vision his disturbed imagination had raised. Her reproving and angry looks, which glanced towards Macbeth at the same time were mixed with angry marks of inward vexation and uneasiness. When at last, as if unable to support her feelings any longer, she rose from her seat, and seized his arm, and with a half whisper of terror, said 'Are you a Man!' she assumed a look of such anger, and contempt, as cannot be surpassed."[78]

Not every performance was perfect. A reviewer in 1759 caught a performance when Garrick had a cold, and urged the actor to rest and recover before attempting another such part. Mrs Pritchard, however was fine.[79] Another reviewer in 1769, fearing that Garrick might not perform Macbeth again, hoped that he would train up others to express more surprise and disappointment in the scene where the witches prophesy that Banquo's issue will succeed ultimately to the throne, and to think about more appropriate costuming. Thomas Wilkes, in 1759, in his *A General View of the Stage*, was complimentary as usual, but nevertheless *was* impressed with the whole flow of the play: He thought the characterization extremely difficult, but that Garrick did it with ease. "It is curious to observe in him the progress of guilt from the intention to the act. How his ambition kindles at the distant prospect of a crown, when the witches prophesy! And with what reluctance he yields, upon the diabolical persuasions of his wife, to the perpetuation of the murder! How finely he does show his resolution staggered, upon the supposed view of the air-drawn dagger, until he is roused to action by the signal, viz. the ringing of the closet bell. It is impossible to convey an adequate idea of the horror of his looks, when he returns from having murdered Duncan with the bloody daggers, and hands stained in gore. How does his voice chill the blood when he tells you 'I've done the deed!' and then looking on his hands, 'this is a sorry sight!' How expressive is his manner and countenance during Lenox's knocking at the door, of the anguish and confusion that possesses him;

and his answer 'twas a rough night' shows as much self-condemnation, as much fear of discovery, as much endeavour to conquer inquietude and assume ease, as ever as infused into, or intended for, the character. What force, what uncontroulable spirit does he discover in his distresses, when he cries out, 'They have tied me to a stake—I cannot fly; / But bear-like I must fight my course.' In short he alone, methinks, performs the character."[80] Wilkes's exercise in a dozen rhetorical exclamations suggests, beyond the praise, a sense of the whole character, not just the conveyance of *fear, remorse, fright, inquietude,* and *courage*—abstractions all.

In Garrick's mid-career with Macbeth, spectators began to write letters about points of breath pause, pronunciation, meaning related to character concept, and the like. H. H., who had written about pauses in *Hamlet*, came on politely but strongly about a seeming break in the line "Shakes so my single state of man" after *single*, and in the line "That his virtues will plead like Angels trumpet-tongud against, &c" a break after *angels* instead of a pause for breath after *tongued*; an over-emphasis on *was* in the line "and such an instrument I was to use," etc. Garrick replied with care to each: "*Shakes so my single*—If I stop at y$^e$ last word, it is a glaring fault, for the Sense is imperfect—but my Idea of the passage is this—Macbeth is absorb'd in thought, & struck with y$^e$ horror of y$^e$ murder, tho but in Idea (*fantastical*) and it naturally gives him a slow—tremulous—under tone of voice, & tho it might appear that I stopp'd at Every word in y$^e$ Line more than Usual, yet my intention, was far from dividing the Substantive from its adjective, but to paint y$^e$ horror of Macbeth's Mind, & keep y$^e$ voice suspended a little. . . . I am sorry to differ with You about the joining *Angels & Trumpet-tongud*, togeather. I really think y$^e$ force of those Exquisite four Lines & a half would be Partly lost for want of an Aspiration after *Angels*—the Epithet may agree with Either of y$^e$ Substantives, but I think it more Elegant to give it to the *Virtues*, & y$^e$ Sense is y$^e$ same" (281). And as to placing emphasis on *was* Garrick thought *was* and *use* should share equal emphasis. H. H. had also objected to Garrick's enunciation of the "Out, out, brief candle" line. "You give two starts, and accompany each with a strong action of the hands: is not this wrong? I should suspect it is; for the whole train of Macbeth's reasoning tends to enforce the insignificence of life. . . . [It] should be spoken with philosophical contempt." Garrick replied "I quite agree with you about—*out, out, brief Candle*—but surely I must have spoke those words quite y$^e$ reverse of my own Ideas, if I did not express with them the most contemptuous indifference of life"

(281).[81] In contrast to a philosophical contempt for life Samuel Nott wrote that he had once heard Garrick deliver the lines in "the softest voice that ever drew pity from the heart of man," and they affected him beyond expression.[82] Garrick's acting was inspiring people to match speaking with a character concept, and consider text with the care Garrick was giving to action.

Murphy, long interested in *Macbeth* had disagreed with Garrick's pronunciation of "making the green-one red," referring to the blood imagery and the sea in the play. He noted that Garrick did adopt his thought that the hint for pronunciation lay in the concept "the multitudinous seas incarnidine," and afterwards spoke the line "making the green one red," meaning universally red.

When Garrick played Macbeth after his return from France Murphy wrote, just after a moving performance, that he had been stimulated to read the whole play over again, and thought on balance that Garrick had been too easy and free with Banquo in the scene preceding the air-drawn dagger one, and that he had not given a burst of melancholy to the line "Doctor, the thanes fly from me." Garrick responded "The next best thing to saying y^r Prayers, was certainly reading Macbeth," and agreed that he should alter a bit the Banquo scene. As to the other, however, "You are certainly right in your account of my speaking— *Doctor the Thanes fly from me*—but I differ a little with You in opinion, that I formerly spoke it in a *burst of melancholy*: Macbeth is greatly heated, & Agitated with News of the English Force coming upon him—His Mind runs from one thing to another—all in hurry, & confusion: Would not his Speaking in a Melancholy manner in y^e midst of his distraction, be too calm—? *Come put my Armor on—Give me my Staff—Seyton send out—Doctor the Thanes fly from me. come Sir dispatch—pluck it off—bring it after* me &c You have flatter'd me much by Your very Obliging letter—& I shall profit by Y^r Criticisms" (485).

Recall of each of these little incidents bespeaks a Garrick thoroughly on top of every detail of the characterization he wished to present, delivering it in a professional manner, but not with a cemented and thoroughly fixed opinion that his every phrase, pause, accent was "right," able, however, to justify each action, and intonation, and ready to change and make more precise the offering of any line from a request backed by justification equally strong. Such was part of his resilient creativity.

Lord North requested that Garrick perform the play in 1772, but Garrick wrote "I am really not yet prepar'd for Macbeth, 'tis the most violent part I have," and he played it no more (726). Readers of the papers were amused, however, by 20 lines of verse appearing under the title:

### Macbeth: Eight Kings appear in Order

Old *Quin*, ere fate suppress'd his labouring breath
In studied accents grumbled out Macbeth:
Next *Garrick* came, whose utt'rance truth impress'd
While every look the tyrant's guilt express'd.
Then the cold *Sowdon* half froze the part
Yet what he lost by Nature, sav'd by Art.
Tall *Barry* now advanc'd towards Birnam wood
Nor ill perform'd the scenes—he understood—
Grave *Mossop* next to Fores shaped his march
His words were minute guns, his action starch.
Rough *Holland* too—but pass his errors o'er
Nor blame the actor when the man's no more!
Then heavy *Ross* essay'd the tragic frown,
But beef and pudding kept all meaning down.
Next careless *Smith* try'd on the horrid mask
While o'er his tongue light tripp'd the horrid task.
Hard *Macklin* late guilt's feelings strove to speak
While sweats infernal drench'd his iron cheek.
Like Fielding's kings, his fancy'd triumph's past
And all he boasts is, that he was the last.[83]

The play was quite popular at both theatres, but the deep impression on Londoners came from Garrick and Mrs Pritchard. Garrick's dying scenes, so successful in Richard, Lothario, Pierre, Hamlet, and King John, held one thing in common which fascinated London spectators—communication of inner agony rather than of bodily pain. Each death differed according to the character, and quality of guilt peculiar to each individual. Actors had felt that Macbeth was a difficult role in which to sustain interest until the final curtain. Garrick had accepted the challenge of holding attention throughout the play, not only by his restoration of the Shakespeare text, but also by providing a death scene for the tyrant King, in a speech which, incidentally, was preserved by actors well into the nineteenth century. We know how he performed it from the minute description left by Jean Georges Noverre —one of those mightily impressed by seeing it.

"I have seen him represent a tyrant," wrote Noverre, "who, appaled at the enormity of his crime, dies torn with remorse. The last act was given up to regrets and grief, humanity triumphed over murder and barbarism; the tyrant obedient to the voice of conscience denounced his crimes aloud; they gradually became his judges and his execution-ers; the approach of death showed each instant on his face; his eyes became dim, his voice could not support the efforts he made to speak his thoughts. His gestures without losing their expression revealed the approach of the last moment; his legs gave way under him, his face lengthened, his pale and livid features bore the signs of suffering and repentence. At last he fell, at that moment his crimes peopled his thoughts, with the most horrible forms; terrified at the hideous pictures which his past acts revealed to him, he struggled against death; nature seemed to make one supreme effort. His plight made the audience shudder, he clawed the ground and seemed to be digging his own grave, but the dread moment was nigh, one saw death in reality, everything expressed that instant which makes all equal. In the end he expired. The death rattle and the convulsive movements of his features, arms, and breast gave the final touch to this terrible picture."[84] For the Frenchman this death upon stage was moving, as it was for the magnetized shuddering audience—many of whom watched death on Tyburn hill. Garrick brought the play to a new life on the London stage—in text, in personal acting, and in ensemble performance.

## OTHELLO AND IAGO

Henry Aston asked an acquaintance "how he had been entertained by my friend Garrick, in the character of Othello? His answer was—*Sunt quaedam mediocria, sunt bona plura*: no mention at all of any *mala*."[85] Aston's letter was a friendly warning for Garrick to think twice before going on with this role, which was, indeed, a kind of defeat for him amid a swirl of success, and his hopes for it had been high. The performing never rose to the full flood of persuasiveness that his others did. He took the advice and performed it only four times—but even those generated comment.

The play, teeming with passion and sexual overtones, horrifying in its display of opportunistic manipulation of a frank and credulous mind by a resourceful and guileful one—a drama terse and insistent in action yet rich in poetry, had caught on quickly after the Restoration, and had lasted as one of the most frequently performed of Shakespeare's plays. Several generations of versatile actors triumphed in it. Betterton and Booth were great Othellos.[86] Both the major and minor theatres had frequently acted it, and 18 well-known actors beside the two early leaders in the profession had played Othello; 11, including Cibber and Macklin, undertook Iago; 16 actresses loved and perished in Desdemona; and nearly a dozen played the catalyst Emelia. The play merited "new dresses, and new scenes" on a number of occasions. More often than not it had been received "with universal applause." Performances were commanded by both George I and George II, and it was given special performances to entertain the ambassadors from Morocco. It was often used, for its drawing power, by actors for their benefit performances. Its stage popularity created a market for a dozen shilling editions advertising "as it is performed in the theatres." In the periodical press, wherever discussions of "jealousy" or "reputation" occurred, *Othello* was quoted, and the lines, "Good name in man or woman / Is the immediate jewell of our souls, / Who steals my purse steals trash, &c.," was the *most often* quoted passage from all Shakespeare from 1700 to 1740.[87]

Against this background one is not surprised to find the young Garrick in the first flush of his stage success writing with excitement to his brother Peter (December 1741) I "shall soon be ready in Bayes in y^e Rehearsal & in y^e Part of Othello—Both which I believe will do Me & Giffard great Service" (20). Performance was delayed for nearly three years to 7 March 1745, and did neither him nor his then manager James Lacy "great service." He played it again on 9 March, and once the following February in Ireland, and for the last time on 20 June 1746 at Covent Garden. In the meantime he had switched to the role of Iago (26 February 1745 in Dublin) which he repeated 9 March 1749 in England for Spranger Barry's benefit. During the following season he played Iago five times to Barry's Othello. His last performance came 2 April 1753 at the benefit of Henry Mossop, who did Othello.[88]

Garrick's involvement with *Othello* was serious. His study for the leading role was long. In December 1744, three months before he played it he wrote to John Hoadly, "I rise or fall by Othell⟨o ver⟩y soon: *oh it comes o'er my ⟨Memory⟩*—but Man or Mouse you shall have as Impartial an Account (as my Vanity will permit me) of my Success in y^e Character" (29). The box receipts were high on all occasions of his performing either the role of Othello or Iago.[89] Why then did he not capitalize on the role? Lines from both roles stuck in his memory and came out in fragmentary apt quotations throughout his vast correspondence—more frequently than from any other play. He was straining at first to supersede Quin in the part of the sooty-bosomed Moor, and he provided a different characterization indeed. He knew the text was his basic guideline, and so his first innovation was the restoration to the play of the "trance scene." The obdurate attitude of the other players of the time is seen in Macklin's comment. He grudgingly describes the competition with Quin in this scene, but notes that the restoration was actually applauded: "Garrick himself was a diminutive mean figure for the Moor; therefore he knew that Quin could not fall suddenly on the ground, as it were in a fit, without greatly hurting himself, and perhaps raising laughter in the audience; but that he might with his insignificant person do it without risk of either; and therefore introduced that shameful scene of epilepsy in the fourth act, which instead of being applauded, ought to have been exploded with indignation and contempt for his impudence in the first place, in offering such an absurd passage to a thinking and supposed judicious public; and for the next place in restoring a passage which in the records of the theatre had never been acted, and which on and off stage must be looked upon as an excrescence of the worst sort, of the great genius that produced it."[90]

One learns more about a soured Macklin than about a consistent Garrick in such remarks. Although the text of *Othello* had been less modified since Restoration times than had any other Shakespeare text (save *Julius Caesar*), Garrick even at the age of 28 was moving (as we have noted elsewhere) toward fresh concepts in Shakespeare, mainly by restoring original scenes and language. Quin watched Garrick's performance and left satisfied with his own superiority—in size and dignity. There seemed to be substance, however, to the criticism of Garrick that he was seeking too hard to differentiate between himself and Quin in performance, rather than to concentrate on giving a particularized and different Othello.

Henry Aston's "friend," who had reported on Garrick's first performance, noted that the speech before the Senate was "delivered with such exact propriety of emphasis and accent, as he had scarce ever heard; but that [his] *action* was, in his opinion, a little exceptionable." It had pomp, but lacked dignity and modesty, although the "modulations of your voice in that recital, (which required many) were observed with a justness greatly beyond any thing he had known." He objected also, in the display of Garrick's jealousy, to the wincings and gesticulations of body.[91]

Richard Rigby, a close friend, disliked the costume Garrick wore, thought he outdid Quin in only a single instance—where Iago gives him his first suspicion about Desdemona. He concluded, "He endeavoured throughout to play everything different from Quin, and failed, I think, in most of his alterations."[92] Benjamin Victor liked the

Senate presentation and the trance, but had misgivings on other points. He had watched closely, he said, fearing most the address to the Senate, "but there, even there you excelled your rival, whose merit lies chiefly in declamation—I found that *you* had applied very judiciously your study to the great and striking passages in the character—the trance had a fine effect, your manner of falling into it and recovering from it was amazingly beautiful." He explained, however, that in the scene with Desdemona and Emelia, Garrick should address Desdemona with anger, and Emelia with peevishness and contempt, as he pushes her from the room. "This you did last night not only in a wrong tone of voice, but in too much hurry." Overall Victor urges Garrick to be less violent in his gestures. "As you have the happiness of a most expressive countenance, you may safely trust to that, which with your proper and pathetic manner of speaking would charm more successfully if those violent and seeming artful emotions of body were a little abated."[93] Quin in the role seemed still dominant, but according to one J. T. he was "ill-suited for the delicate tenderness which the poet has interwoven with the soul of the black warrior."[94] Soon in London, therefore, Barry, the tall, graceful, soft voiced Irishman, who had learned much from Garrick, became the favorite Othello. Some Garrick innovations seem to have come before their time.

Basically Garrick saw the play as a company rather than an individual performance. He spelled out his best sense of the whole in his suggestions to Francis Hayman for an appropriate painting from the play. He chose the climax, and his disposition of the characters tells how he envisioned the performance, and perhaps how he did it in 1745: "The Scene . . . [for] the best Picture, is that point . . . in the last Act, when Emilia discovers to Othello his Error about the Handkerchief *Emil*—Oh Thou Dull Moor! That Handkerchief, &c. Here at once the Whole Catastrophe of the play is unravell'd & the Groupe of Figures in this Scene, with their different Expressions will produce a finer Effect in painting, than perhaps Any other in all Shakespeare. . . . The back Ground . . . must be Desdemona murder'd in her bed; the Characters upon Stage are Othello, Montano, Gratiano & Iago: Othello (y$^e$ Principal) upon y$^e$ right hand (I believe) must be thunderstruck with Horror, his Whole figure extended, w$^{th}$ his Eyes turn'd up to Heav'n & his Frame sinking, as it were at Emilia's Discovery. I shall better make you conceive My Notion of this Attitude & Expression when I see You; Emilia must appear in the utmost Vehemence with a Mixture of Sorrow on Account of her Mistress & I⟨think⟩ should be in y$^e$ Middle. Iago on y$^e$ left hand should express the greatest perturbation of Mind, & should Shrink up his Body, at y$^e$ opening of his Villainy, with his Eyes looking askance . . . on Othello, and gnawing his Lip in anger at his Wife. . . . The other less capital Characters must be affected according to y$^e$ Circumstances of the Scene, & as they are more or less concern'd in y$^e$ Catastrophe" (47).

Garrick actually played Iago twice as many times as he did Othello —and even that was not much. John Hill's long discussion of *Othello* is revealing for its testimony of Garrick as Iago. He makes much of the point that a great actor must interpret the text, not just recite the lines: "The great thing in which players distinguish themselves, is in expressing to the audience such sentiments as are not deliver'd in the play, yet are not only agreeable but necessary to be understood of the character they represent under the situation in which it is when they do it. Whoever has seen Mr Garrick play Iago, or Macklin the Jew of Venice, and has before or after read the plays . . . will find that there are many instances of this kind of merit in both representations." He instances the native ease, and quiet naturalness of tone which Garrick uses to heighten his "finesse" [supplemental by-play] in acting . . . in a soliloquy of Iago . . . in which after an infinite deal of finesse . . . he delivers plainly and without ornament a speech in which we have been used to see a world of unnatural contortion of face and absurd by-play. The place we allude to is this—'If I can fasten but one cup upon him [Cassio] with that which he hath drunk tonight already, He'll be as full of quarrel and offense as my young Mistress' dog.'" [95]

Garrick spoke the 17 lines outlining this plan with casual naturalness, as he revealed the character of Cassio, and developed a plan to turn the lieutenant's weakness to his own advantage. Such a process of showing the mind-at-work in Iago and his pouncing upon opportunities for exploiting occur so frequently in the play that they offered just the avenue for Garrick's deadly effective naturalness of acting. No "heavy" villain he. Seemingly the earlier criticism of his Othello had taken root so that he modified his gestures in the secondary role.

He toyed, occasionally, with the idea of taking up Othello again. George Steevens urged him to do so 31 December 1773. But Garrick dashed his hopes by writing two weeks later "I have no thoughts of othello" (815).[96] But a nagging desire to have another try seized him in his final year. He wrote to Colman (11 October 1775), "I have been rehearsing Othello, as Bensley will tell you, & my head shakes" (945). Probably it was wise that his head shook a negative, as he ruminated. Ill with the gout and the stone, perhaps the thought of doing the trance scene—which would be expected of him—dissuaded him. He decided to depart via Richard, Hamlet, and Lear. After all he had shown his contemporaries a new factor in the developing jealousy of Othello, and the double effectiveness of a plain-speaking, under-played Iago.

## LUSIGNAN IN 'ZARA'

The role of the old and noble Lusignan was the eighth in number of performances of tragic parts by Garrick. He did it 54 times, appearing in it every year from the time he undertook it (25 March 1754) until he left the stage. The play is another one which has a female lead, one in which Mrs Cibber as early as 1736 had established her reputation as a great tragic heroine, not just a stage singer. The tragedy is a translation by Aaron Hill of Voltaire's *Zaire*, and it persisted on the London stage at least until 1796. The tale of noble ideals and fatal passions both by Christians and Muhammadans shows young Zara a slave in the seraglio of Osman, the Sultan of Jerusalem, and chastely loved by him. She knowing herself to be a Christian, but ignorant of her birth, has fallen deeply in love with Osman, even to the point of accepting his religion. Osman generous and humane, has let young Nerestan, a captive about the same age as Zara journey to Paris to raise a ransom to free the Christian captives in Jerusalem—all but Lusignan (the former Christian King of Jerusalem) and Zara. Lusignan has been kept in dungeon dark for many years. Nerestan returns with the ransoming funds just at the time of the proposed marriage between Zara and Osman. He discovers from old Chatillon that Lusignan, at the time of his fall had two surviving babes, Chatillon urges Zara to have Osman release Lusignan for a brief interview. When the old man appears he recognizes a cross (which Zara wears) to be the one he gave to his daughter, and sees a scar on the breast of Nerestan, which is the mark his son bore. He is returned to his dungeon to die happily in the conviction that both will be freed and that Zara will remain a Christian. She, however, wishes to stay with Osman, and will reveal to him her relationship to Nerestan and her father only when Nerestan is safe at sea. A letter making an appointment with him is interrupted in passage and misinterpreted by Osman. He watches for the meeting of the two, and in semidarkness stabs Zara (the first arrival) thinking the meeting to be one between lovers. Discovering too late that Nere-stan is her brother, and not his rival, overcome with grief at his rage and mistake he, Othello-like, stabs himself to death. So both the noble Saracen and the honorable pathetic woman, torn between loyalties, succumb to the clutch of circumstances ironically beyond their control.

The popularity of this play, especially for charitable benefit performances bespoke the power which Garrick and Mrs Cibber (and later Mrs Yates) gave it. It had lain dormant at Drury Lane for 17 years when Garrick worked over the text and revived it. He took on a crucial but very short role, speaking in all no more than 136 lines. A feeble, elderly man emerging from prison, he is strong in the memory of his past powers, and of the tragic loss of his wife, son, and daughter. Garrick's prompt copy, now in the Folger Library, demonstrates the way in which Garrick streamlined the long declamations of the basic Hill text, and restored in subtle ways emphases and lines from Voltaire's original. In arrangements for his own part he occasionally cut declamation down to an almost conversational style.[97] This acting copy was probably made for the performance of 23 January 1766, when Garrick had returned from France, and had received a request from Their Majesties to see the play. Rousseau was in Garrick's box that night. Garrick played Lusignan in the main piece and his Lord Chalkstone in *Lethe* in the farcical after piece. The French visitor is said to have complimented the actor by saying: "I have cried all through your tragedy, and laughed all through your comedy without at all being able to understand the language."[98]

The durability of Garrick's performance in this favorite part is attested further by the appearance of two prints of Garrick and Mrs Yates in the identification scene, one anonymous, and one by J. Roberts in 1770 and 1776, respectively. There she in elegant stage costume hands him the cross. He in furred robe tries to focus his gaze, and arm extended with fingers outspread, gestures surprise.

Davies provides scant information on Garrick's performance. He outlined, however, for his contemporaries (while discussing Garrick's dealing with the play) the essential difference between French and English neoclassical stage drama, a distinction which Garrick knew well. "The Frenchman," writes Davies, "when he goes to a play, seems to make his entertainment a matter of importance. The long speeches in the plays of Corneille, Racine, Crébillon, and Voltaire, which would disgust an English ear, are extremely pleasing to our light neighbors: they sit in silence, and enjoy the beauty of sentiment and energy of language; and are taught habitually to cry at scenes of distress. The Englishman looks upon the theatre as a place of amusement; he does not expect to be alarmed with terror, or wrought upon by scenes of commiseration; but he is surprised into the feelings of these passions,

and sheds tears because he cannot avoid it. The theatre, to most Englishmen, becomes a place of instruction by chance, not by choice."[99]
Garrick's revisions led to active interpretations which counted more for
English instruction, as well as aesthetic amusement, than the French
stage declamation of pious precepts.

But again the troubles and joys of the aged Lusignan became touchstones of quality in performing. Hannah More grew ecstatic in the
spring of 1774 about Garrick in the role. "Yes I have seen Him! I
have heard Him!—& the Music of his Voice, & the Lightening of his
eyes still act so forcibly on my imagination, that I see, & hear Him
still. He play'd *Lusignan* last Night, & we had the good Fortune to
get Places about the Middle of the Pit. . . . The Part was most bar-
barously short;—but the 'excess compensated the Date.' His Pro-
nouncing the little Pronoun *you* in a certain doubtful, apprehensive,
tremulous interrogatory Tone gave me a more precise Idea of Perfection, than all the Elocution I ever heard from the *Stage*:—yet divinely,
as he speaks, Speech is almost superfluous in Him, & I would undertake to translate his Looks and Attitudes into words, tho' perhaps
with some Abatement of the Author's Poetry, & *his* Expression.—No
Rant, no Pomp. . . . What an enchanting Simplicity! What an eter-
nally varying Cadence, yet without one Stop, one Inequality!—I could
have murder'd half the audience with great Composure for the inef-
fable *Non-chalence*, with which some of them behav'd. They took the
Liberty to breathe, to look at the other Actors, nay even to blow their
Noses, & fan themselves. . . . Nor was *He* clappd more than that insipid Vegetable, the unpungent *Reddish*, unless indeed on his first
Entrance. . . . Miss Young play'd *Zara* well" (app. D, p. 1357).

So much for girlish idolatry as she watched the fulfillment of all her
built-up expectations. A year later cold, analytical, and often antagonistic George Steevens saw the play. "I think you never played Lusignan so happily," he wrote, "at least you never affected me in it so
much before." However, thoroughly schooled in the Garrick concept
of the ensemble performance, he looked at the other characters and
found them perilously wanting.[100] A writer for the *London Chronicle*
18 years earlier seems to have had eyes for Garrick only. He disliked
the Osman role but "Lusignan is very well sketched, and receives
infinitely more beautiful touches from the exquisite pencil of Mr. Garrick, than it owes to the hand of the poet." In a quieter moment,
Hannah More felt that Garrick's Lusignan was but a sketch, "the
*Dawning* of the intolerable Lustre, with which He shone in Lear"
(app. D, p. 1358).[101]

This triumph in a small part, one which he originally worked up for

Bell's British Theatre
Garrick and Mrs Yates as Lusignan and Zara in *Zara*.
Engraving by W. Walker, 1776.

Mossop's benefit night, Garrick maintained after his return from France as a not very exacting role, but one which he found the public liked immensely. His reviving the play at Drury Lane was to meet competition from Covent Garden, but in his generosity Garrick gave it more often than not to benefits.

## ROMEO

Garrick revived *Romeo and Juliet* for Drury Lane and established the acting text for the rest of the century on 29 November 1748, coaching Barry and Mrs Cibber in the leading roles. Under the challenging pressure of theatrical competition later (since Barry and Mrs Cibber had crossed over to Covent Garden), he undertook the part of Romeo himself on 28 September 1750, after a two-month rehearsal with Mrs Bellamy as Juliet.[102] He entered the acting fray again to perform Mercutio for three benefit performances in April 1761. But in the ten-year period from 1750 to 22 March 1760 he made the star-crossed lover one of his major tragic roles, performing it to delighted audiences some 60 times.[103]

His adaptation of the Shakespearean play, retrieved from the Otway version of *Caius Marius*, had a most touching dying sequence in which Juliet awakens in the tomb before Romeo expires. Each has a look and a word before catastrophe engulfs them. A 75-line death scene was added by Garrick. It thrilled audiences on at least the 60 occasions of Garrick's performing:

> *Romeo*: Soft, soft, she breathes, she stirs—
> *Juliet*: Where am I? Defend me powers—
> *Romeo*: She speaks, she lives; and we shall still be bless'd!'

But Romeo has already drunk the poison, not having received word, through the quirk of fate, of Friar Lawrence's plan for a drugged deception and counterfeit death for Juliet.[104] Even Garrick's stern opponent MacNamara Morgan acknowledged the pathos of this scene, thus complimenting Garrick on his imagination and creativity: "Nothing was ever better calculated to draw tears from an audience . . . The circumstance of Juliet's awaking . . . is perhaps the finest touch of nature in any tragedy ancient or modern."[105]

No theatrical competition throughout the century quite matched that of the months of September and October 1750, when both theatres played this same play for 12 nights running. Garrick won technically, for Mrs Cibber fell ill after the twelfth performance, while Garrick and Mrs Bellamy carried on for a thirteenth. The story may be familiar to readers of theatre history. Suffice it to say that they caught the imagination of the town and amused it mightily at first. Comparisons were drawn between the two Romeos and the two Juliets. Barry the tender lover seemed to dominate the first three acts, while Garrick the passionate actor carried off honors in the last two. People were even said to shift theatres after the third act (when entrance prices halved) and nip over from Covent Garden to Drury Lane to see Garrick end the play and do the dying scene. But after a week, the tradition of having truly repertory theatres in London was so great that sameness palled, and squibs appeared in the newspapers calling a "plague on both the houses" for interrupting variety of performance for this struggle.[106]

But the real interest of the public carried on for years in the purchase of three editions (1748, 1750, 1753) of Garrick's adaptation, and a printing every three years thereafter until 1787.[107] The play ranked second only to *The Beggar's Opera* in total number of performances throughout the century. Garrick's text and his acting started it on its long modern career.

The period of competition was both tiring and exhilarating to Garrick. He wrote to the Countess of Burlington, 4 October 1750, "I have been acting y$^e$ Part of Romeo & a very fatiguing one it is" (95). Ten days later victory was in sight, and he wrote her again, "I have receiv'd great favour from y$^e$ Town in y$^e$ Character of Romeo; & I am so extremely well, that no fatigue hurts Me, & I have not once lost my Voice or Powers for thirteen Nights togeather, which is amazing" (96). He assured her that the cause lay in his great happiness at home with his new wife Eva Maria. He was especially cheered to have seen Barry and Mrs Cibber in his audience that last night, enjoying the performance, and amazed at the excellence of Mrs Bellamy (96).

Thomas Wilkes cast a sober look of evaluation at Garrick's performance, years after his particular battle had cooled: "All through the character of Romeo, I think him at least equal to any one who ever performed; and where other passions besides love are to be displayed he is vastly superior. This is evidenced particularly in the last act; his transition from the settled satisfaction of his presages, to silent horror and despondency, on receiving news of Juliet's death, that despair which he ever after maintains thro' the character, are as strong proofs as I know of his judgment and abilities. The attitude into which he throws himself, when disturbed by Paris in the Churchyard, is very

Garrick and Mrs Bellamy as Romeo and Juliet in *Romeo and Juliet*.
Engraving by T. Stayner from the painting by Benjamin Wilson, 1753.

striking. . . . In the dying scene he is particularly happy; his manner of expressing this single line—'Parents have flinty hearts, and children must be wretched,' carries with it so much of that sort of frenzy proper to Romeo's melancholy situation, and is delivered in a tone so affecting, *so different* from anything we before heard him express, that it makes one's blood run cold."[108]

The acting prompted William Popple to consult the text again, and determine to his own satisfaction whether "the passion of Romeo should be represented with the warmth and violence of a young man (as Garrick presented it) or the passionate tenderness of a fond lover (Barry's way). He concluded from close examination of a Theobald text that "Romeo is the tenderly passionate languishing lover."[109]

The editor of the *Gentleman's Magazine* had joined the evaluators of the competing pairs (October 1750), sensing that the play turned on the performing well of *many* roles: "Upon the whole Romeo is better perform'd by Garrick; Juliet, tho' not better at least more affectingly by Mrs Cibber. Mercutio in the New House (CG) is not acted but burlesqued by Macklin; Paris is better done at the New; Capulet and Tibalt better in the Old; and Shakespeare is under greater obligation to the Old than to the New House—'At Covent Garden I saw Juliet and Romeo; and at Drury Lane Romeo and Juliet.'"

Francis Gentleman, of course, 20 years after the event, still operating under the judicial theory of balancing maximum beauties versus maximum faults, prepared a balance scale between Barry and Garrick, adding nothing of great insight, but confirming the separate good qualities of each.[110] The point one sees so clearly now 200 years later, is that Garrick's creativity picked up an idea, perhaps from the abortive text prepared by Theophilus Cibber for a short run in 1744, which launched another very good Shakespearean text (and a fascinating way of performing it) on a course that has lasted. He had such joy in it that he used the play and the part as a fine training ground for young upcoming actors; and so not only Barry, but Ross, Fleetwood, Holland, Cautherley, Reddish, and Diamond went to school to him in the role, and Mrs Cibber, Miss Bellamy, Miss Haughton, Mrs Pritchard, Miss Bride, Mrs Barry, Miss Younge, and Miss Morland had his coaching in the role of Juliet. Garrick, always interested in the success of a play rather than of a single part, often played several parts in the same play, perhaps to exemplify to his company the necessity of seeing the play as a totality, and of getting a feeling for the possibilities of all the parts—Pierre and Jaffier, the Ghost and Hamlet, Faulconbridge and King John, Iago and Othello, Archer and Scrub. So in this play, though Woodward was his best Mercutio, he took on the role himself, playing to Holland's Romeo thrice in the early 1760s.[111] For novelty, Rich at Covent Garden had developed a funeral procession and a solemn dirge for Juliet. Garrick matched it, commissioning William Boyce to compose a similar dirge for his play, in which the rich voices of his singers increased the pleasure of the evening.[112]

This detailed review from eyewitness impressions, confirms Garrick the tragic actor compounding greatness in the profession not just by acting in great tragic roles, but by individualizing each, by giving an appropriate and different interpretation of the jealousy, say, of Othello from that of Chamont, of the ambition of Richard from that of Macbeth; of the passion of Romeo from that of Lothario, of the old man's bleakness of Lear from that of Lusignan, of the soul-shattering decision-making of Hamlet from that of Jaffier. Freshness and difference made for quality. Study, understanding, imagination, judgment, control and practice made for performance. And the magnetic quality coming from the genius of this performance drew into its field—*Ion*-like—emulation from his fellow actors, appreciation and discovery from his thousands of spectators. The facts lead nowhere else.

Selection has confined itself, as noted, to recorded firsthand impressions of but a dozen great roles in Garrick's tragic repertory. The 31 others unmentioned here were all followed with interest, whether performed but once (Orestes), or 25 times (Dorilas in *Merope*), nine times (Demetrius in Johnson's *Irene*), or six times each (Regulus in Havard's *Regulus*, and Antony in *Antony and Cleopatra*).[113] Each was watched for its different interpretation if the play were old and familiar, or for its sharp individualism if the play were contemporary. Many contemporary efforts were short-lived—at both theatres. Garrick sensed, as did his spectators and intelligent critics that the century was not one given to great creative tragic drama—though it did exceedingly well in comedy and farce. The imitations of Shakespeare, Corneille, or Voltaire taken from classical story, Gothic times, or the Orient lacked the fresh insights that a Shakespeare, an Otway, or a Rowe had left as theatrical legacies. Garrick was comfortable with this knowledge. He knew what imagination and and artistic excellence could do with the latent powers of the older plays. As they passed through study in the greenroom they, like their counterparts in comedy, emerged in active, exciting forms, making long-lasting impressions upon their audiences, and indelible ones upon the critics. Nothing matching the quantity and little matching the quality of theatrical criticism appeared in the century before Garrick blazed forth in his Richard III in 1741!

# Part Seven
## *The Close*

.

# Exit the Manager

REBUILDING THE Drury Lane company was a continuing process. Garrick watched here and chose there, but other events, excitements, and decisions enlivened this final period of management. Mention of Mrs Siddons's perception of heated rivalry among the actresses at Drury Lane in 1775 suggests the climax of some problems with personnel which became major during Garrick's last years. A few troubles came from the very young, but most from that middle group in age and experience chafing under real or imaginary restraint. Perhaps a quarter century has always marked a too-long period for one man, or even a team of two, to remain in effective command and to operate with peace on *all* fronts. The hint of conditions to come appeared soon after Garrick's return from France. He, though sensing the need for new infusions in the ranks, first had to come to terms with existing members of the company. James Love, whom he had brought from Edinburgh in 1762, a valuable supporter of the troupe, sought a raise in salary in midsummer of 1766. George Garrick, as personnel manager, replied to Love negatively and formally: the managers "think that you are fully rewarded according to the rate of other actors."[1] Love, afraid a breach was opening between himself and Garrick, furthered, perhaps, by his having baulked at helping Cautherly during the preceding summer at his Richmond theatre, asked for an appointment with the manager. Garrick invited him to breakfast, asked him to forget the Cautherly affair, but reminded him that any salary adjustment must go through proper channels, and at proper times, involving brother George and partner Lacy. He would not undercut the dictum of his associates, and urged Love to "accept or refuse the proposals as he thinks will best suit his circumstances" (410). Love left accepting a three-year contract at the old salary scale. Garrick had maintained a firm managerial attitude, and its success encouraged continued firmness.

The manager's basic point lay in the words "you are fully rewarded according to the rate of other actors." For by long tradition relative standing in the pay scale was all important because it normally determined sequence in assigning benefit nights during each spring season. And a benefit night, in turn, could bring to an actor amounts equal to his whole annual salary. Place in the scale was thus less a matter of pride than of economic well-being. Were an actor to receive a raise after the period for making adjustments had passed (late spring) his place on the pay scale changed. That would create either a "ripple" effect (as we now call it) necessitating possible adjustments all along the line, or would likely break harmony, precipitate endless arguments and multiple dissatisfactions among the other actors. So ran the theoretical argument. To seek a change at the wrong time was to court disapproval. The "articles of agreement" on this matter were documents of importance. Some, which have survived in letter form, seem rather casual, but were not so. Garrick had regularized personnel management, but had not yet bureaucratized by imposing legal printed forms in triplicate.

Articles of agreement signed in the early years by Garrick are lacking, save for the terms agreed upon with the dancer Georges Jean Noverre (1755), but Garrick's correspondence with actors later yields the points that must have been mutually understood in such documents. Articles were usually drawn up in May or June of the year preceding first employment, so that the treasurer and managers could anticipate the size of the weekly payroll. Made ordinarily for periods of three years, agreements sometimes included a reasonable salary escalation clause, sometimes not. William Brereton was offered in 1775 a three-year term with a salary increase of £4.0.0 a week during the final year. He preferred an annual raise of a pound a week beginning the second year because, as he stated, "It would give me a kind of rank in the theatre." Rank indeed counted, for payroll rank was the basis for the scheduling of benefit nights for the actors.[2]

If an actor wished a raise, or wished to move before his contract ended he was by custom and by reason to arrange with the managers in the months of May or June, so that they, in turn, would have ample time to recruit a replacement before the next season commenced. Mostly such negotiations were approved orally, but when the articles were drawn, accountability was arranged for by penalties for nonfulfillment on both sides. Garrick, as he told Pritchard 11 June 1747 that first season, wanted the company to work together as a unit. "I shall Engage the best Comp$^y$ in England if I can & think it y$^e$ Interest of the best Actors to be together; I shall to the best of my Ability, do Justice to All" (51).[3] The actors could confer with him, and indeed did meet with top management—Lacy and himself—face to face. The process at times brought on wearing series of arguments. Effort expended in such negotiating was to increase despite the high salary levels in force at Drury Lane.[4]

Late in the 1768–69 season, however, a major diversion from routine absorbed much of Garrick's energy and administrative skill. The affair of a Shakespeare Jubilee at Stratford, with its vision of the role of drama on a national scale, and its ultimate launching of Shakespeare in an international way, had repercussions which have continued for centuries. Jubilees in the middle ages emanating from the church had involved whole communities and states. A Shakespeare jubilee might underscore, as in no other way it could, the national cultural heritage of the best in English drama and honor England's top dramatist.

In December 1767 the Corporation of Stratford, rebuilding its Town Hall, wrote to Garrick that the members would be pleased to have a suitable picture to hang in it of the actor who best interpreted Shakespeare's plays. After a visit to Stratford, in Garrick's mind the concept of a magnificent tribute to the "god of his idolatry" began to form. The complicated problems of carrying out the tribute gave him, if at all, only momentary hesitation. Problems could always be solved. The challenge to his instincts as manager, producer, creative dramatist, and to his combined abilities, quickened his desire to dramatize a jubilee in Shakespeare's native town.

Time passed as he thought out some plans. For such an event he mapped out a three-day schedule, each day of which was to end with a major event to focus the interests of the crowd that might be expected to attend—not this time at a London theatre that seated under a thousand, but a crowd drawn from town and countryside and from abroad, interested spectators all, who as he planned it, would likewise be participants. He announced the project on 9 May 1769, and thereafter until 6 September, when the jubilee opened, Garrick, and George, and Lacy, the musicians, carpenters, actors and wardrobe-keepers of Drury Lane were busily engaged with their responsibilities for putting this affair together. Some few in the theatre were skeptical, acting only under orders, others were cheered and simply caught up by the magnitude and novelty of the occasion. All eventually came under the spell of enthusiasm communicated by the actor.

Garrick's illness that spring made coordination and execution of plans at times difficult. But he was able to delegate, sending his scene-maker, John French, and brother George to take lodgings in Stratford and to supervise *in situ*. George, as it turned out, seems to have supervised mostly from a tavern. The complexities of the production unfolded as the summer months progressed. Garrick gave him a com-

577

prehensive checklist of 20 items—from limiting prices-to-be-set for rooms, to the details of the pageantry, to arrangements for the fireworks, to ticket prices, to expression of his willingness to support half of any losses incurred by the corporation, to sharing with it any profits that might arise (app. C, pp. 1353–55).

Of first importance was the building of a rotunda in the fields along the Avon, one modeled in form and size upon the new pavillion at Ranelagh Gardens. A day-and-evening program in that building had to be developed for all—balls, masquerades, and dedicatory ceremonies. In addition breakfasts, processions through the town (participated in by all attendees), singing of catches and glees and madrigals to ancient tunes, bands and marching music, overtures new-written, background music, the air filled with song were all seen as parts of the celebration. For outdoor shows transparencies were to catch the eye and generate the awe of the country folk. A horse race for a jubilee cup worth £50 was conceived. Fireworks were to brighten the sky each night. Associated enterprises, and objects to preserve the memory multiplied and were made in quantity—ribbons, souvenirs, and wood carvings from the remains of Shakespeare's mulberry tree. Garrick gave friend Thomas Becket the concession for books, pamphlets, brochures, programs, and song sheets. Then there was the publicity. Journalists and the watchful articulate commented on the preparations. In the aftermath the flow of print increased—much praise, much blame, much irony, much sport: adulation mingled with vituperation, as might be expected. The magnitude and comprehensive theatricality jolted the countryside and rocked the town. Modern studies of the program continue to abound 200 years after the event.[5] The remarkable feature from all the words flowing from the public press and private letters of the time is the record of the calm, but actual and sustained enthusiasm of Garrick, coupled with his diplomatic manner in meeting problems head on and solving them.

He wished above all for a spirit of jollity to prevail, coming from general participation by those present, so music, music, music became important. A general assembly hall became important. A controversy which would stimulate discussion became important. For this controversy Garrick played the tune of cultural nationalism as an easy stimulus to polarize the boundless imagination of Shakespeare on the one hand against the constricted but precise dramatic theory and practice of France. He planned to set up such discussion in the broadest terms where he could control it best. With a sense of drama he planned it to occur as an outgrowth of his own recitation of the Ode dedicating the building, which was to be the high point of the ceremonies. Thus he prepared a script for the actor Tom King as the counter irritant for the sentiments in the *Ode*. The script in unsubtle fashion set up opposition from a hypothetical Anti-Goth Society—twelve pages (in Hopkins's fair copy) of a diatribe against Shakespeare and pro-French.[6] After the *Ode* Garrick was to open the floor for discussion, that is for anyone to speak anything for or against Shakespeare. Tom King, dressed as a fashionable Frenchified fop, was to decry Shakespeare's writing, and to condemn a jubilee to commemorate him. The magic would work, he thought, and he was right; for the journalists were entrapped, and repercussions of their side-taking even caused Horace Walpole to blush in Paris when the papers came over, as he said, "crammed with Garrick's nonsense about Shakespeare."[7]

Garrick had expressed himself several times on earlier occasions— in his *Prologue* to the opening of Drury Lane in 1750, and in the *Prologue* to his version of *The Winter's Tale*—that he wished to lose no drop of the immortal Shakespeare, hence dedicated his theatre as sacred to Shakespeare's plays. In both he was thinking of Shakespeare living on the stage, rather than studied on the page. Hence a goodly portion of the publicity now loosed in anticipation of the Stratford Jubilee linked the actor and the dramatist. In fact a pair of articles printed anonymously in the *London Magazine* for August 1769, recalled in many columns the glories and varieties of Shakespeare's plays, then gave in seven more columns the first full-length biographical sketch of Garrick. Five of the columns prepared all readers for the forthcoming event. "Having thus given our readers a cursory history of the first dramatic poet, *and* of the first dramatic performer this country has ever produced, we now come to the very liberal institution projected by the latter to celebrate the memory of the former; an institution which does honour to the age, and entitles Mr. Garrick to a generous regard from the sons of genius, and the friends of humanity."[8]

The piece dwelt upon Garrick's ability to show new beauties in Shakespeare's characters, and paid tribute to his thoughtful planning "to do an essential service to the birthplace of Shakespeare." That Garrick had a hand in this release ("puff") or at least sanctioned the copy comes clear—for the factual details of his life therein are correct. Its tone calmly gets at those elements of the events that Garrick wished to stress—highlighting the dedication, the musicians, the singers, the purveyor of the fireworks, and the race.

Bigness began to dominate, and Garrick dominated the bigness of the production. One hundred and seventy participants were in the cast —including the singers, the full Drury Lane orchestra, and many,

579

*Folger Shakespeare Library*
Garrick Standing with the Bust of Shakespeare.
Painting by Thomas Gainsborough, 1769.

many actors from Drury Lane and Covent Garden. Garrick as Steward set the tone of combined gaiety and seriousness for the various events. The September weather, and the weak logistic support actually given by the town for the unexpectedly large crowds (over which Garrick lacked control) defeated in some measure the full enjoyment of the occasion. Housing was meagre, prices seemed exorbitant, food supplies insufficient, and the heavens opened to a three-day downpour which flooded the race-course, wet down the improvised ball-room floor, and extinguished Domenico Angelo's fireworks. But in customary fashion the show went on, and Garrick kept spirits up as he moved about town smiling and cheerful, led processions, and finally recited his dedicatory *Ode*.

Garrick well knew how impressive the speaking of the *Ode* could be. He also calculated the reception it would have in various quarters when it would later be published to be read, not heard. When, therefore, he had Becket print it, somewhat after the September event, he included testimonials to Shakespeare's greatness from some 30 poets and writers, adding 18 moderns to those he had quoted in the *Ode* itself—from Gray to Voltaire, to George Steevens, to Mrs Montagu. Thus in the print-out they also became participants, as it were, whether they wished it or not. The "impudence and good understanding" and the merry twinkle of the actor revives in Garrick's advertisement for the published poem: "As to the Ode itself, he presents it to the public as an object of their good nature,—to his friends as an exercise of their partiality—to his enemies, as a lucky opportunity of venting their wit, humour, criticism, spleen, or whatever else they please, should they think it worthy of their notice."[9]

And it stares at us today from the page, not particularly rich in poetry. But for those who heard the actor recite it the event was breathtaking, even for his severest critics. "Gentleman" William Smith, from Covent Garden, who considered himself Garrick's rival, and who was overly concerned about the quality of his own costume in the procession, and who argued endlessly about employment at Drury Lane with Garrick later, was so impressed that he wrote on his copy of the *Ode* 40 years later (in an unpublished manuscript note, now in the Folger Shakespeare Library) "I heard with rapture the great genius, author of the Ode recite it at the Jubilee in Stratford upon Avon, amidst admiring multitudes. . . . I loved, honoured and respected his virtues and his talents, and ever thought one of the most fortunate circumstances of my life was living in the days of Garrick!"

We accept the testimony of a participant, but seek to enter the thoughts, possible doubts, yet overriding self-assurance that prompted

Garrick that day. To sense the setting in a way we have Arne's music and a print from the *Town and Country Magazine* to call upon. The overture continues to be played and is beautiful. The print shows part of the 100 singers of the chorus, stylishly groomed, seated behind the balustrade about the statue of Shakespeare, with Garrick commencing the recitation. Fears earlier in the day that the event would be canceled on account of heavy rain proved groundless. At high noon the cannon sounded, Garrick entered a rotunda packed with 2,000 spectators—damped by the downpour, and doubtless quizzical about what they might hear. The success of the Jubilee seemed to depend on the performance of the succeeding half hour. Expectancy quickened. The overture quieted the crowd, even as in a theatre. As it ended Garrick rose, and spoke in his marvelous tones, "To what blest genius of the isle / Shall Gratitude her tribute pay?" And the answer followed with a bid to:

> Swell the choral song,
> Roll the tide of harmony along,
> Let Rapture sweep the strings,
> Fame expand her wings,
> With her trumpet-tongues proclaim
> The lov'd, rever'd, immortal name,
> *Shakespeare! Shakespeare! Shakespeare!*[10]

The cry was picked up by the chorus rising from softness to crescendo. The effect was electrifying, for Garrick had devised an antiphonal performance, new, and abandoning the expected long-drawn-out recitative. Surprise at the innovation, astonishment at the quality of the voices—both speaking and singing—riveted interest and evoked thunderous applause at the close. The discussion period followed, led by Tom King's speech planted in opposition, and the rain for a time was forgot.

The evening ball was enjoyable, though soggy, for those who attended. The race was run, but none asked what the horses thought as they splashed along.[11] On the final day the crowds disbanded, along roads cluttered with every sort of vehicle which could be pressed into service, though some folk remained to see the fizzle of the fireworks. Both Garrick's friends and foes had their sport, as he had anticipated. Squibs and playlets appeared by the dozen, but his attitude throughout took away any sting from the comments, and must have made even the astringent Samuel Foote, the angry Charles Dibdin, and the scornful William Kenrick look foolish. But the mind, the inner feelings of Garrick as he coped with the occasion and faced the crowds? He put on no long face. His professionalism sustained him; his purposefulness buoyed him. He had been through riots and mob violence, but here he knew most people wanted the affair to succeed. He had to be superior to events. In such crises an innate calm prevailed. He wrote to the Reverend Richard Kaye shortly afterwards, "You flatter Mrs Garrick and your humble servant about the Jubilee—if the Heavens had favoured us—we should have returned to town in triumph—but it is over, and I am neither mad, or in a fever, both of which threatened me greatly." [12]

Lacy, of course, was perturbed by the cost undertaken by the theatre to transport the costumes, and by other expenses including George Garrick's time for three months in Stratford. Garrick, in fact, had to lay out his own money for expenses, but *en route* to London, in conversation with fellow-passenger Benjamin Wilson, he bethought him of a way to recoup. [13] Making dramatic capital out of the excessive crowding, the obvious price-gouging, and the unfortunate weather, he plotted his scenario of his *Jubilee*, which with its grand procession of Shakespeare's characters, and spoofing of Stratford logistics achieved success a month later as an after piece on the stage at Drury Lane. It had the longest continuous run of any play yet performed in the eighteenth century—some 90 performances in a single season! [14]

The plot of the playlet as Garrick conceived it centered upon an Irishman who had made the trip to Stratford, ignorant but eager, who could find lodging only in an empty stagecoach by the roadside. Exhausted he slept there—and slept right through the ceremonies. Richard Yates was the actor for the part, and his brogueish comments created by Garrick provided the counterpoint (to audience after audience for the rest of the season) for the elegance of the procession. The procession consisted of nineteen pageants moving across the stage depicting high points of Shakespeare plays including *Much Ado, Twelfth Night, Richard III, Romeo and Juliet, Hamlet, Henry IV, Antony and Cleopatra*, and *The Merchant of Venice*. Hopkins wrote of it: "It was receiv'd with bursts of Applause the Procession of Shakespear's Characters &c. is the most Superb that ever was Exhibited or I believe ever will be. there never was an Entertainment produc'd that gave so much pleasure to all degrees Boxes pit, and Gallery."

Even on the limited stage at Drury Lane Garrick achieved something of the massive effect attained at Stratford. His enthusiasm for preparing this bubbled over as he wrote, in the same letter to Richard Kaye, "I am in the midst of players, musicians and machinists to consult about bringing the Jubilee to Drury Lane." The choric splendor, led again by the soaring voices of Joseph Vernon, Mrs Baddeley, and Charles Bannister, rang in the house. The Larpent manuscript of the

*Folger Shakespeare Library*
Garrick as Steward of the Shakespeare Jubilee, 1769.
Engraving by J. Saunders from a painting by Benjamin Van der Gucht.

after piece closes with the direction, "Every character, tragic and comic, join in the chorus and go back, during which guns fire, bells ring, &c. and the Audience applaud—Bravo, Jubilee, Shakespeare forever!"[15] Again he conceived a total participation, including spectators, in the spectacular.

Garrick's career both as actor and as manager had paralleled that of the questionable friend and competitive personality of Samuel Foote, who gave a "Devil's definition" of the Jubilee at Stratford for the *Town and Country Magazine* underscoring all its misfortunes, "celebrating a great poet whose works have made him immortal, by an Ode without poetry, etc." As an actor Foote would brook no mimicking or imitation of himself by another actor, but indulged in the mimicking practice himself. Garrick would not, after his first season on stage, make sport of another actor on stage, even of Foote. When Henry Woodward got into a dispute with Foote (back in 1750) and planned to take him off in a performance of Otway's *Friendship in Fashion* (22 January), Foote appealed to Garrick to restrain him, threatening reprisal on Garrick and on Woodward (Boaden, I, 55), and insinuating that Garrick was passively behind the Woodward move. Foote actually had started the skirmish against Woodward, which embraced several stage episodes in the spring of 1749. Garrick's reply was calm and rational: "Sir, wou'd you have me (supposing he has a design to be pleasant with *you*) interfere in the Affair while there is a Mimical War betwixt you, & first declar'd on your side? if I did, wou'd he not justly complain of unfair treatment, & say that I am holding his hands, while you are beating him?" Garrick added "He has desir'd to be free with *me*, as other folks have been, & so little sensible am I of the Consequence, that he has an unlimited power to use *me* as he pleases" (85).[16]

Foote, angered, shied at Garrick again and again thereafter in the circles in which he traveled. Foote, the so-called English Aristophanes, was a witty genius in writing farcical afterpieces and in acting those of his own creation, and his farces were some of the best in the whole century. Dr Johnson characterized him as a very comical dog "For loud obstreperous, broad-faced mirth, I know not his equal."[17] Garrick was in Foote's company a good deal, and a dozen of his letters to Foote are still extant. All are kindly and good tempered. He invited Foote to visit him, and always included Mrs Garrick's good wishes, and both of them visited Foote,[18] yet Foote seems to have abused, or threatened abuse frequently. His acrimony became sharper after 1766 when he had received a license to operate the Little Theatre in the Haymarket, which the Duke of York had procured for him as a result of his misfortune in losing a leg.[19]

Seemingly, though not really, Foote and Garrick then became competing managers. Not really because Foote's license was only for operating during the summer season, which competed neither with the schedules of Drury Lane nor of Covent Garden. Foote had probably wanted a full-scale third London theatre.

The dominant strain of humanity in Garrick's attitude towards the man and his troubles of amputation appears in the press and in a serious set of verses. First, he sent a paragraph to the papers correcting the false impression abroad that Foote was down and defeated: "Mr. Foote is now supposed by his physicians to be out of danger; the amputation was made three inches below the knee. He still keeps his vivacity and wonted spirits" (388 n.5). Then he sent Foote a 12-line epigram (which Foote graciously acknowledged) answering "some weak attempts (weak as inhuman) to jest upon Foote's late accident:

> The Ass once bold—threw out his heel
> And made a bed-rid Lion feel;
> For *fools* are ever rash;
> And so You think, Y$^e$ scribbling Crew,
> As Foote is down, that valient *you*
> Will give him *dash for dash*.
>
> O let your desp'rate folly rest;
> Approach not with a ribbald jest
> Misfortune's scared bed;
> What tho' the Wit a Limb has lost,
> You soon will find it to your cost;
> He has not lost his head" (394 n.4).

In 1770 Foote in a prologue criticized Garrick's stage performance of *The Jubilee*. At this Paul Hiffernan, a writer of plays, took umbrage and made a broadside attack upon Foote (*Foote's Prologue Detected*), ostensibly in defense of Garrick. Foote retaliated by threatening to write Hiffernan's life in scurrilous fashion, whereupon Hiffernan prepared a letter for the papers urging spectators to pull down the Haymarket house because Foote also was refusing to take half price for entering after the third act—a custom in vogue at the other houses. Foote, alarmed, asked Garrick in the interests of all theatres to use his influence to have the letter quashed. To whom Garrick: "You do me great Justice in supposing that I should think of the attack you mention in your Letter as your Freind and well wisher.—It is indeed a most wicked & alarming one and should be put an end to directly. I have written to D$^r$ Morris for whom I have great regard and who knows the Culprit and I doubt not but it will have a proper effect. . . . I hope to see you soon at Hampton" (598). and the Hiffernan letter was not published.

In 1771 Francis Gentleman, a member of Foote's company at the Haymarket was the supposed author of an anonymous poem *The Theatres, a Poetical Dissection* which, though abusing Garrick especially, shied also at Foote. Foote, riled, was about to dismiss the actor. Garrick, seeing the document, dismissed it as nonsense, but wrote to Foote: "As to y$^r$ being angry with one of y$^r$ Company, who has been suppoz'd y$^e$ Author of y$^e$ Poem, You ought not in justice discharge him; the Author is as yet unknown, and You had much better exert y$^r$ humanity towards a hundred undeserving people, than injure one innocent Man" (668).

The unaccountable Foote responded little to the civilized treatment Garrick gave him life-long. Thomas Davies, unable to account for Garrick's objective and gentle treatment of Foote, deduced that Garrick was nervously afraid of him, that Foote knew it, and consequently baited Garrick whenever he could. He further concluded that all praises which Garrick bestowed upon Foote were therefore suspicious. William Cooke, writing the *Memoirs of Samuel Foote* in 1805, a quarter of a century after the demise of both Foote and Garrick, developed further this ascribed fear-syndrome to account for Garrick's politeness, and Foote's latest biographer elaborates, finding Garrick in contemptible fashion trying to manipulate others against Foote, while on the surface writing to him pleasantly and praising him openly. "Garrick lived in fear," says he, "of Foote's ridicule, and timidly tried to soften the blows before they were delivered, by propitiating his tormentor."[20] One reading all of Garrick's letters, however, especially those written in the heat of managerial problems or of author attacks, and those to convivial acquaintances, can find no deviation in style or treatment in Foote situations from Garrick's rational diplomatic manner toward all. The charge has little merit and no substantiation.

Garrick regretted, as did everyone, when Foote's horse shied and unseated him, the fall from which broke his leg and necessitated amputation. Garrick helped where he could in Foote's subsequent managing of the Haymarket theatre. Three years later (1769) he bespoke a room especially for Foote at the Stratford jubilee. Foote responded after the event by planning "Drugger's Jubilee," a mock performance with a procession in which a ragamuffin was to address Garrick (in the words of Laureate Whitehead's earlier lines), "A nation's taste depends on you / Perhaps a nation's virtue too," whereupon the representer of Garrick was to flap hands and cry "Cock-a-Doodle Do."

Foote made no effort to conceal the plan. The managers met, writes Davies, "at a nobleman's door; significant looks were exchanged before they spoke. Mr. Garrick broke silence first, 'What is it, war or peace?' 'Oh peace by all means,' said Foote, and the day was passed in seeming cordiality." The Drugger performance was not staged, only the *Prologue*, which had so riled Hiffernan. Garrick's flash of anger then, his admonishing Foote to let humanity surpass irritation in the Francis Gentleman episode, seem not to be acts inspired by fear. Perhaps the best account of the relationship, professional and personal, was laid forth by Garrick in a verse letter to Foote of 25 April 1770. It refers to the *Prologue* under dispute:

> I've call'd, and call'd, & call'd again,
> To gossip with You, but in vain:
> What tho' in Prologue you will lick me,
> Why of Your Conversation trick me?
> Shall all Enjoy Your Wit but Me,
> Who more than all delight in Thee?
> Tho' w$^{th}$ the Manager You War,
> Let not, my Friend, our heart-strings jar.
> You're right to lash me, I confess,
> The Town expects it, more or less:
> In publick wound, in private love me;
> The polish'd lancet cannot move me. (581)

Amiable enough. Perhaps Garrick understood Foote better than have successive writers. Far from being as thin skinned to mockery, and as nervous about Foote's jibes as some of his biographers have claimed,[21] Garrick had become inured, and at the same time was perceptive of the sparkling conversation which the "comical dog" according to all of his contemporaries put forth. Garrick, having passed continually through the bath of Grub Street vituperation, counted, one suspects, manifestations of raillery for what they were worth, and preserved a cool professionalism in the tug of wars of the mid-century theatres. Foote he treated, save for one outbreak of anger, with steady consistency, perhaps the only way to deal with one who according to Dr Johnson had "one species of wit in an eminent degree, that of escape. You drive him into a corner with both hands, but he's gone. You think you have got him—like an animal that jumps over your head. Then he has a great range for his wit, he never lets truth stand between him and a jest, and he is sometimes mighty coarse."[22]

Despite the strident satiric voicings of Foote, or Steevens, and others[23] Garrick's idea and accomplishment at Stratford planted a seed which grew and still grows. Shakespeare's local habitation then became associated with a name as it had never fully been before. The

Continent got the word. The Stratfordians were, upon balance, delighted. Jubilees continued there. The "Shakespeare industry," as a side effect, has grown, and grown, and grown, with now a permanent theatre there, and satellites in Canada and the United States. What would have pleased Garrick most—the actors continue to carry on, astonishing onlookers with fresh performances and new adaptations of what *The London Magazine* in August 1769 called "that absolute original" whose works have "perpetually rais'd and confounded the emulation of his successors."

Certain common denominators, but no real sameness appeared in the personnel problems that came up to Garrick. With them he coped, now with concealed exasperation, now with severity, now with conciliation, always with shrewd understanding, and almost always with a display of human sympathy. But he was no ombudsman. He was the manager upon whom the whole company depended for a well-run theatre, hence for stability and steady employment. Many pages of his published and unpublished correspondence seem to deal *ad infinitum* with some company grievances. But put in proper perspective these pages, often generating considerable heat, are in fact few, considering the extent of overall human relations Garrick dealt with. During 27 years of active management he saw, interviewed, and worked with a beginning company of 68 and ultimately with 517 new performers— an average of about 20 each year—who brought to full complement (after 1765) his company of about 86 each season.[24] Yet his major disputes resulted in correspondence (extant at least) with fewer than a dozen actors and actresses.[25] One can only marvel at what his "regularization" of procedures had accomplished—with easy-going and likeable George as chief personnel man, with diplomatic William Hopkins as head prompter, with Pritchard, Benjamin Victor, and Evans as treasurers.

One can never weigh by statistics the wearing and irritation factor involved, say, in the 13 letters in answer to those of Mrs Abington, but amid 1,362 extant Garrick letters they should take their proper place. The quality of argument and seriousness of the problems are what count. The flavor of a number of the letters dealing with major actors of his company (and the concentration seems greater after 1770 than before) gives insight into the character of Garrick as manager in his later years.

He kept four standards in mind—but certainly subconsciously rather than as a formal yardstick of measurement—as he dealt with complaints. First was a vivid memory of his own acting schedule in the past, and his major efforts to support every member of his company throughout the benefit seasons. Second was his insistence that a strong company should act together with artistic perfection. Such perfection demanded attendance at rehearsals even from the best, and for himself. Third his evaluation of the particular strengths and weaknesses (for the sake of the company) of each performer counted. Fourth was the comparative value of each relative to the pay scale. In this last his own acting and salary (which had risen only £100 over a period of 25 years) was tucked in the back of his mind. The matter comes to an issue, as mentioned, because a few actors (and more probably urged by their wives) sought salary increases at awkward times. Garrick was not averse to paying well for talent. De Loutherbourg received a salary equal to his own, and Mrs Cibber received annually £700 to his £500. His payroll expenses rose from 50 percent of his total annual expenses (1747) to 65 percent in 1776. No raises were automatic. His contracts often indicated increments over the term of the contract, but he wanted to reward merit when he could, and he had to gauge audience reaction in the process.[26]

Garrick knew the advantages of having for himself a reputation for astringency, and even of a temper in his managerial capacity. In the "Occasional Epilogue" spoken by Mrs Clive (and written by Garrick) at the opening of the theatre in 1750, she had commented:

> 'Tis true he's of a choleric disposition,
> And fiery parts make up his composition.
> How often have I seen him rave when things miscarried!

The audience laughed, because he was so affable and genial, but the reputation for disciplined severity was useful. And in-house he occasionally had his tyrannical moments. A quarter of a century later (11 December 1774) Hopkins wrote to George at Bath, "Your Brother . . . has not forgot to scold." And added, "Good God what an angel He would be if he would do his business with good temper but that's impossible" (app. F, p. 1360). The date is important, for Garrick was then engaging in a serious quarrel with Mrs Yates and Mrs Abington, and the stress upon him was severe.

Temper he had, but controlled by a greater instinct for diplomacy. Though his temper flared, it cooled in action. In February 1767 he wrote severely to George, and rashly commented on his old friend Mrs Pritchard. The circumstances were that he was ill at Hampton but received a note for a "command" performance as Oakly in Colman's *The Jealous Wife*, a part he had turned over to Holland, and wanted not to resume. George had failed to send him the whole promptbook so he could re-study the part before rehearsal. He knew he might come to rehearsal a bit rusty, knew that Mrs Pritchard had had been playing Mrs Oakly well since the play had opened in October of that season. He wanted not his own lines (lengths) only (which George had sent him) but the whole acting copy so he could get the feel of the play. "The Deuce is in *You* for not sending Me the Prompter's Book—how could You Mistake it so. . . . The Part you sent me is a false one. . . . I can't do without the book, *y<sup>e</sup> Stage Book*, I have forgot it all, & am very uneasy indeed. . . . I must be a[t] London (which I'm sorry for) on Tuesday to run over my Scenes on *Wednesday Morning*—this damn'd Oakly is a crust for Me indeed, I wish it don't prove too hard for my Gums. . . . I have not play'd Oakly these three Years—Sick—Sick—Sick—& M<sup>rs</sup> P[ritchar]<sup>d</sup> will make me Sicker—great Bubbies, Noddling head, & no teeth—O Sick—Sick" (445). And yet, and yet, and yet—how sure he was in his composure, overcoming the moment's irritation! For Sylas Neville saw the performance about which Garrick had worried, "Never saw Garrick, Pritchard and Clive in perfection before, and I think none of the characters were ill performed." The house was jammed. The actor-manager's professionalism conquered. He coped superbly.

That same spring he wrote sharply about young William Powell, whose career he had sought to further and to whom he had written a long, thoughtful, cogent letter of advice urging him to study and read things outside of theatrical materials, to broaden himself as a cultured man so he could bring grace thus gained to his acting (345). Powell had defected to Covent Garden to share management with Colman. "He is a sc[oundrel]," wrote Garrick to George, "and C[olman] will repent his conjunction in every vein." But as the letter reveals Garrick was also at the time irritated with partner Lacy, "Just give me a clue to walk into the labyrinth of Lacy's brain, that I may be upon my guard" (459). For Powell in going to Colman had breached his contract and (wrote Garrick), "I hope to God my partner has not talk'd with Powell of an agreement, or friendly intercourse between the houses, that would be ruin indeed." Garrick was remembering the sort of cartel which Fleetwood, Lacy and Rich had enjoyed in the mid 1740s, which had enraged Macklin, Mrs Clive, and himself at the time of their walkout. He wanted no revival of that sort of bond, and his instincts were right.

Failure in communications, illnesses, inattendance at rehearsals, and refusals to act assigned parts raised tempers between the Barrys and Garrick in October 1769. Mrs Barry wished no longer to walk in the procession of the ongoing performances of the *Jubilee*, and even refused to go on the night when Garrick, as author, was to have a benefit.[27] Garrick remembering in how many actors' benefits he had played thought her refusal outrageous. He concluded his letter to her husband, "I can lay my hand upon my heart, & say, when I Acted in common, I never refus'd y$^e$ favor in all my Life; and indeed this is y$^e$ first time, & shall be y$^e$ last, that Ever I will run y$^e$ risk of having it refus'd to." Communications had come to Garrick through the channel of prompter Hopkins, who showed Garrick the delinquent record of the Barrys at rehearsals. In response they both pleaded illness. But they remained with Drury Lane through the 1773–74 season, when they went over to Covent Garden upon Garrick's firmly demanding they perform more often in view of the salaries they were making (630).

Not all was tenseness. Garrick welcomed Elizabeth Younge back from Ireland with delight. Her sweet and elegant voice pleased audiences everywhere. "I am sincerely Glad You are again amongst Us, & I hope & trust that You will have no cause to repent" (637). This was in 1771. She had been a Garrick pupil, and he hoped she would—should any grievance arise—bring the matter to him directly and speedily.

Garrick's favorite actor, Thomas King, seemed to be breaking ranks in November 1772 at the insistence of his wife, who thought his salary was not quite up to that of his rival "Gentleman" Smith at Covent Garden. "Had you fir'd a long Gun at me it could not have been w$^{th}$ more astonishment on my part" (713), wrote Garrick (6 November). "I have had my say," wrote King in reply, "where you think I have been wrong . . . excuse it. You *must indeed*, my dear Garrick, give in to my proposals . . . say you will be glad to see me, and I shall be again in my own element." Garrick came quickly to a decision (no "ripple" was involved since King was top-salaried) "Dear Tom You shall have Y$^r$ Terms, or I won't be a Manager—I shall, as I always was, be Ever glad to see You. . . . We must scheme some business togeather, I have a Whim—but that When I see You—God bless You—good Night" (713–16).[28]

The affair in the spring of 1772 with Thomas Weston, whom Garrick prized as a comedian but was exasperated with as a man drinking himself deep into debt, proved more amusing than serious. Garrick had to prepare an apology for the papers explaining Weston's nonappearance (24 April) in a part, only to have him appear in the upper gallery the night the apology was given, accompanied by two constables who had released him from debtor's prison for that evening only. He was in debt to the managers, a fact which he called out from the gallery. The audience complained so the matter had to be handled by Garrick himself, who gave George a rough draft of a letter for the press (686).[29]

The same year Henry Mossop returned from Ireland without a contract, and his great supporter William Shirley published a wild, unfounded, 39-page packet accusing Garrick "of depreciating the merits and magnifying the faults of your contemporaries on stage." Garrick's cool, well-tempered reply, which he had the grace to send Shirley privately and not display in the press, is a model of exemplary reprimand (710,882).[30]

With deaths and retirements of the old guard, major roles were coming up for reassignment. They became counters for argument, grievance, dispute, and some frustrated ambitions—but Garrick's shrewdness in casting surmounted any real problems in this area. Yet Joseph Vernon, whom Garrick had supported through a period of audience disapproval (because of his youth and excellent singing voice), agitated for a salary raise at an inappropriate time of year.[31] Francis Aickin, another very good actor, for behavior apparently nagging and unpleasing to the prompter was dismissed. But Garrick was most displeased with Samuel Cautherly (whom he had much indulged) who breached actor etiquette by accepting a part, holding it nine days, then returning it. To him Garrick wrote his severest reprimand letter extant, docked his pay, and reminded him of his obligation to his profession. "You talk'd to my Brother of being *Just to your Self*, a foolish conceited phrase—You had better take care to be Just to other people, & to your duty" (803). Cautherly departed Drury Lane at the close of the following season.

Three rather prima-donna actresses generated considerable correspondence in Garrick's last two years—Miss Pope, Mary Ann (Graham Yates, and Frances Abington. Garrick recommended Miss Pope (who had talked herself out of a job at Drury Lane in 1775 to her great surprise, as she had felt safe as a protégée of Mrs Clive) to Thomas Sheridan, and she was able after a season in Ireland to return to Drury Lane in 1776–77 (936,982).[32] Mrs Yates had developed after Mrs Cibber's death into a remarkable actress in tragic roles. Garrick brought her over in 1774 from Covent Garden, paid her a salary of £700, plus £50 for providing herself with stylish and modish clothes. She grew temperamental, was over frequently "indisposed," letting down audiences who had come especially to see her. In this Garrick sensed an upcoming problem of insubordination prejudicial to the theatre. He met it quickly and firmly, yet with characteristic whimsey and patience. "It is my greatest pleasure," he wrote, "to live in the greatest Harmony with my Capital performers, and more particularly with M[r] & M[rs] Yates.—But if they persist to distress us . . . I shall be oblig'd to do, what I would most wish to avoid" (949). Mrs Yates capitulated before being fired, but not without at least one more assertion of independence—seeking to drop the role of Almeria in *The Mourning Bride*. Garrick patiently heard this one out and lamented "that our theatrical affairs require so much writing about them." She objected also to performing in benefits. Garrick reprimanded her for considering herself more than the public. "Why is not the Publick at large to be as well entertain'd [at benefits], as the Friends of any Single actor?" He had posted in the greenroom strict regulations about actor obligations. He demonstrated to her how other grumblers had come round to what constituted professional conduct (957).

Before his contretemps with Mrs Abington he had to settle affairs with "Gentleman" William Smith, who after finally being engaged at Drury Lane in September 1775, had immediately abused a brief leave of absence granted by Garrick. In November he baulked at walking in the revived performance of the *Jubilee*, thinking the assignment better for a super than for a star performer. This Garrick could not tolerate. The cool scorn of his comment disabused Smith of the idea that walking in that procession was a menial job "Sir . . . Would your wearing a domino & Mask to take turn about with *Me* walking down y$^e$ Stage, be an injury to your Importance?—I hope not—it would have been of Consequence to y$^e$ Jubilee, which is got up at great expense to support your & other Performers importance, which without it has suffer'd, & may Suffer more. . . . I am likewise in a great hurry, for *I* am oblig'd to make one at y$^e$ Jubilee (969).

If Garrick carried a cross during his last years, it may have borne the name of Frances Abington. One detects through the long flurry of letters between them an undercurrent of increasing irritation on Garrick's part, but it seldom surfaces, for he consistently applied to her complaints the guidelines he had set up for all actors. Yet one letter to Peter Fountain reveals the depth of his feeling about Mrs Abington. "That most Worthless Creature . . . she is below the thought of an honest Man or Woman—she is as *Silly* as she is *false* & treacherous" (1038). In the 1774–75 season she had dropped a role six hours before a play was to go on. She thought Miss Pope was getting better casting, and she complained of overwork. "Your mention of *your great fatigue*," wrote Garrick, 28 January 1775, "What is the Stage come to, if I must continually hear of your *hard labour*, when from the beginning of the season to this time, you have not play'd more than *twice* a Week" (890).

In the spring of 1776, when Garrick was preparing to retire, her jockeying for a benefit position ahead of Miss Younge (after refusing to take hers in due order of priority because it would fall on a night when the opera competed) forced the managers to place her complaint in the hands of lawyers. When it appeared that judgment would favor the managers, she declared that she, too, was going to retire at the close of the season, and asked Garrick to play in her final benefit. He could not refuse, nor did he, and so he played Archer to her Mrs Sullen in *The Stratagem* on 7 May 1776. The crowd was tremendous. She, of course, did not retire, but played on at Drury Lane for six more seasons (1038,890,893,894).[33]

For actor grievance Garrick had set guidelines, generally agreed upon, then treated each major plea individually, considered in detail the salary-benefit structure in any complaints about the pay scale, and considered merit (as judged by past performance and cooperation) in all cases. He also considered the marketplace. He was being deluged with applications for jobs, and had been since 1767. Pressure was being brought by friends. Bennet Langton urged him to employ a Mrs Vernsberg. "Our Theatre at present is so cramm'd with unemployed Actors," he replied, "that we shall be oblig'd at y[e] End of this Season to discharge Some, who are a mere Weight upon the property—others, whom we keep because they have been sometime w[th] Us, have very little to do, & are waiting to be of more Use to us—thus circumstanc'd We cannot open our Doors but to first-rate capital performers" (680). He had resisted similar pressure from the Duchess of Portland in 1767, who was sponsoring John Collins (for similar reasons of the fullness of the company), but he gave the actor a trial to see what he could do. Then he wrote to the Duchess: "If Your Grace will permit me to speak my Mind, I think he has the most unpromising Aspect for an Actor I ever saw—a small pair of unmeaning Eyes stuck in a round unthinking face are not the most desirable requisites for a Hero, or a fine Gentleman—however I will give him a Tryal if he is unemployed [at this time next year]" (476).

The greatest and most perceptive tribute, however, to Garrick's evenhanded justice, firmness, effectiveness, and aspirations as a manager appears in Mrs Clive's letter of 23 January 1776 when news got to her that Garrick was going to retire. "Is it really true, that you have put an end to the glory of Drury-lane theatre? *if it is so*, let me congratulate my dear Mr. and Mrs. Garrick. . . . In the height of the public admiration for you, when you were never mentioned with any other appelation but the Garrick, the charming man, the fine fellow, the delightful creature, both by men and ladies; when they were admiring everything you did, and every thing you scribbled—at this time, I . . . was a living witness that they did not know, nor could they be sensible, of half your perfections. I have seen you, with your magical hammer in your hand, *endeavouring* to beat your ideas into the heads of creatures who had none of their own—I have seen you, with lamb-like patience, endeavouring to make them comprehend you; and I have seen you when that could not be done—I have seen your lamb turned into a lion: by this your great labour and pains the public was entertained; *they* thought they all acted very fine,—they did not see you pull the wires." [34]

By "pulling the wires" Garrick was making stage history by the force and tact of his personality, and the soundness of his judgment.

Not counting his own plays, farces, and adaptations, Garrick during his last ten years of management produced some 32 main pieces written by 18 contemporary authors, and 40 new after pieces by 23 (with some overlap) different writers. All in some way met his standards, and were, he thought, suitable for the talents of his company. To the production of each play he added the touch of artistry that made for success. Letters with each of the authors, except for about five, are amicable and constructive. What a pleasure it was for Garrick to deal with George Colman, Richard Glover, Thomas Francklin, Hugh Kelly, Alexander Dow, Richard Cumberland, William Whitehead, Dorothea Celisia, and Hannah Cowley, William O'Brien, Francis G. Waldron, General Burgoyne, and Robert Jephson. He accepted three by Kelly, and three by Cumberland, but never compromised his principles of selection—a good blend of plot, character, and dialogue. He produced Jephson's *Braganza* but rejected his "Vitellia" out of hand as a hodge-podge unworthy of the dramatist's rising reputation. He had the reading of Goldsmith's manuscript for *She Stoops to Conquer*, but Goldsmith, assured of its being performed at Covent Garden, asked for its return.

The managers at Covent Garden put on somewhat fewer new pieces in each category, but chose most of them from the same contemporary group whose plays Garrick had accepted. They were the best England could write. From Covent Garden *She Stoops to Conquer*, and Sheridan's *Rivals* and operatic *Duenna* (perhaps) have managed to surmount the decays of time. From Garrick's theatre *The West Indian*, *The Clandestine Marriage*, and *The Suspicious Husband* likewise survive. Yet a number of others, such as Murphy's *Grecian Daughter* (first put on at Drury Lane) carried well into the nineteenth century. Yet the total yield seemed to please eighteenth-century audiences, as the box receipts indicate, but the enduring crop was not large. The century was, after all, an age of great acting rather than of great creative drama—except for farce.

Garrick as reader and selector of plays in the 1770s was not much

*National Portrait Gallery*
Garrick at the Breakfast Table.
Pencil sketch by George Dance, 1771.

different from what he had been before he took the two-year period abroad. But the pressures from authors and their sponsors increased in number and mounted in persistence. Arthur Murphy, who seemingly had abandoned playwriting for the law, sensed a renewal of ambition to write heavy drama upon Garrick's return. So two thorny negotiations (for his *Zenobia*, 27 February 1768, and *The Grecian Daughter*, 26 February 1773) were in store for the manager. Garrick in order to fit these plays of strained heroism and long suffering female triumph to the stage insisted upon cutting and rearranging. Murphy continued to quarrel with Garrick's procedures, and thought his reading the manuscripts to his players in the greenroom was not a serious exercise. In December 1767 he dickered for staging his tragedy *Alzuma*, which Garrick fended off, only to have it appear at Covent Garden. When Garrick put on his *Zenobia* Murphy fretted that it lasted only six nights. He wrote to Barry that only his *Grecian Daughter* was ever staged for him with peace of mind. "Upon every other occasion Mr. Garrick has been a thorn in my side." He was trying to engage Barry's support for having Garrick revive his earlier play *The Way to Keep Him*, reviewing at great length the high points of his former battle with Garrick in delaying the production of *The Orphan of China*. Garrick read and listened, and chose only what he wanted of Murphy's new creations, and wrote: "I am too much indispos'd to write long Letters, & too old, & too happy to love Altercation—I had written the enclosed to M^r Barry—I really have no more to say upon the Occasion, & am sorry you have renewed your old Way of making War, when I thought we had concluded a lasting Peace" (737). Peace was patched up, but not a very congenial one.[35]

Elizabeth Griffith's appeals, trials, rejections, and encouragements run through the Garrick correspondence year after year. He had put off her play *The Double Mistake* in 1766 which she finally got produced at Covent Garden. She was badly in need of funds, and anxious to write for a living. Garrick tried to help by sending her French plays to translate and perhaps adapt. She thought her improved version of *Eugenia* (1768) was playable. Garrick disagreed, but he did alter her draft of *The School for Rakes*, and asked for her statement in writing as to whether she thought *he* had improved *it*. She agreed and had her husband countersign the statement. Garrick produced it for a fair success in February 1769. Four years later she accused him of being predetermined not to produce any of her plays. This Garrick denied, so she wrote a long, tedious justification of her works. What comes through the correspondence is Garrick's basic sympathy but actual skill at putting his finger on what was good theatre and rejecting what was not.[36]

Garrick had once produced Joseph Reed's *The Register Office*, a very amusing farce, topical and apt, satirizing the abuses of one of London's first attempts (in the 1750s) to set up a clearing house of information about employment opportunities for all seekers. Reed, the ropemaker, continued to write and send drafts of plays to Garrick. He was most eager to have his tragedy *Dido* performed at Drury Lane. He thought it to be "in the manner of Shakespeare." Garrick resisted for a long, long time, but finally yielded and gave it to Holland for his benefit in the spring of 1767. It received three performances, and despite Garrick's comment to George, "Great God, does *Dido* please!" he scheduled it for a performance the following season. But Reed, who had had seven prominent people read the play, so cherished it that he withdrew the manuscript until the Barrys could take over the major roles. They ultimately refused, so Reed put all the correspondence of the years together in a manuscript called "Theatrical Duplicity" (now in the Folger Library), in which he damned all managerial dealings with authors.[37]

Garrick rejected Benjamin Victor's *Altamira* (September 1766), and was cheered to find that Victor finally agreed that the judgment had been a good one. Richard Cumberland ran the gamut of rejection, acceptance after-improved-alteration, employment as a deputy reader, and later as a severe critic of Garrick. Their happiest relationship came with the very successful performance of *The West Indian* (1771). Garrick had read the manuscript and sent Cumberland suggestions act by act to make it stageable. Cumberland gratefully accepted each, and made the play a huge success.

But the band of would-be dramatists were at Garrick again: John Cleland (of *Fanny Hill* notoriety); Charlotte Lennox (notable for her *Female Characters of Shakespeare's Plays*); the Reverend Charles Jenner (novelist of *The Placid Man*); Francis Gentleman (editor, journalist, poet, playwright, and sometimes severe Garrick critic); Dr Thomas Francklin (the plagiarist); William Elsdon (quartermaster-general of His Majesty's Forces in Lisbon), whose play based on *Don Quixote* might, he said, be tossed in the fire if unacceptable for the stage; and Thomas Augustine Arne, who in 1775 offered a comic opera. Garrick's comment is still legible on Arne's accompanying letter. "Designed for Dr. Arne, who sold me a horse, a very dull one; and sent me a comic opera, ditto."[38] He kept the horse and returned the script. Dozens of others sent texts. Many sent an act or two, as feelers, or as Hugh Kelly (24 November 1768) asked for a hint of promise about whether Garrick would produce a play the following season *if* the author could ready one by that time. Garrick recognized these as questions impossible of answer. An encouraging reply, even a favorable hint could elate the author but produce a grave letdown were the piece ultimately rejected, and could thus breed endless acrimonious correspondence. Garrick continued his forthright and firm negatives to all such.

One instance of such correspondence, and one with which to terminate discussion of Garrick's growing weariness with playreading, as well as to demonstrate the quiet intelligence yet spirited tone of the manager, is that to William Hawkins, who succeeded Robert Lowth as professor of poetry at Oxford. Garrick had graciously but firmly turned down five of his plays. In 1774 in a somewhat pompous letter Hawkins asked Garrick to reread his new-altered "Alfred," noting that since the manager had rejected so many of his plays he must be harboring a nonliterary prejudice against him. In fact he blasted Garrick for pride, rancor, and "Evil designs" against him. Garrick disposed of the matter quickly, coolly putting the clergyman down. "Ought You not as a Gentleman, and a Clergyman, & in justice, reason, & Good Manners, to have waited for my answer before you had been guilty of such outrageous behavior" (864)? He added that Hawkins's approach was hardly calculated to persuade.

Garrick readily accepted his public duty (as patentee of a royal theatre) to read, or have carefully read and reported on by responsible people, all submissions that came to him, to reply without undue delay and according to his best judgment. He was a sociable, friendly man, but pragmatic in all that he deemed good for the theatre, a man having no wish to alienate anyone, especially authors whose works might furnish the theatre with entertaining materials—if not this time, maybe next. He took friend Goldsmith's words (of 1759) to heart. "Is the credit of our own age nothing? Must our present times pass away unnoticed by posterity" in the production of drama, as characteristic of our days as Shakespeare was to his? But sift as he might, the chaff of his own day outweighed the grain.

Goldsmith had felt the plight of contemporary playwrights as an inescapable falling between two unsympathetic forces—the managers and the critics. "The managers and all who espouse their side, are for decoration and ornament; the critic, and all who have studied French decorum, are for regularity and declamation. Thus it is almost impossible to please both parties; and the poet by attempting it finds himself often incapable of pleasing either. If he introduces stage pomp, the critic consigns his performance to the vulgar; if he indulges in recital and simplicity, it is accused of insipidity and affectation."[39] Garrick recognized the dilemma—the confrontation of values on the stage versus the page. He, however, worked as a manager simultaneously on all fronts—stage decoration, selection of plays, recruiting of company, training of actors, acting himself, carrying on good public relations at all levels in London. He also read with care those critics whose views opposed his, those who were unattentive to the varied needs of the whole show. But he and his productions were making an impact upon an upcoming brand of criticism.

In the 1770s theatrical criticism arrived at a respectable position in English journalism. The dailies and weeklies carried departments with some regularity under rubrics, such as *The Theatre*, or *The British Theatre*, or *Theatrical Intelligence*. New *Theatrical Reviews* and *Theatrical Registers* sprang up and endured for a season. Serious writers, such as Boswell, contributed essays on the acting profession to the monthlies.[40] Commentators described new plays and adaptations, recorded pleasures in the enchantments of the new trends in scenic design and effect, and in the quality of the musical accompaniment of performances. They began thus (there had been isolated attempts earlier by Steele and Aaron Hill) to bring ephemeral theatre production into the realm of permanent critical literature. They described how actors opened up new insights into characterization. By comparing one actor with another and both with the critic's concept of the role, they gave a quality of lastingness to a fleeting art.

"Compilers of scandal and defamation" in the papers mounted an attack on Garrick the manager in what, for him, must have seemed a long hot summer of 1772. Word seems to have got about London that Garrick's health was again not good. From a pre-France average of 95 performances each year he had reduced his appearances to an average of 27 per season, not from indolence, but from necessity. His fierce concentration on performing well—with freshness, spirit, and gusto—continued to take much out of him in the Hamlets, and Richards, the Lears and Lusignans that he kept. Mention has been made of William Combe's *Sanitas*, (1772). He hoped "health for a gentleman who by his personal exhibitions, his literary productions, and his close attention to the morality of the stage, has so blended the most liberal instruction with the most exquisite entertainment."

Garrick needed all the robustness Mistress Sanitas could bring to help him preserve his equanimity under the scurrilous bombardment of William Kenrick, whose *Love in the Suds, a Town Eclogue* reached five printings that year. Its subtitle, "Being the Lamentation of Roscius for the Loss of His Nyky," alerted curious readers to the association, which the content made in semilibelous fashion, between Garrick and the unfortunate Isaac Bickerstaff. Garrick had been kind to Bickerstaff, had commissioned him to ready *The Plain Dealer* for the stage, and in 1766 had given him a letter of introduction to Madam Riccoboni in Paris. "The Bearer of this is a Gentleman who has written with great Success for the Stage" (402). In 1772 Bickerstaff had fled the country upon being charged with homosexual solicitation of a marine guard.[41] He had prepared half a dozen plays for Drury Lane. But his big successes had been with the five musicals he had prepared for Covent Garden. Kenrick's *Love in the Suds* was published 27 June 1772. It was preceded by a scurrilous set of couplets appearing anonymously in *The Public Ledger* nine days earlier called *Leap Frog.* Kenrick's motive to bespatter Garrick can easily be traced to pent up animosities over the years resulting from the lack of success of his play manuscripts with Garrick. He compounded the irritant and brought on his own defeat by publishing a two-page folio "Preface to the Poem" entitled "Letter to David Garrick, Esq. from William Kenrick, LLD," affecting surprise that Garrick should assume that the Roscius of the poem referred to him. "Does your modesty," mocked he, "think no man entitled to the application of Roscius but yourself?" Garrick called Kenrick's bluff and took him to court. Kenrick backed off from the accusation of libel, stating that he was just ridiculing Roscius harmlessly "from having encouraged a wretch whom he must have had reason to detest," or at least cautiously shun as a man.

On 12 November Francis Newbery, printer of the *Public Ledger*, published his own apology for having printed the *Leap Frog* verses. "Most sincerely sorry that the lines—containing malignant reflection on Mr. Garrick—were inserted without his privity, and takes this public method of begging Mr Garrick's pardon." Garrick, quick to forgive, thereupon wrote to Peter Fountain, "I shall not suffer Mr. Newbery to pay my costs." He was referring to the printing contract which newspaper proprietors made with their printers about inserting libelous items.

As the court case against Kenrick neared, the author got cold feet, and published his apology in the *London Evening Post*. "He had no ground for casting an imputation, or even harboring a suspicion of the kind against his [Garrick's] character . . . further apologizes . . . etc." After these public apologies Garrick dropped the matter. But a spate of pamphlets, cards, squibs, columns—about equally balanced between outrage against Kenrick, and those using the occasion of easy access to the press to snipe at the manager—provided reading through the summer and into the fall for the interested followers of Grub Street tactics.[42]

Grub Street was alive and thriving. The pamphlet warfare of the 1760s seemed about to revive as Thomas Ryder (whose play *The Politician Reformed* Garrick had rejected) went to press in an *Appeal to the Public from the Judgment of a Certain Manager* (1774). Firmly and politely Garrick replied by private letter to the disgruntled author, "I have read the piece you put into my hands with great care, and it is my sincere opinion that it will not succeed in the representation: the subject has been already most successfully treated by the author of the *Upholsterer*" (778). Ryder told the public that Garrick had not convinced him, that the piece had been approved by "some of the first people of the kingdom for learning and ability!—Were I to use my power and influence." (779 n.2). To which Garrick sent Ryder his compliments, "He can only repeat his former opinion, that it is not calculated for the stage" (779).

Yet the long summer of 1772, and the incipient controversies of 1774 seem actually not to have unduly riled Garrick. In the first instance he moved calmly, kept a low profile, raged not in the press. In the second he won points, as he always had, by replying in private, replying to the point, and not in the press. He seems amazingly consistent in this way of handling troublesome comment. In his public relations right from 1747 on through the end he operated from the strength of his convictions, and his instincts for civilized behavior.

Tasks of managing intensified from the third week in January 1774 when Garrick's longtime partner Lacy died at his estate in Isleworth. Their relationship, though becoming strained from time to time, had been businesslike, civil, and valuable for the theatre. To fund the coal mine which Lacy was searching out on his estate in Oxfordshire, he had mortgaged his share in the patent to Garrick. At his death his son Willoughby Lacy became Garrick's co-partner, inheriting his father's debts, including interest on the mortgage (1162 n.2).

Willoughby aspired to be an actor. Garrick indulged him, but the young man made no great success in performing. He insisted, however, upon having all the perquisites of, and in involving himself in the management that his father had held. Garrick cooperated where he could, but soon Lacy and Garrick were communicating through their lawyers—Lacy busily, Garrick tolerantly, seeming somewhat amused, somewhat patronizing, but in the spirit of letting the young man go his own way (822). Garrick's later letters to him show the kindliness of fatherly advice, especially two years later when Lacy, uneasy with his new partners (Ford, Linley, and Sheridan), had hinted to Garrick that he would like to sell his share, yet have some control in the theatre. Garrick having himself retired by that time opened to him warmly with friendly advice, warning him of the folly of such an action. "I cou'd not have slept quietly, had I not said so much to you, because I most sincerely wish you well & the theatre which I have quitted" (1029).

But to return to the year 1774—major responsibilities devolved upon Garrick, the senior partner. He worked with de Loutherbourg— judging, approving, and mounting the spectacular scenery which the Alsatian artist had worked out in miniature. One remarkable produc- tion was that for General Burgoyne's *The Maid of the Oaks* (November 1774) in which Garrick developed the fête champêtre (in the masque which Burgoyne had put on at the wedding of Lord Stanley and Lady Betty Hamilton at Stanley's estate at Epsom) to a full-length play. The play was slight, the music by Barthélemon fine, the scenes and decora- tions simply remarkable. "This piece," wrote Hopkins in his *Diary* "is got up in a most Superb manner. The Scenery is beyond description fine—& the whole Performance tho the most complicated upon the stage went off with uncommon Applause. Mrs Abington play'd finely [as Lady Bab]. Mr Slingsby & Sga Hidou danc'd for the first time & were amazingly well rece'd. The ballets are very Grand."[43] Garrick was in his element—manager, actor, creator concerned not with any narrow specialty, but with total coordination of excellence. What an impression his dream in France of improved scenic effects was having! *The Westminster Magazine* attributed the whole success to de Lou- therbourg's "excellent scenery." In former days James Lacy would have had a major role in this department. Willoughby was young, raw, and inexperienced. Garrick and de Loutherbourg took over.

In the summer of 1775 George had fallen ill and went to recover at Bath for an extended period. Troubles, already noted, with Cautherly and Miss Pope became vexing. Mrs Griffith was writing again. Nego- tiations were afoot for Mrs Siddons, and in the fall in-house disputes with actresses resumed their wearying rounds. With these increased burdens came Garrick's own declining health—in March, April, May, August, and October he had had severe bouts of illness with the "stone." In December the disorder seemed to him to be increasing. He had turned 58 the preceding February. Time seemed to have come for him to depart. He wrote to his good friend John Hoadly, five days after his decision to retire had been made: "I will not stay to be Sixty with my Cap & bells—Active as I am, & full of Spirit, with the draw- back of a *gravel-complaint*" (976).

His first obligation, once the decision had been reached, was to

George Colman, to whom he had long ago offered to sell when the time came. Hence on 29 December 1775 he sent Becket with a special message to Colman. "I must now seriously acquaint You that I shall most certainly part with it [the patent]—I Saw a Gentleman Yesterday of great property, & who has no Objection to the price Viz: 35,000" (971). Colman replied that he would consider purchase *only* if the two of them could be joint managers—"I told you at the time [of our former conversation] . . . that you were the only man in the kingdom I would suffer to govern me, and I did not know a man in the kingdom who would suffer me to govern him." [44]

Garrick settled the sale with R. B. Sheridan, Thomas Linley, Simon Ewart, and Dr James Ford on 19 January 1776. The news appeared officially in the papers that day. Garrick had written about the change-over to his friends Peter Fountain, Hoadly, Richard Rigby, and James Clutterbuck before the matter became public. He was satisfied in spirit, for he could see the sound condition in which he was leaving the theatre and his company.

Just the preceding September he had, as manager, spent £4,000 refurbishing the Drury Lane house, according to plans devised by the Adam brother architects. News notices stated that it "is now fitted up in the most elegant manner possible . . . and is the most compleat of any theatre in Europe." This in the *Public Advertiser* may, of course, have been prepared by Garrick's staff. But the detailed description of the internal changes appears to be that of an observer who attended the first performance therein. Great and spontaneous applause " for the auditorium" broke forth on opening night. The verses commenting on the "New Front of Drury Lane Theatre," which appeared in *Lloyd's Evening Post* (25 September 1775) have the grace of a Garrick "puff," but suggest the range of Garrick's aesthetic interests. [45] He was sure his large company of 100 compared favorably with that at Covent Garden. His singers and dancers were superb. His scenic department was attracting universal attention. He had seven new pieces in rehearsal for the season.

He could sell at a great capital gain and bow out of acting while he still had the power to move audiences and to entertain in top form. His letter to Hoadly on 3 January 1776 is somewhat wistful, a trifle astringent about the inevitable generation gap, somewhat self-assuring, and somewhat relieved. "M$^{rs}$ Garrick & I are happy w$^{th}$ the thoughts of my *Strutting & fretting no more upon y$^e$ stage*, & leaving to Younger Spirits the present race of Theatrical Heroines with all their Airs, indispositions, tricks & importances which have reduc'd the Stage to be a dependent upon the Wills of our inslent, vain, & let me add in-

David Garrick.
Portrait by Robert Edge Pine, 1778.

significant female trumpery—there must be a revolution, or my Successors will Suffer much." The preceding season with Mrs Yates, Mrs Abington, and the Barrys still clung to his memory. But the future had some assurances in it nevertheless. "Linley will be of great Service— Sing Song is much the Fashion, & his knowledge of Musick & preparing fit Subjects for the Stage, will be a Strength that the Proprietors may depend upon, when the Heroines are prankish" (976). He was recalling the astounding run of Sheridan's opera *The Duenna* at Covent Garden. He thought finally and practically that Dr Ford's money would also be a great mainstay.

We now see, what he must himself have mused over during that Christmas and post-Christmas period of decision, namely, his four remarkable managerial accomplishments. He had cleared the stage at all times of loungers, making it a quiet place for fine acting and uncluttered performance, well-rehearsed, where a hint of a gesture, a look, a modulation of voice could count more than ever before toward fine character delineation. He had vastly improved stage lighting, costume, and scenic design, and with it had brought music to Drury Lane finer than ever before. He had regularized and stabilized management, so as to furnish a good livelihood for a large acting company and its corps of supporting workers, strict in application and with payrolls met. He had established and was about to gain parliamentary sanction for an insurance fund well-invested for the "support of those performers who through age infirmity, or accident should be retired from the stage; and also for the relief and support of the widows and children of deceased performers."

He was proud of his part in establishing this fund. To secure it and perpetuate its operation he used what persuasion he had among members of the Houses of Parliament to establish it by law, and thus prevent misappropriation of the monies. He paid from his own pocket for the printing of 150 copies of the resolution, so that each member could read, ponder, and judge knowledgeably about the Bill. The plan had actually been suggested by Thomas Hull, an actor at Covent Garden while Garrick was in France. He picked up the idea immediately. The fund was to be augmented by annual contributions on a fixed scale from the participating actors (proportioned to their salaries) and by profits from an annual benefit performance. Garrick had acted in each of these, and was to arrange for two of them on the eve of his own departure. He was to be elected the fund's first steward, and was advised by an elected board of directors composed of 13 actors.

But the fund marked only the climax of Garrick's sympathetic attitude toward causes requiring theatre sponsorship. *Actor* benefits had been in progress since 1660. But with the increasing sensibility operating in the second half of the eighteenth century the record of *charity* benefits in the theatres grew markedly. Garrick took a lead in this sort of social responsibility on the part of his theatre giving 107 charity benefits during his regime. They helped individuals in distress, hospitals, churches, orphanages, colleges, and debtors cast into prison. Obviously his art, in all that he touched, had no flavor of art for art's sake, but rather art for the benefit of individuals and institutions, both for personal and social satisfaction, and for professional fulfillment. And in these matters his artistry was never labored. Finally he outstripped his rivals in number and variety of entertainments for 29 years.[46]

Yet his accomplishments had none of them been gained by a wish and a wand. They had come out of 29 years of involvement, commitment, exercise of special talents amounting to management genius in the performing arts. By one stroke of the Jubilee at Stratford (though it is now fashionable to call it Garrick's folly) he had blown the trumpet for Shakespeare with a new note heard on two continents. His vision was no folly.

An influence discussed herein throughout his managing and acting careers needs documentation, namely, the long shadow that Garrick cast before him in the change in dramatic criticism during the second half of the century. It received bold statement in 1795 from Percival Stockdale in his *Lectures on the Truly Eminent English Poets.* "Let the researches which have thrown light on the works of Shakespeare have their just value . . . but let them have no more . . . let them not usurp the commanding station of the great generalissimo of his forces . . . all the various genius of our inimitable bard was thrown into complete action and display by Garrick."[47] Garrick he thought had breathed heart and soul into the characters of the plays. Edmund Malone in that final decade felt the same. But evidences for a shift from major concern with the story of plays, and the beauties of individual phrases and speeches, to character revelation and the total impact of performance appeared early in Garrick's career, and built as he continued on stage and dominated productions.

For Shakespeare alone the newspapers and periodicals from the time of Garrick's first appearance to the close of the century presented seven times as much in the way of critical observation as can be found in their counterparts for the first 40 years.[48] And in them a change of focus from the judicial criticism, which weighed and balanced a play's beauties against its faults, gave way to an interpretive criticism focusing upon character delineation.

The course of the change is highlighted in a number of statements. In September 1745 the *London Magazine* saw a new stage-force establishing itself, but the writer clung to generalization about the "beauties" of Shakespeare. "And Shakespeare the mortal enemy of all unnatural productions, is more the delight of the nation than ever; which to do justice to Mr. Quin and Mr. Garrick is very much owing to the judgment and spirit with which those great actors enter into the beauties of the poet." In April 1746 an article on "Correctness" appeared in Dodsley's *Museum* comparing French and English writings on the preservation of unity and truth in drama. The author admitted French superiority in unity of plot. "But," continued he, "in my opinion the unity of character is prior in dignity, and there I think we exceed them." With Garrick on stage, bringing character interpretation to life, rather than applause from "aria" display, such a statement had a meaning for the multitude, and the following February a writer for the *Museum* coupled the names of Garrick and Shakespeare in a way which was to become common practice thereafter: "As for Garrick, he has given me so many new ideas in acting that I am not sure you will understand what I now write to you till you have seen him. He does not in later tragedies appear to half the advantage as in Shakespeare, probably because our modern poets abound more in description and exclamation, and have fewer of those strokes of passion which are so astonishing yet natural. His action is an excellent comment upon Shakespeare and with all the pains you have taken with your favorite author, you don't understand him so well as if you knew the supplemental lights which Garrick throws upon him."

In the same year the author of *An Examen of the New Comedy Called the Suspicious Husband* commenting, inter alia, on Garrick's Lear, pointed out that "The more essential and noble rules of the drama are always regarded by Shakespeare, *the preservation and consistency of character*, the working up of the passions, their rise, progress, and effects." Samuel Foote in his *Roman and English Comedy Considered and Compared* elaborated the idea: "I do not believe that it was ever in the power of man to furnish out a more elegant, pleasing and interesting form of entertainment than Shakespeare has, in many instances, given us without observing any one unity but that of character."

In 1748 appeared Peter Whalley's *An Enquiry into the Learning of Shakespeare* with its praise of eighteenth-century taste for preferring Shakespeare to other dramatists. "And this seems to proceed," he declares "from the labours of his several editors, and from the inimitable propriety with which his chief characters are represented by an in-comparable actor, whose excellent expression is an admirable com-ment upon the plays of our author."

In 1754 *The Gray's Inn Journal* analyzed many Shakespeare char-acters on the basis of Garrick's acting, and noted the crucial shift in no. 94 for 3 August: "Aristotle was certainly mistaken when he called the fable the life and soul of tragedy; the art of constructing the dra-matic story should always be subordinate to the exhibition of character, our great Shakespeare has breathed another soul into tragedy, which has found the way of striking an audience with sentiment and passion at the same time."

In the 1760s Thomas Whateley began writing his *Remarks on the Characters of Shakespeare*, in which he noted that the "rules" of drama implying strict regularity of form are "by no means the first requisite . . . there is a subject for criticism more worthy of attention. . . . I mean the distinction and preservation of character, without which the piece is but a tale, not an action." And he analyzes Richard III and Macbeth as Garrick played them. In 1777 Maurice Morgan's *Essay on the Dramatic Character of Falstaff* rang clearly the bell for the new criticism, and he inscribed a presentation copy of it to Garrick: "When the hand of time shall have brushed off his present editors and commentators, and when the very name of Voltaire, and even the memory of the language in which he has written shall be no more, the Appalachian Mountains, the banks of the Ohio, and the plains of Scotia shall resound with the accents of this barbarian: in his native tongue he shall roll the genuine passions of nature. Nor shall the griefs of Lear be alleviated, nor the charms and wit of Rosalind be abated by time. There is indeed nothing perishable about him, except that very learning which he is said so much to want."

The drum beating is less important than the evidence of a kind of character study which treats and assumes a real life, a youth, a set of motivations, an aliveness to the individuals as played on stage. And critics inevitably associated this phenomenon with Garrick. He was not working in competition with editors, but affording insights and illumi-nations which perpetually afforded renewed inspiration to critics.

Garrick did not conceive of helping in this shift alone. Though he was himself outstanding in every performance, he sought for a total blending and ensemble performance. And this he achieved, for in periodical after periodical in the 1770s the acting of his associates on stage is likewise commented upon, as it was not earlier. Together they shaped a new criticism.[49]

Dr Johnson and Sir Joshua Reynolds thought of Garrick as a "diffused man"—expending his energy and vivacity on many things, a man with no friends but with many acquaintances, but Johnson saw him as "no common man." [50] Nor indeed was he, for in all his diffused activities in the manifold aspects of his profession he showed a buoyant temperament (under control) that set him apart not only in accomplishment but also in attitude. He may have harbored contempt for his Grub Street assailants—but it seldom shows. He may have burned inwardly at petty attacks from company members—but the heat seldom surfaced. Yet he was anything but a cold, indifferent businessman. He thought well of himself, nearly everyone sensed it, and his first biographers emphasized his more than a modicum of vanity. But the understandable vanity was combined with an engaging warmth of personality. His ability to laugh at himself was healthy and enduring, yet he could and did, as we have seen, explode upon occasion.

If style gives some insight into the man, what impression emerges from his voluminous business correspondence? As one reads into the first volume (of three) of Garrick letters one feels that he is viewing through Garrick's eyes the endless oddity of human behavior displayed in the century. Garrick is looking outward. By the end, and on into the next, the revelation turns inward, where focus is drawn to the seemingly predictable responses from the manager. A pattern develops akin to defensive explosion in vocabulary and phraseology—"I was shocked that. . . . I was hurt by. . . . I could not have been more amazed had you shot me with a long gun. . . . I was surprised to receive yours complaining of . . ."—followed by assurances of patent understanding and possible justifications of both his actions and those of the correspondent. Appeals to pride, to friendship, to gratitude, to loyalty, to "the best interests for the profession" have long been staples in the managerial approach to those disagreeing with one's action. Garrick early mastered such approaches, which put the recipient on the defensive, but his turn of phrase was just as often witty and charming. He declared early to Frank Hayman (and doubtless believed it true) "I have no luke-warmness in my Temper, & as I am naturally open & Impetuous, it is a necessary prudence in me to shun Company I am doubtful of" (47). Yet his sense of humor about his moods broke through and showed often how with a laugh at himself he could take a slight with a grain of salt—"I am continually fighting of Shadows, & am like poor Shirly in y$^e$ Rehearsal—'Hey, ho! hey day!— / I know not what to do, or what to say'" (231).

He was firm—to Joseph Reed, "I can very readily *excuse* your Doubts of my Judgment for I am as great a Skeptick in that point as Yourself, but your Doubts of my Integrity oblige me to abide by y$^e$

Opinion which I have before given *you* of y^r Tragedy of Dido" (275). He could be conciliatory—yet still firm as he put down Arthur Murphy, "I am sorry that You gave Y^rself so much trouble to convince Me of the insufficiency of my Remarks; My advice & fears were submitted to You w^th great good will & Sincerity. . . . Without Entering into any further discussion of this matter, I beg that you will follow y^r own Interest and Inclinations . . . no attention to the Theatre sh^d obstruct y^r pursuits of greater moment" (254).

He bore no grudge for long. His appetite for keeping informed on what was going on in all fields was voracious. Resourcefulness combined with alertness and a sort of extrovert daring animated him. By alertness we mean an observable quickness to pick up a germinal idea when he sensed it, and by resourcefulness his aptness to carry it out boldly. He was quick to develop and implement hints from everyone, when he deemed them productive. Witness the germinal idea of a structure for the Theatrical Fund; the hint of a stage production of the Jubilee given by Benjamin Wilson; ideas for stage lighting gained from Monnet and Boquet in Paris; of scenic design from Messink and de Loutherbourg; seminal directions and examples of natural acting from Macklin; ideas for after pieces from French farces. In these he was alert and derivative in the best sense—creatively so—for he developed each with imagination and effectiveness. He did indeed, as Mrs Clive observed, have a magic hammer in his hand. His genius lay (in management at least) in knowing how, when, and where to use it.

Reynolds thought that Garrick calculated his every act, on stage or off, that he foresaw and planned the outcome well before he entered into any enterprise. Possibly so, for he was an actor and always aware of his public figure, but he was just as remarkable for acting upon a hint, and responding, as we have seen again and again, spontaneously to a piece of good advice on his acting or management.

"I have a whim—we must scheme some business together," he wrote to Tom King in 1772. What the scheme was we cannot tell precisely, but the whim seems to have had something to do with Garrick's sense that the time had come to reemphasize "laughing" comedy. Farce had always laughed on the eighteenth-century stage, but some comedy had become over delicate, serious, and even lachrymose. He was thinking at the time about accommodating Tomkis's *Albumazar* for the stage, which he got up for King as Trincalo in it, and King as the laughing prologuist early the following season:

> Some smiles from Tony Lumpkin, if you spare
> Let Trincalo of Tot'nham have his share . . .
> Each sister muse a sep'rate shop should keep

Comedy to laugh. Tragedy to weep,
And sentimental laudanum to make you sleep . . .
Do laugh, pray laugh—'tis your best cure when ill
The grand specific, universal pill!
What would I give to set a tide a-going
A spring-tide in your hearts with joy o'erflowing.

For two years before Goldsmith's *She Stoops to Conquer* Garrick had been shoring up comedy—laughing at sentiment (as in his epilogue to the *West Indian*) and preparing in *his* way to "set a tide a-going" for emphasis upon laughter. He was at the time still turning over in his mind, and had been since 1771, his spoof on stodgy routines still lingering in theatre corners in London. The spoof appeared early in the 1774 season, as *The Meeting of the Company*. He picked up the idea, of course, from Buckingham's play (*The Rehearsal*); let the members of his company act in it under their own names; and turned acting values topsy-turvy as he gave directions for success on the stage in his last ironical jibe at hackneyed acting style:

Shakespeare has said—a silly empty creature!
"Never o'er step the modesty of Nature."
I say you *must*, to prove it I engage
Whate'er your sex, or character, or age
No modesty will do upon the stage.

And Garrick's Bayes compares his theory of acting to "the *Iliad* in a nutshell." The whim was spontaneous, the playlet—he called it an interlude—was calculated, the effect was applauded.

Much has been made of Garrick's vanity both as actor and manager. Churchill in his *Apology* (1761) condemned him for it:

Let the vain tyrant sit amidst his guards,
His puny-Green Room wits and venal bards
Who meanly tremble at a puppet's frown,
And for a playhouse freedom sell their own.

Walpole suspected Garrick of writing puffs for himself to bolster his vanity. Goldsmith's "Retaliation" verses (1774) impaled the actor:

Of praise a mere glutton, he swallowed what came,
And the puff of a dunce, he mistook it for fame,
Till his relish grown callous, almost to disease
Who peppered him highest was surest to please.

Hard texts these, taken out of their context of motivation—all were retaliations of sorts. Humility was not a flaunted attribute for either the actor or the manager in Garrick, nor was obsessive vanity a characteristic. He was, to be sure, the most be-pictured man in the eighteenth century, with more portraits and prints (in the roles he played, and at his home at Hampton) than even an Alexander Pope or a Voltaire. Yet portraits and replicated prints are the furniture of actors. Most prints served as professional advertising and we are indebted to their extensiveness for graphic insights into the life and theatre of the times. How does a public figure and actor avoid, even if he wished to do so, picturization and consequent accusations of vanity? Customary exhibitions of the trait—currying favor, eschewing subordinates fawning for praise—one finds lacking in Garrick. Most of his associates experienced other dimensions in his character in their dealings with him. Recipients of his letters read them with the image in mind and the presence at hand of a lively person, of a penetrating glance with which they were familiar, concentrated upon them as they read, and of a man often seeing the next move possibly way ahead of them. So much of his success lay in his genuine sense of humor, possession of which contradicts vainglory.

# The Social Rounds

.

From the intimacies of long standing with a diversity of early friends, often their seniors, the private and social lives of the Garricks expanded with the increase in Garrick's fame into the social circles, more generally of his contemporaries, of those who visited and returned visits, who shared weekends of sociability at their country estates and banquets together in London. With the decline perhaps in intimacy, such social life was more mixed and fashionable than intellectual and personal. The drawing rooms and galleries with pictures, books, handsome furnishings, porcelains, tapestries, moulded ceilings and marble fireplaces were for the groups that gathered in them not just for display but created the settings in which they lived and entertained. Why else the building of mansions, the restorations of old houses, the laying out of gardens, the ceremony of the hunt, the music in the drawing room, the rich fabrics, the wit of the dialogue. None were better qualified than the Garricks at Hampton or the Adelphi to welcome and respond to invitation after invitation, to become some of the dramatis personae of the magnificent pageantry of English art during one of its richest periods.

Aroused by Garrick's later dramatic triumphs in Drury Lane, more and more people of all classes sought the distinction of his acquaintance and company, with the result that Garrick had less and less time for friends of his own choosing. We shall here ignore most of these strangers, almost half the names in his correspondence, who addressed him on business, patronage, charity, in vanity, envy, or admiration. Yet in these later years in face of all the attention and flattery, Garrick continued to control his private life and find time and resources for old and new friends, perhaps more discriminating than ever before in the choice of the new and often younger. Gradually, as was the social pattern of the day, he became a member of different coteries, clubs, "circles" for occasional gatherings where he conversed with many but was intimate with only one or two.

Early and late Garrick sought the company of solicitors and judges. One of such a group was Sir Grey Cooper (d. 1801), secretary of the treasury (1765–82). From 1770 on, when Lord North was appointed first lord of the treasury, Cooper became his agent or assistant in public affairs and his companion in attending the theatre. Garrick came to know him well enough to seek and obtain from him a grant of leave for Richard Burke from the post as collector of the port of Jamaica in the West Indies (625).[1] The men in this group were often mutually helpful; hence Garrick made bold to seek through him, by verse petition to Edward Stanley, secretary to the commissioners of the customs, release of some chintz sent to Garrick by admirers in India. The request granted, Mrs Garrick sent the chintz to Chippendale to decorate a bed he was making for her (912,915).[2] At Garrick's further request in 1776, Grey Cooper, as a member of Parliament introduced and supported, with aid from Burke and Lord North, a bill for establishing the Theatrical Fund. "As I am quitting the Sock & Buskin," Garrick wrote, "I cannot help continuing my Care to the Old & helpless of the profession—We have got a fund towards their support of near 5000, & with care & good Management, we shall make it of Some Consequence to the Invalids of $y^e$ Stage" (979,981). Lord and Lady North delegated Cooper, because of his friendship with Garrick, to obtain box seats for them at the theatre, and often suggested parts they wished the actor might play (726,1018).[3] Understandably Garrick was flattered when Cooper and Lord North called at the Adelphi, and wittily and with charm lamented his absence (820).[4] The Norths and Garricks were neighbors near Bushy Park, Lady North being appointed "Ranger" (1771), and it was through the Steward, Samuel Martin, that Garrick petitioned that a neighbor might purchase a small piece of wasteland adjoining his property (1009).[5]

Another in this circle was Henry Wilmot (1710–94) who had accumulated a fortune as a solicitor of Grey's Inn, and acquired a town house in Bloomsbury Square and a country estate at Farnsborough in Hampshire. A large man physically, nicknamed "Giant Wilmot," he was fond of reading Shakespeare aloud to his friends and depicting the character of Falstaff. Garrick thought him a "most Engaging, Worthy, natural Man" (423,593). Garrick petitioned him in behalf of a living in Wales for his friend Evan Lloyd, for Wilmot was on cordial terms with the Bishop of Asaph (558,570,670).[6] The Garricks with friends Joseph Cradock and Hannah More visited at Farnsborough a number of times, and Mrs Wilmot busied herself in seeking out some Hampshire sheep for the Garricks at Hampton. Garrick, of course, entertained the Wilmot children, writing verses for each on the death of a favorite cat (826,1114,1177,1238).[7]

From a group of politicians in the 1750s Garrick made the acquaintance of George Hay (later, 1773, Sir George), who became one of the most active and effective lawyers and politicians, notably as an orator, Garrick later professing he had passed some of the "happiest hours" in his life with him, dining together and on one occasion before 1757 making a holiday expedition to Oxford.

In June, 1766 Hay invited Garrick to meet Camden at the Doctors' Common, of which both Hay and Camden were members. Sometime before 1773, Garrick wrote Hay, "My regard for You is greater than my vanity . . . I had not rather have you with that charming Rigby at $y^e$ opera than with Garrick at Drury Lane" (1308). In response to Garrick's rather embarrassed and awkward support of the solicitations of an old friend, Hay replied: "You are grown formal in your old age, my dear friend. . . . Kiss the blooming wrinkles of my ancient love for my sake, and believe me always yours and hers."[8] And as late as March 1778 Garrick was scheduled to dine with Hay, Edward Thurlow, and Rigby, and at the last moment had to decline because of illness. Only because through the years the two men were near each other in London are the records fragmentary of Garrick's friendship and enjoyment of Hay as one of the protagonists in the current political drama (108,319,411,1020,1161,1307).

Garrick did not meet Charles Pratt (1714–94), baron Camden of Camden Place in the County of Kent (17 July 1765), until the summer of 1766. In the preceding ten years, Camden, then Pratt, had come forward as an able and effective counsel, member of Parliament, King's counsel, attorney general, chief justice of the Court of Common Pleas, defender of Wilkes, and second only to Wilkes as a nationally popular figure. In June 1766 Garrick on Hay's invitation "din'd . . . with some Rakes, & they kept me till 10 o'Clock . . . Lord Camden among them —but Mum—for my Lord chief Justice" (412). Shortly thereafter he had "the Honour of Your Commands," Lord Camden's for Sunday evening, an invitation he was unable to accept having "Engag'd some french Gentlemen, whose Friends Entertain'd me most hospitably at Paris. . . . This disappointment is of too much consequence to Us, not to feel it most Sensibly" (411). About a month later, Garrick wrote his brother Peter (18 August): "I had $M^r$ Wilmot $w^{th}$ Me for two Days the Secretary to $y^e$ last and to the present Chancellour. . . . He has plagu'd my Soul out to call upon my Lord Camden on his taking the great Seal, but I won't stir from Hampton, & have given $y^e$ reason in a Sort of Dialogue between him. . . . L$^d$ Camden admires it, & swears if I won't come to him, he will dine with Me some time this Month. . . .

1

Wil:—You should call at his door, or sh$^d$ send him a Card,
   Shall Garrick alone be so cold?
Gar:—For Me a poor Play'r, and Still poorer Bard,
   To Wish *Camden* joy would be bold:

2

What Joy can I wish him? dear Wilmot, declare,
   No Changes new honours can bring;
To Him twill be labour, Attention, & Care,
   The Joy's for our Country & King (423).[9]

For several years Garrick had been endeavouring to obtain an additional living for his good friend the Reverend Thomas Beighton, who had been serving the parish of Egham, Surrey, ever since 1725. In June, 1767, apparently at Garrick's instigation, Beighton addressed a petition to Lady Camden, which Garrick then dispatched to her ladyship with a covering letter. She in turn presented both letters to Camden, who begged her to inform them that it "would give him infinite pleasure to have it in his power to give any addition to Mr. Beighton's happiness,"[10] appointing Beighton vicar of Wexham in Buckinghamshire, presumably before the year was out. Garrick wrote Burke on 12 July 1768, "On Saturday L$^d$ & L$^y$ Camden are to dine with Us, & they have been so kind to my friend Beighton, I could not put them off" (513). In gratitude, Beighton in 1771 willed to Garrick and Camden and a book dealer his rather exceptional library, especially rich in foreign books, sales catalogues, early English books and engravings, apparently in the hopes of having part or all preserved intact. The Camdens and Garricks journeyed to Egham on 7 July 1771, immediately on Beighton's death, to look over his estate that consisted mostly of his library. Between the possible conflicts in a division and the wish to increase the cash residue in his estate, Camden and Garrick agreed on a sale comprising 2,695 items for a gross of £778.8.9—a very remarkable library for a country vicar. Garrick prepared an epitaph concluding with a reference to Camden that was widely published at the time (466–68,638).[11] Some years later, in 1777, in destitution Beighton's niece solicited Camden, who sent her to Garrick with a guinea in her pocket, and Garrick in turn found a "little place" for her in the India House. Of more biographical consequence, the two men, brought together in disposing of Beighton's library, may have found a mutual taste for the old romances, Camden a great reader of them, and Garrick adding quite a number to his collection of early English drama (780,815).

On 17 January 1770 the great seal was transferred to the Honorable Charles Yorke, whom Garrick had earlier consulted on legal matters and with whom he had exchanged visits. Thereafter Camden lived mostly at Camden Place in Kent, retiring from London and politics, only occasionally coming forward in defense of Wilkes, the Americans, and of personal interest to Garrick in the appeal of *Donaldson* v. *Becket* on the Booksellers' Copyright Bill, at issue the copyright to Shakespeare's plays. In his retirement Camden wrote Garrick 28 letters, clearly treasured by Garrick, mostly taken up with arranging visits of the Garricks to Camden Place, the Garricks being so often already engaged, for which Camden often admonished them. "You and Mrs Garrick are two restless people, whose minds are always upon the stretch for conversation at home and abroad, and are strangers to the pleasure of one day's solitude," and again, in 1777: "I know too well the courtship you receive from the first families in this kingdom to be either surprised or displeased with the multiplicity of your engagements; but it so happens that the importunity of those who, to gratify their own vanity, are content to see you once in a year . . . do so engage your time, that others, whose better motive of friendship makes them wish to see you often, are almost totally deprived of your company. Not that I consider your visit at Mistley among those frivolous engagements I have been alluding to; that is a party that both Socrates and Alcibiades would envy, for it would equally suit the wisest and the most voluptuous." [12]

As for the content of their friendship, the Camdens had a son and three daughters, the youngest Jane, "Jenny," attending Mme Descombes boarding school in Paris with Garrick's nieces, and on the prospects of a visit to Camden Place, Garrick was "tantaliz'd with y$^e$ Young Ladies Harpsicord, Guittar, viol de Gamba . . . I know y$^e$ feast to be real & Exquisite" (703). [13] Each man was concerned for the declining health of the other; they communicated on current politics and books. Familiar with Garrick's admiration for Shakespeare, Camden wrote him: "I have been employed since I saw you in reading Ben Jonson. . . . I make no comparison, but I do assure you I am beyond expression charmed with the dramatic powers of that author, and, in my opinion, the genius of the writer is equal to his art; nay, so far is he from being deficient in the first, that his own fund would have supplied him with every faculty of wit, humour, and nature, though he had been no scholar. His principal fault, in my judgment, arises from a pedantic imitation of the ancients. His prose dialogue is elegant; his

619

verse hard and too much laboured, but by no means difficult or obscure. Read him again, as I have done, without prejudice, and forget Shakespeare while you are doing it, which is but just; for, to say the truth, he that reads an author with *proper attention*, has no *leisure*, while he is so employed, to think of any other." To this Garrick responded in a letter not preserved, and Camden in turn continued his excellent critical evaluation of Jonson in a second letter. On the report in the papers of Garrick's illness, which proved to be serious, Camden wrote Garrick, 15 September 1778: "I have arrived at a time of life when the loss of an old friend is irreparable; and however it has happened that we have not lately met as often as formerly, my friendship is as warm as ever, and I am sure there is not one among your large catalogue of friends who is more affectionately yours than Camden," endorsed by Garrick, "Lord Camden—most affectionate."

None of what must have been an extensive correspondence of Garrick's letters to the Camdens survives, only the drafts or copies of six in Garrick's private file; on the other hand Garrick refers often to visits, engagements with the Camdens in other letters. Only the frequency and not the tone implies that Garrick was proud of the friendship. Proud he was indeed to introduce Camden to Gibbon, whose *History* Camden praised to Garrick. *"The Author is y<sup>e</sup> Only Man to write History of the Age—such depth—such perspicuity—such language force variety"* (991).[14] Garrick had every reason to be gratified in Camden's friendship, to be proud that he had won the admiration and intimacy of a really great public figure, who like Garrick, short in stature, had risen professionally and socially, and in turn Camden's admiration was a measure of Garrick the individual. His appointment by Garrick as an executor, by Sheridan as a pall bearer were founded not on worldly prestige, but confidence and affection.

On their circuit of country visits, the Garricks were occasionally the guests of Sir William Young (1725–98) and his wife, Lady Elizabeth (1729–1801). He was born in the West Indies but settled in England, and became the governor of Jamaica in 1769. They resided in England in a country mansion, Standlich, in Wiltshire, where he overspent in improvements, and had to sell to Delaford in 1768. But there in the summer of 1758 he staged an elaborate dramatic production for which Garrick loaned some properties from Drury Lane, but could not let his Roman "shapes" go, for his *Antony and Cleopatra* was about to be in production. A misunderstanding resulted, but was cleared up, though it became rather distressing to Garrick at the time. Young was much interested in painting and employed Cipriani for a fresco, and was on friendly terms with Benjamin Wilson. Garrick introduced Lady Young to Joseph Lambert, the painter, who had recently given lessons to Mrs Garrick and to his nieces. Garrick congratulated him, in a letter of many flourishes, upon the marriage of his eldest daughter Sarah Elizabeth in June 1770, excusing himself for his belated note on the hurry and confusion involved in "half a dozen visits, made by my Wife & Me into y$^e$ Several Counties of Hertfordshire, Bucks & Essex," which delayed his hearing of the event. Garrick thought well enough of Young's friendship to confide in him in January 1773 about his venture of having produced "Hamlet with alterations," and his hopes for doing Macbeth "in y$^e$ old dresses." The friendship was peripheral, but genuine because of Sir William's passion for drama and theatre, and Garrick's cordiality extended to the wife and children (203,209,231,549,596,726,733,1142).

Camden and Johnson were not alone in admonishing Garrick and deploring his waste of his energies and failing health in a dissipation of house parties at country estates, fashionable social gatherings in London, and the welcoming at Hampton and the Adelphi of new acquaintances at home and from abroad. Yet the Garricks, their hosts, and guests were all as much a part of the fine arts as were the drawing rooms, the galleries, the gardens, the pageantry and wit, a setting as essential to the portrait as the portrait was to the setting. But emerging from this flow of social activity and its personalities, three individuals moved to closer friendship than the others: Sir William Young, Richard Rigby, and Richard Berenger.

The key to Garrick's temperament, however, both in his personal and in his professional relations, was best sensed, perhaps, by Morellet when he remarked that Garrick "Chez le baron d'Holbach, lorsqu'il me voyait aux prises avec Diderot ou Marmontel, il s'assèyait les bras croisès, et nous regardait comme un dessinateur observant une figure qu'il veut saisir."[15] Here is the essence of drama: a confrontation to be resolved by competence, by wit, by dynamics in dialogue, with the spectator, not necessarily detached or objective, but attentive and even responsive. Emphatically the confrontation is in dialogue with the words animated by action, and the spectator endeavoring to grasp and carry over into his own life, not primarily the ideas, but the animation, the artistry of the protagonists.

The heat of political debate, in fact the whole political process, intrigued Garrick, and especially current political personalities. His long friendship with Richard Rigby (1722–88) is a case in point and demonstrates again the wide and varying range (even in a relatively small group of close friends) of Garrick's interest. By professed modern standards Rigby was most corrupt, "an unblushing placeman during the worst period of parliamentary corruption," and Garrick rejoiced when Rigby attained the goal of all his jobbery, corruption, his appointment as paymaster of the forces, 1768 (510,511).[16] In turn it was to Rigby that Garrick first announced, in confidence, his decision to retire from Drury Lane. Nathaniel Wraxall described Rigby in action as a politician: "When in his place [in the House of Commons, Rigby] was invariably habited in a full-dressed suit of clothes, commonly of a purple or dark colour, without lace or embroidery, close buttoned, with his sword thrust through the pocket. His countenance was very expressive, but not of genius; still less did it indicate timidity or modesty. All the comforts of the pay office seemed to be eloquently depicted in it. . . . His manner, rough, yet frank, bold but manly, admirably set off whatever sentiments he uttered in parliament. . . . Whatever he meant, he expressed indeed without circumlocution or declamation. There was a happy audacity about his forehead which must have been the gift of nature; art could not attain to it by any efforts. He seemed neither to fear nor even respect the House, whose composition he well knew, and to the members of which assembly he never appeared to give credit for any portion of virtue, patriotism, or public spirit. Far from concealing these sentiments, he insinuated, or even pronounced them without disguise, and from *his* lips they neither excited surprise nor even commonly awakened reprehension."[17]

The personality, the effectiveness of a politician in confrontations counted for more than all else in public life, and for two reasons. Political power both in church and in state was in the hands and was the prerogative of individuals by inheritance or appointment. Secondly, the national political dialogue was in the House of Parliament—in debates such as Samuel Johnson reported. Rigby's political career, therefore, has little bearing on the relations of Garrick and Rigby; what counts was Rigby's personality. The "nice discrimination in Rigby's behaviour in the House of Commons" accounts for Garrick's frequent attendance on Parliament. It was in style or manner, though to be sure not in details, a sort of delineation of Garrick on the stage and in social gatherings.

In private life, in personal relations, Rigby was courteous, considerate, generous, frank yet modest, with many admiring and devoted friends, men and women. He may have played the political game catch-as-catch-can, but his integrity was not questioned in personal relations. For example, he wrote Garrick once in response to Garrick's petition for a preferment, an appointment for a petitioner: "You shall command Me in any thing that is reasonable when I have it in my power to comply with your requests; but I cannot gratify You for your friend Sparkes; I disapprove totally of supernumerary Clerks in pub-lick offices, and will put none into mine, I have found one there al-ready put in by Charles Townshend; it is too cruel to remove Him & yet I had thoughts of it" (363 n.3).

As early as the summer of 1744, Garrick may have been a guest of Rigby's at Mistley Hall, in Essex on the Stour, an estate and mansion inherited from his father, which Rigby continued to enlarge, redeco-rate, and furnish, employing the Adam brothers, until he had one of the more magnificent country estates near London.[18] How they met is not known, perhaps through the Duke of Bedford, whom Garrick had assisted with properties for a dramatic production, Drury Lane being part of the Bedford estate and who was to become, if not already, Rigby's patron and intimate friend. The next year, 1755, Rigby was MP from Castle Rising; 1747, from Sudbury; and 1754–84, from Tavistock. Garrick's interest in Rigby may have increased when during the min-istry of the Duke of Devonshire, Bedford was appointed (1758) lord lieutenant of Ireland and Rigby his secretary. By 1765 the visits of the Garricks to Mistley of a week or so became an annual affair, where they enjoyed the company and correspondence, among others of Martha Rigby "Haly Paly," his sister, and her husband, Captain Ber-nard Hale, who became in 1773 lieutenant governor of Chelsea Hos-pital (322,363,1114). On the early death in 1773 of his eldest son, Bernard, the Hales begged Garrick, who had been often kind to the boy at Hampton, to compose the epitaph which was inscribed on the boy's tombstone (783,322,1114).[19]

At Mistley or in London or elsewhere, Rigby and the Garricks were joined by such friends as Christopher Anstey, John Calvert, Richard Cox, Edward Thurlow, Sir George Hay, Hannah More, the Duke of Newcastle, the Cadogans, Lady Glyn, and Anthony Chamier. Gar-rick's ultimate tribute to Rigby was a wish to introduce Rigby to Lady Spencer at a party at Hampton; this failing because of Rigby's illness, Garrick arranged for Rigby "to pay his devoirs at Wimbleton" in May 1777. In return, Lady Spencer, accompanied by the Duchess of Dev-onshire, who was seeing her off to France, and with Rigby in atten-dance, stopped by at Mistley in August. In anticipation of the visit, Garrick wrote Lady Spencer, "Let me ardently wish, that the Pleasures of Mistley were not Exaggerated by my passion for the Place, and master; but that for once, Lady Spencer hath seen with my Eyes, and tasted with my palate. If she is happy at Mistley, I shall be happy." Earlier on 11 October 1776, Rigby wrote Garrick: "You are going to the first woman in the world. The only rub in my political life has been, that it has frequently set me at a distance from more acquaintance with her," a letter which Garrick endorsed; "Mr. Rigby and Lady Spencer. All gospel."[20]

Garrick and all others relished the excellent table and wine at Mistley, which was always matched with witty conversation, and sometimes turns of verse. In the summer before his death Garrick visited Rigby, even though his health was precarious. "The eternal Vivacity of our Right Honourable Host disperses almost Every gloom" (1185, 511).[21] Rigby was an executor of Garrick's will, a pallbearer at his funeral, and a thoughtful, quiet host to Lady Spencer on the occasion, offering her a warm room in the Pay Office from which to witness the funeral procession.[22]

From the fragmentary information that has survived covering Garrick's associations with Richard Berenger (1720–82) for at least 30 years, one can only wish for more. His father, Moses Berenger, was a rich London merchant, his mother the youngest sister of Sir Richard Temple, baron Cobham, with whom Garrick was acquainted as early as 1749 (63,64,1229). Professionally he was a horseman and in 1754 published a translation from the French of Bourgelat, *A New System of Horsemanship*. Sometime after 1760 he was appointed gentleman of the equerry to George III, and in that capacity, Garrick wittily begged Berenger, from Bath 19 March 1766: "If a Phoenix should come across you, or rather if you should come across a Phoenix . . . I will certainly be proud to mount a palfrey of thy appointment" (393).[23]

Garrick had counted on his suave and diplomatic aid years before in resolving an argument with Arthur Murphy over *The Orphan of China* production, in an altercation with Lord Lyttleton, and to defend Garrick against a hostile press (175,218,266,399,784).[24] Berenger, a member of the royal entourage, carried to Garrick requests for command performances, and occasionally Garrick asked his assistance in picking an appropriate epigram, such as that for the bust of Shakespeare, presented by Garrick to the Corporation of Stratford (373,393,399,784).[25]

In private life, Berenger was very much like the characters in Congreve; as Johnson remarked, he was "the standard of true elegance." Hannah More, who frequently met him at Mrs Boscawen's, liked him "prodigiously."—"Everybody's favourite even Johnson's. . . . all chivalry, and blank verse, and anecdote."[26] And like the gentleman in Congreve and in the fashionable society, Berenger's tastes exceeded his means, and fortunately he resided in the Royal Mews where by royal prerogative he was safe from bailiffs. Garrick urged him to seek preferment: "It is the most astonishing thing, that you should be $y^e$ friend & Relation of all the great men of great interest & that you $sh^d$ not have a rasher of $y^e$ Gammon" (418). The Garricks and Berenger dined together and with friends, once in the following manner: "But think you, my merry wag, that I will so ill requite y$^r$ Kindness to me as to bring you down this bliteing weather to Hampton?—what shall I draw you from those fragrant Dunghills which are plac'd so near you, & to the breath of which, you open your enraptur'd nostrils, to sniff at my Hyacinths, Gillyflowers, Violets, Snowdrops and Polyanthoses? —Shall the sweet Musick of Hackney Coaches, Muffins & Teddydoll be exchang'd for the chirping of Birds, the cackling of Hens, the gobbling of Turkeys, and the grunting of hogs? Heavens forfend No my dear Richard, I love you too well to bring you from the Lap of noise & Luxury, to repose your high-tune'd spirits sub tegmine fagi [under my spreading beech's covert—Virgil, *Eclogues*, I, i]" (1228,230,526, 697).

By the spring of 1778, Berenger had fallen so deeply in debt that he dared not venture out from the Royal Mews. In March his family and friends came to his aid raising £2,600 to pay off his creditors. On 29 March Garrick wrote: "Dear Berenger I did not hear till last Night—, and I heard it with the greatest pleasure, that Your Friends have generously contributed to your, & their own happiness—No one can more rejoice at this circumstance than I do, and as I hope We shall have a Bonfire upon the Occasion, I beg that You will light it with the inclos'd," Berenger's bond for £280.10.0 dated 2 February 1762 (1168). Garrick added a bank note for £300 and gave a grand dinner in celebration when he had the honor of setting alight all the notes and bonds which had been purchased from the creditors, throwing "them into the grate, and setting the pile on fire" (1168 n.2). Berenger responded (in part) on the same day as Garrick's letter: "Though I can never be *surprised* at any mark of your compassion and generosity to me, yet, my dearest Sir, I was so struck when I opened your letter, that for awhile I could only thank you with my tears. . . . My heart is too full to allow me to say more than that I still owe, and must ever owe, the debt which your bounty has cancelled; for nothing shall ever cancel the remembrance of your kindness, nor my respect, affection, and gratitude to you, my honoured friend and benefactor."[27]

During Garrick's lifetime, thanks largely to the success and qualities in his professional and private life, the social status of the theatrical community improved, and Garrick not only negotiated with dramatists at Drury but he encountered them in social gatherings, even such old perennial irritants as Foote and Murphy. Later, two in particular prominent in the annals of eighteenth-century drama involved Garrick in the inevitable conflicts between social courtesies and pressures and his exacting professional standards and obligations.

The first was the socially established and engaging George Colman (1732–94), who perhaps second only to Garrick was the ablest manager-dramatist in the century. Garrick's 63 extant letters, plus 45 allusions in letters to mutual acquaintances, and as many in reply, cover only in part their diverse and often intimate relations, in and out of the theatre for 21 years. Born in Florence, where his father was for many years envoy to the Grand Duke of Tuscany, Colman was brought to London, on the death of his father, when Colman was a year old. The government supplied a house to his mother, whose brother-in-law, William Pulteney, the earl of Bath, assumed a dominating guardianship. Pulteney insisted that George excel at Westminster School and Oxford, and on Pulteney's insistence Colman matriculated in Lincoln's Inn, was called to the bar in 1757, and in a desultory fashion practised law, all the while, however, devoting himself to literature and the drama. Throughout these early years he sought to remain in Bath's favor, who, it was assumed, intended to leave Colman a sizable inheritance, an expectation that was defeated when Colman persisted in a liaison with the actress Sarah Ford, former mistress of Henry Mossop, and whom Colman later, in two years, married. The Earl disapproved sharply on grounds that she had neither a fortune nor charm; Garrick's private opinion was that she was an idiot (1057).

Colman was at first one of a group, including his Oxford friends Robert Lloyd and Bonnell Thornton, witty, intelligent young men-about-town who came to the fore in the 1750s with their periodical *The Connoisseur*. He first came to Garrick's attention in 1757, at about the time when Goldsmith observed in *The Bee* that "all Grub Street was preparing its advice to the managers," when he published an open *Letter of Abuse of D— G—, Esq.*, actually in praise of Garrick, who was much pleased.[28] Colman went on to share with Garrick an interest in the older drama. He wrote with insight on the quality of Massinger's plays; he edited Ben Jonson and Beaumont and Fletcher; he translated Terence. The knowledge so gained supported his success as a dramatist in his plays, such as *Polly Honeycombe* (1760), *The Jealous Wife* (1761), and in his collaboration with Garrick in *The Clandestine Marriage* (1766). Such accomplishments won Garrick's respect, and he could find no better or more trusted dramatist to take over the management of Drury Lane while he was abroad for two years. In his absence from London, Garrick wrote Colman in full confidence and intimacy. The two became stockholders with others in the *St. James Chronicle*. Understandably as in all business ventures, differences occasionally arose, which they resolved reasonably and amicably.[29]

When, however, on Garrick's return to Drury Lane, Colman bought into and became the manager of Covent Garden in open competition with Garrick, an estrangement arose briefly. Eventually Garrick promised Colman that when he himself gave up managing Drury Lane that the first option to buy into the patent would be given to Colman. He concluded his letter of 29 December 1775, in which he made the offer, "Once again Many happy Years to you—I am Dear Colman Most Af-fec[ly] Yours" (971), to which Colman replied the next day: "I would not for worlds again sit on the throne of Brentford with any assessor, except it were yourself."[30] Eventually, it might be recalled, Drury Lane passed to Richard Brinsley Sheridan and partners, much to Garrick's increasingly bitter disappointment. After Garrick's retirement, and when Colman had taken on the management of the little theatre in the Haymarket, Garrick wrote Colman: "I wish You most sincerely Success & Every pleasure from your new Engagement—I am truly partial to the *Old* Spot, from an Old habitual liking, but likewise from a principle of honesty that make me Attach'd to people, who have bought my property, & behave so Well to me—were You Manager at the other house [Covent Garden], I should have been much distress'd for then *honour would say, do this, & tender Love say nay*. . . . God bless you my dear Friend" (1057).

In Richard Cumberland Garrick encountered no obscure ambitious hack writer, but an heir in education and social position to scholars, gentry, and the church. His father was Bishop of Clonfert in Ireland, and Cumberland himself was patronized by Lord Halifax, who provided him with sinecures, first in Ireland, later in London. He had some knowledge of music, as well as painting and contemporary letters. His classical education was sound, and he contemplated writing a treatise on Greek drama.[31] Although much of his perhaps too facile verse, prose and drama (some 40 plays in the same number of years) was written and published after Garrick's death, he early on attained the reputation as a versatile writer and major dramatist, the latter owing in great measure to Garrick's guidance and production of some of the early plays.

Though his first two plays, *The Summer's Tale* (a comic opera) and *The Brothers* were first produced at Covent Garden, his next, and most successful, *The West Indian*, as he acknowledged, profited greatly from Garrick's criticism before being produced at Drury Lane, 19 January 1771. Later the same year Garrick put on his *Timon of Athens*, which he had earlier rejected.[32] Cumberland asked Garrick year in and year out to offer criticism, and suggest revisions. Cumberland accepted all, and Garrick hoped he would improve, but he seemingly came to dislike the man, and to condemn his outpouring of sentimental comedies.[33] But socially and personally Garrick could not ignore the younger dramatist. As early as 1761 Lord Halifax brought Cumberland over to Hampton to introduce him, and to seek support for his first play *The Banishment of Cicero*. Within two days Garrick turned it down. Cumberland accompanied Halifax to Ireland, where he became acquainted with Burke and with members of the Dublin theatre. Upon his return he became acquainted with Foote, Reynolds, and Goldsmith, Boswell, and Johnson at the British Coffee House, and assiduously called on Garrick both at Southampton Street and at Hampton.

Garrick attended the opening performance of *The Brothers* at Covent Garden (2 December 1769) where Cumberland flattered him in the epilogue. Cumberland records, thereupon, in his *Memoirs*, "From this time Mr. Garrick took pains to cultivate an acquaintance, which he had hitherto neglected, and after Mr Fitzherbert had brought us together at his house we interchanged visits."[34] One wonders a bit just who pursued whom. Garrick did ask him to appear with Faulkner in a magistrate's court in Dublin to straighten out a possible case of Irish plagiarism of Garrick's *The Jubilee* (635).[35] Cumberland's letters, effusive and flattering, gradually put Garrick off. After the success of *The West Indian* he wrote Garrick, "The solitude I am going into naturally disposes my mind to take leave of those friends which the world's society have bestowed upon me . . . my chief accession lies in your breast, and when 'The West Indian' gave me your regard, and bestowed all mine upon you, it did more for me than the best production ever did for its author before."[36] During the correspondence over the production of *The Battle of Hastings*, he continued in the same vein: "I considered myself doubly honoured to be heard by such an audience [as you] and read by such a master: I expect your correction with impatience, for though your applause would highly flatter me, your emendations would profit me; and in my present situation, I cannot scruple which to prefer."[37] Of such effusions Garrick noted, "a true picture of the man." If surviving correspondence is any indication, Cumberland's 50 long letters against Garrick's six, the most laconic he ever wrote, confirm a sustained initiative on Cumberland's part to cultivate the actor. Both his letters and his *Memoirs* give the impression, however, that a mutual friendship prevailed.

Garrick became visibly annoyed when Cumberland pushed aggressively for the manager's taking on John Henderson, the Bath actor. Correspondence terminated for a time (857,879,900).[38] But professional as well as social relations were restored when Garrick read, criticized, and wrote a prologue for, and produced *The Choleric Man*.

Even Garrick's friends noted in Cumberland a rather broad streak of vanity atop a very thin skin, where public criticism was concerned.[39] Garrick in good spirits wrote William Woodfall, characterizing Cumberland, 1 February 1777. "Always in fermentation, & Ever Sore about himself . . . very near being a good Man, and a good Writer, but that cursed leaven Vanity spoils y^e Whole" (1078).[40]

The theatre also was the initial medium of the long friendship of James Boswell and Garrick. Boswell was an ardent admirer of Garrick by reputation before he met the actor; later the friendship was personal and mutual covering much in English and Scottish life. Further, after Garrick's death, by the inclusion of biographical material on Garrick in *The Life of Johnson* and the survival of Boswell's correspondence and journals, he now bids fair to be not simply a source but also perhaps the best contemporary biographer of Garrick's private life.

The affinity of Boswell for Garrick was that of one who was fascinated by acting and he himself was temperamentally an actor. As a boy Boswell was drawn to the theatre in Edinburgh; congenitally all his life he endeavored to play one role after another, impelled by a consciousness of the dilemmas in his own life. He could "think of himself only in terms of other people. . . . His private memoranda contain a perpetual series of admonitions in this form: 'Be Erskine.' 'Be Sir D. Dalrymple.' 'Be Digges.' 'Be Johnson (You resemble him).'" From observing the diversity, the idiosyncrasies of human personality, he assiduously cultivated mimicry at which he became most adept and practiced with gusto.[41] In Edinburgh, to be sure, Boswell knew Garrick only by reputation—"the god." It was all to Boswell's credit that he admonished himself "Be Digges," that is West Digges, one of the most accomplished, sophisticated, and well-mannered actors, who, as Boswell later wrote Garrick, "was the first actor that I ever saw . . . who threw open to me the portals of Theatrical Enchantment."[42]

Boswell heard much about Garrick before he first met him in London in 1760, from several men who had earlier known Garrick in Dublin and in London: Francis Gentleman and Samuel Derrick, Dubliners who failing as actors became hack writers in London patronized by Garrick. In 1758, Garrick wrote John Home recommending "M^r Gentleman, born & Educated a Gentleman . . . now going to try his fortune upon the Edinburgh Stage" (213), failing in which he moved to Glasgow, where Boswell was much in his company. Of Samuel Derrick, Boswell later communicated to Johnson: "I was much obliged to [Garrick] in my days of effervescence in London, when Derrick was my gouvernor"; he "shewed me the town in all its variety of departments, both literary and sportive. . . . Poor Derrick! I remember him with kindness."[43] The third, James Dance, alias Love, was the longest and most intimate mutual friend of Boswell and Garrick. Born in London of an able family, educated at Oxford, Love first acted in Dublin in the 1740s, then long in the Edinburgh company, until in 1762, he joined Garrick at Drury Lane, and later at Covent Garden, where he continued successfully until his death in 1774. While in Edinburgh, Boswell spoke of him as "my second best friend."

But of all of Boswell's acquaintances in Edinburgh and later in London, none was better qualified by experience and knowledge to stabilize Boswell in his pursuit of the drama, to inform him about Garrick's attainments as an actor-manager, to prepare him for his adventures in the London theatre and literary circles, to tell him in his early days about Garrick and Johnson, than Thomas Sheridan, gentleman, scholar, and actor-producer, long and intimately associated as actor and manager with Garrick in Dublin and London. Dissensions and conflicts in the Dublin theatre, of which he was manager, led him to abandon acting and the theatre and to become a teacher of elocution in Edinburgh, Boswell becoming one of his pupils. Boswell later recalled Sheridan's kindness to him in Edinburgh; they were much together in London, and though Sheridan became adversely critical of Garrick's acting, both Boswell and Garrick shared his friendship.

These men not only introduced Boswell to Garrick, by reputation, but prepared him for the London theatres. Later, along with Scotsman David Ross, who after a long career with Garrick in London Garrick recommended to Boswell as manager of the Canongate Theatre in Edinburgh, these actors, writers, and managers, became enduring ties between Boswell and Garrick, their long associations a chapter in Boswell's biography without Johnson. It should be recalled, however, that Boswell's interest in the theatre was in the personalities of actors, and only secondarily in the literature of the drama. Garrick sensed this and made a special point, nevertheless, in encouraging Boswell in writing about and for the theatre in his *Critical Strictures on the New Tragedy of "Elvira,"* written by David Malloch, "Here are half a dozen clever things . . . as I have ever read," and in his several prologues. Boswell in turn was eager for Garrick's commendation of his three essays on the art of acting in the *London Magazine* (1770).[44]

To return now to 1762–63, to Boswell's longer and second visit to London. Shortly after he arrived he saw Garrick and Love at Drury Lane, and by 18 January 1763, he was calling on Garrick in his home, where Garrick treated him with great civility and kindness. The climax of years of anticipation came on 20 January when Garrick invited Boswell to breakfast, and with a twinkle in his eye remarked, "Then the cups shall dance and the saucers skip." "I was quite in raptures with Garrick's kindness," wrote Boswell, "to find him paying me so much respect! . . . I was this day with him what the French call *un etourdi*. I gave free vent to my feelings. Love was by to whom I cried, 'This, Sir, is the real scene.' And taking Mr. Garrick cordially by the hand, 'Thou greatest of men,' said I, 'I cannot express how happy you make me.' This upon my soul, was no flattery. He saw it was not. And the dear great man was truly pleased with it." At breakfast the next morning, presided over by Mrs Garrick, James Love was again present, but Garrick had to attend shortly a rehearsal. "He asked me to come whenever I could. I rejoiced. This is really establishing myself in a charming Place. I shall there see all the men of genius of the age."[45] Boswell, as most of his acquaintances would have been, was rather overwhelmed by Garrick's extraordinary reception. Boswell's fame, even notoriety, all were attained later in life; he had as yet not met Johnson and at the time he was little known outside the London Scottish colony. The key to Garrick's reception of Boswell is to be found in the presence of James Love, who did not drop out of the later friendship but was often with Garrick and Boswell in the ten ensuing years.

The communications between Garrick and Boswell, so promisingly launched in 1762–63, lapsed during the ensuing four years, except for an incident in Strasbourg where Boswell followed Garrick on a grand tour. Garrick in Strasbourg in 1764 had written some verses "On Seeing Strasbourg Cathedral" and the shops built round it. They were communicated to Boswell by Felix-Louis Gayot, who had been entertained both by Garrick and by Boswell, and Boswell wrote some verses in reply, which he sent later to Garrick.[46] Garrick responded 25 November 1767, most cordially: "Had I been happy enough to have Met You in my ramble abroad, I sh[o]uld have had, I speak sincerely, a great addition to my pleasure there: I wanted now and then a Man of fire, to kindle up my fancy, & set my Electrical Matter afloat; I have often been rais'd to rapture at the remains of Antiquity, but the continuance of the fit, can only be supported by social intercourse, &, as our friend Johnson would call it, by an *animated reciprocation of Ideas*" (479). This characteristic Johnsonian phrase, which Garrick may have recalled or approximated, set the mood for the ensuing correspondence. Not until late 1767, nearly five years after the Strasbourg encounter, when Boswell returned to Edinburgh to practice law, to search out a wife, to put in press his *Account of Corsica*, all the while rallying support for Ross in the Royal Theatre, did Boswell seek to renew the acquaintance by soliciting a correspondence with Garrick that was sustained until Garrick's death.[47]

Boswell professed that "in writing to Garrick, I felt particles of vivacity rise by a sort of contagion of fancy." Garrick addressed Boswell as an equal; perhaps Boswell was overly self-conscious in his gratitude for Garrick's kindness. As might be anticipated, the correspondence was much taken up with theatrical matters and actors in Edinburgh and London, informed but not always in agreement. They complimented each other on their respective literary productions, Boswell notably on Garrick's prologues and epilogues, and Garrick on Boswell's *Account of Corsica*, in which "You have paid Me a great Compliment . . . that You should chuse my hurly burly Song of *Hearts of Oak*, to spirit up the Corsicans" (493). The two turned often to the writings of friends, such as Gray, Goldsmith, and Johnson, with occasional references to the Club. As pointed out earlier, Boswell sent Garrick book sale catalogues from Edinburgh and made purchases for him. Later, on an introduction from Boswell, Garrick welcomed Hugo Arnot to consult his collection of early plays, a favor graciously acknowledged by Arnot. Boswell never for long, in all his relations with Englishmen, neglected the good qualities of Scottish life and letters, urging Garrick to visit Scotland and accept for production the plays of Mickle, both rejected by Garrick frankly and in good humor. Boswell was proud of his wig from Garrick's wigmaker. They warmly felicitated each other on their married lives. Both consciously cultivated the epistolary art in elaborations and style. Boswell seldom wrote Garrick without one or more classical allusions or tags in compliment to Garrick's ability to recognize and recall the passage, and Garrick returned the compliment. "Mr. Johnson is ready to bruise any one who calls in question your classical knowledge and your happy application of it."[48] They wrote as equals; they "waited" on each other. Garrick challenged the best that was in Boswell, and Boswell was ever grateful.

Above all else, the exchanges between Garrick and Boswell in their mutual devotion to Johnson are especially welcome; some of the incidents were later incorporated in the *Life*. On 31 March 1772, Boswell recorded in his Journal: "I have a constant plan to write the life of Mr. Johnson. I have not told him of it yet." In May he obtained from Bishop Percy a copy of a bibliography of Johnson's writings that Percy had been compiling. Boswell must have communicated his plan to Garrick, who, thereupon, solicited a copy of the bibiliography, which with Percy's permission, Boswell sent to Garrick, with some queries, on 10 September.[49] Garrick thereupon responded on 17 November: "Your list of Johnson's Works was most agreeable, tho incorrect and incompleat—I will tell you in What when I see You" (717).[50] Garrick was one of the earliest, if not the first along with Percy who assisted

Boswell in assembling the primary material upon which Boswell drew for the *Life*. There is more in the correspondence in admiration and affection for Johnson than on any other subject. Nothing could have been more apposite than that Boswell should write his long famous letter, incorporated in the *Tour of the Hebrides* of 29 August 1773, from Scotland: "In coming to [Forres], in the dusk of the evening we passed over the bleak and blasted heath where Macbeth met the Witches. Your old Preceptor repeated with much solemnity the Speech 'How far is't called to Forres? What are these So wither'd and so wild in their attire? etc.' This day we visited the ruins of Macbeth's Castle at Inverness. . . . I have a rich Journal of his [Johnson's] conversation. Look back, Davy, to Lichfield,—run up through the time that has elapsed since you first knew Mr. Johnson,—and enjoy with me his present extraordinary Tour." Later, on 11 April 1774, Boswell wrote Garrick on their return from the Hebrides to Inverness where "for the first time *after many days* [we] renewed our enjoyment of the luxuries of civilized life, one of the most elegant I could wish to find, was lying for me—a letter from Mr. Garrick. It was a Pine apple of the finest flavour."[51]

In these later days, endowed as we are by the munificent riches of Boswell's wide correspondence and his many journals, we can not only trace, as in the Garrick letters, Boswell's sources for the *Life of Johnson*, but we can pursue Garrick's biography, to whom Boswell devoted more space in the *Life*, second only to Goldsmith, Reynolds (to whom he dedicated it), and the Thrales. In Boswell's journals we catch glimpses of his encounters with Garrick in society, of their hours together, of Garrick as a companion and a host. An early example of the flavor of such comments is that of 8 May 1772: "Garrick called on me ere dressed. He had called before and left [his name as] 'Rantum Scantum.' Entered again: 'Here's Rantum Scantum.' Took me out to walk in St. James's Park: Fifteen guineas to [Francis] Gentleman. Took off Johnson: 'Davy is futile.' Then on Thames, where we talked of language, repeated, 'Hast thou a medicine for a mind diseased,' from *Macbeth*, ending, 'Throw physic,' etc. Great,"[52] Boswell revealed, established his primary thesis or purpose as regards Garrick when he wrote Garrick as early as 10 September 1772, sending Garrick the bibliography of Johnson's writings: "If I survive Mr. Johnson, I shall publish a life of him, for which I have a store of materials. I can with pleasure record many of his expressions to your honour; and I think I can explain with truth, and at the same time with delicacy, the coldness with which he has treated your Publick Merit."[53]

During Boswell's succeeding visits and sojourns in London, he tirelessly pursued his friendship with Garrick, recording their conversations alone and in company in journals, the awareness of which made Garrick at times a bit nervous. Ashamed of his intemperance, Boswell resolved to drink water only, but on one public occasion (10 May 1776), with Paoli and others, Garrick persuaded Boswell to join the company in a glass of wine. Two years later Boswell recalled the incident in the following passage from his Journal, 9 April 1778: "Garrick said to Johnson, 'Here, Sir, is the great Boswell from Scotland, as sublime as ever' (ridiculously). I was a *little* angry. However, down on settee beside them, Johnson and he agreeing that most men worse for drinking. I mentioned to Garrick his being my tempter two years ago. . . . GAR-RICK. 'It gave all the company a better opinion of you that you yielded.' (To Johnson.) 'Sir, there was he drinking water, with his book to take down our conversation. . . . Let it be a law of The Club, either drink or we'll search him, that he mayn't have book. If he won't let wine search him, we will.' Nonsense: as if I had book and wrote in company and could not carry in my *head*.'" [54]

In the pursuit and elaboration of these two subjects and others in the relations of Garrick and Johnson, though he was loyal to both men, Boswell accepted Johnson's dictum in the analysis of personalities: "Every attack produces a defense; and so attention is engaged. There is no sport in mere praise, when people are all of a mind." [55] What may appear to be an obsession with personalities, was actually a literary genre, a "sport," in which the speaker and the theme dominated, controlled the selection of anecdote and interpretation of the biographical content. The focus was a controversial evaluation, no better examples being than Sir Joshua Reynolds's *Portraits* of Goldsmith, Johnson, and Garrick, recently found among Boswell's papers, [56] or Goldsmith's *Retaliation* of antithetic epitaphs as a set "sport" one evening at the Club.

Boswell became remarkably adept at challenging, even irritating Johnson on some controversial issue, to "bring him out" in current parlance, with such gambits as "I have heard it said," or "Garrick's name was introduced." In his later years and posthumously Garrick became a set subject for controversial depreciation or eulogy; actually "he would not have had so much reputation, had he not been so much attacked." [57]

From long association, the enduring attitudes of master and pupil, the license of familiarity, both Johnson and Garrick treated each other with greater freedom than others. Reynolds summed it all up when he wrote "that Johnson considered Garrick to be as it were his *property*. He would allow no man either to blame or to praise Garrick in his presence, without contradicting him."[58] Less than a year before Garrick's death, Boswell remarked to Johnson that Garrick "thinks you do not love him as he loves you. He says you will let nobody else abuse him but you do it yourself. Johnson (smiling), 'Why, that's true.'"[59] The result of this habit is a heightened, often false sense of conflict, even alienation, between Garrick and Johnson. On the other hand Garrick's proclivity, as with all actors, to mimic Johnson for the entertainment of guests, even in Johnson's presence has been misinterpreted as a lampooning of Johnson. The occasions are often recited: Johnson retiring with Mrs Johnson, borrowing a rare and handsome volume of Petrarch from Garrick, squeezing a lemon in a punch bowl and calling out "Who's for *poonsh*?", reciting from Ovid's *Metamorphoses*, "Davy has some convivial pleasantry about him, but 'tis a futile fellow."[60] All such mimicry was more in the spirit of caricature, the heightening of an idiosyncrasy out of affection.

The recurring, even dominant, theme of Johnson's references to Garrick was Johnson's derogation of the actor as against the playwright, in which he did not always distinguish between the actor and the man. He considered acting as affording little more than gaiety and harmless pleasure, yet he praised Garrick's versatility on the stage, the uniformity of his private life, and his advancing the dignity of his profession. Johnson rated his conversational powers at the head of a table, perhaps even greater than his acting, all the while objecting to Garrick's tendency to dominate in the parlor or club as he did on the stage. While on a visit to Lichfield and Peter Garrick with Boswell, Johnson reminisced: "Garrick's conversation . . . is gay and grotesque. It is a dish of all sorts, but all good things. There is no solid meat in it. There is a want of sentiment, not but that he has sentiment sometimes, and sentiment, too, very powerful and very pleasing; but it has not its full proportion in his conversation."[61] He condemned Garrick's vanity on the one hand and often, and on the other hand praised him for his modesty uncorrupted by the applause that resounded in his ears season in and season out in Drury Lane. He emphatically rejected all accusations of parsimony, yet recognized Garrick's early frugality. Finally he regretted rather than deplored that Garrick's great capacity for friendship was dissipated with the many rather than cultivated with the few. Actually Johnson's portraiture of Garrick reveals as much if not more about Johnson than Garrick. Quite simply, Johnson was piqued at his early failure as a playwright; failing eyesight denied him the pleasure of attending the theatre, and in the English tradition he rated the writer above the artist, the actor. In the later years Johnson was more and more isolated and lonely, more than ever dependent on friends who would continue in his company for hours, while Garrick was more and more a man of affairs, of many obligations, sought by many in all walks of life. When Hannah More once enquired of Garrick why Johnson was so often harsh and unkind in his speeches, both of him and to him; "Why," he replied, "it is very natural; is it not to be expected he should be angry, that I, who have had so much less merit than he, should have so much greater success?"[62]

Another who was temperamentally ambivalent in his frequent remarks and his "Portrait" of Garrick, was Sir Joshua Reynolds. He and Garrick must have met at about the same time that Reynolds met Johnson, in the mid-'50s. In the succeeding years Reynolds painted seven portraits of Garrick, which means that they were often together in Reynolds's studio. With Reynolds as president of the Society of Artists and Garrick a supporter, they shared common interests outside the theatre. Finally they were often guests in each other's homes, and in the homes and society of friends. Reynolds was unqualified in his enjoyment and praise of Garrick's acting, and respected his critical evaluations of plays submitted to him. On the other hand, however, Reynolds like Johnson, forced into retirement and loneliness by failing eyesight, sought to spend long hours in the company of only a few friends. Most of all he sought to bring friends together, with no specific subject of conversation in mind, but rather wishing that out of the gathering an animated conversation would spontaneously develop. He objected to the brevity of Garrick's visit, but more to Garrick's anticipating subjects for conversation, and most of all for contriving his exit, as on the stage, of leaving nothing to chance, to the inspiration of the moment.

The culmination, the fulfillment for Garrick and Johnson of their club life over the years with many friends, was the founding by Sir Joshua Reynolds with Johnson's concurrence of a club in the spring of 1764 that met weekly until 1776 at the Turk's Head, Gerard Street, Soho, and was limited at first to nine founding members. Subsequent additions were by unanimous election only. The members originally and later, though often friends of other members, were selected and elected in recognition, not of fame or public office, but professional diversity and conversational and social talents. Any two members could keep each other company. Very shortly after founding, election to the Club was a much sought after honor, especially by Boswell. Johnson generally resisted the expansion of numbers, but by Garrick's death some 30 had been elected.

Garrick was abroad when the Club was founded and for the ensuing

*Folger Shakespeare Library*
David Garrick, Esq.
Portrait by Sir Joshua Reynolds, ca. 1776.

eight years was so heavily committed at Drury Lane that he was not at liberty to attend weekly meetings. Not very long after the institution of the Club, however, Sir Joshua Reynolds spoke of it to Garrick. "'I like it much, (said he,) I think I shall be of you.' When Sir Joshua mentioned this to Dr Johnson, he was much displeased with the actor's conceit. '*He'll be of us*, (said Johnson) how does he know we will *permit* him? The first Duke in England has no right to hold such language.'"[63] With eight of the nine founding members, Garrick had long been acquainted: Reynolds, Johnson, Burke, Beauclerk, Langton, Nugent, Goldsmith, and Hawkins. Of the four elected in 1768, he had close ties with Percy and Colman. Of the five added in 1773, Garrick was the second and Boswell the fifth. Johnson was indeed most cordial to Garrick, supporting his election and warmly welcoming him.[64] Before his death in January 1779 others of his friends were elected, among them George Steevens, who was proposed by Johnson and elected the same evening (24 February 1774) that Edward Gibbon was blackballed; later elected, (823),[65] Joseph Warton (1777), Richard Brinsley Sheridan (1777), George John Spencer, second earl Spencer (1778), John Fitzpatrick, second earl of Upper Ossory (1777). One afternoon (25 August 1773) during their *Tour* to Scotland, Boswell proposed to Johnson: "'If . . . our club should come and set up in St. Andrews, as a college, to teach all that each of us can, in the several departments of learning and taste, we should rebuild the city: we should draw a wonderful concourse of students.' Dr. Johnson entered fully into the spirit of the project. We immediately fell to distributing the offices"—'a set of Professors in every Branch of Literature'—'fifteen in all and each quite distinct: Garrick, the art of publick speaking,'" there being as yet no chairs of drama.[66] The analogy of the Club and a faculty may be only an amusing fantasy, yet dramatizes a measure of the diversified intellectual pursuits and achievements of the members, a tribute to Garrick in the company of his intellectual peers. On Garrick's death, Johnson proposed in mourning and tribute to his memory that no one be elected for a year to succeed Garrick.

Of all of Garrick's diverse and devoted friends, Edmund Burke (1729–97), more than any other, associated with Garrick in the full range of their professional, intellectual, and social lives, in family, mutual acquaintances, and as close friends. They associated both as individuals and as members of closely integrated groups or circles of able and prominent public and historical figures. So direct and intimate were their associations and communications that their correspondence was slight and occasional, Burke in particular being inclined to destroy, certainly not preserve, letters in a private correspondence.

For 20 years and more of their close friendship, both were resident in London; hence much must be interpolated from the biographical records of their contemporaries.

As a resident in Dublin and a student in Trinity College, 1743–48, Burke attended the Smock Alley theatre, perhaps first seeing Garrick there in the summer of 1742. At first Burke joined the scholars of Trinity College in supporting and defending Sheridan in the Kelly riots, but after 1747, when Sheridan had rejected a play he submitted, he became critical of the Dublin manager in a personal journal he published entitled *The Reformer*.[67] Once Burke had settled in London, studying law in the Middle Temple, he "often attended the theatre, and acknowledged that he derived very great benefit in the art of speaking from Mr. Garrick."[68]

The exact date when Burke first met Garrick off stage has not been established—perhaps as early as 1752 through Arthur Murphy, who may have drawn Burke into the circle of actors gathering at the Grecian Coffee House off the Strand, or perhaps through Dodsley, whose shop and bookselling Garrick knew much about.[69] Certainly their acquaintance was not recent when Garrick invited Johnson, Murphy, and Burke to his home for Christmas dinner in 1758, and again in 1760. Friendship was solid enough in 1759 for Garrick to consult Burke about which of two drafts of a letter he might best reply to an attack by Dr John Hill (226). The two had in common memories of Dublin and Smock Alley, a devotion to literature and the drama, a long though unsettled friendship with Thomas Sheridan, and acquaintance with many actors in London. Off and on in the Burke household was his brother Richard and kinsman William, with whom over the years Garrick associated, corresponded, and supported in their political and financial ventures.[70] He was close enough to Richard to be able to assert once and for all to Sir Grey Cooper that Richard was not the author of the *Junius Letters*.[71] Burke was a regular member of the circle including Mrs Montagu, Reynolds, and Johnson, who were socially guests of one another during Garrick's last ten years.[72]

Burke the potential literary man became Burke the busy politician when he went with Hamilton, secretary to the Earl of Halifax, to Ireland (1761–63). Hamilton wrote Garrick about Burke, 6 December 1761: "Burke will bear ample testimony how much we talk of you, and you yourself will judge how often you are present to my memory, when I assure you I never laugh in anybody's face, without wishing for you . . . I have strong expectations that it will soon be in my power to serve him [Burke] and I hope I shall be able to make one of the worthiest men in the world one of the happiest" with a pension of

£300 a year on the Irish establishment.[73] In 1765 Burke broke sharply with Hamilton, and was appointed private secretary to Charles Watson-Wentworth, second marquis of Rockingham, first lord of the treasury, whom Garrick knew through his friendship with Lord Hartington (333,88,128–30,365 nn.). Garrick wrote congratulating him, and Burke replied: "You have made me perfectly happy by the friendly and obliging satisfaction you are so good to express on this little gleam of prosperity. . . . When will you call to see your Mecenas atavis and praise this administration of Cavendishes and Rockinghams in Ode, and abuse your enemies in Epigram?"[74] Garrick immediately responded: "My dear Burke. You have no friend who rejoices more at Your happiness than I do. . . . Enjoy the Gleam, as you so modestly call it, that now falls upon your fortune & don't let y$^e$ least cloud pass over it, by any disagreeable reflections—I will insure You, my good friend, that this gleam of Yours will very quickly become a fixed Sunshine—Your Merit cannot vary, tho administration may: when once you are known, by the first People, they will for their own Sakes offer their Sunshine, & you must take care that it is not Moonshine, for there are great ones among 'em has dealt in both" (365).

Burke in turn responded with a series of invitations for Garrick and Mrs Garrick to dine. The turn of the tide for Burke came 26 December 1765, when he obtained his first seat in Parliament. The next month he made his maiden speech in Westminster Hall; Garrick was present and wrote how successful the speech had been and how much he was pleased (385).[75] After 1766, when Burke had to be in attendance at Parliament during hours when plays were performed, he had less leisure for the theatre, but made a special point of attending Garrick's final appearances in the spring of 1776.[76] Burke submitted a play of his own and plays of friends, which Garrick duly read and with customary candor rejected (433,470,709,859).[77] In 1770 Garrick was able to clear Richard Cumberland of a false imputation in the eyes of Burke, doubtless about a low opinion of the Irish shown in some of his plays.[78]

In April 1768 Burke purchased an estate of 600 acres in Buckinghamshire, near Beaconsfield, with a handsome house called Gregories, but only with financial assistance from William Burke and friends—an indebtedness from which he was never free. A year later he sought and obtained from Garrick a loan of £1,000, never repaid, and the interest later being in arrears.[79]

Once established, however, somewhat in the style of his parliamentary and political associates on 13 June 1768, Burke and his brother Richard wrote: "My dear David, We have now got a little settled in our new Habitation. When will you and Mrs Garrick come and make it complete to us by your Company for a day or two? you have promised us. . . . You shall have fowls from our own Poultry Yard, and such Beef and Mutton as our next market Town yields; and to make it complete, we will assure you it is our own feeding; and then you will find it very good."[80] Garrick responded postponing the visits until after a previous engagement to visit Rigby (511)[81]; Burke accepted the excuse, remarking, "You first sate yourself with Wit, jollity, and Luxury; and afterwards retire hither to repose your person and understanding on early hours, boild Mutton, drowsy conversation, and a little Clabber Milk."[82]

Garrick returned from Rigby's "tormented with a fever in my head . . . ever since I left his honour's Claret at Mistley" (513), and had to postpone the visit because of earlier engagements to visit Lord Delaware, Lord and Lady Camden, and a command performance for the King of Denmark, until the first week in August (514).[83] In the vein and manner of the Rigby-Garrick hospitality and wit, Burke perhaps both chided and flattered Garrick in a letter of 1769. "Dear Garrick, I send you a Rose sera, a *late* Turtle [Horace, *Odes*, I, xxxviii, 3–4] an entertainment at least as good for the palate, as the other for the nose. Your true Epicureans are of the opinion, you Know, that it contains in itself all Kinds of flesh, fish and fowl. It is therefore a dish fit for one who represents all the solidity of flesh, the volatility of fowl, and the oddity of fish. As this entertainment can be found no longer any where but at your Table, let the Type and shadow of the Master grace his board. A little *pepper* he can add himself. The *wine* likewise he will supply—I do not know whether he still retains any friend who can finish the dressing of his Turtle by a gentle squeeze of the Lemon. Our best regards to Madam, Ever Dear Garrick Most faithfully your obedient Servant Edm. Burke."[84]

Although Burke because of his demanding political commitments was unable to attend Garrick's Stratford Jubilee, September 1769, he followed the progress and near disaster of that project that distressed even harrowed Garrick more than any other in his later years, and certainly no one was more thoughtful or a greater comfort to Garrick than Burke, who failing to meet Garrick in London, wrote him 18 September a most gracious and thoughtful letter of consolation, "Enjoy your applause and your abuse together."[85]

In the final ten years of Garrick's life, season in and season out, the two men were in each other's company in the city, in the homes of friends, at Hampton and Gregories, occasioning no correspondence except the semiofficial solicitations of patronage. On 3 May 1771, Garrick wrote Burke soliciting his support in the appointment of Theodore Aylward as a professor of music at Gresham College (631). Later in 1776, Garrick wrote Burke desiring, "Your Concurrence" in the passing of an act of Parliament *for Securing the Money we have got towards a fund for the relief of decay'd Actors"* (981).

Finally as regards patronage, in March-April 1777, at Garrick's solicitation Burke initially supported in Parliament Richard Yates's project for a licensed playhouse in Birmingham, but later under pressure from his constituents he felt obliged to vote against the petition. In response to Burke's letter of explanation and regrets of 29 April, Garrick wrote: "Ten thousand thanks my dear Burke for Your very kind Letter—God forbid that all y$^e$ Patents in the World should injure Your Interest, where you are so much in Duty & kindness ⟨bound⟩" (1096, 1087).[86]

Though not substantiated in the *Journal of the House of Commons*, a final episode in Burke's devotion to Garrick has the authority of both Garrick's letter to Hannah More (1184) and that of Thomas Davies. In May 1778 the debating in Parliament became so sharp that Charles Baldwyn (Baldwin), the Shropshire member "happened to observe that Mr. Garrick was sitting in the gallery, and immediately moved to clear the House." "Mr. Burk rose, and appealed to the honourable Assembly, whether it could possibly be consistent with the rules of decency and liberality, to exclude from the hearing of their debates, a man to whom they were all obliged; one who was the great master of eloquence; in those school they had all imbibed the art of speaking, and be taught the elements of rhetoric. For his part, he owned that he had been greatly indebted to his instructions. Much more he said in commendation of Mr. Garrick, and was warmly seconded by Mr. Fox and Mr. T. Townshend, who very copiously displayed the great merit of their old preceptor, as they termed him; they reprobated the motion of the gentleman with great warmth and indignation. The House almost unanimously concurred in exempting Mr. Garrick from the general order of quitting the gallery."[87] Garrick responded more in vanity than good taste in some verses, which he read, for their approval, to Lords North, Gower, Weymouth, and Mr. Rigby, asserting his "Peculiar joy I felt that day in the oratory of Fox, Burke, Barre, North, Rigby, and Thurloe." "For most of these I call my friends" (1184).[88]

Other than social hours together at Hampton, in London, or at the Gregories and in the homes of mutual friends, both Burke and Garrick were prevented by their necessary presence at Drury Lane and Parliament, from attending frequently the Club. Outside gatherings of the

Club, Burke and Garrick were often together in the company of other members, as for example not long before Garrick's death, a gathering at Hampton, recalled by Reynolds, included besides Reynolds and Burke, also Fox, Gibbon, Sheridan, and Beauclerk. Burke was selected as one of the four representatives of the Club at Garrick's funeral, for which he returned from a very pressing engagement in the country.

Happy in his friendships to the end, Garrick died on 20 January 1779. At his elaborate funeral some mourned, many observers were grave, some were appalled, some laughed wryly, but hundreds watched. Horace Walpole was disgusted at the elaborateness. Boswell and Burke wept, along with Dr Schomberg, Hannah More, Frances Cadogan, and many other close friends. A public figure of wide-ranging prominence had passed away, but the impact of the professional man and the engaging private companion lingered.

About the solemn ceremony which took place on 1 February 1779, biographers have written much. It was contrived and supervised by Richard Brinsley Sheridan. "The body was most magnificently interred in Westminster Abbey under the monument of his beloved Shake-speare. He was attended to the grave by persons of the first rank; by men of illustrious genius, and the famous for science; by those who loved him living, and lamented his death. Twenty-four of the principal actors of both theatres were also attendants at the funeral; and with unfeigned sorrow regretted the loss of so great an ornament to their profession, and so manifest a benefactor to their charitable institution."[89] Sheridan, chief mourner, now primary master of Drury Lane theatre, knew that audiences who had seen Garrick act would wish to watch, and stand in silence as the funeral cortege passed from the Adelphi to the Abbey. He inserted in the *Morning Post*, 29 January, a listing of the carriages and their order in the procession. Nearly 50 coaches (with Garrick's family carriage empty) accompanied by pages, and horsemen in black followed the hearse which bore the casket covered with crimson velvet and silver nails. The bells tolled that afternoon. The procession leaving the Adelphi about one o'clock was several hours in its passage and in the alighting of dignitaries at the Abbey. The service was read by the Bishop of Rochester, and the music was Purcell's grand funeral service, accompanied by the choir and the organ. Garrick was buried in the Poets' Corner.

Later the statue erected in his memory by his executor Albany Wallis, which stands there still, carried on its base lines written by Samuel Jackson Pratt, which voiced for Garrick's generation appreciation of years of enjoyment which the actor had provided in breathing life anew into Shakespeare's unforgettable characters, and prophesied that "Shakespeare and Garrick like twin stars shall shine / And Earth irradiate with a beam divine."

Verse tributes to Garrick appeared in the press for the ensuing three months. The one which impressed most and lasted longest was the *Monody to the Memory of Mr. Garrick*, by Sheridan. It was set to music by Thomas Linley, and spoken by Mrs Yates at Drury Lane theatre on the night of 11 March 1779, with vocal and instrumental accompaniment. A new scene had been designed by de Loutherbourg for the occasion, and the performers were dressed in black. The theme dealt with the ephemeral art of acting, "The actor Only shrinks from Time's award / Feeble tradition is his mem'ry's guard," and memorialized Garrick's grace of action, expressive glance, use of gesture, his fine use of silences, his harmonious speech, his passion and tenderness as his roles required, and paid tribute to his "Naturalness." *The Monody* was called for and continued to be given until 1783, for audiences remembered the actor, and the descriptions of his talents were meaningful to them.

Although the American Revolutionary War was still in progress, *The Independent Chronicle* of Boston on 23 December 1779, printed Sheridan's *Monody* in three columns on its front page. Philomusis, who sent it to the editor, remarked: "It is perhaps the first copy of that performance that has arrived in the United States. . . . We Americans have no quarrel with the Arts and Sciences. We cherish them. We only lament that a nation in which they have so long flourished, a nation from whose eyes Garrick has so often drawn floods of tears . . . should have carried on a war against America in so relentless and so barbarous a manner."

Garrick in death knew nothing of the elaborate ceremonies: he knew, however, in June of 1776 the triumph of life, his life and his chosen career—when he retired from the stage amid the plaudits and tears of friends and anonymous spectators from all classes, when crowds overflowed the capacity of his Drury Lane as he played the aged Lear, and when the actresses playing Regan and Goneril did so (sensing their loss) with streaming eyes and heaving bosoms. And he knew it when similar crowds witnessed his departure forever after playing Don Felix in Mrs Centlivre's comedy of *The Wonder*, after which he had spoken his farewell address to the public choked up emotionally, but relieved. In the public image lived a vivacious but considerate man who enjoyed life in its broadest spectrum and who relished his selected friends with deep pleasure.

Shortly before his death Garrick told Boswell, "It has been my way always amongst friends to *heal*." [90] Five years later, almost to the day (20 April 1781), Boswell epitomized the intrinsic nature of Garrick's private life surviving in the memory of friends, in one incident, the particulars more revealing than any eloquent generalizations, more meaningful with each repetition: "Mrs Garrick . . . had this day, for the first time since his death, a select party of his friends to dine with her. The company was Miss Hannah More . . . Mrs Boscawen, Mrs Elizabeth Carter, Sir Joshua Reynolds, Dr. Burney, Dr. Johnson, and myself. We found ourselves very elegantly entertained at her house in the Adelphi, where I have passed many a pleasing hour with him 'who gladdened life.'" . . . [Garrick's portrait hung over the chimney piece.] The very semblance of David Garrick was cheering. Mr. Beau-clerk, with happy propriety, inscribed under the fine portrait of him . . . the following passage from his beloved Shakespeare:

> — — A merrier man
> Within the limit of becoming merth,
> I never spent an hour's talk withal.
> His eye begets occasion for his wit;
> For every object that the one doth catch,
> The other turns to a mirth-moving jest;
> Which his fair tongue (Conceit's expositor)
> Delivers in such apt and gracious words,
> That aged ears play truant at his tales,
> And younger hearings are quite ravished;
> So sweet and voluble is his discourse
> (*Loves Labours Lost*, ii, i).

"We were all in fine spirits; and I whispered to Mrs Boscawen, 'I believe this is as much as can be made of life.' [Later in the evening after a dinner party with other friends . . . Johnson] and I walked away together; we stopped a little while by the rails of the Adelphi, looking on the Thames, and I said to him with some emotion that I was now thinking of two friends we had lost, who once lived in the buildings behind us, Beauclerk and Garrick. 'Ay, Sir, (said he, tenderly) and two such friends as cannot be supplied.'" [91]

Albany Wallis invited Burke to draw up an epitaph and to work jointly with William Windham, son of Garrick's great and early friend. When in 1797 the epitaph proved to be too long for the space on the monument, Burke defended its length saying that an epitaph on Garrick "ought to account why it is fit that an actor should have a place in so solemn a temple, among legislators, heroes, saints, and the ornaments of science, erudition and genius." [92] Of all Garrick's gifted

Garrick's Farewell Appearance, 1776.
Painting by Robert Edge Pine.

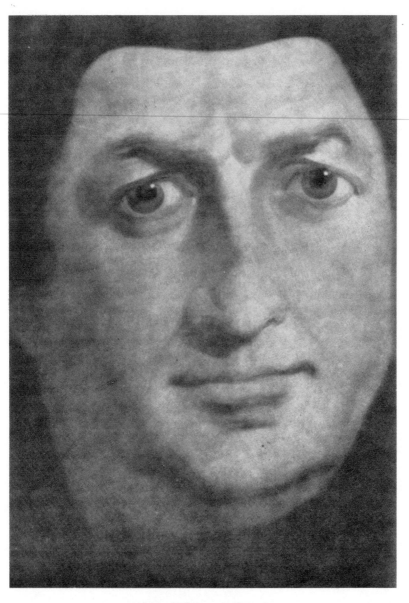

*Harvard Theatre Collection*
Garrick's Death Mask(?), eyes inserted
from an engraving of the Pine portrait.

friends none was better qualified by long intimacy, insight, gratitude, and superior cultural values, to enunciate for the century, and for all subsequent ones, in his epitaph, the eulogy of Garrick in his professional and in his private life.

> To the Memory of David Garrick
>
> Whose remains lie interred near the monument of Shakespeare and close to the body of Samuel Johnson . . . .
>
> Under him the English dramatic representation took a new form; he brought it nearer to the standard of nature, and to the expression of real passion.
>
> Shakespeare was the chosen object of his study: in his action, and in his declamation he expressed all the fire, the enthusiasm, the energy, the facility, the endless variety of that great poet. Like him he was equally happy in the tragic and the comic style.
>
> He entered into the true spirit of the poets, because he was himself a poet, and wrote many pieces with elegance and spirit.
>
> He raised the character of his profession to the rank of a liberal art, not only by his talents, but by the regularity and probity of his life and the elegance of his manners.
>
> His friendships were sincere, his manners were amiable. He excelled in all relations of domestic and social life. His conversation was gay, cheerful, and ingenious. His wit was without levity, affection, or malice, and as inoffensive as it was pointed. His society was therefore courted and cultivated by all those who were the most distinguished by their taste and erudition.
>
> His memory will be long honoured by all who are sensible how much a solid, refined, and moral taste, in its public pleasures, contributes to the improvement and glory of a great nation.[93]

To come to know Garrick, critically and imaginatively, through the multitude of extant primary records, affords an opportunity to observe the versatility and creativeness of an artist of transcendent ability, a very complex personality—now tentative, now confident, now cautious, now daring, always animated and engaging in the company of others, a man of laughter and a genuine sense of humor, occasionally reflective even brooding, as manifest in his manuscript notes and drafts of his correspondence, remarkably creative on the stage having always a professional command of his art, a writer of more depth than has usually been conceded, a manager concerned about the welfare of his company, from doorkeeper, to prompter, scene painter, prima ballerina, and the leading actors. He was a cultivated, intelligent, civilized person, interested in economics, politics, religion, science, the art of the past and present, and in England's cultural heritage, in gossip and the transient pleasures of daily life, the travels of Englishmen abroad, and the lives of men and women, his good friends at home.

Quietly and unobtrusively he forwarded scholarship in the drama by lending to scholars of his acquaintance books out of his extensive private library. Later generations are in his debt for his Collection of Early English Drama, which he bequeathed to the British Museum. His personal charm and his professional abilities gave the theatre the stability and qualities that vitalized it; he projected dozens of reforms that enhanced it; he trained a generation of actors and managers who founded and supported flourishing provincial theatres throughout Great Britain. He brought fresh ideas to the stage, and his creativeness and personality dominated the English theatre for a third of a century.

He learned from others and saw the present and future implications of new ideas for his profession: stage lighting, ensemble acting, a stage cleared of spectators, the potentials in dancing, in musical productions. He preserved the excellence of the past drama and helped create the range and excellence of contemporary plays. In costuming and scenic design he made significant advances. In the financing and organization of a theatre, none could equal him. He early instituted collective bargaining and was sympathetic for the destitute in the profession, and to remedy or supplement irregular pensions he established the Fund for Decayed Actors, supported by an annual benefit performance by Garrick, and by the actors with a small percentage of their salaries.

He was a realist and a pragmatist, yet was creative and imaginative. It is difficult to separate his personal values from his professional accomplishments. He loved children and entertained them with mimicry at his Hampton estate and at their homes. He relished being lionized, and repaid all such compliments given him in Paris and Rome by acting out scenes in the drawing rooms of his hosts. He sometimes seemed abrasive, and indecisive to some among the many people he dealt with, but even those who at times were antagonistic—articulate persons such as Thomas Davies and Arthur Murphy—sought to be his first biographers and to pay tribute to the man they knew best and honored most. Garrick was constantly in the fray, yet always capable of rising above the animosities of smaller men and women, determined as he was to demand (but graciously) excellence in the performance of every task. It would have been a pleasure to have known him in life, as it is a privilege to know him through his works, in his legacies to us and to the future.

# Appendixes
# References and Notes
# Index

.

# Appendix A

## DAVID GARRICK'S ANCESTRY AND
## PERTINENT FAMILY RELATIONSHIPS

AS THE ACCOMPANYING chart indicates David Garrick, descended from the Hugenot grandfather David Garric, a refugee from French persecution after the revocation of the Edict of Nantes, was born into a family that continued to proliferate. Childless himself he kept up with his relatives—aunts, uncles, brothers, sisters, nephews, nieces, and cousins—and enjoyed doing so. The sturdy French stock from the Bordeaux area settled in London and Lichfield and prospered as citizens of repute, marrying into the English families of the Bailyes, Cloughs, Carringtons, Battiscombes, Schaws, Harts, Egertons, Paynes, Dockseys, and Grays. David alone of his generation married outside the English gentry, taking the lovely Eva Maria Veigel (the accomplished Viennese dancer and protégée of Lady Burlington) to be his bride. Of his brothers and sisters, Peter, Magdalene, and Jane never married. William, who went into the navy seems early to have dropped out of the family correspondence. Merrial married and had a daughter. George married twice and proved to be as prolific as his father, Peter, and his grandfather, David the Hugenot, had been, siring eight children.

DAVID GARRICK'S ANCESTRY AN

I

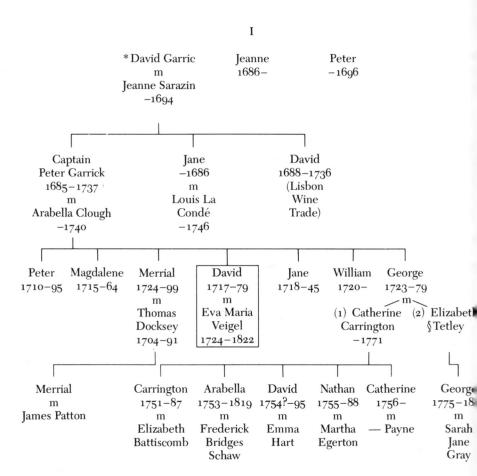

\* David also had 2 sons, one named Stephen (1687–90) and one named John (1693), both of whom died in infancy.

† Mary Magdalene and Peter? Fermignac had a son David (1722) and a daughter Marie (1723), both of whom died in infancy.

ERTINENT FAMILY RELATIONSHIPS

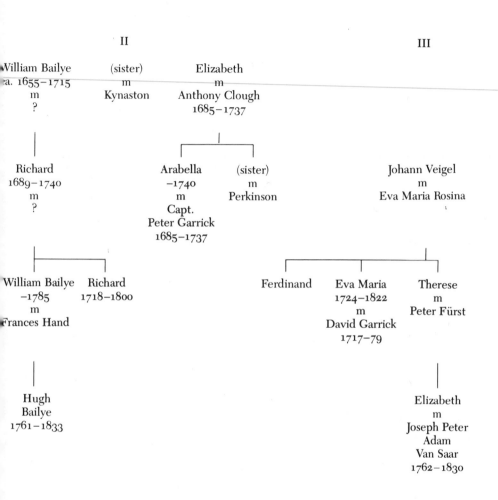

II                                                    III

William Bailye       (sister)        Elizabeth
a. 1655–1715            m                m
     m               Kynaston      Anthony Clough
     ?                                1685–1737

Richard                          Arabella      (sister)              Johann Veigel
1689–1740                         –1740           m                         m
     m                              m          Perkinson         Eva Maria Rosina
     ?                            Capt.
                              Peter Garrick
                               1685–1737

William Bailye   Richard                      Ferdinand   Eva Maria      Therese
   –1785       1718–1800                                  1724–1822         m
     m                                                        m        Peter Fürst
Frances Hand                                             David Garrick
                                                            1717–79

   Hugh                                                                  Elizabeth
   Bailye                                                                    m
 1761–1833                                                            Joseph Peter
                                                                          Adam
                                                                        Van Saar
                                                                       1762–1830

‡ William Bailye and Frances Hand had a son Richard (1762), who died in infancy.
§ George Garrick and Elizabeth Tetley (actress) also had 2 daughters, Sarah (1776) and
Elizabeth (1777), who died in infancy.

# Appendix B

·

| | | | |
|---|---|---|---|
| Benedict | *Much Ado About Nothing* (as a walk-on in the pageant procession in his *Jubilee*) | E | 153 |
| Ranger | *The Suspicious Husband* | C | 121 |
| Benedict | *Much Ado about Nothing* | C | 113 |
| Sir John Brute | *The Provoked Wife* | C | 105 |
| Archer | *The Beaux Stratagem* | C | 100 |
| Bayes | *The Rehearsal* | C | 91 |
| Hamlet | *Hamlet* | T | 90 |
| Lear | *King Lear* | T | 85 |
| Richard III | *King Richard III* | T | 83 |
| Lothario | *The Fair Penitent* | T | 82 |
| Kitely | *Every Man in His Humour* | C | 81 |
| Abel Drugger | *The Alchemist* | C | 80 |
| Don Felix | *The Wonder* | C | 70 |
| Chamont | *The Orphan* | T | 66 |
| Hastings | *Jane Shore* | T | 60 |
| Romeo | *Romeo and Juliet* | T | 60 |
| Fribble | *Miss in Her Teens* | F | 59 |
| Lusignan | *Zara* | T | 54 |
| Sharp | *The Lying Valet* | F | 39 |
| Leon | *Rule a Wife and Have a Wife* | C | 38 |
| Macbeth | *Macbeth* | T | 37 |
| Oakly | *The Jealous Wife* | C | 35 |
| Lord Chalkstone | *Lethe* | F | 35 |
| Don John | *The Chances* | C | 31 |

| | | | |
|---|---|---|---|
| Heartly | *The Guardian* | F | 25 |
| Dorilas | *Merope* | T | 25 |
| Osmyn | *The Mourning Bride* | T | 24 |
| Posthumus | *Cymbeline* | C | 23 |
| Branville | *The Discovery* | C | 23 |
| Leontes | *The Winter's Tale* | C | 23 |
| Biron | *The Fatal Marriage* | T | 23 |
| Jaffier | *Venice Preserved* | T | 20 |
| Tancred | *Tancred and Sigismunda* | T | 20 |
| Jack Smatter | *Pamela* | C | 19 |
| Horatius | *The Roman Father* | T | 19 |
| Young Belmont | *The Foundling* | C | 19 |
| Achmet | *Barbarossa* | T | 18 |
| Fondlewife | *The Old Batchelor* | C | 17 |
| Lovemore | *The Way to Keep Him* | C | 17 |
| Townly | *The Provoked Husband* | C | 16 |
| King Henry IV | *King Henry IV, Part 2* | H | 15 |
| Dorilant | *The School for Lovers* | C | 14 |
| Marplot | *The Busy Body* | C | 14 |
| Lysander | *Agis* | T | 13 |
| Don Carlos | *The Mistake* | C | 13 |
| Alonzo | *Elvira* | T | 13 |
| Capt Plume | *The Recruiting Officer* | C | 13 |
| Aletes | *Creusa* | T | 12 |
| Scrub | *The Beaux Stratagem* | C | 12 |
| Beverly | *The Gamesters* | T | 12 |
| Clodio | *Love Makes a Man* | C | 12 |
| Faulkenbridge | *King John* | H | 12 |
| Pamphlet | *The Upholsterer* | F | 11 |
| Pierre | *Venice Preserved* | T | 11 |
| Virginius | *Virginia* | T | 11 |
| Zamti | *The Orphan of China* | T | 11 |
| Frenchman | *Lethe* | F | 10 |
| Aemilius | *The Siege of Aquilea* | T | 9 |
| Demetrius | *Irene* | T | 9 |
| Dumnorix | *Boadicea* | T | 9 |
| Farmer | *The Farmer's Return from London* | I | 9 |
| Athelstan | *Athelstan* | T | 9 |
| Iago | *Othello* | T | 9 |
| Edward | *Edward the Black Prince* | T | 9 |
| King John | *King John* | H | 9 |
| Gil Blas | *Gil Blas* | C | 9 |

| | | | |
|---|---|---|---|
| Alfred | *Alfred, a Masque* | M | 9 |
| Demetrius | *The Brothers* | T | 8 |
| Oronooko | *Oronooko* | T | 8 |
| Duretete | *The Inconstant* | C | 7 |
| Ode | On Dedicating a Building to Shakespeare | | 7 |
| Wilding | *The Gamesters* | C | 7 |
| Loveless | *Love's Last Shift* | C | 6 |
| Antony | *Antony and Cleopatra* | T | 6 |
| Hotspur | *King Henry IV, Part 1* | H | 6 |
| Mercour | *Eugenia* | T | 6 |
| Millamour | *The Wedding Day* | C | 6 |
| Regulus | *Regulus* | T | 6 |
| Chorus | *King Henry V* | P | 5 |
| Schoolboy | *The Schoolboy* | F | 5 |
| Poet | *Lethe* | F | 5 |
| Drunken Man | *Lethe* | F | 5 |
| Periander | *Eurydice* | T | 4 |
| Witwou'd | *The Way of the World* | C | 4 |
| Wildair | *The Constant Couple* | C | 4 |
| Zaphna | *Mahomet the Imposter* | T | 4 |
| Lord Foppington | *The Careless Husband* | C | 3 |
| Ghost | *Hamlet* | T | 3 |
| Mercutio | *Romeo and Juliet* | T | 3 |
| Othello | *Othello* | T | 3 |
| Fine Gentleman | *Lethe* | F | 3 |
| Aboan | *Oronooko* | T | 2 |
| Sciolto | *The Fair Penitent* | T | 2 |
| Capt. Brazen | *The Recruiting Officer* | C | 1 |
| Sir Harry Gubbins | *The Tender Husband* | C | 1 |
| Coster Pearmain | *The Recruiting Officer* | C | 1 |
| Orestes | *Orestes* | T | 1 |

# Appendix C

.

| | |
|---|---|
| 1741 | 169 |
| 1742 | 98 |
| 1743 | 71 |
| 1744 | 73 |
| 1745 | (In Smock Alley, Dublin) |
| 1746 | 86 |
| 1747 | 106 |
| 1748 | 116 |
| 1749 | 83 |
| 1750 | 103 |
| 1751 | 96 |
| 1752 | 94 |
| 1753 | 95 |
| 1754 | 83 |
| 1755 | 101 |
| 1756 | 73 |
| 1757 | 111 |
| 1758 | 95 |
| 1759 | 90 |
| 1760 | 91 |
| 1761 | 109 |
| 1762 | 111 |
| 1763–64 | (On grand tour in France and Italy) |
| 1765 | 10 |
| 1766 | 21 |
| 1767 | 30 |

| | |
|---|---|
| 1768 | 25 |
| 1769 | 30 (plus 90 walk-ons in *The Jubilee*, as Benedict) |
| 1770 | 14 (plus 20 walk-ons in *The Jubilee*, as Benedict) |
| 1771 | 30 |
| 1772 | 29 |
| 1773 | 35 |
| 1774 | 22 |
| 1775 | 50 (plus 43 walk-ons in *The Jubilee*, as Benedict) |

As the figures indicate (taken from the pages of *The London Stage*), the actor performed in regular season activity about 2,500 times. A count for the Dublin summer season of 1742 would add another 30. Before he took his grand tour (1763–65) he averaged 94+ appearances *each* season despite several rather long and severe illnesses. The theatres then averaged about 175 nights each season of operation. After his return from France (1765) and until he retired from the stage (1776) he averaged about 27 performances annually, plus some walk-ons in the procession of Shakespeare's plays featured in *The Jubilee*, during which time his theatre averaged 190 nights of operation each year. Garrick's performances during his last 11 years, therefore, became rather special occasions.

During his long span of 33 years on stage he undertook 96 different roles in tragedy, comedy, farce, and processional, gracefully moving from one type to another. On many occasions he played a double bill of tragedy in the main piece and comedy in the petite farce with which the night's offering closed. He rehearsed carefully for all of his 2,530 performances. The energy he devoted to his profession was simply amazing.

# Appendix D

GARRICK'S TOTAL COMPANY STRENGTH IN PERFORMERS
1747–1776
(FIGURES IN PARENTHESES SIGNIFY NEW PERFORMERS
WHOM HE INTERVIEWED AND ENGAGED.)

| Season | Basic company | New acting personnel | Actors | | Actresses | | Dancers | | Singers | | Specialty Musicians |
|---|---|---|---|---|---|---|---|---|---|---|---|
| 1747–48 | 68 | | 31 | | 21 | | 14 | | 2 | | |
| 1748–49 | 81 | (36) | 33 | (12) | 20 | (12) | 25 | (9) | 3 | (3) | |
| 1749–50 | 83 | (27) | 31 | (3) | 18 | (2) | 30 | (19) | 4 | (3) | |
| 1750–51 | 82 | (20) | 33 | (9) | 18 | (4) | 24 | (4) | 7 | (3) | |
| 1751–52 | 74 | (15) | 34 | (9) | 14 | (1) | 21 | (3) | 5 | (2) | |
| 1752–53 | 87 | | 38 | (10) | 19 | (7) | 24 | (8) | 6 | (3) | |
| 1753–54 | 88 | (19) | 38 | (4) | 22 | (6) | 22 | (6) | 3 | | (3) |
| 1754–55 | 75 | (12) | 33 | (5) | 19 | (1) | 18 | (3) | 6 | (3) | 1 |
| 1755–56 | 104 | (43) | 45 | (10) | (19) | (5) | 35 | (24) | 1 | | (4) |
| 1756–57 | 95 | (20) | 43 | (5) | 28 | (6) | 14 | (1) | 5 | (3) | (5) |
| 1757–58 | 79 | (13) | 38 | (3) | 25 | (1) | 15 | (5) | | (1) | (3) |
| 1758–59 | 78 | (14) | 36 | (8) | 23 | (3) | 16 | (3) | 3 | | |
| 1759–60 | 81 | (13) | 38 | (5) | 23 | (4) | 16 | (3) | 4 | (1) | |
| 1760–61 | 86 | (23) | 38 | (8) | 24 | (7) | 20 | (5) | 4 | (3) | |
| 1761–62 | 94 | (20) | 38 | (5) | 26 | (4) | 20 | (6) | 7 | (3) | 3 (2) |
| 1762–63 | 91 | (23) | 36 | (6) | 25 | (6) | 24 | (10) | 4 | (1) | 2 |
| 1765–66 | 73 | (13) | 36 | (8) | 22 | (4) | 11 | (1) | 4 | | |
| 1766–67 | 81 | (14) | 36 | (2) | 24 | (3) | 18 | (8) | 2 | | (1) |
| 1767–68 | 86 | (19) | 41 | (9) | 26 | (5) | 15 | (4) | 4 | (1) | |
| 1768–69 | 94 | (20) | 43 | (4) | 25 | (5) | 18 | (7) | 8 | (4) | |
| 1769–70 | 97 | (18) | 46 | (6) | 24 | (4) | 18 | (9) | 7 | (2) | (2) |
| 1770–71 | 91 | (8) | 47 | (3) | 25 | (4) | 14 | (1) | 5 | | |
| 1771–72 | 101 | (21) | 45 | (3) | 27 | (6) | 16 | (4) | 9 | (5) | 4 (3) |
| 1772–73 | 103 | (21) | 51 | (6) | 28 | (7) | 17 | (5) | 5 | (1) | (2) |
| 1773–74 | 98 | (13) | 46 | (3) | 25 | (3) | 18 | (4) | 5 | (1) | 4 (2) |
| 1774–75 | 93 | (21) | 42 | (7) | 28 | (5) | 13 | (4) | 6 | (2) | 4 (3) |
| 1775–76 | 97 | (22) | 45 | (8) | 25 | (5) | 14 | (4) | 9 | (3) | 4 (2) |
| | 2,360 | (517) | | | | | | | | | |

The average complement of the performing company during this period was 86. Garrick, or Garrick and Lacy, or Garrick and Lacy and George Garrick seem to have interviewed over the years some 517 performers whom they accepted. He and/or they had twice as many applicants in addition whom they turned down, or recommended some years of seasoning in the provinces. This aspect of managerial obligation has heretofore been underplayed by Garrick biographers. The activity required application, shrewdness, diplomacy, and tact.

# Appendix E

(AP, after piece; B, burletta; BO, ballad opera; C, comedy; E, entertainment; F, farce; I, interlude; M, masque; MP, main piece; Mus, Musical; O, opera; P, pantomime; Pas, pastoral; T, tragedy)

| | Drury Lane | Covent Garden |
|---|---|---|
| 1747–48 | *The Foundling*, E. Moore, C, MP | *The Perplexed Husband*, anon., P, AP |
| | *George Dandin*, from Molière, F, AP | |
| | *The Club of Fortune Hunters*, Macklin, F, AP | |
| | *A Will and no Will*, Macklin, F, AP | |
| 1748–49 | *Irene*, Johnson, T, MP | *Coriolanus*, Thomson, T, MP |
| | *Merope*, Hill, T, MP | *The Gentleman Gardner*, from Dancourt, BO, AP |
| | *The Triumph of Peace*, Dodsley, M, AP | *Henry and Emma*, H. Bate, I, AP |
| | *Tit for Tat*, Woodward, F, AP | |
| 1749–50 | *Edward the Black Prince*, Shirley, T, MP | *The Fair*, Rich, P, AP |
| | *The Roman Father*, Wm. Whitehead, T, MP | |
| | *Don Saverio*, Arne, Mus. (damned) AP | |

|  | Drury Lane | Covent Garden |
|---|---|---|
|  | *The Chaplet*, Mendez, Mus, AP | |
|  | *Bayes in Petticoats*, Clive, F, AP | |
| 1750–51 | *Gil Blas*, E. Moore, C, MP | *Zara*, A. Hill, T, MP |
|  | *Alfred*, Thomson-Mallet, M, MP | |
|  | *Robin Hood*, Mendez, Mus AP | |
|  | *Queen Mab*, Woodward, P, AP | |
|  | *A Lick at the Town*, Woodward, F, AP | |
| 1751–52 | *Eugenia*, P. Francis, T, MP | *Covent Garden Theatre*, Macklin, F, AP |
|  | *Harlequin Ranger*, Woodward, P, AP | *Triumphs of Hibernia*, Pasquale, M, AP |
|  | *The Sheperd's Lottery*, Mendez, Mus, AP | |
| 1752–53 | *The Gamester*, E. Moore, T, MP | *The Earl of Essex*, Jones, T, MP |
|  | *The Brothers*, E. Young, T, MP | *The Englishman in Paris*, Foote, F, AP |
|  | *The Genii*, Woodward, P, AP | *A Pastoral Dialogue*, anon., E, AP |
|  | *Harlequin Enchanted*, Leviez, P, AP | |
| 1753–54 | *Boadicea*, R. Glover, T, MP | *Philoclea*, Mac. Morgan, T, MP |
|  | *Creusa Queen of Athens*, Wm. Whitehead, T, MP | *Constantine*, P. Francis, T, MP |
|  | *Virginia*, H. Crisp, T, AP | *Gli Amanti Gelosi*, Cocci, B, AP |
|  | *Fortunatus*, Woodward, P, AP | *Lo Studente a la Mode*, Pergolesi, B, AP |
|  | *The Humourists*, T. Cibber, T, AP | *La Cameriera Accorta*, Galuppi, B, AP |

|  | Drury Lane | Covent Garden |
|---|---|---|
|  | *The London Prentice*, C. Clive, E, AP | *L'Amour Costante*, Leo, B, AP |
| 1754–55 | *Barbarossa*, J. Brown, T, MP | Revived 20 old plays. |
|  | *Britannia*, Mallet, M, AP |  |
|  | *Harlequin in China*, Woodward, P, AP |  |
|  | *The Schemers*, Wm. Bromfield, F, AP |  |
| 1755–56 | *Athelstan*, J. Brown, T, MP | *The Englishman Returned from Paris*, Murphy, F, AP |
|  | *Love and Duty*, John Slade, T, MP (1 night) | *La Comediante Cantatricce*, anon., B, AP |
|  | *Chinese Festival*, Noverre, E, AP |  |
|  | *The Apprentice*, Murphy, F, AP |  |
|  | *The Englishman Returned from Paris*, Murphy, F, AP |  |
|  | *The Mock Orators*, anon., F, AP |  |
|  | *The Maiden Whim*, J. Hill, F, AP |  |
|  | *Harlequin Mountebank*, anon., P, AP |  |
| 1756–57 | *Eliza*, R. Rolt, O, MP | *Douglas*, Home, T, MP |
|  | *Lilliput*, Garrick, F, AP |  |
|  | *Mercury Harlequin*, Woodward, P, AP |  |
|  | *The Reprisal*, Smollett, F, AP |  |
|  | *The Author*, Foote, F, AP |  |
|  | *The Male Coquette*, Garrick, F, AP |  |
| 1757–58 | *Agis*, Home, T, MP | *The Anniversary Sequel to Lethe*, anon., F, AP |
|  | *The Upholsterer*, Murphy, F, AP |  |

|  | Drury Lane | Covent Garden |
|---|---|---|
|  | *No Matter What*, anon., F, AP | *Madrigal and Truletta*, J. Reed, Mock T, MP |
| 1758–59 | *The Orphan of China*, Murphy, T, MP | *Cleone*, Dodsley, T, MP |
|  | *Arden of Feversham*, Hoadly-Lillo, T, MP | *The Lady's Choice*, P. Hiffernan, F, AP |
|  | *Antony and Cleopatra*, Shakespeare, T, MP |  |
|  | *Diversions of a Morning*, Foote, F, AP |  |
|  | *The Rout*, J. Hill, F, AP |  |
|  | The Heiress, T. Mozeen, F, AP |  |
| 1759–60 | *The Desert Island*, Murphy, E, AP | *The Spirit of Contradiction*, anon., F, AP |
|  | *The Siege of Aquilea*, Home, T, MP | *The English Sailors in America*, anon., F, AP |
|  | *Love a La Mode*, Macklin, F, AP | *The Siege of Quebec*, anon., E, AP |
|  | *The Tutor*, anon., B, AP |  |
|  | *Harlequin's Invasion*, Garrick, P, AP |  |
|  | *The Way to Keep Him*, Murphy, F, AP |  |
|  | *Every Woman in Her Humour*, Clive, F, AP |  |
| 1760–61 | *The Minor*, Foote, C, MP | *The Married Libertine*, Macklin, C, MP |
|  | *The Jealous Wife*, Colman, C, MP | *Thomas and Sally*, Bickerstaff, Mus, AP |
|  | *Tears and Triumphs of Parnassus*, Lloyd, M, AP |  |
|  | *Polly Honeycombe*, Colman, F, AP |  |
|  | *The Enchanter*, Garrick, Mus, AP |  |
|  | *Edgar and Emmeline*, Hawkesworth, F, AP |  |

| | Drury Lane | Covent Garden |
|---|---|---|
| | *The Island of Slaves*, C. Clive, F, AP | |
| | *The New Hippocrates*, P. Hiffernan, F, AP | |
| | *Taste and Modern Tragedy*, Foote, E, AP | |
| | *The Register Office*, J. Reed, F, AP | |
| 1761–62 | *Hecuba*, Delap, T, MP | *Artaxerxes*, Arne, O, MP |
| | *The School for Lovers*, Wm. Whitehead, C, MP | *The Lyar*, Foote, C, MP |
| | *Arcadia or the Shepherd's Wedding*, Lloyd, Pas, AP | *The Love Match*, anon., F, AP |
| | *The Musical Lady*, Colman, F, AP | |
| | *The Farmer's Return*, Garrick, I, AP | |
| 1762–63 | *Elvira*, Mallet, T, MP | *Love in a Village*, Bickerstaff, O, MP |
| | *The Discovery*, F. Sheridan, C, MP | |
| | *Spring*, J. Harris, F, AP | |
| | *Witches; or, Harlequin Cherokee*, Love, P, AP | |
| | *Magician of the Mountain*, anon., P, AP | |
| | *The Fine Lady's Return from a Rout*, C. Clive, F, AP | |
| | *The Elopement*, Havard, F, AP | |
| 1763–64 | Garrick in France | |
| 1764–65 | Garrick in France | |
| 1765–66 | *Falstaff's Wedding*, Kenrick, E, MP | A Summer's Tale, Cumberland, C, MP |

|  | Drury Lane | Covent Garden |
|---|---|---|
|  | *The Clandestine Marriage*, Garrick-Colman, C, MP | *The Double Mistake*, E. Griffiths, T, MP |
|  | *The Hobby Horse*, Edw. Thompson, F, AP | *All in the Right*, Hull, F, AP |
|  | *The Hermit*, Love, F, AP | *Midas*, O'Hara, B, AP |
| 1766–67 | *The Country Girl*, Garrick, C, MP | *The Accomplished Maid*, Toms, C, MP |
|  | *The Earl of Warwick*, T. Francklin, T, MP | *School for Guardians*, Murphy, C, MP |
|  | *Cymon*, Garrick, E, MP | *Love in the City*, Bickerstaff, O, MP |
|  | *The English Merchant*, Colman, C, MP | *The Fairy Favour*, Hull, M, AP |
|  | *Medea*, R. Glover, T, MP |  |
|  | *Dido*, J. Reed, T, MP |  |
|  | *Neck or Nothing*, Garrick, F, AP |  |
|  | *The Cunning Man*, C. Burney, C, AP |  |
|  | *The Young Couple*, Jane Pope, F, AP |  |
|  | *Marriage a La Mode*, Murphy, F, AP |  |
|  | *Linco's Travels*, Garrick, I, AP |  |
| 1767–68 | *The Widowed Wife*, Kenrick, C, MP | *The Good Natured Man*, Goldsmith, C, MP |
|  | *False Delicacy*, H. Kelly, C, MP | *Lionel and Clarissa*, Bickerstaff, O, MP |
|  | *Zenobia*, Murphy, T, MP | *The Oxonian in Town*, Colman, F, AP |
|  | *A Peep Behind the Curtain*, Garrick, F, AP | *Amelia*, Cumberland, Mus, AP |
|  | *The Absent Man*, Bickerstaff, F, AP | *The Irish Fine Lady*, Macklin, F, AP |
|  | *The National Prejudice*, P. Hiffernan, F, AP |  |
|  | *Wit's Last Stake*, T. King, F, AP |  |

|  | Drury Lane | Covent Garden |
|---|---|---|
| 1768–69 | *Zingis*, A. Dow, T, MP | *Cyrus*, Hoole, T, MP |
|  | *The School for Rakes*, E. Griffiths, C, MP | *Tom Jones*, J. Reed, O, MP |
|  | *The Fatal Discovery*, Home, T, MP | *The Sister*, Ch. Lennox, C, MP |
|  | *The Padlock*, Bickerstaff, Mus, AP | *Orestes*, T. Francklin, T, MP |
|  | *No Wit Like a Woman's*, anon., F, AP | *The Royal Garland*, Bickerstaff, I, AP |
| 1969–70 | *The Jubilee*, Garrick, F, AP | *Man and Wife*, Colman, C, MP |
|  | *A Word to the Wise*, Kelly, C, MP | *The Brothers*, Cumberland, C, MP |
|  | *Three Old Women Weatherwise*, G. S. Carey, I, AP | *Timanthes*, Hoole, T, MP |
|  |  | *The Court of Alexander*, G. A. Stevens, F, AP |
| 1770–71 | *'Tis Well 'tis no Worse*, Bickerstaff, C, MP | *Clementina*, Kelley, T, MP |
|  | *Almida*, D. Celisia, T, MP | *The Portrait*, Colman, B, AP |
|  | *The West Indian*, Cumberland, C, MP |  |
|  | *The Capricious Lady*, J. H. Pye, F, AP |  |
|  | *The Noble Pedlar*, G. S. Carey, B, AP |  |
| 1771–72 | *The Fashionable Lover*, Cumberland, C, MP | *Zobeide*, J. Cradock, T, MP |
|  | *The Grecian Daughter*, Murphy, T, MP | *A Wife in the Right*, E. Griffiths, C, MP |
|  | *Institution of the Garter*, Garrick, I, AP | *The Fairy Prince (Garter)*, Colman, C, AP |
|  | *Newmarket or Humours of the Turf*, anon., F, AP | *An Hour Before Marriage*, Colman, C, AP |
|  | *Amelia*, Cumberland, Mus, AP |  |
| 1772–73 | *The Duel*, O'Brien, C, MP | *Elfrida*, Mason, T, MP |
|  | *Alonzo*, Home, T, MP | *Alzuma*, Murphy, T, MP |

|  | Drury Lane | Covent Garden |
|---|---|---|
|  | *The Maid of Kent*, Waldron, C, MP | *She Stoops to Conquer*, Goldsmith, C, MP |
|  | *The Irish Widow*, Garrick, F, AP | *Cross Purposes*, O'Brien, F, AP |
|  | *The Rose*, Arne, Mus, AP | *The Golden Pippin*, O'Hara, F, AP |
|  | *The Pigmy Revels*, anon., P, AP |  |
| 1773–74 | *The School for Wives*, Kelly, C, MP | *The Duelist*, Kenrick, C, MP |
|  | *A Christmas Tale*, Garrick, E, MP | *The Man of Business*, Colman, C, MP |
|  | *Sethona*, Dow, T, MP | *The South Briton*, anon., C, MP |
|  | *The Heroine of the Cave*, Dow, T, MP | *Sylphs; or, Harlequin's Gambols*, anon., P, AP |
|  | *The Deserter*, Dibdin, Mus, AP |  |
|  | *A Note of Hand*, Cumberland, F, AP |  |
|  | *The Swindlers*, Baddeley, E, AP |  |
|  | *The Conjuror*, M. P. Andrews, F, AP |  |
| 1774–75 | *The Maid of the Oaks*, Burgoyne, Mus, MP | *The Rivals*, Sheridan, C, MP |
|  | *The Choleric Man*, Cumberland, C, MP | *Cleonice*, Hoole, T, MP |
|  | *Matilda*, T. Francklin, T, MP | *Edward and Eleanora*, T. Hull, T, MP |
|  | *Braganza*, R. Jephson, T, MP | *Romance of an Hour*, Kelly, C, AP |
|  | *The Meeting of the Company*, Garrick, I, AP | *Two Misers*, K. O'Hara, Mus, AP |
|  | *The Election*, M. P. Andrews, F, AP | *St Patrick's Day*, Sheridan, F, AP |
|  | *The Cobbler; or, A Wife in a Thousand*, Dibdin, Mus, AP |  |

| Drury Lane | Covent Garden |
|---|---|

*Harlequin's Jubilee*,
  anon., P, AP
*The Rival Candidates*,
  Bate, Mus, AP
*Bon Ton*, Garrick, F, AP
*The Contrast*, Waldron,
  F, AP

1775–76

*The Runaway*, Hannah
  Cowley, C, MP
*The Theatrical Candi-
  dates*, Garrick, I, AP
*May Day*, Garrick, F, AP
*The Sultan*, Bickerstaff,
  Mus, AP
*Blackamoor Washed
  White*, H. Bate, Mus,
  AP
*The Spleen; or, Islington
  Spa*, Colman, F, AP
*Valentine's Day*, Wm.
  Heard, F, AP

*The Man of Reason*,
  Kelly, C, MP
*The Duenna*, Sheridan,
  O, MP
*The Weathercock*,
  Forrest, E, AP
*Prometheus*, anon., P, AP
*The Syrens*, Capt
  Thompson, M, AP
*Imposters*, J. Reed, F, AP

## THE RECORD

Garrick put on 61 new main pieces and 96 new after pieces. *The Jealous Wife*, *The Clandestine Marriage*, and *The West Indian* have lasted.

Covent Garden put on 49 new main pieces and 42 new after pieces. *Douglas*, *She Stoops to Conquer*, and *The Rivals* have lasted.

# Appendix F

.

GARRICK'S HEALTH RECORD
DURING HIS PROFESSIONAL CAREER

| Date/Place | Ailment/Source of Information |
|---|---|
| | (Source references are to *Letters* except when otherwise noted.) |
| 1742–43 | Fever (reported in Ireland). |
| 1745 | Fever (36). |
| May 1746 | Cold and sore throat (44). |
| July 1747 | Cold from damp sheets. Goes to Tunbridge, Bath, Cheltenham for waters. Takes quinine, abandons malt liquor (51, 52). |
| March 1748 | Fever |
| April 1748 | Ague (54). |
| October 1749 | Nausea (81). |
| March 1750 at Bath | Stomach pains (99). |
| July 1751 | Gout (105). |
| October 1751 | Cold (112). |
| February 1758 | Gravel (205). |
| November 1758 | Generally ailing (215). |
| May 1759 | Bilious colic (231). |
| November 1764 in Paris | Chills (343). |
| August 1764 in Munich | Wasting fever (336, 337). |
| January 1766 at Bath | Gout (386). |
| April 1766 in London | Gout (397). |
| April 1766 at Bath | Bile (399). |
| July 1766 | Dizziness (414). |
| May 1768 | Gout (504). |
| July 1768 | Headaches (513). |
| January 1769 | Fever (528). |

| Date/Place | Ailment/Source of Information |
|---|---|
| March 1769 | Stone, gout, jaundice (532). |
| December 1769 | Stone (568). |
| April 1770 | Generally ill (580). |
| November 1770 | Gout, so to Bath (695 n.8). |
| March 1771 | Generally ill (624) and gout (625). |
| April 1771 | Gout (627, 628). |
| May 1771 | Flatulence and gout (632). |
| August 1771 | Fever (644) and cold (649). |
| October 1771 | Generall ill (656). |
| November 1771 | Stone (658, 670). |
| February 1772 | Stone (676). |
| March 1772 | Stone (678). |
| May 1772 | Cold (689). |
| November 1772 | Headaches (714). |
| January 1773 | Stone (738). |
| February 1773 | Stone and sore throat (745, 748). |
| March 1773 | Gout (753). |
| April 1773 | Gout (755). |
| May 1773 | Gravel (767) and gout (768). |
| September 1773 | Gout (799). |
| December 1773 | Gout in hands (811). |
| January 1774 | Cold (816) and gout (817). |
| March 1774 | Fever and cold (823). |
| May 1774 | Gout (833). |
| June 1774 | Generally ill (846). |
| July 1774 | Gout (850). |
| August 1774 | Bile (855). |
| September 1774 | Gout (838; Boaden, II, 38). |
| January 1775 | Gout (882). |
| March 1775 | Stone (895). |
| April, May 1775 | Stone, so to Bath (905, 906, 909). |
| August 1775 | Stone (936). |
| October 1775 | Stone (943). |
| December 1775 | Disorders increase (971). |
| January 1776 | Indisposed (Boaden, II, 126). |
| February 1776 | Gravel, gout, and sore throat (984). |
| March 1776 | Gout (Boaden II, 134, 138, 142). |

# Appendix G

.

GARRICK LOVED LIFE, but knew he was not eternal. He saw his worldly wealth and possessions increase, but knew that without prudent care
they could quickly dissipate. He held his intimate family in great
regard—his wife, Eva Maria, his brothers, Peter and George; his sister Merrial (Docksey); George's three sons, David, Carrington, and
Nathan; his two daughters, Arabella and Catherine. His cousins the
Bailyes and Fermignacs existed outside of his close family, although he
was ever cordial to Richard Bailye (who became a partner with Peter
Garrick in the Lichfield wine trade) and with Peter Fermignac.[1] Concern for his extended family, his acting company, and for a few friends
lay just beyond that for his close relatives. As thoughts of mortality
crept into his mind now and again he sought, practical man that he
was, to enable the inner group to continue to enjoy his possessions,
and live with some margins that he could provide after his death. Most
of his other close friends were well enough off to need no monetary
bequests.

The serious illness in Munich in 1764, and subsequent bouts of ailments in the next few years prompted him to consult lawyers and make
out a will, which is now extant in manuscript form in the Harvard Theatre Collection, and dated 23 March 1767.[2]

The first five provisions of this early will dealt with particular and
generous concern for Eva Maria, his wife. He then provided for brother Peter an annuity of £100, and one of £50 for sister Merrial (plus
another of £50 should she be widowed). To brother George he left his
effects at Hampton and Hendon (after Eva's death), and entailed them
to nephew Carrington, and on to his eldest male heir, and the heir's
eldest, and so on. But for George he set up a trust, so that the estates
could not fall due until after Eva Maria's demise. Should nephew Carrington have no male issue, the trust was to go to David (George's sec-

674

ond son) and should he not have a male heir, all was to go on to Nathan (George's third son). Should Nathan have no male issue the trust was to revert to Arabella, George's eldest daughter and her male issue. If none such appeared the trust was to devolve upon Catherine (George's second daughter), and if no male heir was produced by her, thence to any son produced by George subsequent to Garrick's death. If no male heir came by this route the trust was left to any male issue of Merrial. Brother Peter was a bachelor, so no succession seemed probable there. A proviso, should the trust be handed on to Arabella, Catherine, or Merrial, stated that within a month after receiving the trust the male recipient should adopt the surname Garrick. The trust also allowed the recipient to expand up to but not exceeding £5,000 for the education of daughters bred from second sons along the line.

Eva was to have Hampton and all its appurtenances during her life, plus the sum of £400 immediately upon Garrick's death, and an annuity of another £1,000 (paid quarterly), plus £5,000 to dispense with as she saw fit. Should she be hindered from living at Hampton (possibly by marrying and moving elsewhere, or by illness) she was to receive an extra £300 in annuities added to the original £1,000. These benefits were calculated to balance the value of interest over the years received from her £10,000 dowry. Garrick willed that should his estate at death not be capable of managing all the bequests, the executors were to fulfill completely those to Eva, then dispense the rest porportionally. Legally she was to sign an agreement of acceptance of her bequests within three months after her husband's death, or the sums specified would sink into his personal estate.

Trusts were also to be set up in amounts of £2,000 each for nephews David and Nathan, and like sums for nieces Arabella and Catherine, with payments to come when they (the girls) became 21 or were legally married. The proviso, however, was that any advances which Garrick might make to the nephews or nieces beforehand were to be deducted from their bequests so as not to diminish the sums for the others. A second proviso stated that if, at the time the bequest was due, nephew George was already in possession of a fortune of £5,000 his portion should be abated and be added to Nathan's bequest. Annuities for Peter and Merrial were to come from rents at Hendon.

All Garrick's debts were to be paid, and the executors were not to press for payment of a debt of £400 specifically owed by the upcoming Irish playwright Robert Jephson, until he was amply able to repay.[3]

Garrick's "Collection of Early English Plays" was to go to the British Museum (for the time being) for the benefit of the public. The property at Hampton was to be kept in repair, and the library there was not to be sold. It should remain for the enjoyment of the inhabitants.

To the four executors John Paterson (lawyer), Richard Smallbrook (lawyer), Jacob Tonson (publisher), and James Clutterbuck (mercer) he left £10 each for the purchase of memorial seal rings. Finally he made provision for the succession of trustees. A clear but complicated document this in its entailment of his real and personal property. He emphasized legal preciseness, and (considering the statutes extant re primogeniture) was scrupulously fair, equitable, and considerate for those his closest family.

As the years passed Garrick's wealth increased. His real estate increased, for the manor at Hendon, which Clutterbuck had managed, was conveyed to him two months after this first will was signed. Jacob Tonson died a week after the will was drawn. In 1771 Garrick purchased the house in the Adelphi Terrace. Jephson's loan had been repaid out of his receipts from his play *Braganza* (in 1775). James Clutterbuck had died in 1776. Nephew Nathan, his maternal grandfather's favorite, had been provided with a commision in the guards worth £6,000, and presumably had fortune enough. Eva's niece Elizabeth Fürst had come to live with the Garricks and should be provided for.

It seemed the time had arrived by September 1778 for drafting a new will. This second will, signed 24 September 1778, and his last one, was probated on 2 February 1779. It was shorter and simpler.[4] The new executors and trustees became John Paterson, Richard Rigby, Charles Townsend (Lord Camden), and Albany Wallis (attorney).

Eva received life tenure in Hampton, a bequest of £1,000 to be paid immediately upon Garrick's death, and £5,000 to be paid her twelve months later with its interest, plus an annuity of £1,500 to be paid quarterly and to be free of any "intermeddling husband" she might marry. Garrick wished her to stay in England and make Hampton and the Adelphi her residences. Were she to leave the kingdom the provisions became void and were to be replaced by an annuity of £1,000 during her natural life. After her death (or forfeiture of her legacies by not signing an acceptance of them within three months of her husband's demise) the executors were to sell all the real estate, save Hampton (and the collection of plays and Garrick's Roubillac Statue of Shakespeare, which were to go to the British Museum for the enjoyment of the public), the monies to be invested in government or other securities at interest, and the proceeds to establish the following trusts:

The Hampton estate was entailed to nephew David, its library to go to nephew Carrington along with a trust of £6,000.

The houses Garrick had bought of the Theatrical Fund in Drury Lane were to be returned to the fund for its use.

To brother George he left a legacy of £10,000. To Peter one of £3,000. To sister Merrial £3,000. Nephew David besides Hampton was to receive £5,000, plus what was agreed to be given him on his marriage.

To niece Arabella Schaw he left in trust the sum of £6,000, and one of equal amount to niece Catherine when she came of age, or was legally married. To Mrs Garrick's niece Elizabeth Fürst he left £1,000.

The cash outlay, including the portions for Eva Maria, came to about £47,000. Should his estate not cover this sum, the legacies to Eva were first to be paid in full, and the others abated proportionally. After Eva's death the contents of Hampton, and the Adelphi house and its contents were to be sold and the proceeds applied to fulfilling the terms of all the bequests.

The calculation of nearly £50,000 was a reasonable one, since Garrick had sold his part of the Drury Lane patent for £35,000[5] and had sufficient investments and valuables in property and furnishings to match nearly that amount. His concern for family members' welfare after his death, his prudence and fairness, his desire through bequests to perpetuate enjoyment of the good things he had assembled in this life, at least for a generation or two, speak through the turgid and repetitious legalisms of the documents. His last days were sometimes painful, often silent, but in lucid intervals his cheerfulness and sense of humor prevailed. He joked with the servant who brought him his medicine. Mrs Garrick's entry in her diary for the morning of 20 January 1779 reads "At a quarter before eight my husband sighed and died without one uneasy moment, the Lord be praised." His last thoughts were probably not on his will, but after he had signed it four months earlier its tidyness and simple comprehensiveness gave him a certain peace of mind in regard to his worldly possessions and care for those closest to him.

# References and Notes

.

DOCUMENTATION OF all references in the text is made in the notes to each chapter by short title and/or identifying author—e.g., Davies, *Memoirs*, for Thomas Davies, *Memoirs of the Life of David Garrick, Esq., Interspersed with Characters and Anecdotes of His Theatrical Contemporaries*, 2 vols. (London, 1831); or *Letters*, 134, for David M. Little and George M. Kahrl, eds., and Phoebe deK. Wilson, associate editor, *The Letters of David Garrick*, 3 vols. (The Belknap Press of Harvard University Press, 1963); or Spencer, *Letters*, for Earl Spencer and Christopher Dobson, eds., *The Letters of David Garrick and Georgiana Countess Spencer* (Cambridge, 1960). References to *The Letters of David Garrick* are made to letter numbers therein rather than to dates. All such references to printed materials are fully listed in the following sources:

Account Books, Covent Garden, MSS 1746–47, 1749–50, 1760–61, 1766–70, 1771–74. British Museum Add. MSS, Egerton 2268–78.
*Accounts of Chippendale, Haig & Co. for the Furnishing of David Garrick's House in the Adelphi.* London, 1920.
Adams, C. K. *Catalogue of the Pictures at the Garrick Club.* London, 1936. Supplement, 1947.
*Adventurer, The.* Edited by John Hawkesworth. London, 1752–54.
Alexander, Ryllis Clair. *The Diary of David Garrick, 1751.* Oxford, 1928.
Alleman, G. S. *Matrimonial Law and the Materials of Restoration Comedy.* Philadelphia, 1942.
Allen, Ralph G. "The Stage Spectacles of Philip James De Loutherbourg," Ph.D. dissertation, Yale, 1950.
Almon, John, ed. *The Correspondence of the late John Wilkes.* London, 1805.
Anglesea, Martyn. "David Garrick and the Visual Arts," M.Lit. dissertation, University of Edinburgh, 1971.
*Annals of the Club, 1764–1914.* London, 1914. *See also* Grant-Duff, M. E.
*Annual Register, The.* London, 1759.
*Antique Collector, The.* Vol. 44, December–January, 1973–74.
*Apollo, a Journal of the Arts.* London, 1725–.
*Appeal to the Public on Behalf of the Manager, An.* London, 1763.

Appleton, William W. *Charles Macklin, an Actor's Life*. Cambridge, Mass., 1960.

Aristotle, *Poetics, VI*. Translated by Ingram Bywater. Oxford, 1920 and 1929.

Avery, Emmett L. "Dancing and Pantomime on the English Stage, 1700–1737," *SP*, June 1934.

———. "The Shakespeare Ladies Club," *SQ*, Spring 1936.

Baker, George Pierce. *Some Unpublished Correspondence of David Garrick*, Boston, 1907.

Baker, Herschel. *John Philip Kemble*. Cambridge, Mass., 1942.

*Baldwin's London Journal; or, British Chronicle*. London, 1762–92.

Barker, Kathleen. *The Theatre Royal Bristol, 1766–1966*. London, 1974.

Barton, Margaret. *Garrick*. New York, 1949.

*Bath Chronicle, The*. Bath, 1761–.

*Bath Journal, The*. Bath, 1773–.

*Battle of the Players, The, In Imitation of Swift's Battle of the Books* . . . . London, 1762.

*Bayes in Council; or, A Picture of the Green Room*. Dublin, 1751.

*Beauties of Shakespeare Regularly Selected, The*. Edited by William Dodd. 3 vols. London, 1752.

Benezit, Emmanuel, *Dictionnaire critique et documentaire des peintres, sculpteurs, et graveurs*. 10 vols. Paris, 1976.

Bergmann, Frederick L. "David Garrick and *The Clandestine Marriage*," *PMLA* March 1952.

———. "David Garrick Producer, A Study of Garrick's Alterations of·Non-Shakespearean Plays," Ph.D. dissertation, The George Washington University, 1953.

———. "Garrick's *Zara*," *PMLA*, June 1969.

Bertelson, Lance. "David Garrick and English Painting," *ECS*. Spring 1978.

Betterton, Thomas. *The History of the English Stage from the Restoration to Present Time, Including the Lives, Characters and Amours of the Most Eminent Actors and Actresses; with Instructions for Public Speaking Wherein the Action and Utterances of the Bar, Stage and Pulpit Are Distinctly Considered*. Edited by William Oldys. London, 1741.

*Biographia Dramatica; or, A Companion to the Playhouse*. By David Erskine Baker, Isaac Reed, and Stephen Jones. 2 vols. in 4 pts. London, 1812.

*Biographical Dictionary of Actors, Actresses, &c., A*. Philip H. Highfill, Jr, Kalman A. Burnim, and Edward A. Langhans. Carbondale, 1975–.

Bisset, R. *The Life of Edmund Burke*. 2 vols. London, 1800.

Blunt, Reginald. *Mrs Montagu, Queen of the Blues*. London, 1923.

Boaden, James. *Memoirs of the Life of John Philip Kemble, Esq*. 2 vols. London, 1825.

———, ed. *The Private Correspondence of David Garrick with the Most Celebrated Persons of his Time*. 2 vols. London, 1821.

Boswell, Eleanore. "Young Mr. Cartwright," *MLR*, XXIV, April, 1929.

Boswell, James. *Boswell for the Defence, 1769–1774*. Edited by William K. Wimsatt, Jr, and Frederick A. Pottle. New York, 1959.

———. *Boswell: The Ominous Years*. Edited by Charles Ryskamp and Frederick A. Pottle. New York, 1963.

———. *Boswell in Extremes, 1776–1778*. Edited by Charles McC. Weiss and Frederick A. Pottle. New York, 1970.

————. *Boswell's Correspondence Relating to the Making of the "Life of Johnson."* Edited by Marshall Waingrow. 2 vols. New York, 1970.

————. *Boswell's London Journal, 1762–63.* Edited by Frederick A. Pottle. New York, 1950.

————. *Boswell's Notebook, 1776–77, Recording Particulars of Johnson's Early Life Communicated to Him by Others.* Edited by R. B. Adam. London, 1925.

————. *James Boswell on the Grand Tour.* Edited by Frank Brady and Frederick A. Pottle. New York, 1955.

————. *Life of Johnson.* Edited by G. B. Hill and L. F. Powell. 6 vols. Oxford, 1934–50.

————. "Remarks on the Profession of a Player," *London Magazine*, August, September, and October 1770.

————. See also Pottle, Frederick; Fifer, Charles.

Brown, John. *An Estimate of the Manners and Principles of the Times.* Dublin, 1757.

Bryant, Donald C. *Edmund Burke and His Literary Friends.* St. Louis, 1939.

Burke, Edmund. *A Philosophical Inquiry into the Origin of Our Ideas of the Sublime and the Beautiful.* London, 1757.

————. *See also* Bisset, R.; Copeland, Thomas W.; Morley, John; Samuels, A. P. I.; and Wecter, Dixon.

Burke, Joseph. *English Art, 1714–1800*, The Oxford History of English Art Series, IX (1976).

Burney, Charles. *Dr. Charles Burney's Continental Travels, 1770–1772.* Compiled by Cedric H. Glover. London, 1927.

————. *An Eighteenth-Century Musical Tour in Central Europe and the Netherlands, Being Dr Charles Burney's Account of His Musical Expenses.* Edited by Percy A. Scholes. 2 vols. London, 1959.

————. *Memoirs of Dr Burney Arranged from His Own Manuscripts and Family Papers, and from Personal Recollections by Madam d'Arblay.* Edited by Edward Moxon. 3 vols. London, 1832.

Burney, Fanny. *The Early Diary of Frances Burney, 1768–78.* Edited by Annie R. Ellis. 2 vols. Rev. ed. London, 1907. See Hemlow, Joyce.

Burnim, Kalman A. *David Garrick, Director.* Pittsburgh, 1961.

————. "David Garrick's Early Will," *ThR* 7 (1965), 26–44.

Burrell and Sons. See *Catalogue of the Late David Garrick's Effects,* (*a*) at Hampton, (*b*) in the Adelphi.

Burton, John Hill, ed. *The Autobiography of Alexander Carlyle.* London and Edinburgh, 1860.

Byrne, Muriel St Claire. "The Stage Costuming of *Macbeth* in the 18th Century." *Studies in English Theatre History.* London, 1952.

Bysshe, Edward. *The Art of English Poetry.* London, 1702.

Capell, Edward. *Notes and Various Readings to Shakespeare.* 3 vols. London, 1779–83. (vol. 3 of this work is entitled "The School of Shakespeare, to Which Is Appended 'Notitia Dramatica; or Tables of Ancient Plays from Their Beginning to the Restoration of Charles II.'") *See also* Walker, Dame Alice.

————, ed. *Mr. William Shakespeare, His Comedies, Histories, and Tragedies.* London, 1765.

Carlyle, Alexander. *See* Burton, John Hill, ed.

Case, Arthur E. *A Bibliography of English Poetical Miscellanies, 1521–1750.* Oxford, 1935.

*Case of the Stage in Ireland, The.* . . . *Wherein the Qualifications , Duty, and Importance of a Manager Are Carefully Considered.* Dublin, n.d.

*Catalogue of a Valuable and Highly Interesting Collection of Engravings, Consisting of English and Foreign Portraits . . . the Property of the Late David Garrick, Esq. May 5th, 1825. by Christie* [Christie II], A. [London, 1825.]

*Catalogue of the Late David Garrick's Effects in the Adelphi . . . To Be Sold at Auction, by Messrs. Burrell and Sons, on the Premises. No 5 on the Royal Terrace, on Thursday July 3, and the Following Day,* A. [London, 1823.]

*Catalogue of the Miscellaneous Assemblage of Valuable Property of Mrs Garrick, Dec'd . . . Removed from the Residence in the Adelphi Terrace and Hampton. . . . Sold at Auction by Messrs Robins . . . Covent Garden . . . 22 May 1823,* A. [London, 1823.]

*Catalogue of Pictures at the Garrick Club.* See Adams, C. K.

*Catalogue of the Library of Splendid Books and Prints of David Garrick, Sold at Auction 23 April 1823,* A. By Robert Saunders. London, 1823.

*Catalogue of the Small, but Valuable Collection, of Italian, French, Flemish, Dutch, and English Pictures . . . to Be Sold by Auction, by Mr. Christie* [Christie I] *in His Great Room, in Pall Mall, on Monday, June the 23rd, 1823,* A. [London, 1823.]

*Catalogue of the Valuable and Curious Effects of the Late David Garrick at Hampton . . . To Be Sold at Auction, by Messrs. Burrell & Sons, on the Premises at Hampton . . . Monday, July 21* [1823] *and the Two Following Days,* A. [London, 1823.]

*Champion, The.* Edited by James Ralph. London, 1739–43.

Charlton, John. *Chiswick House and Gardens.* London, 1958.

Chetwood, William Rufus. *A General History of the Stage.* London, 1749.

Christie. *See Catalogue* listings

Churchill, Charles. *The Rosciad.* London, 1761. *See also* Grant, Douglas.

Cibber, Colley. *An Apology for the Life of Colley Cibber.* London, 1740. Edited by B. R. S. Fone. Ann Arbor, Michigan, 1968.

Cibber, Theophilus. *Theophilus Cibber to David Garrick, Esq., With Dissertations on Theatrical Subjects.* London, 1759.

———. *An Epistle from Theophilus Cibber to David Garrick.* London, 1755.

Clifford, James L. *The Young Sam Johnson.* New York, 1955.

Clive, Catherine. *The Case of Mrs. Clive.* London, 1744. Augustan Reprint, no. 159.

*Club, The:* See Fifer, Charles; Grand-Duff, M. E.

Collé, Charles. *Journal et Mémoires.* 3 vols. Paris, 1868.

Colman, George, the Younger. *Random Records.* 2 vols. London, 1830.

Combe, William. *Sanitas Daughter of Aesculapius to David Garrick, Esq.* London, 1772.

*Complete Peerage of England, Scotland, Ireland and the United Kingdom.* Edited by Vicary Gibbs, London, 1910–.

Conolly, Leonard W. *Censorship of English Drama, 1737–1824.* San Marino, 1976.

Cooke, Thomas. *The Comedian; or, Philosophical Enquirer, 1732.* Augustan Reprint, nos. 85–86. Edited by John Loftis. Clark Library, Los Angeles, 1960.

Cooke, William. *Memoirs of Charles Macklin.* London, 1804.

# References

――――. *Memoirs of Samuel Foote, Esq.* 3 vols. London, 1805.

Copeland, Thomas W. *The Correspondence of Edmund Burke.* 2 vols. to date. Chicago, 1958–.

――――. *Our Eminent Friend Edmund Burke.* New Haven, 1949.

*Covent Garden Journal, The.* Edited by Henry Fielding. London, 1752.

*Critical Balance of Performers at Drury Lane Theatre, A.* London, 1765.

*Critical Review, The.* Edited by Tobias Smollett. London, 1759.

Crosby, Emily A. *Une Romancière Oubliée, Madame Riccoboni.* Paris, 1924. Reprint, Geneva, 1970.

Cross, Richard, and William Hopkins. *Diaries, 1747–76.* Folger Shakespeare Library MSS. Also fully transcribed in *The London Stage, 1660–1800,* pt. 4.

Cumberland, Richard. *Memoirs of Richard Cumberland.* London, 1806. *See also* Williams, Stanley T.

*Dancers Damned; or, The Devil to Pay at the Old House, The.* London, 1755.

Dapp, Kathryn G. *George Keate, Esq., Eighteenth-Century Gentleman.* Philadelphia, 1939.

Davies, Thomas. *Dramatic Miscellanies.* 3 vols. Dublin, 1784.

――――. *Memoirs of the Life of David Garrick, Esq.* 2 vols. London, 1780. 1808 ed. *Interspersed with Characters and Anecdotes of His Theatrical Contemporaries. The Whole Forming a History of the Stage.* Edited by Stephen Jones.

Deelman, Christian. *The Great Shakespeare Jubilee.* London, 1964.

Delany, Mary Granville. *Autobiography and Correspondence of Mary Granville, Mrs Delany.* Edited by Lady Llanover. 2d series, 3 vols. London, 1862.

Derrick, Samuel. *The Dramatic Censor.* London, 1752.

Descartes, René. *A Trestise on the Passions of the Soul.* 1649, Translated by Elizabeth Haldane. Cambridge, 1931.

*Dialogue in the Green Room, A.* London, 1763.

Dibdin, Charles. *The Professional Life of Mr. Dibdin, Written by Himself.* 4 vols. London, 1803.

Diderot, Denis. *L'Encyclopédie.* Paris, 1758–72.

――――. *Le Paradoxe sur le comédien.* Paris, 1770.

Dilke, Charles Wentworth. *Papers of a Critic Selected from the Writings of the Late Charles Wentworth Dilke, with a Biographical Sketch by His Grandson, Sir Charles Wentworth Dilke.* 2 vols. London, 1875.

Dircks, Phyllis T. "Garrick's Fail-Safe Musical Venture, *A Peep Behind the Curtain,* an English Burletta," forthcoming from the Clark Library Seminar, "The Stage and the Page," held on 18 February 1977.

Dircks, Richard J. "Garrick and Gentleman: Two Interpretations of Abel Drugger," *RECTR* (November, 1968).

Docksey, Merrial: *The Trial between Mrs Docksey (Sister of the Late David Garrick, Esq.) Plaintiff and Mr. Stephen Panting, . . . Stafford Lent Assizes.* Stafford, [1796].

Dodsley, Robert.*The Museum, or Literary and Historical Register.* London, 1746–.

――――, and J. Dodsley. *London and Its Environs Described.* 6 vols. London, 1761.

Donohue, Joseph W., Jr. *Dramatic Character in the English Romantic Age.* Princeton, 1970.

Downer, Alan S. "Nature to Advantage Dressed," *PMLA,* December, 1943.

*Dramatic Censor: Being Remarks on the Conduct, Character, and Catastrophe of Our Most Celebrated Plays, The*. By Several Hands. London, 1752. No. 1 by Samuel Derrick. *See* Gentleman, Francis

*Dramatic Execution of Agis, The*. London, 1759.

*Drury Lane Playhouse Broke Open, in a Letter to Mr. G—*. London, 1748.

*Dublin Journal, The*. Edited by George Faulkner. Dublin, 1746.

*Dublin Newsletter*. Dublin, 1737–44.

Dunbar, Howard. *The Dramatic Career of Arthur Murphy*. New York, 1946.

Emery, John Pike. *Arthur Murphy: An Eminent English Dramatist*. Philadelphia, 1946.

England, Martha W. *Garrick and Stratford*. New York, 1962.

Enthoven, Gabrielle. "Collection," Victoria and Albert Museum.

Esdaile, Katherine E. *Life and Works of François Roubillac*. London, 1928.

*Essay on the Present State of the Theatre in France, England, and Italy, An*. London, 1760.

*Essay on Satirical Entertainments, An*. 3d ed. London, 1772.

*European Magazine, The*. London, 1782–.

*Examen of the New Comedy Called The Suspicious Husband*. London, 1747.

Falconer, A. F., ed. *The Correspondence of Thomas Percy and David Dalrymple, Lord Hailes*. London, 1954.

Favart, A. P. C., *Mémoires et correspondence de G. F. Favart*. Paris, 1808.

Fielding, Henry. *See Covent Garden Journal, The*

Fifer, Charles, ed. *Correspondence of James Boswell with Certain Members of the Club*. London, 1976.

Fiske, Roger, *English Theatre Music in the Eighteenth Century*. London, 1973.

Fitzgerald, Percy H. *The Life of Mrs Catherine Clive*. London, 1888.

———. *The Life of David Garrick*. London, 1868. Rev. ed. London, 1899.

———. *Samuel Foote, A Biography*. London, 1910.

*Fitzgig; or, The Modern Quixote, a Tale; Relative to the Late Disturbances at Drury Lane and Covent Garden Theatres*. London, 1763.

Fitzpatrick, Thaddeus. *An Enquiry into the Real Merits of a Certain Popular Performer*. London, 1760.

Folger Shakespeare Library, Washington, D.C. "Scrapbook Collection," Garrick MSS, and "News Clippings."

Foot, Jesse. *The Life of Arthur Murphy, Esq*. London, 1811.

Foote, Samuel. *The Roman and English Comedy Considered and Compared*. London, 1747.

———. *A Treatise on the Passions, So Far As They Regard the Stage, with a Critical Inquiry into the Theatrical Merit of Mr. G—k, Mr. Q—n, and Mr. B—y, the First Considered in the Part of Lear, the Last Opposed in Othello*. London, 1747.

Forster Collection. Victoria and Albert Museum, London. "News Clippings" and pertinent volumes relating to Garrick's correspondence.

Forster, John. *The Life and Times of Oliver Goldsmith*, 2d ed. 2 vols. London, 1854.

*Fortune, a Rhapsody, Inscribed to Mr. Garrick*. London, 1751.

Gainsborough, Thomas. *See* Hayes, John; Woodfall, Mary, ed.

Galbraith, Laetitia. "Garrick's Furniture at Hampton." *Apollo Magazine*, July 1972, pp. 45–65.

Garat, Dominic J. *Mémoires historiques sur la vie de M. Suard, sur ses ecrits, et sur le XVIII<sup>e</sup> siècle.* 2 vols. Paris, 1820.

Garrick, David. *Mr. Garrick's Answer to Mr. Macklin's Case.* London, 1743.

———. *Diary, 1751.* See Alexander, Ryllis Clair

———. *Dramatic Works of David Garrick, Esq., The.* 3 vols. London, 1798. Reprint, Farnsborough, 1969.

———. *Essay on Acting, An, in Which Will Be Considered the Mimical Behaviour of a Certain Fashionable, Faulty Actor.* London, 1744.

———. Household Furniture. *See* Inventories

———. *The Journal of David Garrick, Describing His Visit to France and Italy in 1763.* Edited by G. W. Stone, Jr. New York, 1939.

———. *Letters of David Garrick, The.* Edited by David M. Little and George M. Kahrl, with associate editor Phoebe deK. Wilson. 3 vols. Cambridge, Mass., 1963.

———. *Letters of David Garrick and Georgiana Countess Spencer, 1759–1779. See* Spencer, Earl

———. *Letters. See also* Boaden, James; Baker, George Pierce

———. *Poetical Works of David Garrick, Esq., The.* Edited by George Kearsley. London, 2 vols. 1785.

———. Garrick Scrapbook Collection, Folger Shakespeare Library.

———. *Three Plays: Harlequin's Invasion; The Jubilee; The Meeting of The Company, or, Bayes's Art of Acting.* Edited by Elizabeth P. Stein, 1926. Reprint New York, 1967.

*Mr. Garrick's Conduct as Manager of the Theatre Royal in Drury Lane Considered in a Letter Addressed to Him.* Signed E. F., London, 1747.

*Gazetteer and London Daily Advertiser, The.* London, 1741–96.

Genest, John. *Some Account of the English Stage from the Restoration in 1660 to 1830.* 10 vols. Bath, 1832.

Gentleman, Francis. *The Dramatic Censor; or, Critical Companion.* 2 vols. London, 1770.

———. *The Theatres, a Poetical Dissection.* By Sir Nicholas Nipclose. London, 1771.

*Gentleman's Magazine, The.* Edited by E. Cave. London, 1731–.

Gibbon, Edward. *Gibbon's Journal.* Edited by D. M. Low. London, 1929.

Gilbert, T. *Some Reflections on the Management of a Theatre.* London, 1760.

Gildon, Charles. *The Life of Mr. Thomas Betterton.* London, 1710.

———. *The Lives and Characters of the English Dramatic Poets.* London, 1699.

Girouard, Mark. "English Art and the Rococo," *Country Life*, 13 January 1966.

Glover, Cedric H. *See* Burney, Charles

Goldsmith, Oliver. *The Collected Works of Oliver Goldsmith*, Edited by Arthur Friedman. Oxford, 1966.

———. "Essay on Laughing and Sentimental Comedy," *Westminster Magazine*, January 1773.

———. *Miscellaneous Works of Oliver Goldsmith, The.* Edited by James Prior. 4 vols. New York, 1850.

———. *See* Forster, John

Gottesman, Lillian. "Garrick's *Institution of the Garter, RECTR*, November 1967.

Granger, James. *A Biographical History of England*. 2 vols. in 4 pts. London, 1769.

Grant, Douglas. *The Poetical Works of Charles Churchill*. Oxford, 1956.

Grant-Duff, M. E. *The Club, 1784–1905*. London, 1905.

Graves, Algernon. *The Society of Artists of Great Britain, 1760–1791; The Free Society of Artists, 1761–1783, a Complete Dictionary of Contributors and Their Work from the Foundation of the Society to 1791*. London, 1907.

Gray, Charles H. *Theatrical Criticism in London to 1795*. New York, 1931.

Green, F. C. "Robert Liston et Marie Riccoboni," *Revue de littérature comparée*. October–January 1964.

Green, John Richard. *A Short History of the English People*. New York, 1916.

Grimm, F. R. *Correspondance littéraire*. Paris, 1765. Edited by Maurice Tourneau. Paris, 1878.

Haig, R. L. *The Gazetteer, 1715–1797*. Carbondale, 1960.

Harbage, Alfred. "Elizabethan Acting," *PMLA*, September 1939.

Harwood, Thomas. *The History and Antiquities of the Church and City of Lichfield*. Gloucester, 1806.

Hawkesworth, John. *See Adventurer, The*

Hawkins, Sir John. *The Life of Samuel Johnson, LL.D.* London, 1787.

Hayes, John. *The Drawings of Thomas Gainsborough*. 2 vols. New Haven, 1971.

Haywood, Charles. "William Boyce's Solemn Dirge in Garrick's *Romeo and Juliet, SQ* XI (1960).

Hedgcock, F. A. *David Garrick and His French Friends*. Paris, 1911.

Hemlow, Joyce. *The History of Fanny Burney*. Oxford, 1958.

Henderson, John. *Letters and Poems by the Late Mr. John Henderson*. Edited by John Ireland. London, 1786.

Herford, C. H., and Percy Simpson. *Ben Jonson*. 10 vols. London, 1925–37.

Heywood, Thomas. *Apology for Actors*. 1612. Reprint. New York, 1941.

Hill, Aaron. *The Art of Acting*. London, 1753.

———. *The Prompter: A Theatrical Paper*. London, 1734–36. Edited by William W. Appleton and Kalman A. Burnim. New York, 1966.

Hill, John. *The Actor, a Treatise on the Art of Playing. Interspersed with Theatrical anecdotes, Critical Remarks on Plays, and Occasional Observations on Audiences*. London, 1750.

Hilles, Frederick W. *The Literary Career of Sir Joshua Reynolds*. New York, 1936.

———, ed. *Portraits by Sir Joshua Reynolds*. New York, 1952.

Hind, Arthur M. *Engraving in England in the Sixteenth and Seventeenth Centuries*. 3 vols. Cambridge, 1952–64.

*Historical and Succinct Account of the Late Riots at the Theatres Royal of Drury Lane and Covent Garden*. London, 1763.

Huchon, René Louis. *Mrs Montagu, 1780–1800*. New York, 1907.

Hudson, Derek, and Kenneth Luckhorst. *The Royal Society of Arts, 1754–1954*. London, 1954.

Hughes, Leo. "The Actor's Epitome," *RES* 20, 1944.

———. *The Drama's Patrons*. Austin, Tex., 1971.

Howard, Henry. *A Visionary Interview at the Shrine of Shakespeare. Inscribed to Mr. Garrick*. London, 1756.

Hunt, F. Knight. *The Fourth Estate: Contributions Towards a History of Newspapers*. London, 1850.

*Index to The London Stage, 1660–1800*. Compiled by Ben Ross Schneider. Carbondale, 1979.

Inventories: I. "A Descriptive Inventory of the Household Furniture and Pictures, Together with a Schedule of Fixtures Belonging to the Late Country Seat of David Garrick, Esq. Deceased, at Hampton, Taken This 1st Day of March 1779 and the Five Following Days." MS. Victoria and Albert Museum.

——. II. "An Inventory of the Royal Terrace Adelphi . . . of the 18th Day of February 1779 and the Five Following Days." [28 folio pages.] MS. Victoria and Albert Museum.

Johnson, Samuel. *The Letters of Samuel Johnson with Mrs Thrale's Genuine Letters to Him*. Edited by R. W. Chapman. Oxford, 1952.

——. *The Letters of Samuel Johnson*. Edited by G. B. Hill. London, 1892.

——. *Life. See* Boswell, James; Hawkins, Sir John; and Reade, Aleyn Lyell

Jones, Claude E. "Dramatic Criticism in the *Critical Review*," *MLQ*, June 1959.

——, ed. *Isaac Reed Diaries, 1762–1804*. Berkeley, 1946.

Joseph, B. L. *Elizabethan Acting*. Oxford, 1934.

Kahrl, George M. "Smollett as a Caricaturist." In *Tobias Smollett*, edited by G. S. Rousseau and P. G. Boucé. Oxford, 1971.

——. *See* Garrick, *The Letters of David Garrick*

Kelly, Hugh. *Thespis: or, A Critical Examination of the Merits of all the Principal Performers Belonging to Drury Lane Theatre*. London, 1766.

Kelly, John A. *German Visitors to English Theatres in the Eighteenth Century*. Princeton, 1936.

Kenrick, William. *Love in the Suds, a Town Eclogue, Being the Lamentations of Roscius for the Loss of His Nyky*. London, 1772.

——. *A Poetical Epistle to George Colman*. London, 1748.

——. *The Town, a Satire*. London, 1748.

Ketton-Cremer, R. W. *The Early Life and Diaries of William Windham*. London, 1930.

King, Alexander Hyatt, *Some British Collectors of Music, c. 1600–1960*. Cambridge, 1963.

Kirkman, James T. *Memoirs of the Life of Charles Macklin, Esq.* 2 vols. London, 1799.

Klinger, Mary F. "William Hogarth and 18th-Century Drama. A Study of Dramatic Forms and Themes in Hogarth's Theatrical Works and Four Narrative Cycles." Ph.D. dissertation, New York University, 1970.

Knapp, Mary E. *David Garrick: A Checklist of His Verse*. Charlottesville, Va., 1955.

——. "Garrick's Last Command Performance," *The Age of Johnson: Essays Presented to Chauncy B. Tinker*. New Haven, 1949.

——. Garrick's Verses to the Marquis of Rockingham, *PQ*, January 1950.

——. *Prologues and Epilogues of the Eighteenth Century*. New Haven, 1961.

Knapp, J. Merrill, Jr. "Theatrical Music in Garrick's *The Enchanter*, and *May Day*." Forthcoming. Clark Library Seminar, "The Stage and the Page," held February 1977.

Knight, Joseph. *David Garrick*. London, 1894.

Kors, Alan Charles. *D'Holbach's Coterie*. Princeton, 1976.

Lacy, James. "Memoirs of James Lacy, Esq., Late Patentee of the Theatre Royal Drury Lane," *European Magazine*, LV (1809).

*Lady's Magazine, The*. London, 1770–.

Lairesse, Gerard. *The Art of Painting in All Its Branches*. 2 vols. London, 1778.

Laithwaite, Percy. *The History of the Lichfield Conduit Lands Trust*. Lichfield, 1947.

[Lancaster, Nathaniel.] *The Pretty Gentleman, or Softness of Manners Vindicated from the False Ridicule Exhibited under the Character of William Fribble, Esq*. London, n.d. Available in *Bibliotheca Curiosa*, edited by Edmund Goldsmid. Edinburgh, 1885.

Langbaine, Gerard. *An Account of the English Dramatic Poets*. Oxford, 1691.

———. *A New Catalogue of English Plays*. London, 1688.

Larpent, John. Collection of Plays [in manuscript] Submitted to the Licenser. Huntington Library. See *Catalogue of the Larpent Plays in the Huntington Library*, by Dougald MacMillan. San Marino, 1939.

Le Brun, Charles. *A Method to Learn to Design the Passions*. Paris, 1698. English trans. London, 1701.

Lees-Milne, James. *Earls of Creation, Five Great Patrons of Eighteenth-Century Art*. London, 1962.

*Lethe Rehearsed: A Critical Discussion of the Beauties and Blemishes of That Performance*. London, 1749.

*Letter of Abuse to D—d G—k, Esq., A*. London, 1757.

*Letter of Complaint to the Ingenious Author of a Treatise on the Passions so far as They Regard the Stage, A*. London, 1747.

*Letter to Mr. Garrick on the Opening of the Theatre, with Observations on the Conduct of Managers to Actors, Authors and Audiences. Particularly the New Performers, A*. London, 1758.

*Letter to the Honourable Author of* The Rout. *To Which is Subjoined an Epistle to Mr. Garrick upon That and Other Theatrical Subjects. With an Appendix Containing Some Remarks upon the New Revived Play of* Antony and Cleopatra, *A*. London. 1759.

*Library, The: Transactions of the Bibliographical Society*. 3d ser., vol. XIX, edited by D. G. Neill. London, 1964.

Lichfield: Subscription Books in the Lichfield Cathedral Library. Deeds and Other Papers in the Muniment Room, Guild Hall, Lichfield, are MSS in the William Salt Library, Stafford.

Lichtenberg, Georg Christian. *Lichtenberg's Visits to England, As Described in His Letters and Diaries*. Edited and translated by Margaret L. Mare, and W. H. Quarrell. Oxford, 1938.

Lincoln, Stoddard. "Barthélemon's Setting of Garrick's *Orpheus*." Forthcoming from the Clark Library Seminar, "The Stage and the Page," held February 1977.

*Literary Magazine, The*. London, 1756.

Lloyd, Evan. *An Epistle to David Garrick*. London, 1773. *See also* Price, Cecil

Lloyd, Robert. *The Actor: A Poetical Epistle to Bonnel Thornton*. London, 1760.

Lodge, John. *The Peerage of Ireland*. 7 vols. London, 1789.

*London Chronicle, or Universal Evening Post, The*. London, 1757–.

Little, David Mason. Collection. Harvard College Library. Harvard University.

*London Evening Post, The*. London, 1727–

*London Magazine; or Gentleman's Monthly Intelligencer, The*. London, 1732–85.

*London Stage, 1660–1800, The*. Pt. 3, edited by Arthur H. Scouten, and Pt. 4, edited by G. W. Stone, Jr. 5 vols. Carbondale, 1961, 1962.

Lonsdale, Roger H. *Dr. Charles Burney; a Literary Biography*. Oxford, 1965.

Lovejoy, Arthur O. *Essays in the History of Ideas*. Baltimore, 1948.

———. "Nature as an Aesthetic Norm." *MLN* (1927).

Lowe, Robert. *English Theatrical Literature: A Bibliography*. Edited by J. F. Arnott and J. W. Robinson. London, 1970.

Lynham, Deryck. *The Chevalier Noverre*. London, 1950.

Macklin, Charles. *The Case of Charles Macklin, Comedian*. London, 1743.

———. *Mr Macklin's Reply to Mr. Garrick's Answer*. London, 1743.

———. *See also* Cooke, William; Appleton, William W.; and Kirkman, James T.

Madan, Martin. *A Letter to David Garrick Occasioned by the Intended Representation of* The Minor *at the Theatre Royal in Drury Lane*. London, 1760.

Mander, Raymond, and Joe Mitchenson. *The Artist and the Theatre. The Story of the Paintings Collected and Presented to the National Theatre by W. Somerset Maugham*. London [1955].

Mayer, Dorothy Moulton. *Angelica Kaufmann, R. A., 1741–1807*. London, 1972.

Merchant, W. Moelwyn. *Shakespeare and the Artist*. Oxford, 1959.

*Midwife, The*. London, 1750–53.

Montagu, Elizabeth. *Essay on the Writings and Genius of Shakespeare*. London, 1769.

———. *See also* Huchon, René Louis; Blunt, Reginald.

*Monthly Review, The*. Edited by E. Griffiths. London, 1749–.

More, Hannah. *See* Roberts, William.

Morgan, MacNamara. *A Letter to Miss Nossiter Occasioned by her First Appearing on the Stage, in Which Is Contained Remarks on Her Playing the Character of Juliet*. London, 1753.

Morellet, André. *Mémoires (inédite) de l'abbé Morellet*. 2 vols. Paris, 1822.

Morley, John. "Edmund Burke." In *English Men of Letters*. London, 1882.

*Morning Chronicle and London Advertiser, The*. London, 1769–.

Murphy, Arthur. *Gray's Inn Journal*. London, 1753–54.

———. *Life of David Garrick*. 2 vols. London, 1801.

*Muses' Address to D. Garrick, The*. London, 1761.

*Museum, The*. See Dodsley, Robert

Nangle, Benjamin C. *Index to Contributors to the* Monthly Review, *First Series, 1749–89*. Oxford, 1934.

Nash, Mary. *The Provoked Wife: The Life and Times of Susannah Cibber*. Boston, 1977.

Naudeus, Gabriel. *Instructions Concerning Erecting of a Library . . . New Interpreted by Jo. Evelyn*. London, 1661.

Neville, Sylas. *The Diary of Sylas Neville, 1767–1788*. Edited by Basil Cozens-Hardy. Oxford, 1950.

Newbery, John. *The Art of Poetry on a New Plan*. 2 vols. London, 1762.

"News Cuttings." *See* Folger Shakespeare Library, Forster Collection.

Nicholls, James C. *Mme Riccoboni's Letters to David Hume, David Garrick, and Sir Robert Liston*. Oxford, 1976.

Nicholls, James, and J. Taylor. *Bristol Past and Present*. Bristol, 1881–82.

Nichols, John. *Literary Anecdotes of the Eighteenth Century*. 9 vols. London, 1812–16.

———. *Illustrations of the Literary History of the Eighteenth Century*. 8 vols. London, 1817–58.

Noverre, Jean Georges. *Letters on Dancing and Ballet, 1760*. Translated by Cyril Beaumont. London, 1930. *See also* Lynham, Deryck.

Noyes, Robert Gale. *Ben Jonson's Plays on the English Stage, 1660–1776*. Cambridge, Mass., 1936.

Odell, George C. D. *Shakespeare from Betterton to Irving*. 2 vols. London, 1920.

Oldys, William. *The History of the English Stage from the Restoration to the Present Time, Including the Lives, Characters, and Amours of the Most Eminent Actors and Actresses; with Instructions for Public Speaking, Wherein the Action and Utterance of the Bar, Stage and Pulpit are Distinctly Considered*. By Mr. Betterton. London, 1741.

Oman, Carola. *David Garrick*. London, 1958.

Osborn, James M. Collection of Books and Manuscripts, Yale University.

———. "Edmund Malone: Collector-Scholar," *The Library*, XIX, 1964.

———. *John Dryden: Some Biographical Facts and Problems*. New York, 1940.

Osborne, Thomas. *Catalogue of the Collection of Manuscripts and Autograph Letters Formed by the Late William Upcott*, London, 23 June 1846.

Page, Eugene R. *George Colman, the Elder*. New York, 1935.

Paulson, Ronald. *Hogarth, His Life, Art, and Times*. 2 vols. New Haven, 1971.

———. *Hogarth's Graphic Works*. New Haven, 1965.

Pedicord, Harry W. "Mr and Mrs Garrick: Some Unpublished Correspondence," *PMLA* (September 1945), 775–83.

———. *The Theatrical Public in the Time of Garrick*. New York, 1954.

Pegge, Samuel. "Brief Memoirs of Edward Capell." In Nichols, *Illustrations of Literary History . . . .* London, 1817.

Pentzell, Raymond J. "Garrick and Costuming," *Theatre Survey* (May 1969).

Percy, Thomas. *The Percy Letters*. Edited by David N. Smith and Cleanth Brooks. 7 vols. Baton Rouge, 1944–77. Vol. 3, *The Percy-Farmer Correspondence*, edited by Cleanth Brooks; Vol. 4, *The Percy-Warton Correspondence*, edited by M. G. Robinson and Leah Dennis, Baton Rouge, 1951.

———. *Reliques of Ancient English Poetry*. London, 1765. *See also* Falconer, A. F., ed.

Pickering, Roger. *Reflections upon Theatrical Expression in Tragedy*. London, 1755.

Pine-Coffin, R. B. *Bibliography of British and American Travel in Italy*. Florence, 1974.

Pitt, William. *The Correspondence of William Pitt, Earl of Chatham*. 4 vols. Edited by W. S. Taylor and J. H. Pringle. London, 1838–40.

Pittard, Joseph [Samuel Jackson Pratt]. *Observations on Mr Garrick's Acting.* London, 1758.

Planché, J. R. *A Cyclopedia of Costume.* 2 vols. London, 1876–79.

*Poetical Epistle from Shakespeare in Elysium to Mr. Garrick at Drury Lane Theatre, A.* London, 1752.

Pope, Alexander. *An Essay on Criticism.* London, 1711.

Pottle, Frederick A. *James Boswell, the Earlier Years, 1740–69.* New York, 1950, 1966.

————. *The Literary Career of James Boswell.* Oxford, 1929.

Powel, John. "Tit for Tat," MS (1749). Harvard Theatre Collection.

Powell, L. F. "Percy's Reliques," *The Library,* 4th ser., IX, 1929.

Price, Cecil. *Theatre in the Age of Garrick.* Oxford, 1973.

————, ed. "Unpublished Letters of Evan Lloyd." In *The National Library of Wales Journal.* Winter 1954.

Prior, Sir James. *The Life of Edmund Malone, Editor of Shakespeare.* London, 1860.

*Public Advertiser, The.* London, 1752–.

*Public Ledger, The.* London, 1760–.

Purdon, Edward. *A Letter to David Garrick on the Opening of the Theatre in 1759.* London, 1759.

*Queries upon Queries to Be Answered by the Male-Content Actors, for the Satisfaction of the Public in Regard to the Present Dispute Between Them and the Managers.* London, 1743.

*Questions to Be Answered by the Manager of Drury Lane, for the Satisfaction of the Public in Regard to the Present Disputes Between Him and the Actors.* London, 1743.

Quintilianus, M. Fabius. *Institutiones Oratoriae.* Loeb Classical Library.

Ralph, James. *The Case of the Authors by Profession or Trade Stated. With Regard to Booksellers, the Stage, and the Public.* London, 1758. *See also The Champion.*

Reade, Aleyn Lyell. *Johnsonian Gleanings.* 11 vols. London, 1909–52.

Reed, Isaac. *Select Collection of Old Plays.* London, 1780. *See also* Jones, Claude E.

Reynolds, Graham. *English Portrait Miniatures.* London, 1952.

Reynolds, Sir Joshua. *See* Hilles, Frederick W.

Riccoboni, Mme. *See* Crosby, Emily; Green, F. C.; Nicholls, James C.; and Stewart, Joan H.

Richardson, Jonathan. *An Essay on the Theory of Painting.* London, 1715.

Riely, John C. "Horace Walpole and 'the Second Hogarth,'" *ECS* XL (Spring 1978).

Ripley, Henry. *The History and Topography of Hampton-on-Thames.* London, 1885.

Roberts, William. *Memoirs of the Life and Correspondence of Hannah More.* 4 vols. London, 1834.

————. *Memorials of Christie's.* 2 vols. London, 1897.

Robins, Messrs. *See Catalogue of the Miscellaneous Assemblage . . . Hampton.*

Rogal, Samuel J. "David Garrick at the Adelphi," *Journal of the Rutgers University Library* XXXVII (January 1974).

Rogerson, Brewster. "The Art of Painting the Passions," *JHI*, 1953.

Rosenfeld, Sybil. "Foreign Theatrical Companies in Great Britain in the 17th and 18th Centuries," *Society for Theatre Research Pamphlet Series*, no. 4 (1954–55).

*Royal Magazine, The*. London, 1759.

St Albine, Ramón. *Le Comédien*. Paris, 1747.

*St James's Chronicle; or, British Evening Post*. London, 1761–.

*St James's Evening Post*. London, 1755.

*St. James's Magazine*. London, 1762–64; 1774.

Samuels, A. P. I. *The Early Life, Correspondence, and Writings of the Rt. Hon. Edmund Burke*. LL.D. Cambridge, 1923.

*Satirical Dialogue Between a Sea Captain and a Friend in Town. Humbly Addressed to the Gentlemen Who Deformed the Play* Othello. . . , A. London, 1751.

Saunders, Robert. *See Catalogue of the Library of Splendid Books . . . .*

Sawyer, Paul. "Joseph Reed and Dido," *RECTR*, November 1967, May 1968.

Scholes, Percy. *See* Burney, Charles

Scouten, Arthur H. "Shakespeare's Plays in the Theatrical Repertory When Garrick Came to London." *University of Texas Studies in English*, 1945.

Seward, Anna. *The Letters of Anna Seward*. 6 vols. Edinburgh, 1811.

Seward, Thomas, and John Sympson. *The Works of Mr Francis Beaumont and Mr John Fletcher*. London, 1750.

Sheldon, Esther K. *Thomas Sheridan of Smock Alley*. Princeton, 1967.

Sherbo, Arthur. *New Essays by Arthur Murphy*. East Lansing, Mich., 1963.

Sheridan, Thomas. *An Humble Appeal to the Public Together with Some Considerations on the Present and Dangerous State of the Stage in Ireland*. Dublin, 1758.

Shirley, William. *A Bone for the Chroniclers to Pick; or, A Take-Off Scene from Behind the Curtain. A Poem*. London, 1758.

———. *Brief Remarks on the Original and Present State of the Drama*. London, 1758.

———. *Hecate's Prophecy, Being a Characteristic Dialogue Betwixt Future Managers and their Dependents*. London, 1758.

———. *A Letter to David Garrick on His Conduct as a Principal Manager and Actor at Drury Lane*. London, 1772.

———. *See also* Telltruth, Stentor

Siddons, Sarah. *The Reminiscences of Mrs Sarah Siddons, 1773–1785*. Edited by W. B. VanLennep. Cambridge, Mass. 1942.

Smart, Alastair. "Dramatic Gesture and Expression in the Age of Hogarth," *Apollo*, August 1965.

Smith, John Thomas. *Nollekens and his Times*. 2 vols. London, 1828.

Spencer, Earl Edward John, and Christopher Dobson. *The Letters of David Garrick and Georgiana, Countess Spencer*. Cambridge, 1960.

Spencer, Hazleton. *Shakespeare Improved*. Cambridge, Mass., 1927.

Sprague, Arthur Colby. *Shakespeare and the Actors*. Cambridge, Mass., 1944.

Staffordshire: *Collections for a History of Staffordshire*. Edited by William Salt. Birmingham, 1880–.

Steele, Joshua. *An Essay Towards Establishing the Melody and Manners of Speech to Be Expressed and Perpetuated by Peculiar Symbols*. London, 1775.

Stein, Elizabeth P. *David Garrick, Dramatist*. New York, 1938.
———. *Three Plays by David Garrick*. New York, 1926, reissued 1967.
Sterne, Lawrence: *The Works of Lawrence Sterne*. 6 vols. New York, 1813–14.
Stewart, Joan Hinde. *The Novels of Mme Riccoboni*. Chapel Hill, 1976.
Stochholm, Johanne M. *Garrick's Folly*. New York, 1964.
Stone, Geo. Winchester, Jr. "Bloody, Bold, and Complex Richard: Garrick's Interpretation." In *On Stage and Off*. Pullman, Wash., 1968.
———. "A Century of *Cymbeline*; or Garrick's Magic Touch." *PQ*, Winter 1975.
———. "David Garrick's Significance in the History of Shakespearean Criticism," *PMLA* March 1950.
———. "Garrick and Othello," *PQ* 45 (January 1966).
———. "Garrick's Handling of *Macbeth*," *SP*, January 1948.
———. "Garrick's Handling of Shakespeare's Plays, and His Influence on the Changed Attitude Towards Shakespearean Criticism During the Eighteenth Century." Ph.D. dissertation, Harvard University, 1940.
———. "Garrick's Long Lost Alteration of *Hamlet*," *PMLA*, September 1934.
———. "Garrick's Presentation of *Antony and Cleopatra*," *RES*, January 1937.
———. "Garrick's Production of *King Lear*," *SP*, January 1948.
———. *The Journal of David Garrick, 1763*. New York, 1939.
———. "A Midsummer Night's Dream in the Hands of Garrick and Colvan," *PMLA* June 1939.
———. "The Repertory and Its Making." In *The London Theatre World*, edited by R. D. Hume. Carbondale; in press.
———. "*Romeo and Juliet*: The Source of Its Modern Career," *SQ*, Spring 1964.
———. "Shakespeare in the Periodicals, 1700–1740," *SQ*, July 1951 and October 1952.
———. "Shakespeare's *Tempest* at Drury Lane During Garrick's Management," *SQ*, Winter 1956.
———. "An Unknown Operatic Version of *Love's Labours' Lost*," *RES*, July 1939.
Strauss, Ralph. *Robert Dodsley, Poet, Publisher and Playwright*. London, 1910.
Strong, Roy C. *Tudor and Jacobean Portraits*. 2 vols. London, 1969.
Suard, Mme Amelie. *Essais de Mémoires sur M Suard*. Paris, 1820.
*Survey of London: The Strand*. London, 1937 [chap. 14, "Adelphi Terrace"].
T. J. *Letter of Complaint to the Ingenious Author of a Treatise on the Passions*. London, 1747.
Taite, Hugh. "Garrick, Shakespeare, and Wilkes." *British Museum Quarterly* XXIV (1961), 100–107.
Talma, François. *Mémoires de Henri LeKain*. Paris, 1801.
Tasch, Peter A. *The Dramatic Cobbler: The Life and Works of Isaac Bickerstaff*. Lewisburg, Pa., 1971.
Taylor, Edward. *Cursory Remarks on Tragedy*. London, 1774.
Taylor, George. "The Just Delineation of the Passions: Theories of Acting in the Age of Garrick." In *The Eighteenth Century Stage*, edited by Kenneth Richards and Peter Thompson. *Proceedings of a Symposium at Manchester*. London, 1972.
Taylor, John. *Records of My Life*. 2 vols. London, 1832.

Telltruth, Stentor [William Shirley]. *The Herald, or Patriot Proclaimer*. London, 1758.

Tepper, Michael. "Occasional Verse in the Poetical Miscellanies of Augustan England." Ph.D. dissertation, New York University, 1970.

*Theatrical Examiner, The*. London, 1757.

*Theatrical Manager; A Dramatic Satire, The*. London, 1751.

*Theatrical Monitor; or, The Green Room Laid Open, The*. London, 1767–.

*Theatrical Review, Containing Critical Remarks on the Principal Performers of Both Theatres, The*. London, 1757–58; 1763.

*Three Original Letters to a Friend in the Country: An Appeal to the Public in Behalf of the Managers*. London, 1763.

*Tottel's Miscellany*. Edited by Hyder E. Rollins. 2 vols. Cambridge, Mass., 1928–29.

*Town and Country Magazine, The*. London, 1769–.

*Treasurer's Books, Drury Lane*, MSS, 1749–50, by George Garrick; 1766–67, 1771–76, by Benjamin Victor. Folger Shakespeare Library.

Treffman, Samuel. *Sam Foote, Comedian*. New York, 1971.

Turberville, Arthur S. ed. *Johnson's England: An Account of the Life and Manners of His Age, by Various Authors*. 2 vols. Oxford, 1933.

*Universal Magazine, The*. London, October 1776.

*Universal Visitor, The*. London, 1756–.

Vertue, George. *Notebooks*. Oxford, 1934.

Walch, Peter. "David Garrick in Italy," *ECS* III (1970).

Walker, Dame Alice. "Edward Capell and His Edition of Shakespeare," *British Academy Lecture*, London, 1960.

Walpole, Horace. *Catalogue of the Pictures of the Duke of Devonshire, . . . .* Strawberry Hill, 1760.

———. *Correspondence with George Montagu, 1736–1770*. 2 vols. Edited by W. S. Lewis, and Ralph S. Brown, Jr. *Yale Edition of the Walpole Correspondence*. New Haven, 1941.

———. *Correspondence with Sir Horace Mann, 1740–1789*. 11 vols. Edited by W. S. Lewis, et al. New Haven, 1954–71.

———. "Visits to Country Seats," *Walpole Society* XVI (1928).

Warner, Richard. *A Letter to David Garrick, Esq. Concerning the Glossary to the Plays of Shakespeare on a More Extensive Plan Than Has Hitherto Appeared. To Which is Annexed a Specimen*. London, 1768.

Warton, Joseph. *An Essay on the Writings and Genius of Pope*. London, 1756.

Warton, Thomas. *History of English Poetry*. 2 vols. London, 1781.

———. *Observations on the Poetry of Spenser*, 2d ed. 2 vols. London, 1762.

Wasserman, Earl R. "The Sympathetic Imagination in Eighteenth-Century Theories of Acting," *JEGP*, 1947.

Watkin-Jones, A. "Langbaine's Account of the *English Dramatic Poets* (1691)," *Essays and Studies by Members of the English Association*, XXI, collected by Herbert Read, Oxford, 1936.

Watson, F. B. "Thomas Patch (1725–1782): Notes on his Life, Together with a Catalogue of His Known Works," *Walpole Society* XXVIII (1940).

Wecter, Dixon. *Edmund Burke and His Kinsmen*. Boulder, 1939.

*Weekly Magazine, The*. London, 1760.

Werkmeister, Lucyle. *The London Daily Press, 1772–1792*. Lincoln, Neb., 1963.

*Westminster Magazine; or, The Pantheon of Taste, The*. London, 1773–85.

Westminster Parish Registers. MSS. London.

Wheeler, G. W., ed. *Letters of Thomas Bodley to Thomas James*. Oxford, 1926.

*Whitehall Evening Post, The*. London, 1718–1800.

Whitley, William T. *Artists and Their Friends in England, 1700–1799*. 2 vols. London, 1928.

––––––. "An Eighteenth-Century Art Chronicle, Sir Henry Bate Dudley, Bart." *Walpole Society* XIII (1924–25).

Wilkes, John. See Almon, John.

Wilkes, Thomas. *A General View of the Stage*. London, 1759.

Wilkinson, Tate. *Memoirs of His Own Life*. 4 vols. York, 1790.

Williams, John. *A Method to Learn to Design the Passions Proposed in a Conference on Their General and Particular Expression*. London, 1743.

Williams, Stanley T. *Richard Cumberland: His Life and Dramatic Works*. New Haven, 1917.

Windham, William. *The Diary of the Right Hon. William Windham, 1784–1810*. Edited by Mrs Henry Baring. London, 1866.

*World, The*. Edited by E. Moore. London, 1753–54.

Woodall, Mary, ed. *The Letters of Thomas Gainsborough*. New York, 1963.

Wooll, John. *Biographical Memoirs of the Rev. Joseph Warton*. London, 1806.

Wraxall, Sir Nathaniel N. *Historical Memoirs of My Own Times* [1772–84]. 2 vols. London, 1884.

Notes

All references to David M. Little and George M. Kahrl, eds., *The Letters of David Garrick*, 3 vols. (Cambridge, Mass., 1963), are cited in the text by letter number. References to other editions of Garrick letters are cited by author and/or short title.

## Chapter 1
## The Lichfield Years

1. Boswell, *Life*, II, 462.
2. Davies, *Memoirs*, I, 3; see also *Letters*, 11.
3. The property remained in possession of the choral vicars until 1857, when it was appropriated by the ecclesiastical commission and became the site of the probate registry.
4. Forster Collection; see also Reade, *Gleanings*, IV, 150–53.
5. The catalogue of Walmesley's library, sold in 1756 by Thomas Osborne, has been searched for in vain. See Nichols, *Anecdotes*, III, 650; Osborne, *Catalogue*, 23 June 1846, no. 34.
6. *Catalogue*, Saunders, no. 1190.
7. Davies, *Memoirs*, chap. 1; see also a letter from John Swifen to Peter Garrick, 20 October 1751, on Garrick and Johnson's attending dramatic performances in the Guildhall in Lichfield in Forster Collection.
8. Thomas's brother, Andrew Newton, lived in Lichfield, a wealthy bachelor whose mansion became something of a museum, for which Garrick sent him in 1773 a portrait head of himself by Nathaniel Dance.
9. Boaden, I, 9.
10. Ibid., 3.
11. Boswell, *Life*, I, 101–2n.
12. See especially Docksey. We are indebted to Herman W. Liebert, of Yale University, for the privilege of reading his unpublished study of Peter Garrick and his manuscript of the accounting of the brothers when they began their partnership.
13. William Salt Library.
14. Ibid.
15. Seward, *Letters*; see also A.l.s. from Erasmus Darwin to Richard Green, 25 February 1796, in William Salt Library.
16. Johnson, *Letters* (Hill), II, 198.
17. Alexander, *Diary*, pp. 2, 41.
18. Dibdin, *Professional Life*.
19. Boswell, *Life*, I, 81–82.

## Chapter 2
### Garrick and the Acting Tradition

1. See Conolly, *Censorship*, p. 14.
2. *London Stage*, pt. 3. II, 995, hereafter, *L.S.*
3. Colley Cibber, *Apology*, p. 60.
4. *L.S.*, pt. 4, III, 1984.
5. His reputation for this became international. See Grimm, *Correspondance littéraire* (July, 1765): "Le grand art de David Garrick consiste dans la facilité de s'aliener l'esprit, et de se mêttre dans la situation du personnage qu'il doit representer: et lorsq'il s'en est une fois penètre il cesse d'être Garrick, et il devient le personnage dont il est chargé."
6. Hedgcock, *French Friends*, p. 43, quoting Mantzius, *History of Theatrical Art*.
7. Cumberland, *Memoirs*, pp. 59–60; see also *L.S.*. pt. 3, II, CG, 14 November 1746.
8. See Aaron Hill, *Prompter*, no. 92 of 26 September 1735.
9. Cumberland, *Memoirs*.
10. Davies, *Memoirs*, I, 135.
11. *The Rosciad*, a satiric poem on the players.
12. See Harbage, "Elizabethan Acting," p. 698. *The Cyprian Conquerer* is a play in manuscript (British Museum MS, Sloane 3709); see Joseph, *Elizabethan Acting*; see George Taylor, "The Just Delineation"; see Downer, "Nature to Advantage Dressed," pp. 1002–1037; see Wasserman, "Sympathetic Imagination," pp. 264–72; see Donohue, *Dramatic Character*, chap. IX; see Rogerson, "Art of Painting the Passions," pp. 68–94; and Smart, "Dramatic Gesture," pp. 90–97.
13. *Prompter*, No. 64.
14. Quintilianus, *Institutiones*, bk. I, chap. 11; bk. II, chap. 19.
15. Heywood, *Apology for Actors*. The tradition extended to an unknown writer for Thomas Cooke's *The Comedian*, whose advice on elocution extended to players: "The player, therefore who would charm the ears of an audience should first . . . consider well the character which he represents, and after having maturely deliberated on the circumstances in which the character is represented, he should by the strength of the imagination suppose how he himself would be affected in such a situation, by which means he will become almost as interested in the fortunes of the character as if he was acting a real part on the stage of the world," p. 9.
16. See Harbage, "Elizabethan Acting," p. 698.
17. See Le Brun, *Method to Learn*, which Hogarth called the common drawing book; see also Alastair Smart's discussion, in "Dramatic Gesture." The psychology of Descartes seemed an important base for French writers. In his *Treatise on the Passions of the Soul* (1649) he distinguished between the body (man's active part) and the soul (man's contemplative part), and attempted to demonstrate rationally their interaction. Movements depend on the muscles, which depend on the nerves, which resemble small filaments or little tubes which all proceed from the brain, and thus contain (as it contains) a very subtle air or wind called animal spirits. It does the thinking, the animal spirits stimu-

late the acting, for some thoughts terminate in the soul itself, others in bodily action. Six primitive passions emanate from the soul: wonder, love, hatred, desire, joy, sadness. The many others are gradations or combinations of these.

18. John Williams again "Englished" Le Brun in 1743, conveying his sketches for all to view, see *Method to Learn*; see also Richardson, *Essay on the Theory of Painting*; St. Albine, *Le Comédien*; and Lairesse, *The Art of Painting*.

19. See note 14, above.

20. Gildon, *Betterton*, pp. 25–35. He was considering action and utterance of "the Stage, Bar, and Pulpit."

21. Oldys, *History of the English Stage*, pp. 65, 101, 103.

22. No. 64.

23. Hill, *The Art of Acting*, pt. I, and vol. IV of *The Works of Aaron Hill* (London, 1753). Three stages of the poem on the subject were printed in *The Prompter*, see (in the Appleton and Burnim edition) Introduction, xiii, and p. 175n.4; see also Leo Hughes, "The Actor's Epitome," *RES* 20 (1944) 306–7.

24. Quotations are from the Aaron Hill essay incorporated in *The Actor*.

25. As late as the summer of 1773 John Henderson bore witness that country players were still moving in mechanical fashion—hardly becoming the "characters personated": "To learn words, indeed, is no great labor, and to pour them out no difficult matter. It is done on our stage almost every night. . . . The generality of performers think it enough to learn the words, and hence all that uniformity, and unvaried manner which disgraces the theatre." See his letter to John Palmer, 3 August 1773, in Henderson, *Letters*.

26. "A Memoir of David Garrick Esq.," *The Universal Magazine* (October, 1776) p. 187. Garrick, after all, had begun his training with Henry Giffard in a milieu dominated by the "conventional" rhetorical theory. That he himself was thoroughly informed of what the books had to say may be judged from holdings on the subject in his own library—some dozen titles dating from the late 1720s to 1775, numbered from the Saunders *Catalogue*: 38, *The Art of Delivering Written Language*; 333, J. Buchanan, *Towards Establishing Standard English Pronunciation* (1766); 20, Hutcheson, *On the Passions* (1728); 543, J. Cooper, *Letters on Taste* (1755); 849, *Essais sur les passions et sur leur caractères* (2 vols., 1748); 935, Gilbert, *La Rhetorique ou les règles de l'eloquence* (1730); 1052, T. Heywood, *Actor's Vindication*; 2371, Joshua Steele, *Melody and Measure in Speech* (1775); 2252, John Walker, *Exercises in Elocution* (1771); 2195, T. Sheridan, *Lectures on the Art of Reading* (1775); and 2646, Tra[?], *Art of Acting, a Poem* (1746).

27. 16 December 1741, Boaden, I, 3, 4, when Newton had come from Lichfield to see several Garrick performances.

28. Colley Cibber gives glowing accounts of audience reception of Betterton's declaiming (*Apology*), but Betterton for him seemed to be the epitome of a "natural" actor.

29. *An Essay on Acting*, pp. 7–11.

30. Quoted in Kirkman's *Memoirs*, I, 293–94. One of Macklin's papers identified by Kirkman as "The Art and Duty of an Actor," emphasizes that the actor is "to know the passion and humour of each character so correctly, so intimately, and (if you will allow me the expression) to feel it so enthusiastically as to be able to describe it as a philosopher." *Memoirs*, I, 363–64. See also Appleton, *Macklin*, chap. II.

31. Wasserman, see n. 12, above.
32. Robert Lloyd, *The Actor*.
33. *Essay on Criticism*, ll. 299–300.
34. Ibid., ll. 245–46.
35. *Theatre in the Age of Garrick*, p. 3.
36. See *Letter of Complaint*, where the anonymous author contradicts Foote's statement that when Garrick was on stage no one else is seen. Writes he, "When Macbeth has seen the horrid shadow of his murdered friend. . . . I have seen the refuse of the theatre, Macbeth's company, creatures who seldom betray any idea of nature, or feeling, behave in the justest manner in the scene from the infection they have caught from the countenance of their Roscius" (p. 16). On 14 January 1755 Garrick played in *The Suspicious Husband*. A clipping in the Forster collection notes, "Mr Garrick inimitable in Ranger, and throws a vivacity into it that not only inspirits the character but the whole play."
37. John Hill, *The Actor*, pp. 248–49.
38. *The Theatres, a Poetical Dissection*. See also *L.S.*, pt. 4, I, cci.
39. March, pp. 169–70.
40. *The Actor*, p. 22.
41. Chap. 15, below.
42. Papers on King Lear contributed to John Hawkesworth's *Adventurer*, Nos. 113 (4 December 1753), 116 (15 December 1753), and 122 (5 January 1754).
43. Boaden, I, 217 (27 December 1765).
44. Pittard, *Observations*, pp. 5–6.
45. *Letters on Dancing and Ballet*, pp. 82, 85.
46. *Lichtenberg's Visits to England*, pp. 6–8.
47. The Westminster Parish Registers, London.
48. Thomas Wilkes, *View of the Stage*, p. 257.
49. *Essay on Acting*, pp. 7–10.
50. Ibid., p. 10.
51. Pasted in Joseph Knight's *David Garrick* (extra-illustrated) in the Folger Shakespeare Library, I, i.
52. Perhaps related to the "finesse" spoken of so glowingly by John Hill, or the "grace beyond the reach of art" noted by Pope in his *Essay on Criticism*, or the *je ne sais quoi* so often mentioned by French writers.
53. Pt. IV, sec. iii, iv; pt. V, sects. ii, v.
54. Stein, *Three Plays*, pp. 139–40.
55. Ed. James Ralph. See no. 455.
56. See *Essay on the Present State of the Theatre*, chap. XXXII, p. 209.
57. Ranger, Benedict, Sir John Brute, Archer, Bayes, then Hamlet. See app. B.
58. See chaps. 15 and 16, below, and *Letters*, 726.
59. See suggestions of Lovejoy, "Nature As an Aesthetic Norm," *MLN* (1927), pp. 444–50, and chap. V in his *Essays in the History of Ideas*.
60. Forster Collection, "News Clippings," No. 203, referring to Mrs Cibber's benefit night of 18 March 1762.
61. Ibid., referring to Garrick's Hastings in the performance of *Jane Shore* 2 November 1758. One who saw him play Sir Anthony Branville (see *St. James's Chronicle* 23 January 1776) remembered him as so lifelike that he thought him to be an old acquaintance of his from Germany.

62. See Barker, *Theatre Royal Bristol*, 1766–1966, pp. 9–10, and *Letters*, 404.

63. Davies, *Memoirs*, II, 30–31.

## Chapter 3
### The Beginning Manager

1. Appleton, *Macklin*, p. 7.
2. Ibid., p. 14.
3. Ibid., pp. 30–33.
4. William Cooke, *Memoirs*, p. 107.
5. Boaden, I, 15.
6. Sheldon, *Sheridan*, chaps. 1, and 2.
7. Appleton, *Macklin*, p. 59.
8. William Cooke, *Memoirs*, p. 120.
9. Nash, *Provoked Wife*, p. 318.
10. Ibid., p. 181, from the *Dublin Newsletter*, 21–24 August 1742.
11. Barton, *Garrick*, p. 94.
12. Boaden, I, 39.
13. Ibid., I, 167.
14. Genest, *English Stage*, IV, 640.
15. Davies, *Memoirs*, II, 110.
16. Nash, *Provoked Wife*, p. 318.
17. *L.S.* pt. 1, xliii; 439–40; and Colley Cibber, *Apology*, pp. 106–7.
18. Colley Cibber, *Apology*, p. 107.
19. *L.S.*, pt. 3, xciii–xcv.
20. William Mills, Elizabeth Mills, F. Lee, William Havard, William Pritchard, Hannah Pritchard, E. Berry, E. Woodburn, and Catherine Clive.
21. *L.S.*, pt. 3, I, xciv; Lowe, *English Theatrical Literature*, items 2829–33. The cartoon is in the Folger Shakespeare Library, accompanied by a 16-line doggerel verse, with a letter-key identifying the actors involved:

> Behold the mimic monarchs of the stage
> Against oppression (patriot-like) engage,
> Heroes and heroines combin'd unite
> T'oblige the Patentee to do 'em right,
> Vow no vile slavish, late-contriv'd cartel
> Shall bind a Richard (B) Shylock (C), or a Nell (D) &c.

22. The "Cases" of Macklin and Garrick are printed in full in Davies, *Memoirs*. Garrick offered to take £200 less in salary if Fleetwood would relent and rehire Macklin. He also offered to find Mrs Macklin a job at Covent Garden at £3 per week, and to subsidize Macklin at £6 per week until he could find proper employment. He offered to make up any difference between what Giffard would offer him in Ireland to make Macklin's salary equal to what it would have been at Drury Lane. At Macklin's request he delayed as long as he possibly could before returning to Fleetwood, but felt he simply could not abandon the other actors. See Davies, *Memoirs*; Appleton, *Macklin*, chap. IV.

23. *Macklin's Reply to Garrick's Answer.*

24. London, 1743.

25. Ibid.

26. Ibid., 1744.

27. See Garrick's Letter to Mrs Noverre (*Letters*, 200), which explains clearly the husband's prerogative in England: "Tho' we honor the Ladies as much in England as in France, & I particularly have the greatest Regard for You, Yet Business of this Nature is always transacted with the Husband, and by the Laws of our Country, the Act & Deed of the Wife, in such Cases pass for Nothing."

28. See John Powel's testimony, though he was a hostile witness, in his "Tit for Tat" manuscript (*L.S.*, pt. 4, I, 122–28) of Garrick's worth to the Box Office: "In my opinion Mr. Garrick is such a rarity, that he needs no embellishment and I hope I shan't be thought too lavish in his praise when I say that with his great condescension in playing oftener since he has been manager (almost in spite of his sickness) than he did when he was under management, is such an obligation conferr'd on the Town, that it is questionable whether the salary he now receives as an actor is equivalent." Garrick was the *sine qua non* for Lacy.

29. It is difficult to assess the skills which Garrick as a young actor picked up from observing the management practices of Giffard and Sheridan. He was always quick to profit from any situation in which he found seeds for future use. With Sheridan he was responsible for some of the staging, and for coaching actors in parts. His acumen was particularly valuable in casting, though his efforts were often countered by a pushing of favorites by politicians and great ladies outside the confines of Smock Alley. Yet during the season he observed Sheridan's handling of crowds (by creating one-way traffic lanes on benefit nights), by placing restrictions on the servants' gallery, by attempting to diminish stage lounging by the gallants—actions all of which Garrick later carried out when *he* managed Drury Lane. He also noted Sheridan's way of mollifying top actors by giving them alternating roles in the same play (one night Iago, the next Othello) and by noting their appearance in large capitals in the play notices. Such items seem small details, but later correspondences between operating procedures at Drury Lane and Smock Alley suggest that Garrick absorbed in Ireland a great deal which would qualify him for his management to come. See Sheldon, *Sheridan*, chap. III.

30. See his Dedication of *The Spanish Fryar* to Lord Houghton.

31. *Biographical Dictionary of Actors*, s.v. Delane.

32. *L.S.*, pt. 3, 1253.

33. *Biographia Dramatica*, I, s.v. Havard.

34. Ibid., Woodward.

35. Boswell, *Life*, IV, 243. He also, contrary to the opinion of his peers, thought her acting, though good, somewhat mechanical and affected, as though she had some former player in mind which occasioned it. V, 126.

36. Gibbon, *Journal*, p. 186; and *Letters*, 51n.4.

37. Davies, *Memoirs*, II, chap. XLIII.

38. Joseph Knight in *DNB* article (from Davies) on Mrs Pritchard.

39. Letter from Rome, 11 April 1764, to Colman expressing irritation that William Powell should waste his talents on such a character as Alexander ( in *The Rival Queens*): "He might have serv'd Mrs Pritchard & himself too in some good *natural* character: I hate your Roarers—Delane was once a fine Alexander—damn y$^e$ part." See also *Letters*, 337, in which Garrick writes to

George from Munich: "How do Holland and Powell agree?—Jealous—Clive, I suppose more fussocky than ever, and Pritchard often ailing."

40. See Churchill, *Rosciad*: "Original in spirit and in ease, / She pleased by hiding all attempts to please; / No comic actress ever yet could raise / on humour's base, more merit or more praise."

41. Available in Augustan Reprint Society Publication No. 159 (1973), ed. Richard C. Frushell.

42. "The Rehearsal; or Bayes in Petticoats" (1753); "Every Woman in Her Humour" (1760); "Sketch of a Fine Lady's Return from a Rout" (1763); and "The Faithful Irishwoman" (1765). See Larpent Collection.

43. See note 39, above, in ref. to Clive.

44. Boaden, I, 320. The full series of letters may be found in Fitzgerald, *Clive*, p. 70. She insisted that the date specified by Lacy in her "Articles" be hers, and that neither Barry nor Mrs Hopkins should precede her in the benefit series that year.

45. Boaden, I, 341.

46. Ibid., 610.

47. Fitzgerald, *Clive*, pp. 100–101.

48. *L.S.*, pt. 4, I, pp. 121–28.

49. Ibid., xl.

50. Boswell, *Life*, 1, 233, presumably in 1749 when Johnson was age 40.

51. Siddons, *Reminiscences*, p. 5.

52. See *L.S.*, pt. 4, I, xxxvii.

53. Ibid., clxxiv; also Pedicord, *Theatrical Public*, and Hughes, *Drama's Patrons*.

54. See Stone, "Repertory."

55. The best viewpoint was from the pit, where MacNamara Morgan noted he could see the color change along Miss Nossiter's throat and breast as she played Juliet (*Letter to Miss Nossiter*), and where Sylas Neville "was squeez'd dreadfully, but rewarded by seeing Mr. Garrick play Hamlet. the expression in his features, his eyes particularly, surpasses anything I every saw." Neville, *Diary*, 28 May 1767.

56. Boaden, I, 343.

57. No. 15, of 22 February 1752.

58. *L.S.*, pt. 4, I, cxlv.

59. See Lacy, "Memoirs," pp. 273–78.

60. *L.S.*, pt. 4, I, app. D, and pp. 121–29.

61. Ibid., pt. 3, II, 11 April 1747.

62. Ibid.

63. Gay wrote in his Preface (1715) "I would have critics consider when they object against it as a *Tragedy*, that I designed it something of a *Comedy*; when they cavil at it as a *Comedy*, that I had partly in a view a *Pastoral*; when they attack it as a *Pastoral*, that my endeavours were in some degree to write a *Farce*; and when they would deny its character as a *Farce*, that my design was a *Tragi-Comi-Pastoral*: . . . Yet that I might avoid the cavils and misinterpretations of severe critics, I have not call'd it a *Tragedy*, *Comedy*, *Pastoral*, or *Farce*, but left the name entirely undetermined in the doubtful appelation of the *What D'Ye Call It*."

64. See app. E.

65. See chap. 17, n.3.

66. The occasion of *The Chinese Festival* (1755) with over 50 dancers alone.

67. Davies, *Memoirs*, I, 193.

68. See Alexander, *Diary*, 4–6.

69. Ibid., p. 31.

70. Ibid., p. 30.

71. See Oman, *David Garrick*, pp. 140–50; also Hedgcock, *French Friends*, pp. 111, 415.

72. Davies, *Memoirs*, I, 163.

73. See app. E.

74. These box receipts were the only pay the author received, but usually as a courtesy he received the freedom of the house, i.e., a free seat thereafter. He might sell his manuscript to a publisher later for the standard fee of £100.

75. The *Diaries* are printed in full in the comment sections of the *L.S.* on pertinent dates.

76. Boaden, I, 203–4.

77. Dodsley's reply was peevish, reflecting the pent-up animosities of a once-rejected author. On balance Garrick's motives for offering to cooperate seem genuine. Boaden, I, 79.

78. April [?] 1763, Boaden, I, 156.

79. 2 November 1775, Ibid., II, 109.


## Chapter 4
### David Garrick, Esquire

1. His social life at the time was predominantly personal and transient, leaving much to be inferred, since only fragmentary records exist.

2. See Paulson, *Hogarth Life*, and Klinger, "William Hogarth and 18th-Century Drama."

3. Paulson, *Hogarth Life*, II, 22.

4. An anecdote (Paulson, *Hogarth, Life*, II, 35) that the two men first met at a performance staged by Garrick of Fielding's *Mock Doctor* in Cave's quarters over St. John's Gate, with Samuel Johnson present, has more imaginative appropriateness than authority. See Hawkins *Johnson*, p. 45.

5. Paulson, *Hogarth Life*, II, 22 and 31 n. 58.

6. Houghton Library, Harvard University; Paulson, *Hogarth Life*, II, 85.

7. Paulson, *Hogarth Life*, II, 234–35 and notes.

8. Ibid., pp. 235, 344.

9. Ibid., p. 242.

10. Ibid., pp. 343–44.

11. Ibid.

12. A huge armchair now in the Folger Shakespeare Library. For illustration see *Apollo* (July, 1972) p. 47.

13. 1756 edition, I, 122.

14. Acknowledged by Hoadly, Boaden, I, 470. See also Johnson, *Letters* (Hill), II, 289.

15. Garrick, *Poetical Works*, II, 483.

16. Garrick preserved 42 of Hoadly's letters (38 of which are printed in Boaden). Curiously enough all 42 are after 1763 (17 dated 1773). There is no

evidence that Hoadly wrote more often this year than in any other, or that Garrick had any special reason for saving those of 1773. Presumably Hoadly wrote thrice as many letters to Garrick as have survived. In turn only ten of Garrick's to Hoadly survive haphazardly in several sources, half before 1751. See Boaden, I, 170.

17. Boaden, I, 550.
18. Ibid., 466.
19. Ibid. 490.
20. Ibid., 466, 489.
21. Ibid., II, 93–94. Again not produced. It had been written in 1737, and published in 1745. Hoadly was now trying to turn it into a musical.
22. Ibid., I, 191.
23. Ibid., I, 583, referring to Goldsmith's *Essay on Laughing*, in the *Westminster Magazine* (January, 1773).
24. Boaden, I, 457.
25. Ibid., 546, 551.
26. Ibid., 583. Another piece of evidence (Boaden, II, 124) suggested that Jonson's *The Silent Woman* (DL 13 January 1776) should be produced with the character Epicene played by a "smooth-face" young man, which Garrick did on the fourth performance (23 January 1776), when the play was not drawing many spectators.
27. Boaden, I, 200.
28. Ibid., 470.
29. Ibid., 433.
30. John Home, "The Surprise; or Who Would Have Thought It," found un-acted and unpublished in Home's papers after his death.
31. Boaden, II, 139–40.
32. Hawkins, *Johnson*, p. 106.
33. Boaden, I, 70 n. He addressed two letters to Garrick from Luckman House, Boaden, I, 205, 422.
34. *L.S.*, pt. 4, comment section.
35. Boaden, I, 422.
36. *L.S.*, pt. 4, I, xxxii, xlvii, 377; and III, p. 1566. See a 13-page document in the Harvard Theatre collection. It stipulates that Garrick and Lacy will operate at no other location in London, and that any arrears in payment can be made from Drury Lane profits.
37. Boaden, I, 206–7.
38. Boaden, I, 206; see also *Letters*, 337, 339, 522, 997.
39. After the mortgage (if indeed it was executed) Clutterbuck had access by it to a theatre seat wherever and whenever he wished. See *L.S.* Note 59 above.
40. Boaden, II, 127.
41. Ibid., I, 207.
42. Ibid., I, 422, 548; II, 127.
43. Ibid., I, 548, and 422.
44. Ibid., II, 127–28.
45. Boswell, *Life*, II, 62.
46. Fitzgerald, *Garrick*, 217.
47. Boaden, II, 421–22.
48. Boaden, I, 196.
49. Ibid., I, 549.

50. Boaden, I, 223, 310, 312; *Letters*, 46, 84, 1350.
51. Boaden, I, 223, 310, 312.
52. Knapp, Mary, *Checklist*, no. 184; see also *Letters*, 552, 1161, 1252.
53. See Oman, *Garrick*, 302–3, 369, 373.
54. Preserved in the family, most recently, of Col and Mrs Rex Solly.
55. Murphy, *Garrick*, p. 67.
56. Ketton-Cremer, *Early Life and Diaries*, p. 134.
57. Ibid., p. 150. Nothing on this head has been identified as coming from Windham, though Hogarth later removed Townshend's name from *The Bench*.
58. Ibid., p. 143.
59. Ketton-Cremer, *Early Life and Diaries*, p. 144, 150; see also *Letters*, 127, 143, 1295.
60. Ibid., p. 150.

## Chapter 5
## Problems of Management

1. *Poetics*, sec. VI: "There are six parts, consequently, of every tragedy as a whole, that is of such and such quality, viz: a Fable or plot, Characters, Diction, Thought, Spectacle, and Melody; two of them arising from the means, one from the manner, and three from the objects of the dramatic imitation; and there is nothing else besides these six." (Ingram Bywater trans., Oxford, 1920, 1929).
2. Boaden, I, 56–59.
3. Goldsmith, *Miscellaneous Works*, I, 455.
4. P. 63.
5. Reynolds thought painters and players to be poor judges of their own work, but excepted Garrick and Mrs Cibber. See Hilles, *Literary Career*, p. 29, n.2.
6. *In a Letter Addressed to Him*. London, 18 October 1747.
7. Pp. 7–9.
8. See *A Satirical Dialogue*. See also *L.S.*, pt. 4, I, 240, for an account of the performance. The same season brought forth *Bayes in Council*. It was a dramatic poem purporting to give the speeches of Garrick, Havard, John Sowdon, Woodward, Mrs Clive, and Mrs Pritchard a few days before the theatre was opened. It recalls Satan's Council with the fallen angels in Book II of *Paradise Lost*, for in it Garrick is supposed to be regrouping his decimated troops to inspire them to acceptable efforts for the 1751–52 season: "Stung to the heart and raging to behold / His mortal foes so elevate and bold, / Thus G—k spoke, amid a motley crew / Which he together as a Council drew." For 40 lines Garrick is made to praise himself as a leader, commenting on his piercing eyes, fine face, delicate fingers, beautiful walk, striking and startling attitudes. Havard suggests he will write a tragedy for Garrick to act in, and the Council determines to wage war on the opposition at Covent Garden. The vein is amusing but not kindly.
9. It added a "View from Heymon Hill near Shrewsbury," and a "Solitudinarian Ode." Four years later Henry Howard produced a similar Visionary Interview at the Shrine of Shakespeare (1756), wherein Shakespeare discovers Gar-

rick amid a crowd of worshippers, and Garrick rededicates himself to "lose no drop of that immortal man."

10. Garrick had also hoped to have Noverre produce his equally famed *La Fontaine de Jouvence*, wherein the garments of senility "disappear with desirable promptitude" in an elegant dance on several tiers of staging. See Lynham, *Noverre*, p. 23.

11. The descriptions are from Lynham, *Noverre*, p. 21. The designer was Louis Boquet. The details of the negotiation are recorded in Boaden, II, 379–90. Briefly Noverre required a year's contract with 350 guineas for himself, 100 for his dancing sister, transportation costs, a third-night benefit, and an additional one in a preferred spot the following spring, with Garrick participating in the performance. Scenes and clothes were to be designed by M. Boquet, who was to accompany him and dress out the theatre and lighting according to his taste. See Hedgcock, *French Friends*, chap. IV.

12. *L.S.*, pt. 4, II, 505, for the playbill, and for the quotations from the Cross *Dairy*.

13. Witty but semi-serious throughout.

14. Boswell, *Life*, II, 398–99, though the context seems to refer to patriotism as a cover-up for political dishonesty, rather than as a manifestation of super fervor and prejudice.

15. An eight-page brochure. The Folger Library copy bears an MS reply from a player.

16. All quotations from prologues and epilogues are from the *Poetical Works*, ed. Kearsley. "The Recipe," p. 510.

17. The form brought to prominence by Dryden became an art indeed, for the writer had to master the skill of saying about the same things over and over again, but with charming and attractive differences each time. Contemporary opinion, despite the voice of the author of *Drury Lane Playhouse Broke Open*, had it that Garrick excelled in his reciting as well as in composing these introductory and valedictory pieces. Common denominators in his were three—British nationalism, stage history, and critics as attackers but not real spokesmen for appreciative audiences.

18. One of Garrick's triumphs in overcoming a sense of sameness in the prologues lay in his varying the form—now using iambic pentameter couplets, now Swiftean tetrameters, now singing, jogging anapests, now brief prose dialogues. He mastered the genre, but turned it to public relations as a managerial necessity. Not even his Grub Street enemies (only aristocratic Horace Walpole) doubted his prowess here.

19. The group was pleased with the artistic and dramatic achievements Garrick had wrought. See Page, *George Colman*, chaps. III, IV.

20. P. 15.

21. An anonymous pamphleteer (perhaps Nathaniel Lancaster) had published a 32-page piece of *double entendre* but really patent satire: *The Pretty Gentleman*. The preface, in a letter to Garrick, sets the tone: "Surely Sir, It must have been a secret admiration of their elegant and refined manners that called forth your spleen to turn into ridicule those soft accomplishments you despaired to equal. . . . Your farce was most prodigiously laughed at, a plain truth that it was judged to be ridiculous." The author's history of elegance proves to be a description of the characteristics of the stage Fop, the stock

character which reached its epitome in VanBrugh's Lord Foppington in *The Relapse*, half a century earlier. "Elegance," he defines as "the absence or debilitation of masculine strength and vigor—or rather the happy metamorphosis of the Gentleman turn'd Lady." He calls mockingly for demolishing a theatre that ridicules this, noting that the pretty gentlemen have now revived. "They are determined to push on their designs and polish the British manners" (p. 26).

22. It contained critical remarks on the principal performers of both theatres and observations on the plays (new and revived) produced therein, along with an evaluation scale of comparative merit as to actors.

23. Pp. 11–13.

24. Boaden, I, 212.

25. It hoped to concentrate particularly on new performers.

26. Seventy-six pages. It appeared anonymously as "No Matter by Whom."

27. Boaden, I, 455.

28. Complains that Garrick papers his house so that popularity is somewhat specious.

29. Particularly during the period under discussion by the Reverend John Brown (Boaden, I, 154) in the spring of 1763, who wrote a critique "upon Mr. Johnston's play I desired him to read"; by William Whitehead (Boaden, I, 97, 98) who was asked to read Murphy's *Orphan of China* in several stages during February 1759. Later he asked the views of Hoadly, proposed reader for Mrs Griffith and for Joseph Reed. Some in-house reports were made by Lacy, and William Hopkins and Richard Cross (prompters): See MS in Forster Collection (213 F 48 F6), in which Garrick writes, "I am much dissatisfy'd with the first act. Act 2—some well imagined speeches, but the dismissal of Clementina unnatural and most ridiculous. Act 3, p. 34 good and feeling." Then follows in Garrick's hand comments on Acts 4 and 5: "The first scene between the Duke and Julio ill managed—Julio does not endeavour to cloak his rage, but bursts out at once, &c." Garrick also sought secondary support from Warburton's judgment, sending him for comment Hawkesworth's *Amphitryon* (Boaden, I, 76); his own *Gamester* (Boaden, I, 78); his revised *Winter's Tale* (Boaden, I, 88, 12 January 1758); his *Antony and Cleopatra* as worked on by Edward Capell (Boaden, I, 92, 3 January 1759). He offered to bring in Dr. Johnson as arbiter about a Murphy play (Boaden, I, 106). When authors themselves noted that current great scholars had "approved their pieces," Garrick more often than not relied upon his own judgment as a man of the theatre.

30. For a listing of Murphy's plays, see *Index to L.S.*

31. See Emery, *Murphy*.

32. Emery, *Murphy*, pp. 13–14.

33. Boaden, I, 66.

34. Ibid., p. 67.

35. Emery, *Murphy*, p. 47.

36. Ibid., p. 97.

37. John Taylor, *Records*, I, 194.

38. II, p. 15.

39. Emery, *Murphy*, p. 162.

40. Fitzpatrick, a pamphleteer, elusive as an actual individual despite the trouble he caused in 1763, was the Irishman Thomas Fitzpatrick. Garrick had caricatured him in this poem in response to Fitzpatrick's *Enquiry* (1760). Chur-

chill drew a menacing portrait of him in an addition to the original *Rosciad*. His lines in the 8th ed. of the *Rosciad* (see modern ed. by Douglas Grant, 1956) begin at line 117. The tone is devastating:

> With that low cunning which in fools supplies,
> And amply too, the place of being wise . . .
> With that smooth falsehood, whose appearance charms
> And reason of each wholesome doubt disarms,
> Which to the lowest depth of guile descends
> By vilest means pursues the vilest ends;
> Wears friendship's mask for purposes of spite,
> Fawns in the day, and butchers in the night . . .
> Came simpering in; to ascertain whose sex
> Twelve sage impanneled matrons would perplex.
> Nor *male* nor *female*; neither and yet both*
> Of neuter gender, tho' of Irish growth.
> A six-foot suckling, mincing in his gait—
> Affected, peevish, prim, and delicate.

41. *In a Series of Letters first Publish'd in the Craftsman: or Gray's Inn Journal with an Introduction to D—d G—k.* Two of the letters came from *The London Chronicle*, and one from the *St. James Evening Post*. Others were from *The Craftsman*. Some were signed X.Y.Z., some Theatricus. One for 7 May 1760 gives a mock speech by one purportedly reared in the Garrick method— some 20 lines botched up by 31 dashes, marking hesitancy, parenthetic over-kill, contradiction, as well as by broken emphases. Concentration is on Garrick's playing Pierre (in *Venice Preserved*) and Hamlet. Garrick had not played Pierre for six years.

42. See Madan, *Letter*.

43. Which the author thought was obviously put on stage by Garrick's *will*, not by his *judgment*. But Harlequin is always allowed a response in the essay. He notes that the audience always comes to strict attention when he performs—an attitude not so likely to obtain when talking-plays are in progress. Satire here shifts from Garrick to the audience which relishes retouched old plays and harlequinade.

44. Another "impartial estimate" of the respective merit of actors. It deals with 55 belligerents. In it Garrick finds himself beloved by the people, "for he caused the laws to be justly and strongly administered." Rich was likewise beloved until he sought to dethrone Garrick.

45. P. 52.

46. "As the Admittance of Persons behind the Scenes has occasioned a general Complaint on Account of the frequent Interruptions in the Performance, 'tis hop'd Gentlemen won't be offended, that no Money will be taken there for the future." Some Gentlemen complained the following February, and from time to time the rule seems to have been relaxed. See *L.S.*, pt. 4, I, 31, where Cross complains of a near riot during performance of Moore's *The Foundling*, "I believe the main cause of this anger, in spite of their Excuses, was their being

*A line from the *Fribbleriad*. Dr. Johnson defined a *fribble* as "one who professes rapture for the woman and dreads her consent." To fribble for him was to trifle.

refus'd admittance behind the Scenes." A public correspondent berated Garrick for occasionally relaxing the rule. See *Drury Lane Playhouse Broke Open*, p. 18.

47. *L.S.*, pt. 4, II, 983.

48. This includes the letters *pro* and *con* which the occasion stimulated. See also *An Historical and Succinct Account of the Late Riots at the Theatres of Drury Lane and Covent Garden, January 25, 1763*, which includes a humorous description of the handbill circulated by the Fitzpatrick group.

49. Sold by J. Williams, London, 1763.

50. Included in *Poetical Works*, pp. 492–99.

51. See *An Appeal to the Public in Behalf of the Managers*, in which the author claims his objectivity, since he had not spoken three words to Garrick in his life. He suggests that *A Dialogue in the Green Room* was written by Fitzpatrick, that all so-called facts are fictions, for Garrick was in the theatre and did appear. It was done "for personal pique and private revenge." The author also wondered why, if as Fitzpatrick stated Garrick was blocking his expression in the press, X.Y.Z. was so busy publishing in the papers his detractions on the actor? Claims for censorship seemed negated by the facts.

52. See *Biographical Dictionary of Actors, Actresses . . .*

53. Boaden, I, 167.

54. See Noverre, *Letters on Dancing*, pp. 82–85.

55. *L.S.*, pt. 3, II, under dates.

56. See Garrick's Fever Chart, app. F.

57. "A deposit of small calculous concretions in the kidneys and urinary bladder" (Webster), also referred to as "the stone."

58. The MS in the Folger Shakespeare Library, but published in *The Journal of David Garrick*, pp. 58–59.

59. "Study hard, my friend for Seven Years, & you may play the rest of your life,—I would advise You to read at Your leisure other books besides the plays in which you are concern'd—our friend Colman will direct You in these matters, and as he loves, and is a good Judge of Acting, consult him as often as you can upon your Theatrical Affairs—But above all, never let your *Shakespear* be out of your hands, or your Pocket—Keep him about you as a Charm—the more you read him, the more you'll like him, & the better you'll Act him—one thing more, And then I will finish my preaching; Guard against *the Splitting the Ears of the Groundlings who are capable of Nothing but dumb Shew, & noise*,—don't sacrifice your taste and ffeelings to the Applause of Multitude; a true Genius will convert an Audience to His Manner."

## Chapter 6
### The Literary World of Scholarship

1. II, 197, 201.
2. Wheeler, *Letters of Bodley*, pp. 221–22.
3. Naudeus, *Instructions*, p. 64.
4. Eleanore Boswell, "Young Mr. Cartwright," pp. 124–42.
5. Watkin-Jones, "Langbaine's Account," pp. 75–85.
6. *Catalogue*, Saunders, No. 1269.

7. Osborn, "Malone," p. 16.

8. Herschel Baker, *Kemble*, pp. 22–25.

9. For Garrick's will see *Letters*, III, app. G.

10. Foreword to *Catalogue*, Saunders.

11. John Nichols, *Illustrations*, I, 465–76; Pegge's "Memoirs of Capell." See also Walker, *Capell and his Edition*; and *Biographia Dramatica*.

12. See Capell, *Shakespeare*, I, 19–20. Capell entered title, author, date, and printer, assigned a number to each entry (in red ink for duplicate titles) and gave the pressmark of each of the bound gatherings of quartos, all in six marked columns. Titles in collected editions were marked with an asterisk. At the foot of each folio were numerous annotations, and following the catalogue 19 folio pages of an alphabetical index to titles by number, and ten more of an alphabetical index of authors. Capell professed to have worked "from the piece's own title-page, from Langbaine, or from certain old catalogues that accompany some of them, or from recent sales catalogues," to which should be added James Ames's *Typographical Antiquities*, 1749. See "Notitia Dramatica," preface, p. 1, in vol. III.

13. Folger Shakespeare Library.

14. Considerable confusion arose in passing to the Museum the collected editions that were not bound and marked to conform with the quarto gatherings. Further, Garrick's later purchases and gifts from friends after about 1763, not so bound and marked by Capell and Garrick, did not pass to the Museum but were later sold in the sale of his general library. Perhaps aware of the confusion in the transfer of the Garrick Collection to the British Museum in 1778–80, Capell undertook to control the accession of his collection of Shakespeariana by Trinity College, Cambridge, by preparing a catalogue, later published by George Steevens, and supervising the transfer himself. His collection consisted of 245 volumes, bound and indexed, with "E C" and the pressmarks on the spine, the largest collection of Shakespeare quartos to date, 55 in all, with nine apocryphal plays. Garrick had only 44 with five or six accredited to Shakespeare. Capell's library of 296 titles, of which only 40 were of plays, embraced an extraordinary assemblage of early poetry and prose, such as were to be found in Garrick's general library. Capell's benefaction to Trinity College has ever since been one of the most valued and consulted collections in that great library.

15. Also from Capell to Lord Dacre, 26 December 1776, Osborn Collection, Yale.

16. Appended to his *Memoirs of the Life and Writings of Ben Jonson, Esq.*, 1756.

17. Seward and Sympson, eds., *Beaumont and Fletcher*, I, i, 372. Seward married Elizabeth, the daughter of the Reverend John Hunter, the headmaster of the Lichfield school that Johnson and Garrick attended, and begat the still more famous daughter, Anna Seward.

18. Forster Collection, vol. XXVI.

19. For a recent account of the Whalley edition, see Herford and Simpson's edition of *Jonson*, vol. IX (1950), *passim*.

20. See Osborn, *Dryden*, p. 21.

21. *Percy-Warton Correspondence*, p. 85; John Nichols, *Anecdotes*, III, 74–75.

22. BM add MS 10544, 1464, 543.

23. The legacy remained in Garrick's estate until Mrs Garrick's death in 1823, when it was presented to the British Museum by Thomas Racket, Jr., one of the executors, who apparently retained several of the volumes of the Warner bequest, which by subsequent sale went to the Osborn Collection in Yale University.

24. One example gives some measure of the quality and the neglect. *The Works of Ben Jonson*, 1640, with "Richard Warner, 1755" (Warner generally dated his purchases), on the reverse side of the binding, also with Warner's and Wadham College's bookplates, was "once the property of Mr. Lewis Theobald . . . and the MSS notes are in his handwriting." This was the copy loaned Whalley by Warner in 1756, doubtless at Garrick's suggestion. It was sold by Wadham College through Dobell in 1925 (Catalogue 47, No. 495), and is now in the Folger Shakespeare Library.

25. Warner's *Letter* further acknowledges Garrick's aid: "The intimate acquaintance you have with [Shakespeare's] writings: the very minutiae of which you have made your study . . . will it is hoped, induce you to give sanction to a work, not of Genius indeed, but her Handmaid Industry; without whose assistance, even your genius, as well as that of Shakespeare, must have appear'd with imperfect beauty" (p. 92).

26. Like Hawkins, Steevens was re-editing Johnson's edition of Shakespeare and borrowing many if not all of Garrick's Collection to be transported to his study in Hampstead. Also, out of a "course of reading the productions of our first dramatic writers" for the sources of Shakespeare's plays, he prepared for John Nichols to publish in two volumes in 1779, *Six Old Plays, on which Shakespeare Founded his Measure for Measure, Comedy of Errours, The Taming of a Shrew, King John, Henry IV, and King Lear*. In his preface Steevens recognized Hawkins's work in these words: "These volumes were given in a size corresponding with that of the three Volumes of Antient English Drama published by the late Mr. Hawkins, and may be considered as supplemental to his work" (I, vii–viii). The texts of the four English plays were in the Garrick Collection.

27. *Catalogue*, Saunders, No. 2269; Boaden, I, 80.

28. Boaden, I, 64.

29. Warburton had covered the "the rise and progress of the modern stage" in a long footnote in his edition of Shakespeare, V, 275.

30. "Memorandum," BM Add MS 32336.

31. *Percy-Warton Correspondence*, p. 9.

32. Folger, Garrick MS No. W.b.475.

33. See Falconer, ed., *Percy-Hailes Correspondence*, p. 1.

34. Watkin-Jones, "Langbaine's Account," pp. 75–85.

35. Powell, "Percy's *Reliques*," pp. 75–85; see also BM Add MS 32336, I, 24 verso; also Percy MS in the Osborn Collection.

36. Garrick's manuscript collection of his own prologues and epilogues is in the Folger Library.

37. *Percy-Warton Correspondence*, pp. 84–85.

38. *Tottel's Miscellany*, ed. Hyder Edward Rollins, 1929, II, 12. In the Sotheby sale of Percy's library, 1969, No. 507, was a copy of Surrey's *Poems*, 1717, pp. 1–194 only with Percy's insertion and corrections, now in Queen's College, Belfast. See also *Percy-Farmer Correspondence*, I, 191–99.

39. I, 123.

40. Boaden, I, 355, 369.

41. *History of English Poetry*, III (1781), 355.

42. Ibid., II (1770), 363 in Sec. xv, 336–65.

43. Boaden, I, 216–17.

44. February, 104, 113–14. Reprinted in the Johnson-Steevens edition of *Shakespeare*, 1773, K7v–K8r.

45. Boaden, I, 500–1.

46. Boswell, *Life*, II, 192.

47. Johnson, *Letters* (Hill), nos. 168, 189, 1127.1.

48. In addition to 42 published by Boaden there are unpublished letters of Steevens in the British Museum, Forster Collection, the Folger and Huntington libraries, the Osborn Collection at Yale, and elsewhere.

49. Folger (C. b. No. 163); see also Boaden, I, 430; and *Letters*, 848.

50. In the Bodleian Library the Steevens Collection is now Malone 158–211 of small quartos, mostly plays before 1600, and Malone 39–103, the larger post-Restoration quartos—155 volumes in all. The Bodleian has preserved as far as possible, the original bindings.

51. Osborn Collection; Boaden, I, 450–51.

52. 20 January 1763, courtesy of the Boswell Papers at Yale University.

53. Ibid.

54. Wooll, *Memoirs of Warton*, p. 32; *Letters*, 645.

55. Scholes, *Burney's Musical Tours*, p. 22.

56. Jones, *Reed Diaries*.

57. *Select Collection of Old Plays*, 1780, I, xvii.

58. I, pt. 2, 283–384.

59. *Biographical History of England*, 1768, I, 288 n. In more recent times Henry Clay Folger, persuaded that Garrick had done more for Shakespeare, than any other actor or scholar assembled along with his magnificent collection of Shakespeare, the largest recent collection of Garrickiana, and thereby Shakespeare repaid his debt to Garrick.

## Chapter 7
### Garrick's own Plays

1. *L.S.*, pt. 3, II, 802.

2. It was played again in April 1741 for Giffard's benefit, and repeated a week later "for the entertainment of the Masons," and for five more benefits that season (20, 24, 27, 30 April, and 4 May). On one occasion "the Music Room [at Goodman's Fields] being too small to contain the additional number of hands, several select pieces were performed on stage," the popular songs, that is, which Garrick had written for Beard and Mrs Clive. The piece, modified a number of times later, was essentially written for the public stage. When Garrick acted it at Court (after retiring in 1777), court etiquette prevailed and applause was damped. See Mary Knapp, "Garrick's Last Command Performance," pp. 61–71.

3. The very popular after pieces during the period received more perfor-

mances than did the main pieces in the regular repertory, save for the most popular play of the century, *The Beggar's Opera*, with its more than 1,000 performances. See *L.S.*, pt. 4, and introduction, clix.

4. The playlet crossed the sea in 1778, when it was printed for R. Bell in Philadelphia, "at the desire of some officers of the American Army who intend to exhibit at the playhouse for the benefit of families who have suffered in the war for American liberty." See copy in Folger Library.

5. *L.S.*, pt. 3, II, 1280, and pt. 4, I, 12–54. For all subsequent statistics on performance records of the plays see *Index* and pertinent volumes.

6. See *The Male Coquette*; *Fribbleriad*; the Fitzpatrick riots; and the Kenrick affair, pp. 214, 149–51, 603–4.

7. *Correspondance littéraire*, quoted in Hedgcock, *French Friends*, p. 224.

8. February, 1747, pp. 71–72; *L.S.*, pt. 3, II, p. 1284.

9. Cross, *Diary*, *L.S.*, pt. 4, II, p. 709, comment.

10. For full discussion of this play, and of all Garrick's plays, see Elizabeth P. Stein, *Dramatist*. One may note also the resemblance between *The Guardian* and Swift's "Cadenus and Vanessa" poem.

11. Act I, i, 5–6.

12. Stein, *Dramatist*, p. 102.

13. Book IV, "A Voyage to the Houyhnhnms," chap. 6.

14. See Brown, *Estimate*; Lancaster, *The Pretty Gentleman*; chap. 6, above, pp. 142, and 706.

15. *L.S.*, pt. 4, II, 568.

16. *L.S.*, pt. 5, I, 84.

17. *Poetical Works*, Kearsley, I, 154.

18. *The Westminster Magazine*, March, 1775, pp. 124–25.

19. See Avery, "Dancing and Pantomime," especially his discussion of the two most popular early pantomimes, *Harlequin Dr. Faustus* and *The Necromancer*, viewed by critics in *The Weekly Journal* (7 December 1724), and *The Daily Journal* (of 9 December 1724).

20. *Harlequin Ranger*, 1751; *The Genii*, 1752; *Queen Mab*, 1752; *Fortunatus*, 1753; *Proteus*, 1755, 1756.

21. See Stein, *Dramatist*, pp. 115–17; idem, *Three Plays*. In a transparency "part or all of the back scene is painted, *not* upon canvas, but upon linen or calico, and executed *not* in opaque size-paint, but in transparent dye. The appearance of the painting is normal when lit from the front, but as lights are brought up from behind, the subject fades or becomes supplemented by further painting on the back of the linen, until the whole effect is changed, and a normal building, for instance, appears given over to the ravages of fire, or a quiet country landscape blossoms into the glow of a lurid sunset," See *Oxford Companion to the Theatre* (1951–57), s.v. "Trick-work," p. 801.

22. See *L.S.*, *Index*, s.v. *Harlequin's Jacket*, and *Lun's Ghost*.

23. See Jones, "Dramatic Criticism," p. 135.

24. *L.S.*, pt. 4, introduction, cxxvii–cxxxiv.

25. Such as *Alfred* (1751, and 1773), *The Fairies* (1755), *The Tempest* (1756), *The Enchanter* (1760), *Cymon* (1767), *The Jubilee* (1769), *King Arthur and Emmeline* (1770), *The Institution of the Garter* (1771), the operatic version of *Love's Labours' Lost* (1773), and *A Christmas Tale* (1773).

26. See Mary Knapp, *Checklist*.

27. Theatre fires doubtless destroyed the Drury Lane music scores, but their popularity was so great that printed versions came quickly from the music publishing houses soon after the plays were performed. The melodies, at least, appeared if not the whole orchestration. Pieces lie scattered in the British Museum, The Royal College of Music, The Folger Shakespeare Library, the Library of Congress, and the Bodleian. The most fetching songs appeared in the Poetry Sections of *The London Magazine*, with one or two bars of musical accompaniment, 1749–76.

28. *Poetical Works*, I, 32.

29. Boaden, I, 146, 147.

30. *Poetical Works*, I, 198.

31. Boaden, I, 262.

32. See particularly Stein, *Dramatist*, concluding chapter.

33. *English Theatre Music*, chap. VI, p. 205.

34. L.S., pt. 5, III, 2065. For the quality of the music in *The Enchanter* and in *May Day* see the forthcoming article by Merrill Knapp, "Theatrical Music."

35. Stein, *Dramatist*, p. 133, who discusses two MSS (Barton-Ticknor Collection in the Boston Public Library, and the full copy in the Larpent Collection at the Huntington Library, which she printed in *Three Plays*. A partial third MS is in the Folger Shakespeare Library, which differs somewhat as to the procession of pageants.

36. Stein, *Dramatist*, p. 136.

37. Boaden, I, 248–49.

38. *Poetical Works*, II, 289.

39. Stein, *Dramatist*, p. 142.

40. Boaden, I, 611 (23 January 1774).

41. See full account in Stein, *Dramatist*, pp. 161–63. One Parsons in revenge for being sent to debtor's prison by one William Kent (whose mistress Fanny had died suddenly of small pox, had word spread about town that Fanny's ghost, restless and troubled, manifested itself to his daughter by knockings and scratchings in the wall of her lodgings in Cock Lane. The fashionable gentry, according to Horace Walpole, went in parties to witness the phenomenon, and the rage prompted both Rich and Garrick to revive at the theatres Addison's old play *The Drummer; or, the Haunted House*.

42. See Phyllis T. Dircks, "Two Burlettas of Kane O'Hara" (Ph.D. dissertation, New York University, 1967) and her forthcoming "Garrick's Fail-Safe Musical Venture."

43. See Lincoln, "Barthélemon's Setting."

44. See full study of text in Bergmann, "David Garrick Producer," pp. 314–32.

45. L.S., pt. 4, III, the 1771–72 season.

46. Quotations from Licenser's copy in the Larpent Collection, Huntington Library. See a study by Lillian Gottesman, "Garrick's Institution."

47. See Bergmann, "*Clandestine Marriage*," pp. 148–62. He has also discovered Garrick's earliest version of the play, called "The Sisters" which has long lain in an exhibit case in the Garrick Club.

48. L.S., pt. 4, II, 1153.

49. Partially quoted from G. S. Alleman, *Matrimonial Law*, p. 38.

## Chapter 8
### Garrick's Adaptations of Older Plays

1. See Odell, *Shakespeare from Betterton to Irving*, and Spencer, *Shakespeare Improved*.
2. Colley Cibber, *Apology*, chap. 4.
3. *L.S.*, pt. 3, I, cxlix–cliv; and Avery, *Shakespeare Ladies' Club*, pp. 153–58; and Scouten, "Shakespeare's Plays in the Theatrical Repertory," pp. 257–68.
4. See Murphy, *Life*, I, 71; and Stone, "Garrick's Handling *Macbeth*."
5. See Stone, "*Romeo and Juliet*"; and Burnim, *David Garrick, Director*.
6. Knight, David Garrick, pp. 115–17.
7. 1748, 1750, 1753, 1756, 1758, 1763, 1766, 1770, 1774, 1775, 1778, 1780, 1784, 1787.
8. See Haywood, "William Boyce's Solemn Dirge," pp. 173–88.
9. See Stone, "Garrick and *Othello*."
10. In his notes for Bell edition of *Shakespeare's Plays*, 1774, p. 40 n.
11. Full account in Stone, "Bloody, Cold, and Complex Richard."
12. *Gray's Inn Journal*, No. 65.
13. Ibid., No. 87. Full study in Stone, "Garrick's Production of *King Lear*."
14. London, 1756.
15. Dr. Johnson had struggled with the mixture of genres in three *Rambler* essays.
16. *L.S.*, pt. 4, II, 630.
17. Full study in Bergmann, "David Garrick Producer," pp. 189–207.
18. See Bergmann, "Garrick's *Zara*," pp. 225–32.
19. *Dramatic Miscellanies*, III, 86.
20. Foot, *Life of Murphy*, pp. 252–74.
21. *Kemble*, I, 110–13.
22. *Biographia Dramatica*, II, 278.
23. *Life of David Garrick*, II, 288.
24. Wilkinson, *Memoirs*, IV, 360.
25. For the Act, and full treatment of the text see Stone, "Garrick's *Hamlet*," pp. 890–921.
26. Henry N. Paul, unpublished article, see Stone, "Garrick's *Hamlet*," p. 896 n.29.
27. *Shakespeare Improved*, p. 19.
28. An example in point is the dialogue between Polonius and Ophelia, to which Claudius is also a party:

*Pol:* 'Tis too much prov'd that with devotion's visage, and pious action, we do sugar o'er the Devil himself!
*King:* O 'tis true. How smart a lash this speech doth give my conscience.

This part, immediately preceding the "To be or not to be" soliloquy had been cut since the time of Betterton. A comparison of the cuts made in the acting copies of *Hamlet* from 1703 to 1772 is revealing as showing Garrick's desire for stage freshness. It is printed in full in Stone, "Garrick's *Hamlet*," p. 903.
29. See Bergmann, "David Garrick Producer," pp. 100–119.

30. *L.S.*, pt. 4, II, 704.

31. See Stone, "Garrick's *Antony and Cleopatra*."

32. Bergmann, "David Garrick Producer," pp. 238–58.

33. See full studies of all these plays: the Shakespearean ones by Stone in his Harvard dissertation, the non-Shakespearean by Bergmann in his George Washington University dissertation. Copies of each are also in the Folger Shakespeare Library.

34. See chap. 15, below, for Garrick's acting of Kitely.

35. See discussion of the play in Noyes, *Ben Jonson's Plays on the English Stage*.

36. Bergmann, "David Garrick Producer," p. 133.

37. See indexes in *Letters*, and in Boaden.

38. *Correspondance littéraire* (Tourneau ed.), VI, 318.

39. *The London Chronicle*, 16 January 1772, from "News Clippings" in the Forster Collection.

40. Copies in the Larpent Collection, Huntington Library.

41. Thomas Warton, *Observations*, I, 54.

42. See Mrs Montagu to Garrick: "In private life, who so beloved and respected as Mr. Garrick!" (Boaden, II, 374). The breath of scandal so often clouding others in the period scarcely touched Garrick.

43. Boaden, I, 80 (21 December 1757). It would have been difficult for the actor, addressed with such adulation coupled with high sentiments, not to have responded positively to the mood of his correspondents and the public. The Duke of Newcastle wrote 15 September 1761, "You, Sir, I hope, will continue, as far as may be agreeable to you, to give (sometimes at least,) the public such representations of human nature, as must encourage and promote love of virtue and virtuous actions" (Boaden, I, 130). Warburton had written him again on 9 November 1759 (Boaden, I, 105), "I find you will not be content with being the greatest performer that ever trod the stage, which is no mean fame, but you will be the reformer too. This was only wanting to give lasting lustre to your incomparable talents; and therefore I say, *macte nova virtute tua*. I call it *new*, because the greatest of your predecessors contented themselves with being what the French call *honest men*. You think, and justly, that, as a good citizen, more is required from the advantages of your talents and situation,— the reform of those follies which the laws cannot punish; for which, what the poet would have done, posterity will do—place you among these

> Who, from the task obscene, reclaim our youth,
> And set the passions on the side of truth."

These sentiments Warburton presumably got from reading Garrick's plays, or from hearsay about his acting, since we cannot determine that Warburton ever went to the theatre. The Reverend Evan Lloyd wrote (23 April 1772), "Is it a sin, is it a heresy to prefer Shakespeare to Tillotson? Will the imprudence to confess that my heart pants more ardently after virtue when you are Lear than when I hear the opiate lullabies of Dr. Dod?" See "Unpublished Letters of Evan Lloyd," ed. Cecil Price, p. 437.

44. George Lillo's "Dedication to Sir John Eyles" of his *The London Merchant*, generally printed with the play.

45. Boaden, I, 82.

46. And the audience liked it.

47. See Tasch, *The Dramatic Cobbler*, pp. 93–94. Garrick did at times call upon others, whose skill he trusted, to work on alterations, which he then approved, added to, or belayed. Bickerstaff was one, Arthur Murphy another, Cumberland also, Capell, and Captain Edward Thompson. But Garrick accepted the major responsibility of alterations for himself. Copious advice was often given by John Hoadly.

## Chapter 9
## *David Garrick Abroad: An Heir to the Classical Traditions*

1. Garat, *Mémoires historique*, Book IV; also Hedgcock, *French Friends*, p. 219.
2. See Boaden, II, 383–85, the first only of ten; Hedgcock, *French Friends*, pp. 309–14; and Boaden, II, 463, 476, respectively.
3. Talma, *LeKain*, p. 275.
4. Boaden, II, 464; and Favart, A. P. C., *Mémoires et correspondance*, III, 9.
5. Alexander, *Diary*.
6. *Diary*, pp. 10, 14; Collé, *Journal et mémoires*, I, 324, III, 2; *Letters*, 107, 300, 354.
7. *Diary*, p. 33.
8. Walpole, "Visits to Country Seats," p. 23.
9. *Diary*, p. 15.
10. Ibid., p. 26.
11. Huchon, *Mrs Montagu*, pp. 112–14.
12. *Works*, VI (1814), 65.
13. *Journal to France and Italy*, pp. 7, 39, 58; *Letters*, 314, 317 n. 4.
14. Garrick knew something of such comment from C. N. Cochin's *Voyage d'Italie*, given him by Charles Burney; *Letters*, 322.
15. *Journal*, pp. 12, 11.
16. Ibid., p. 15.
17. Ibid., p. 17.
18. Boaden, II, 423; *Letters*, 325, 327.
19. Boaden, I, 171. William Cavendish, fourth duke of Devonshire.
20. See Walch, "David Garrick in Italy," pp. 525–26; Boaden, I, 183; *Letters*, 322.
21. See Anglesea, "Garrick and the Visual Arts," pp. 163–64. The painting now in the Folger Shakespeare Library.
22. See Walch, "David Garrick in Italy," pp. 523–24; Anglesea, 154–55; *Letters*, 382.
23. John Thomas Smith, *Nollekens and His Times*, p. 6.
24. Portrait now in the Exeter Collection. See Mayer, *Angelica Kauffman*, p. 17; and *Boswell on the Grand Tour*, p. 50.
25. Now in the Royal Albert Memorial Museum, Exeter. See Watson, *Thomas Patch*, pp. 6–9; and Kahrl, "Smollett as a Caricaturist," pp. 177–79.
26. Recounted in a letter ca. June 1774, *Letters*, 335. See also Walch, pp. 527–30; Anglesea, pp. 239–40; Murphy, *Life*, II, 15, 18. Painting now in the Lever Collection.

27. Anglesea, pp. 155–56.
28. Ibid., p. 187.
29. *Journal*, pp. 19–35. Not all listings are in Garrick's hand.
30. Garrick engaged Richard Brompton, the painter, to assist him in purchases. See *Letters*, 356, and Boaden, I, 176.
31. *Journal*, pp. 48–49; Mary Knapp, *Checklist*, No. 49.
32. As proposed by M Camp (banker from Lyons), Boaden, II, 421; *Letters*, 325. In November Francis Tronchin, Voltaire's Swiss friend had obtained an invitation for Garrick to stop by Ferney, *Letters*, 325, 328, 340; and Boaden, I, 196.
33. Boaden, II, 579–636; Forster Collection, unpublished materials.
34. Kors, *D'Holbach's Coterie*, especially the chapter on "The Membership of the coterie Holbachique."
35. Boaden, II, 613; *Letters*, 787, 789.
36. Hedgcock, *French Friends*, p. 233; Grimm, *Correspondance littéraire*, p. 318.
37. Boaden, II, 438, 513, 552, 583.
38. Amelie Suard, *Essais de Mémoires sur M Suard*, pp. 44–47.
39. Boaden, II, 608.
40. The record is to be found in part in Talma, *Le Kain*, but see also *Letters*, 368, 386, 395, 396, 442; Boaden, II, 439, 443, 473, 474, 482, 537, 557.
41. Boaden, II, 429; *Letters*, 346n.
42. Hedgcock, *French Friends*, p. 395.
43. A cataloguing alone, much less a summary of the subjects covered in Monnet's letters, generally long and almost invariably detailed, is out of the question here. He scouted for and contracted with actors and dancers for Garrick; engaged artists, such as de Loutherbourg (designer), F. H. Barthélemon (musician, composer); and he sent new stage properties, such as the licopodium torch. See chapter 10, below.
44. Hedgcock, *French Friends*, p. 422. See Forster Collection Add XXI [48e 15], 194.
45. *Correspondence*, Mann, VI, 164, the italics are Walpole's.
46. *Memoirs*, II, 99.

## Chapter 10
### Garrick's Theatrical Innovations

1. Alexander, *Diary*, p. 37; and Oman, *Garrick*, p. 394 n.1.
2. See Rosenfeld, "Foreign Theatrical Companies."
3. Hedgcock, *French Friends*, pp. 102–7.
4. Ibid., p. 394.
5. Ibid., chap. VI, pp. 371–402.
6. Boaden, II, 578, March 1771.
7. Hedgcock, *French Friends*, p. 393.
8. Ibid., pp. 235–37.
9. Ibid., p. 243.
10. Ibid., pp. 233, 234.
11. Ibid., p. 163.

12. Ibid., p. 407.
13. P. 7.
14. Hedgcock, *French Friends*, p. 272.
15. Ibid., p. 339.
16. Ibid., p. 276.
17. Ibid., pp. 281–82.
18. Boaden, I, 488 (Murphy to Garrick 21 October 1772).
19. Hedgcock, *French Friends*, pp. 285–86.
20. Ibid., pp. 291–94.
21. Ibid., pp. 300, 301.
22. Ibid., p. 301.
23. Ibid., p. 304.
24. Ibid., p. 288.
25. Forster Collection; Boaden, I, 186–88; Hedgcock, *French Friends*, pp. 264–67.
26. See *Critical Balance of Performers*, Huntington Library E 79680.
27. *L.S.*, pt. 4, I, app. D.
28. Boaden, I, 205, 223. A similar quarrel erupted in 1767 (*Letters*, 481), and Boaden, I, 279), but shortly subsided.
29. Alexander, *Diary*, p. 5.
30. *Journal*, pp. 6, 7.
31. Boaden, II, 441, 446.
32. See Burnim, *David Garrick, Director*, pp. 78–83.
33. Comment in *The Case of the Stage in Ireland*, pp. 35–37.
34. Expenditure for this department increased heavily. See *L.S.*, pt. 4, I, app. D, also year-end accounts for several years. Messink's notes for mounting the pageants for Garrick's *Jubilee* (1769) are extant, and apparently Garrick adopted most of his suggestions, see *MS* in Folger Library.
35. Forster Collection, vol. II, 213 F.48.F6, pp. 3–6.
36. Folger Library MS.
37. For possible cross-over influences of operatic scenery to that of the comic and tragic stage, see Cecil Price, *Theatre in the Age of Garrick*, pp. 64 and 82, where he quotes at length from the *London Chronicle* 11–14 November 1758, a description of the scenery at the first presentation of Galuppi's opera *Attolo* at the King's Theatre: "The prospect is that of a rock which being open in two or three different places dicovers a wide river, and, in appearance at least half a mile long, the transparency of the water is so well imitated, that we see the shadows of several flags and bulrushes which grow upon it." Professor Price notes the prevailing attitude that "scenery and costume should be as magnificent as possible because opera, ballet, and pantomime appeared to be rather superficial entertainments that needed to please the eye." A major Garrick contribution, however, was the experimental and gradual use of scenic effect to enhance the solid forms of comedy and tragedy, first through pantomime, then through entertainment, then in the stricter forms. By 1761 he was opening the back stage to the street, so the audience could see real people and a bonfire back there in his coronation procession and celebration for George III (disastrously, to be sure, because of the inflow of fog and smoke). In 1769 he was using people from the street in droves for scenic effects in his *Jubilee*, with a touch, so to speak, of actualism. In 1774, as Professor Price quotes from the *Morning Chronicle* (11 December) "At Drury Lane whenever

they make an Apartment they always lower down a suitable ceiling to it [prefiguring the Box Set of 1841?]; not so at Covent Garden . . . Our correspondent would advise *them* to get proper sets of ceilings painted."

Though Garrick often advertised plays with "new Dresses and New Scenes," especially for historical plays, in the 1750s and 1760s, his real interest seems to have followed his return from France. He had written to Sir William Young in 1758 (*Letters*, 209) that he was using his scenes over and over. "We have no Useless scenes—what we have, are in constant Wear, & take their turns as the different Plays & Entertainments are exhibited." His scene painters, French and Messink were constantly busy, and did wonders for his *Jubilee*, but before the 1770s Covent Garden seems to have laid out more on prominent painters George Lambert, Nicholas Dahl, Servandoni, Cipriani, Pierre Royer, and John Clayton than did Garrick. His engagement of de Loutherbourg was novel and exciting. See *L.S.*, pt. 4, I, cix.

38. See Boaden, II, 592; and Merchant, *Shakespeare and the Artist*, pp. 60–61.

39. See Allen, "Stage Spectacles of De Loutherbourg," chap. II–V. Such plays as *Alfred*, *Pigmy Revels* (pantomime for child actors), *Cymon*, *The Fair Quaker of Deal*, *The Christmas Tale*, *Sethona*, *The Maid of the Oaks*, *The Election*, *Harlequin's Jacket*, *Matilda*, *Braganza*, *Queen Mab*, *The Runaway*, and *The Spleen*.

40. See Woodall, *Gainsborough*, pp. 75–76.

41. In January 1773 both the *London* and *Westminster* magazines reported the scenic effects of the *Pigmy Revels*, since "pantomimes are designed for the eye, not for the ear": "The beginning discovers a winter scene . . . then a Register Office . . . then a variety (during the chase) of well-known places in the Metropolis—St. George's in Hanover Square, the west front of St. Paul's, Mews stables, the door of Drury Lane Theatre (viewed from the stage) with people in the boxes . . . Covent Garden Church and Market next appear . . . then Windsor Castle, St. Paul's churchyard, a view of Blackfriar's Bridge, a street scene, a wild heath where the Pigmy King appears to Harlequin; a superb garden scene, a cascade—many admirably executed, and Mr. Dibdin's music characteristic" (*London Magazine*). Blackfriar's Bridge was begun in 1760 and was still a novel sight. The *Westminster Magazine* described the same scenes along with notes on the pleasing Dibdin music. In February 1774 the *Westminster* commented on *Sethona*—"The dresses, scenery and decorations of the play were equal, if not superior, to those of any modern tragedy. The scenes of the Temple of Osiris, and the view of the Egyptian catacombs did great credit to Mr. Loutherbourg." In November it commented on the marvels of *The Maid of the Oaks* and in November 1775 on de Loutherbourg's accomplishments in *Queen Mab*.

42. Aaron Hill in *The Prompter*; Roger Pickering, *Reflections*, app.; the author of *The Dramatic Execution of Agis*; J. R. Planché in his *Cyclopedia of Costume*; among others have scored the age for inconsistencies in costuming. They have found anachronisms similar to those in Shakespeare's plays and medieval paintings unthinkable in the "age of enlightenment." But audiences were unperturbed.

43. See *L.S.*, pt. 4, I, cix–cxxvi, on costuming and scenery.

44. See Pentzell, "Garrick and Costuming." *L.S.*, pt. 4, II, 1137.

45. Garrick's personal library, as revealed in *Catalogue*, Saunders, lists the

following titles on costuming: 660, *Desseins de differens habits de costume de théâtre français*, in colors drawn by J. L. Faesch, 3 vols. 1765; 767, *Dresses of Different Nations . . . Also the Principal Characters of the English Stage*, 2 vols., with 240 plates; M. Darly, *Comic Prints of Characters, Caricatures, Macaronies, &c*. London, 1776, dedicated to Garrick; 1042, *Habillements de plusieur nations representez au naturel, en 137 figures*, n.d.; 1074, J. B. Breuze, *divers habillements suivant costume d'Italie*, 1768. Special attention has often been drawn to the costuming of *Macbeth*, which Garrick played in contemporary regimentals, and for which Macklin sought innovations in the 1770s. Macklin's innovations failed to take hold because of his many other troubles, but see Appleton, *Macklin*, pp. 170–82; Byrne, "Stage Costuming of *Macbeth*", pp. 52–64.

46. *L.S.*, pt. 4, II, 1137.

47. Ibid., p. 1148.

48. Kenrick had long been unpleased with Garrick. His *The Town* published when Garrick was bending every effort to make his new management agreeable, deplored the evening's offering, the entr'acte dancing, and the custom of having an after piece, then turned on the actor himself, and his influence on the coxcombs of London:

> Hail mighty Garrick, chief amongst the throng
> Of leading nonsense, and of apish song.
> To thee with joy the herd of fools submit,
> And curse-me fellows' current coin for wit . . .
> Pleasing the character you set to view [Fribble in
> Garrick's *Miss in Her Teens*]
> (For fools are ever plea'd with what is new)
> The mean infection catches through the street,
> And see a Fribble in every fop we meet . . .
> First taught by thee they boast the strange pretense
> To satire coxcombs, while they murder sense.

The Fribble in Garrick's play, obnoxious to Kenrick, was doubly so in his *Fribbleriad* (1761). Kenrick's gall-dipped pen was poisonous to Colman too, in his *Poetical Epistle to George Colman*, in 24 raw, six-line stanzas.

49. Unpublished, in Forster, vol. XXIV, 213 F.48, F38, pp. 18–20.

50. The musical is in the Royal College of Music, London. XXVI. A 27 (5).

51. See Fiske, *Theatre Music*, chap. 6: "He worked far harder in the cause of English opera than Rich in the fourteen years they were rivals. . . . He also believed that quiet background music could heighten the emotion of such scenes as the one in *King Lear* when the King and Cordelia are reunited." The quality of voices that Garrick recruited was remarkable, over and above the fact that all actors and actresses were supposed to be able to carry tunes: *Bassos*, Samuel Champness, James Kear, Frederick Reinhold, Charles Bannister; *tenors*, Thomas Norris, John Beard (until he left to manage Covent Garden), Joseph Vernon, James Wilder; counter tenor, Daniel Sullivan; sopranos, Mary Young (Mrs Barthélemon), Sophia Baddeley, and Elizabeth Young (as a mezzo-soprano) and Harriet Abrams (as a *lyric soprano*).

52. Settings by John Frederick Lampe and Samuel Howard, and with one yet to come by William Russell.

53. *L.S.*, pt. 4, I, cxxvii–cxxxiv.

54. See Kelly, *Thespis*, who reiterated the point of Garrick's versatility, shining equally and excellently in characters from Sharp to King Lear. He was only disappointed when Garrick on stage at times turned his wondrous face away from the audience. The author was uncomplimentary to Miss Pope, who for him revelled in boistrous scenes:

> And like Clive, too, in those superior spheres
> Where ease delights and elegance endears,
> That shapeless form to grace so unally'd
> That roaring laugh, and manliness of stride,
> In spite of pity force us to be just
> And all we feel is hatred and disgust.

55. *L.S.*, pt. 4, II, January-May, 1767.
56. See *L.S.*, pt. 4, III, under the year 1767; also Page, *Colman*, chap. v.
57. The charge cropped up again in *The Morning Chronicle* (19 October 1772) claiming that the managers (now including Colman) obligated the *Public Advertiser* and *Gazetteer* (by giving them a monopoly for printing accurate play notices) to insert all "puffs" for their own plays and to exclude critical remarks reflecting in any way upon the theatres—simply not a fact. A letter the following month (5 November 1772) praised Woodfall of the *Public Advertiser* for his impartiality.
58. *The Adventurer*, sw, J. Hawkesworth (1752–54); *The Critical Review* m, T. Smollett (1756–); *The Gentleman's Magazine* m, (1731–); *Gray's Inn Journal*, w, A. Murphy (1752–54); *The Monthly Review* m, R. Griffiths (1749–); *The Museum, or Literary and Historical Register* sm, R. Dodsley (1746–47); *The Theatrical Monitor, or the Green Room Laid Open* m, (1767–68); *The Theatrical Review* (1757–58, 1763, 1772); *The Town and Country Magazine* m, (1769–96); *The World*, m, E. Moore (1753–56); and probably *The London Magazine* and *The Westminster Magazine*.
59. *Annual Register, European Magazine, Lady's Magazine, Literary Magazine, The Midwife, The Royal Magazine, St James's Magazine, Universal Magazine, Universal Visitor, Baldwin's London Journal; Bath Chronicle, Bath Journal; Weekly Magazine; London Evening Post, Public Ledger, Whitehall Evening Post.* "Opinion-making" may perhaps be related to the size of the print orders, hence number of papers issued and presumably read. Statistics from the MS accounts of *The Public Advertiser*, from January 1765–December 1771 (British Museum Add. MSS, 38169), when multiplied by the number of different papers published, are suggestive. The print order came to about 1,900–2,000 daily, or 47,515 a month. Advertising brought in about £303, and the street sale of the 47,515 brought in about £380. Monthly income, therefore, came to about £683. Print orders rose that year in December to 55,050, and when the books closed, expenses (paper, press-work, composition, etc.) came to £7,354, offset by income of £7,800. Profit was £446. In the following December the print order had risen to 65,525, and the year's expense came to £8,178, out of an income of £9,128. The profit came to nearly £950. See Dilke, *Papers of a Critic*, II, 28.
60. See Hunt, *Fourth Estate*, II, 97.
61. See Werkmeister, *The London Daily Press*, p. 7.
62. Ibid., p. 4.
63. *L.S.*, pt. 4, I, lxxii.

64. See Haigh, *Gazetteer*, p. vi, and for details on printers' contracts and liabilities, app. B, pp. 270–80.
65. *L.S.*, pt. 4, I, lxxii–lxxvii.
66. He also knew and corresponded with the famous printers and booksellers of the day: Dryden Leach, Paul Vaillant, Thomas Becket, Thomas Evans, John Payne, and Francis Newbery. See index to *Letters*.
67. See Nangle, *Index*. The Garrick items are nos. 534, 535, 855, 4653.
68. Boaden, II, 136.
69. Page, *Colman*, chap. III, and pp. 226–30.
70. Ibid., p. 67.
71. Ibid., p. 70.
72. Ibid., p. 71.
73. Ibid., p. 210.
74. *Checklist*. Professor Knapp traces specific contributions (during Garrick's lifetime alone) in 36 periodicals: 14 monthlies, nine dailies, seven weeklies, and six miscellaneous.
75. Turberville, *Johnson's England*, II, 344.
76. Boaden, I, 443.
77. Mary Knapp, "Verses to Rockingham," pp. 78–81; Boaden, I, 205.
78. Davies, *Memoirs*, II, 117–19.
79. In the late 1760s Mrs Cibber, Mrs Pritchard, Mrs Clive, William Havard, John Palmer, Richard Yates, Mary Ann Yates, Elizabeth Bennett, Henry Vaughan, Elizabeth Hippisley, Prudence Prtichard, and a few others vanished from the scene. New strengths came on under Garrick's recruitment campaign then and in the early 1770s—William Brereton, John Hartry, Thomas and Sophia Baddeley, the Barrys, Francis and James Aickin, James Love, Robert Bensley, James Dodd, John (the younger), Robert, and Wingfield Palmer, James and Mary Ann Wrighten, Frances Abington, Jane Pope, Elizabeth Millidge, and Mrs S. J. Platt.
80. Each was managed by former associates of his at Drury Lane, who had set out (usually with Garrick's help) on their own ventures. See *L.S.*, pt. 4, I, xcix.
81. Walpole, *Montagu*, I, 74.
82. Colman, *Random Records*.
83. William O'Brien, a promising young actor training with Garrick, had married the Earl of Ilchester's daughter. The family forced him to quit the acting profession. See *L.S.*, pt. 4, I, xcviii.
84. Boaden, II, p. 74.
85. The relationship of Cautherly to Garrick remains a minor mystery. In the late 1750s Garrick had invested in India stocks through the advice of Charles Selwyn, his banker in Paris. These and the interest they bore he left in Paris where the value rose to 70,168 livres by 1759. The Forster Collection contains the correspondence between Garrick and his French bankers, in which it appears that in June 1763 he laid out 934 livres for Cautherly and his tutor, young Cautherly having been sent to France for further education. From September 1763 to November 1764 Garrick expended another 18,740 livres for Cautherly [and his tutors]. Cautherly had a room in Garrick's house in London (*Letters*, 393), and lived with the Garricks when they returned from France at least through 1766. Garrick treated him with affection, but hardly of the fatherly kind. He helped him as an actor (*Letters*, 450, 452, 455) in 1767. He

dressed him down rigorously for nonprofessional action when Cautherly abandoned a part which he had kept for nine days, demanding that he think about other people and his duty to the theatre, rather than to his personal interests. (*Letters*, 803).

86. *The Country Girl, L.S.*, pt. 4, II, 1191.

87. Henderson failing to get an engagement with Colman at Covent Garden, renewed his articles with John Palmer at Bath for three years. He then went up to London with Colman, who was managing the Haymarket theatre. Henderson gradually moved on to success at Drury Lane and died, aged 38, in 1785.

88. Henderson *Letters*, pp. 101, 134.

89. Ibid., p. 139.

90. Boaden, II, 45, 52, 63.

91. *L.S.*, pt. 4, III, p. 1941.

92. *Reminiscences*, pp. 5–6.

93. *L.S.*, pt. 4, I, app. D.

## Chapter 11
## London Social Life

1. Boaden, I, 35.

2. Oman, *Garrick*, p. 266, from the Solly Collection.

3. Forster Collection, XXXV, 20, 23.

4. Oman, *Garrick*, p. 72, [Solly Collection.]

5. The copy of *The Fables* is now in the Tinker Collection, Yale University Library. The verses were forth with published in the *London Magazine* (February, p. 95) and later by Dodsley in *Collection of Poems by Various Hands*, II, 327 (Mary Knapp, *Checklist*, p. 267). The inscription reads: "To Lucy Countess of Rochford her Book, D. Garrick, Easton. Aug$^{st}$ 1744."

6. *Catalogue*, Saunders, p. 267.

7. Mary Knapp, *Checklist*, p. 78.

8. Forster Collection, XXXV, 27.

9. Boaden, II, 301.

10. Two of those letters, 20 July and 27 August, which Garrick answered, are in the Berg Collection, New York Public Library. See *Letters*, 63, 70.

11. *L.S.*, pt. 3, II, 1280 (16 January 1747), Drury Lane, Comment.

12. Thirty-four in all, plus four to Lady Hartington. Garrick did not strictly keep to his word to Devonshire: "Nobody knows but my Wife that I have the honor of corresponding w$^{th}$ Y$^r$ Lord$^p$ & I burn Y$^r$ Letters y$^e$ moment that I receive them & have read them" (155). This was written in 1755 when Hartington was in Ireland and applied presumably only to letters with political content. The 19 shorter and more personal extant letters from Hartington cover only a small part of their frequent and long associations in London and at Chiswick, Chatsworth, and Londesburgh.

13. Again from Albano, near Padua, Garrick acknowledged a letter he received from Venice, *Letters*, 334.

14. Boaden, I, 171.

15. Three years later (21 September 1767) in writing the Duke of Newcastle, Garrick referred to "my best friend the late Duke of Devonshire" (474).
16. *Complete Peerage*. See also Pitt, *Correspondence*, II, 206.
17. Boaden, I, 89.
18. Ibid., p. 440.
19. Eight letters to Garrick are in the Harvard Theatre Collection, and one is in the Folger Shakespeare Library.
20. Boaden, I, 285–86. Further he reassured Garrick when his production of Beaumarchais's *Barber of Seville* was attacked by the libelous Charles Theveneau de Morande (Boaden, I, 416–17; II, 235).
21. See Harvard Theatre Collection for Pembroke's letter of 13 February 1773.
22. Forster Collection, vol. XXXII, p. 30; also *Letters*, 730, 742.
23. Fitzmaurice's reply of 20 April is in the Forster Collection, vol. XXXII, p. 42.
24. Forster Collection, XXXII, F.15. See also F.12.
25. *Mémoires*, I, 216; see also Hedgcock, *French Friends*, p. 341.
26. Morellet, *Mémoires*, I, 205–6.
27. Ibid., I, 208–9.
28. Boswell, *Life*, III, 64–79.
29. Paulson, *Hogarth Life*, II, 465.
30. Boaden, I, 250.
31. The translation was eventually made and published by Suard in 1774. Morellet, *Mémoires*, I, 209; *Letters*, 730, 735, 787; Boaden, II, 605; Lonsdale, *Burney*, pp. 111–12.
32. Garrick recommended Hawkesworth to publish Fulke Greville's *Maxims, Characters, and Reflections* (Boswell, *Life*, IV, 535).
33. Boaden, I, 535, 536.
34. Lonsdale, *Burney*, p. 454.
35. Fanny Burney, *Memoirs*, I, 36–46.
36. Ibid., I, 170.
37. Lonsdale, *Burney*, p. 61; *Letters*, 321, 322, 324, 331.
38. Lonsdale, *Burney*, p. 62; *Letters*, 414.
39. Lonsdale, *Burney*, p. 87, and Osborn Collection.
40. Boaden, II, 403; see also *Burney's Continental Travels* (Glover), p. 13; *Burney's Musical Tours* (Scholes), I, 17, 21, 22, 25.
41. *Early Diary*, I, 109.
42. A *General History of Music from the Earliest Ages to the Present Period*, vol. I, 1776 (vols. II, III, IV, followed in 1782–89). The *History* as well as the several tours were published by Becket and promoted among friends by Garrick (Lonsdale, *Burney*, pp. 128, 173; Fanny Burney *Early Diary*, I, 216, 221; Charles Burney, *Memoirs*, I, 271–74).
43. Lonsdale, *Burney*, p. 454.
44. *Memoirs*, I, 166.
45. Fanny Burney, *Early Diary*, I, 144; see also, 168, 197, 212, 253–55; idem, II, 31.
46. For these four plays see Fanny Burney, *Memoirs*, I, 157, 178, 191, 255.
47. See also *Letters*, 1232; *Early Diary*, I, 255.
48. *Early Diary*, I, 254.

49. *L.S.*, pt. 5, I, 96.
50. *Early Diary*, II, 277–84.
51. Ibid., pp. 28–31.
52. *Memoirs*, I, 344–54, 360.
53. *Early Diary*, II, 277–84.
54. Lonsdale, *Burney*, p. 351.
55. *Early Diary*, II, 277–84.
56. Hemlow, *History of Fanny Burney*, 1958, pp. 71–76.
57. *Memoirs*, II, 203–4.
58. Ibid.

## Chapter 12
### Garrick the Occasional Poet

1. Boswell, *Life*, I, 398; idem, II, 325; Mary Knapp, *Prologues*, pp. 11, 13–18.
2. See Mary Knapp, *Checklist*.
3. Introduction, p. 13; and see the preface to the 1974 rev. ed.
4. See Case, *Bibliography*.
5. See Tepper, "Occasional Verse," pp. 239–40.
6. *Poetical Works*, Kearsley, II, 365.
7. They became very popular in the sheet music trade.
8. *Poetical Works*, Kearsley, II, 368, 369.
9. Ibid., p. 374.
10. Ibid., p. 388.
11. Ibid., p. 472.
12. Ibid., p. 483.
13. Ibid., p. 484.
14. Ibid., p. 485.
15. Ibid., p. 514; and Mary Knapp, *Checklist*, no. 4; and idem, "Verses to Rockingham," pp. 78–81.
16. *Poetical Works*, Kearsley, II, 511.
17. Ibid., p. 490; Mary Knapp, *Checklist*, no. 153.
18. *Poetical Works*, II, 489; Mary Knapp, *Checklist*, no. 32.
19. Green, *Short History*, pp. 753–57.
20. Barton, *Garrick*, p. 293.
21. *Poetical Works*, Kearsley, II, 506; Mary Knapp, *Checklist*, no. 220. It appeared (unascribed) in the Dublin issue of *The London Magazine* (April, 1755, p. 221) as an advertisement for the *Dictionary*.
22. *Poetical Works*, Kearsley, II, 532–33.
23. Barton, *Garrick*, p. 290.
24. Oman, *Garrick*, p. 328.
25. *Poetical Works*, Kearsley, II, 532; Mary Knapp, *Checklist*, no. 215.
26. Riddle (*London Chronicle*, 1757); *Poetical Works*, Kearsley, I, 137; Embroidery (*Gentleman's Magazine*, 1740); *Poetical Works*, Kearsley, I, 198; Picture (*Whitehall Evening Post*, 1773); *Poetical Works, Kearsley*, I, 93; House (*St James's Chronicle*, 1769); *Poetical Works*, Kearsley, II, 516; Gothic Prophecy (*St James's Chronicle*, 1769); *Poetical Works*, Kearsley, II, 518.

27. *Poetical Works*, Kearsley, I, 3; Mary Knapp, *Checklist*, no. 101.
28. *Poetical Works*, Kearsley, I, 127–29; Mary Knapp, *Checklist*, no. 282.
29. *Poetical Works*, Kearsley, I, 132; Mary Knapp, *Checklist*, no. 309.
30. *Poetical Works*, Kearsley, I, 134; Mary Knapp, *Checklist*, no. 285.
31. Mary Knapp, *Prologues*, p. 313.
32. *Poetical Works*, Kearsley, I, 80–81; Mary Knapp, *Checklist*, no. 382.
33. *Poetical Works*, Kearsley, I, 84; Mary Knapp, *Checklist*, no. 335.
34. *Poetical Works*, Kearsley, I, 85; Mary Knapp, *Checklist*, no. 390.
35. *Poetical Works*, Kearsley, I, 102; Mary Knapp, *Checklist*, no. 350. The vaulting Turk referred to the acrobatic team of Caratha, employed at Covent Garden.
36. *Poetical Works*, Kearsley, I, 150; Mary Knapp, *Checklist*, no. 280.
37. *Poetical Works*, Kearsley, I, 158.
38. Ibid., 192; Mary Knapp, *Checklist*, no. 357.
39. *Poetical Works*, Kearsley, I, 171; Mary Knapp, *Checklist*, no. 356.
40. *Poetical Works*, Kearsley, II, 281; Mary Knapp, *Checklist*, no. 400.
41. *Poetical Works*, Kearsley, II, 327; Mary Knapp, *Checklist*, no. 377.

## Chapter 13
### Garrick's Friendships with Women of Distinction

1. *L.S.*, pt. 3, II, 1224. For a fuller biography and primary sources, see *Letters*, I, xxxv–xxxvii, *and* III, app. A.
2. *Autobiography of Carlyle*, pp. 192–93.
3. Walpole, *Montagu*, I, 28.
4. *L.S.*, pt. 3, II, 1268.
5. Ibid., p. 1275.
6. *L.S.*, pt. 3, II, 1280: "Mademoiselle Violette humbly begs leave to acquaint the Publick, that she is very much concern'd to hear that she is charg'd with having been the occasion for the Noise at the Playhouse in Drury Lane on Wednesday night. That she was entirely ignorant that three dances had been advertised, until it was too late to prepare herself; and as she cannot possibly be guilty of any Intention to disoblige, or give offence to an English Audience (from whom she has receiv'd so much applause) she presumes to hope they will not impute to her a fault which she is not capable of committing, and especially where she has met with so much indulgence, for what she retains all possible gratitude."
7. Ibid., p. 1287.
8. *Correspondence with Mann*, II, 42: "Plays only are in fashion at one house, the best company that perhaps ever were gathered together, Quin Garrick, Mrs Pritchard, Mrs Cibber; at the other Barry, a favorite young actor, and the Violette, whose dancing our friends don't like: I scold them but all their answer is, 'Lord, you are *so* English.'"
9. For a copy of the marriage contract, see George Pierce Baker, *Unpublished Correspondence*, pp. 16–22.
10. Paulson, *Hogarth, Life*, I, 85.
11. From the little known of Mrs Garrick's family with the passing of years, they neither merited nor won Garrick's respect. Apparently her father had died

before the marriage, but the mother, Eva Rosina, lived on for many years, pathetically expressing her gratitude and dependence in her own letters and those of her children. A sister Therese Fürst, dictated on 26 February 1752 a distressing letter to a father confessor announcing the death at birth of a son, and detailing domestic bickerings of a family hard pressed for money. There was also a brother, Ferdinand Charles, who visited Mrs Garrick "twice in England not much to her satisfaction." One of his letters survives, dated from Vienna, 12 December 1772, in which he acknowledges receiving £80, and refers to his mother as still living. Several years later Elizabeth (Liserl) Fürst, daughter of Peter Fürst, a retired Viennese municipal inspector, and Therese, Mrs Garrick's sister, came to live with her aunt in June 1777 (*Letters*, 1134 n.3). After the death of Garrick, who left her £1000 in his will, she returned to Vienna, and on 2 July 1781, married Joseph Peter Adam von Saar (1762–1830), imperial royal councillor of finance in the Austrian Postal Service. The Garricks did not visit Vienna when they were traveling on the Continent. Other than for one or two benefactions (mentioned above), none of Mrs Garrick's family are named in the will. Garrick specified if Mrs Garrick resided abroad after his death she was no longer to receive the income provided for her in his will. On the other hand Mrs Garrick seems to have saved out of income (notably after Garrick's death) funds she gave to her family.

12. Folger Shakespeare Library; Mary Knapp, *Checklist*, p. 261.

13. Folger Shakespeare Library.

14. For a description, see the deed in the David Mason Little Collection, Harvard University Library.

15. *The Letters of Laurence Sterne*, ed. L. P. Curtis (Oxford, 1935, p. 157).

16. Boaden, I, 173.

17. *Autobiography*, I, 284.

18. James C. Nicholls, *Riccoboni's Letters*, p. 18.

19. F. C. Green, "Robert Liston et mme Riccoboni," 550–58; James C. Nicholls, *Riccoboni's Letters*, p. 28.

20. Luigi Riccoboni was also the ablest historian of continental drama, six of whose books in French and English translation Garrick sooner or later had in his library.

21. James C. Nicholls, *Riccoboni's Letters*, pp. 226–28.

22. See Crosby, *Une Romancière Oubliée*, pp. 175–83.

23. *DNB*; James Nicholls, *Riccoboni's Letters*, passim.

24. James C. Nicholls, *Riccoboni's Letters*, pp. 50, 101, 229.

25. Ibid., p. 52.

26. Ibid., p. 128.

27. Presumably to passages, such as the following: "La traduction des premiers ouvrages de ce poète [Shakespeare] nous révolta. Les Français frémirent en lisant Richard III; tant de morts entassés dans Hamlet, nous firent penser (un peu légrèment, à la verité) que sur les bords de la Tamise, on se plaisoit à voir répandre le sang. Le temps a dissipé cette errour, mais san en effacer absolument la trace. . . . A Londres, les personnes distinguées vont raremont à la comedie; l'emploi leur temps et l'heure de leurs repas, ne leur permettant guère d'être libres quand elle commence. C'est donc a la bourgeoisie, même au peuple que l'on est obligé de plaire." Pp. ii–iii.

28. "Pardon, mon ami, pardon. J'ai tort, un grand tort." James C. Nicholls,

p. 149. Vol. I: Edward Moor, *The Foundling* (1747); Arthur Murphy, *The Way to Keep Him* (1760); vol. II: Hugh Kelly, *False Delicacy* (1768); and George Colman, *The Jealous Wife* (1761) and *The Deuce is in Him* (1763).

29. James C. Nicholls, *Riccoboni's Letters*, p. 152.
30. Ibid., p. 103.
31. Ibid., p. 81, also pp. 70, 80, 123.
32. Ibid., pp. 135–36.
33. Ibid., p. 81.
34. Ibid., p. 153.
35. Ibid., p. 155. See also, Hedgcock, *French Friends*, p. 360.
36. James C. Nicholls, *Riccoboni's Letters*, p. 268.
37. Ibid., p. 154.
38. Ibid., p. 228.
39. Ibid., pp. 263, 267; Boaden, II, 279.
40. Stewart, *Riccoboni*, p. 122.
41. James C. Nicholls, *Riccoboni's Letters*, p. 406.
42. Boswell, *Life*, IV, 64.
43. Ten surviving in the Museum at Stratford and one in the Folger Shakespeare Library.
44. Boaden, I, 376.
45. Blunt, *Mrs Montagu*, I, 356.
46. Boaden, I, 389.
47. He flattered her also: "wishing You would as secretly a play, as you did a certain Essay [*On the Genius and Writings of Shakespeare*], & that I, as Manager, might partake of yᵉ plot and yᵉ Profits" (597). The stillborn effort of this "Bon Ton" is not to be confused with Garrick's *Bon Ton; or, High Life Above Stairs* (1760).
48. Boaden, I, 394–95.
49. Ibid., I, 385. Her *Essay on the Genius and Writings of Shakespeare, Compared with the Greek and French Dramatic Poets, with Some Remarks upon the Misrepresentations of Mons. de Voltaire* (London, 1769, 1770, 1772, 1777 and Paris, 1777, in translation), deals with "Dramatic Poetry," "Historic Drama," "The First Part of King Henry IV," "The Second Part of Henry IV," "Preternatural Beings," "The Tragedy of Macbeth," "The *Cinna* of Corneille," and "The Death of Julius Caesar." In the initial chapter she paid tribute to Garrick, observing "Shakespeare's very spirit seems to come forth and to animate his characters as often as Mr. Garrick who acts with the same inspiration with which he wrote, assumes them on the stage" (2d ed., pp. 15–16).
50. 23 August 1776. The attack was later published as *A Lettre de M. de Voltaire à l'Academie Française* (Genoa, 1776), a copy of which she sent to Garrick (Boaden, II, 183, 20 October 1776).
51. To the invitation she responded: "I remember 60 years ago in the same Academy old Homer had met with the same treatment with Shakespeare; but that they now did justice to Homer, I did not doubt but they would do so to Shakespeare; for that Great Geniuses survived those who set up to be their critics, or more absurdly to be their rivals. . . . Indeed everything but the paper on Voltaire was very ingenious, and such as did honour to the speaker and the Assembly." (Blunt, *Mrs Montagu*, I, 330–31). See also her letter to Garrick 3 November 1776 (Boaden, II, 188).

52. Boswell, *Life*, IV, 275, n.3.

53. Ibid., p. 275.

54. As examples of Mrs Montagu's judgment, Blunt cites "Her just appreciation of Falstaff's charm; her chaff of Mrs. Carter; her laughing letters from Spa; her criticisms of the pompous Gray; the infatuated Hanway, the amazing Chudleigh; her love of Monsey's foolery; her appreciation of Tristram and of his fretful spouse; her efforts to evoke the best out of Tom Lyttleton; her love of adventurous Emin . . . are good to remember." (*Mrs Montagu*, II, 364).

55. Johnson, *Letters*, 443.

56. Ibid., p. 445.

57. *Mrs Montagu*, II, 362–63.

58. Ibid., I, 350.

59. Boaden, I, 397.

60. William Roberts, *More*, I, 51.

61. Mary Knapp, *Checklist*, pp. 362, 363.

62. Her comments and insights were shrewd: of Percy, "quite a sprightly modern, instead of a rusty antique, as I expected." Of Johnson's *Tour of the Hebrides*, "It is an agreeable work, though the subject is sterility itself. He knows how to avail himself of the commonest circumstances, and trifles are no longer trifles when they have passed through his hands" (William Roberts, *More*, I, 49 and 391).

63. William Roberts, *More*, I, 46.

64. Stonhouse had submitted it a year earlier in MS. The text was printed by Cadell in Bristol 1774. The play was based on Metastasio's *Attolo Regolo*.

65. William Roberts, *More*, I, 52, 53.

66. Ibid., I, 56.

67. Ibid., p. 68.

68. Ibid., pp. 68, 69.

69. Ibid., p. 78.

70. Ibid., p. 84.

71. Ibid., p. 87.

72. Garrick's nickname for Hannah More, because she was the epitome of the Nine Muses.

73. Boaden, II, 159.

74. William Roberts, *More*, I, 111, 112; also *Letters*, 1114.

75. Boaden, II, 163–64.

76. Ibid., p. 229.

77. Ibid., p. 267.

78. Ibid., p. 278.

79. Fitzgerald, *Life of Clive*, p. 101. From original in Forster Collection.

80. Spencer and Dobson, *Garrick and Spencer*, p. 119.

81. Boaden, II, 295.

82. See William Roberts, *More*, I, 146; Boswell, *Life*, III, 256–60; *Letters*, 1163.

83. She had sent him three acts to which he replied with careful criticism 23 November 1778 (Boaden, II, 314; *Letters*, 1184 and 1209), but Garrick died in January 1779 without having seen the full MS. Harris eagerly sought to produce it with Sheridan's help for an epilogue, but the play lasted only three nights late in 1779.

84. Boswell, *Life*, III, 293 n.5. Mrs Montagu was flowry in her praise: "Let me beg you my dear to allow your muse still to adorn British names and British places. Wherever you lead the fairy dance, flowers will spring up. Your rock will stand unimpaired for ages, as eminent as any in Grecian Parnassus" (William Roberts, *More*, I, 60).

85. William Roberts, *More*, I, 70. Garrick later printed in the *Public Advertiser* and the *Morning Chronicle* his answer to Chesterfield's contention that women had genius, namely six sportive verses "Upon Reading *Sir Eldred of the Bower*, by a Lady" (Garrick, *Poetical Works*, p. 535, and Mary Knapp, *Checklist*, p. 239).

86. Mary Knapp, *Checklist*, 255.

87. William Roberts, *More*, I, 133–34.

88. Ibid., p. 147.

89. Ibid., p. 149.

90. Spencer and Dobson, *Garrick and Spencer*, p. 5 n.1.

91. Ibid., p. xvi.

92. Ibid., pp. 3–5.

93. Ibid., pp. 9–11.

94. Ibid., p. 15. Pascal Paoli, the Corsican patriot landed in England in September 1769 and was thereafter much entertained.

95. Ibid., pp. 51, 73.

96. Ibid., p. 75.

97. Ibid., pp. 59, 61, 63; see also pp. 19, 39, 89.

98. Ibid., pp. 119, 158.

99. Ibid., p. 134.

100. Ibid., p. 133, 137.

101. Ibid. All in all 58 letters from Garrick, four from Mrs Garrick, and 14 from Lady Spencer; no letters are acknowledged that have not survived. While the Spencers were abroad in the summer of 1777, Garrick wrote Lady Spencer ten letters to her one in reply and acknowledgment.

102. Ibid., p. 89.

103. Ibid., pp. 27, 55, 71: also such notations as, "Lady Spencer is a divine woman" (*Letters*, 1052); "Heavenly Lady Spencer to me" (Spencer, p. 37); "Celestial Duchess" (Ibid., p. 39). In his letters to her, however, he never dropped the formalities of salutation, complimentary close, the terms of Lady or Lord, and Mr, and the titles of formal address, nor did she.

104. Ibid., p. 33.

105. Ibid., p. 123.

106. Ibid., p. 49.

107. Ibid., p. 17.

108. Ibid., pp. 143–44.

109. Ibid., 131. Incidentally and yet characteristically, in late 1778, Garrick ordered from Anne Louise Lane, who with her sister had for several years produced hair pictures (exhibited annually at the Society of Artists), a copy of Reynolds's portrait of John Campbell (later Lord Cawder) as well as pictures of himself and Shakespeare done in the hair of Lady Spencer and the Duchess of Devonshire, as well as of Mrs Garrick and his own.

110. Ibid., p. 161; *Letters*, 1221.

111. Spencer and Dobson, *Garrick and Spencer*, p. xviii.

## Chapter 14
## Patron of the Arts

1. The annotations in this chapter are limited to primary sources and quotations. The history of eighteenth century art has been pursued in the many standard studies of the various genre and artists, fully and authoritatively covered by Joseph Burke, *English Art, 1714–1800*, with full critical bibliography, and by Roy C. Strong, *Tudor and Jacobean Portraits*, 1969. In particular we wish to thank Martin Anglesea, of the Ulster Museum, Belfast, for the great favor of xerox copy of his "David Garrick and the Visual Arts" (279 pages), M.Lit. dissertation, University of Edinburgh, 1971, which has long since merited publication. In part III, "Catalogue of Representations of Garrick in Contemporary Painting and Sculpture," Mr Anglesea has assembled alphabetically authors, a description, the provenance, number of copies, successive owners, exhibitions, engravings, later reproductions, and the pertinent bibliography for each picture and sculpture. General Acknowledgments are also made to: Merchant, *Shakespeare and the Artist*, esp. chaps. III, IV; Mander and Mitchenson, *The Artist and the Theatre*; Bertelson, "Garrick and Painting," 308–24; Adams, *Catalogue*; Benezit, *Dictionnaire*; Graham Reynolds, *Miniatures*, esp. pp. 126–27; Hind, *Engravings*.

2. Dodsley and Dodsley, *London Environs*; pp. 1–10, I, 112–13, 224–32; Lees-Milne, *Earls of Creation*, pp. 140–56; Charlton, *Chiswick House*. William Kent, the leading architect-gardener, designed the ticket for the Violette's benefit performance; it was engraved by George Vertue.

4. Vertue, *Notebooks*, III, 91; Girouard, "English Art"; 13 January 1966; Paulson, *Hogarth's Graphic Works*; Esdaile, *Roubillac*.

4. Whitley, *Artists and Their Friends*, I, 158.

5. John Forster, *Goldsmith*, I, 239.

6. Enthoven Collection, 4 June 1771.

7. Whitley, *Artists and Their Friends*, I, 282.

8. Algernon Graves, *The Society of Artists*; Hudson and Luckhurst, *The Royal Society of Arts*.

9. *Catalogue*, Saunders [781–83]. Hereafter to avoid confusion with data in parentheses, all references, by number only, to the catalogues and inventories are enclosed in brackets.

10. The building was still standing in 1978 with some survival of the old elegance of the paneling (*Letters*, 60).

11. The David Mason Little Collection, Harvard College Library.

12. Later removed to the British Museum after Mrs Garrick's death. Several of the green and white hall chairs are now in the Victoria and Albert Museum. Another chair, on exhibition on the front stairs of the Garrick Club, is of painted pine with gold lining on a Chinese red background, upholstered with Garrick's arms. The most distinctly Garrickian room designed by Mrs Garrick, was the Chinese Drawing Room, on the second floor east. The antechamber for the drawing room was a gallery for drawings and prints. From the drawing room one passed into the bedroom and dressing room, from which has survived the japanned and decorated furniture, with the famous chintz (*Letters*, 912), on display in the Victoria and Albert Museum. In addition to the 1779 in-

ventory, see Galbraith, "Garrick's Furniture at Hampton," pp. 45–65. On the furniture in the Garrick Club, see *The Antique Collector*, December 1973, pp. 283–91.

13. In his will Garrick specified that an inventory shall be taken of "all and every . . . Pictures Household Goods and Furniture of and in both the said Houses at Hampton and Adelphi at the time of my decease" (app. G, p. 1663). In 1970, the two inventories became the property of the Victoria and Albert Museum. We wish to make grateful acknowledgment to Allan Millar, the librarian, for the privilege of examining, and assistance in deciphering xerox copies of the two inventories. I (Hampton): The furniture, 252 items, is listed in 36 rooms; the fixtures in 35 rooms and areas, followed by a catalogue by rooms and in 87 entries (many listing two pictures totaling ca. 144 pictures in all, 40 folio pages in all, plus an additional two folios in Mrs Garrick's hand of items overlooked. II (Royal Terrace Adelphi): Room by room, of 128 pictures, plus an addenda of one folio page in Mrs Garrick's hand, 29 pages in all.

Both inventories are basic to any examination, notably of the pictures, in Garrick's possession at his death. The several auction catalogues of 1823 have been carefully checked against these inventories. In general Mrs Garrick made few changes by gift and by will, between 1779 and 1822, her death, notably in disposing to heirs a number of family portraits. References are made to the published catalogues, therefore, as more accurate in the identification of the pictures, and more generally available. *Catalogue*, Burrell, for Hampton, describes all in all, 37 rooms, the pictures in one category.

14. Delany, *Autobiography*, I, 284.

15. Ripley, *Hampton-on-Thames*, p. 14.

16. When the Garricks moved into their house, no. 5, Royal Terrace, in March 1772, the entire project was not yet completed. Later the Garricks had as neighbors their friend Topham Beauclerk in no. 3; Robert Adam in no. 4; Dr John Turton (who had attended Garrick in his illness in Munich) in no. 7; and at Garrick's request, Thomas Becket, his personal bookseller and publisher, who leased a corner house for his bookshop. For some comment on the furnishings, see Rogal, "David Garrick at the Adelphi"; *Survey of London*, chap. 14, "The Adelphi Terrace."

17. See *Catalogue*, Robins.

18. See *Catalogue*, Christie II, 5 May 1825, entries 151–73, 156-A.

19. *Catalogue*, Burrell, p. 12, no. 4, p. 6, no. 9; *Catalogue*, Christie II, nos. 70, 170, 171; Taite, "Garrick," 100–7.

20. Of interest, no doubt, were the copious illustrations therein depicting the stage mechanics of French theatres.

21. Christie I. A full and accurate listing of the Garrick collection of pictures, statuary, and the like, is thwarted in the inventories of 1779 by the scant nature of the entries in the order of location, the unfamiliarity of the appraisers of the collection, occasionally corrected by Mrs Garrick (?), frequent failure to identify artists, and an incompleteness filled out by Mrs Garrick in several additional folio pages. The catalogues of Christie and Burrell of some 40 years later, though fuller in describing pictures, vary from the inventories in ascription of painters, omit other items, but add some valuable biographical information not found in the inventories. We have not been able to examine a copy of Burrell's catalogue for the sale of the furnishings of the Adelphi, 1823.

22. His famous *View of the Eruption of Mt Vesuvius*, done under Hamilton's direction was for a time on display at Hampton. No. 23, 24, 27, 34, 35; Christie I, 24. See also Roberts, *Memorials*, I, ix, 108.

23. Boaden, II, 172 now in possession of G. M. Kahrl; Inventory II, 106, Christie I, 76.

24. In *Letters*, 47 (also 33) Garrick elaborates carefully his pictorial analysis of the scene. Although the project of the six pictures was not carried through, Hayman did complete the one on *Othello*, later used by Charles Jennens as a frontispiece of his edition of *Othello*.

25. Christie I, 45. A. L. S., Hayman to Garrick, ca. Oct. 15, 1745, Folger. Sooner or later Garrick obtained and exhibited *A Whole Length Portrait of Mr. Wyndham in a Military Dress* [Inventory II, Christie I, 47].

26. Anglesea, "David Garrick," p. 226.

27. Ibid., p. 230; for his friendship with Garrick see Dapp, *George Keate*, pp. 59–74.

28. Mrs Garrick's will of 1822; Anglesea, *David Garrick*, pp. 233–34.

29. Hilles, *Portraits*, p. 87.

30. Woodall, *Gainsborough*.

31. Ibid.

32. Ibid.; Boaden, I, 472.

33. John Hayes, *The Drawings of Thomas Gainsborough*, II, 90; Whitley, "Art Chronicle," pp. 25–66.

34. Woodfall, *Gainsborough*, nos. 44, 45.

35. *The Idler*, 45 (1759).

## Chapter 15
## Garrick's Great Comic Roles

1. See chap. 2, above.

2. Count made from *L.S.*, pts. 3 and 4.

3. Under the pseudonym Sir Nicholas Nipclose. See Gentleman, *Theatres*, p. 46.

4. See Stone, "Garrick's Significance," pp. 183–99.

5. Boaden, I, 216–17.

6. Ibid., I, p. 385.

7. Davies, *Dramatic Miscellanies*, III, 180.

8. Murphy, *Life*, I, 32.

9. Ibid., p. 33.

10. Davies, *Dramatic Miscellanies*, III, 179–80.

11. Thomas Wilkes, *General View*, pp. 256–57.

12. Pp. 169–70.

13. Folger, "Scrapbook."

14. *L.S.*, pt. 4, III, 1833. See unfavorable review in *Westminster Magazine*, 1774, p. 472.

15. With some 187 performances at both theatres in Garrick's time alone, outdoing the popularity earlier of *The Recruiting Officer*.

16. Thomas Wilkes, *General View*, pp. 254–55.

17. John Hill, *The Actor*, pp. 21–22.

18. Gentleman, *Dramatic Censor*, I, 138.
19. Lichtenberg, *Visits*, pp. 66–67.
20. Ibid., pp. 25–27.
21. Thomas Wilkes, *General View*, p. 258.
22. Davies, *Dramatic Miscellanies*, II, 67–68.
23. Davies, *Memoirs*, I, 61.
24. Lichtenberg, *Visits*, pp. 3–4.
25. Lichtenberg noted that in this boxing scene, "Garrick runs about and skips from one neat leg to the other with such admirable lightness one would dare swear he was floating in the air" (*Visits*, p. 7).
26. See above, chap. 2, pp. 42–43.
27. See Richard Dircks, "Garrick and Gentleman," pp. 48–55.
28. *The London Chronicle*, 14 October 1758.
29. Ibid.
30. Forster Collection, "News Clippings," no. 319.
31. Murphy, *Life*, I, 100.
32. This sequence, like that of air-drawn daggers in Macbeth, Garrick gave in the salons of Paris to demonstrate English acting.
33. See discussion in Bergmann, "David Garrick, Producer," pp. 73–97.
34. See (448) to Sir John Delaval, where Garrick says that "Fix'd attention to the Business of y^e Scene . . . is the Sine qua non of Acting." The most complete discussion of the *Provoked Wife* promptbook and its stage implications is in Burnim, *David Garrick, Director*, pp. 174–88.
35. Lichtenberg, *Visits*, pp. 18–19.
36. Ibid., 17–18.
37. *L.S.*, pt. 4, III, 1924.
38. Murphy, *Life*, I, 118.
39. Foote, *Roman and English Comedy Compared*.
40. For March 1747, pp. 133–39.
41. Davies, *Memoirs*, I, 140.
42. Murphy, *Life*, 123–24.
43. *Poetical Works*, Kearsley, I, 93.
44. Telltruth, *Herald*, II, p. 56. As a member of Garrick's extreme opposition he objected in general to his voice, his pauses, his deportment, and his "fidgiting."
45. *Dramatic Censor*, II, 347.
46. In the fictional *Dialogue in the Shades Between the Celebrated Mrs Cibber, and the no less Celebrated Mrs Woffington* (London, 1766) p. 4, Garrick's "charm in Ranger was by nature formed to please the sex; and I believe there was scarce a woman off or on the stage who saw him, who did not wish to be Mrs. Strictland."
47. Prologue to the Opening of the Theatre, 1750.
48. *L.S.*, pt. 4, I, clxii.
49. Benedict, Leontes, Posthumus.
50. Thomas Wilkes, *General View*, p. 259.
51. *L.S.*, pt. 4, I, 140.
52. Thomas Wilkes, *General View*, p. 259.
53. T. Cibber *To David Garrick*, p. 64.
54. Henderson, *Letters and Poems*, p. 122.
55. Murphy, *Life*, I, 155.

56. Davies, *Memoirs*, II, 99.

57. Gentleman, *Dramatic Censor*, II, 318–19.

58. *Morning Chronicle*, 4 November 1772.

59. See Sprague, *Shakespeare and the Actors*, p. 17.

60. Lichtenberg, *Visits*, p. 7.

61. Thomas Wilkes, *General View*, p. 261.

62. *The London Chronicle*, 1–3 February 1775, noted the paltry dialogue of Mrs Centlivre, concluding, "This play is a proof what what the players call business will succeed without writing when it is in the hands of such excellent performers."

63. Thomas Wilkes, *General View*, p. 258.

64. *Life*, I, 205–6.

65. Ibid., p. 207.

66. Davies, *Dramatic Miscellanies*, II, 43.

67. Felix, disguised, seeks to leave under pretext of drunkenness, and scampers away as Don Pedro asks him to smoke a pipe and share a bottle with him. The escape takes nine lines in the Centlivre text. In the 1776 Garrick acting text (substantiated by the manuscript elaboration now in the Folger Shakespeare Library, YD.147 in Garrick's hand) the scene is expanded to 26 lines of comic byplay in which Don Felix maneuvers Pedro into becoming an adversary urging him to leave, not just allowing him to scamper out. Much more comic, and much more dramatic!

68. *Essay on Satirical Entertainments*, p. 8.

## Chapter 16
### Garrick's Great Tragic Roles

1. See Hilles, *Portraits*, p. 118.

2. Edward Taylor, *Cursory Remarks*, p. 16.

3. Forster Collection, "News Clippings," no. 64.

4. Count made from *L.S.*, pts. 3 and 4.

5. Davies, *Dramatic Miscellanies*, I, 57 and 63.

6. For the number and variety of Garrick's performances of tragic characters, see app. B. Parts from Shakespeare's plays far outran those of other dramatists.

7. Davies, *Memoirs*, I, 40–44.

8. William Cooke, *Memoirs*, p. 99.

9. Boaden, I, 3, 4.

10. Ibid., p. 4.

11. T. Cibber, *To David Garrick*, p. 56.

12. Ibid., p. 63.

13. Thomas Wilkes, *General View*, p. 237.

14. Ibid., pp. 236–39.

15. Murphy, *Life*, I, 22–24.

16. By one who signed himself D. H.

17. In the Bell edition of Shakespeare's plays, 1774. See also Stone, "Bloody Bold, and Complex Richard."

18. *L.S.*, pt. 4, III, 1982.

19. Ibid., pp. 1984–85.

20. Davies, *Memoirs*, I, 54.

21. Gentleman, *Dramatic Censor*, II, 57.

22. Ibid., I, 73–74.

23. Cumberland, *Memoirs*, pp. 59–60.

24. Thomas Wilkes, *General View*, p. 252.

25. Garrick wrote to Richard Penn (773) that it was unseemly for him at an advanced age to play the young rake. He advised Charles Yorke (438) not to engage a box for the command performance: "When by order of the Duke of York I shall be oblig'd to Act a Character, not well suited to my time of life, which is Lothario . . . I would rather wish that Mrs. Yorke did not see me in that part which I would willingly have excused myself from but his Rl Highness would not be said nay."

26. She performed in similar fashion at Rooker's benefit (Ophelia in *Hamlet*, 29 April 1763) as noted in *The Theatrical Review* (1 May 1763): "I hope you will not let such a flagrant outrage to the decorum of the stage as the following pass unnoticed. As [Mrs Cibber] sat upon the stage, with Hamlet at her feet in the third act, she rose up three several times, and made as many courtsies, and those very low ones, to some ladies in the boxes. Pray good Sir, ask her in what part of the play it is said that the Danish Ophelia is acquainted with so many British ladies?" *L.S.*, pt. 4, II, 993.

27. Davies, *Dramatic Miscellanies*, III, 145.

28. Murphy, *Life*, I, 139.

29. Ibid., pp. 149–50.

30. Ibid., p. 143.

31. Boaden, I, 110.

32. Derrick, *Dramatic Censor*, p. 8; and Gentleman, *Dramatic Censor*, I, 313. The first number seems to have been done by Samuel Derrick and redone by Gentleman 20 years later.

33. Derrick, *Dramatic Censor*, p. 41.

34. Thomas Wilkes, *General View*, pp. 241–43.

35. Gentleman, *Dramatic Censor*, I, 327–35.

36. Forster Collection, "News Clippings," no. 126.

37. See Stone, "Garrick's Production of *King Lear*," 89–103.

38. London, 1747.

39. *The Adventurer*, no. 113.

40. During the years 1753–54, *Gray's Inn Journal*, nos. 65–67.

41. Ibid., p. 67.

42. Boaden, I, 158.

43. James Beattie in a letter to Garrick, 20 May 1773 (Boaden, I, 539) wrote: "Whether I can outlive the distresses of Lear when personated by you, is uncertain; for once in the character of Macbeth you almost murdered me as well as Duncan;—but I wish to make a trial, and if I fall a martyr to Garrick and Shakspeare, I shall from that circumstance have some chance of being remembered as a person who had had feelings of a man, and the imagination of a poet."

44. *General View*, pp. 234–35.

45. *Visits*, pp. 32, 68.

46. See n.40.

47. I, 27–28.
48. See Gray, *Theatrical Criticism*, p. 113.
49. *Dramatic Miscellanies*, II, 180–81.
50. Boaden, I, 539. See also Edward Taylor's *Cursory Remarks* on the effect of instant communication of Lear's feelings to the author.
51. *L.S.*, pt. 4, III, 1977.
52. 21–23 May 1776.
53. Boaden, II, 617.
54. *L.S.*, pt. 4, III, 1980.
55. Boaden, I, 13–14.
56. Ibid., p. 11.
57. Ibid., p. 23.
58. Ibid., p. 25.
59. Ibid., p. 26.
60. Ibid., p. 28.
61. Ibid., p. 109.
62. Murphy, *Life*, I, 46–47.
63. Davies, *Memoirs*, I, 64.
64. For full discussion see Burnim, *David Garrick, Director*, pp. 168–69.
65. Lichtenberg, *Visits*, p. 17.
66. See John Kelly, *German Visitors*, p. 61.
67. Lichtenberg, *Visits*, pp. 9–11.
68. Ibid., p. 16.
69. The purity and effectiveness of Garrick's enunciation of the "To be, or not to be" soliloquy, and its familiarity to thousands of Englishmen prompted the rhetorician Joshua Steele to use it as a model for fine speech in his *Essay*. Therein he established a set of markings over the syllables by which pitch and quantity could be noted: "There is a perfection in the pronunciation of the best speakers (which was remarkable in the late Mrs Cibber and is the same in Mr Garrick) they are distinctly heard even in the softest sounds of their voices, while others are scarcely intelligible though offensively loud. The essential is chiefly owing the speaker's dwelling with nearly uniform loudness on the whole length of every syllable, and adopting a deliberate instead of a rapid manner."
70. I, 34.
71. See Stone, "Garrick's Alteration of *Hamlet*."
72. *L.S.*, pt. 4, III, 1983.
73. Boaden, II, 148.
74. Davies, *Dramatic Miscellanies*, II, 105.
75. Ibid., p. 73.
76. For full discussion of the text, restored passages, and scholarly cooperation with Warburton and Johnson see Stone, "Garrick's Handling of *Macbeth*," 609–28.
77. Forster Collection, "News Clippings," no. 191.
78. Davies, *Dramatic Miscellanies*, II, 105–6.
79. Forster Collection, "News Clippings," 11 October 1759.
80. Thomas Wilkes, *General View*, pp. 248–49.
81. Boaden, I, 132–38.
82. Ibid., pp. 377–78.
83. Forster Collection, "News Clippings," no. 21.
84. Noverre, *Letters on Dancing*, pp. 84–85.

85. Boaden, I, 30.
86. Colley Cibber, *Apology*, p. 65.
87. For documentation see Stone, "Garrick and *Othello*," pp. 305–20, and "Shakespeare in the Periodicals," pp. 327–28.
88. *L.S.*, pt. 4, 362.
89. See Stone, "Garrick and *Othello*," pp. 306–7.
90. See Kirkman, *Memoirs*, II, 260.
91. Boaden, I, 30.
92. Published in *The Edinburgh Magazine*, LXXX (1884), 5.
93. See Genest, *English Stage*, IV, 147–48.
94. See *Letter of Complaint*, p. 16.
95. See John Hill, *The Actor*, pp. 248, 249, 283.
96. Boaden, I, 592.
97. See Bergmann, "Garrick's *Zara*," 225–32.
98. Ibid.
99. Davies, *Memoirs*, I, 178.
100. Boaden, II, 35.
101. *London Chronicle*, 27–29 January 1757.
102. He had begun preparations in July 1750, as he wrote to Lacy, *Letters*, 93.
103. *L.S.*, pt. 4, II, and III, under dates of performance.
104. For discussion of text alteration and stage history, see Stone, "*Romeo and Juliet*," 191–206.
105. Morgan, *Letter to Miss Nossiter*, pp. 50–56.
106. See verses of I. H—tt, in *The Daily Advertiser*, 12 October 1750:

> "Well What's tonight?" says angry Ned,
>    As up from bed he rises.
> "Romeo again!" and shakes his head,
>    A plague on both your houses!

107. See Stone, "*Romeo and Juliet*," p. 195.
108. Thomas Wilkes, *General View*, p. 251.
109. Forster Collection, MS vol. XXII, pp. 243–46, letter from Popple to Garrick 30 October 1753.
110. Gentleman, *Dramatic Censor*, I, 171.
111. On 6, 13, and 20 April 1761.
112. See Haywood, "Boyce's Solemn Dirge," pp. 173–88.
113. Garrick could be pressured by none, but when a play had a chance, for friendship's sake (as with Johnson and Havard) he gave all the support he could.

## Chapter 17
### Exit the Manager

1. Boaden, I, 229.
2. Boaden, II, 67, 379–89.
3. Unfortunately no copies of the actual articles of agreement between managers and actors seem to be extant for this period. But from letters about the negotiations with Noverre, with Signora Paccini, and with the clear account

of Garrick's argument with Lacy in 1745, before he became a patentee, see (36), we can reconstruct the points and guarantees which actors expected, and which managers were aware of. By the turn of the nineteenth century Articles, like modern contracts, became printed forms with space allowed for exceptions agreed upon by both parties. But even as late as 1775 when Garrick wrote the agreement with Signora Paccini (Boaden, II, 63) articles seemed more in the vein of letters, with one copy for the recipient, and one to be filed presumably in the business office of the theatre. George Garrick must have presided over these files. Eight major points were basic to the articles for actors, dancers, and singers, though not all (apparently) were included in every contract. Each of the eight included alternatives with choices to be determined. The eight were followed by three which were not spelled out, but were left to gentlemanly agreement and rational understanding. Hypothetically the points were:

1. *Length of contract*: (a) for one season, (b) for more than one.
2. *Salary*: (a) fixed (weekly, or seasonal rate), (b) escalating, (c) a percentage of overall profit (such as ¼ of profit in excess of the first £100, made on the nights when the performer acted): Barry, Macklin, Lee negotiated such, (d) allowances for clothing, &c.
3. *Roles*: (a) major (and their complexity), (b) minor, (c) taking on new ones.
4. *Frequency of performing*: (a) actor's stipulation, (b) manager's assignment, (c) successive fatiguing ones, (d) relief in performing minor ones.
5. *Accountability*: (a) obligation not to play at competing theatres in the kingdom during the season, (b) manager's bond, (c) actor's forfeit, (d) due notice of intent to article elsewhere.
6. *Benefit night*: (a) clear (i.e., without paying house charges), (b) house charge, (c) sequence in the season, (d) full or partial.
7. *Rank*: (a) in proper slot in the salary scale, (b) advertised (valuable to dancers, i.e., ballet master, or first dancer).
8. *Renewal*: (a) automatic (presumably at same salary), (b) new negotiation, (c) time for negotiating (i.e., before mid-June annually).

Customary understandings not spelled out included: (a) sick leave and temporary leave with pay, (b) attendance at rehearsals (understood to be compulsory with a pay stoppage—forfeit—for nonappearance), and (c) release from articles by mutual understanding. See *L.S.*, pt. 4, I, introduction.

4. Especially from husband and wife teams. Negotiations were always then made with the husbands. When children were involved negotiations were made with the parent—father if he were alive. See *L.S.*, pt. 4, I, xc.

5. See particularly *Garrick and Stratford*; Stochholm, *Garrick's Folly*; and Deelman, *Jubilee*.

6. Folger Shakespeare Library MS, "Garrick Attack on Shakespeare" W.b 460. See Deelman, *Jubilee*, chap. 10; and Stochholm, *Garrick's Folly*, pp. 88–92.

7. Walpole, *Correspondence with George Montagu*, I, 10; II, 298.

8. Pages 406–7, and 532.

9. *Poetical Works*, Kearsley, I, 56.

10. Ibid., p. 58.

11. The list of horses (and owners) entered in the race appears in a broadside, Folger Shakespeare Library [PR 2923, 1769, R2, Cage].

12. Unpublished letter advertised as Item 192 in Quaritch sale Catalogue No. 931. Present location unknown.

13. Painter Benjamin Wilson became Garrick's artistic adviser at Stratford. He painted the picture of Shakespeare for the Town Hall, *Letters*, 560; and Deelman, *Jubilee*, pp. 69 and 159.

14. *L.S.*, pt. 4, III, 1429. First performance 14 October 1769.

15. Huntington Library. See also Stein, *Three Plays*, p. 103.

16. See items recorded under *Taste, Auction of Pictures, Tit for Tat*, and *Chocolate* in *L.S.*, pt. 4, during the season 1748–49; and Boaden, I, 55.

17. Boswell, *Life*, III, 69, 70 n.

18. *Letters*, 394, "A very heavy task for my heart, to pass by Newbury without calling upon You; and I most joyfully Accept of S$^r$ Francis's [Dalaval] & your kind invitation to visit You on my return" (March 1766). Also *Letters*, 506, "I hope you will not forget next Sunday Sen'night perhaps M$^r$ Fitzherbert will venture here, when he is Sure of having a pleasant Companion in a post chaise—the Bargain is, you know, that I am in retirn to attend You in y$^e$ Country upon demand." (June 1766). Also *Letters*, 516:

> Dear Foote, I love Your Wit, & Like your Wine,
> And hope, when next with you I dine,
> Indeed I do not care how soon,
> I hope—nay beg it as a boon,
> That You will get Decanters six,
> (Your various Wines that number fix:). . . .
> Your liquor then each Taste will hit,
> Pure, clear & sparkling as Your Wit.

Garrick had left without taking some geese which Foote had given him. See also *Letters*, 653, to Foote in Paris, "My wife sends her best wishes." And *Letters*, 790, "Mr Garrick returns his best comp$^{ts}$ to M$^r$ Foote, He has too long lamented the loss of his Society, not to accept of his invitation with Pleasure." Mrs Garrick was anxious to join hom (August, 1773).

19. Foote had been at a house party (3 February 1766) of Lord and Lady Mexborough's at Cannon Park in Hampshire, at which the Duke of York was present. Guests urged Foote, who by his own admission was not a good rider, to try the Duke's spirited horse. Knowing he was being baited, he insisted on facing down the sports, so mounted, and was quickly thrown. The sobered crowd found he had a compound fracture below the knee. The Duke's own physician, Dr Bromfield was summoned. He had to amputate above the knee, and, in those days, without anesthesia, so Foote could wear a peg leg. The Duke in compassion and recompense procured the license of the Haymarket theatre for him. See Treffman, *Sam Foote*, p. 148.

20. Treffman, *Sam Foote*, p. 158, 179. Tate Wilkinson, 13 years after both Garrick and Foote were dead, and 40 years after the events he purports to describe, contributed to the "nervous fear" theory about Garrick's relationship with Foote, in his *Memoirs of His Own Life*, I, 238–39. All seems surmise. Garrick was prudent enough not to provoke trouble with the unpredictable Foote, but his letters are in no sense placating. One suspects he could have devastated Foote at the game of mimicry had he been so disposed, but he well knew that mimicry would soon wear itself out of popularity, and would in gen-

eral be unfair to the actors. It was unprofessional, and he had a company to maintain. Isaac Sparks complained to Garrick in the early 1750s that "imitations" by Foote and Wilkinson were destroying his career. As for the charge that Garrick kept calm on the surface but manipulated persons behind the scenes against Foote, no evidence is adduced, save reliance upon Howard Dunbar's deductions, supposes, and web of innuendos (in his *The Dramatic Career of Arthur Murphy* pp. 106–21) that Garrick in effect forced Murphy to drop playwriting and turn to the law by working deviously against him through the writings of Colman, Robert Lloyd, Bonnell Thornton, and Charles Churchill. No case.

21. See Percy Fitzgerald, *Samuel Foote*, p. 82, "Garrick had in his character a certain dread of opponents, a lack of courage in confronting them. Nervousness together with a sort of jealousy thus disturbed his repose."

22. Boswell, *Life*, III, 70.

23. The puckish George Steevens and William Kenrick, as well as many anonymous writers took aim. See Deelman, and Stochholm.

24. He interviewed as job seekers about 200 actors, 135 actresses, 170 dancers, 40 singers, and 32 musicians. See app. D, and headnotes to each year recorded in *L.S.*, pt. 4, I, II, and III.

25. With Barry, Weston, Powell, King, Mossop's sponsor, Vernon, Cautherly, Miss Pope, Mrs Yates, William Smith, and Frances Abington.

26. *L.S.*, pt. 4, I, introduction and app. C.

27. *L.S.*, pt. 4, III, 1431.

28. Boaden, I, 490–99.

29. *L.S.*, pt. 4, III, 1626–30; and *Letters*, 686.

30. See also Shirley, *Letter to Garrick*.

31. Garrick had first employed him as a child actor (Master Vernon) for his voice (1751). In the 1754–55 season he married without her parents' consent the girl dancer Jenny Poitier. The minister who performed the illegal ceremony was jailed, and Vernon was hissed off the stage in 1755 in the part of Palemon in *The Chaplet*. Hissed on his second attempt he had to be replaced by Edward Rooker, but Garrick carried him on, until the ruckus blew over and he was again accepted by the audience.

32. Boaden, II, 57–59.

33. Ibid., pp. 140–42.

34. Ibid., p. 128.

35. Ibid., I, 519; See particularly Emery, *Murphy*; Dunbar, *Dramatic Career*, and Sherbo, *New Essays*. Sherbo traces Murphy's essays in the periodicals.

36. Boaden, I, 226–33, 366, 322.

37. See Sawyer, "Joseph Reed" November 1967, pp. 44–51, and May 1968, pp. 18–51.

38. Boaden, II, 112.

39. *Miscellaneous Works*, Prior, I, 454, in "The Present State of Polite Learning."

40. *The London Magazine* for August, September, and October 1770, "Remarks on the Profession of a Player."

41. See Peter A. Tasch, *The Dramatic Cobbler*.

42. Among them *An Epistle to David Garrick, Esq.* by the Reverend Evan Lloyd in a 295-line poem, suggesting that Garrick not be hurt by the Grub

Street scribblers, to remember that the sun shines on good and evil alike, each plum and pear is attacked by gnats, &c. "The world of Letters more prosp'rous still / Is but one scene of good purg'd by ill." This bred a retort by a Kenrick supporter entitled "A Whipping for a Welsh Parson." Also appeared *The Kenrickiad*, an anonymous poem, but possibly by Frances Brooke, the novelist (1772):

> All men must follow, Sir, their Trade
> Yours is at present much in use
> Head scavenger for rank abuse.

43. *L.S.*, pt. 4, III, 1846.
44. Boaden, II, 118.
45. 
> Not surely meaning to give o'er
> His Art, and make no faces more,
> Yet, fair as 'tis, I'd have him know
> If 'tis the last he means to show.
> This face [of the building] will never make amends,
> For turning tail upon his friends;
> Who own, by general consent,
> His face the best Stage ornament. (*L.S.*, pt. 4, III, 1913.)

46. See app. E, and *L.S.*, pt. 4, I, cvii.
47. Stone, Garrick's Significance," pp. 183–97.
48. See Stone, "Shakespeare in the Periodicals," *SQ*, July 1951, pp. 221–31; and idem, October 1952, pp. 313–28.
49. Gray, *Theatrical Criticism*. Perfection had not come in a flash and remained. As late as October 1759 Goldsmith in his *The Bee* (nos. 1 and 2) reminded his reading and theatre-going public to demand stage attention on the part of all actors. For him even the children who held up the princesses' trains should not let their eyes wander from their business, and young actors should not look out into the audience until the final line of the epilogue. Garrick worked by example, and by rigid rehearsals.
50. See Hilles, *Portraits*, p. 108.

## Chapter 18
### The Social Rounds

1. Boaden, I, 417, 418.
2. The chintz and bed are on exhibit in the Victoria and Albert Museum.
3. Boaden, I, 442; II, 147, 152, 155, 367.
4. Ibid., I, 611.
5. Garrick also showed to North and others his verse on the occasion of being allowed to remain in the House of Commons when others were asked to leave. *Letters*, 1184; Mary Knapp, *Checklist*, 255.

> When Barre stern, with accents deep
> Calls up Lord North, and murders sleep;
> And if his Lordship rise to speak,
> Then wit and argument awake.

6. Boaden, I, 407, 410; II, 357; Forster Collection.

7. Boaden, II, 228, 314; Mary Knapp, *Checklist*, pp. 45, 174.

8. Boaden, II, 158.

9. Mary Knapp, *Checklist*, p. 265.

10. Boaden, I, 190–91.

11. For sources on Beighton, see Boaden, I, 263, 408–9; Mary Knapp, *Checklist*, p. 48.

12. Boaden, I, 565; II, 231. For exchange of visits, see *Letters*, 370, 438, 481, 496, 525 and Boaden, I, 241, 246, 279, 320, 413.

13. Boaden, I, 482, 649; also *Letters*, 777, 850, 899 to nieces Arabella and Catherine.

14. Boaden, II, 1–2, 4–5. 310–11.

15. *Mémoires*, I, 205–6.

16. DNB.

17. Wraxall, *Memoirs*, I, 539–41.

18. See *Manningtree, Mistley, and Lawford, Official Guide issued by the Combined Parish Commitee*. Carshalton, 1970, pp. 13–14. See also *Letters*, 414, 511–13, 530, 556, 768, 921, 1184, 1299.

19. Mary Knapp, *Checklist*, p. 37.

20. Spencer and Dobson, *Garrick and Spencer*, p. 99, also pp. 83, 85, 101; Boaden, II, 180.

21. See an incident related on 16 December 1776, when Garrick wrote Lady Spencer (*Garrick and Spencer*, pp. 67, 69, 151) and *Letters*, 1326; and Mary Knapp, *Checklist*, p. 252, when Rigby's butler ran out of Vin de Grave—Garrick's extempore verse was published about it:

> What! & did Rigby's Butler cry no more!
> Is that tide stop'd, which overflowed before?
> Did ere this Mortal call for wine in vain?
> The sea is sunk—Chaos is come again!

22. Spencer and Dobson, *Garrick and Spencer*, p. xviii.

23. French books that Garrick imported for Berenger have not been identified. Garrick did help him to get his *History and the Art of Horsemanship* published by Becket in 1771 (ibid., 575).

24. Boaden, I, 73.

25. This was a replica of Scheemaker's bust. "Have you nothing to say about him," wrote Garrick, "no Song—no Epigram, Frisk, or fun or flibertygibbet upon the Occasion?" (Ibid., 547). The verses eventually inscribed from *A Midsummer Night's Dream* (v, i, 12–17) may have been suggested by Berenger.

26. *Memoirs*, 1832, I, 74, 77, 175.

27. Boaden, II, 297–98.

28. Page, *George Colman*.

29. Ibid., chap. 7.

30. Boaden, II, 118.

31. Forster Collection, xv, 53.

32. *The Summer's Tale* produced 6 December 1765. *The Brothers*, 2 December 1769 had been rejected by Garrick (Boaden, I, 293; *Letters*, 632). *Timon* had been rejected in first draft (*Letters*, 483). Cumberland tried another "Salome" hoping to serve their mutual fame (Boaden, I, 381), but Garrick rejected it and it was never produced or published under this title.

33. Davies thought Garrick disliked Cumberland, but kept trying to help him. He recommended his pasticcio *The Battle of Hastings* to Sheridan, and it met with great applause. When Garrick was pressed to comment on the quality of the play, he replied only, "Sir, what all the world says must be true." The noncommittal sentiment baffled Davies (*Memoirs*, 1808), p. 301, and his chap. 49.

34. P. 138; and ALS 24 June 1770, Folger Library; *Letters*, 1100.

35. Boaden, I, 425–26.

36. Ibid., I, 430.

37. Ibid., II, 283–86.

38. Cumberland also pressured Garrick on Goldsmith's *She Stoops to Conquer*; *Letters*, 781, 889.

39. See the character Sir Fretful Plagiary in Sheridan's *The Critic* (1779), and Garrick's letter to Colman in Bath (1774), "It was impossible for you to satisfy Cumberland, had y$^e$ rack forc'd from you as much falsehood, as he has vanity" (*Letters*, 875).

40. One is tempted to set off against this relationship that which Garrick had with a minor dramatist, producer of but a single tragedy *Zobeide*, Joseph Cradock (1743–1826), who came to London from Leicester, was a Cambridge graduate, and friend of Richard Farmer, who dedicated to him his essay on *The Learning of Shakespeare*. He was welcomed to London's critical, musical, and literary circles, wrote travel books, and a valuable (later) *Literary and Miscellaneous Memoirs*—a mine for seekers of biographical anecdotes re eighteenth-century people. He was fond of Garrick, attended the Stratford Jubilee and helped Garrick there greatly—"Your . . . kind assistance to Me at y$^e$ Ball, I shall ever remember with gratitude" (*Letters*, 560). Eleven Garrick letters suggest the cordial relationship with the Cradocks, for Mrs Cradock was included in the association (*Letters*, 527, 560, 651, 816, 933, 939, 950, 975, 1163, 1196, and 1253) stretching over a ten-year period.

41. James Boswell, *The Private Papers of James Boswell from Malahide Castle in the Collection of Lt.-Colonel Ralph Heyward Isham*, eds. Geoffrey Scott and Frederick A. Pottle, 1828–34, V, 7.

42. Yale MS L 569.

43. Boswell, *Life*, I, 456; III, 371.

44. Yale MS C 1337; Pottle, *Literary Career of Boswell*, passim.

45. *Boswell's London Journal*, Pottle, pp. 161, 163.

46. Mary Knapp, *Checklist*, 243; Boswell, MS Journal, 21–22 November 1764.

47. Yale MS C 1336; Journal, 21 December 1775. Thirteen of Boswell's letters survive (11 in copies) and 16 from Garrick, all now in the Boswell Papers in Yale University, to whom we wish gratefully to thank for the privilege to quote and refer to. Judging from the acknowledgments in the letters, the correspondence is complete except for an initial letter from Boswell.

48. Journal, 21 December 1775; *Boswell Papers*, XI, 44; *Letters Between the Honourable Andrew Erskine and James Boswell, Esq.* (1763), p. 124; Boswell, *Life*, II, 377. On "Hearts of Oak," see Yale MS C 1337; Yale MS L 564.

49. Wimsatt and Pottle, eds., *Boswell for the Defence*, p. 83; Marshall Waingrow, *Boswell's Correspondence Relating to the Making of the Life of Johnson* (1969), I, 5–9. Does not include the Boswell-Garrick correspondence.

50. Yale MS C 1346.

51. Yale MS L 563, 564; the letter L 563 is printed in Boswell, *Life*, v, 347–48.
52. *Boswell for the Defence*, p. 133.
53. Yale MS L 560.
54. *Boswell in Extremes*, p. 257.
55. Boswell, *Life*, v, 273.
56. Frederick W. Hilles, ed.
57. Boswell, *Life*, v, 273.
58. Hilles, *Portraits*, p. 105; Boswell, *Life*, I, 393.
59. *Boswell in Extremes*, p. 263.
60. Boswell, *Life*, II, 326 n.3.
61. Journal, 23 March 1776; *Boswell: The Ominous Years*, p. 292.
62. William Roberts, *Memoirs*, II, 16.
63. Boswell, *Life*, I, 480.
64. Records of attendance were not kept until 1775; in the last three years of his life Garrick attended the meetings. See also *Annals of the Club, 1764–1914*, by Jones and Fifer, *Correspondence*.
65. Boswell, *Life*, II, 273.
66. *Tour*, v, 108; see also Fifer, *Correspondence*, p. 208.
67. Samuels, *Early Life*, which includes an introduction and supplementary chapters on Burke's contributions to *The Reformer*.
68. R. Bisset, *Life*, I, 113; Copeland, *Correspondence*, Vol 1 (1958), I, 360–61; Burke's professional ambitions were not in law, or the theatre, but in literature. He had early written "Hints for an Essay on the Drama," not published until after his death, and his essays in *The Reformer* were often on the literature of the drama. Dodsley published for him in 1756 his *Vindication of Natural Society*, and in 1757 his *Philosophical Enquiry into the Origin of Our Ideas of the Sublime and the Beautiful*, both of which went through many printings, a copy of the latter being in Garrick's library, as well as the 1770 edition in "calf gilt." In 1758 he contracted with Dodsley at £100 per year to edit *The Annual Register*, 1759–88. See Copeland, *Our Friend Burke*, pp. 94–98; idem, *Correspondence*, I, xvii.
69. See Strauss, *Dodsley*, p. 254; Bryant, *Burke*, p. 133.
70. Garrick introduced by letter Richard to Mme Riccoboni on his visit to Paris in 1766, the resulting encounters being reported by Mme Riccoboni with mixed reactions. See James C. Nicholls, *Riccoboni's Letters*.
71. Boaden, I, 484.
72. Wecter, *Burke*.
73. Harry W. Pedicord, "Mr and Mrs Garrick," pp. 781–82.
74. Copeland, *Correspondence*, I, 211–12.
75. Ibid., 233.
76. Morley, "Burke," p. 106.
77. Copeland, *Correspondence*, II, 333–34.
78. Bryant, *Burke*, p. 142.
79. Copeland, *Correspondence*, II, 31, 438, 443; VII, 551; VIII, 284; IX, 306.
80. Ibid., I, 353–54.
81. Ibid., pp. 354–56.
82. Ibid., p. 356.
83. Ibid., II, 1–3.
84. Ibid., IX, 451; Bryant, *Burke*, pp. 141–42.

746

85. Copeland, *Correspondence*, II, 83–84.
86. Copeland, *Correspondence*, II, 335–36; Bryant, *Burke*, pp. 144–45.
87. Davies, *Memoirs*, II, 359–60; Mary Knapp, *Checklist*, p. 255.
88. Davies, *Memoirs*, II, 361.
89. Details about those who filled the carriages appear in Davies, *Memoirs*, pp. 485–91.
90. Journal, 24 April 1776.
91. Boswell, *Life*, IV, 96–99.
92. Copeland, *Correspondence*, IX, 360–61; see also VII, 560–61; VIII, 115; IX, 323; and Murphy, *Life*, II, 151–52.
93. Windham, *Diary*, p. 361.

## Appendix G
### Garrick's Two Known Wills in Summary

1. When Peter died in 1770 George Garrick became the rather slow-moving executor of his affairs and estate. See *Letters*, index, s.v. Fermignac, Jr., Peter.
2. Thirteen pages bound into extra-illustrated Vol. IV of Murphy's *Life*, (TS 937.3). For discussion, see Burnim, "Garrick's Early Will." Neither this nor his later will is punctuated.
3. The correspondence in Boaden, I, and in the *Letters*, and in the accounts for Jephson's play *Braganza* in *L.S.*, pt. 4, III, spell out the relationship. Garrick was friendly with the playwright-to-be and judged him able, possibly from the author's benefits in future plays, to repay the loan. His *Braganza* of 17 February 1775 amply justified Garrick's faith. Its 14 performances that season grossed for the house £2,563, and from his three benefits Jephson received something over £474. Presumably out of this his debt was paid, for no mention is made of it in Garrick's second will.
4. The will is printed in full in *Letters*, app. G.
5. See *Letters*, 978, to Clutterbuck.

# General Index

.

Note: It has been impossible to supply first names for a number of the persons listed, especially of artists whose pictures the Garricks hung in their residences. The pictures have been dispersed, and the auction catalogues are general rather than specific in their descriptions.

Caballé, Mme Montserrat: "aria tech-
nique," 31–32
Cadell, Thomas, 430
Cadogan, Frances, 403–4, 438, 623, 643
Cadogan, William, 403–4
Cahusac, Louis de: *Zeneide*, 296
Cailhava d'Estandoux: *Le Tuteur dupé*,
318
Calvert, Frederick. *See* Baltimore, Fred-
erick Calvert, Lord
Calvert, John (MP), 623
Cambridge, Richard Owen, 392
Camden, Charles Pratt, Lord, 173, 370,
617, 620–21
Camden, Lady Elizabeth Jeffreys, 370,
618
Capell, Edward: inventories Garrick's
dramatic library, 174–75, 176, 182; men-
tioned, 190–91, 193
Car, Lord (Mark Kerr), 6
Caramontelle, 303
Carara, Antonio, 119, 300, 351, 380
Caravaggio, Polidoro da, 450
Carlyle, Dr Alexander, 405
Caroline (queen), 358
Carracci, 450
Carrington, Catherine (Mrs George Gar-
rick), 20
Carrington, Nathan (George Garrick's
father-in-law), 20
Carter, Elizabeth, 99, 367, 424, 431,
645
Cartwright, William, 168, 172
Castiglione, Giovanni Benedetto, 456
Caswell, Richard, 451
Cautherly, Samuel, 57, 88, 286, 349–50,
575, 593, 604, 723
Cave, Edward, 15, 99, 342
Cazalets (Garrick's cousins), 99, 294
Celisis, Dorothea, 596
Centlivre, Susannah, 282, 511, 644
Cervantes, Miguel de, 460
Chambers, Robert, 436
Chamier, Anthony, 623
Champness, Samuel Thomas, 88, 223
Changuion, Philip, 299, 414
Chapone, Mrs Hester, 431
Charles I, king, 455
Chastellux, François Jean de, 307–8
Chatsworth House, 296, 361–62, 448
Chaucer, Geoffrey, 232
Chaussée, Nivelle de La. *See* La Chaus-
sée, Nivelle de
Chesterfield, Lord Philip Stanhope, 195,
357

Chetwood, William Rufus, 176–78
Chippendale, Thomas, 453, 616
Chiswick Manor, 296, 359–62, 448
Christie (auctioneer), 456
Chudleigh, Elizabeth (duchess of Kings-
ton), 433
Church, early influence on Garrick, 4
Churchill, Charles: *Apology*, 374, 613;
*Epistle to Hogarth*, 105; *The Rosciad*,
30, 322, 373, 480, 494, 702, 708; mentioned, 104, 343, 373–74, 402
Cibber, Colley, 25, 28, 35, 53, 61, 86, 248,
477, 485, 493, 518–19, 560
Cibber, Susanna Maria: bears children to
Sloper, 59; in Handel's *Messiah*, 60; pa-
tronized by Quin and Handel, 58; seeks
to join Garrick as joint patentee, 59;
trained well by Colley, 59; mentioned,
25, 53, 54, 66, 159, 251, 266–68, 320–
21, 330, 357, 403, 527–28, 544, 565,
568–69, 590, 735 n.46, 737 n.26
Cibber, Theophilus: seeks a theatre
license, 62; mentioned, 25, 58, 68,
137–38, 261, 477, 480, 487, 505–6,
519–20, 571
Cicero: *De Oratore*, 31
Cipriani, Giovanni Battista, 454, 620
Clairon, Claire Josèphe, 45, 89, 298, 308,
314, 417, 458
Cleland, John, 127, 599
Clive, Catherine: plays by, 702; tribute to
Garrick, 595; mentioned, 24–25, 53,
64, 75–78, 223–24, 320–21, 332, 389,
403, 407, 435, 593, 612
Clive, Robert, 393
Clough, Anthony, 7
Club, The, 192, 638, 642
Clutterbuck, James, 83, 110, 113, 115–18,
323, 467, 605
Collé, Charles, 295, 307
Collier, Jeremy, 474
Collins, John, 595
Colman, George, *Clandestine Marriage*,
109; *Jealous Wife*, 282; *Letter of Abuse*,
142; mentioned, 83, 105, 163, 185, 188,
239, 242–44, 272, 298, 303, 309, 316,
321, 323, 343, 350, 374, 379, 417, 432,
458, 523, 563, 591, 596, 605
Colson, John, 9, 13, 14
Combe, William: *Sanitas, Daughter of
Aesculapius*, 164, 601
Comédie-Française, 295, 315, 324
Comédie-Italienne, 295, 414
Comédie Larmoyante, 129
Congreve, William, 246, 442, 460, 624

579, 581, *Othello*, 255–56, 561, *A Peep Behind the Curtain*, 236–38, *Prologue at opening of the theatre*, 1750, 399, "Ragandjaw," 100, 123, *Richard III*, 256–63, *Romeo and Juliet*, 251–55, "On Seeing Strasbourg Cathedral," 631, *The Sick Monkey*, 322, 336, 396, *Theatrical Candidates*, 241–42, *Zara*, 269; youth of, 4, 5, 10, 11, 24

Garrick, Eva Maria (Mrs David): apologizes to English audiences, 727; broken English of, 409; first appearance in London of, 359–61; first entertains five years after Garrick's death, 645; as Garrick's most acute adviser, 409; health of, 160, 162, 297, 300; as Hilverding's most successful dance pupil, 405; mentioned, 84, 89, 173, 180, 296, 310, 333, 334, 362–63, 365, 367, 369, 404–12, 415, 420, 432, 434, 437, 447, 453, 456, 458, 461, 463, 467, 569, 616

Garrick, David (Garrick's nephew), 20, 458

Garrick, George (Garrick's brother), 20–21, 120, 403, 437, 458, 487, 575, 577, 583, 589, 590–91

Garrick, Jane (Garrick's unmarried sister), 19

Garrick, Mary Magdelene (Garrick's eldest sister), 19

Garrick, Merrial (Mrs Thomas Docksey), 19

Garrick, Nathan Egerton (Garrick's nephew), 21, 463

Garrick, Captain Peter (Garrick's father), 4, 5, 14

Garrick, Peter (Garrick's elder brother), 5, 7, 12, 14–17, 26, 209, 296, 362, 364, 477, 560, 617

Garrick, William (Garrick's youngest brother), 20

Gastrell, Francis, 15

Gay, John: *Beggar's Opera*, 713 n.3; *The What D'Ye Call It*, 87, 702 n.63

Gayot, Felix Louis, 631

Gentleman, Francis, 38, 134, 181, 251–52, 474, 507, 522, 525–26, 530, 547, 571, 587, 599, 629

Geoffrin, Mme Marie Thérèse Rodet, 306, 419

George I (king), 560

George II (king), 360, 364, 439, 560

George III (king), 449, 458

Ghezzi, Pier Leone, 450

Gibbon, Edward, 72, 375, 433, 436, 515, 620

Giffard, Henry, 23–24, 272, 541

Gilbert, T., 150

Gildon, Charles, 33, 169, 474

Giordani family, 236

Glover, Richard, 596

Glover, William Frederick, 359

Glyn, Lady Elizabeth (Carr), 623

Goldsmith, Oliver: pleads for literary content for plays rather than performance promise, 130–31; *Retaliation*, 395; solicits secretaryship of Society of Artists, 448; mentioned, 109, 121, 234, 377, 381, 383, 528, 596, 600, 613, 626, 628, 632, 704

Goltzius, Hendrick, 456

Gonzalo (painter), 457

Goupy, Joseph, 457

Gower, Granville Leveson-Gower, second earl Gower, 5, 239, 642

Grafton, Charles Fitzroy, second duke of, 174, 359, 451

Grandval, Charles François Racot de, 89

Gravelot, Hubert François, 448, 459, 465

Gray, Thomas, 390–92, 632

Green, Richard, 61–65

Greville, Fulke, 195

Griffin, William, 171

Griffith, Elizabeth, 129, 321, 598, 707

Griffiths, Ralph, 342

Grignion, Charles, 100

Grimm, F. M., Baron, 210, 282, 298, 307–8, 315, 417

Guercino (Giovanni Francesco Barbieri), 450

Guido (painter), 457

Gunderode, Frederick, 544

Gunst, Pieter (?), 450

Gwatkin, Mrs Edward Lovell, 429

H. H.: On stops and pauses in *Hamlet*, 543; word pronunciation in *Macbeth*, 556

Hale, Captain Bernard, 623

Hale, Sacheverel, 477

Half-price riots. *See* Fitzpatrick, Thaddeus

Halifax, George Montagu Dunk, second earl of, 360, 465, 627

Halifax, George Saville, first marquis of, 357, 458, 639

Hall (engraver), 459

Hallam, Charles, 330

Hallam, Thomas, 53

# Index to Titles

771